CONSTITUTIONAL LAW FOR

A CHANGING AMERICA

CONSTITUTIONAL LAW FOR A CHANGING AMERICA

INSTITUTIONAL POWERS AND CONSTRAINTS

LEE EPSTEIN
WASHINGTON UNIVERSITY

THOMAS G. WALKER
EMORY UNIVERSITY

PRESS

A DIVISION OF CONGRESSIONAL QUARTERLY INC.

WASHINGTON, D.C.

Copyright © 1992 Congressional Quarterly Inc.
1414 22nd Street, N.W.
Washington, D.C. 20037

Book design by Kachergis Book Design, Pittsboro, North
Carolina.

Printed in the United States of America.

Permissions for copyrighted materials not credited on the
page where they appear are listed in the "Acknowledg-
ments" section beginning on page 528. This section is to
be considered an extension of the copyright page.

Library of Congress Cataloging-in-Publication Data
Epstein, Lee, 1958–
    Constitutional law for a changing America :
institutional powers and constraints / Lee Epstein,
Thomas G. Walker.
        p.   cm.
    Includes bibliographical references and index.
    ISBN 0–87187–612–4
    1. United States—Constitutional law.   I. Walker,
Thomas G.
II. Title.
KF4550.E67   1992
342.73—dc20
[347.302]   91–46712
                                                CIP

CONTENTS

TABLES AND FIGURES

PREFACE

Constitutional Law for a Changing America makes its debut in a discipline already supplied with many fine books. Over the years, law professors, historians, and political scientists have produced numerous casebooks and related materials. Given the choices currently available, is there room and, more to the point, a need for yet another?

To this question, naturally, we answer yes. As political science professors who regularly teach courses on public law and as scholars who are concerned with judicial processes, we saw a growing disparity between what we were teaching and what our research taught us. We adopted books for our classes that focused primarily on Supreme Court decisions and how the Court applied the resulting legal precedents to subsequent disputes, but as scholars we know that the law is only one slice of the pie. A host of political factors—internal and external to the Court—influence judicial decisions and shape the development of constitutional law. Among the more significant forces at work are the ways that lawyers and interest groups frame legal disputes, the ideological and behavioral propensities of the justices, the politics of judicial selection, public opinion, and the positions taken by elected officials, to name just a few.

Because we thought no existing book adequately combined the lessons of the legal model with the influences of the political process, we decided to write one. We do not veer significantly from the traditional approaches to the study of constitutional law. Professors will find, for example, that we include the classic cases that best illustrate the development of constitutional law. But our focus—and even the appearance of this volume—is different. We emphasize the arguments raised by lawyers and interest groups, and we include tables and figures on Court trends, profiles of influential justices and organizations, and other materials that bring out the rich political context in which decisions are reached. As a result, students and instructors will find this work both similar to and different from casebooks they may have used before.

Integrating traditional teaching and research concerns was only one of our goals. Another was to animate the subject of public law. As instructors, we find our subject inherently interesting. To us public law is exciting stuff. The typical constitutional law book, however, could not be less inviting in design, presentation, or prose. That kind of book seems to dampen enthusiasm. We have written a book that we hope mirrors the excitement we feel for our subject. Along with cases excerpted in the traditional manner, we have included photographs of litigants and the situations they disputed, relevant exhibits from the cases, and full descriptions of the events that led to the suits. We hope these materials demonstrate to students that Supreme Court decisions are more than just legal names and citations, that they involve real people engaged in real disputes. Readers will also find appendices designed to aid in understanding the law—information on the Supreme Court decision-making process, the structure of the federal judiciary, material on briefing court cases, a glossary of legal terms, and biographical information on the justices.

This book has been in the works for some time, and with time we have accumulated debts. We owe much to the folks at CQ Press, especially Joanne Daniels. She helped develop this project from a concept to a proposal to a book. In doing so, she exhibited patience and faith in us and the work. When Joanne left Washington, David Tarr, Margaret Benjaminson, and Brenda Carter took over. They too remained extraordinarily enthusiastic and committed. Jeanne Ferris solicited reviews and summarized them in a way that made it impossible for us to miss the forest for the trees. The manuscript editor, Carolyn Goldinger, was nothing short of a saint. She went above and beyond the call of duty, viewing the project from both a professional and student perspective and suggesting changes when we failed on either score. Production editors Ann O'Malley and Jamie Holland tracked down photographs and other materials with creativity and perseverance, and Jenny Philipson provided editorial assistance.

We also thank our many colleagues who reviewed and commented on this volume: Judith A. Baer, Ralph Baker, Lawrence Baum, John Brigham, Gregory A. Caldeira, Robert A. Carp, Phillip J. Cooper, John B. Gates, Wayne McIn-tosh, John A. Maltese, Richard L. Pacelle, Jr., C. K. Rowland, and Donald R. Songer. Special thanks go to Joseph A. Kobylka of Southern Methodist University, who served as a sounding board for so many ideas included in (and excluded from) the book.

Our home institutions provided substantial support, not complaining in the face of astronomical telephone bills, postal fees, and copying expenses. Epstein conducted her work at Washington University and Southern Methodist University, where Tracey George, Leslie Moss, and Eric Parkinson provided valuable research assistance. June Manton typed parts of the manuscript from almost unreadable handwritten versions. Walker is particularly grateful to Harvey Klehr, the chair of his department, and to his colleagues on the staff and faculty, who make Emory University's Political Science Department such an enjoyable place to teach and study.

Finally, we acknowledge the support of our friends and families. We are forever grateful to our former professors for instilling in us their genuine interest in and curiosity about things judicial and legal, and to our parents for their unequivocal support. Walker expresses his special thanks to Aimee and Emily for always being there; and Epstein to her husband Jay for enduring all that he does not have to (but does, anyway), without complaining (much).

Any errors of omission or commission remain our sole responsibility. We encourage students and instructors alike to comment on the book and to inform us of any errors.

PART I

THE U.S. CONSTITUTION

**AN INTRODUCTION TO THE
U.S. CONSTITUTION**

**I. APPROACHES TO CONSTITUTIONAL
INTERPRETATION**

AN INTRODUCTION TO THE
U.S. CONSTITUTION

According to President Franklin Roosevelt, "Like the Bible, it ought to be read again and again."[1] Henry Clay said, it was "made not merely for the generation that then existed, but for posterity—unlimited, undefined, endless, perpetual posterity."[2] And William Gladstone once wrote, "I have always regarded [it] as the most remarkable work . . . to have been produced by the human intellect, at a single stroke . . . , in its application to political affairs."[3] Justice Hugo Black carried one with him virtually all the time. The object of all this admiration? The United States Constitution. To be sure, the Constitution has its flaws and its share of detractors, but most Americans take great pride in their charter. And why not? It is, after all, the world's oldest written constitution.

Here we provide a brief introduction to the U.S. Constitution—in particular the circumstances under which it was written, the basic principles underlying it, and some controversies surrounding it. While this material will not be new to you, we think it is worth reviewing. Because the balance of this book is devoted to Supreme Court interpretation of the Constitution it is important to have some understanding of it.

The Road to the U.S. Constitution

While the fledgling United States was fighting for its independence from England, it was being run (and the war conducted) by the Continental Congress. Although this body had no formal authority, it met in session from 1774 through the end of the war in 1781, establishing itself as what C. Herman Pritchett called a "de facto" government.[4] But it may have been something more than that. About a year into the Revolutionary War, Congress took steps toward nationhood. On July 2, 1776, it passed a resolution declaring the "United Colonies free and independent states." Two days later, on July 4, it formalized this proclamation in the Declaration of Independence, in which the nation's Founders used the term *United States of America* for the first time.[5] But even before the adoption of the Declaration of Independence, the Continental Congress had "designated a group of delegates to make recommendations for the formation of a national gov-

1. Quoted in Michael Kammen, ed., *The Origins of the American Constitution* (New York: Penguin Books, 1986), vii.
2. Speech to the Senate, January 29, 1850.
3. Letter to the Committee for the Centennial Celebration of the American Constitution, July 20, 1887.

4. C. Herman Pritchett, *Constitutional Law of the Federal System* (Englewood Cliffs, N.J.: Prentice-Hall, 1984), 4.
5. See J. W. Peltason, *Corwin & Peltason's Understanding the Constitution,* 11th ed. (New York: Holt, Rinehart and Winston, 1988), 1.

ernment after independence was achieved."[6] Composed of representatives of each of the thirteen colonies, this committee labored for several months to produce a proposal for a national charter, the Articles of Confederation. Congress passed the proposal and submitted it to the states for ratification in November 1777. Ratification was achieved in March 1781, when Maryland—a two-year holdout—gave its approval.

The Articles of Confederation represented the nation's first written charter, but it changed the way the government operated very little; it merely "codified the structure and procedures that had emerged in practice in the years since 1774."[7] For example, rather than provide for a compact between the people and the government, the 1781 charter institutionalized "a league of friendship" among the states, one that rested "expressly on state sovereignty."[8] This is not to suggest that the Articles failed to provide for a central government. As we can see in Figure I-1, which depicts the structure and powers of government, the Articles created a national governing apparatus, however weak and simple. There was a one-house legislature, but no formal federal executive or judiciary. And while the legislature had some power, most notably in the area of foreign affairs, it derived its authority from the states that had created it, not the people.

The Articles of Confederation was a much-maligned document. Analysts have pointed out its weaknesses, which included the following:

–Because it allowed Congress only to "requisition" funds and not to tax, the federal government was virtually broke. Between 1781 and 1783 the national legislature requested $10 million from the states and received only $1.5 million.[9] Given the foreign debts the United States had accumulated during the war, this problem was particularly troublesome.

–Because Congress lacked any concrete way to regulate foreign commerce, "treaties between foreign countries and the Confederation were of little value." Some European nations (for example, England and Spain) took advantage by imposing "trade restrictions that narrowed the markets for American exports."[10]

–Because the government lacked any coercive power over the states, mutual cooperation among them quickly dissipated. They engaged in trading practices that hurt one another economically. In short, the states acted more like thirteen separate countries than a union or even a confederation.

–Because the exercise of most national authority required the approval of nine states and the passage of amendments required unanimity, the Articles stymied Congress. One scholar has noted, "Given the divisions among the states at the time, the approval of nine states for any action of substance was rare, and the required unanimity for amendment[s] was never obtained."[11]

Clearly, the United States had problems under the Articles. But scholar Lance Banning points out that "historians have long since given up the old idea that the Confederation years were a period of governmental folly and unmixed disaster."[12] Indeed, under the Articles, the government accomplished many notable objectives: it brought the Revolutionary War to a successful end and paved the way for the 1783 Treaty of Paris, "which gave the United States de jure the status of a nation."[13] Moreover, the charter

6. Thomas G. Walker, *American Politics and the Constitution* (North Scituate, Mass.: Duxbury Press, 1978), 10.

7. Lance Banning, "From Confederation to Constitution: The Revolutionary Context of the Great Convention," in *This Constitution—Our Enduring Legacy* (Washington, D.C.: Congressional Quarterly, 1986), 30.

8. Peltason, *Understanding the Constitution*, 9.

9. Pritchett, *Constitutional Law of the Federal System*, 6.

10. Daniel A. Farber and Suzanna Sherry, *A History of the American Constitution* (St. Paul, Minn.: West Publishing, 1990), 24-25.

11. Walker, *American Politics*, 11.

12. Banning, "From Confederation to Constitution," 30.

13. Peltason, *Understanding the Constitution*, 10.

Figure I-1. *The Structure and Powers of Government Under the Articles of Confederation*

The States

Congress

Had the Power to

Declare war and make peace
Enter into treaties and alliances
Establish and control armed forces
Requisition men and money from states
Regulate coinage
Borrow money and issue bills of credit
Fix uniform standards of weight and
  measurement
Create admiralty courts
Create a postal system
Regulate Indian affairs
Guarantee citizens of each state the rights
  and privileges of citizens in the several
  states when in another
Adjudicate disputes between states upon
  state petition

Lacked Power to

Provide for effective treaty-making
  power and control of foreign relations;
  it could not compel states to respect
  treaties
Compel states to meet military quotas;
  it could not draft soldiers
Regulate interstate and foreign commerce;
  it left each state free to set up its own tariff
  system
Collect taxes directly from the people; it had
  to rely on states to collect and forward
  taxes
Compel states to pay their share of government costs
Provide and maintain a sound monetary
  system or issue paper money; this was
  left up to the states, and monies in
  circulation differed tremendously in value

Committee of the States

(Composed of representatives of all
the states to act in the name of
Congress between sessions)

Officers

(Congress appointed officers to do some of
the executive work)

Source: Adopted from Steffen W. Schmidt, Mack C. Shelley II,
and Barbara A. Bardes, *American Government and Politics Today*
(St. Paul, Minn.: West Publishing, 1989), 34, 35.

served an important purpose. It "preserved the idea of a federal national union until national wisdom could adopt a more efficient system."[14]

Nevertheless, the shortcomings of the Articles were more and more apparent to some citizens. By the mid-1780s, in fact, several dissidents, including James Madison of Virginia and Alexander Hamilton of New York, had held a series of meetings to arouse interest in revising the system of government. At one such meeting in Annapolis in September 1786, they urged the states to send delegations to another meeting scheduled for the following May in Philadelphia. Their plea could not have come at a more opportune time. Just the month before, in August 1786, a former Revolutionary War captain, Daniel Shays, led disgruntled and armed farmers to rebellion in Massachusetts. They were protesting the poor state of the economy, which was taking its toll on farmers, who were jailed for not paying their debts.

Shays's Rebellion was suppressed by state forces, but it was seen as yet another sign that the Articles needed amending. Congress formalized

14. J. T. Keenan, *The Constitution of the United States* (Chicago: Dorsey Press, 1988), 11.

the Annapolis call in February 1787 when it "passed a resolution calling for a convention to reevaluate the state of the national government."[15] It was quite clear, however, that Congress did not want a whole new charter; in fact, it stated that the delegates were to meet "for the sole and express purpose of revising the Articles of Confederation."

Despite these words, the fifty-five delegates who gathered in Philadelphia quickly realized that they would be doing more than "revising" the Articles: they would be framing a new charter. After examining the records of the convention, scholars Daniel Farber and Suzanna Sherry concluded "that many delegates were contemplating more than merely revising or amending the Articles is clear throughout the Convention."[16]

We can attribute this, at least in part, to the Virginia delegation. When it arrived in Philadelphia on May 14, 1787, the day the convention was supposed to start, only it and the Pennsylvania delegation were there. Although lacking a quorum, the Virginia contingent "took advantage of an eleven-day delay in the opening of the convention . . . to prepare a series of proposals."[17] And, as illustrated in Table I-1, its "hopes" for the meeting represented far more than just a revision in the existing structure. The Virginians called for a wholly new one, composed of a strong three-branch national government empowered to lead the nation.

Called the Virginia Plan, this series of proposals was formally introduced to the delegates May 29, just four days after the convention began. And, although it was the target of a counterproposal submitted by the New Jersey delegation, the Virginia Plan set the tone for the convention. It served as the basis for many of the ensuing debates and, as we shall see, for the Constitution itself.

The delegates had much to accomplish during the four-month convention period. Arguments between large states and small states and over the structure of the new government and its relationship to the states threatened to deadlock the meeting. In fact, it is almost a miracle that the delegates were able to frame a new constitution and do so in just a few months. One can speculate that the Founders succeeded in part because they were able to close their meetings to the public, a feat almost inconceivable today. A convention of the states today would be a media circus. Moreover, it is hard to imagine that delegates from fifty states could agree even to frame a new charter, much less do it in four months.

The difficulties facing such an enterprise lead to an important issue. A constitutional convention held today would be hard pressed to reach consensus because the delegates would bring with them diverse interests and aims. What about back in 1787? Who were the Framers and what were their motives? If, as had been recorded, they were such a fractious bunch, how could they have reached accord so rapidly?

These questions have been the subject of lively scholarly debates. Many agree with historian Melvin I. Urofsky who wrote of the Constitutional Convention, "Few gatherings in the history of this or any other country could boast such a concentration of talent." And, "despite [the Framers'] average age of forty-two [they] had extensive experience in government and were fully conversant with political theories of the Enlightenment."[18] The Framers were, indeed, an impressive group. Among them were many future leaders: two U.S. presidents, sixteen governors, and two Supreme Court chief justices. Thirty-three had served in the Revolutionary War, forty-two had attended the Continental Congress, and

15. Walker, *American Politics*, 13.
16. Farber and Sherry, *A History of the American Constitution*, 37.
17. Peltason, *Understanding the Constitution*, 12.

18. Melvin I. Urofsky, *A March of Liberty* (New York: Knopf, 1988), 89.

Table I-1   The Virginia Plan, the New Jersey Plan, and the Constitution

Item	Virginia Plan	New Jersey Plan	Constitution
Legislature	Two houses	One house	Two houses
Legislative representation	Both houses based on population	Equal for each state	One house based on population; one house with two votes from each state
Legislative power	Veto authority over state legislation	Authority to levy taxes and regulate commerce	Authority to levy tariffs and regulate commerce; authority to compel state compliance with national policies
Executive	Single; elected by legislature for a single term	Plural; removable by majority of state legislatures	Single; chosen by electoral college; removable by national legislature
Courts	National judiciary elected by legislature	No provision	Supreme Court appointed by executive, confirmed by Senate

Source: Paul Johnson et al., *American Government* (Boston: Houghton-Mifflin, 1990), 47.

two had signed the Declaration of Independence.[19]

Others would take issue with Urofsky's statement. Because the Framers were a relatively homogeneous lot—all white men, many of whom had been educated at the country's best schools—some suggest that the document they produced was biased in various ways. For example, in 1987 Justice Thurgood Marshall said that the Constitution was "defective from the start," that its first words—"We the People"—excluded "the majority of American citizens," because it left out blacks and women. He further alleged that the Framers "could not have imagined, nor would they have accepted, that the document they were drafting would one day be construed by a Supreme Court to which had been appointed a woman and the descendent of an African slave."[20] Another point of view is expressed by historian Charles Beard in his controversial work, *An Economic Interpretation of the Constitution of the United States,* which depicts the Framers as self-serving. Beard says the Constitution was an "economic document" devised to protect the "property interests" of those who wrote it.

Various scholars have refuted these allegations; Beard's work, in particular, has been largely negated by other studies.[21] Still, by today's standards it is hard to deny that the original Constitution was a racist and sexist document or that the Framers did not write it in a way that benefited them.

Given these charges, how has the Constitution survived for so long, particularly as the U.S. population has become increasingly heterogeneous? In part, the answer lies with the Supreme Court, which generally has analyzed the document in light of its contemporary context. That is, some justices have viewed the Constitution as a living document and have sought to adopt it to the times. In addition, the Founders provided for an amending process to keep their document alive. That we can alter the Constitution to fit changing needs and expectations is obviously important. The original document held a slave to be three-fifths of a person for the purposes of repre-

19. Paul E. Johnson et al., *American Government* (Boston: Houghton Mifflin, 1990), 43.

20. Quoted in the *Washington Post,* May 7, 1987.

21. See, for example, Robert E. Brown's *Charles Beard and the Constitution* (Princeton, N.J.: Princeton University Press, 1956). Brown concludes that "we would be doing a grave injustice to the political sagacity of the Founding Fathers if we assumed that property or personal gain was their only motive." (Page 198).

sentation; as a citizen, a slave had no rights at all. In the aftermath of the Civil War, the country recognized the outrageousness of such a provision and added three amendments to alter the status of blacks and provide full equality under law.

This is not to suggest that controversies surrounding the Constitution no longer exist. To the contrary, charges abound that the document has retained an elitist or otherwise biased flavor. Some argue that the amending process is too cumbersome, that it is too slanted toward majority will. Others point to the Supreme Court as the culprit, asserting that its interpretation of the document—particularly at certain points in history—has reinforced the biases and motives of the Framers.

Throughout this volume, you will have many opportunities to evaluate this controversy. It will be especially prominent in cases involving economic liberties—those that ask the Court, in some sense, to adjudicate claims between the privileged and the underdogs in society. For now, let us consider some of the basic features of that controversial document—the U.S. Constitution.

The Underlying Principles of the Constitution

Table I-1 sets forth the basic proposals considered at the convention and how they got translated into the Constitution. What it does not show are the fundamental principles underlying, though not necessarily explicit in, the Constitution. Three are particularly important: the separation of powers/checks and balances doctrine, federalism, and individual rights and liberties.

Separation of Powers/Checks and Balances

One of the fundamental weakness of the Articles of Confederation was its failure to establish a strong and authoritative federal government. To be sure, it created a Congress, but that body had few powers and those it did have were kept in check by the states. The new Constitution overcame this deficiency by creating a national government with three branches—the legislature, the executive, and the judiciary—and by providing each with significant power and authority over its sphere. Moreover, the three newly devised institutions were "given constitutional and political independence from one another."[22] As Urofsky wrote, "Perhaps the most striking feature of the Constitution was how extensively it implemented the prevailing notions of separation of powers. Unlike the Articles and most state constitutions, clear lines divided the executive, legislative, and judicial functions."[23]

Certainly, Articles I, II, and III of the Constitution outlined the specific powers that each branch was given. Section 8 of Article I is especially explicit, empowering Congress to lay and collect taxes, to regulate commerce, and so forth. Nonetheless, many questions have arisen over the scope of these powers as they are wielded by all three institutions. Consider a few examples:

–Article I provides Congress with various authority over the U.S. military, for example, to provide and maintain a navy, to raise and support armies. But it does not specifically empower Congress to initiate and operate a draft. Does that omission mean that Congress may not do so?

–Article II provides the president with the power to "nominate, and by and with the Advice and Consent of the Senate, [to] appoint . . . Officers of the United States," but it does not specifically empower the president to fire such officers. May the president dismiss appointees or is the "advice and consent" of the Senate also necessary?

–Article III provides the federal courts with

22. Peltason, *Understanding the Constitution*, 21.
23. Urofsky, *A March of Liberty*, 94.

Figure I-2. *The Separation of Powers / Checks and Balances*

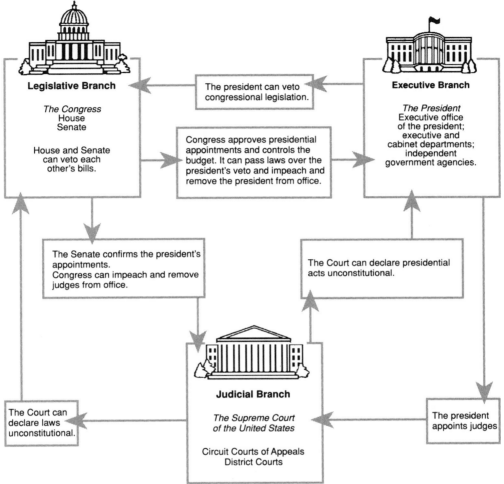

Source: Janet A. Flammang et al., *American Politics in a Changing World* (Pacific Grove, Calif.: Brooks/Cole, 1990), 41.

the authority to hear cases involving federal laws. But it does not specifically empower these courts to strike down such laws if they are incompatible with the Constitution. Does that mean federal courts lack the power of judicial review?

These examples present just a handful of the questions involving institutional powers that the U.S. Supreme Court has addressed.

Institutional powers constitute only one concern within constitutional law. The flip side also is worthy of consideration—constraints on those powers. As depicted in Figure I-2, the Framers not only gave each branch distinct authority, but also they worked out an intricate system of checks and balances. Because they "feared concentration of powers in a single branch," they provided each with mechanisms to rein in the others' authority.[24] Moreover, they made the institutions responsible to different sets of constituencies.

Although this system has worked successfully, it too has produced numerous constitutional questions, many of which become apparent when we have a politically divided government, such as a Republican president and a Democratic Congress, and one or the other is seeking to assert its authority. What is truly interesting about such cases is that they continue to appear at the Court's doorstep; despite the passage of 200 years, the justices have yet to resolve all the "big" constitutional questions. During the 1970s and 1980s the Court addressed many, including:

–May Congress call for the creation of a commission (whose members, including judges, would be appointed by the president) that would create mandatory sentencing guidelines for federal judges and that would be located within the judicial branch?
–May Congress write into laws legislative veto provisions by which to nullify actions of the executive branch?
–May Congress pass legislation requiring the attorney general to appoint a special prosecutor to investigate allegations of wrongdoing within the executive branch?

Federalism

Another weakness of the Articles of Confederation was the way it envisioned the relationship between the federal government and the states. As already noted, the national legislature was not only weak, it was more or less an apparatus con-

trolled by the states. They had set up the Articles of Confederation and, therefore, they empowered Congress.

The U.S. Constitution overcame this liability in two ways. First, it created three branches of government, all with significant authority. Second, it set out a plan of operation for the exercise of state and federal power. Called *federalism*, it works under the following constitutional guidelines:

–The Constitution grants certain legislative, executive, and judicial powers to the national government. Those not granted to the national government are reserved to the states.
–The Constitution makes the national government supreme. The Constitution, all laws passed in pursuance thereof, and treaties are the supreme law of the land. American citizens, most of whom are also state citizens, owe their primary allegiance to the national government; officers of the state governments owe the same allegiance.
–The Constitution denies some powers to both national and state governments, some only to the national government, and still others only to the state governments.[25]

By making the national government supreme in its spheres of authority, the Constitution corrected a flaw of the Articles of Confederation. Nevertheless, and in spite of the best efforts of the Framers to spell out the nature of federal-state relations, the Constitution left open many questions. Does the national government, particularly Congress, have powers beyond those that are enumerated in the text? For example, the Constitution authorizes Congress to lay and collect taxes, but does not explicitly empower it to create banks. Does that mean that Congress has no power to do so? Further, the Constitution is unclear as to whether the states also may exercise powers that are reserved to the federal govern-

24. Peltason, *Understanding the Constitution,* 21.

25. Adapted from Peltason, *Understanding the Constitution,* 16-17.

ment. For instance, states are not expressly prohibited from collecting taxes. Therefore, may Congress and the states both operate taxing systems?

As you know, the answer to both questions is yes. However, why that is the case is not explicitly answered by the Constitution. As a result, it has been left largely to elected government bodies through legislation and to the courts through interpretation to define the specifics of state-federal relations. The Supreme Court, in particular, by defining the boundaries of federal and state power, has helped shape the contours of American federalism.

Individual Rights and Liberties

For many of the Framers, the most important purpose of the new Constitution was to safeguard individual rights and liberties. That is why they created a limited government that would wield only those powers delegated to it and would be checked by its own component parts—the states and the people. The majority of the Founders felt it unnecessary to load the Constitution with specific individual rights. As Alexander Hamilton put it, "The Constitution is itself . . . a Bill of Rights." Under it the government could exercise only those functions specifically bestowed upon it; all other rights remained with the people. He and others felt that a laundry list of such rights might even be dangerous because it inevitably would leave some out.

For this reason and possibly others—for example, some argue that the Framers were too exhausted to draw up a list of rights—the Constitution was sent to the states without a bill of rights. That omission became the source of major controversy and served as the vehicle by which states exacted a compromise over the Constitution's ratification. The trouble started in January 1788. Although four states already had ratified the Constitution by this time, "the pace . . . slowed

considerably."[26] A movement opposed to ratification was growing in size and depth and was marshaling arguments to deter state convention delegates. These opponents, the so-called Anti-Federalists, most of all feared the Constitution's new balance of powers. They believed that strong state governments "provided the only sure defense of their liberties against a potentially tyrannical central authority"[27] and that the Constitution tipped the scales in favor of federal power. These fears were countered by the self-labeled Federalists, who favored passage of the Constitution. Although their arguments and writings took many forms, among the most important was a series of eighty-five articles published in New York newspapers under the *nom de plume* Publius. Written by John Jay, James Madison, and Alexander Hamilton, *The Federalist Papers*—as we shall see throughout this book—continue to provide great insight into the objectives and intent of the nation's Founders.

Debates between the Federalists and their opponents were often highly philosophical in tone, with emphasis on the appropriate roles and powers of national institutions. Yet, within the states, ratification drives were full of the stuff of ordinary politics. Massachusetts provides a case in point. According to one account, the following events transpired there:

Of the 355 delegates, 60 percent or more probably came to Boston on January 9 opposed. If the Federalists were to have any chance at all, they would need the hearty support of Samuel Adams, their already legendary Revolutionary hero, and of governor John Hancock, of Declaration immortality. Adams was tepid; Hancock, aloof and cool, preferring to wait and see which way the political tides might flow.

After three weeks of heated debate a delegation headed by Adams climbed Beacon Hill to knock on the door of the wealthy and gouty Hancock. They proposed that the governor declare for ratification on con-

26. Farber and Sherry, *A History of the American Constitution*, 177.
27. Urofsky, *A March of Liberty*, 97-98.

dition that a series of amendments be tacked on for the consideration of the Congress.

The price for Hancock's support? The presidency, if Virginia failed to ratify or if Washington declined to serve. Otherwise, the vice presidency or, some say, the promise of Bowdoin's support in the governor's race.

Hancock agreed to the bribe and, his feet swathed in bandages, was carried theatrically to the rostrum to make his "Conciliatory Proposition" as though it were his own brainchild. Adams, still the darling of both sides, seconded the resolution to consider the amendments, and a few days later added several of his own.

The Constitution carried on February 6, 187 to 168, making Massachusetts the sixth state to ratify.[28]

This compromise—the call for a bill of rights—caught on. One scholar has noted, "It worked so well that Madison now advocated its use wherever the vote promised to be close." As it turned out, Madison and other Federalists needed to use it quite often: of the nine states ratifying after January 1788, seven recommended that the new Congress consider amendments. New York and Virginia probably would not have agreed to the Constitution without such an addition; the latter actually called for a second constitutional convention for this purpose. Other states began revising their own wish lists of specific rights they wanted put into the document.[29]

The Federalists realized that if they did not accede to state demands, either the Constitution would not be ratified or a new constitutional convention would be necessary. Since neither alternative was particularly attractive, it was agreed to amend the document as soon as the new government came into power. And with that promise came the ratification of the Constitution by the requisite number of states a year after it had been drafted.

28. Joseph T. Keenan, *The Constitution of the United States* (Chicago: Dorsey Press, 1988), 32-33.
29. Alpheus T. Mason, *The States Rights Debate,* 2d ed. (New York: Oxford University Press, 1972), 92-93.

The eventual ratification of the Bill of Rights, on December 15, 1791, quieted those who had voiced objections. But the guarantees it contained continue to serve as fodder for debate and, most relevant here, for Supreme Court litigation. Many of these debates involve the construct of specific guarantees, such as free speech, free exercise of religion, and equal protection, under which individuals seek relief when governments allegedly infringe upon their rights. But, by the same token, they also often involve clashes between the authority of the government and the rights of individuals. Government has the power to protect the safety, health, morals, and general welfare of citizens, but individuals may not be deprived of their liberty without due process of law. For example, may government force employers to pay their employees a certain wage? Or does that infringe on the employer's liberty? The answers to this question and others like it are of obvious importance. They reveal the contours of government power in relation to individual rights.

READINGS

Beard, Charles A. *An Economic Interpretation of the Constitution.* New York: Macmillan, 1935.

Brown, Robert E. *Charles Beard and the Constitution.* Princeton, N.J.: Princeton University Press, 1956.

Farber, Daniel A., and Suzanna Sherry. *A History of the American Constitution.* St. Paul, Minn.: West Publishing, 1990.

Farrand, Max. *The Framing of the Constitution of the United States.* New Haven, Conn.: Yale University Press, 1913.

Jensen, Merrill. *The New Nation: A History of the United States During the Confederation, 1781-1789.* New York: Knopf, 1950.

Kramnick, Isaac, ed. *The Federalist Papers.* New York: Penguin Books, 1987.

McDonald, Forrest. *E Pluribus Unum.* Boston: Houghton Mifflin, 1965.

Roche, John P. "The Founding Fathers: A Reform Caucus in Action." *American Political Science Review* 55 (1961): 799-816.

Smith, David G. *The Convention and the Constitution.* New York: St. Martin's Press, 1965.

Warren, Charles. *The Making of the Constitution.* Boston: Little, Brown, 1928.

APPROACHES
TO CONSTITUTIONAL
INTERPRETATION

The balance of this book is devoted to narrative and case excerpts that reveal the interpretation of the Constitution by the U.S. Supreme Court. As a student approaching constitutional law, perhaps for the first time, you may think it is odd that the subject requires a 471-page book. After all, in length, the Constitution could fit easily into many Court decisions. Moreover, the document itself—its language—seems so clear.

As we hinted in the introduction to this book, however, first appearances can be deceiving. Even apparently clear constitutional scriptures do not necessarily lend themselves to clean constitutional interpretation. For example, according to Article I, Section 2, the president "shall be Commander in Chief of the Army and Navy of the United States." Sounds simple enough, doesn't it? But could you, based on those words, answer the following questions, all of which have been posed to the Court?

–May a president, during times of war, order a blockade of certain American ports?
–May Congress delegate to the president the power to order an arms embargo against nations at war?
–May a president, during times of war, order

that "traitors" be tried by military tribunals, rather than civilian courts?
–May a president, during times of international crisis, authorize the creation of military camps to intern potential "traitors" to prevent sabotage?

What these questions and others arising from different sections of the Constitution illustrate is that a gap often exists between the document's words and reality. Although its language may seem quite explicit, its meaning can be elusive and difficult to apply to actual circumstances.

In the final analysis, it is the gap between what the Constitution says (or does not say) and the kinds of concrete questions litigants ask the Court to address that explains why we devote a book to constitutional law. Because the meaning of the powers of government and the constraints on government are less than crystal clear, the institution charged with interpreting and applying them—the Supreme Court of the United States—has approached its task in a somewhat erratic way. Throughout the Court's history, justices of different political and ideological stripes have brought various modes of interpretation to constitutional mandates, which in turn have affected significantly the way the government—all branches and at all levels—operates. In this chapter, we review some of the major modes of interpretation, strains of which appear in justices' opinions in the chapters that follow.

The Doctrine of Original Intent

In *Marbury v. Madison* (1803) Chief Justice John Marshall enunciated the view that the Supreme Court has the power to strike down laws passed by Congress. He reasoned in part that the Framers of the Constitution intended for the Court to do so. About 200 years later, Chief Justice Warren E. Burger used the same grounds to find that Congress is constitutionally prohibited from attaching legislative veto provisions to laws.

Undoubtedly, between Marshall and Burger and now William H. Rehnquist, many chief justices and associate justices have looked to the intent of the Framers of the Constitution to reach conclusions about the disputes before them. But why? What possible relevance could their intentions have for today's controversies? Advocates of this approach, sometimes called *originalism,* offer several answers. First, they assert that the Framers acted in a calculated manner, that they obviously knew what they were doing, so why should we disregard their precepts? One adherent, former attorney general Edwin Meese III, wrote, "Those who framed the Constitution chose their words carefully; they debated at great length the most minute points. The language they chose meant something. It is incumbent upon the Court to determine what that meaning was."[1]

Second, by scrutinizing the intent of the Framers, justices can deduce certain "constitutional truths" that they can then apply to cases. Doing so, defeated Supreme Court nominee Robert Bork (and others) argue, would produce neu-

tral principles of law and thus eliminate value-laden decisions.[2] To understand what is meant by a value-laden decision, suppose the federal government enacted legislation forcing states to pay their employees a minimum wage. Justices could look at such a law in several ways. A justice who favors states' rights might conclude that the Tenth Amendment, which states, "The Powers not delegated to the United States by the Constitution . . . are reserved to the States," bars the federal government from interfering with the state-employee relationship, while a jurist who favors a strong national government might reach the opposite conclusion. They disagree because their policy orientations dictate different outcomes. Neither, however, is using proper jurisprudence, according to this school of thought; policy or ideological preferences should not creep into the law. Therefore, originalists favor an examination of the Framers' intent as a way to keep the law value free. Meese wrote,

[T]he Court [has] displayed . . . an inaccurate reading of the text of the Constitution and a disregard for the Framers' intention that state and local governments be a buffer against the centralizing tendencies of a national Leviathan. . . . In considering [this] area of adjudication—Federalism . . . —it seems fair to conclude that far too many of the Court's opinions were, on the whole, more policy choices than articulations of constitutional principle. The voting blocs, the arguments, all reveal a greater allegiance to what the Court thinks constitutes sound public policy than a deference to what the Constitution—its text and intention—may demand.[3]

Finally, supporters of this mode of analysis argue that it fosters stability in law. They feel the law today is far too fluid; it changes with the ideological whims of the justices, which, in turn, wreaks havoc for all those who must implement

1. Edwin Meese III, Address Before the American Bar Association, July 9, 1985, Washington, D.C.

2. See Robert Bork, "Neutral Principles and Some First Amendment Problems," *Indiana Law Journal* 47 (1971): 1-35.
3. Meese, Address.

and interpret Court decisions. Lower court judges, attorneys, and even average citizens do not know if rights existing today will be there tomorrow. Following a jurisprudence of original intent would eliminate such confusion because, Meese wrote, "[b]y seeking to judge policies in light of principles, rather than remold principles in light of policies, the Court could avoid both the charge of incoherence and the charge of being either too conservative or too liberal."[4]

Although many Supreme Court opinions contemplate the original intent of the Framers and the arguments in favor of such an approach seem to have merit, this view has come under attack. One reason for the increased controversy is that the philosophy became politicized during the Reagan presidency. Those who advocated it, particularly Meese and Bork, were widely viewed as conservatives using the doctrine to attain their own ideological ends. Others, however, have raised more concrete objections to this jurisprudence. Some argue that if justices employed only this approach, the Constitution would lose its applicability and be rendered useless. Justice William J. Brennan, Jr., wrote:

We current justices read the Constitution in the only way that we can: as Twentieth Century Americans. We look to the history of the time of framing and to the intervening history of interpretation. But the ultimate question must be, what do the words of the text mean in our time. For the genius of the Constitution rests not in any static meaning it might have had in a world that is dead and gone, but in the adaptability of its great principles to cope with current problems and current needs. What the constitutional fundamentals meant to the wisdom of other times cannot be their measure to the vision of our time. Similarly, what those fundamentals mean for us, our descendants will learn, cannot be the measure to the vision of their time.[5]

In short, Brennan argues that we must view the Constitution as a living document, flexible enough to adapt to the needs of today's citizens.

A second criticism is that the Constitution embodies not one intent, but many. Again, as Brennan wrote,

Faith in democracy is one thing, blind faith quite another. Those who drafted our Constitution understood the difference. One cannot read the text without admitting that it embodies substantive value choices; it places certain values beyond the power of any legislature. . . .

To remain faithful to the content of the Constitution, therefore, an approach to interpreting the text must account for the existence of these substantive value choices, and must accept the ambiguity inherent in the effort to apply them to modern circumstances.[6]

Historian Arthur Schlesinger, Jr., provided a poignant example of this ambiguity when he noted that Meese attacked the Dred Scott decision, which held that blacks did not enjoy the same constitutional status as whites, "as a violation of original intent. Yet Chief Justice Roger B. Taney [the opinion's author] based his decision squarely on 'original intent.'" In Taney's words:

[The Constitution] speaks not only in the same words, but with the same meaning and intent with which it spoke when it came from the hands of its framers, and was voted on and adopted by the people of the United States. Any other rule of construction would abrogate the judicial character of this court, and make it the mere reflex of the popular opinion or passion of the day.[7]

Such a discrepancy led Schlesinger to ask, "Whose version of original intent are we to believe: Roger Taney's in 1857 or Edwin Meese's in 1985?"[8]

Finally, from which sources should justices divine the original intentions of the Framers? Obviously, they could look at the records of the

4. Meese, Address.
5. William J. Brennan, Jr., Address to the Text and Teaching Symposium, Georgetown University, October 12, 1985, Washington, D.C.

6. Brennan, Address.
7. *Dred Scott v. Sandford,* 19 How. 393 at 426 (1857).
8. Arthur Schlesinger, Jr., "On 'Original Intent,'" *Wall Street Journal,* January 17, 1986, 18.

constitutional debates and the Founders' journals and papers. But far too often those documents fail to provide a single, clear message. Justice Robert H. Jackson wrote,

Just what our forefathers did envision, or would have envisioned had they foreseen modern conditions, must be divined from materials almost as enigmatic as the dreams Joseph was called upon to interpret for Pharoah. A century and a half of partisan debate and scholarly specification yields no net result but only supplies more or less apt quotations from respected sources on each side of any question. They largely cancel each other.[9]

Literalism

On the surface, literalism resembles the doctrine of original intent: it puts a premium on the Constitution. But that is where the similarity ends. In an effort to prevent the infusion of new meanings from sources outside the text of the Constitution, Bork, Meese, and other original intent adherents seek to deduce constitutional truths by examining the intended meanings behind the words. Literalists, however, consider only the plain or literal meaning of the words in the Constitution and apply that meaning to disputes. This distinction can lead to some extraordinary differences in case outcomes. Consider, for example, a case dealing with congressional hearings on subversive activity aimed at the overthrow of the U.S. government. In particular, let us say that during the course of investigating the extent of communist infiltration into the United States, Congress orders a witness to answer questions about his activities and those of others. The witness declines to do so on First Amendment grounds. Originalists would hold that "speech advocating violent overthrow is . . . not [protected] 'political speech' as that term must be defined by a Madisonian system of govern-

ment."[10] They would argue that Congress could compel the witness to testify. Literalists would scrutinize the words of the First Amendment—"Congress shall make no law . . . abridging the freedom of speech"—and read them literally: "no law" means "no law." Therefore, any government action infringing on speech, even that which prohibits expression advocating the overthrow of the government, would violate the First Amendment.

Although strains of literalism run through the opinions of many justices, Hugo L. Black is most closely associated with this view. During his nearly thirty-five-year tenure on the Court, Black continually reiterated the literalist philosophy. His own words best describe his position:

My view is, without deviation, without exception, without any ifs, buts, or whereases, that freedom of speech means that government shall not do anything to people . . . either for the views they have or the views they express or the words they speak or write. Some people would have you believe that this is a very radical position, and maybe it is. But all I am doing is following what to me is the clear wording of the First Amendment. . . . As I have said innumerable times before I simply believe that "Congress shall make no law" means Congress shall make no law. . . . Thus we have the absolute command of the First Amendment that no law shall be passed by Congress abridging freedom of speech or the press.[11]

As this statement indicates, Black applied literalism most often to cases involving the First Amendment, but he also invoked it to examine other kinds of constitutional disputes. In *Youngstown Sheet & Tube Co. v. Sawyer* (1952) the Court was asked to determine whether President Harry S. Truman could issue an order directing the secretary of commerce to seize the nation's steel mills, which, because of an impending strike, were under threat of being shut down.

9. *Youngstown Sheet and Tube Co. v. Sawyer,* 343 U.S. 579 at 634 (1952).

10. Bork, "Neutral Principles," 31.

11. Hugo L. Black, *A Constitutional Faith* (New York: Knopf, 1968), 45-46.

Truman argued that because the country was at war in Korea, the action was necessary "to avert a national catastrophe." Even so, Black refused to relent. Indeed, his response for the majority was classic literalism: "It is clear that if the President had the authority to issue the order he did, it must be found in some provision of the Constitution. . . . The order cannot properly be sustained [because] . . . the Constitution limits his functions in the lawmaking process to the recommending of laws he thinks wise and the vetoing of laws he thinks bad."

Why did Black advocate literalism? Like those favoring original intent, Black saw literalism as a value-free form of jurisprudence. If justices looked only at the words of the Constitution, their decisions would not reflect ideological or political values, but rather those of the document. Following this philosophy, Black almost always supported claims of free speech against government challenges, but he refused to extend constitutional protection to expression that was not precisely speech. He asserted that activities such as flag burning, even if designed to express political views, fell outside the speech protected by the First Amendment.

Despite the high regard scholars have for Black, many have attacked his jurisprudence. John Hart Ely asserts that it led Black to "quixotic" views, particularly of the coverage of the First Amendment.[12] For example, most analysts and justices—even liberals—agree that obscene material falls outside of First Amendment protection and that states can prohibit its dissemination. But in opinion after opinion, Black clung to the view that no publication could be banned on the grounds that it was obscene. In *Smith v. California* (1959) Black wrote separately, primarily to express his displeasure with the use of legal standards that may allow for the suppression of obscene material. He asserted:

Certainly the First Amendment's language leaves no room for inference that abridgments of speech and press can be made just because they are slight. That Amendment provides, in simple words, that "Congress shall make no law . . . abridging the freedom of speech, or of the press." I read "no law . . . abridging" to mean *no law abridging*. The First Amendment, which is the supreme law of the land, has thus fixed its own value on freedom of speech and press by putting these freedoms wholly "beyond the reach" of *federal* power to abridge. No other provision of the Constitution purports to dilute the scope of the unequivocal commands of the First Amendment. Consequently, I do not believe that any federal agencies, including Congress and the Court, have power or authority to subordinate speech and press to what they think are "more important interests." The contrary notion is, in my judgment, court-made, not Constitution-made.[13]

Even those who *generally* agreed with literalism thought such a view went a bit too far.

A second objection is that literalism can result in wholly inconsistent outcomes. For example, is it really sensible for Black to hold that obscenity is constitutionally protected, while the desecration of the flag is not? Moreover, there were times when even Black could not abide by his own approach. During World War II he allowed President Franklin D. Roosevelt to issue an order "excluding all persons of Japanese descent" from certain designated areas on the West Coast, but he held that President Truman lacked the authority to seize the nation's steel mills. How did he justify the earlier decision? He said, "[B]ecause we are at war with the Japanese Empire . . . and . . . because Congress, reposing its confidence in this time of war in our military leaders—as inevitably it must—determined that they should have the power to do just this."[14] The decision may been reasonable in the context of the times, but certainly it is difficult to justify under a literal reading of the Constitution.

12. See John Hart Ely, *Democracy and Distrust* (Cambridge, Mass.: Harvard University Press, 1980).

13. *Smith v. California,* 361 U.S. 147 at 157-158 (1959).
14. *Korematsu v. United States,* 323 U.S. 214 at 223 (1944).

Meaning of the Words

The "meaning of the words" approach to constitutional interpretation, most associated with W. W. Crosskey, has its roots in both literalism and originalism.[15] It emphasizes the words of the Constitution at the time the Framers wrote them. But differences exist. Whereas literalists stress the words themselves, this mode emphasizes their meaning; whereas originalism "places a premium upon reasoning that is historically grounded, the meaning of the words focuses upon lexicographic skill."[16] In other words, "the 'meaning' mode attempts to define the words of the Constitution according to what they meant at the time the document or its amendment was written."[17]

The merits of this approach are quite similar to those of literalism and originalism. By focusing on how the Framers defined their own words and then applying their definitions to disputes over those constitutional provisions containing them, this approach seeks to generate value-free and ideology-free jurisprudence. Of even greater importance, its adherents argue, is that it attempts to "preserve some sense of stability and continuity in the agreement and understandings on which legitimate governmental power is based."[18]

Chief Justice Marshall's opinion in *Gibbons v. Ogden* (1824), which, in part, involved a dispute over the congressional power to regulate interstate commerce, provides a particularly good illustration of the value of this approach. As part of his decision, Marshall felt it necessary to deter-

mine the meaning of the word *commerce*. Rather than fashion his own definition, Marshall turned to how the Framers defined it at the time they wrote it:

America understands, and has uniformly understood, the word "commerce," to comprehend navigation. It was so understood, and must have been so understood, when the constitution was framed. The power over commerce, including navigation, was one of the primary objects for which the people of America adopted their government, and must have been contemplated in forming it.

Like the other modes we have examined, the meaning of the words approach is not without its criticisms. One objection is similar to that often leveled at originalism: it is too static. C. Herman Pritchett noted that like originalism, it can "make a nation the prisoner of its past, and reject any method of constitutional development save constitutional amendment.[19] Because seafaring vessels were the primary instruments of commerce in 1787, it was rather easy for Marshall to conclude in *Gibbons* that commerce "comprehend[s]" navigation. Although one could try to make an equally compelling case today for airplanes, it would be a far more difficult task.

Another criticism is that the "original meaning may be as difficult to establish as original intent."[20] In our discussion of originalism, we pointed out that it was often hard, for many reasons, to determine the intent of the Framers. Attempting to understand what they meant by each word can be just as rigorous, requiring the development of a specialized dictionary, which could take years of research to compile and still not have any value—determinate or otherwise. Even Marshall seemed to recognize this problem when he wrote:

A Constitution . . . [which] would partake of the prolixity of a legal code . . . could scarcely be em-

15. See W. W. Crosskey, *Politics and the Constitution in the History of the United States* (Chicago: University of Chicago Press, 1953).

16. David W. Rohde and Harold J. Spaeth, *Supreme Court Decision Making* (San Francisco: W. H. Freeman, 1976), 41.

17. Ibid.

18. C. Herman Pritchett, *Constitutional Law of the Federal System* (Englewood Cliffs, N.J.: Prentice-Hall, 1984), 37.

19. Ibid.
20. Ibid.

braced by the human mind. It would probably never be understood by the public. Its nature, therefore, requires that only its great outlines should be marked, its important objects designated, and the minor ingredients which compose those objects be deduced from the nature of the objects themselves.[21]

Logical Reasoning

Unlike originalism or the meaning of the words approach, logical reasoning is not dependent on historical interpretations of particular constitutional provisions. Rather, it suggests that judges do "what all intelligent people do when obliged to interpret a document: analyze its terms, then try to discern the premises of its arguments and the conclusions to which they lead."[22] Logical analysis often takes the form of a syllogism, consisting of a major premise, which "sets forth a proposition"; a minor premise, which "contains an assertion related to the major premise"; and a conclusion, which logically follows from both major and minor premises.

Chief Justice Marshall's opinion in *Marbury v. Madison* provides an oft-cited example of logical reasoning in action:

MAJOR PREMISE: A law repugnant to the Constitution is void.
MINOR PREMISE: This law is repugnant to the Constitution.
CONCLUSION: Therefore, this law is void.

The beauty of logical analysis, as this example illustrates, is that the resulting decision takes on an objective, perhaps even a scientific, aura. In other words, Marshall's syllogism suggests that anybody with a logical mind would reach the same conclusion. But is this necessarily so? Consider another syllogism:

MAJOR PREMISE: Sweden has many storks.
MINOR PREMISE: Storks deliver babies.
CONCLUSION: Therefore, Sweden has many babies.

We know that storks do not deliver babies, and therein lies the problem with logical analysis: it "exists independently of factual or empirical analysis." Therefore, "almost any conclusion can be given logical form."[23] To understand why this assertion is correct, compare the two syllogisms. If we assume that the major premises of both are accurate, then "the soundness of [their] conclusion[s] depends upon whether the minor premise is *factually* true."[24] Obviously, storks do not deliver babies, but is Marshall's minor premise any more believable or, more to the point, logically driven? Put another way, can logic reveal whether a particular law is repugnant to the Constitution?

To many the answer is no. David Rohde and Harold Spaeth suggest that logical reasoning "enables judges to make decisions compatibly with their personal policy preferences and at the same time causing their opinions and decisions to exhibit a semblance of order and a quality of connectedness."[25] Justice Oliver Wendell Holmes, Jr., put it this way:

The life of the law has not been logic: it has been experience. The felt necessities of the time, the prevalent moral and political theories, intuitions of public policy, avowed or unconscious, even the prejudices which judges share with their fellow-men, have had a good deal more to do than the syllogism in determining the rules by which men should be governed.

Stare Decisis

Translated from Latin, the term *stare decisis* means "to abide by, or adhere to, decided cases."

---

21. *McCulloch v. Maryland,* 4 Wheat. 316 (1819).
22. Walter F. Murphy, James E. Fleming, and William F. Harris II, *American Constitutional Interpretation* (Mineola, N.Y.: Foundation Press), 302-303.
23. Ibid., 43.
24. Pritchett, *Constitutional Law of the Federal System,* 38.
25. Rohde and Spaeth, *Supreme Court Decision Making,* 43.

What the term suggests is that, as a general rule, judges and justices should decide cases on the basis of previously established precedent. In shorthand terms, judicial tribunals should "honor prior rulings."[26] Many assert that Chief Justice Earl Warren did just that in *Watkins v. United States* (1957) to resolve one of Watkins's claims, that some questions put to him by a congressional committee violated his First Amendment rights. Grounding his ruling at least in part on a related Supreme Court case, Warren wrote:

The Court recognized the restraints of the Bill of Rights upon congressional investigations in United States v. Rumely. . . . It was concluded that, when First Amendment rights are threatened, the delegation of power to [a] committee [to conduct investigations] must be clearly revealed in its charter.[27]

The benefits of this approach are fairly evident. Ralph Rossum and G. Alan Tarr wrote, "Reliance on precedent . . . adds stability, continuity, and predictability to the entire legal enterprise."[28] Chief Justice Harlan F. Stone acknowledged the value of precedent in a somewhat more ironic way: "The rule of *stare decisis* embodies a wise policy because it is often more important that a rule of law be settled than that it be settled right."[29] The message, however, is the same: if the Court adheres to past decisions, it provides some direction to all who labor in the legal enterprise. Lower court judges know how they should and should not decide cases; lawyers can frame their arguments in accord with the lessons of past cases; legislatures understand what they may and may not enact or regulate, and so forth. In addition, as Sheldon Goldman notes, the

"rule of precedent symbolizes that we are dealing with a court of law as distinguished from a legislative body."[30] It is one of the features that makes the judiciary unique.

Precedent, then, is an important and useful factor in Supreme Court decision making. It is interesting to note that not only does the Court rarely reverse itself (only 175 times over its entire history), but also it almost always cites previous rulings in its decisions.[31] But we should not necessarily take these statements to mean that the justices follow this approach. Many allege that judicial appeal to precedent often is mere window dressing, used to hide their ideologies and values, rather than a substantive form of analysis. There are several reasons for this allegation.

First, courts have generated so much precedent that it is usually possible to find support for any conclusion. By way of proof, turn to any page of any case in this book and you probably will find the opinion writer citing precedent.

Second, it may be difficult to "locate" the rule of law, the *ratio decidendi,* emerging in a majority opinion, and "technically, a court is bound to follow not everything stated in a relevant precedent, but only the rule of law that was necessary for decision in that case, what is called the holding."[32] Other language in a given opinion—*obiter dicta*—has no legal weight, and judges are not bound by it. It is up to courts to separate the *ratio decidendi* from *dicta.* Doing so can be a difficult task, but it provides a way for justices to skirt precedent with which they do not agree. All they need to do is declare "portions of the reasoning upon which the previous decision was based to be *dicta.*"[33] By the same token, justices can

26. Louis Fisher, *Constitutional Dialogues* (Princeton, N.J.: Princeton University Press, 1988), 80.

27. *Watkins v. United States,* 354 U.S. 178 at 198 (1957).

28. Ralph A. Rossum and G. Alan Tarr, *American Constitutional Law,* 3d. ed. (New York: St. Martin's Press, 1991), 4.

29. *United States. v. Underwriters Association,* 322 U.S. 533, 579 (1944).

30. Sheldon Goldman, *Constitutional Law,* 2d ed. (New York: HarperCollins, 1991), 13.

31. Stephen L. Wasby, *The Supreme Court in the Federal Judicial System,* 3d ed. (Chicago: Nelson-Hall, 1988), 269.

32. Lawrence Baum, *The Supreme Court,* 4th ed. (Washington, D.C.: CQ Press, 1992), 132.

33. Rohde and Spaeth, *Supreme Court Decision Making,* 36.

brush aside even the *ratio decidendi* when it suits their interests. Because the Supreme Court, at least today, is so selective about the cases it chooses to decide, it probably would not take one for which clear precedent existed. Even in the past, two cases that were precisely identical would not be accepted. What this means is that justices can always deal with "problematic" *ratio decidendi* (that which they dislike) by distinguishing the case at hand from those that have already been decided. The Court's later interpretation of the *Watkins* decision provides a good example. As we describe in some detail in Chapter 3, just two years after it ruled in favor of John T. Watkins, the Court heard *Barenblatt v. United States* (1959) in which it looked again at whether a congressional committee could question an individual about his political beliefs and associations. Like Watkins, Lloyd Barenblatt alleged that he could refuse to answer such questions because they infringed on his First Amendment rights. But the Court "distinguished the *Watkins* precedent by authorizing investigating committees to 'balance' the competing . . . interests."[34]

Third, and most interesting, many justices recognize the limits of *stare decisis* in cases involving constitutional interpretation. As Justice William O. Douglas once wrote, a judge should support the Constitution, "not the gloss which his predecessors may have put on it."[35] But Justice Black may have said it best:

Ordinarily it is sound policy to adhere to prior decisions but this practice has quite properly never been a blind, inflexible rule. Courts are not omniscient. Like every other human agency, they too can profit from trial and error, from experience and reflection. As others have demonstrated, the principle commonly referred to as *stare decisis* has never been thought to extend so far as to prevent the courts from correcting

their own errors. . . . Indeed, the Court has a special responsibility where questions of constitutional law are involved to review its decisions from time to time and where compelling reasons present themselves to refuse to follow erroneous precedents; otherwise its mistakes in interpreting the Constitution are extremely difficult to alleviate and needlessly so.[36]

Balancing Approaches

So far we have examined five modes of analysis that are not case specific, meaning that conclusions reached by literalists and original intent advocates, for example, on points of law would not waiver with the facts of a given case. Presumably, originalists always would hold that the First Amendment does not protect speech advocating the violent overthrow of the government, and literalists always would reach precisely the opposite conclusion, regardless of the specific controversy at hand. Supporters of a balancing approach take a position that is more case specific than philosophical; that is, in each case they balance the interests of the individual against those of the government. Their decisions can vary because at times an individual's activity outweighs the government's interest in prohibiting it, while at other times the reverse holds true.

Justices invoking this approach, however, have not done so monolithically. Some take a very strict view of balancing, giving the interests of individuals and governments precisely equal weight. They justify doing so on constitutional and philosophical grounds, saying, for example, that while the First Amendment protects individual speech, the text of the Constitution gives legislatures the power to enact laws, which may sometimes interfere with such speech. The Court, according to this view, should initially give equal weight to both and then balance them to determine which should fall. Justice John Marshall Harlan's

34. Ibid., 37.
35. William O. Douglas, "Stare Decisis," *Columbia Law Review* 49 (1949): 736.
36. *Green v. United States*, 356 U.S. 165, 195 (1958).

opinion in *Barenblatt* demonstrates this theory in practice. To Barenblatt's allegation that he could refuse to answer questions about his political beliefs and associations, Harlan responded:

Where First Amendment rights are asserted to bar governmental interrogations, resolution of the issue always involves a balancing by the courts of the competing private and public interests at stake in the particular circumstances shown.

He held that, in this instance, the scale favored the government over the individual.

Balancing also can take at least two other forms. While some opinions, such as Harlan's in *Barenblatt,* weigh equally the claims of the government and the individual, others give preference to one or the other. In accordance with a philosophy of judicial restraint, Justice Felix Frankfurter often balanced government versus individual interests, but with a finger on the scale: he gave preference to the state over the individual. He did so out of the belief that a body made up of unelected judges should not readily overturn laws passed by legislatures composed of representatives elected by the populace. In his view,

the framers of the Constitution denied . . . legislative powers to the federal judiciary. They chose instead to insulate the judiciary from the legislative function. They did not grant to this Court supervision over legislation. . . . [T]he removal of unwise laws from the statute books . . . lies, not to the court, but to the ballot and to the processes of democratic government.[37]

In contrast to Frankfurter's perspective is one that tips the balance to favor individual rights and liberties.[38] Although this approach is most often associated with First Amendment freedoms, Courts also have invoked it to adjudicate disputes involving economic liberties. For example, in *Lochner v. New York* (1905) the justices examined a state law that established maximum work hours for bakery employees. New York defended its law as a valid exercise of its police powers, its ability to legislate in the best interests of its citizens. An employer challenged it as a violation of his liberty to enter into a contract with his employees. Writing for the majority, Justice Rufus W. Peckham acknowledged the need for the Court to balance these interests, but to do so with a bias in favor of the individual. He wrote:

Statutes of the nature of that under review, limiting the hours in which grown and intelligent men may labor to earn their living, are mere meddlesome interferences with the rights of the individual, and they are not saved from condemnation by the claim that they are passed in the exercise of the police power.

The holding in *Lochner* has since been overruled, and now the government may regulate employee work hours. But the logic of balancing rights with a bias in favor of the individual is still invoked, only today more often in conjunction with rights and liberties contained in the first ten amendments. Justice Jackson explained:

The very purpose of a Bill of Rights was to withdraw certain subjects from the vicissitudes of political controversy, to place them beyond the reach of majorities and officials and to establish them as legal principles to be applied by the courts. One's right to life, liberty, and property, to free speech, a free press, freedom of worship and assembly, and other fundamental rights may not be submitted to vote; they depend on the outcome of no elections.[39]

Critiques of the various forms of balancing often are less pointed than those we have already examined, and more philosophical in orientation.[40] Debates over this mode of analysis gener-

---

37. *West Virginia v. Barnette,* 319 U.S. 624 (1943).
38. As C. Herman Pritchett wrote, "Advocates of the preferred position . . . also allowed for balancing, but [put] freedom's thumb on the scales." *Constitutional Civil Liberties* (Englewood Cliffs, N.J.: Prentice-Hall, 1984), 30.

39. *West Virginia v. Barnette,* 319 U.S. 624 (1943).
40. But, for more specific criticisms of balancing, see Laurent B. Frantz, "The First Amendment in the Balance," *Yale Law Journal* 71 (1962): 1424-50. On the preferred freedoms approach, see Felix Frankfurter's dissent in *Kovacs v. Cooper,* 336 U.S. 77 (1949).

ally have centered on views about the role of the Supreme Court in a democratic society. Those opposed to the equal balancing of Harlan and to the judicial restraint of Frankfurter contend that each ignores the Court's role of protecting minority interests. According to this argument, justices, because they are not elected officials, are in the best position to protect those who represent unpopular views. As Justice Brennan wrote in *NAACP v. Button* (1963):

Groups which find themselves unable to achieve their objectives through the ballot frequently turn to the courts. Just as it was true of the opponents of New Deal legislation during the 1930s, for example, no less is it true of the Negro minority today. *And under the conditions of modern government, litigation may well be the sole practicable avenue open to a minority to petition for redress of grievances. . . . For such a group, association for litigation may be the most effective form of political association* (emphasis added).

Brennan opposed doctrines like absolute balancing because they almost always lead to decisions in favor of the majority. In *Barenblatt,* for example, would it have been possible for Justice Harlan to weigh the interests of society, the whole population of the country, against one person and reach any other conclusion?

Using the reverse logic, Frankfurter and others chastise adherents of a position giving special treatment to individual rights and liberties. In Frankfurter's view, that posture is "mischievous" because its application gives the Court too much power. When Congress and other legislative bodies enact laws that reflect the will of the people, why should the Court strike them down?

In this light, the Court should be seen as part of the ruling regime, willing to reflect its wishes.

As you read the narrative and cases that follow, try to keep these different approaches in mind. They and variations of them show up in many opinions. Two questions inevitably arise: Do the justices use certain modes of analysis to reach decisions? Or do they reach conclusions first and then invoke interpretative approaches to justify them?

READINGS

Baum, Lawrence. *The Supreme Court,* 4th ed. Washington, D.C.: CQ Press, 1992.

Bickel, Alexander. *The Least Dangerous Branch of Government.* Indianapolis: Bobbs-Merrill, 1962.

Brigham, John. *Constitutional Language: An Interpretation of Judicial Decision.* Westport, Conn.: Greenwood Press, 1978.

Crosskey, W. W. *Politics and the Constitution in the History of the United States.* Chicago: University of Chicago Press, 1953.

Ducat, Craig R. *Modes of Constitutional Interpretation.* St. Paul, Minn.: West Publishing, 1978.

Fisher, Louis. *Constitutional Dialogues.* Princeton, N.J.: Princeton University Press, 1988.

Garvey, John H., and T. Alexander Aleinikoff. *Modern Constitutional Theory.* St. Paul, Minn: West Publishing, 1989.

Holmes, Oliver Wendell. *The Common Law.* Boston: Little, Brown, 1881.

O'Neill, Timothy J. "The Language of Equality in a Constitutional Order." *American Political Science Review* 75 (1981): 626-635.

Rohde, David W., and Harold J. Spaeth. *Supreme Court Decision Making.* San Francisco: W. H. Freeman, 1976.

Shapiro, Martin. "Stability and Change in Judicial Decision Making: Incrementalism or Stare Decisis." *Law in Transition Quarterly* 2 (1965): 134-157.

Wasby, Stephen L. *The Supreme Court in the Federal Judicial System,* 3d ed. Chicago: Nelson-Hall, 1988.

PART II

INSTITUTIONAL AUTHORITY

THE SEPARATION OF POWERS

One of the first things anyone learns in an American government course is that the Constitution prescribes a government consisting of three branches: the legislative, the executive, and the judicial. Each plays a distinct role: the legislature makes the laws, the executive implements those laws, and the judiciary interprets them.

This initial view of the American political system remains apt, but it is an overly simplified version. It tells us of the relative powers of the branches of government, but not of their limits. It ignores the fact that policy in the United States emanates not from the separate actions of the branches of government, but from the interaction among them.

To move beyond the basics of the powers and constraints of institutions requires a consideration of two important subjects. First, we must understand the separation of powers doctrine and why the Framers adopted it, a subject we take up in the following pages. Second, because of the unique role played by the judiciary in the American government system, we must grasp the importance of the Supreme Court's decisions relating to the authority of the three branches of government as well as the constitutional constraints placed upon those institutions. We consider these matters in the next three chapters.

The Origins of the Separation of Powers Doctrine

Even a casual comparison of the Articles of Confederation with the Constitution reveals major differences in the way the two documents structured the national government. Under the Articles, the powers of government were concentrated in the legislature, a unicameral Congress, with the states having equal voting powers. There was no executive or judicial branch separate and independent from the legislature. Issues of separation of powers and checks and balances were not particularly relevant to the Articles, largely because the national government had little power that might be abused. The states were capable of checking anything the central government proposed and provided whatever restraints the newly independent nation needed.

The government under the Articles failed for the most part because it lacked sufficient power and authority to cope with the problems of the day. The requirements for amending the document were so restrictive that fundamental change within the Articles proved impossible. When the Constitutional Convention met in Philadelphia in 1787, the delegates soon concluded that the Articles had to be scrapped and replaced with a charter that would provide more effective power for the national government. The Framers had experienced conditions of economic decline, crippling taxation policies, interstate barriers to commerce, and isolated but alarming insurrections among the lower economic classes. A newly structured national government was seen as the only method of dealing with the problems besetting the nation in the aftermath of the Revolution.

But allocating significant power to the national government was not without its risks. Many of the Framers feared the creation of a federal power capable of dominating the states and abusing individual liberties. It was apparent to all that the new government would have to be structured in a way that the potential for abuse and excess would be minimized. The concept of the separation of powers and its twin, the idea of checks and balances, appealed to the Framers as the best way to accomplish these necessary restraints.

The theory of separation of powers was not new to the Framers. They were introduced to it by the political philosophy of the day and by their own political experiences. The theories of James Harrington and Charles de Montesquieu were particularly influential in this respect. Harrington (1611-1677) was an English political philosopher whose emphasis on the importance of property found a sympathetic audience among the former colonists. Harrington's primary work, *Oceana*, published in 1656, was a widely read description of a model government. Incorporated into Harrington's ideal state was the notion that government powers ought to be divided into three parts. A Senate made up of the intellectual elite would propose laws; the people, guided by the Senate's wisdom, would enact the laws; and a magistrate would execute the laws. This system, Harrington argued, would impose an important balance that would maintain a stable government and protect rights to property.

Harrington's concept of a separation of powers was less well developed than that later proposed by Montesquieu (1689-1755), a French political theorist. His *Spirit of the Laws* (1748), widely

circulated during the last half of the eighteenth century, is considered the classic treatise on the separation of powers philosophy. Montesquieu was concerned about government abuse of liberty. In his estimation, liberty could not long prevail if too much power accrued to a single ruler or a single branch of government. He flatly warned, ''When the legislative and executive powers are united in the same person, or the same body of magistrats, there can be no liberty. . . . Again, there is no liberty if the judicial power be not separated from the legislative and executive.'' Although Montesquieu's message was directed at the citizens of his own country, he found a more receptive audience in the United States.

The influence of these political thinkers was reinforced by the political experiences of the Framers. The settlers came to the New World largely to escape the abuses of the European governments. The treatment of the colonies by George III taught them that executives were not to be trusted with too much power. They also feared an independent and powerful judiciary, especially if it were not answerable to the people. While the legislature was undoubtedly the institution in which the Framers had the most confidence, they knew it too had the potential of exceeding proper bounds. The English experience during the reign of Oliver Cromwell was lesson enough that muting the power of the king did not necessarily lead to the elimination of government abuse. What the Framers sought was balance, a system in which each branch of government would be strong enough to stop excessive power flowing into the hands of any other single branch. This necessary balance, as John Adams pointed out in his *Defense of the Constitutions of Government of the United States of America,* would also have the advantage of being able to keep the power-hungry aristocracy in check and prevent the majority from taking the rights away from the minority.

Separation of Powers and the Constitution

The debates at the Constitutional Convention and the various plans that were presented for the delegates' consideration all focused on the issue of dividing government power among the three branches as well as between the national government and the states. A general fear of a concentration of power permeated all the discussions. James Madison noted, "The truth is, all men having power ought to be distrusted to a certain degree." The Framers' solution to the exceedingly difficult problem of expanding government power, while at the same time reducing the probability of abuse, was found in their proposed new Constitution of the United States.

Although the term *separation of powers* is nowhere to be found in the document, the Constitution plainly adopts the central tenets of the theory. A reading of the first lines of each of the first three articles makes this point clearly.

–All legislative Powers herein granted shall be vested in a Congress of the United States, which shall consist of a Senate and House of Representatives. [Article I]

–The executive Power shall be vested in a President of the United States of America. [Article II]

–The judicial Power of the United States, shall be vested in one supreme Court, and in such inferior Courts as the Congress may from time to time ordain and establish. [Article III]

In the scheme of government incorporated into the Constitution, the legislative, executive, and judicial powers each resided in a separate branch of government. Unless otherwise specified in the document, each branch was limited to the political function granted to it, and that function could not be exercised by either of the other two branches. In addition to the separation concept, the Framers placed into the Constitution a number of mixed powers. That is, while the document reserves certain functions for specific branches, it also provides explicit checks on the exercise of those powers. As a consequence, each branch of government imposes limits on the primary functions of the others. A few examples illustrate this point:

–Congress has the right to pass legislation, but the president may veto those bills.

–The president may veto bills passed by Congress, but the legislature may override that veto.

–The president may make treaties with foreign powers, but the Senate must ratify those treaties.

–The president is commander in chief of the army and navy, but Congress must pass legislation to raise armies, regulate the military, and declare war.

–The president may nominate federal judges, but the Senate must confirm them.

–The judiciary may interpret the law and even strike down laws as being in violation of the Constitution, but Congress may pass new legislation or propose constitutional amendments.

–Congress may pass laws, but the executive must enforce them.

In addition to these offsetting powers, the Framers structured each branch so that the criteria and procedures for selecting the officials of each institution differed, as did their tenures. Consequently, each branch has a slightly different source of political power. In the original scheme these differences were even more pronounced than they are today.

In the original version of the Constitution, for example, the two houses of Congress were politically dependent upon different selection processes. Members of the House were, as they are today, directly elected by the people, and the seats were apportioned among the states on the basis of population. With terms of only two years, the representatives were required to go back to the people for review on a frequent and regular basis.

Senators, on the other hand, were, and still are, representatives of whole states, with each state having two members in the upper chamber. But senators originally were selected by the state legislatures, a system that was not changed until the Seventeenth Amendment, which imposed popular election of senators, was ratified in 1913. The six-year, staggered terms of senators were intended to make the upper house less immediately responsive to the volatile nature of public opinion.

The Constitution dictated that the president be selected by an Electoral College, a group of political elites selected by the people or their representatives who would exercise judgment in casting their ballots among presidential candidates. Although the electors over time have ceased to perform any truly independent selection function, presidential selection remains a step away from direct popular election. The president's four-year term places the office squarely between the tenures conferred on representatives and senators. The original Constitution placed no limits on the number of terms a president could serve, but a traditional two-term limit was observed until 1940 and was then imposed by constitutional amendment in 1951.

Differing altogether from the other two branches is the judiciary, which was assigned the least democratic selection system. The people have no direct role in the selection or retention of federal judges. Instead, the president nominates individuals for the federal bench, and the Senate confirms. Once in office, federal judges serve for terms of good behavior, removable against their will only through impeachment. The intent of the Framers was to make the judiciary independent. To do so they created a system in which judges would not depend on the mood of the masses nor on a single appointing power. Furthermore, judges would be accountable only to their own philosophies and consciences, with no periodic review or reassessment required.

Through a division of powers, an imposition of checks, and a variation in selection and tenure requirements, the Framers hoped to achieve the balanced government they desired. This structure, they thought, would be the greatest protection against abuses of power and government violations of personal liberties and property rights. Many delegates to the Constitutional Convention considered this system of separation of powers a much more effective method of protecting civil liberties than the formal pronouncements of a bill of rights.

Most political observers would conclude that the Framers' invention has worked remarkably well. As the government has evolved through the years, the relative strengths of the branches have changed back and forth. At certain times, for example, the judiciary was exceptionally weak, such as during the pre-Marshall era and before the Civil War. At other times, however, the judiciary has been criticized as being too powerful such as when it repeatedly blocked New Deal legislation in the 1930s or expanded civil liberties during the Warren Court era. The executive also has led the other branches in political power. Beginning with the tenure of Franklin Roosevelt, for example, and extending into the 1970s, one often heard references to the "imperial presidency." But when one branch gains too much power and abuses occur, as in the case of Richard Nixon and the Watergate crisis, the system tends to reimpose the balance intended by the Framers.

In the next three chapters we explore the constitutional separation of powers, reviewing the basic grants of authority extended to each branch of the government and the limitations placed on those powers. We also examine the significant political and legal clashes among the executive, legislative, and judicial branches, focusing on how the justices of the Supreme Court have interpreted and applied the Constitution to settle these disputes. Throughout these constitutional controversies fundamental issues of institutional powers and the constraints placed on those powers have taken center stage.

READINGS

Fisher, Louis. *The Constitution between Friends*. New York: St. Martin's Press, 1978.

Gwyn, William B. *The Meaning of the Separation of Powers*. New Orleans, La.: Tulane University, 1965.

Knight, Barbara B. *Separation of Powers in the American Political System*. Fairfax, Va.: George Mason University Press, 1989.

Kurland, Philip B. *Watergate and the Constitution*. Chicago: University of Chicago Press, 1978.

Pocock, J. G. A. *The Political Works of James Harrington*. New York: Cambridge University Press, 1977.

Richter, Melvin. *The Political Theory of Montesquieu*. New York: Cambridge University Press, 1977.

Vanderbilt, Arthur T. *The Doctrine of the Separation of Powers and its Present Day Significance*. Lincoln: University of Nebraska Press, 1953.

Vile, M. J. C. *Constitutionalism and the Separation of Powers*. Oxford: Clarendon Press, 1967.

CHAPTER 2

THE JUDICIARY

Between 1932 and 1983 Congress attached legislative veto provisions to more than 200 laws. Although these provisions took different forms, among the more common were those that authorized one house of Congress to invalidate a decision of the executive branch. For example, under the Immigration and Nationality Act, Congress gave the U.S. attorney general power to suspend the deportation of aliens. However, it reserved the authority to veto, by a majority vote in either house, any such suspension.

In *Immigration and Naturalization Service v. Chadha* (1983), the U.S. Supreme Court found this device violative of specific clauses and of general principles contained in the U.S. Constitution. In doing so, as Justice Byron R. White wrote in his dissent, the Court sounded the "death knell" for the legislative veto.

In many ways, the Court's action was less than startling. For nearly two centuries federal courts have exerted the power of judicial review, the power to review acts of government to determine their compatibility with the U.S. Constitution. And, despite the fact that the Constitution does not explicitly give them such power, the courts' authority to do so has rarely been challenged. Indeed, today we take for granted the notion that federal courts will review government actions and will strike them down if they violate constitutional mandates.

Nevertheless, when courts do exert this power, as the U.S. Supreme Court did in *Chadha,* they provoke controversy. Look at it from this perspective: Congress, composed of officials we *elect,* passed these legislative veto provisions, which were then rendered invalid by a Supreme Court of nine *unelected* judges. Such an occurrence strikes some people as quite odd, perhaps even antidemocratic. Why should Americans allow a branch of government, over which we have no electoral control, to review and nullify the actions of government officials whom we elect, who represent us?

The alleged antidemocratic nature of judicial review is just one of many controversies surrounding the practice. In this chapter, we review others—both in theory and in practice. Before we do, however, we explore the development of judicial review in the United States. Many of the early justifications for the practice are still fueling contemporary debates.

Judicial review is the primary weapon, the check that federal courts have over other branches of government. Because this power could be awesome in scope, many tend to emphasize it to the neglect of factors that constrain its use, as well as other checks on the power of the Court. In the second part of this chapter, we explore the limits on judicial power.

Judicial Review

Even though judicial review is the most powerful tool of federal courts, it is not, for reasons we discuss later, a power contained within the Constitution, although there is evidence to suspect that the Framers intended for courts to have it (*see pages 50–51.*) Quite early in our history, federal courts claimed it for themselves. In *Hylton v. United States* (1796), Daniel Hylton challenged the constitutionality of a 1793 federal tax on carriages. According to Hylton, the act violated the constitutional mandate that direct taxes must be apportioned on the basis of population. With only three justices participating, the Court upheld the act. But even by considering it, the Court in effect used its authority to review acts of Congress.

Not until 1803, however, did the Court invoke judicial review to strike down legislation deemed incompatible with the U.S. Constitution. That decision came in the landmark case *Marbury v. Madison.* How does Chief Justice John Marshall justify the Court's power to strike down legislation in light of the failure of the newly framed Constitution to confer on it judicial review?

Marbury v. Madison

1 Cr. 137 (1803)

Vote: 4 (Chase, Marshall, Paterson, Washington)
   0
Opinion of the Court: Marshall
Not participating: Cushing, Moore

When the presidential election of 1800 resulted in a tie between Republican candidate Thomas Jefferson and his running mate, Aaron Burr, the election had to be settled in the House of Representatives. Although it was apparent that Federalist president John Adams had lost after a long and bitter campaign, it was not known who had won. In February 1801 the House elected Jefferson. Because the Federalists had lost both the presidential election and their majority in Congress, they took steps to gain control of the third branch of government, the judiciary. The lame-duck Congress enacted the Circuit Court Act of 1801, which created six new circuit courts and several district courts to accommodate the new states of Kentucky, Tennessee, and Vermont. These new courts required judges and support staff such as attorneys, marshalls, and clerks. As a result, during the last six months of his term in office, Adams made more than 200 nominations, with sixteen judgeships (the "midnight appointments") approved by the Senate during his last two weeks in office.

An even more important opportunity arose in December 1800, when the third chief justice of the U.S. Supreme Court, Federalist Oliver Ellsworth resigned so that Adams—not Jefferson—could name his replacement. Adams first offered the post to John Jay, who had served as the first chief justice before leaving to take the more prestigious office of governor of New York. When Jay refused, Adams turned to his secretary of state, John Marshall. Marshall, also an ardent Federalist, was confirmed by the Senate in January 1801, while he continued as secretary of state.

In addition, the Federalist Congress passed the Organic Act, which authorized Adams to appoint forty-two justices of the peace for the District of Columbia. It was this final, seemingly innocuous, law that set the stage for the dramatic case of *Marbury v. Madison.* In the confusion of the Adams administration's last days in office, Marshall, the outgoing secretary of state, failed to deliver at least four of these commissions. When the new administration came into office, James Madison, the new secretary of state, acting under orders from Jefferson, refused to deliver the commissions.

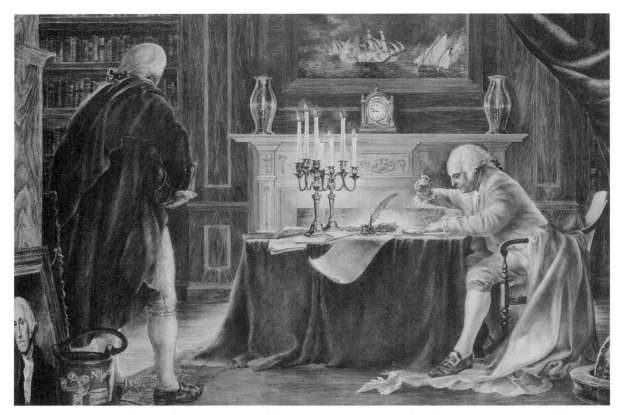

President John Adams signing judicial commissions, the so-called "midnight appointments," on his last night in office. Several appointees, including William Marbury, did not receive their commissions. The Jefferson administration's refusal to deliver them led to the famous case of Marbury v. Madison *(1803) in which the Supreme Court clearly asserted its power of judicial review.*

As a result, in 1801 William Marbury and three others who were denied their commissions went directly to the Supreme Court and asked it to issue a writ of mandamus, ordering Madison to deliver the commissions. Under Section 13 of the 1789 Judiciary Act, Congress presumably had given the Court the power to do so:

The Supreme Court . . . shall have power to issue . . . writs of mandamus, in cases warranted by the principles and usages of law, to any courts appointed, or persons holding office, under the authority of the United States.

In this volatile political climate, Marshall, now serving as chief justice, was perhaps in the most tenuous position of all. On the one hand, he had been a major supporter of the Federalist party, which now looked to him to "scold" the Jefferson administration. On the other, Marshall wanted to avoid a confrontation between the Jefferson administration and the Supreme Court, which not only seemed imminent, but also could end in disaster for the struggling nation. Note the year in which *Marbury* was handed down by the Court; the case was not decided until two years after Marbury filed suit because the Jefferson administration had abolished the 1802 term of the Court!

Chief Justice Marshall delivered the opinion of the Court:

The peculiar delicacy of this case, the novelty of some of its circumstances, and the real difficulty attending the points which occur in it, require a complete exposition of the principles, on which the opinion to be given by the court, is founded.

These principles have been, on the side of the applicant, very ably argued at the bar. In rendering the opinion of the court, there will be some departure in form, though not in substance, from the points stated in that argument.

In the order in which the court has viewed this subject, the following questions have been considered and decided.

1st. Has the applicant a right to the commission he demands?

2dly. If he has a right, and that right has been violated, do the laws of his country afford him a remedy?

3dly. If they do afford him a remedy, is it a *mandamus* issuing from this court?

The first object of enquiry is,

1st. Has the applicant a right to the commission he demands? . . .

In order to determine whether he is entitled to this commission, it becomes necessary to enquire whether he has been appointed to the office. For if he has been appointed, the law continues him in office for five years, and he is entitled to the possession of those evidences of office, which, being completed, became his property. . . .

These are the clauses of the constitution and laws of the United States, which affect this part of the case. They seem to contemplate three distinct operations:

1st. The nomination. This is the sole act of the President, and is completely voluntary.

2d. The appointment. This is also the act of the President, and is also a voluntary act, though it can only be performed by and with the advice and consent of the senate.

3d. The commission. To grant a commission to a person appointed, might perhaps be deemed a duty enjoined by the constitution. "He shall," says that instrument, "commission all the officers of the United States." . . .

This is an appointment made by the President, by and with the advice and consent of the senate, and is evidenced by no act but the commission itself. In such a case therefore the commission and the appointment seem inseparable; it being almost impossible to shew an appointment otherwise than by proving the existence of a commission; still the commission is not necessarily the appointment; though conclusive evidence of it.

But at what stage does it amount to this conclusive evidence? . . .

If it should be supposed, that the solemnity of affixing the seal, is necessary not only to the validity of the commission, but even to the completion of an appointment, still when the seal is affixed the appointment is made, and the commission is valid. No other solemnity is required by law; no other act is to be performed on the part of government. All that the executive can do to invest the person with his office, is done; and unless the appointment be then made, the executive cannot make one without the co-operation of others. . . .

In considering this question, it has been conjectured that the commission may have been assimilated to a deed, to the validity of which, delivery is essential.

This idea is founded on the supposition that the commission is not merely *evidence* of an appointment, but is itself the actual appointment; a supposition by no means unquestionable. But for the purpose of examining this objection fairly, let it be conceded, that the principle, claimed for its support, is established.

The appointment being, under the constitution, to be made by the President *personally,* the delivery of the deed of appointment, if necessary to its completion, must be made by the President also. It is not necessary that the livery should be made personally to the grantee of the office: It never is so made. The law would seem to contemplate that it should be made to the secretary of state, since it directs the secretary to affix the seal to the commission *after* it shall have been signed by the President. If then the act of livery be necessary to give validity to the commission, it has been delivered when executed and given to the secretary for the purpose of being sealed, recorded, and transmitted to the party.

But in all cases of letters patent, certain solemnities are required by law, which solemnities are the evidences of the validity of the instrument. A formal delivery to the person is not among them. In cases of commissions, the sign manual of the President, and the seal of the United States, are those solemnities. This objection therefore does not touch the case.

It has also occurred as possible, and barely possible, that the transmission of the commission, and the acceptance thereof, might be deemed necessary to complete the right of the plaintiff.

The transmission of the commission, is a practice directed by convenience, but not by law. It cannot therefore be necessary to constitute the appointment which must precede it, and which is the mere act of the President. If the executive required that every person appointed to an office, should himself take means to procure his commission, the appointment would not be the less valid on that account. The appointment is the sole act of the President; the transmission of the commission is the sole act of the officer to whom that duty is assigned, and may be accelerated or retarded by circumstances which can have no influence on the appointment. A commission is transmitted to a person already appointed; not to a person to be appointed or not, as the letter enclosing the commission should happen to get into the post-office and reach him in safety, or to miscarry. . . .

If the transmission of a commission be not considered as necessary to give validity to an appointment; still less is its acceptance. The appointment is the sole act of the President; the acceptance is the sole act of the officer, and is, in plain common sense, posterior to the appointment. As he may resign, so may he refuse to accept: but neither the one, nor the other, is capable of rendering the appointment a non-entity.

That this is the understanding of the government, is apparent from the whole tenor of its conduct.

A commission bears date, and the salary of the officer commences from his appointment; not from the transmission or acceptance of his commission. When a person, appointed to any office, refuses to accept that office, the successor is nominated in the place of the person who has declined to accept, and not in the place of the person who had been previously in office, and had created the original vacancy.

It is therefore decidedly the opinion of the court, that when a commission has been signed by the President, the appointment is made; and that the commission is complete, when the seal of the United States has been affixed to it by the secretary of state. . . .

The discretion of the executive is to be exercised until the appointment has been made. But having once made the appointment, his power over the office is terminated in all cases, where, by law, the officer is not removeable by him. The right to the office is *then* in the person appointed, and he has the absolute, unconditional, power of accepting or rejecting it.

Mr. Marbury, then, since his commission was signed by the President, and sealed by the secretary of state, was appointed; and as the law creating the office, gave the officer a right to hold for five years, independent of the executive, the appointment was not revocable; but vested in the officer legal rights, which are protected by the laws of his country.

To withhold his commission, therefore, is an act deemed by the court not warranted by law, but violative of a vested legal right.

This brings us to the second enquiry; which is,

2dly. If he has a right, and that right has been violated, do the laws of his country afford him a remedy?

The very essence of civil liberty certainly consists in the right of every individual to claim the protection of the laws, whenever he receives an injury. One of the first duties of government is to afford that protection. . . .

The government of the United States has been emphatically termed a government of laws, and not of men. It will certainly cease to deserve this high appellation, if the laws furnish no remedy for the violation of a vested legal right.

If this obloquy is to be cast on the jurisprudence of our country, it must arise from the peculiar character of the case. . . .

The conclusion . . . is, that where the heads of departments are the political or confidential agents of the executive, merely to execute the will of the President, or rather to act in cases in which the executive possesses a constitutional or legal discretion, nothing can be more perfectly clear than that their acts are only politically examinable. But where a specific duty is assigned by law, and individual rights depend upon the performance of that duty, it seems equally clear that the individual who considers himself injured, has a right to resort to the laws of his country for a remedy.

If this be the rule, let us enquire how it applies to the case under the consideration of the court.

The power of nominating to the senate, and the power of appointing the person nominated, are political powers, to be exercised by the President according to his own discretion. When he has made an appointment, he has exercised his whole power, and his discretion has been completely applied to the case. If, by law, the officer be removable at the will of the President, then a new appointment may be immediately made, and the rights of the officer are terminated. But as a fact which has existed cannot be made never to have existed, the appointment cannot be annihilated; and consequently if the officer is by law not removable at the will of the President; the rights he has acquired are protected by the law, and are not resumable by the President. They cannot be extinguished by executive authority, and he has the privilege of asserting them in like manner as if they had been derived from any other source.

The question whether a right has vested or not, is, in its nature, judicial, and must be tried by the judicial authority. If, for example, Mr. Marbury had taken the oaths of a magistrate, and proceeded to act as one; in consequence of which a suit had been instituted against him, in which his defence had depended on his being a magistrate; the validity of his appointment must have been determined by judicial authority.

So, if he conceives that, by virtue of his appointment, he has a legal right, either to the commission which has been made out for him, or to a copy of that commission, it is equally a question examinable in a court, and the decision of the court upon it must depend on the opinion entertained of his appointment.

That question has been discussed, and the opinion is, that the latest point of time which can be taken as that at which the appointment was complete, and evidenced, was when, after the signature of the presi-dent, the seal of the United States was affixed to the commission.

It is then the opinion of the court,

1st. That by signing the commission of Mr. Marbury, the president of the United States appointed him a justice of peace, for the county of Washington in the district of Columbia; and that the seal of the United States, affixed thereto by the secretary of state, is conclusive testimony of the verity of the signature, and of the completion of the appointment; and that the appointment conferred on him a legal right to the office for the space of five years.

2dly. That, having this legal title to the office, he has a consequent right to the commission; a refusal to deliver which, is a plain violation of that right, for which the laws of his country afford him a remedy.

It remains to be enquired whether,

3dly. He is entitled to the remedy for which he applies. . . .

The act to establish the judicial courts of the United States authorizes the supreme court "to issue writs of mandamus, in cases warranted by the principles and usages of law, to any courts appointed, or persons holding office, under the authority of the United States."

The secretary of state, being a person holding an office under the authority of the United States, is precisely within the letter of the description; and if this court is not authorized to issue a writ of mandamus to such an officer, it must be because the law is unconstitutional, and therefore absolutely incapable of conferring the authority, and assigning the duties which its words purport to confer and assign.

The constitution vests the whole judicial power of the United States in one supreme court, and such inferior courts as congress shall, from time to time, ordain and establish. This power is expressly extended to all cases arising under the laws of the United States; and consequently, in some form, may be exercised over the present case; because the right claimed is given by a law of the United States.

In the distribution of this power it is declared that "the supreme court shall have original jurisdiction in all cases affecting ambassadors, other public ministers and consuls, and those in which a state shall be a party.

In all other cases, the supreme court shall have appellate jurisdiction.''

It has been insisted, at the bar, that as the original grant of jurisdiction, to the supreme and inferior courts, is general, and the clause, assigning original jurisdiction to the supreme court, contains no negative or restrictive words; the power remains to the legislature, to assign original jurisdiction to that court in other cases than those specified in the article which has been recited; provided those cases belong to the judicial power of the United States.

If it had been intended to leave it in the discretion of the legislature to apportion the judicial power between the supreme and inferior courts according to the will of that body, it would certainly have been useless to have proceeded further than to have defined the judicial power, and the tribunals in which it should be vested. The subsequent part of the section is mere surplussage, is entirely without meaning, if such is to be the construction. If congress remains at liberty to give this court appellate jurisdiction, where the constitution has declared their jurisdiction shall be original; and original jurisdiction where the constitution has declared it shall be appellate; the distribution of jurisdiction, made in the constitution, is form without substance.

Affirmative words are often, in their operation, negative of other objects than those affirmed; and in this case, a negative or exclusive sense must be given to them or they have no operation at all.

It cannot be presumed that any clause in the constitution is intended to be without effect; and therefore such a construction is inadmissible, unless the words require it.

If the solicitude of the convention, respecting our peace with foreign powers, induced a provision that the supreme court should take original jurisdiction in cases which might be supposed to affect them; yet the clause would have proceeded no further than to provide for such cases, if no further restriction on the powers of congress had been intended. That they should have appellate jurisdiction in all other cases, with such exceptions as congress might make, is no restriction; unless the words be deemed exclusive of original jurisdiction.

When an instrument organizing fundamentally a judicial system, divides it into one supreme, and so many inferior courts as the legislature may ordain and establish; then enumerates its powers, and proceeds so far to distribute them, as to define the jurisdiction of the supreme court by declaring the cases in which it shall take original jurisdiction, and that in others it shall take appellate jurisdiction; the plain import of the words seems to be, that in one class of cases its jurisdiction is original, and not appellate; in the other it is appellate, and not original. If any other construction would render the clause inoperative, that is an additional reason for rejecting such other construction, and for adhering to their obvious meaning.

To enable this court then to issue a mandamus, it must be shewn to be an exercise of appellate jurisdiction, or to be necessary to enable them to exercise appellate jurisdiction.

It has been stated at the bar that the appellate jurisdiction may be exercised in a variety of forms, and that if it be the will of the legislature that a mandamus should be used for that purpose, that will must be obeyed. This is true, yet the jurisdiction must be appellate, not original.

It is the essential criterion of appellate jurisdiction, that it revises and corrects the proceedings in a cause already instituted, and does not create that cause. Although, therefore, a mandamus may be directed to courts, yet to issue such a writ to an officer for the delivery of a paper, is in effect the same as to sustain an original action for that paper, and therefore seems not to belong to appellate, but to original jurisdiction. Neither is it necessary in such a case as this, to enable the court to exercise its appellate jurisdiction.

The authority, therefore, given to the supreme court, by the act establishing the judicial courts of the United States, to issue writs of mandamus to public officers, appears not to be warranted by the constitution; and it becomes necessary to enquire whether a jurisdiction, so conferred, can be exercised. . . .

If an act of the legislature, repugnant to the constitution, is void, does it, nothwithstanding its invalidity, bind the courts, and oblige them to give it effect? Or, in other words, though it be not law, does it constitute a rule as operative as if it was a law? This would be to overthrow in fact what was established in theory; and would seem, at first view, an absurdity too gross to be insisted on. It shall, however, receive a more attentive consideration.

It is emphatically the province and duty of the judicial department to say what the law is. Those who apply the rule to particular cases, must of necessity expound and interpret that rule. If two laws conflict with each other, the courts must decide on the operation of each.

So if a law be in opposition to the constitution; if both the law and the constitution apply to a particular case, so that the court must either decide that case conformably to the law, disregarding the constitution; or conformably to the constitution, disregarding the law; the court must determine which of these conflicting rules governs the case. This is of the very essence of judicial duty.

If then the courts are to regard the constitution; and the constitution is superior to any ordinary act of the legislature; the constitution, and not such ordinary act, must govern the case to which they both apply.

Those then who controvert the principle that the constitution is to be considered, in court, as a paramount law, are reduced to the necessity of maintaining that courts must close their eyes on the constitution, and see only the law.

This doctrine would subvert the very foundation of all written constitutions. It would declare that an act, which, according to the principles and theory of our government, is entirely void; is yet, in practice, completely obligatory. It would declare, that if the legislature shall do what is expressly forbiden, such act, notwithstanding the express prohibition, is in reality effectual. It would be giving to the legislature a practical and real omnipotence, with the same breath which professes to restrict their powers within narrow limits. It is prescribing limits, and declaring that those limits may be passed at pleasure.

That it thus reduces to nothing what we have deemed the greatest improvement on political institutions—a written constitution—would of itself be sufficient, in America, where written constitutions have been viewed with so much reverence, for rejecting the construction. But the peculiar expressions of the constitution of the United States furnish additional arguments in favour of its rejection.

The judicial power of the United States is extended to all cases arising under the constitution.

Could it be the intention of those who gave this power, to say that, in using it, the constitution should not be looked into? That a case arising under the constitution should be decided without examining the instrument under which it arises?

This is too extravagant to be maintained.

In some cases then, the constitution must be looked into by the judges. And if they can open it at all, what part of it are they forbidden to read, or to obey?

There are many other parts of the constitution which serve to illustrate this subject.

It is declared that "no tax or duty shall be laid on articles exported from any state." Suppose a duty on the export of cotton, of tobacco, or of flour; and a suit instituted to recover it. Ought judgment to be rendered in such a case? ought the judges to close their eyes on the constitution, and only see the law.

The constitution declares that "no bill of attainder or *ex post facto* law shall be passed."

If, however, such a bill should be passed and a person should be prosecuted under it; must the court condemn to death those victims whom the constitution endeavours to preserve?

"No person," says the constitution, "shall be convicted of treason unless on the testimony of two witnesses to the same overt act, or on confession in open court."

Here the language of the constitution is addressed especially to the courts. It prescribes, directly for them, a rule of evidence not to be departed from. If the legislature should change that rule, and declare *one* witness, or a confession *out* of court, sufficient for conviction, must the constitutional principle yield to the legislative act?

From these, and many other selections which might be made, it is apparent, that the framers of the constitution contemplated that instrument, as a rule for the government of *courts,* as well as of the legislature.

Why otherwise does it direct the judges to take an oath to support it? This oath certainly applies, in an especial manner, to their conduct in their official character. How immoral to impose it on them, if they were to be used as the instruments, and the knowing instruments, for violating what they swear to support!

John Marshall
(1801-1835)

T he eldest of fifteen children, John Marshall was born September 24, 1755, in a log cabin on the Virginia frontier near Germantown. His father, descended from Welsh immigrants, was an assistant surveyor to George Washington and member of the Virginia House of Burgesses. His mother was the daughter of an educated Scottish clergyman.

As a youth, Marshall was tutored by two clergymen, but his primary teacher was his father, who introduced him to the study of English literature and Blackstone's *Commentaries on the Laws of England.*

During the Revolutionary War, young Marshall participated in the siege of Norfolk as a member of the Culpeper Minute Men and was present at Brandywine, Monmouth, Stony Point, and Valley Forge as a member of the third Virginia Regiment. In 1779 he returned home to await another assignment but was never recalled. He left the Continental Army with the rank of captain in 1781.

Marshall was self-taught in the law; his only formal instruction came in 1780 when he attended George Wythe's course of law lectures at the College of William and Mary. He was admitted to the bar that same year and gradually developed a lucrative practice, specializing in defending Virginians against their pre–Revolutionary War British creditors.

On January 3, 1783, Marshall married Mary Willis Ambler, daughter of the Virginia state treasurer, and established a home in Richmond. The couple had ten children, only six of whom survived to maturity. Marshall spent many years attending to the needs of his wife, who suffered from a chronic illness and accompanying nervousness. She died December 25, 1831.

From 1796 until about 1806, Marshall's life was dominated by the pressures of meeting debts incurred by a land investment he had made in the northern neck of Virginia. It has been speculated that his need for money motivated him to write *The Life of George Washington,* which appeared in five volumes from 1804 to 1807. He later condensed the work into a schoolbook, but it proved not to be the answer to his financial difficulties.

The leisurely pace of the Supreme Court in its early days was well suited to Marshall's personality; as a boy he had learned to appreciate relaxation and the outdoors. The chief justice enjoyed socializing in the clubs and saloons of Richmond and accumulated a fine collection of wines. He is said to have excelled at the game of quoits (similar to horseshoes), and was also known to take a turn at whist, backgammon, and tenpins.

Marshall was master of his Masonic lodge in Richmond and served as Masonic grand master of Virginia for several years. He was a member of the American Colonization Society, which worked toward the transfer of freed slaves to Africa, and belonged to the Washington Historical Monument Society and several literary societies.

Marshall was elected to the Virginia House of Delegates from Fauquier County in 1782 and 1784. He reentered the House in 1787 and was instrumental in Virginia's ratification of the new U.S. Constitution. At the state ratifying convention his primary attention was directed to the need for judicial review. By 1789 Marshall was considered to be a leading Federalist in the state.

Marshall refused many appointments in the Federalist administrations of George Washington and John

Adams, including U.S. attorney general in 1795, associate justice of the Supreme Court in 1798, and secretary of war in 1800. In 1796 he refused an appointment by President Adams as minister to France, but the following year agreed to serve as one of three special envoys sent to smooth relations with that country. This mission, known as the "XYZ Affair," failed when French diplomats demanded a bribe as a condition for negotiation. Congress, however, was greatly impressed by the stubborn resistance of the American emissaries, and Marshall received a generous grant as a reward for his participation.

In 1799 Washington persuaded Marshall to run for the U.S. House of Representatives as a Federalist from Richmond. His career in the House was brief, however, for in 1800 he became secretary of state under Adams. When Adams retired to his home in Massachusetts for a few months that year, Marshall served as the effective head of government.

Chief Justice Oliver Ellsworth resigned in 1800, and Adams offered the position to John Jay, who had been the Court's first chief justice. Jay declined, and the Federalists urged Adams to elevate Associate Justice William Paterson. But on January 20, 1801, Adams nominated Marshall instead. The Senate confirmed Marshall January 27 by a voice vote.

As the primary founder of the American system of constitutional law, including the doctrine of judicial review, Marshall participated in more than 1,000 Supreme Court decisions, writing more than 500 of them himself. In 1807 he presided over the treason trial of Aaron Burr in the Richmond circuit court, locking horns with Thomas Jefferson, who sought an absolute conviction. Burr was acquitted.

In 1831, at age seventy-six, Marshall underwent successful surgery in Philadelphia for the removal of kidney stones. Three years later, he developed an enlarged liver, and his health declined rapidly. When Marshall died in Philadelphia on July 6, 1835, three months short of his eightieth birthday, the Liberty Bell cracked as it tolled in mourning.

Source: Adapted from Elder Witt, *Guide to the U.S. Supreme Court,* 2d ed. (Washington, D.C.: Congressional Quarterly, 1990), 810-811.

The oath of office, too, imposed by the legislature, is completely demonstrative of the legislative opinion on this subject. It is in these words, "I do solemnly swear that I will administer justice without respect to persons, and do equal right to the poor and to the rich; and that I will faithfully and impartially discharge all the duties incumbent on me as according to the best of my abilities and understanding, agreeably to *the constitution,* and laws of the United States."

Why does a judge swear to discharge his duties agreably to the constitution of the United States, if that constitution forms no rule for his government? if it is closed upon him, and cannot be inspected by him?

If such be the real state of things, this is worse than solemn mockery. To prescribe, or to take this oath, becomes equally a crime.

It is also not entirely worthy of observation, that in declaring what shall be the *supreme law* of the land, the *constitution* itself is first mentioned; and not the laws of the United States generally, but those only which shall be made in *pursuance* of the constitution, have that rank.

Thus, the particular phraseology of the constitution of the United States confirms and strengthens the principle, supposed to be essential to all written constitutions, that a law repugnant to the constitution is void; and that *courts,* as well as other departments, are bound by that instrument.

The rule must be discharged.

Despite controversy over the opinion (*see pages 49–53)* many scholars consider Marshall's opinion in *Marbury* absolutely stunning, even brilliant. Think about the way the chief justice dealt with a most delicate political situation. By ruling against Marbury, he avoided a potentially devastating clash with the new president; but, by exerting the power of judicial review, he sent a clear signal to Jefferson that the Court had a major role to play in the American government.

The decision helped to establish John Marshall's reputation as perhaps the greatest justice in Supreme Court history. As will be shown throughout this book, *Marbury* was just the first in what would be a long line of seminal Marshall decisions.

But most important, *Marbury* firmly established the Court's authority to review and strike government actions that were incompatible with the Constitution. In Marshall's view, such authority, while not explicit in the Constitution, was clearly intended by the Framers of that document. Was he correct? His opinion makes a plausible argument, but some judges and scholars have suggested otherwise. We review their assertions later in this chapter.

For now, note that in *Marbury*, the Court addressed only the power to review acts of the federal government. Could it exert judicial review over the states? According to Section 25 of the 1789 Judiciary Act, indeed, it could. In that provision, Congress expanded the Supreme Court's appellate jurisdiction to encompass appeals from the highest state courts if those tribu-

nals upheld a state law against challenges of unconstitutionality or denied some claim based on the U.S. Constitution, federal laws, or treaties. But the mere existence of this statute did not necessarily mean that either state courts or the Supreme Court would follow it. Because Section 25 expanded the Supreme Court's jurisdiction, it was always possible that the justices might question Congress's authority to do so, even though it involved appellate, not original, jurisdiction.

More important was the potentially hostile reaction from the states. In the 1780s and 1790s, they zealously guarded their power from federal encroachment. Even if the Court were to take advantage of its ability to review state court decisions, it was more than likely that such tribunals would disregard its rulings. Keep these issues in mind as you read *Martin v. Hunter's Lessee,* an important case in which the Court firmly asserted its power to review state court decisions.

Martin v. Hunter's Lessee

1 Wheat. 304 (1816)

Vote: 6 (Duvall, Johnson, Livingston, Story, Todd, Washington)

0

Opinion of the Court: Story
Concurring opinion: Johnson
Not participating: Marshall

Prior to the Revolutionary War, Lord Fairfax, a British loyalist, inherited a large tract of land in Virginia. When the war broke out, Fairfax, too old and frail to make the journey back to England, remained in Virginia and died there in 1781. He left the property to his nephew, Denny Martin, a British subject residing in England, with the stipulation that Martin change his name to Fairfax. The inheritance was complicated by a 1781 Virginia law, which specified that no "enemy" could inherit land. Virginia confiscated Fairfax's

(also known as Martin's) property and began proceedings to sell it. Because he believed he had rightfully inherited the land, Martin also began to sell off tracts—among the purchasers were John Marshall and his brother—resulting in a suit contesting title.

A lower Virginia state court upheld Martin's claim, but the highest court in Virginia reversed. When the case, *Fairfax's Devisee v. Hunter's Lessee* (1813), was appealed to the U.S. Supreme Court, only four justices heard it; Chief Justice Marshall recused himself due to the potential conflict of interest. In a 3-1 decision the Court upheld Fairfax's claim, finding that the Virginia statute was unconstitutional because it conflicted with the 1783 Treaty of Paris in which Congress promised to recommend to the states that they restore confiscated property to the loyalists.

The Supreme Court ordered the Virginia Supreme Court to carry out its ruling. In response, the Virginia court, which did not consider itself subordinate to the Supreme Court, held hearings to determine whether it should comply with the order. Eventually, it not only declined to follow the order but also struck down Section 25 of the Judiciary Act of 1789 as unconstitutional. The Virginia Supreme Court's decision was then appealed to the U.S. Supreme Court in the case of *Martin v. Hunter's Lessee.*

Justice Joseph Story delivered the opinion of the Court:

The questions involved in this judgment are of great importance and delicacy. Perhaps it is not too much to affirm, that, upon their right decision, rest some of the most solid principles which have hitherto been supposed to sustain and protect the constitution itself. The great respectability, too, of the court whose decisions we are called upon to review, and the entire deference which we entertain for the learning and ability of that court, add much to the difficulty of the task which has so unwelcomely fallen upon us. It is, however, a source of consolation, that we have had the assistance of most able and learned arguments to aid our inquiries; and that the opinion which is now to be pronounced has been weighed with every solicitude to come to a correct result, and matured after solemn deliberation.

Before proceeding to the principal questions, it may not be unfit to dispose of some preliminary considerations which have grown out of the arguments at the bar.

The constitution of the United States was ordained and established, not by the states in their sovereign capacities, but emphatically, as the preamble of the constitution declares, by "the people of the United States." There can be no doubt that it was competent to the people to invest the general government with all the powers which they might deem proper and necessary; to extend or restrain these powers according to their own good pleasure, and to give them a paramount and supreme authority. As little doubt can there be, that the people had a right to prohibit to the states the exercise of any powers which were, in their judgment, incompatible with the objects of the general compact; to make the powers of the state governments, in given

cases, subordinate to those of the nation, or to reserve to themselves those sovereign authorities which they might not choose to delegate to either. The constitution was not, therefore, necessarily carved out of existing state sovereignties, nor a surrender of powers already existing in state institutions, for the powers of the states depend upon their own constitutions; and the people of every state had the right to modify and restrain them, according to their own views of policy or principle. On the other hand, it is perfectly clear that the sovereign powers vested in the state governments, by their respective constitutions, remained unaltered and unimpaired, except so far as they were granted to the government of the United States.

These deductions do not rest upon general reasoning, plain and obvious as they seem to be. They have been positively recognised by one of the articles in amendment of the constitution, which declares, that "the powers not delegated to the United States by the constitution, nor prohibited by it to the states, are reserved to the *states* respectively, or *to the people.*"

The government, then, of the United States, can claim no powers which are not granted to it by the constitution, and the powers actually granted, must be such as are expressly given, or given by necessary implication. On the other hand, this instrument, like every other grant, is to have reasonable construction, according to the import of its terms; and where a power is expressly given in general terms, it is not to be restrained to particular cases, unless that construction grow out of the context expressly, or by necessary implication. The words are to be taken in their natural and obvious sense, and not in a sense unreasonably restricted or enlarged.

The constitution unavoidably deals in general language. It did not suit the purposes of the people, in framing this great charter of our liberties, to provide for minute specifications of its powers, or to declare the means by which those powers should be carried into execution. It was foreseen that this would be a perilous and difficult, if not an impracticable, task. The instrument was not intended to provide merely for the exigencies of a few years, but was to endure through a long lapse of ages, the events of which were locked up in the inscrutable purposes of Providence. It could not be foreseen what new changes and modifications of power might be indispensable to effectuate the general objects of the charter; and restrictions and specifications, which, at the present, might seem salutary, might, in the end, prove the overthrow of the system itself. Hence its powers are expressed in general terms, leaving to the legislature, from time to time, to adopt its own means to effectuate legitimate objects, and to mould and model the exercise of its powers, as its own wisdom, and the public interests, should require.

With these principles in view, principles in respect to which no difference of opinion ought to be indulged, let us now proceed to . . . the consideration of the great question as to the nature and extent of the appellate jurisdiction of the United States. . . . [A]ppellate jurisdiction is given by the constitution to the supreme court in all cases where it has not original jurisdiction; subject, however, to such exceptions and regulations as congress may prescribe. It is, therefore, capable of embracing every case enumerated in the constitution, which is not exclusively to be decided by way of original jurisdiction. But the exercise of appellate jurisdiction is far from being limited by the terms of the constitution to the supreme court. There can be no doubt that congress may create a succession of inferior tribunals, in each of which it may vest appellate as well as original jurisdiction. The judicial power is delegated by the constitution in the most general terms, and may, therefore, be exercised by congress under every variety of form, of appellate or original jurisdiction. And as there is nothing in the constitution which restrains or limits this power, it must, therefore, in all other cases, subsist in the utmost latitude of which, in its own nature, it is susceptible.

As, then, by the terms of the constitution, the appellate jurisdiction is not limited as to the supreme court, and as to this court it may be exercised in all other cases than those of which it has original cognizance, what is there to restrain its exercise over state tribunals in the enumerated cases? The appellate power is not limited by the terms of the third article to any particular courts. The words are, ''the judicial power (which includes appellate power) shall extend *to all cases*,'' &c., and ''in all other cases before mentioned the supreme court shall have appellate jurisdiction.'' It is the *case*, then, and not *the court*, that gives the

jurisdiction. If the judicial power extends to the case, it will be in vain to search in the letter of the constitution for any qualification as to the tribunal where it depends. It is incumbent, then, upon those who assert such a qualification to show its existence by necessary implication. If the text be clear and distinct, no restriction upon its plain and obvious import ought to be admitted, unless the inference be irresistible.

If the constitution meant to limit the appellate jurisdiction to cases pending in the courts of the United States, it would necessarily follow that the jurisdiction of these courts would, in all the cases enumerated in the constitution, be exclusive of state tribunals. How otherwise could the jurisdiction extend to *all* cases arising under the constitution, laws, and treaties of the United States, or *to all cases* of admiralty and maritime jurisdiction? If some of these cases might be entertained by state tribunals, and no appellate jurisdiction as to them should exist, then the appellate power would not extend to *all,* but to *some,* cases. If state tribunals might exercise concurrent jurisdiction over all or some of the other classes of cases in the constitution without control, then the appellate jurisdiction of the United States might, as to such cases, have no real existence, contrary to the manifest intent of the constitution. Under such circumstances, to give effect to the judicial power, it must be construed to be exclusive; and this not only when the *casus faederis* should arise directly, but when it should arise, incidentally, in cases pending in state courts. This construction would abridge the jurisdiction of such court far more than has been ever contemplated in any act of congress.

On the other hand, if, as has been contended, a discretion be vested in congress to establish, or not to establish, inferior courts at their own pleasure, and congress should not establish such courts, the appellate jurisdiction of the supreme court would have nothing to act upon, unless it could act upon cases pending in the state courts. Under such circumstances it must be held that the appellate power would extend to state courts; for the constitution is peremptory that it shall extend to certain enumerated cases, which cases could exist in no other courts. Any other construction, upon this supposition, would involve this strange contradiction, that a discretionary power vested in congress, and which they might rightfully omit to exercise, would defeat the absolute injunctions of the constitution in relation to the whole appellate power. . . .

It must, therefore, be conceded that the constitution not only contemplated, but meant to provide for cases within the scope of the judicial power of the United States, which might yet depend before state tribunals. It was foreseen that in the exercise of their ordinary jurisdiction, state courts would incidentally take cognizance of cases arising under the constitution, the laws, and treaties of the United States. Yet to all these cases the judicial power, by the very terms of the constitution, is to extend. It cannot extend by original jurisdiction if that was already rightfully and exclusively attached in the state courts, which (as has been already shown) may occur; it must, therefore, extend by appellate jurisdiction, or not at all. It would seem to follow that the appellate power of the United States must, in such cases, extend to state tribunals; and if in such cases, there is no reason why it should not equally attach upon all others within the purview of the constitution.

It has been argued that such an appellate jurisdiction over state courts is inconsistent with the genius of our governments, and the spirit of the constitution. That the latter was never designed to act upon state sovereignties, but only upon the people, and that if the power exists, it will materially impair the sovereignty of the states, and the independence of their courts. We cannot yield to the force of this reasoning; it assumes principles which we cannot admit, and draws conclusions to which we do not yield our assent.

It is a mistake that the constitution was not designed to operate upon states, in their corporate capacities. It is crowded with provisions which restrain or annul the sovereignty of the states in some of the highest branches of their prerogatives. The tenth section of the first article contains a long list of disabilities and prohibitions imposed upon the states. Surely, when such essential portions of state sovereignty are taken away, or prohibited to be exercised, it cannot be correctly asserted that the constitution does not act upon the states. The language of the constitution is also imperative upon the states as to the performance of many duties. It is imperative upon the state legislatures to make laws prescribing the time, places, and manner of holding elections for senators and representatives,

and for electors of president and vice-president. And in these, as well as some other cases, congress have a right to revise, amend, or supercede the laws which may be passed by state legislatures. . . . The courts of the United States can, without question, revise the proceedings of the executive and legislative authorities of the states, and if they are found to be contrary to the constitution, may declare them to be of no legal validity. Surely the exercise of the same right over judicial tribunals is not a higher or more dangerous act of sovereign power.

Nor can such a right be deemed to impair the independence of state judges. It is assuming the very ground in controversy to assert that they possess an absolute independence of the United States. In respect to the powers granted to the United States, they are not independent; they are expressly bound to obedience by the letter of the constitution; and if they should unintentionally transcend their authority, or misconstrue the constitution, there is no more reason for giving their judgments an absolute and irresistible force, than for giving it to the acts of the other co-ordinate departments of state sovereignty.

The argument urged from the possibility of the abuse of the revising power, is equally unsatisfactory. It is always a doubtful course, to argue against the use or existence of a power, from the possibility of its abuse. It is still more difficult, by such an argument, to ingraft upon a general power a restriction which is not to be found in the terms in which it is given. From the very nature of things, the absolute right of decision, in the last resort, must rest somewhere—wherever it may be vested it is susceptible of abuse. In all questions of jurisdiction the inferior, or appellate court, must pronounce the final judgment; and common sense, as well as legal reasoning, has conferred it upon the latter. . . .

It is further argued, that no great public mischief can result from a construction which shall limit the appellate power of the United States to cases in their own courts: first, because state judges are bound by an oath to support the constitution of the United States, and must be presumed to be men of learning and integrity; and, secondly, because congress must have an unquestionable right to remove all cases within the scope of the judicial power from the state courts to the courts of the United States, at any time before final judgment, though not after final judgment. As to the first reason—admitting that the judges of the state courts are, and always will be, of as much learning, integrity, and wisdom, as those of the courts of the United States, (which we very cheerfully admit,) it does not aid the argument. It is manifest that the constitution has proceeded upon a theory of its own, and given or withheld powers according to the judgment of the American people, by whom it was adopted. We can only construe its powers, and cannot inquire into the policy or principles which induced the grant of them. The constitution has presumed (whether rightly or wrongly we do not inquire) that state attachments, state prejudices, state jealousies, and state interests, might sometimes obstruct, or control, or be supposed to obstruct or control, the regular administration of justice. Hence, in controversies between states; between citizens of different states; between citizens claiming grants under different states; between a state and its citizens, or foreigners, and between citizens and foreigners, it enables the parties, under the authority of congress, to have the controversies heard, tried, and determined before the national tribunals. No other reason than that which has been stated can be assigned, why some, at least, of those cases should not have been left to the cognizance of the state courts. In respect to the other enumerated cases—the cases arising under the constitution, laws, and treaties of the United States, cases affecting ambassadors and other public ministers, and cases of admiralty and maritime jurisdiction—reasons of a higher and more extensive nature, touching the safety, peace, and sovereignty of the nation, might well justify a grant of exclusive jurisdiction.

This is not all. A motive of another kind, perfectly compatible with the most sincere respect for state tribunals, might induce the grant of appellate power over their decisions. That motive is the importance, and even necessity of *uniformity* of decisions throughout the whole United States, upon all subjects within the purview of the constitution. Judges of equal learning and integrity, in different states, might differently interpret a statute, or a treaty of the United States, or even the constitution itself: If there were no revising authority to control these jarring and discordant judgments, and harmonize them into uniformity, the laws, the treaties, and the constitution of the United States would be different in different states, and might, perhaps, never have precisely the same construction, obligation, or efficacy, in any two states. The public mischiefs that would attend such a state of things would be truly deplorable; and it cannot be believed that they could have escaped the enlightened convention which formed the constitution. What, indeed, might then have been only prophecy, has now become fact; and the appellate jurisdiction must continue to be the only adequate remedy for such evils. . . .

On the whole, the court are of opinion, that the appellate power of the United States does extend to cases pending in the state courts; and that the 25th section of the judiciary act, which authorizes the exercise of this jurisdiction in the specified cases, by a writ of error, is supported by the letter and spirit of the constitution. We find no clause in that instrument which limits this power; and we dare not interpose a limitation where the people have not been disposed to create one. . . .

It is the opinion of the whole court, that the judgment of the court of appeals of Virginia, rendered on the mandate in this cause, be reversed, and the judgment of the district court, held at Winchester, be, and the same is hereby affirmed.

With these words, the justices may have presumed that the issue was settled. But after they announced *Martin,* Virginia continued its assaults on the authority of the Supreme Court to review state actions. The issue was not fully resolved until the case of *Cohens v. Virginia* (1821), in which Chief Justice Marshall wrote for the majority. How does his opinion here compare with *Marbury*? Does he invoke the same logic to assert the Court's power to review state decisions as he did for federal actions?

Cohens v. Virginia

6 Wheat. 264 (1821)

Vote: 6 (Duvall, Johnson, Livingston, Marshall, Story,
  Todd)
       0

Opinion of the Court: Marshall
Not participating: Washington

The Cohen brothers were tried and convicted in Virginia for selling tickets for the District of Columbia lottery, a lottery that was authorized by an act of Congress but not by Virginia law. When the Cohens alleged that the federal law superseded the Virginia statute, the Supreme Court was again compelled to review a Virginia court's interpretation of a congressional act.

As it was in *Marbury,* the Court was faced with a difficult political situation. Virginia refused to comply with the Court's earlier decision in *Martin.* The state's attorneys, including Philip P. Barbour, who later would serve on the U.S. Supreme Court, continued to argue that the Court could not review state court decisions because the states were sovereign entities.

Chief Justice Marshall delivered the opinion of the Court:

The first question to be considered is, whether the jurisdiction of this Court is excluded by the character of the parties, one of them being a State, and the other a citizen of that State? . . .

The counsel for the defendant . . . have laid down the general proposition, that a sovereign independent State is not suable, except by its own consent.

This general proposition will not be controverted. But its consent is not requisite in each particular case. It may be given in a general law. And if a State has surrendered any portion of its sovereignty, the question whether a liability to suit be a part of this portion, depends on the instrument by which the surrender is made. If, upon a just construction of that instrument, it shall appear that the State has submitted to be sued, then it has parted with this sovereign right of judging in every case on the justice of its own pretensions, and

has entrusted that power to a tribunal in whose impartiality it confides.

The American States, as well as the American people, have believed a close and firm Union to be essential to their liberty and to their happiness. They have been taught by experience, that this Union cannot exist without a government for the whole; and they have been taught by the same experience that this government would be a mere shadow, that must disappoint all their hopes, unless invested with large portions of that sovereignty which belongs to independent States. Under the influence of this opinion, and thus instructed by experience, the American people, in the conventions of their respective States, adopted the present constitution.

If it could be doubted, whether from its nature, it were not supreme in all cases where it is empowered to act, that doubt would be removed by the declaration, that "this constitution, and the laws of the United States, which shall be made in pursuance thereof, and all treaties made, or which shall be made, under the authority of the United States, shall be the supreme law of the land; and the judges in every State shall be bound thereby; any thing in the constitution or laws of any State to the contrary notwithstanding."

This is the authoritative language of the American people; and, if gentlemen please, of the American States. It marks, with lines too strong to be mistaken, the characteristic distinction between the government of the Union, and those of the States. The general government, though limited as to its objects, is supreme with respect to those objects. This principle is a part of the constitution; and if there be any who deny its necessity, none can deny its authority.

To this supreme government ample powers are confided; and if it were possible to doubt the great purposes for which they were so confided, the people of the United States have declared, that they are given "in order to form a more perfect union, establish justice, ensure domestic tranquillity, provide for the common defence, promote the general welfare, and secure the blessings of liberty to themselves and their posterity."

With the ample powers confided to this supreme government, for these interesting purposes, are connected many express and important limitations on the sovereignty of the States, which are made for the same purposes. The powers of the Union, on the great subjects of war, peace, and commerce, and on many others, are in themselves limitations of the sovereignty of the States; but in addition to these, the sovereignty of the States is surrendered in many instances where the surrender can only operate to the benefit of the people, and where, perhaps, no other power is conferred on Congress than a conservative power to maintain the principles established in the constitution. The maintenance of these principles in their purity, is certainly among the great duties of the government.

One of the instruments by which this duty may be peaceably performed, is the judicial department. It is authorized to decide all cases of every description, arising under the constitution or laws of the United States. From this general grant of jurisdiction, no exception is made of those cases in which a State may be a party. When we consider the situation of the government of the Union and of a State, in relation to each other; the nature of our constitution; the subordination of the State governments to that constitution; the great purpose for which jurisdiction over all cases arising under the constitution and laws of the United States, is confided to the judicial department; are we at liberty to insert in this general grant, an exception of those cases in which a State may be a party? Will the spirit of the constitution justify this attempt to control its words? We think it will not. We think a case arising under the constitution or laws of the United States, is cognizable in the Courts of the Union, whoever may be the parties to that case.

Had any doubt existed with respect to the just construction of this part of the section, that doubt would have been removed by the enumeration of those cases to which the jurisdiction of the federal Courts is extended, in consequence of the character of the parties. In that enumeration, we find "controversies between two or more States, between a State and citizens of another State," "and between a State and foreign States, citizens, or subjects."

One of the express objects, then, for which the judicial department was established, is the decision of controversies between States, and between a State and individuals. The mere circumstance, that a State is a party, gives jurisdiction to the Court. How, then, can it

be contended, that the very same instrument, in the very same section, should be so construed, as that this same circumstance should withdraw a case from the jurisdiction of the Court, where the constitution or laws of the United States are supposed to have been violated? The constitution gave to every person having a claim upon a State, a right to submit his case to the Court of the nation. However unimportant his claim might be, however little the community might be interested in its decision, the framers of our constitution thought it necessary for the purposes of justice, to provide a tribunal as superior to influence as possible, in which that claim might be decided. Can it be imagined, that the same persons considered a case involving the constitution of our country and the majesty of the laws, questions in which every American citizen must be deeply interested, as withdrawn from this tribunal, because a State is a party? . . .

The second objection to the jurisdiction of the Court is, that its appellate power cannot be exercised, in any case, over the judgment of a State Court.

This objection is sustained chiefly by arguments drawn from the supposed total separation of the judiciary of a State from that of the Union, and their entire independence of each other. The argument considers the federal judiciary as completely foreign to that of a State; and as being no more connected with it in any respect whatever, than the Court of a foreign State. If this hypothesis be just, the argument founded on it is equally so; but if the hypothesis be not supported by the constitution, the argument fails with it.

This hypothesis is not founded on any words in the constitution, which might seem to countenance it, but on the unreasonableness of giving a contrary construction to words which seem to require it; and on the incompatibility of the application of the appellate jurisdiction to the judgments of State Courts, with that constitutional relation which subsists between the government of the Union and the governments of those States which compose it.

Let this unreasonableness, this total incompatibility, be examined.

That the United States form, for many, and for most important purposes, a single nation, has not yet been denied. In war, we are one people. In making peace, we are one people. In all commercial regulations, we are one and the same people. In many other respects, the American people are one, and the government which is alone capable of controling and managing their interests in all these respects, is the government of the Union. It is their government, and in that character they have no other. America has chosen to be, in many respects, and to many purposes, a nation; and for all these purposes, her government is complete; to all these objects, it is competent. The people have declared, that in the exercise of all powers given for these objects, it is supreme. It can, then, in effecting these objects, legitimately control all individuals or governments within the American territory. The constitution and laws of a State, so far as they are repugnant to the constitution and laws of the United States, are absolutely void. These States are constituent parts of the United States. They are members of one great empire—for some purposes sovereign, for some purposes subordinate.

In a government so constituted, is it unreasonable that the judicial power should be competent to give efficacy to the constitutional laws of the legislature? That department can decide on the validity of the constitution or law of a State, if it be repugnant to the constitution or to a law of the United States. Is it unreasonable that it should also be empowered to decide on the judgment of a State tribunal enforcing such unconstitutional law? Is it so very unreasonable as to furnish a justification for controling the words of the constitution?

We think it is not. We think that in a government acknowledgedly supreme, with respect to objects of vital interest to the nation, there is nothing inconsistent with sound reason, nothing incompatible with the nature of government, in making all its departments supreme, so far as respects those objects, and so far as is necessary to their attainment. The exercise of the appellate power over those judgments of the State tribunals which may contravene the constitution or laws of the United States, is, we believe, essential to the attainment of those objects. . . .

This opinion has been already drawn out to too great a length to admit of entering into a particular consideration of the various forms in which the counsel who made this point has, with much ingenuity, presented his argument to the Court. The argument in all its forms is essentially the same. It is founded, not on the words of the constitution, but on its spirit, a spirit extracted, not from the words of the instrument, but from his view of the nature of our Union, and of the great fundamental principles on which the fabric stands.

To this argument, in all its forms, the same answer may be given. Let the nature and objects of our Union be considered; let the great fundamental principles, on which the fabric stands, be examined; and we think the result must be, that there is nothing so extravagantly absurd in giving to the Court of the nation the power of revising the decisions of local tribunals on questions which affect the nation, as to require that words which import this power should be restricted by a forced construction. The question then must depend on the words themselves: and on their construction we shall be the more readily excused for not adding to the observations already made, because the subject was fully discussed and exhausted in the case of *Martin* v. *Hunter*.

Judicial Review: Some Controversies

Marbury, Martin, and *Cohens* firmly established the power of federal courts to exert judicial review over national and state actions. What they did not do, and perhaps could not do, was put an end to the controversies surrounding judicial review. Although most Americans accept the fact that courts have this power, many legal analysts still debate whether they should. Let us, then, consider some of the theoretical debates surrounding judicial review, debates that political scientist David Adamany puts into five categories: Framers' intent, judicial restraint, democratic checks on the Court, public opinion, and protection of minority rights.[1]

Framers' Intent. Perhaps the oldest debate concerns whether the Framers intended the federal courts to exercise judicial review. Chief Justice Marshall's affirmative view was the major justification in *Marbury* and *Cohens*, and there is some historical evidence to support it. Most important is that the Framers had knowledge of judicial review. Although Marshall often is credited with its first full enunciation, there is evidence that the concept originated in England in *Dr. Bonham's Case* (1610). At issue here was an act of Parliament that enabled physicians of the London College to authorize medical licenses and to punish those practicing without one. Convicted of violating the act, Dr. Bonham appealed his case to England's high court, the King's Bench. Writing for the court, Lord Chief Justice Sir Edward Coke struck down the act, noting in *dictum,* "It appears in our books, that in many cases, the common law will control acts of Parliament, and sometimes adjudge them to be utterly void." Coke's resounding declaration of the authority of the court to void parliamentary acts came at a critical point in British history. At a time when King James I was claiming tremendous authority, the court, in an otherwise trivial case, took the opportunity to assert its power.

By the early 1700s the concept of judicial review fell out of favor in England. Coke's writings, however, had a profound impact on the development of the American legal system, as best illustrated by the *Writs of Assistance Case* (1761), involving the legality of sweeping search warrants issued by the British Parliament in the name of the king. In arguing against such writs, James Otis, a Boston lawyer, relied on Coke's opinion in *Bonham* as precedent for his request.

1. David Adamany, "The Supreme Court," in *The American Courts: A Critical Assessment,* ed. John B. Gates and Charles A. Johnson (Washington, D.C.: CQ Press, 1991).

Otis lost the case, but his argument was not forgotten. Between 1776 and 1787, eight of the thirteen colonies incorporated judicial review into their constitutions, and by 1789 various state courts had struck down as unconstitutional eight acts passed by their legislatures.

This background makes the question of why the Framers left judicial review out of the Constitution even more perplexing. Some historians argue that they omitted it because Article III was the source of division at the constitutional convention and the insertion of judicial review would only have heightened their differences. By the same token, many of these same analysts claim that several factors point to the view that the Framers implicitly accepted the notion of judicial review. First, historians have established that well over half the delegates to the Constitutional Convention approved of the concept, including those generally considered to be the most influential. Second, in *The Federalist Papers,* Alexander Hamilton adamantly defended judicial review, arguing that one branch of government must safeguard the Constitution and that the courts would be in the best position to undertake that important responsibility. He wrote:

There is no position which depends on clearer principles than that every act of a delegated authority, contrary to the tenor of the commission under which it is exercised, is void. No legislative act, therefore, contrary to the Constitution, can be valid. To deny this would be to affirm that the deputy is greater than his principal; that the servant is above his master; that the representatives of the people are superior to the people themselves; that men acting by virtue of powers may do not only what their powers do not authorize, but what they forbid.

If it be said that the legislative body are themselves the constitutional judges of their own powers and that the construction they put upon them is conclusive upon the other departments it may be answered that this cannot be the natural presumption where it is not to be collected from any particular provisions in the Constitution. It is not otherwise to be supposed that the Constitution could intend to enable the representatives of the people to substitute their *will* to that of their constituents. It is far more rational to suppose that the courts were designed to be an intermediate body between the people and the legislature in order, among other things, to keep the latter within the limits assigned to their authority. The interpretation of the laws is the proper and peculiar province of the courts. A constitution is, in fact, and must be regarded by judges as, a fundamental law. It therefore belongs to them to ascertain its meaning as well as the meaning of any particular act proceeding from the legislative body. If there should happen to be an irreconcilable variance between the two, that which has the superior obligation and validity ought, of course, to be preferred; or, in other words, the Constitution ought to be preferred to the statute, the intention of the people to the intention of their agents.

Even with all this evidence, many still argue that the Framers did not intend for courts to review acts of the other branches. As Adamany summarizes, "The Constitutional Convention rejected a proposed Council of Revision, including judges, to reject or revise laws that did not conform to the Constitution."[2] Furthermore, even though some states adopted judicial review, their courts rarely exercised the power. And "the outrage that followed some of those [state] decisions showed that judicial review was not widely accepted."[3] What, then, can we conclude about the intent of the Framers? Perhaps legal scholar Edward S. Corwin said it best: "The people who say the framers intended it are talking nonsense, and the people who say they did not intend it are talking nonsense."[4]

Judicial Restraint. Another controversy surrounding judicial review involves the notion of judicial restraint. Many legal analysts and justices have asserted that courts generally should defer to the elected institutions of government and "avoid conflicts" with those branches. An early state-

2. Ibid., 13.
3. Ibid.
4. Quoted in ibid.

ment of this position came in *Eakin v. Raub* (1825) in which a Pennsylvania Supreme Court justice took issue with the *Marbury* decision. Justice John Gibson wrote:

The constitution and the *right* of the legislature to pass [an] act may be in collision; but is that a legitimate subject for judicial determination? If it be, the judiciary must be a peculiar organ, to revise the proceedings of the legislature, and to correct its mistakes. . . [I]t is by no means clear, that to declare a law void which has been enacted according to the forms prescribed in the constitution, is not a usurpation of legislative power. It is an act of sovereignty; and sovereignty and legislative power are . . . to be convertible terms. It is the business of the judiciary to interpret the laws, not scan the authority of the law giver; and without the latter, it cannot take cognizance of a collision between a law and the Constitution. So that to affirm that the judiciary has a right to judge the existence of such collision, is to take for granted the very thing to be proved.

The use of judicial review belies this notion of judicial restraint for which Justice Gibson clamors. Recall, for example, the legislative veto case described in the introduction to this chapter. By even considering the issue, the Court placed itself squarely in the middle of an executive-legislative dispute; when it nullified the veto, it showed no deference to the wishes of the legislature. To this argument, supporters of judicial review point to Marshall's decision in *Marbury,* Hamilton's assertion in *The Federalist Papers,* and so forth. They suggest that the goverment needs an umpire who will act neutrally and fairly in interpreting the constitutional strictures.

Again, the question of which posture is correct has no absolute answer, only opinion. But what we do know is that U.S. Supreme Court justices—with a few exceptions, such as Felix Frankfurter—have not taken seriously the dictate of judicial restraint or, at the very least, have not let it interfere in their voting. Even those who profess a basic commitment to judicial deference have tended to allow their attitudes and values to dictate their decisions.[5] Still, a tendency exists even today to equate judicial restraint with conservatism and judicial activism with liberalism. Former president Ronald Reagan often asserted the need for judicial restraint, saying that, if he could, he would appoint a Court of Felix Frankfurters. But many note that what Reagan really wanted was a Court that would defer to legislatures if the laws in question reflected conservative values and would overturn them otherwise.

Democratic Checks. A third controversy involves what Adamany calls "democratic checks on the Court." According to one side of this debate, judicial review is defensible on the grounds that the Supreme Court—while lacking an explicit electoral connection—is "subject to potential checks by the elected branches." That is, if the Court exercises judicial review in a way repugnant to the best interests of the people, Congress, the president, and even the states have a number of recourses. Acting in different combinations they can, for example, ratify a constitutional amendment to overturn a decision, change the size of the Court, or remove the Court's appellate jurisdiction. The problem with these checks, in the eyes of some analysts, is that they are very rarely invoked: only four amendments have explicitly overturned Court decisions; the Court's size has not been changed since 1870; and only once has Congress removed the Court's appellate jurisdiction.

We do not mean to imply that Congress, in particular, has no control over the federal courts and their decisions. As recently as 1989, in *Mistretta v. United States,* the Supreme Court scrutinized a congressional act that sought to minimize judicial discretion in sentencing. The law created a sentencing commission charged with promul-gating guidelines for federal judges to follow in handing down criminal sentences. Although some lower court judges refused to adopt the guidelines, arguing that they undermined judicial independence, the Supreme Court upheld the law. *(For a full account of Mistretta, see Chapter 3.)*

Public Opinion. A fourth debate surrounding judicial review concerns public opinion and the Court. Those who support judicial review argue that Court decisions usually are in harmony with public opinion; that is, even though the Court faces no real pressure to do so, it generally "follows the elections." Therefore, Americans need not fear that the Court will usurp their power. Empirical evidence, however, is mixed. After conducting an extensive investigation of the relationship of public opinion and the Court, Thomas Marshall concluded that "the evidence suggests that the modern Court has been an essentially majoritarian institution. Where clear poll margins exist, three-fifths to two-thirds of Court rulings reflect the polls."[6] Yet, as he and others concede, the Court at times has handed down decisions well out of line with public preferences, such as its prohibition of prayer in school and its short-lived ban on the death penalty.[7]

Another aspect of this controversy involves the "legitimacy-conferring" power of the Court. According to this view, when the Court reviews and upholds legislation, it plays the role of republican schoolmaster, educating the public and conferring some measure of acceptance for government policies. Again, evidence suggests that the Court does not and cannot serve this function, that too few people actually know about any given Court decision and, even if they do know, they do not necessarily shift their ideas to conform to the Court's opinions.

5. See, for example, Harold Spaeth and Stuart Teger, "Activism and Restraint," in *Supreme Court Activism and Restraint,* Stephen Halperin and Charles Lamb, eds. (Lexington, Mass.: Lexington Books, 1982).

6. Thomas R. Marshall, *Public Opinion and the Supreme Court* (Boston: Unwin Hyman, 1989), 192.

7. For an excellent review of this literature, see Gregory A. Caldeira, "Courts and Public Opinion," in *The American Courts.*

Role of the Court. A final controversy—arguably the most hotly debated—concerns what role the Supreme Court should play in our system of government. Those who support judicial review assert that the Court must have this power if it is to fulfill its most important constitutional assignment: protector of minority rights. By their very nature, the fact that they are elected, legislatures and executives reflect the interests of the majority. But those interests may take action that is blatantly unconstitutional. So that the majority cannot tyrannize a minority, it is necessary for the one branch of government that lacks any electoral connection to have the power of judicial review. This is a powerful argument, the truth of which has been demonstrated many times throughout our history. For example, when the legislatures of southern states continued to enact segregation laws, it was the U.S. Supreme Court that struck them down as violative of the Constitution.

This position also has its share of problems. One is that this view conflicts with the notion of the Court as a body that defers to the elected branches. Another is that empirical evidence suggests that some Supreme Courts have not used judicial review in this manner. According to Robert Dahl, many of the acts struck down by the Supreme Court before the 1960s were those that harmed a "privileged class," not disadvantaged minorities.[8] We have seen similar decisions by the Rehnquist Court as well. For example, in *City of Richmond v. J. A. Croson Co.* (1989), the justices struck down a city affirmative action program designed to help minority interests.

Judicial Review in Action

These controversies are important to the extent that they place the subject of judicial review into a theoretical context for debate. But they present debates that probably never will be resolved: as one side finds support for its position, the other always seems to follow suit.

Let us consider instead several issues arising from the way the Court actually has exercised the power of judicial review: the number of times it has invoked the power to strike laws, and the significance of those decisions. As Lawrence Baum suggests, investigation of these issues can help us achieve a better understanding of judicial review and place it in a realistic context.[9] First, how often has the Court overturned a federal, state, or local law or ordinance? In Figure 2-1, we depict those numbers over time. The data seem to indicate that the Court has made frequent use of the power, striking down close to 1,500 government acts since 1790. However, as Baum notes, those acts are but a "minute fraction" of the laws enacted at various levels of government. Between the 1790s and 1990s, for example, Congress passed more than 60,000 laws, with the Court striking far less than 1 percent of them.

The more important question, then, may be one of significance: Does the Court tend to strike down important laws or relatively minor laws? Using the case of *Dred Scott v. Sandford (see Chapter 5)* as illustration, some argue that the Court, in fact, often strikes significant legislation. Undoubtedly, that opinion had major consequences. By ruling that Congress could not prohibit slavery in the territories and by striking down a law, the Missouri Compromise, that had already been repealed, the Court fed the growing divisions between the North and South, providing a major impetus for the Civil War. The decision also tarnished the prestige of the Court and the reputation of Chief Justice Roger B. Taney.

But how representative is *Dred Scott*? Some other Court opinions striking down government acts have been almost as important; those nullifying state abortion and segregation laws, the fed-

8. Robert Dahl, "Decision-Making in a Democracy: The Supreme Court as a National Policy-Maker," *Journal of Public Law* 6 (1957): 279-295

9. Lawrence Baum, *The Supreme Court,* 3d ed. (Washington, D.C.: CQ Press, 1989), 175-180.

Figure 2-1. *Provisions of Federal, State, and Local Laws and Ordinances Held Unconstitutional by the Supreme Court*

Number Held
Unconstitutional

Source: Adapted from Lawrence Baum, *The Supreme Court,* 4th ed. (Washington, D.C.: CQ Press, 1992), 188, 190.

eral child labor acts, and many pieces of New Deal legislation come to mind. Yet, as Baum astutely notes, "A good many of the Court's decisions declaring [state and federal] measures unconstitutional, perhaps a majority . . . were minor."[10] Following are two examples:

Monongahela Navigation Co. v. United States (1893) in which the Court struck down, on Fifth Amendment grounds, a law concerning the amount of money to be paid to the United States by companies for the "purchase or condemnation

10. Ibid., 176.

of a certain lock and dam in the Monongahela River."

Coyle v. Smith (1911) in which the Court struck down, on Article IV ground, part of the Oklahoma Enabling Act, which prohibited the relocation of the state's capital until 1913.[11]

Despite the rather murky record, we can reach two conclusions about the Court's use of judicial review. First, "while judicial review has helped the Court to play a major role in policy making, it certainly has not made the Court the dominant national policy maker."[12] Second, it is not necessarily the Court's use of judicial review that is significant. Rather, like the presidential veto, the threat of its invocation may be its power. In either case, it has provided federal courts with their most significant political weapon.

Constraints on Judicial Power

Given all the attention paid to judicial review, it is easy to forget that the power of courts to exercise it and their judicial authority, more generally, has substantial limits. Article III—or the Court's interpretation of it—places three major constraints on the ability of federal tribunals to hear and decide cases: the court must have authority to hear a case (jurisdiction); the case must be appropriate for judicial resolution (justiciability); and the appropriate party must be bringing the case (standing).[13] In what follows, we review doctrine surrounding these constraints. As you read this discussion, consider not only the Court's interpretation of its own limits but also the justifications it offers. Note, in particular, how fluid these can be: some Courts tend towards loose

11. For a list of federal laws struck down by the Court, see Elder Witt, *Guide to the U.S. Supreme Court,* 2d ed. (Washington, D.C.: Congressional Quarterly, 1990), 1001-09.

12. Baum, *The Supreme Court,* 181.

13. See Stephen L. Wasby, *The Supreme Court in the Federal Judicial System,* 3d ed. (Chicago: Nelson-Hall, 1988), 165.

constructions of the rules, while others are anxious to enforce them. What factors might explain these different tendencies?

Jurisdiction

According to Chief Justice Salmon P. Chase, "Without jurisdiction the court cannot proceed at all in any cause. Jurisdiction is power to declare the law, and when it ceases to exist, the only function remaining to the court is that of announcing the fact and dismissing the cause."[14] In other words, a court cannot hear a case unless it has the authority—the jurisdiction—to do so.

Article III, Section 2, defines the jurisdiction of U.S. federal courts. It gives lower courts the authority to hear disputes involving particular parties and subject matter. The U.S. Supreme Court's jurisdiction is divided into two types: original and appellate. The former are classes of cases that originate in the Court; the latter are those that it hears after a lower court.

To what extent does jurisdiction actually constrain the federal courts? *Marbury v. Madison* provides some, albeit contradictory, answers to this question. Chief Justice Marshall informed

14. *Ex parte McCardle*, 7 Wall. 506 (1869).

Congress that it could not alter the original jurisdiction of the Court. Having reached this conclusion, Marshall could have merely dismissed the case on the grounds that the Court lacked authority to hear it, but that is not what he did.

Marbury remains the most important ruling on original jurisdiction. What other Supreme Courts have dealt with is the issue of appellate jurisdiction. This area is a bit more complex because Article III explicitly states that for those cases over which the Court does not have original jurisdiction, it "shall have appellate Jurisdiction . . . with such Exceptions, and under such Regulations as the Congress shall make." In other words, this Exceptions Clause seems to give Congress authority to alter the Court's appellate jurisdiction.

Has the Supreme Court allowed Congress to do so? The short answer to this question is yes. Recall that the Court relied on the addition to its appellate jurisdiction, under Section 25 of the 1789 Judiciary Act, to review the decisions of the Virginia Supreme Court. In *Ex parte McCardle* (1869) it also allowed Congress to use its power under the Exceptions Clause to remove the Court's appellate jurisdiction over a particular category of cases.

Ex parte McCardle

7 Wall. 506 (1869)
Vote: 10 (Bradley, Chase, Clifford, Davis, Field, Grier, Miller, Nelson, Strong, Swayne)[15]
0
Opinion of the Court: Chase

After the Civil War the radical Republican Congress imposed a series of restrictions on the South. Known as the Reconstruction laws, they in

15. In 1863 Congress enlarged the Court's size to ten, providing President Lincoln with an opportunity to appoint four Supreme Court justices within a two-year period.

effect placed the region under military rule. Journalist William McCardle wrote editorials opposing these measures and urging resistance to them. As a result, he was arrested for publishing allegedly "incendiary and libelous articles" and held for a trial before a military tribunal, established under Reconstruction.

Because he was a citizen, not a member of any militia, McCardle alleged that he was being illegally held. He petitioned for a writ of habeas corpus—an order issued to determine if a person held in custody is being unlawfully detained or imprisoned—under an 1867 act, which "gave federal judges power to grant habeas corpus to any person restrained in violation" of the U.S. Constitution.[16] When this effort failed, McCardle appealed to the U.S. Supreme Court.

In early March 1868 *McCardle* "was very thoroughly and ably [presented] upon the merits" to the U.S. Supreme Court.[17] But before the justices could meet in conference to decide the case, Congress, on March 27, 1868, enacted a law repealing the 1867 Habeas Corpus Act and removing the Supreme Court's authority to hear appeals emanating from it. This move was meant to punish the Court or, at the very least, to send it a strong message. Two years before *McCardle,* in 1866, the Court had invalidated Lincoln's use of military tribunals in certain areas, and Congress did not want to see the Court take similar action in this dispute. The legislature felt so strongly on this issue that after President Andrew Johnson vetoed the 1868 act, Congress overrode the veto.

The Court responded by redocketing the case for oral arguments in March 1869. During the arguments and in its briefs, the government made its position clear: "When the jurisdiction of a court to determine a case or a class of cases depends upon a statute and that statute is repealed, the jurisdiction ceases absolutely." In short, the government contended that the Court no longer had authority to hear the case and should dismiss it.

Chief Justice Salmon P. Chase delivered the opinion of the Court:

16. C. Herman Pritchett, *The American Constitution* (New York: McGraw-Hill, 1959), 109.
17. See *McCardle,* 7 Wall. 506.

It is unnecessary to consider whether, if Congress had made no exceptions and no regulations, this court might not have exercised general appellate jurisdiction under rules prescribed by itself. From among the earliest Acts of the first Congress, at its first session, was the Act of September 24th, 1789, to establish the judicial courts of the United States. That Act provided for the organization of this court, and prescribed regulations for the exercise of its jurisdiction. . . .

The exception to appellate jurisdiction in the case before us . . . is not an inference from the affirmation of other appellate jurisdiction. It is made in terms. The provision of the Act of 1867, affirming the appellate jurisdiction of this court in cases of habeas corpus, is expressly repealed. It is hardly possible to imagine a plainer instance of positive exception.

We are not at liberty to inquire into the motives of the Legislature. We can only examine into its power under the Constitution; and the power to make exceptions to the appellate jurisdiction of this court is given by express words.

What, then, is the effect of the repealing Act upon the case before us? We cannot doubt as to this. Without jurisdiction the court cannot proceed at all in any cause. Jurisdiction is power to declare the law, and when it ceases to exist, the only function remaining to the court is that of announcing the fact and dismissing the cause. And this is not less clear upon authority than upon principle. . . .

It is quite clear, therefore, that this . . . court cannot proceed to pronounce judgment in this case, for it has no longer jurisdiction of the appeal; and judicial duty is not less fitly performed by declining ungranted jurisdiction than in exercising firmly that which the Constitution and the laws confer. . . .

The appeal of the petitioner in this case must be dismissed for want of jurisdiction.

As we can see, the Court acceded and declined to hear the case. *McCardle* suggests that Congress has the authority to remove the Court's appellate jurisdiction as it deems necessary. Since *McCar-* dle, however, Congress has only considered and not enacted legislation to do so. Table 2-1 lists some of the proposals members of Congress have offered. As noted, many involve controversial

Table 2–1   A Sample of Congressional Proposals Aimed at Eliminating the U.S. Supreme Court's Appellate Jurisdiction

Issue	Supreme Court Decision Provoking Proposal	Proposal
Communist infiltration/Security programs	*Schware v. Board of Bar Examiners* (1957) in which the Supreme Court refused to allow states to use "inferences regarding moral character" (i.e., past association with a subversive cause) to exclude applicants for admission to the bar.	1958 proposal that would have eliminated the Court's appellate jurisdiction over any "regulation pertaining to the admission of persons to the practice of law."
Criminal confessions	*Miranda v. Arizona* (1966) in which the Court required police to read those under arrest a series of rights.	1968 proposal that removed the Court's jurisdiction to hear state cases involving the admissibility of confessions.
School busing	*Swann v. Charlotte-Mecklenburg County* (1971) in which the Court permitted district courts to fashion their own school desegregation plans, which may include the busing of students to other schools.	During the 1970s and 1980s many proposals were offered to curb the Court's authority to hear busing cases and to limit the authority of courts to order busing.
School prayer	*Engel v. Vitale* (1962) and *Abington School District v. Schempp* (1963), which eliminated voluntary and mandatory prayer in school.	Several proposals, with a major effort coming in 1979, that would have eliminated the Supreme Court's as well as all other federal courts' ability to hear any cases involving voluntary school prayer.
Abortion	*Roe v. Wade* (1973) in which the Supreme Court struck down state laws criminalizing abortion. *Roe* legalized abortion during the first two trimesters of pregnancy.	During the 1970s and 1980s several proposals to remove the Court's authority to hear abortion cases.

Adopted from Gerald Gunther, *Constitutional Law* (Mineola, N.Y.: Foundation Press, 1985), 48–49.

issue areas—abortion, prayer in school, busing—leading to the conclusion that modern Congresses are no different from the one that passed the 1867 act: they would like to use the Exceptions Clause as a political tool, as a way to restrain the Court, but they have yet to do so successfully.

In spite of *McCardle,* there are several reasons to believe that the Court might not uphold the sorts of proposals depicted in Table 2-1. One is that *McCardle* was something of an odd case. According to many scholars, the Court had no choice but to acquiesce to Congress if it wanted to retain its legitimacy in post–Civil War America. The pressures of the day, rather than the Constitution, may have led to the decision. Another reason

is that a case subsequent to *McCardle* cast some doubt on the precedent it seemed to set. In *United States v. Klein* (1872) the Court considered an 1870 law in which Congress sought to impinge on the president's authority to issue executive amnesties. In particular, it required those who wished to recover property taken by the government during the Civil War to prove their loyalty, even if they had received a presidential pardon. Moreover, the law withdrew the U.S. Supreme Court's (and a lower appellate court's) jurisdiction to hear such cases. Although the justices acknowledged that the Exceptions Clause gave Congress the right to remove their appellate jurisdiction "in a particular class of cases," it could not do so only as "a means to an end." That is, in previous cases, the Court had stated that the president had the power to grant pardons. Therefore, Congress was using the Exceptions Clause to skirt those decisions. If the Court allowed this, it would then permit Congress to "prescribe rules of decision to the Judicial Department . . . in cases pending before it," in violation of constitutional mandates requiring the separation of powers.[18]

Still, *Klein* did not settle the issue. Compare, for example, the views of two twentieth century justices. In 1948 Justice Frankfurter wrote, "Congress need not give this Court any appellate power; it may withdraw appellate jurisdiction once conferred and it may do so even while a case is *sub judice.*"[19] Thirteen years later, Justice William O. Douglas remarked, "There is a serious question whether the *McCardle* case could command a majority view today."[20]

Whether the Court would allow Congress to use the Exceptions Clause remains an open question until such litigation occurs. Until then, Chief Justice Chase summed up the situation best when he noted, after *McCardle* had been decided, that use of the Exceptions Clause was "unusual and hardly to be justified except upon some imperious public exigency."[21]

Justiciability

According to Article III, judicial power of the federal courts is restricted to "cases" and "controversies." Taken together, these words mean that a litigation must be justiciable—appropriate or suitable for a federal tribunal to hear or to solve. As Chief Justice Earl Warren asserted, cases and controversies

are two complementary but somewhat different limitations. In part those words limit the business of federal courts to questions presented in an adversary context and in a form historically viewed as capable of resolution through the judicial process. And in part those words define the role assigned to the judiciary in a tripartite allocation of power to assure that the federal courts will not intrude into areas committed to the other branches of government. Justiciability is the term of art employed to give expression to this dual limitation placed upon federal courts by the case-and-controversy doctrine.[22]

Although Warren also suggested that "justiciability is itself a concept of uncertain meaning and scope," he elucidated several characteristics of litigation that would render it nonjusticiable. In this section, we treat five of these characteristics: advisory opinions, collusion, mootness, ripeness, and political questions. In the following section we deal with another concept related to justiciability, standing to sue.

Advisory Opinions. Put simply, federal courts will not issue advisory opinions. They will not render advice in hypothetical suits because if litigation is abstract, it possesses no real controversy.

The language of the Constitution does not prohibit advisory opinions as opinions. Quite early on, however, the Supreme Court read the case-or-controversy restriction to prohibit it from rendering them. In July 1793 Secretary of State Thomas Jefferson asked the justices if they would be willing to address questions concerning the appropriate role America should play in the ongoing British-French war. In particular, Jefferson wrote that President George Washington "would be much relieved if he found himself free to refer questions [involving the war] to the opinions of the judges of the [Court], whose knowledge . . . would secure us against errors dangerous to the peace of the United States."[23] Less than

18. See, generally, Gerald Gunther, *Constitutional Law,* 11th ed. (Mineola, N.Y.: Foundation Press, 1985), 43.
19. *National Mutual Insurance Co. v. Tidewater Transfer Co.,* 337 U.S. 582 (1949).
20. *Glidden Co. v. Zdanok,* 370 U.S. 530 (1962).
21. *Ex parte Yerger,* 8 Wall. 85 (1869).

22. *Flast v. Cohen,* 392 U.S. 83 (1968).
23. Quoted in Gunther, *Constitutional Law,* 1535.

a month later the justices denied Jefferson's request:

[The] three departments of government [being] in certain respects checks upon each other, and our being judges of a court in the last resort, are considerations which afford strong arguments against the propriety of our extrajudicially deciding the questions alluded to, especially as the power given by the Constitution to the President, of calling on the heads of departments for opinions, seems to have been *purposely* as well as expressly united to the *executive* departments.[24]

With these words, the justices sounded the death knell for advisory opinions: they would violate the separation of powers principle embedded in the Constitution. The subject has resurfaced only a few times in U.S. history; in the 1930s, for example, President Franklin Roosevelt considered a proposal that would require the Court to issue advisory opinions on the constitutionality of federal laws. According to Gerald Gunther, "That plan was soon abandoned, partly because of its obvious unconstitutionality."[25]

Nevertheless, scholars still debate the Court's 1793 letter to President Washington. Some agree with the justices' logic. Others assert that more institutional concerns were at work; perhaps the Court sought to avoid being "thrust" into disputes "too early and too often."[26] Whatever the reason, all subsequent Courts have followed that 1793 precedent: requests for advisory opinions to the U.S. Supreme Court present nonjusticiable disputes.[27]

Collusive Suits. A second corollary of justiciability is collusion. The Court will not decide cases in which the litigants (1) want the same outcome, (2) evince no real adversity between them, or (3) are merely testing the law. Why the Court deems collusive suits nonjusticiable is well illustrated in *Muskrat v. United States* (1911). At issue here were several federal laws involving land distribution and appropriations to Native Americans. To determine whether these laws were constitutional, Congress authorized David Muskrat and other Native Americans to challenge them in court. When the dispute reached the U.S. Supreme Court, it dismissed it. As Justice William Day wrote,

[T]here is neither more nor less in this [litigation] than an attempt to provide for a judicial determination, final in this court, of the constitutional validity of an act of Congress. Is such a determination within the judicial power conferred by the Constitution, as the same has been interpreted and defined in the authoritative decisions to which we have referred? We think it is not. That judicial power, as we have seen, is the right to determine actual controversies arising between adverse litigants, duly instituted in courts of proper jurisdiction. The right to declare a law unconstitutional arises because an act of Congress relied upon by one or the other of such parties in determining their rights is in conflict with the fundamental law. The exercise of this, the most important and delicate duty of this court, is not given to it as a body with revisory power over the action of Congress, but because the rights of the litigants in justiciable controversies require the court to choose between the fundamental law and a law purporting to be enacted within constitutional authority, but in fact beyond the power delegated to the legislative branch of the Government. This attempt to obtain a judicial declaration of the validity of the act of Congress is not presented in a "case" or "controversy," to which, under the Constitution of the United States, the judicial power alone extends. It is true the United States is made a defendant to this action, but it has no interest adverse to the claimants. The object is not to assert a property right as against the Government, or to demand compensation for alleged wrongs because of action upon its part. The whole purpose of the law is to determine the constitutional validity of this class of legislation, in a suit not arising between parties concerning a property right necessarily involved in the decision in question, but in a proceeding against the Government in its sovereign capacity, and concerning which the only judgment required is to settle the doubtful character of the legislation in question.

24. Quoted in ibid.
25. Ibid., 1536.
26. For a discussion of this debate, see ibid., 1536-38.
27. We emphasize the Supreme Court because some state courts do, in fact, issue advisory opinions.

However, the Court has not always followed the *Muskrat* precedent. To the contrary, as C. Herman Pritchett noted, "several significant pieces of constitutional litigation" were the result of collusive suits.[28] Some examples include:

–*Pollack v. Farmers' Loan and Trust Co.* (1895) in which the Court struck down as unconstitutional a federal income tax. The litigants in this dispute, a bank and a stockholder in the bank, both wanted the same outcome—the demise of the tax.
–*Carter v. Carter Coal Co.* (1936) in which the Court struck down as unconstitutional a major piece of New Deal legislation. The litigants in this dispute, a company president and the company, which included the president's father, both wanted the same outcome—the eradication of the New Deal legislation.

By the same token, it is true that the Court has decided a great many disputes brought by interest groups to "test" the constitutionality of specific pieces of legislation, including:

–*Hammer v. Dagenhart* (1918) in which a business-oriented organization, the Executive Committee of Southern Cotton Manufacturers, designed litigation directed at overturning a federal child labor act.
–*National Labor Relations Board v. Jones & Laughlin Steel* (1937) in which an anti–New Deal group, the American Liberty League, sought unsuccessfully to challenge a major piece of New Deal legislation.

Why did the Court resolve these other disputes evincing some sort of collusion when it dismissed *Muskrat?* Elder Witt provides a reasonable explanation: "The Court's decision to hear or dismiss such a test case usually turns on whether it presents an actual conflict of legal rights."[29] In other words, the Court might overlook some element of

28. Pritchett, *The American Constitution,* 144.
29. Witt, *Guide to the U.S. Supreme Court,* 288

collusion if the suit itself presents a real controversy or the potential for one.

Mootness. In general, the Court will not decide cases in which the controversy is no longer live by the time it reaches its doorstep. *DeFunis v. Odegaard* (1974) provides one example. Rejected for admission to the University of Washington Law School, Marco DeFunis, Jr., brought suit against the school, alleging that it had engaged in reverse discrimination, that it had denied him a place, but accepted statistically less qualified minority students. In 1971 a trial court found merit in his claim and ordered that the university admit him. While DeFunis was in his second year of law school, the state's high court reversed the trial judge's ruling. He then appealed to the U.S. Supreme Court. By that time, DeFunis had registered for his final quarter in school. In a per curiam opinion, the Court refused to rule on the merits of DeFunis's claim, asserting that it was moot:

Because [DeFunis] will complete his law school studies at the end of the term for which he has now registered regardless of any decision this Court might reach on the merits of this litigation, we conclude that the Court cannot, consistently with the limitations of Art. III of the Constitution, consider the substantive constitutional issues tendered by the parties.

Still, the rules governing mootness are a bit fuzzier than the *DeFunis* opinion characterized them. A well-known case is *Roe v. Wade* (1973) in which the Court legalized abortions performed during the first two trimesters of pregnancy. Norma McCorvey, also known as Roe, was pregnant when she filed suit in 1970. When the Court handed down the decision in 1973, she had long since given birth and put her baby up for adoption. But the justices did not declare this case moot.

Why not? What differentiated *Roe* from *DeFunis?* The justices provided two legal justifications. First, DeFunis brought suit on his own behalf; *Roe* was a class action, Second, DeFunis had been admitted to law school, and he would "never again be required to run the gauntlet." Roe could become pregnant again; that is, pregnancy is a situation capable of repetition or recurrence. Are these reasonable points? Or is it possible, as some suspect, that the Court developed them to avoid particular legal issues? In either case, it is clear that mootness may be a rather slippery concept, open to interpretation by different justices and Courts.

Ripeness. Related to the concepts of advisory opinions and mootness is that of ripeness. Under existing Court interpretation a case is nonjusticiable if the controversy is premature—has insufficiently gelled—for review. *International Longshoreman's Union v. Boyd* (1954) provides an illustration. In 1952 Congress passed a law mandating that all aliens seeking admission into the United States from Alaska be "examined" as if they were entering from a foreign country. Believing that the law might affect seasonal American laborers working in Alaska temporarily, a union challenged the law. Writing for the Court, Justice Frankfurter dismissed the suit. In his view,

Appellants in effect asked [the Court] to rule that a statute the sanctions of which had not been set in motion against individuals on whose behalf relief was sought, because an occasion for doing so had not arisen, would not be applied to them if in the future such a contingency should arise. That is not a lawsuit to enforce a right; it is an endeavor to obtain a court's assurance that a statute does not govern hypothetical situations that may or may not make the challenged statute applicable. Determination of the . . . constitutionality of the legislation in advance of its immediate adverse effect in the context of a concrete case involves too remote and abstract an inquiry for the proper exercise of the judicial function.

Political Questions. Another type of nonjusticiable suit involves a political question. Chief Justice Marshall stated in *Marbury v. Madison:*

The province of the court is, solely, to decide on the rights of individuals, not to inquire how the executive, or executive officers, perform duties in which they have a discretion. Questions in their nature political, or which are, by the constitution and laws, submitted to the executive, can never be made in this court.

In other words, there is a class of questions that may be constitutional in nature but that the Court will not address because they are better solved by other branches of government.

The major question to consider while reading *Luther v. Borden* is what exactly constitutes a political question?

Luther v. Borden

7 How. 1 (1849)

Vote: 8 (Catron, Daniel, Grier, McKinley, McLean, Nelson, Taney, Wayne)
1 (Woodbury)
Opinion of the Court: Taney
Dissenting opinion: Woodbury

Through the 1840s the state of Rhode Island had no formal constitution, but continued under its charter from King Charles II. Although the state enacted occasional legislation to alter suffrage requirements, it never changed those mandating the ownership of property as a criterion for voting. Eventually, this qualification became "obnoxious"; "it excluded so many adult males of personal worth and possessed of intelligence and wealth, though not of land, and as it made the ancient apportionment of the number of representatives, founded on real estate, very disproportionate to the present population and personal property in different portions and towns of the State."[30]

30. Dissenting opinion of Justice Woodbury, *Luther v. Borden,* 7 How. 1 (1849).

Thomas Wilson Dorr led a rebellion against state authorities in Rhode Island. To suppress it, the governor placed the state under martial law, which in turn led to the Supreme Court case of Luther v. Borden (1849), in which the Court decided that the complaint constituted a "Political question."

Thomas Wilson Dorr
of Rhode Island

As a result, some Rhode Island citizens sought to convince the legislature to change suffrage requirements or to hold a convention for the purpose of writing a constitution. When the government rejected these proposals, Thomas Dorr, an attorney, organized "voluntary societies" which, in 1842, drafted, wrote, and ratified a Constitution—all outside of the existing government structure. Indeed, with Dorr as their governor, the societies set up their own political and judicial apparatus.

The existing government refused to acknowledge the Dorrites or accede to their requests to surrender public documents. Dorr then "made some attempt to get possession of the public arsenal"—a rebellion of sorts—so that he and his followers could take over. When this failed, he disbanded the "military" he had assembled, asserting "that the majority of the friends of the people's constitution disapprove of any further forcible measures for its support." In the meantime, the existing government issued a proclamation placing the entire state under martial law, and the governor warned citizens not to support the new constitution. He even contacted President John Tyler for help in suppressing the rebellion.

After these actions took effect, the state tried and convicted Thomas Dorr of treason. Other followers, including Martin Luther, also were arrested because martial law gave authorities a great deal of leeway in "investigating" offenses against the state; for example, it enabled police to enter and search their houses without warrants.

In an effort to publicize his cause and his belief that the existing Rhode Island government was illegitimate, Luther sued officials for trespassing. He argued that the Rhode Island Charter, which the Dorrites sought to replace with their constitution, denied to citizens of the state a republican form of government, guaranteed in Article IV of the U.S. Constitution. Because the Dorr constitution met that requirement, Luther asserted that it was actually in force at the time he was arrested. He asked the Court to declare the charter government illegitimate and to supplant it with the Dorr constitution.

Chief Justice Taney delivered the opinion of the Court:

The fourth section of the fourth article of the Constitution of the United States provides that the United States shall guarantee to every State in the Union a republican form of government, and shall protect each of them against invasion; and on the application of the Legislature or of the executive (when the Legislature cannot be convened) against domestic violence.

Under this article of the Constitution it rests with Congress to decide what government is the established one in a State. For as the United States guarantee to each State a republican government, Congress must necessarily decide what government is established in the State before it can determine whether it is republican or not. And when the senators and representatives of a State are admitted into the councils of the Union, the authority of the government under which they are appointed, as well as its republican character, is recognized by the proper constitutional authority. And its decision is binding on every other department of the government, and could not be questioned in a judicial tribunal. It is true that the contest in this case did not last long enough to bring the matter to this issue; and as no senators or representatives were elected under the authority of the government of which Mr. Dorr was the head, Congress was not called upon to decide the controversy. Yet the right to decide is placed there, and not in the courts.

So, too, as relates to the clause in the above mentioned article of the Constitution, providing for cases of domestic violence. It rested with Congress, too, to determine upon the means proper to be adopted to fulfill this guarantee. They might, if they had deemed it most advisable to do so, have placed it in the power of a court to decide when a contingency had happened which required the federal government to interfere. But Congress thought otherwise, and no doubt wisely; and by the Act of February 28, 1795, provided, that, "in case of an insurrection in any State against the government thereof it shall be lawful for the President of the United States, on application of the Legislature of such State or of the executive (when the Legislature cannot be convened), to call forth such number of the militia of any other State or States, as may be applied for, as he may judge sufficient to suppress such insurrection."

By this act, the power of deciding whether the exigency had arisen upon which the government of the United States is bound to interfere, is given to the President. He is to act upon the application of the Legislature or of the executive, and consequently he must determine what body of men constitute the Legislature, and who is the governor, before he can act. The fact that both parties claim the right to the government cannot alter the case, for both cannot be entitled to it. If there is an armed conflict, like the one of which we are speaking, it is a case of domestic violence, and one of the parties must be in insurrection against the lawful government. And the President must, of necessity, decide which is the government, and which party is unlawfully arrayed against it, before he can perform the duty imposed upon him by the act of Congress.

After the President has acted and called out the militia, is a circuit court of the United States authorized to inquire whether his decision was right? Could the court, while the parties were actually contending in arms for the possession of the government, call witnesses before it and inquire which party represented a majority of the people? If it could, then it would become the duty of the court (provided it came to the conclusion that the President had decided incorrectly) to discharge those who were arrested or detained by the troops in the service of the United States or the government, which the President was endeavoring to maintain. If the judicial power extends so far, the guarantee contained in the Constitution of the United States is a guarantee of anarchy, and not of order. Yet if this right does not reside in the courts when the conflict is raging, if the judicial power is at that time bound to follow the decision of the political, it must be equally bound when the contest is over. It cannot, when peace is restored, punish as offenses and crimes the acts which it before recognized, and was bound to recognize, as lawful.

It is true that in this case the militia were not called out by the President. But upon the application of the governor under the charter government, the President recognized him as the executive power of the State, and took measures to call out the militia to support his authority if it should be found necessary for the general government to interfere; and it is admitted in the argument, that it was the knowledge of this decision that put an end to the armed opposition to the charter government, and prevented any further efforts to establish by force the proposed constitution. The interference of the President, therefore, by announcing his determination, was as effectual as if the militia had been assembled under his orders. And it should be equally authoritative. For certainly no court of the United States, with a knowledge of this decision, would have been justified in recognizing the opposing party as the lawful government; or in treating as wrong-doers or insurgents the officers of the government which the President had recognized, and was prepared to support by an armed force. In the case of foreign nations, the government acknowledged by the President is always recognized in the courts of justice. And this principle has been applied by the act of Congress to the sovereign States of the Union.

It is said that this power in the President is dangerous to liberty, and may be abused. All power may be abused if placed in unworthy hands. But it would be difficult, we think, to point out any other hands in which this power would be more safe, and at the same time equally effectual. When citizens of the same State are in arms against each other, and the constituted authorities unable to execute the laws, the interposition of the United States must be prompt, or it is of little

value. The ordinary course of proceedings in courts of justice would be utterly unfit for the crisis. And the elevated office of the President, chosen as he is by the people of the United States, and the high responsibility he could not fail to feel when acting in a case of so much moment, appear to furnish as strong safeguards against a willful abuse of power as human prudence and foresight could well provide. At all events, it is conferred upon him by the Constitution and laws of the United States, and must therefore be respected and enforced in its judicial tribunals. . . .

The remaining question is whether the defendants, acting under military orders issued under the authority of the government, were justified in breaking and entering the plaintiff's house. In relation to the act of the Legislature declaring martial law, it is not necessary in the case before us to inquire to what extent, nor under what circumstances, that power may be exercised by a State. Unquestionably a military government, established as the permanent government of the State, would not be a republican government, and it would be the duty of Congress to overthrow it. But the law of Rhode Island evidently contemplated no such government. It was intended merely for the crisis, and to meet the peril in which the existing government was placed by the armed resistance to its authority. It was so understood and construed by the State authorities. And, unquestionably, a State may use its military power to put down an armed insurrection, too strong to be controlled by the civil authority. The power is essential to the existence of every government, essential to the preservation of order and free institutions, and is as necessary to the States of this Union as to any other government. The State itself must determine what degree of force the crisis demands. And if the government of Rhode Island deemed the armed opposition so formidable, and so ramified throughout the State, as to require the use of its military force and the declaration of martial law, we see no ground upon which this court can question its authority. It was a state of war; and the established government resorted to the rights and usages of war to maintain itself, and to overcome the unlawful opposition. And in that state of things the officers engaged in its military service might lawfully arrest anyone, who, from the information before them, they had reasonable grounds to believe was engaged in the insurrection; and might order a house to be forcibly entered and searched, when there were reasonable grounds for supposing he might be there concealed. Without the power to do this, martial law and the military array of the government would be mere parade, and rather encourage attack than repel it. No more force, however, can be used than is necessary to accomplish the object. And if the power is exercised for the purposes of opposition, or any injury wilfully done to person or property, the party by whom, or by whose order, it is committed would undoubtedly be answerable. . . .

Upon the whole, we see no reason for disturbing the judgment of the Circuit Court. The admission of evidence to prove that the charter government was the established government of the State was an irregularity, but is not material to the judgment. A circuit court of the United States sitting in Rhode Island is presumed to know the constitution and law of the State. And in order to make up its opinion upon that subject, it seeks information from any authentic and available source, without waiting for the formal introduction of testimony to prove it, and without confining itself to the process which the parties may offer. But this error of the Circuit Court does not affect the result. For whether this evidence was or was not received, the Circuit Court, for the reasons hereinbefore stated, was bound to recognize that government as the paramount and established authority of the State.

Much of the argument on the part of the plaintiff turned upon political rights and political questions, upon which the court has been urged to express an opinion. We decline doing so. The high power has been conferred on this court of passing judgment upon the acts of the State sovereignties, and of the legislative and executive branches of the federal government, and of determining whether they are beyond the limits of power marked out for them respectively by the Constitution of the United States. This tribunal, therefore, should be the last to overstep the boundaries which limit its own jurisdiction. And while it should always be ready to meet any question confided to it by the Constitution, it is equally its duty not to pass beyond its appropriate sphere of action, and to take care not to involve itself in discussions which properly belong to other forums. No one, we believe, has ever doubted the proposition, that, according to the institutions of this country, the sovereignty in every State resides in the people of the State, and that they may alter and change their form of government at their own pleasure. But whether they have changed it or not by abolishing an old government, and establishing a new one in its place, is a question to be settled by the political power. And when that power has decided, the courts are bound to take notice of its decision, and to follow it.

The judgment of the Circuit Court must therefore be affirmed.

What, then, constitutes a political question? In *Luther*, Taney took the position that the Court should avoid any issue arising out of the Article IV Guarantee Clause. In his view, that article governs relations between the states and the federal government, not governments and courts. For more than 100 years, the Court adopted Taney's position: any case involving the Guarantee Clause constituted a nonjusticiable dispute.

This construction kept the Court out of several areas of the law, including disputes involving an important and controversial issue, reapportionment, the manner in which states draw legislative districts. Under the U.S. Constitution, each state is allotted a certain number of seats in the House of Representatives, a number based on the population of the state. Once that figure has been established, it is up to the state to determine specific congressional districts. Article I specifies,

Representatives . . . shall be apportioned among the several States which may be included within this Union, according to their respective Numbers. . . . The actual Enumeration shall be made within three Years after the first Meeting of the Congress of the United States, and within every subsequent

Term of ten Years, in such Manner as they shall by Law direct. The Number of Representatives shall not exceed one for every thirty Thousand, but each State shall have at Least one Representative.

In other words, Article I makes clear that a ten-year census determines the number of representatives each state receives. But no guidelines exist as to how those representatives are to be allocated or apportioned within a given state.

As population shifts occurred within states in the mid-1900s, some redrew their congressional district lines. For most, the new maps meant creating greater parity for urban centers as citizens moved out of rural areas. Others, however, ignored these shifts and refused to reapportion seats. Over time, their failure to do so became readily apparent. It was possible for two districts within the same state, with large differences in populations, each to elect one member to the House.

Because malapportionment generally had the greatest effect on urban voters, grossly undervaluing their voting power, reform groups representing their interests began to bring litigation to force legislatures to reapportion. In one of the most important of these efforts, *Colegrove v.*

Green (1946), they did so under Article IV. They argued that the failure to reapportion legislative districts deprived some voters of their right to a republican form of government. By way of proof, plaintiffs indicated that a large statistical discrepancy existed between the voting power of urban and rural dwellers because the Illinois legislature had not reapportioned since 1901.

Writing for the Court, Justice Frankfurter dismissed *Colegrove*. He invoked the logic of *Luther v. Borden* to hold that the question of legislative reapportionment within states was one left open by the Constitution. If the Court intervened in this matter, it would be acting in a way "hostile to a democratic system." Put in different terms, reapportionment constituted a "political thicket" into which "courts ought not enter."

Less than two decades later, however, in *Baker v. Carr* (1962), the Court did, in fact, enter this thicket, holding that reapportionment was a justiciable issue. What brought about this change? And, more relevant here, what meaning does *Baker* have for the political question doctrine? In particular, does it overrule *Luther* or does it merely change its interpretative context?

Baker v. Carr

369 U.S. 186 (1962)

Vote: 6 (Black, Brennan, Clark, Douglas, Stewart, Warren)
2 (Frankfurter, Harlan)
Opinion of the Court: Brennan
Concurring opinions: Clark, Douglas, Stewart
Dissenting opinions: Frankfurter, Harlan
Not participating: Whittaker

As a result of the Court's decision in *Colegrove,* many of the states that had not reapportioned since the turn of the century were under no federal constitutional mandate to do so, and disparities between the voting power of urban and

rural citizens continued to grow. Figure 2-2 shows that a rural vote for the Tennessee legislature counted nearly four times as much as an urban vote.

Naturally, many citizens and organizations wanted to force legislatures to reapportion, but under *Colegrove* they could not do so under the Guarantee Clause. They looked, therefore, to another section of the Constitution, the Fourteenth Amendment's Equal Protection Clause, which says, no state shall "deny to any person within its jurisdiction the equal protection of the laws." From this clause, they made the argument that the failure to reapportion led to unequal treatment of voters.

Although this strategy represented a clever legal attempt to reframe the issue of reapportionment, when attorneys sought to apply it to the Tennessee situation, a lower federal district court dismissed their suit.[31] Relying on *Colegrove* and other cases, that court held reapportionment to constitute a political question on which it could not rule.

Justice William J. Brennan, Jr., delivered the opinion of the Court:

[I]t is argued that apportionment cases . . . can involve no federal constitutional right except one resting on the guaranty of a republican form of government, and that complaints based on that clause have been held to present political questions which are nonjusticiable.

We hold that the claim pleaded here neither rests upon nor implicates the Guaranty Clause and that its justiciability is therefore not foreclosed by our decisions of cases involving that clause. . . . Appellants' claim that they are being denied equal protection is justiciable, and if "discrimination is sufficiently shown, the right to relief under the equal protection clause is not diminished by the fact that the discrimination relates to political rights." To show why we reject the argument based on the Guaranty Clause, we must examine the authorities under it. But because there appears to be some uncertainty as to why those cases did present political questions, and specifically as to whether this apportionment case is like those cases, we deem it necessary first to consider the contours of the "political question" doctrine. . . .

The nonjusticiability of a political question is primarily a function of the separation of powers. Much confusion results from the capacity of the "political question" label to obscure the need for case-by-case inquiry. Deciding whether a matter has in any measure been committed by the Constitution to another branch

31. For more on this, see Richard C. Cortner, "Strategies and Tactics of Litigants in Constitutional Cases," *Journal of Public Law* 17 (1968): 287-307; and Cortner, *The Apportionment Cases* (Knoxville: University of Tennessee Press, 1970).

Figure 2-2. *Map of Districts in Tennessee, 1901 and 1950*

1901

Battle of the ballot: In 1901 Memphis, Tennessee, had as many people as eight nearby counties together and elected nearly the same number of representatives.

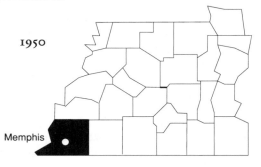

1950

By 1950 Memphis's population equaled that of twenty-four counties. Under the state constitution the city should have gained more representatives, but did not; so the rural vote counted almost four times as much as the urban. Reviewing city voters' complaint that this situation denied them equal protection of the laws, the Court in 1962 held that judges should hear and decide such claims under the Fourteenth Amendment *(Baker v. Carr)*. Chief Justice Earl Warren looked back upon this decision as the most important and influential in his sixteen years on the Court. It opened the way to enunciation (in *Reynolds v. Sims)* of the "one person, one vote" principle and its enforcement by court order in many related cases across the nation.

Source: *Equal Justice Under Law* (Washington, D.C.: Foundation of the Federal Bar Association, 1965), 108.

of government, or whether the action of that branch exceeds whatever authority has been committed, is itself a delicate exercise in constitutional interpretation, and is a responsibility of this Court as ultimate interpreter of the Constitution. To demonstrate this requires no less than to analyze representative cases and to infer from them the analytical threads that make up the political question doctrine. We shall then show that none of those threads catches this case.

Foreign relations: There are sweeping statements to the effect that all questions touching foreign relations are political questions. Not only does resolution of such issues frequently turn on standards that defy judicial application, or involve the exercise of a discretion demonstrably committed to the executive or legislature; but many such questions uniquely demand single-voiced statement of the Government's views. Yet it is error to suppose that every case or controversy which touches foreign relations lies beyond judicial cognizance. Our cases in this field seem invariably to show a discriminating analysis of the particular question posed, in terms of the history of its management by the political branches, of its susceptibility to judicial handling in the light of its nature and posture in the specific case, and of the possible consequences of judicial action. . . .

Dates of duration of hostilities: . . . [H]ere too analysis reveals isolable reasons for the presence of political questions, underlying this Court's refusal to review the political departments' determination of when or whether a war has ended. Dominant is the need for finality in the political determination. . . . But deference rests on reason, not habit. The question in a particular case may not seriously implicate considerations of finality. . . . Further, clearly definable criteria for decision may be available. In such case the political question barrier falls away. . . .

It is apparent that several formulations which vary slightly according to the settings in which the questions arise may describe a political question, although each has one or more elements which identify it as essentially a function of the separation of powers. Prominent on the surface of any case held to involve a political question is found a textually demonstrable constitutional commitment of the issue to a coordinate political department; or a lack of judicially discoverable and

manageable standards for resolving it; or the impossibility of deciding without an initial policy determination of a kind clearly for nonjudicial discretion; or the impossibility of a court's undertaking independent resolution without expressing lack of the respect due coordinate branches of government; or an unusual need for unquestioning adherence to a political decision already made; or the potentiality of embarrassment from multifarious pronouncements by various departments on one question.

Unless one of these formulations is inextricable from the case at bar, there should be no dismissal for non-justiciability on the ground of a political question's presence. The doctrine of which we treat is one of "political questions," not one of "political cases." The courts cannot reject as "no law suit" a bona fide controversy as to whether some action denominated "political" exceeds constitutional authority. The cases we have reviewed show the necessity for discriminating inquiry into the precise facts and posture of the particular case, and the impossibility of resolution by any semantic cataloguing.

But it is argued that this case shares the characteristics of decisions that constitute a category not yet considered, cases concerning the Constitution's guaranty, in Art. IV, § 4, of a republican form of government. A conclusion as to whether the case at bar does present a political question cannot be confidently reached until we have considered those cases with special care. We shall discover that Guaranty Clause claims involve those elements which define a "political question," and for that reason and no other, they are nonjusticiable. In particular, we shall discover that the nonjusticiability of such claims has nothing to do with their touching upon matters of state governmental organization.

Republican form of government: Luther v. Borden, though in form simply an action for damages for trespass was, as Daniel Webster said in opening the argument for the defense, "an unusual case." The defendants, admitting an otherwise tortious breaking and entering, sought to justify their action on the ground that they were agents of the established lawful government of Rhode Island, which State was then under martial law to defend itself from active insurrection; that the plaintiff was engaged in that insurrection; and that they entered under orders to arrest the plaintiff. The case arose "out of the unfortunate political differences which agitated the people of Rhode Island in 1841 and 1842," and which had resulted in a situation wherein two groups laid competing claims to recognition as the lawful government. The plaintiff's right to recover depended upon which of the two groups was entitled to such recognition. . . .

[S]everal factors were thought by the Court in Luther to make the question there "political": the commitment to the other branches of the decision as to which is the lawful state government; the unambiguous action by the President, in recognizing the charter government as the lawful authority; the need for finality in the executive's decision; and the lack of criteria by which a court could determine which form of government was republican.

But the only significance that Luther could have for our immediate purposes is in its holding that the Guaranty Clause is not a repository of judicially manageable standards which a court could utilize independently in order to identify a State's lawful government. The Court has since refused to resort to the Guaranty Clause—which alone had been invoked for the purpose—as the source of a constitutional standard for invalidating state action. . . .

Just as the Court has consistently held that a challenge to state action based on the Guaranty Clause presents no justiciable question so has it held, and for the same reasons that challenges to congressional action on the ground of inconsistency with that clause present no justiciable question. . . .

We come, finally, to the ultimate inquiry whether our precedents as to what constitutes a nonjusticiable "political question" bring the case before us under the umbrella of that doctrine. A natural beginning is to note whether any of the common characteristics which we have been able to identify and label descriptively

are present. We find none: The question here is the consistency of state action with the Federal Constitution. We have no question decided, or to be decided, by a political branch of government coequal with this Court. Nor do we risk embarrassment of our government abroad, or grave disturbance at home if we take issue with Tennessee as to the constitutionality of her action here challenged. Nor need the appellants, in order to succeed in this action, ask the Court to enter upon policy determinations for which judicially manageable standards are lacking. Judicial standards under the Equal Protection Clause are well developed and familiar, and it has been open to courts since the enactment of the Fourteenth Amendment to determine, if on the particular facts they must, that a discrimination reflects *no* policy, but simply arbitrary and capricious action.

This case does, in one sense, involve the allocation of political power within a State, and the appellants might conceivably have added a claim under the Guaranty Clause. Of course, as we have seen, any reliance on that clause would be futile. But because any reliance on the Guaranty Clause could not have succeeded it does not follow that appellants may not be heard on the equal protection claim which in fact they tender. True, it must be clear that the Fourteenth Amendment claim is not so enmeshed with those political question elements which render Guaranty Clause claims nonjusticiable as actually to present a political question itself. But we have found that not to be the case here. . . .

We conclude that the complaint's allegations of a denial of equal protection present a justiciable constitutional cause of action upon which appellants are entitled to a trial and a decision. The right asserted is within the reach of judicial protection under the Fourteenth Amendment.

Baker is significant for a number of reasons. One is that it opened the window for judicial resolution of reapportionment cases. Another, and more relevant here, is that it established a clear doctrinal base for determining political questions.

We demonstrate the vitality of *Baker* in Table

2-2, which depicts how the Court has used that framework. Note that Brennan's opinion did not dismiss the logic of *Luther* entirely; it just reworked it a bit. Nor did *Baker* lead to the demise of the political questions doctrine. Over the years, the Court has used it to dismiss a range of substantive disputes, particularly those involving interna-

Table 2–2 The Supreme Court and the Political Questions Doctrine: Some Examples

Examples of Its Use	*Examples of Its Rejection*
1. *Gilligan v. Morgan* (1973). In the aftermath of the shootings at Kent State, students asked the Court to hold that there was "a pattern of training, weaponry, and orders" in the National Guard that made the events of Kent State inevitable. They asked the Court to restrain the governor from "prematurely ordering Guard troops in civil disorders." The Court found that no justiciable controversy existed. Control of military forces is something the Constitution leaves explicitly to the control of legislatures and executives. In the words of the Court, "It would be difficult to think of a clearer example of the type of governmental action that was intended by the Constitution to be left to the political branches directly responsible . . . to the electoral process."	1. In *Powell v. McCormack* (1969) the Court examined the issue of whether the House of Representatives could vote to exclude a member—Rep. Adam Clayton Powell—on the grounds that he allegedly engaged in unethical activities. Respondents asked the Court to dismiss the suit because it asked a political question, meeting several of the criteria set out in *Baker v. Carr.* The Court refused to do so. In particular, it rejected the contention that the dispute was one which a "textually demonstrable constitutional commitment" to the House existed, enabling it to determine its own membership. Rather, the Constitution permits the House only to judge the "qualifications expressly set forth in the Constitution," which Powell met. It also rejected *Baker's* potentially embarrassing criteria, noting that: "Our system of government requires that the federal courts . . . interpret the Constitution in a manner at variance with a construction given the document by another branch."
2. In *Goldwater v. Carter* (1979), which presented a challenge to President Carter's unilateral termination of a U.S. treaty with Taiwan, Justice Rehnquist held the case presented a political question. In his view, it involved a foreign policy matter on which the Constitution provided no definitive answer. As such, it "should be left for resolution by the Executive and Legislative branches."	2. In *Goldwater v. Carter,* Justice Powell argued that the dispute did not present a political question under *Baker.* In his view, the case only "touched" foreign affairs, with the major issue being "constitutional division of power between Congress and the President." He wrote, "Interpretation of the Constitution does not imply lack of respect for a coordinate branch. If the President and the Congress had reached irreconcilable positions, final disposition of the question presented by this case would eliminate, rather than create, multiple constitutional interpretations."
3. In *O'Brien v. Brown* (1972), the Court refused to get involved in a split in the Democratic party. A national committee of the party excluded certain state delegations. Those excluded then challenged the committee's authority to do so. The Court suggested that the dispute involved a political question. Specifically, it stated that "no case is cited to us in which any federal court has undertaken to inject itself into the deliberative processes" of a national party convention.	3. In *Davis v. Bandemer* (1986) the Court held that political gerrymandering constituted a justiciable issue. Though they had been urged to find that it inherently asked the Court to address a political question, the justices found "none of the identifying characteristics of a nonjusticiable political question" dispute to exist.

tional relations. For example, federal courts often invoked the political question doctrine "as the basis for refusing to decide the validity of the Vietnam War under our own Constitution or international law."[32]

32. Wasby, *The Supreme Court in the Federal Judicial System,* 178.

Standing to Sue

Another constraint on federal judicial power is standing: if the party bringing the litigation is not the appropriate party, the courts will not resolve the dispute. Put in somewhat different terms, "not every person with the money to bring a lawsuit is entitled to litigate the legality or constitutionality of government action in the federal courts.''[33] Rather, as Justice Brennan noted in *Baker,* Article III requires that litigants demonstrate ''such a personal stake in the outcome of the controversy as to assure that concrete adverseness which sharpens the presentation of issues upon which the Court so largely depends for illumination of difficult constitutional questions.''

In most private disputes, the litigants have no difficulty demonstrating a personal stake or injury. The more interesting constitutional questions have arisen in those suits that involve parties wishing to challenge some government action on the grounds that they are taxpayers. Such claims raise an important question: Does the mere fact that one pays taxes provide a sufficiently personal stake in litigation, sufficient enough to meet the requirement for standing?

The Court first addressed this question in *Frothingham v. Mellon* (1923). At issue was the Sheppard-Towner Maternity Act, in which Congress provided federal maternity aid to the states to fund programs designed to reduce infant mortality rates. Although many progressive groups had lobbied for the law, other organizations viewed it as an unconstitutional intrusion into the family.[34] They decided to challenge it and enlisted one among their ranks, Harriet Frothingham, to serve as a plaintiff. She was not receiving Sheppard-Towner Maternity Act aid; she was a taxpayer who did not want to see her tax dollars spent on the program. Her attorneys argued that she had sufficient grounds to bring suit.

It has been held with practical uniformity by the Courts of the various states that a taxpayer has a sufficient interest to entitle him to maintain a suit against a public officer for the purpose of enjoining an unauthorized payment of public funds. . . . The appellant maintains . . . [that if] these payments are made [she] will suffer a direct injury in that she will be subjected to taxation to pay her proportionate part of such unauthorized payments. She, therefore, has an interest sufficient . . . to maintain a proceeding to enjoin the making of these payments. Her relation to these funds is exactly that of a *cestui que trust* [trust beneficiary] to funds held by his trustee. Her injury would be irreparable because it cannot be calculated. She can resort only to equity to maintain her right.

The Court refused to adopt this position. Rather, it held that Frothingham lacked standing to bring the litigation. Justice George Sutherland wrote for the majority:

If one taxpayer may champion and litigate such a cause, then every other taxpayer may do the same, not only in respect of the statute here under review but also in respect of every other appropriation act and statute whose administration requires the outlay of public money, and whose validity may be questioned. The bare suggestion of such a result, with its attendant inconveniences, goes far to sustain the conclusion which we have reached, that a suit of this character cannot be maintained.

He also outlined an approach to standing:

The party . . . must be able to show not only that the statute is invalid but that he has sustained or is immediately in danger of sustaining some direct injury as the result of its enforcement, and not merely that he suffers in some indefinite way in common with people generally.

For the next forty years, *Frothingham* served as a major bar to taxpayer suits. Unless litigants could demonstrate that a government program injured them or threatened to do so—beyond the mere expenditure of tax dollars—they could not bring suit. In *Flast v. Cohen,* however, the Court substantially relaxed that rule. Why? With what did it replace it?

---

33. Pritchett, *The American Constitution,* 145.
34. We adopt this discussion from Lee Epstein, *Conservatives in Court* (Knoxville: University of Tennessee Press, 1985), 31–36.

Flast v. Cohen

392 U.S. 83 (1968)

Vote: 8 (Black, Brennan, Douglas, Fortas, Marshall,
*   Stewart, Warren, White)*
*   1 (Harlan)*
Opinion of the Court: Warren
Concurring opinions: Douglas, Fortas, Stewart
Dissenting opinion: Harlan

Seven taxpayers sought to challenge federal expenditures made under the Elementary and Secondary Education Act of 1965. Under this law, states could apply to the federal government for grants to assist in the education of children from low income families. They could, for example, obtain funds for the acquisition of textbooks, school library materials, and so forth. The taxpayers alleged that some of the funds disbursed under this Act were used to finance "instruction in reading, arithmetic, and other subjects and for guidance in religious and sectarian schools." Such expenditures, they argued, violated the First Amendment's prohibition on religious establishment.

A three-judge district court dismissed their complaint. It reasoned that because the plaintiffs had suffered no real injury and because their sole claim of standard rested "solely on their status as federal taxpayers," they failed to meet the criteria established in *Frothingham*.

Chief Justice Warren delivered the opinion of the Court:

Standing is an aspect of justiciability and, as such, the problem of standing is surrounded by the same complexities and vagaries that inhere in justiciability. Standing has been called one of "the most amorphous [concepts] in the entire domain of public law." Some of the complexities peculiar to standing problems result because standing "serves, on occasion, as a shorthand expression for all the various elements of justiciability." In addition, there are at work in the standing doctrine the many subtle pressures which tend to cause policy considerations to blend into constitutional limitations.

Despite the complexities and uncertainties, some meaningful form can be given to the jurisdictional limitations placed on federal court power by the concept of standing. The fundamental aspect of standing is that it focuses on the party seeking to get his complaint before a federal court and not on the issues he wishes to have adjudicated. The "gist of the question of standing" is whether the party seeking relief has "alleged such a personal stake in the outcome of the controversy as to assure that concrete adverseness which sharpens the presentation of issues upon which the court so largely depends for illumination of difficult constitutional questions." Baker v. Carr (1962). In other words, when standing is placed in issue in a case, the question is whether the person whose standing is challenged is a proper party to request an adjudication of a particular issue and not whether the issue itself is justiciable. . . .

A taxpayer may or may not have the requisite personal stake in the outcome, depending upon the circumstances of the particular case. Therefore, we find no absolute bar in Article III to suits by federal taxpayers challenging allegedly unconstitutional federal taxing and spending programs. There remains, however, the problem of determining the circumstances under which a federal taxpayer will be deemed to have the personal stake and interest that impart the necessary concrete adverseness to such litigation so that standing can be conferred on the taxpayer *qua* taxpayer consistent with the constitutional limitations of Article III.

. . . We have noted that, in deciding the question of standing, it is not relevant that the substantive issues in the litigation might be nonjusticiable. However . . . it is both appropriate and necessary to look to the substantive issues for another purpose, namely, to determine whether there is a logical nexus between the status asserted and the claim sought to be adjudicated. . . .

The nexus demanded of federal taxpayers has two aspects to it. First, the taxpayer must establish a logical link between that status and the type of legislative enactment attacked. Thus, a taxpayer will be a proper party to allege the unconstitutionality only of exercises of congressional power under the taxing and spending clause of Art. I, § 8, of the Constitution. It will not be sufficient to allege an incidental expenditure of tax funds in the administration of an essentially regulatory statute. . . . Secondly, the taxpayer must establish a nexus between that status and the precise nature of the constitutional infringement alleged. Under this requirement, the taxpayer must show that the challenged enactment exceeds specific constitutional limitations imposed upon the exercise of the congressional taxing and spending power and not simply that the enactment is generally beyond the powers delegated to Congress by Art. I, § 8. When both nexuses are established, the litigant will have shown a taxpayer's stake in the outcome of the controversy and will be a proper and appropriate party to invoke a federal court's jurisdiction.

The taxpayer-appellants in this case have satisfied both nexuses to support their claim of standing under the test we announce today. Their constitutional challenge is made to an exercise by Congress of its power under Art. I, § 8, to spend for the general welfare, and the challenged program involves a substantial expenditure of federal tax funds. In addition, appellants have alleged that the challenged expenditures violate the Establishment and Free Exercise Clauses of the First Amendment. Our history vividly illustrates that one of the specific evils feared by those who drafted the Establishment Clause and fought for its adoption was that the taxing and spending power would be used to favor one religion over another or to support religion in general. James Madison, who is generally recognized as the leading architect of the religion clauses of the First Amendment, observed in his famous Memorial and Remonstrance Against Religious Assessments that ''the same authority which can force a citizen to contribute three pence only of his property for the support of any one establishment, may force him to conform to any other establishment in all cases whatsoever.'' The concern of Madison and his supporters was quite clearly that religious liberty ultimately would be the victim if government could employ its taxing and spending powers to aid one religion over another or to aid religion in general. The Establishment Clause was designed as a specific bulwark against such potential abuses of governmental power, and that clause of the First Amendment operates as a specific constitutional limitation upon the exercise by Congress

of the taxing and spending power conferred by Art. I, § 8.

The allegations of the taxpayer in Frothingham v. Mellon were quite different from those made in this case, and the result in *Frothingham* is consistent with the test of taxpayer standing announced today. The taxpayer in *Frothingham* attacked a federal spending program and she, therefore, established the first nexus required. However, she lacked standing because her constitutional attack was not based on an allegation that Congress, in enacting the Maternity Act of 1921, had breached a specific limitation upon its taxing and spending power. . . . In essence, Mrs. Frothingham was attempting to assert the States' interest in their legislative prerogatives and not a federal taxpayer's interest in being free of taxing and spending in contravention of specific constitutional limitations imposed upon Congress' taxing and spending power.

We have noted that the Establishment Clause of the First Amendment does specifically limit the taxing and spending power conferred by Art. I, § 8. Whether the Constitution contains other specific limitations can be determined only in the context of future cases. However, whenever such specific limitations are found, we believe a taxpayer will have a clear stake as a taxpayer in assuring that they are not breached by Congress. Consequently, we hold that a taxpayer will have standing consistent with Article III to invoke federal judicial power when he alleges that congressional action under the taxing and spending clause is in derogation of those constitutional provisions which operate to restrict the exercise of the taxing and spending power. The taxpayer's allegation in such cases would be that his tax money is being extracted and spent in violation of specific constitutional protections against such abuses of legislative power. Such an injury is appropriate for judicial redress, and the taxpayer has established the necessary nexus between his status and the nature of the allegedly unconstitutional action to support his claim of standing to secure judicial review. Under such circumstances, we feel confident that the questions will be framed with the necessary specificity, that the issues will be contested with the necessary adverseness and that the litigation will be pursued with the necessary vigor to assure that the constitutional challenge will be made in a form traditionally thought to be

Standing to Sue in the Aftermath of *Flast*

Examples of Cases Limiting Standing Concepts

Laird v. Tatum (1972)

Question: Do plaintiffs have standing to bring a suit to enjoin the army from surveilling the political activity of civilians, as a violation of the first Amendment?

The Court: No. They were unable to demonstrate a sufficiently direct injury or a particular and concrete constitutional violation.

United States v. Richardson (1974)

Question: Does a taxpayer have standing to challenge a congressional law allowing the CIA to avoid a public "accounting of agency expenditures" as a violation of Article I, Section 9?

The Court: Richardson fails to meet the criteria established in *Flast* and "neatly . . . falls within the *Frothingham* holding." In short, because the law was not enacted under Article I, Section 8, the taxpayer can-not demonstrate a "logical nexus" between his status and the law.

Schlesinger v. Reservists Committee to Stop the War (1974)

Question: Do members of an organization (and taxpayers) have standing to launch an attack on the Vietnam War? In particular, can they challenge the fact that members of Congress have commissions in the military reserves, as a violation of Article I, Section 6?

The Court: No. They have suffered an insufficiently concrete injury. Further, the suit does not meet *Flast's* nexus test because they did not challenge an Article I, Section 8, power.

Warth v. Seldin (1975)

Question: Do individuals and organizations have sufficient standing to sue a town zoning board on the grounds that its regulations discriminate against low and moderate income persons in violation of several constitutional guarantees?

The Court: No. They failed to demonstrate that they each had suffered some personal, actual, or concrete injury.

Valley Forge Christian College v. Americans United for Separation of Church and State (1982)

Question: Can an organization challenge, on First Amendment grounds, a decision by the Department of Health, Education and Welfare—made under a congressional law—to transfer surplus government property to a religious college?

The Court: No. The organization failed to demonstrate some personal injury. And, the "property transfer . . . was not an exercise of authority conferred by the taxing and spending clause of Article I, Section 8." The organization fails the *Flast* nexus test.

Allen v. Wright (1984)

Question: Do parents of black children have standing to challenge the IRS's alleged failure to deny tax-exempt status to schools that engage in racial discrimination on the grounds that such inaction diminished the quality of education their children were receiving and thus constituted a violation of the Equal Protection Clause?

The Court: No. Although an injury existed, the injury was not "fairly traceable" to IRS conduct. Further, it was unclear whether the injury would, in fact, be removed if the policy changed. The majority opinion also expressed concern that the principle of separation of powers might be violated if the Court granted standing in this suit. In its view, federal courts are "not the proper forum for general complaints about how government does its business."

Karcher v. May (1987)

Question: Do public officials (here, former presiding officers of the New Jersey state legislature) "who have participated in a lawsuit solely in their official capacities" have standing to appeal a judgment after they have left office?

The Court: No. Because they no longer hold office, they "lack the authority to pursue [the] appeal on behalf of the legislature."

Examples of Cases Expanding Standing Concepts

Sierra Club v. Morton (1972)

Question: Does an interest group have standing to bring a suit seeking to restrain the federal government from approving the development of a ski resort in a valley of a national park?

The Court: No. The group lacks standing because it failed to demonstrate sufficient injury to it or its members. However, the Court expanded the concept of injury to include harm to "aesthetic and environmental well-being."

United States v. SCRAP (1973)

Question: Does an interest group have standing to challenge an order of the Interstate Commerce Commission on the grounds that the order adversely affected the environment and the economic interests and recreational pursuits of the organization and its members?

The Court: Yes. The allegations made by SCRAP, though unproven, were sufficient to indicate that perceptible harm might occur. Moreover, SCRAP demonstrated a more "attenuated line of causation to the eventual injury" than did the Sierra Club in *Morton.*

Arlington Heights v. Metropolitan Housing Corporation (1977)

Question: Does a developer have standing to challenge a town's refusal to rezone an area (from a single-family to multifamily category) as racially discriminatory, despite the fact that zoning was not the only obstacle to its housing project? Does an individual black plaintiff have standing to challenge the town's decision on the grounds that he would want to live in the proposed housing project?

The Court: Yes to both questions. Both had specific, not "generalized," complaints. And, both had indicated a "fairly traceable" causal link between the injury and the town's denial sufficient to demonstrate an "actionable causal relationship."

capable of judicial resolution. We lack that confidence in cases such as *Frothingham* where a taxpayer seeks to employ a federal court as a forum in which to air his generalized grievances about the conduct of government or the allocation of power in the Federal System.

While we express no view at all on the merits of appellants' claims in this case, their complaint contains sufficient allegations under the criteria we have outlined to give them standing to invoke a federal court's jurisdiction for an adjudication on the merits.

As we can see, *Flast* did not overrule *Frothingham;* in fact, the Court was careful to indicate that had the 1968 ruling been applied to *Frothingham,* the plaintiff still would have been unable to attain standing. But *Flast* substantially revised the 1923 precedent. If taxpayers could indicate a logical link between their status and the legislation, and one between their status and a specific constitutional infringement, then they might have standing.

In theory, this standard appears to be relatively straightforward; in practice, however, it is open to a significant amount of interpretation. The box compares Warren Court and early Burger Court rulings on standing with some later rulings. As we can see, the earlier Court read *Flast* to relax significantly standing barriers. That reading has changed yet again; some suggest doctrine governing standing now resembles *Frothingham* rather than *Flast.*

Those who hold that view may be overstating the case, but it is true that standing, like the other "constraints" on judicial power—jurisdiction and justiciability—is open to interpretation. Article III may place certain limits on the power of the federal judiciary. However, its language is sufficiently vague, allowing for a good deal of judicial latitude.

In the final analysis, then, we are left with many questions centering on judicial power and constraints on its exercise. We shall ask just one.

Justice Brandeis, Concurring in *Ashwander v. Tennessee Valley Authority*

In 1936 Justice Louis D. Brandeis delineated, in a concurring opinion in *Ashwander v. Tennessee Valley Authority,* a set of Court-formulated rules useful in avoiding constitutional decisions. A portion of his opinion setting forth those rules, minus case cites and footnotes, follows:

The Court developed, for its own governance in the cases confessedly within its jurisdiction, a series of rules under which it has avoided passing upon a large part of all the constitutional questions pressed upon it for decision. They are:

1. The Court will not pass upon the constitutionality of legislation in a friendly, non-adversary, proceeding, declining because to decide such questions "is legitimate only in the last resort, and as a necessity in the determination of real, earnest and vital controversy between individuals. It never was the thought that, by means of a friendly suit, a party beaten in the legislature could transfer to the courts an inquiry as to the constitutionality of the legislative act."

2. The Court will not "anticipate a question of constitutional law in advance of the necessity of deciding it." "It is not the habit of the Court to decide questions of a constitutional nature unless absolutely necessary to a decision of the case."

3. The Court will not "formulate a rule of constitutional law broader than is required by the precise facts to which it is to be applied."

4. The Court will not pass upon a constitutional question although properly presented by the record, if there is also present some other ground upon which the case may be disposed of. This rule has found most varied application. Thus, if a case can be decided on either of two grounds, one involving a constitutional question, the other a question of statutory construction or general law, the Court will decide only the latter. Appeals from the highest court of a state challenging its decision of a question under the Federal Constitution are frequently dismissed because the judgment can be sustained on an independent state ground.

5. The Court will not pass upon the validity of a statute upon complaint of one who fails to show that he is injured by its operation. Among the many applications of this rule, none is more striking than the denial of the right of challenge to one who lacks a personal or property right. Thus, the challenge by a public official interested only in the performance of his official duty will not be entertained. . . .

6. (Omitted)

7. "When the validity of an act of the Congress is drawn in question, and even if a serious doubt of constitutionality is raised, it is a cardinal principle that this Court will first ascertain whether a construction of the statute is fairly possible by which the question may be avoided."

In the box on page 76 we excerpt part of Justice Louis D. Brandeis's concurring opinion in *Ashwander v. Tennessee Valley Authority* (1936) in which he outlined the constraints on judicial decision making we reviewed in this chapter. Given the cases and material you have just read, to what extent are those limitations real or open to interpretation?

READINGS

Adamany, David. "Legitimacy, Realigning Elections, and the Supreme Court."*Wisconsin Law Review* (1973): 790-846.

Bickel, Alexander M. "The Supreme Court, 1960 Term-Foreword: The Passive Virtues." *Harvard Law Review* 75 (1961): 40-79.

———. *The Least Dangerous Branch.* New York: Bobbs-Merrill, 1962.

Caldeira, Gregory A. "Courts and Public Opinion," in *The American Courts: A Critical Assessment.* John B. Gates and Charles A. Johnson, eds. Washington, D.C.: CQ Press, 1991.

Casper, Jonathan D. "The Supreme Court and National Policy Making." *American Political Science Review* 70 (1976): 50-63.

Choper, Jesse H. *Judicial Review and the National Political Process.* Chicago: University of Chicago Press, 1980.

Dahl, Robert. "Decision Making in a Democracy: The Supreme Court as a National Policy-Maker." *Journal of Public Law* 6 (1957): 279-295.

Ely, John Hart. *Democracy and Distrust.* Cambridge, Mass.: Harvard University Press, 1980.

Fisher, Louis. *Constitutional Dialogues.* Princeton, N.J.: Princeton University Press, 1988.

Funston, Richard. *A Vital National Seminar.* Palo Alto, Calif.: Mayfield, 1978.

Lasser, William. *The Limits of Judicial Power.* Chapel Hill: University of North Carolina Press, 1988.

Orren, Karen. "Standing to Sue: Interest Group Conflict in the Federal Courts." *American Political Science Review* 70 (1976): 723-741.

Radcliffe, James E. *The Case-or-Controversy Provision.* University Park: Pennsylvania State University Press, 1978.

Strum, Philippa. *The Supreme Court and Political Questions.* Tuscaloosa: University of Alabama Press, 1974.

Wolfe, Christopher. *The Rise of Modern Judicial Review.* New York: Basic Books, 1986.

———. *Judicial Activism.* Pacific Grove, Calif.: Brooks/Cole, 1991.

CHAPTER 3

THE LEGISLATURE

Article I of the U.S. Constitution is its longest and most explicit. The nation's Founders spelled out in great detail the powers Congress did and did not have over its own operations and its authority to make laws. Reading through Article I, we might conclude that it would not have been the source of much litigation. After all, given its clarity, how much room for interpretation could there be?

For cases involving Congress's authority over its internal affairs, this assumption would be accurate. The Supreme Court has heard relatively few cases touching upon the first seven sections of Article I, which deal with the various qualifications for membership in Congress, the ability of the chambers to punish members, and certain privileges enjoyed by the members. In those on which the Court has ruled, it generally, though not always, has given the legislature great latitude over its own business. That assumption, however, is incorrect when we consider cases that deal directly with Congress's most basic power, the enactment of laws, and with its role in American government. Article I, Section 8, enumerates specifically the substantive areas in which Congress may legislate. But is it too specific, failing to foresee how congressional powers might need to be exercised in areas it does not cover? For example, Section 8 provides Congress with the power to borrow and coin money, but not with the "authority to make paper money legal tender for

the payment of debts."[1] Since 1792 congressional committees have held investigations and hearings, but no clause in Section 8 authorizes them to do so. In general, the Supreme Court has had to determine whether legislative action that is not explicitly covered in Article I falls within Congress's authority, and that is why the Court so often has examined statutes passed by Congress.

There is another reason. As we saw in Chapter 1, and as we shall see throughout this book, basic (and purposeful) tensions were built into the design of the government. Sometimes disputes occur between the branches of the federal government; in other instances, between the federal government and the states; and often, between government and individuals. Emanating from the basic principles underlying the structure of government—federalism, the separation of powers, and checks and balances—these conflicts have provided the stuff of myriad legal disputes. And Congress has been right in the middle of many of them.

This chapter examines how the Court has interpreted Article I of the Constitution. It is divided into three sections: the first explores cases involving Congress's authority over its own structure and operations; the second looks at the sources and scope of its lawmaking power; and the third

1. J. W. Peltason, *Understanding the Constitution,* 11th ed. (New York: Holt, Rinehart and Winston, 1988), 17.

Table 3-1   U.S. Supreme Court Justices with Federal or State Legislative Experience

Justice	House	Senate	State	Court Service
		Legislative Service		
		Federal		
John Rutledge			S.C. (1776–78; 98–99)	1789–91
John Blair, Jr.			Va. (1766–70)	1789–96
William Paterson		1789–90	N.J. (1775–76)	1793–1806
Samuel Chase			Md. (1776–84)	1796–1811
Oliver Ellsworth		1789–96	Conn. (1773–76)	1796–1800
Bushrod Washington			Va. (1787)	1798–1829
Alfred Moore			N.C. (1782, 1792)	1799–1804
John Marshall	1799–1800		Va. (1782–85; 87–90; 95–96)	1801–35
William Johnson			S.C. (1794–98)	1804–34
Henry B. Livingston			N.Y. (3 sessions)	1806–23
Joseph Story	1808–09		Mass. (1805–08)	1811–45
Gabriel Duvall	1794–96		Md. (1787–94)	1811–35
Smith Thompson			N.Y. (1800)	1823–43
Robert Trimble			Ky. (1802)	1826–28
John McLean	1813–16			1829–61
Henry Baldwin	1817–22			1830–44
James M. Wayne	1829–35		Ga. (1815–16)	1835–67
Roger B. Taney			Md. (1799–1800; 16–21)	1836–64
Philip P. Barbour	1814–25		Va. (1812–14)	1836–41
John McKinley	1837	1826–31; 1837	Ala. (1820, 1831, 1836)	1837–52
Peter Daniel			Va. (1809–12)	1841–60
Levi Woodbury		1825–31; 41–45	N.H. (1825)	1846–51
Benjamin R. Curtis			Mass. (1849–51)	1851–57
John A. Campbell			Ala. (1837, 1843)	1853–61
Nathan Clifford	1839–43		Maine (1830–34)	1858–81
Noah H. Swayne			Ohio (1830, 1836)	1862–81
David Davis		1877–85	Ill. (1845–47)	1862–77
Stephen J. Field			Calif. (1850–51)	1863–97
Salmon P. Chase		1849–55		1864–73
William Strong	1847–51			1870–80
Ward Hunt			N.Y. (1839)	1873–82
Morrison R. Waite			Ohio (1850–52)	1874–88
William B. Woods			Ohio (1858–62)	1880–87
Stanley Matthews		1877–79	Ohio (1855–58)	1881–89
Lucius Q. C. Lamar	1857–60; 73–77	1877–85	Ga. (1853)	1888–93
Melville W. Fuller			Ill. (1863–64)	1888–1910
Howell E. Jackson		1881–86	Tenn. (1880)	1893–95
Edward D. White		1891–94	La. (1874)	1894–1921
Joseph McKenna	1885–92		Calif. (1875–76)	1898–1925
William Moody	1895–1902			1906–10
Willis Van Devanter			Wyo. (1888)	1910–37
Joseph R. Lamar			Ga. (1886–89)	1910–16
Mahlon Pitney	1895–99		N.J. (1899–1901)	1912–22
George Sutherland	1901–03	1905–17	Utah (1896–1900)	1922–38
Hugo L. Black		1927–37		1937–71
James F. Byrnes	1911–25	1931–41		1941–42
Harold H. Burton		1941–45	Ohio (1929)	1945–58
Fred M. Vinson	1924–29			1946–53
Sherman Minton		1935–41		1949–56
Sandra Day O'Connor			Ariz. (1969–75)	1981–

Source: Adapted from Elder Witt, *Guide to the U.S. Supreme Court*, 2d ed. (Washington, D.C.: Congressional Quarterly, 1990), 171.

examines its role within the larger American government system.

Congressional Authority over Internal Affairs: Institutional Independence and Integrity

Several sections of Article I provide Congress with the means to safeguard the independence and integrity of the institution. Some deal with the ability of the chambers to control who joins them and to punish those who do not behave in accord with their norms. Another section, the Speech or Debate Clause, protects members from "harassment" by other institutions.

Before we discuss how the Court has interpreted these sections, look at the data in Table 3-1, page 79. We often think about the Court and Congress as wholly separate entities, but they are connected in an interesting way. Table 3-1 lists the justices who served in Congress or a state legislature prior to their appointment to the bench. Almost half of all those who have sat on the Supreme Court have had legislative experience. Some might conclude that those justices would empathize with the claims of Congress regarding the need for authority over its own affairs, and, indeed, the Court generally has acceded to legislative wishes—but not always. As you read what follows, think about the reasons the Court offers for its decisions. Further, take note of the various coalitions emerging on different Courts. Do the justices with legislative experience exhibit a greater willingness to defer to Congress than those who never were legislators?

Membership in Congress: Seating and Discipline

Article I contains the requirements that must be met by all prospective members of Congress:

—A senator must be at least thirty years old and have been a citizen of the United States not less than nine years (Section 3, Clause 3).

—A representative must be at least twenty-five years old and have been a citizen not less than seven years (Section 2, Clause 2).

—Every member of Congress must be, when elected, an inhabitant of the state that he or she is to represent (Section 2, Clause 2, and Section 3, Clause 3).

—No one may be a member of Congress who holds any other "Office under the United States" (Section 6, Clause 2).

In addition, Section 3 of the Fourteenth Amendment states that no person may be a senator or a representative who, having previously taken an oath as a member of Congress to support the Constitution, has engaged in rebellion against the United States or given aid or comfort to its enemies, unless Congress has removed such disability by a two-thirds vote of both houses.

With only a few exceptions, these standards *qua* standards have not caused much controversy or litigation. Some legal questions have arisen with respect to their relationship to another Article I provision, Section 5, which reads: "Each House shall be the Judge of the Elections, Returns and Qualifications of its own Members." Several alternative interpretations are possible here. One is that this clause ought to be read in conjunction with the constitutional standards set out above. That is, Congress cannot deny a duly elected person a seat in the institution unless that person fails to meet specified criteria. Another interpretation is that Congress is free to develop additional qualifications, independent of those specified elsewhere.

For the better part of the nation's history, the Court stayed away from such disputes, even though Congress occasionally acted "as if it were entitled to add qualifications as well as wink at

Table 3–2   Duly Elected Members of Congress Excluded

Chamber (Year)	Member-Elect (Party-State)	Grounds for Exclusion
Senate (1793)	Albert Gallatin (D-Pa.)	Citizenship
House (1823)	John Bailey (Ind.-Mass.)	Residence
House (1867)	John Y. Brown (D-Ky.)	Loyalty
House (1867)	John D. Young (D-Ky.)	Loyalty
House (1867)	John A. Wimpy (Ind.-Ga.)	Loyalty
House (1867)	W. D. Simpson (Ind.-S.C.)	Loyalty
Senate (1867)	Phillip F. Thomas (D-Md.)	Loyalty
House (1870)	Benjamin F. Whittemore (R-S.C.)	Malfeasance
House (1900)	Brigham H. Roberts (D-Utah)	Polygamy
House (1919)	Victor L. Berger (Socialist-Wis.)	Sedition
House (1920)	Victor L. Berger (Socialist-Wis.)	Sedition
House (1967)	Adam C. Powell, Jr. (D-N.Y.)	Misconduct

Source: *Guide to Congress,* 3d ed. (Washington, D.C.: Congressional Quarterly, 1982), 823, 825.

failure to meet them."[2] For example, in the wake of the Civil War, Congress enacted the Test Oath Law (1862), which required incoming members to "swear . . . that they had never voluntarily borne arms against the United States." Moreover, as shown in Table 3-2, both the House and the Senate have refused to seat properly elected individuals, sometimes on extraconstitutional grounds. The Senate excluded Phillip Thomas on loyalty grounds when it was discovered that he had "given $100 to his son when the son entered Confederate military service."[3] The House refused to seat Brigham H. Roberts because he had

2. *Guide to Congress,* 3d. ed, (Washington, D.C.: Congressional Quarterly, 1982), 822.
3. Ibid.

been convicted of violating an antipolygamy law.

Investigating the Roberts case, a congressional committee concluded that the Framers "had not foreclosed the right of Congress to establish qualifications for membership other than those mentioned in the Constitution."[4] As Table 3-2 shows, both houses subscribed to this theory. The question of whether the Supreme Court would follow suit remained largely unaddressed until 1969. In that year, the Court decided *Powell v. McCormack* in which it squarely responded to Congress's traditional approach to seating qualifications. What was the nature of that response? Did the Court simply defer to Congress's wishes?

4. Ibid., 824.

Powell v. McCormack

395 U.S. 486 (1969)

Vote: 7 (Black, Brennan, Douglas, Harlan, Marshall, Warren, White)
    1 (Stewart)
Opinion of the Court: Warren
Concurring opinion: Douglas
Dissenting opinion: Stewart

Rep. Adam Clayton Powell, Jr., was "one of the most interesting and controversial figures ever to serve in the United States Congress."[5] As pastor of the Abyssinian Baptist Church in Harlem, one of the nation's largest congregations, Powell had been a force within that New York

5. Thomas G. Walker, *American Politics and the Constitution* (North Scituate, Mass.: Duxbury Press, 1978), 132. We derive our account largely from this source.

In 1967 the House of Representatives voted to exclude Adam Clayton Powell, Jr., from its chambers, even though he had been duly elected to office. In Powell v. McCormack *(1969) the Court held that because Powell met the constitutional standards for membership, the House could not refuse to seat him.*

City community since the 1930s. This influence only increased when he was elected to the House in 1944 (he received nominations from both the Democratic and Republican parties) and continued to be reelected by wide margins for the next twenty-five years.

Powell's problem was never the displeasure of his constituents; rather, it centered on his relations with his colleagues. By the early 1960s he had acquired sufficient seniority to assume the chairmanship of the House Committee on Education and Labor, but he had became unpopular. Other House members disliked his opulent, unconventional lifestyle, his unpredictable leadership, and his use of the media to suit his political ends. Moreover, by that time, Powell had become entangled in various legal controversies; for example, he refused to pay damages assessed against him in a defamation of character suit and actively sought to avert efforts to compel him to pay.

In response to all this the Eighty-ninth Congress (1965-1966) launched an inquiry into Powell's activities. This investigation yielded two major violations of House rules: Powell had used federal monies to fly a woman staff member with him on trips to his vacation home in the Bahamas and to pay his former wife a salary of $20,000, even though she did not work in his district or in Washington, D.C., in accordance with law. The House refused to seat Powell pending further investigation and despite the fact that he had been reelected in November 1966.

Four months later, in March 1967, the new investigation reached two conclusions: (1) from a constitutional standpoint, Powell met the requirements for office; he was older than twenty-five, had been a citizen of the United States for seven years, and he was an inhabitant of New York; and (2) Powell had sought to evade the fine associated with the defamation of character offense, had misused public funds, and filed false expenditure reports. The committee recommended "that Powell be sworn and seated as a member of . . . Congress but that he be censured by the House, fined $40,000 and be deprived of his seniority."[6] The House, however, rejected that recommendation and instead adopted 307-116, a resolution that excluded Powell from the House and directed House Speaker John McCormack to "notify the Governor of New York that the seat was vacant."[7]

Powell, not one to accept this decision lying down, responded. He and thirteen constituents filed a lawsuit against McCormack and other members of Congress, claiming that Congress's refusal to seat him violated the letter of the Constitution. In other words, because he met the requirements for office, the House had no choice but to seat him. In his view, Article I, Section 5—"Each House shall be the judge of the Elections, Returns and Qualifications of its own Mem-

6. *Powell v. McCormack,* 395 U.S. 486 at 492 (1969).
7. Ibid. at 493.

bers''—was not implicated: it gave Congress no authority to exclude members meeting constitutional standards for office.

McCormack's attorneys thought otherwise. In their opinion and in accord with institutional tradition, the Court should read separately the Qualifications Clause and Section 5. They argued that the House has the authority to exclude members, even if they meet constitutional standards.[8]

Chief Justice Earl Warren delivered the opinion of the Court.

Relying heavily on Charles Warren's analysis of the Convention debates, petitioners argue that the proceedings manifest the Framers' unequivocal intention to deny either branch of Congress the authority to add to or otherwise vary the membership qualifications expressly set forth in the Constitution. We do not completely agree, for the debates are subject to other interpretations. However, we have concluded that the records of the debates, viewed in the context of the bitter struggle for the right to freely choose representatives which had recently concluded in England and in light of the distinction the Framers made between the power to expel and the power to exclude, indicate that petitioners' ultimate conclusion is correct.

The Convention opened in late May 1787. By the end of July, the delegates adopted, with a minimum of debate, age requirements for membership in both the Senate and the House. The Convention then appointed a Committee of Detail to draft a constitution incorporating these and other resolutions adopted during the preceding months. . . .

On August 10, the Convention considered the Committee of Detail's proposal that the "Legislature of the United States shall have authority to establish such uniform qualifications of the members of each House, with regard to property, as to the said Legislature shall seem expedient." The debate on this proposal discloses much about the views of the Framers on the

8. McCormack's attorneys also made a number of more procedurally based claims. For example, after Powell initiated the suit, he was reelected to office. This time the House decided to seat him. Thus, they argued that the dispute was moot. The Court, however, disagreed and ruled on the merits of Powell's claims.

issue of qualifications. For example, James Madison urged its rejection, stating that the proposal would vest

"an improper & dangerous power in the Legislature. The qualifications of electors and elected were fundamental articles in a Republican Govt. and ought to be fixed by the Constitution. If the Legislature could regulate those of either, it can by degrees subvert the Constitution. A Republic may be converted into an aristocracy or oligarchy as well by limiting the number capable of being elected, as the number authorized to elect. . . . It was a power also, which might be made subservient to the views of one faction agst. another. Qualifications founded on artificial distinctions may be devised, by the stronger in order to keep out partizans of [a weaker] faction."

Significantly, Madison's argument was not aimed at the imposition of a property qualification as such, but rather at the delegation to the Congress of the discretionary power to establish any qualifications. . . .

In view of what followed Madison's speech, it appears that on this critical day the Framers were facing and then rejecting the possibility that the legislature would have power to usurp the "indisputable right [of the people] to return whom they thought proper" to the legislature. Oliver Ellsworth, of Connecticut, noted that a legislative power to establish property qualifications was exceptional and "dangerous because it would be much more liable to abuse." Gouverneur Morris then moved to strike "with regard to property" from the Committee's proposal. His intention was "to leave the Legislature entirely at large." Hugh Williamson, of North Carolina, expressed concern that if a majority of the legislature should happen to be "composed of any particular description of men, of lawyers for example, . . . the future elections might be secured to their own body." Madison then referred to the British Parliament's assumption of the power to regulate the qualifications of both electors and the elected and noted that "the abuse they had made of it was a lesson worthy of our attention. They had made the changes in both cases subservient to their own views, or to the views of political or Religious parties." Shortly thereafter, the Convention rejected both Gouverneur Morris' motion and the Committee's proposal. Later the same day, the Convention adopted without debate the provision authorizing each House to be "the judge of the . . . qualifications of its own members."

One other decision made the same day is very important to determining the meaning of Art. I, § 5. When the delegates reached the Committee of Detail's proposal to empower each House to expel its members, Madison "observed that the right of expulsion . . . was too important to be exercised by a bare majority of a quorum: and in emergencies [one] faction might be dangerously abused." He therefore moved that "with the concurrence of two-thirds" be inserted. With the exception of one State, whose delegation was divided, the motion was unanimously approved without debate, although Gouverneur Morris noted his opposition. The importance of this decision cannot be over-emphasized. None of the parties to this suit disputes that prior to 1787 the legislative powers to judge qualifications and to expel were exercised by a majority vote. Indeed, without exception, the English and colonial antecedents to Art. I, § 5, cls. 1 and 2, support this conclusion. Thus, the Convention's decision to increase the vote required to expel, because that power was "too important to be exercised by a bare majority," while at the same time not similarly restricting the power to judge qualifications, is compelling evidence that they considered the latter already limited by the standing qualifications previously adopted. . . .

As clear as these statements appear, respondents dismiss them as "general statements . . . directed to other issues." They suggest that far more relevant is Congress' own understanding of its power to judge qualifications as manifested in post-ratification exclusion cases. Unquestionably, both the House and the Senate have excluded members-elect for reasons other than their failure to meet the Constitution's standing qualifications. For almost the first 100 years of its existence, however, Congress strictly limited its power to judge the qualifications of its members to those enumerated in the Constitution.

Congress was first confronted with the issue in 1807, when the eligibility of William McCreery was challenged because he did not meet additional residency requirements imposed by the State of Maryland. In recommending that he be seated, the House Committee of Elections reasoned:

"The committee proceeded to examine the Constitution, with relation to the case submitted to them, and to find that qualifications of members are therein determined, without reserving any authority to the State Legislatures to change, add to, or diminish those qualifications; and that, by that instrument, Congress is constituted the sole judge of the qualifications prescribed by it, and are obliged to decide agreeably to the Constitutional rules. . . ." (1807).

Lest there be any misunderstanding of the basis for the committee's recommendation, during the ensuing debate the chairman explained the principles by which the committee was governed:

"The Committee of Elections considered the qualifications of members to have been unalterably determined by the Federal Convention, unless changed by an authority equal to that which framed the Constitution at first; that neither the State nor the Federal Legislatures are vested with authority to add to those qualifications, so as to change them. . . . Congress, by the Federal Constitution, are not authorized to prescribe the qualifications of their own members, but they are authorized to judge of their qualifications; in doing so, however, they must be governed by the rules prescribed by the Federal Constitution, and by them only. These are the principles on which the Election Committee have made up their report, and upon which their resolution is founded."

The chairman emphasized that the committee's narrow construction of the power of the House to judge qualifications was compelled by the "fundamental principle in a free government," that restrictions upon the people to choose their own representatives must be limited to those "absolutely necessary for the safety of the society." At the conclusion of a lengthy debate, which tended to center on the more narrow issue of the power of the States to add to the standing qualifications set forth in the Constitution, the House agreed by a vote of 89 to 18 to seat Congressman McCreery.

There was no significant challenge to these principles for the next several decades. They came under heavy attack, however, "during the stress of civil war [but initially] the House of Representatives declined to exercise the power [to exclude], even under circumstances of great provocation." The abandonment of such restraint, however, was among the casualties of the general upheaval produced in war's wake. From that time until the present, congressional practice has been erratic; and on the few occasions when a member-elect was excluded although he met all the qualifications set forth in the Constitution, there were frequently vigorous dissents. Even the annotations to the official manual of procedure for the 90th Congress manifest doubt as to the House's power to exclude a member-elect who has met the constitutionally prescribed qualifications.

Had these congressional exclusion precedents been more consistent, their precedential value still would be quite limited. That an unconstitutional action has been taken before surely does not render that same action any less unconstitutional at a later date. Particularly in view of the Congress' own doubts in those few cases where it did exclude members-elect, we are not inclined to give its precedents controlling weight. The relevancy of prior exclusion cases is limited largely to the insight they afford in correctly ascertaining the draftsmen's intent. Obviously, therefore, the precedential value of these cases tends to increase in proportion to their proximity to the Convention in 1787. And, what evidence we have of Congress' early understanding confirms our conclusion that the House is without power to exclude any member-elect who meets the Constitution's requirements for membership.

Had the intent of the Framers emerged from these materials with less clarity, we would nevertheless have been compelled to resolve any ambiguity in favor of a narrow construction of the scope of Congress' power to exclude members-elect. A fundamental principle of our representative democracy is, in Hamilton's words, "that the people should choose whom they please to govern them." As Madison pointed out at the Convention, this principle is undermined as much by limiting whom the people can select as by limiting the franchise itself. In apparent agreement with this basic philosophy, the Convention adopted his suggestion limiting the power to expel. To allow essentially that same power to be exercised under the guise of judging qualifications, would be to ignore Madison's warning, and some of Congress' own post–Civil War exclusion cases, against "vesting an improper & dangerous power in the Legislature." Moreover, it would effectively nullify the Convention's decision to require a two-thirds vote for expulsion. Unquestionably, Congress has an interest in preserving its institutional integrity, but in most cases that interest can be sufficiently safeguarded by the exercise of its power to punish its members for disorderly behavior and, in extreme cases, to expel a member with the concurrence of two-thirds. In short, both the intention of the Framers, to the extent it can be determined, and an examination of the basic principles of our democratic system persuade us that the Constitution does not vest in the Congress a discretionary power to deny membership by a majority vote.

For these reasons, we have concluded that Art. I, § 5, is at most a "textually demonstrable commitment" to Congress to judge only the qualifications expressly set forth in the Constitution. Therefore, the "textual commitment" formulation of the political question doctrine does not bar federal courts from adjudicating petitioners' claims.

Chief Justice Warren's holding in *Powell* is indisputable: because Powell was duly elected and because he met the constitutional standards for membership, the House could not refuse to seat him. As Warren emphatically noted, "Congress is limited to the standing qualifications prescribed in the Constitution."

The Court has been more willing to give Congress latitude in disciplining seated members. According to the Constitution, "Each House may . . . punish its Members for disorderly Behavior, and, with the Concurrence of two thirds, expel a Member." Although the Supreme Court has not dealt directly with any dispute involving the punishment of members, such as censure or expulsion, it has suggested that this is a broad privilege, best left to the judgment of the individual chambers (see, for example, *In re Chapman*, 1897). To be sure, this kind of action is not something Congress takes with any regularity—particularly disciplining through expulsion—but since 1787, it has censured twenty-six members and expelled nineteen.

The Speech or Debate Clause

The Constitution not only provides mechanisms for Congress to discipline its members, but also it contains a safeguard against harassment or intimidation. Article I, Section 6, specifies:

The Senators and Representatives . . . shall in all Cases, except Treason, Felony, and Breach of the Peace, be privileged from Arrest during their Attendance at the Session of their respective Houses, and in going to and returning from the same; and for any Speech or Debate in either House, they shall not be questioned in any other Place.

Called the Speech or Debate Clause, this privilege of membership emanates from British practice. C. Herman Pritchett noted, "Immunity from arrest during sessions of the legislature was one of the protections asserted by the English Parliament in its struggle with the Crown, and embodied in the English Bill of Rights."[9] The importance of the Speech or Debate Clause's protection is undeniable: without it, a president could order the arrest of, or otherwise intimidate, members of Congress who disagreed with the administration. The Framers thought the protection was necessary

9. C. Herman Pritchett, *Constitutional Law of the Federal System* (Englewood Cliffs, N.J.: Prentice-Hall, 1984), 177.

"to protect the integrity of the legislative process by insuring the independence of individual legislators."[10]

The language of Section 6 has generated two kinds of constitutional questions: What is protected and who is protected? Its reach was first addressed by the Court in *Kilbourn v. Thompson* (1881). In *Kilbourn* the Court dealt primarily with the scope of congressional investigations (*see pages 100–101*), but it also noted that the clause extends to

written reports presented . . . by its committees, to resolutions offered, which, though in writing, must be reproduced in speech, and to the act of voting, whether it is done vocally or by passing between the tellers. In short, to things generally done in a session [of Congress] by one of its members in relation to the business before it.

With only some minor modifications, *Kilbourn* remained the Court's most significant statement on the Speech or Debate Clause until 1972, when *Gravel v. United States* was decided. This case had important implications for both dimensions of Section 6: Who and what are protected?

10. *United States v. Brewster*, 408 U.S. at 507 (1972). See Louis Fisher, *American Constitutional Law* (New York: McGraw-Hill, 1990), 235.

Gravel v. United States

408 U.S. 606 (1972)

Vote: 5 (Blackmun, Burger, Powell, Rehnquist, White)
    4 (Brennan, Douglas, Marshall, Stewart)
Opinion of the Court: White
Dissenting opinions: Brennan, Douglas
Dissenting in part: Stewart

On June 29, 1971, Sen. Mike Gravel, D-Alaska, held a public meeting of the Subcommittee on Buildings and Grounds of which he was the chair. Before the hearing began, Gravel made a statement about the Vietnam War, noting that it was

"relevant to his subcommittee . . . because of its effects upon the domestic economy and . . . the lack of federal funds to provide for adequate public facilities."[11] He then read portions of a classified government document, now known as the Pentagon Papers, which provided details of U.S. involvement in the war. After he finished, Gravel introduced the forty-seven-volume document into the committee's record and "arranged, without any personal profit to himself, for its verbatim publication by Beacon Press," a pub-

11. *Gravel v. United States*, 408 U.S. 606 (1972), Brief for Petitioner, 5.

lishing division of the Unitarian Universalist Association.[12]

The Justice Department undertook an investigation to determine how the Pentagon Papers got released. It requested a district court judge to convene a grand jury, which in turn subpoenaed Dr. Leonard Rodberg, an aide to Senator Gravel. Rodberg and Gravel asked the court to quash the subpoena. In their view, U.S. attorneys "intended to interrogate Dr. Rodberg" about "the actions of Senator Gravel and his aides in making available" the Pentagon Papers. Such interrogation, they argued, would violate the Speech or Debate Clause because its scope extended to aides. As Gravel's attorney later noted, "Given the realities of the modern-day legislative process, congressmen must seek the advice and assistance of persons outside the immediate staff." Forcing Rodberg to testify would be tantamount to having Gravel do so: they were both protected. He made a similar claim when prosecutors sought to force the publisher of Beacon Press to testify.

At first, the government rejected all those claims; it even argued that Gravel's actions remained outside of constitutional protections. By the time the case reached the Supreme Court, however, the government had limited its arguments to Gravel's aide and the publisher. It asserted that the language of the Speech or Debate Clause, past precedents, and the intent of the Framers all pointed to the same conclusion: its reach covered neither congressional aides nor third parties.

Justice Byron R. White delivered the opinion of the Court:

[T]he United States strongly urges that because the Speech or Debate Clause confers a privilege only upon "Senators and Representatives," Rodberg himself has no valid claim to constitutional immunity from grand jury inquiry. In our view, both courts below correctly rejected this position. We agree with the Court of

12. Ibid.

Appeals that for the purpose of construing the privilege a Member and his aide are to be "treated as one." . . . [I]t is literally impossible, in view of the complexities of the modern legislative process, . . . for Members of Congress to perform their legislative tasks without the help of aides and assistants; the day-to-day work of such aides is so critical to the Members' performance that they must be treated as the latter's alter egos; and that if they are not so recognized, the central role of the Speech or Debate Clause—to prevent intimidation of legislators by the Executive and accountability before a possibly hostile judiciary—will inevitably be diminished and frustrated. . . .

Rather than giving the clause a cramped construction, the Court has sought to implement its fundamental purpose of freeing the legislator from executive and judicial oversight that realistically threatens to control his conduct as a legislator. We have little doubt that we are neither exceeding our judicial powers nor mistakenly construing the Constitution by holding that the Speech or Debate Clause applies not only to a Member but also to his aides insofar as the conduct of the latter would be a protected legislative act if performed by the Member himself. . . .

The United States fears the abuses that history reveals have occurred when legislators are invested with the power to relieve others from the operation of otherwise valid civil and criminal laws. But these abuses . . . are for the most part obviated if the privilege applicable to the aide is viewed . . . as the privilege of the Senator, and invocable only by the Senator or by the aide on the Senator's behalf, and if in all events the privilege available to the aide is confined to those services that would be immune legislative conduct if performed by the Senator himself. This view places beyond the Speech or Debate Clause a variety of services characteristically performed by aides for Members of Congress, even though within the scope of their employment. It likewise provides no protection for criminal conduct threatening the security of the person or property of others, whether performed at the direction of the Senator in preparation for or in execution of a legislative act or done without his knowledge or direction. Neither does it immunize Senator or aide from testifying at trials or grand jury proceedings involving third-party crimes where the questions do not require testimony about or impugn a legislative act. Thus our refusal to distinguish between Senator and aide in applying the Speech or Debate Clause does not mean that Rodberg is for all purposes exempt from grand jury questioning.

We are convinced also that the Court of Appeals correctly determined that Senator Gravel's alleged arrangement with Beacon Press to publish the Pentagon Papers was not protected speech or debate within the meaning of Art. I, § 6, cl. 1, of the Constitution. . . .

The heart of the Clause is speech or debate in either House. Insofar as the Clause is construed to reach other matters, they must be an integral part of the deliberative and communicative processes by which Members participate in committee and House proceedings with respect to the consideration and passage or rejection of proposed legislation or with respect to other matters which the Constitution places within the jurisdiction of either House. As the Court of Appeals put it, the courts have extended the privilege to matters beyond pure speech or debate in either House, but ''only when necessary to prevent indirect impairment of such deliberations.''

Here, private publication by Senator Gravel through the cooperation of Beacon Press was in no way essential to the deliberations of the Senate; nor does questioning as to private publication threaten the integrity or independence of the Senate by impermissibly exposing its deliberations to executive influence. The Senator had conducted his hearings; the record and any report that was forthcoming were available both to his committee and the Senate. Insofar as we are advised, neither Congress nor the full committee ordered or authorized the publication. We cannot but conclude that the Senator's arrangements with Beacon Press were not part and parcel of the legislative process. . . .

The Speech or Debate Clause does not in our view extend immunity to Rodberg, as a Senator's aide, from testifying before the grand jury about the arrangement between Senator Gravel and Beacon Press or about his own participation, if any, in the alleged transaction, so long as legislative acts of the Senator are not impugned. . . .

Rodberg's immunity . . . extends only to legislative acts as to which the Senator himself would be immune. The grand jury, therefore, if relevant to its investigation into the possible violations of the criminal law, . . . may require from Rodberg answers to questions relating to his or the Senator's arrangements, if any, with respect to republication or with respect to third-party conduct under valid investigation by the grand jury, as long as the questions do not implicate legislative action of the Senator. Neither do we perceive any constitutional or other privilege that shields Rodberg, any more than any other witness, from grand jury questions relevant to tracing the source of obviously highly classified documents that came into the Senator's possession and are the basic subject matter of inquiry in this case, as long as no legislative act is implicated by the questions.

Because the Speech or Debate Clause privilege applies both to Senator and aide, it appears to us that paragraph one of the order, alone, would afford ample protection of the privilege if it forbade questioning any witness, including Rodberg: (1) concerning the Senator's conduct, or the conduct of his aides, at the June 29, 1971, meeting of the subcommittee; (2) concerning the motives and purposes behind the Senator's conduct, or that of his aides, at that meeting; (3) concerning communications between the Senator and his aides during the term of their employment and related to said meeting or any other legislative act of the Senator; (4) except as it proves relevant to investigating possible third-party crime, concerning any act, in itself not criminal, performed by the Senator, or by his aides in the course of their employment, in preparation for the subcommittee hearing.

Gravel provided some guidance for legislators: although the Speech or Debate Clause gave similar protection to the senator and the aide, that protection was not absolute. Both could be questioned for activities that had no direct connection to or ''impinged upon'' the legislative process.

Despite the breadth of the Court's ruling, the Speech or Debate Clause ''has continued to cause

Table 3-3   Speech or Debate Clause Cases after *Gravel*

Case	Legal Question	Court's Response
United States v. Brewster (1972)	Does the Speech or Debate Clause protect members from prosecution for alleged bribery to perform a legislative act?	The Speech or Debate Clause protects members from inquiry into legislative acts; it does not protect them from all conduct relating to the legislative process.
Doe v. McMillan (1973)	Does the Speech or Debate Clause protect members of Congress (and their staff) and other persons who were involved in the investigating, disseminating, and distributing of a report of the D.C. school system, which identified, by name, specific children and did so in a negative way?	The Speech or Debate Clause offers absolute immunity to members of Congress and staff, but not to individuals who, acting under congressional authority, distributed the materials.
Eastland v. U.S. Servicemens' Fund (1975)	Does the Speech or Debate Clause protect members of Congress against a suit brought by an organization to stop the implementation of a subpoena ordering a bank to produce certain records?	The Speech or Debate Clause offers absolute protection because the activities fall within the "legitimate legislative" sphere.
Davis v. Passman (1979)	Does the Speech or Debate Clause protect a member of Congress against charges of sex discrimination?	The Supreme Court decided the case on Fifth Amendment grounds and reached no result on the member of Congress's claim that he was protected by the Speech or Debate Clause.
United States v. Helstoski (1979)	Does the Speech or Debate Clause protect a member of Congress against prosecution (for accepting bribes), when evidence introduced in that action hinges on past legislative acts?	The Speech or Debate Clause does not permit the introduction of evidence involving past legislative acts.
Hutchinson v. Proxmire (1979)	Does the Speech or Debate Clause protect a member of Congress from a civil suit in response to negative statements made about a government grant awardee's research to the press and in newsletters?	The Speech or Debate Clause does not protect a member of Congress from a libel judgment when information is disseminated to the press and the public through newsletters.

difficulties."[13] Indeed, as illustrated in Table 3-3, in the 1970s the Court decided several important issues that were left open by *Gravel*. In *United States v. Helstoski* (1979) the justices refused to allow prosecutors to introduce evidence into a court proceeding against a former member of Congress involving legislative activities.

13. Pritchett, *Constitutional Law of the Federal System*, 179.

Hutchinson v. Proxmire (1979), however, was a defeat for congressional authority. Here the Court examined a dispute arising when Sen. William Proxmire, D-Wis., on the floor of the Senate and later in a newsletter and on television, labeled Ronald R. Hutchinson's federally funded research virtually worthless and a waste of taxpayer money. Hutchinson brought a libel suit against Proxmire, and when the case reached the Court

Table 3-4   The Sources of Congressional Power

Power[a]	Defined	Example
Enumerated powers	Those that the Constitution expressly grants	See Article I, Section 8. Includes the power to borrow money, raise armies, regulate commerce.
Implied powers	Those that may be inferred from power expressly granted	Read Article I, Section 8, Clauses 2–17, in conjunction with Clause 18, the Necessary and Proper Clause. For example, the enumerated power of raising and supporting armies leads to the implied power of operating a draft.
Inherent powers	Those powers that do not depend on constitutional grants but grow out of the very existence of the national government	Encompasses field of foreign affairs. That is, foreign affairs powers are those that the national government would have even if the Constitution was silent, because they are powers that all nations have under international law. For example, the federal government can issue orders prohibiting U.S. businesses from selling arms to particular nations.
Amendment-enforcing powers	Those powers contained in some constitutional amendments that provide Congress with the ability to enforce them	Amendments 13, 14, and 15 state that Congress shall have the power to enforce the article by "appropriate legislation"

Source: Adopted from J. W. Peltason, *Understanding the Constitution,* 11th ed. (New York: Holt, Rinehart and Winston, 1988), 19.
[a] Some analysts suggest Congress also possesses resulting powers (those that result when several enumerated powers are added together) and inherited powers (those that Congress inherited from the British Parliament).

the justices addressed the issue of whether the Speech or Debate Clause immunized the senator from a libel proceeding on the grounds that he had first made the remarks on the chamber's floor. The Court held that it did not:

A speech by Proxmire in the Senate would be wholly immune and would be available to other Members of Congress and the public in the Congressional Record. But neither the newsletters nor the press release was "essential to the deliberations of the Senate," and neither was part of the deliberative process.

The Sources and Scope of Legislative Powers

Article I, Section 8, contains a virtual laundry list of Congress's powers. These enumerated powers, covered in seventeen clauses, establish congressional authority to regulate commerce, to lay and collect taxes, to establish post offices, and so forth. The enumerated powers pose few constitutional problems: those that the Constitution names, Congress clearly has.

But questions have arisen over other aspects of congressional power. First, does the legislative branch have powers beyond those specified by the Constitution? As noted in Table 3-4, the Court has answered that question affirmatively, suggesting that Congress has implied, inherent, and amendment-enforcing powers in addition to those listed in Article I. In this section, we examine the cases in which the Court located those sources.

We also focus on a second, more complex, question: What constraints are there on Congress's ability to exercise these powers? For example, the Court has permitted Congress to conduct hearings and investigations, but it also has asserted that the power is not unlimited, that certain restrictions apply.

As you read the next cases, keep in mind not only the sources of legislative power but also its scope. How has the Court sought to constrain Congress and, more important, why? What pressures have been brought to bear on the justices in making their decisions?

Enumerated and Implied Powers

As noted, the Constitution specifically lists some congressional powers, leaving no doubt that Congress has these powers. In *Gibbons v. Ogden* (1824), when the Court was asked to interpret one of them, the power to regulate interstate commerce, Chief Justice John Marshall said:

The words [of the Constitution] are, "Congress shall have power to regulate commerce with foreign nations, and among the several States. . . ." The subject to be regulated is commerce, and our constitution being . . . *one of enumeration, and not of definition,* to ascertain the extent of the power, it becomes necessary to settle the meaning of the word. [Emphasis added.]

In these two sentences, Marshall asserted that Congress indeed has the enumerated power to regulate commerce, but that the Court needed to define just what that power entails. This point is important because, as we shall see later, the fact that a power is written into the Constitution does not necessarily make the Court's task easier: often it must define how Congress can and cannot make appropriate use of that power. For now, we can conclude that virtually no debate ever occurs over whether, in fact, Congress has the powers contained in Article I, Section 8.

Where debate has occurred is over the question of whether Congress has more powers, or was intended to have more powers, than those specifically granted. And if so, how broad should they

be? Those who look to the plain language of the Constitution or to the intent of the Framers would find few concrete answers, although both camps would point to the same clause. Article I, Section 8, Clause 18, provides that Congress shall have the power

to make all Laws which shall be necessary and proper for carrying into Execution the foregoing Powers, and all other Powers vested by this Constitution in the Government of the United States, or in any Department or Officer thereof.

Called by various names—the Necessary and Proper Clause, the Elastic Clause, or the Sweeping Clause—this provision was the subject of some debate by the Founders. Many affiliated with the Federalist party, which favored a strong national government, argued for a loose construction of the clause. In their view, the Framers inserted it into the Constitution to provide Congress with some "flexibility"; in other words, Congress could exercise powers beyond those listed in the Constitution, those that were "necessary and proper" for implementing legislative activity. In contrast, the Jeffersonians asserted the need for a strict interpretation of the clause; in their view, it constricted congressional powers, rather than expanded them. Louis Fisher notes that they "regard[ed] the American Constitution as one of enumerated [or limited] powers. They oppose[d] . . . any . . . extraconstitutional power not explicitly grounded to one of the three branches."[14] In other words, congressional exercise of power under the Necessary and Proper Clause could be only that power necessary to carry out its enumerated functions.[15]

Which view would the Supreme Court adopt? Would it interpret the Necessary and Proper Clause strictly or loosely? This was one of two major questions at the core of *McCulloch v.*

14. Fisher, *American Constitutional Law,* 220.
15. Pritchett, *Constitutional Law of the Federal System,* 182.

Maryland (1819), which many consider the Court's most important explication of congressional powers.[16] Indeed, some suggest that this

16. The other question involved federalism. See Chapter 5.

opinion was Chief Justice Marshall's finest. As you read this case, consider not only the Court's holding, but also the language and logic of *McCulloch*. Why is it such an extraordinary statement?

McCulloch v. Maryland

4 Wheat. 316 (1819)

Vote: 6 (Duvall, Johnson, Livingston, Marshall, Story, Washington)

0

Opinion of the Court: Marshall
Not participating: Todd

Although we now take for granted the ability of the federal government to operate a banking system—today called the Federal Reserve System—in the 1700s and into the 1800s, this topic was heatedly debated. The first sign of controversy came as early as 1790, when George Washington's secretary of the Treasury, Alexander Hamilton, asked Congress to adopt a series of proposals amounting to a "comprehensive financial and economic" plan.[17] Among the proposals was the creation of a Bank of the United States, which would receive deposits, disburse funds, and make loans. Congress enacted a bill authorizing the founding of the first federal bank.

When the bill arrived at President Washington's desk, however, he did not sign it immediately. He wanted to ascertain whether in fact Congress could create a bank since it lacked explicit constitutional authority to do so. To this end he asked Hamilton, Secretary of State Thomas Jefferson, and Attorney General Edmund Randolph for their opinions on the bank's constitutionality.

The box, pages 93–94, provides excerpts of Hamilton's and Jefferson's responses. We offer them not only because they reached different con-

clusions—Hamilton argued that it was constitutional, Jefferson that it was not—but also because they represent the "classical expositions of divergent theories" of congressional power.[18] Moreover, they illustrate the limits of the Framers' intent mode of constitutional interpretation. Does it seem odd that just four years after the founding of the country, two of its foremost leaders could have such different views? In his argument, Hamilton, in fact, noted that there was a "conflicting recollection" of a convention debate highly relevant to the bank issue.[19] In the end, the president was persuaded by Hamilton and signed the bill. Congress then created the first Bank of the United States in 1791, chartering it for a twenty-year period.

Nevertheless, the bank controversy did not disappear. As we illustrate in Figure 3-1, which superimposes the bank's history (and that of its successor) against political and economic events, it is clear why the bank remained in the spotlight. Most important was that it became a symbol of the loose-construction, nationally oriented Federalist party, which had lost considerable power from its heyday in the 1790s. Indeed, by the turn of the century, "strict construction of congressional authority became a central plank in the opposition platform of the Jeffersonian Republicans."[20] To no one's surprise, and despite the fact that the

18. Pritchett, *Constitutional Law of the Federal System.*
19. One scholar notes that the Framers rejected a proposal that would have allowed Congress to establish corporations; in fact, they did so in part because of the possibility that Congress would create banks. See Lieberman, *Milestones!*, 118. Still Hamilton argued that debate was unclear.
20. Gerald Gunther, *Constitutional Law* (Mineola, N.Y.: Foundation Press, 1985), 86.

17. Jethro Lieberman, *Milestones!* (St. Paul, Minn.: West Publishing, 1976), 117-118.

Opinion on the Constitutionality of a National Bank (1791)

Thomas Jefferson

I consider the foundation of the Constitution as laid on this ground that "all powers not delegated to the U.S. by the Constitution, not prohibited by it to the states, are reserved to the states or to the people." To take a single step beyond the boundaries thus specially drawn around the powers of Congress, is to take possession of a boundless field of power, no longer susceptible of any definition.

The incorporation of a bank, and other powers assumed by this bill have not, in my opinion, been delegated to the U.S. by the Constitution.

I. They are not among the powers specially enumerated, for these are

1. A power to *lay taxes* for the purpose of paying the debts of the U.S. But no debt is paid by this bill, nor any tax laid. . . .

2. "to borrow money." But this bill neither borrows money, nor ensures the borrowing of it. . . .

3. "to regulate commerce with foreign nations, and among the states, and with the Indian tribes." To erect a bank, and to regulate commerce, are very different acts. . . .

II. Nor are they within either of the general phrases, which are the two following.

1. "To lay taxes to provide for the general welfare of the U.S." that is to say "to lay taxes *for the purpose* of providing for the general welfare." For the laying of taxes is the *power* and the general welfare the *purpose* for which the power is to be exercised. They are not to lay taxes ad libitum *for any purpose they please;* but only to *pay the debts or provide for the welfare of the Union.* In like manner they are not *to do anything they please* to provide for the general welfare, but only *to lay taxes* for that purpose. To consider the latter phrase, not as describing the purpose of the first, but as giving a distinct and independent power to do any act they please, which might be for the good of the Union, would render all the preceding and subsequent enumerations of power completely useless. It would reduce the whole instrument to a single phrase, that of instituting a Congress with power to do whatever would be for the good of the U.S. and as they would be the sole judges of the good or evil, it would be also a power to do whatever evil they pleased. . . . Certainly no such universal power was meant to be given them. It was intended to lace them up straitly within the enumerated powers, and those without which, as means, these powers could not be carried into effect. It is known that the very power now proposed *as a means,* was rejected *as an end,* by the Convention which formed the constitution. . . .

2. The second general phrase is "to make all laws *necessary* and proper or carrying into execution the enumerated powers." But they can all be carried into execution without a bank. A bank therefore is not *necessary,* and consequently not authorised by this phrase.

It has been much urged that a bank will give great facility, or convenience in the collection of taxes. Suppose this were true: yet the constitution allows only the means which are "necessary" not those which are merely "convenient" for effecting the enumerated powers. If such a latitude of construction be allowed to this phrase as to give any non-enumerated power, it will go to every one, for there is no one which ingenuity may not torture into a *convenience, in some way or other,* to *some one* of so long a list of enumerated powers. It would swallow up all the delegated powers, and reduce the whole to one phrase as before observed. Therefore it was that the constitution restrained them to the *necessary* means, that is to say, to those means without which the grant of the power would be nugatory.

Opinion as to the Constitutionality of the Bank of the United States (1791)

Alexander Hamilton

In entering upon the argument, it ought to be premised that the objections of the Secretary of State [Jefferson] . . . are founded on a general denial of the authority of the United States to erect corporations. The latter, indeed, expressly admits, that if there be anything in the bill which is not warranted by the Constitution, it is the clause of incorporation.

Now it appears to the Secretary of the Treasury that this *general principle* is *inherent* in the very *definition* of government, and *essential* to every step of the progress to be made by that of the United States, namely: That every power vested in a government is in its nature *sovereign,* and includes, by *force* of the *term,* a right to employ all the *means* requisite and fairly applicable to the attainment of the *ends* of such power, and which are not precluded by restrictions and exceptions specified in the Constitution, or not immoral, or not contrary to the *essential ends* of political society.

This principle, in its application to government in general, would be admitted as an axiom; and it will be incumbent upon those who may incline to deny it, to prove a distinction, and to show that a rule which, in the general system of things, is essential to the preservation of the social order, is inapplicable to the United States.

The circumstance that the powers of sovereignty are in this country divided between the National and State governments, does not afford the distinction required. It does not follow from this, that each of the portion of *powers* delegated to the one or to the other, is not sovereign with *regard to its proper objects*. It will only *follow* from it that each has sovereign power as to *certain things,* and not as to *other things.* To deny that the Government of the United States has sovereign power, as to its declared purposes and trusts, because its power does not extend to all cases, would be equally to deny that the State governments have sovereign power in any case, because their power does to extend to every case. . . .

If it would be necessary to bring proof to a proposition so clear, as that which affirms that the powers of the Federal Government, as to *its objects,* were sovereign, there is a clause of its Constitution which . . . declares that the Constitution, and the laws of the United States made in pursuance of it, and all treaties made, or which shall be made, under their authority, shall be the *supreme law of the land.* The power which can create the *supreme law of the land* in *any case.*

This general and indisputable principle puts at once an end to the *abstract* question, whether the United States have power to erect a corporation; that is to say, to give a *legal* or *artificial capacity* to one or more persons, distinct from the *natural.* For it is unquestionably incident to *sovereign power* to erect corporations, and consequently to *that* of the United States, in *relation* to the *objects* intrusted to the management of the government. . . .

Another argument made use of by the Secretary of State is, the rejection of a proposition by the Convention to empower Congress to make corporations, either generally, or for some special purpose.

What was the precise nature or extent of this proposition, or what the reasons for refusing it, is not ascertained by any authentic document, or even by accurate recollection. . . .

But whatever may have been the nature of the proposition, or the reasons for rejecting it, it includes nothing in respect to the real merits of the question. The Secretary of State will not deny that, whatever may have been the intention of the framers of a constitution or of a law, that intention is to be sought for in the instrument itself, according to the usual and established rules of construction. Nothing is more common than for laws to *express* and *effect* more or less than was intended. If, then, a power to erect a corporation in any case be deducible, by fair inference, from the whole or any part of the numerous provisions of the Constitution of the United States, arguments drawn from extrinsic circumstances, regarding the intention of the Convention, must be rejected. . . .

To establish such a right, it remains to show the relation of such an institution to one or more of the specified powers of the government. Accordingly it is affirmed that it has a relation, more or less direct, to the power of collecting taxes, to that of borrowing money, to that of regulating trade between the States, and to those of raising and maintaining fleets and armies. To the two former the relation may be said to be immediate; and in the last place it will be argued, that it is clearly within the provision which authorizes the making of all *needful rules and regulations* concerning the *property* of the United States, as the same has been practised upon the government.

A bank relates to the collection of taxes in two ways—*indirectly,* by increasing the quantity of circulating medium and quickening circulation, which facilitates the means of paying directly, by creating a *convenient species* of medium in which they are to be paid. . . .

A hope is entertained that it has, by this time, been made to appear, to the satisfaction of the President, that a bank has a natural relation to the power of collecting taxes—to that of regulating trade—to that of providing for the common defence—and that, as the bill under consideration contemplates the government in the light of a joint proprietor of the stock of the bank, it brings the case within the provision of the clause of the Constitution which immediately respects the property of the United States.

Under a conviction that such a relation subsists, the Secretary of the Treasury, with all deference, conceives that it will result as a necessary consequence from the position, that all the specified powers of government are sovereign, as to the proper objects; that the incorporation of a bank is a constitutional measure; and that the objections taken to the bill in this respect, are ill-founded.

Source: Melvin I. Urofsky, ed., *Documents of American Constitutional and Legal History,* vol. I (New York: Knopf, 1989), 132-139.

Figure 3-1. *The History of the First and Second Banks of the United States*

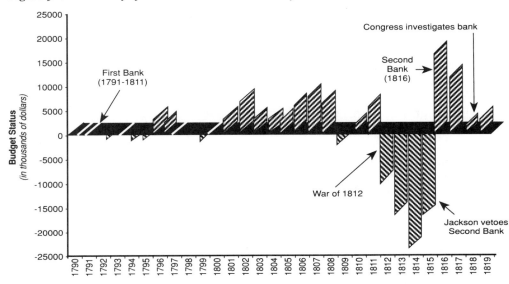

Data source: U.S. Department of Commerce, *Historical Statistics of the United States* (Washington D.C.: U.S. Bureau of the Census, 1975), 1104.

bank "had performed its functions in an orderly [and honest] manner"—the Republican Congress refused to renew its charter in 1811.[21]

After the War of 1812, however, it became apparent even to the Republicans that Congress should recharter the bank. During the war "the administration had been embarrassed by the lack of a national bank, both as a source for borrowing and as a means of transferring funds from one part of the country to another."[22] Moreover, with the absence of a federal bank, state-chartered institutions flooded the market with worthless notes, contributing to economic problems throughout the country. Therefore, amid renewed controversy and cries for strict constructionism, Congress in 1816 created the second Bank of the

United States, granting it a twenty-year charter and $35 million in capital.

According to historian Melvin I. Urofsky, "No one doubted that a court challenge to the new Bank would eventually arise . . . [for] the Supreme Court had never passed on the legitimacy of the first Bank."[23] It is possible, however, that litigation would not have materialized had the second bank performed its function as well as its predecessor did, but it did not. It flourished during the postwar economic boom, mainly because it was fiscally aggressive and encouraged speculative investing.[24] These practices caught up to bank officials when, in 1818, in anticipation of a recession, they began calling in the bank's outstanding loans. As a result, they brought down banks throughout the South and West, which had over-

21. Lieberman, *Milestones!*, 120.
22. Melvin I. Urofsky, *A March of Liberty* (New York: Knopf, 1988), 211.

23. Ibid.
24. Gunther, *Constitutional Law*, 89.

extended themselves.[25] To make matters worse, accusations of fraud and embezzlement were rampant within several of the bank's eighteen branches, particularly those in Maryland, Pennsylvania, and Virginia. Among those most seriously implicated was James McCulloch, the cashier of the Baltimore branch bank and its main lobbyist in Washington.[26] According to some accounts, his illegal financial schemes had cost the branch more than $1 million.

As a result of these allegations, Congress began to hold hearings on the bank. In addition, some states reacted by attempting to regulate branches located within their borders. For example, Maryland mandated that branches of the bank in the state pay either a 2 percent tax on all bank notes or a fee of $15,000. When a state official came to collect from the Baltimore branch, James McCulloch refused to pay and, by refusing, set the stage for a monumental confrontation between the United States and Maryland on not one, but two, major issues. The first involved the bank itself: Did Congress, in the absence of an explicit constitutional authorization, have the power to charter the bank? Second, did the state exceed its powers by seeking to tax a federal entity?

By the time the case reached the Supreme Court, it was clear that something significant was going to happen. The Court reporter noted that *McCulloch* involved "a constitutional question of great importance." The justices waived their rule that permitted only two attorneys per side "and allowed three each."[27] Moreover, oral arguments took nine days.

Both sides were ably represented. Some commentators praise Daniel Webster's oratory for the federal government's side as extraordinary, but it was former attorney general and Maryland senator William Pinkney with whom the Court was most taken. Justice Joseph Story said later, "I never, in my whole life, heard a greater speech."[28] The gist of his arguments (and those of his colleagues) was familiar stuff; Pinkney largely reiterated Hamilton's original defense of the bank, particularly his interpretation of the Necessary and Proper Clause.

Maryland's legal representation may have appeared less astute. According to one account, "it has been rumored" that one of the state's lawyers, Attorney General Luther Martin, "was drunk when he made his two-day-long argument. If he was, it apparently did not affect his acuity."[29] For his side, he reiterated parts of Jefferson's argument against the bank, added some on the subject of state's rights, and "closed his argument by reading from John Marshall's own speeches in the Virginia convention."

Chief Justice Marshall delivered the opinion of the Court:

The constitution of our country, in its most interesting and vital parts, is to be considered; the conflicting powers of the government of the Union and of its members, as marked in that constitution, are to be discussed; and an opinion given, which may essentially influence the great operations of the government. No tribunal can approach such a question without a deep sense of its importance, and of the awful responsibility involved in its decision. But it must be decided peacefully, or remain a source of hostile legislation, perhaps of hostility of a still more serious nature; and if it is to be so decided, by this tribunal alone can the decision be made. On the Supreme Court of the United States has the constitution of our country devolved this important duty.

The first question . . . is, has Congress power to incorporate a bank? . . .

This government is acknowledged by all to be one of enumerated powers. The principle, that it can exer-

25. Urofsky, *A March of Liberty*, 211.

26. Gunther, *Constitutional Law*, 89.

27. Fred W. Friendly and Martha J. H. Elliot, *The Constitution—That Delicate Balance* (New York: Random House, 1984), 256.

28. Quoted in Lieberman, *Milestones!*, 122.

29. Daniel A. Farber and Suzanna Sherry, *A History of the American Constitution* (St. Paul, Minn.: West Publishing, 1990), 251.

cise only the powers granted to it, would seem too apparent to have required to be enforced by all those arguments which its enlightened friends, while it was depending before the people, found it necessary to urge. That principle is now universally admitted. But the question respecting the extent of the powers actually granted, is perpetually arising, and will probably continue to arise, as long as our system shall exist. . . .

Among the enumerated powers, we do not find that of establishing a bank or creating a corporation. But there is no phrase in the instrument which, like the articles of confederation, excludes incidental or implied powers; and which requires that everything granted shall be expressly and minutely described. Even the 10th amendment, which was framed for the purpose of quieting the excessive jealousies which had been excited, omits the word "expressly," and declares only that the powers "not delegated to the United States, nor prohibited to the states, are reserved to the states or to the people;" thus leaving the question, whether the particular power which may become the subject of contest has been delegated to the one government, or prohibited to the other, to depend on a fair construction of the whole instrument. . . . A constitution, to contain an accurate detail of all the subdivisions of which its great powers will admit, and of all the means by which they may be carried into execution, would partake of a prolixity of a legal code, and could scarcely be embraced by the human mind. It would probably never be understood by the public. Its nature, therefore, requires, that only its great outlines should be marked, its important objects designated, and the minor ingredients which compose those objects be deduced from the nature of the objects themselves. That this idea was entertained by the framers of the American constitution, is not only to be inferred from the nature of the instrument, but from the language. Why else were some of the limitations, found in the ninth section of the 1st article, introduced? It is also, in some degree, warranted by their having omitted to use any restrictive term which might prevent its receiving a fair and just interpretation. In considering this question, then, we must never forget that it is a constitution we are expounding.

Although, among the enumerated powers of government, we do not find the word "bank" or "incorporation," we find the great powers to lay and collect taxes; to borrow money; to regulate commerce; to declare and conduct a war; and to raise and support armies and navies. The sword and the purse, all the external relations, and no inconsiderable portion of the industry of the nation, are entrusted to its government. It can never be pretended that these vast powers draw after them others of inferior importance, merely because they are inferior. Such an idea can never be advanced. But it may with great reason be contended, that a government, entrusted with such ample powers, on the due execution of which the happiness and prosperity of the nation so vitally depends, must also be entrusted with ample means for their execution. The power being given, it is the interest of the nation to facilitate its execution. It can never be their interest, and cannot be presumed to have been their intention, to clog and embarrass its execution by withholding the most appropriate means. . . .

The government which has a right to do an act, and has imposed on it the duty of performing that act, must, according to the dictates of reason, be allowed to select the means; and those who contend that it may not select any appropriate means, that one particular mode of effecting the object is excepted, take upon themselves the burden of establishing that exception. . . .

But the constitution of the United States has not left the right of Congress to employ the necessary means for the execution of the powers conferred on the government to general reasoning. To its enumeration of powers is added that of making "all laws which shall be necessary and proper, for carrying into execution the foregoing powers, and all other powers vested by this constitution, in the government of the United States, or in any department thereof."

The counsel for the State of Maryland have urged various arguments, to prove that this clause, though in terms a grant of power, is not so in effect; but is really restrictive of the general right, which might otherwise be implied, of selecting means for executing the enumerated powers. . . .

The word "necessary" is considered as controlling the whole sentence, and as limiting the right to pass laws for the execution of the granted powers, to such as are indispensable, and without which the power would be nugatory. That it excludes the choice of means, and leaves to Congress, in each case, that only which is most direct and simple.

Is it true that this is the sense in which the word "necessary" is always used? Does it always import an absolute physical necessity, so strong that one thing, to which another may be termed necessary, cannot exist without that other? We think it does not. If reference be had to its use, in the common affairs of the world, or in approved authors, we find that it frequently imports no more than that one thing is convenient, or useful, or essential to another. To employ the means necessary to an end, is generally understood as employing any means calculated to produce the end, and not as being confined to those single means, without which the end would be entirely unattainable. . . . This word, . . . like others, is used in various senses; and, in its construction, the subject, the context, the intention of the person using them, are all to be taken into view.

Let this be done in the case under consideration. The subject is the execution of those great powers on which the welfare of a nation essentially depends. It must have been the intention of those who gave these powers, to insure, as far as human prudence could insure, their beneficial execution. This could not be done by confiding the choice of means to such narrow limits as not to leave it in the power of Congress to adopt any which might be appropriate, and which were conducive to the end. This provision is made in a constitution intended to endure for ages to come, and, consequently, to be adapted to the various crises of human affairs. To have prescribed the means by which government should, in all future time, execute its powers, would have been to change, entirely, the character of the instrument, and give it the properties of a legal code. It would have been an unwise attempt to provide, by immutable rules, for exigencies which, if foreseen at all, must have been seen dimly, and which can be best provided for as they occur. To have declared that the best means shall not be used, but those alone without which the power given would be nugatory, would have been to deprive the legislature of the capacity to avail itself of experience, to exercise its reason, and to accommodate its legislation to circumstances. . . .

The baneful influence of this narrow construction on all the operations of the government, and the absolute impracticability of maintaining it without rendering the government incompetent to its great objects, might be illustrated by numerous examples drawn from the constitution, and from our laws. . . .

In ascertaining the sense in which the word "necessary" is used in this clause of the constitution, we may derive some aid from that with which it is associated. Congress shall have power "to make all laws which shall be necessary and proper to carry into execution" the powers of the government. If the word "necessary" was used in that strict and rigorous sense for which the counsel for the state of Maryland contend, it would be an extraordinary departure from the usual course of the human mind, as exhibited in composition, to add a word, the only possible effect of which is to qualify that strict and rigorous meaning; to present to the mind the idea of some choice of means of legislation not straightened and compressed within the narrow limits for which gentlemen contend.

But the argument which most conclusively demonstrates the error of the construction contended for by the counsel for the state of Maryland, is founded on the intention of the convention, as manifested in the whole clause. To waste time and argument in proving that without it Congress might carry its powers into execution, would be not much less idle than to hold a lighted taper to the sun. As little can it be required to prove, that in the absence of this clause, Congress would have some choice of means. That it might employ those which, in its judgment, would most advantageously effect the object to be accomplished. That any means adapted to the end, any means which tended directly to the execution of the constitutional powers of the government, were in themselves constitutional. This clause, as construed by the state of Maryland, would abridge, and almost annihilate this useful and necessary right of the legislature to select its means. That this could not be intended, is, we should think, had it not been already controverted, too apparent for controversy. We think so for the following reasons:

1st. The clause is placed among the powers of Congress, not among the limitations on those powers.

2d. Its terms purport to enlarge, not to diminish the powers vested in the government. . . .

We admit, as all must admit, that the powers of the government are limited, and that its limits are not to be transcended. But we think the sound construction of the constitution must allow to the national legislature that discretion, with respect to the means by which the powers it confers are to be carried into execution, which will enable that body to perform the high duties assigned to it, in the manner most beneficial to the people. Let the end be legitimate, let it be within the scope of the constitution, and all means which are appropriate, which are plainly adapted to that end, which are not prohibited, but consist with the letter and spirit of the constitution, are constitutional.

That a corporation must be considered as a means not less usual, not of higher dignity, not more requiring a particular specification than other means, has been sufficiently proved. If we look to the origin of corporations, to the manner in which they have been framed in that government from which we have derived most of our legal principles and ideas, or to the uses to which they have been applied, we find no reason to suppose that a constitution, omitting, and wisely omitting, to enumerate all the means for carrying into execution the great powers vested in government, ought to have specified this. Had it been intended to grant this power as one which should be distinct and independent, to be exercised in any case whatever, it would have found a place among the enumerated powers of the government. But being considered merely as a means, to be employed only for the purpose of carrying into execution the given powers, there could be no motive for particularly mentioning it. . . .

If a corporation may be employed indiscriminately with other means to carry into execution the powers of the government, no particular reason can be assigned for excluding the use of a bank, if required for its fiscal operations. To use one, must be within the discretion of Congress, if it be an appropriate mode of executing the powers of government. That it is a convenient, a useful, and essential instrument in the prosecution of its fiscal operations, is not now a subject of controversy. All those who have been concerned in the administration of our finances, have concurred in representing the importance and necessity; and so strongly have they been felt, that statesmen of the first class, whose previous opinions against it had been confirmed by every circumstance which can fix the human judgment, have yielded those opinions to the exigencies of the nation. Under the confederation, Congress, justifying the measure by its necessity, transcended perhaps its powers to obtain the advantage of a bank; and our own legislation attests the universal conviction of the utility of this measure. The time has passed away when it can be necessary to enter into any discussion in order to prove the importance of this instrument, as a means to effect the legitimate objects of the government.

But, were its necessity less apparent, none can deny its being an appropriate measure; and if it is, the degree of its necessity, as has been very justly observed, is to be discussed in another place. Should Congress, in the execution of its powers, adopt measures which are prohibited by the constitution; or should Congress, under the pretext of executing its powers, pass laws for the accomplishment of objects not entrusted to the government, it would become the painful duty of this tribunal, should a case requiring such a decision come before it, to say that such an act was not the law of the land. But where the law is not prohibited, and is really calculated to effect any of the objects entrusted to the government, to undertake here to inquire into the degree of its necessity, would be to pass the line which circumscribes the judicial department, and to tread on legislative ground. This court disclaims all pretensions to such a power. . . .

After the most deliberate consideration, it is the unanimous and decided opinion of this court that the act to incorporate the bank of the United States is a law made in pursuance of the constitution, and is a part of the supreme law of the land.

As we can see, Marshall fully adopted Hamilton's reasoning and the government's claims. Some even felt his opinion ''sounded almost like recitations'' of the oral arguments presented by the federal attorneys.[30] Given that Marshall issued *McCulloch* just three days after the case had been

30. Friendly and Elliot, *The Constitution,* 259

presented, it is more likely, as others suspect, that he wrote the opinion the previous summer.

Either way, *McCulloch* stands as a landmark decision. By holding that Congress has powers beyond those enumerated, that it has implied powers, Marshall set into law a largely Hamiltonian version of congressional authority:

> Let the end be legitimate, let it be within the scope of the constitution, and all means which are appropriate, which are plainly adapted to that end, which are not prohibited, but consist with the letter and spirit of the constitution, are constitutional.

And in so doing, he might very well have accomplished his stated objective: to allow the Constitution "to endure for ages to come."

The immediate reaction to Marshall's opinion was interesting in that it focused less on the portion we have dealt with here—congressional powers—and more on the federalism dimension, which we shall take up in Chapter 5. Nonetheless, the long-term effect of his interpretation of the Necessary and Proper Clause has been significant. In particular, Congress now exercises a whole series of powers not enumerated within the Constitution but implied from it.

Congressional Investigations

Of all the implied powers now asserted by Congress, the power to investigate merits close examination. Many think it is one of the most significant congressional powers. Woodrow Wilson's statement is often quoted: "The informing function of Congress should be preferred even to its legislative function." Another president, Harry S. Truman, concurred: "The power of investigation is one of the most important powers of Congress. The manner in which that power is exercised will largely determine the position and prestige of the Congress in the future."[31] In addition, the scope of congressional authority in

this area has been the subject of some rather interesting, perhaps conflicting, and most definitely controversial, Supreme Court opinions.

What never has been controversial, however, is Congress's ability to conduct investigations. Although this is not an enumerated power, there is little question that legislatures can hold inquiries. Some analysts refer to it as an incidental power that legislatures have by virtue of being legislatures.[32] Others call it an inherited power that the British Parliament willed to Congress or, alternatively, an implied power.[33] In any event, Congress took advantage of this privilege virtually from the beginning, holding its first investigation in 1792. Since then "no period of American history has been without" investigations.[34]

Another relatively noncontroversial aspect of congressional investigations is the ability of either house to summon witnesses and to punish, by holding in contempt, those who do not cooperate with the investigating body. Many scholars think these powers may be implied from the inherent nature of legislative authority. Congress is, by definition, *the* lawmaking institution, and an inherent quality of such an institution is the power to investigate. To function, therefore, it is necessary for Congress to have the authority to summon and punish witnesses, and both chambers have always availed themselves of this authority. As early as 1795 Congress jailed for contempt a man who had tried to bribe a member of Congress. Since then, congressional committees have introduced more than 380 contempt citations. When they do so, and if the parent chamber approves by a simple majority, the case is forwarded to a U.S. attorney for possible prosecution. The Supreme Court, theoretically and in fact, approved of the contempt practice as early as 1821.[35]

31. Quoted in *Guide to Congress,* 161

32. Peter Woll, *Constitutional Law* (Englewood Cliffs, N.J.: Prentice-Hall, 1981), 193.

33. Pritchett, *Constitutional Law of the Federal System,* 191.

34. *Guide to Congress,* 161.

35. *Anderson v. Dunn,* 6 Wheat. 204 (1821).

If the power of Congress to investigate and to summon and punish witnesses is so well entrenched, what is controversial about the practice? In general, debates have centered on two interrelated questions: What is the scope of the power—into what subjects may Congress inquire—and what sorts of rights, if any, do witnesses have? Both questions have presented some difficulty for the Court. *Kilbourn v. Thompson* (1881) was one of the Court's first significant rulings on the scope of legislative inquiries. The Court examined a House investigation into a private banking firm. An important witness, Hallett Kilbourn, refused to produce documents demanded by the inquiring committee. By a House order, Kilbourn was held in contempt and jailed. When he was released, he sued various officials and representatives for false arrest. In his view, the investigation was not legitimate because it concerned private, not public matters and, as such, he would resist "the naked, arbitrary power of the House to investigate private businesses in which nobody but [he] and [his] customers have concern."[36]

The Supreme Court agreed. In what some have called a rather narrow ruling on legislative pow-

36. Quoted in *Guide to Congress,* 150.

ers, the justices said that Congress could punish witnesses only if the inquiry itself was within the "legitimate cognizance" of the institution. With this ruling, the Court seemed to establish several limits on the scope of investigations. Inquiries (1) must not "invade areas constitutionally reserved to the courts or the executive"; (2) must deal "with subjects on which Congress could validly legislate"; and (3) must suggest, in the resolutions authorizing the investigation, a "congressional interest in legislating on that subject.[37] In general, then, *Kilbourn* said that Congress could hold inquiries only into subjects that are specifically grounded within its constitutional purview, and in particular that the "private affairs of individuals," where the inquiry could result in "no valid legislation," did not fall into that category.

Four decades later the Court was once again called on to examine the scope of congressional investigative authority. As you read *McGrain v. Daugherty* (1927), consider its ruling in light of *Kilbourn.* Some think that the justices substantially reworked the 1881 holding. Do you agree? If so, what did they change?

37. Pritchett, *Constitutional Law of the Federal System,* 191.

McGrain v. Daugherty

273 U.S. 135 (1927)

Vote: 8 (Brandeis, Butler, Holmes, McReynolds, Sanford, Sutherland, Taft, Van Devanter)
0
Opinion of the Court: Van Devanter
Not participating: Stone

In 1922 Congress began the investigation of the so-called Teapot Dome Scandal, which involved the alleged bribery of public officials by private companies to obtain leasing rights to government-held oil reserves, including the Teapot Dome reserves in Wyoming. Although initial

inquiries centered on employees of the Department of the Interior, Congress soon turned its attention to the Justice Department. In particular, members believed that Attorney General Harry M. Daugherty was involved in fraudulent activities because he failed to prosecute wrongdoers. As part of that inquiry, a Senate committee ordered the attorney general's brother, Mally S. Daugherty, to appear before it and to produce documents. Mally Daugherty was a bank president, and the committee suspected that he was involved in the scandal.

This suspicion grew stronger with the resignation of the attorney general and the subsequent refusal of his brother to appear before the committee. The Senate had Mally arrested. He, in turn, challenged the committee's authority to compel him—through arrest—to testify against his brother. Picking up on one of the limits of investigation emanating from *Kilbourn*, Mally's lawyer argued that "the arrest of Mr. Daugherty is the result of an attempt of the Senate to vest its committee with judicial power."[38]

The U.S. government's brief was written by Attorney General Harlan F. Stone, who had since been appointed a justice on the Court deciding the case. The brief also used *Kilbourn* to frame its arguments: "The investigation ordered by the Senate, in the course of which the testimony of the Appellee [Daughtery] and the production of books and records of the bank of which he is President were required, was legislative in its character."[39]

Justice Willis Van Devanter delivered the opinion of the Court:

We have given the case earnest and prolonged consideration because the principal questions involved are of unusual importance and delicacy. . . .

The first of the principal questions—the one which the witness particularly presses on our attention—is . . . whether the Senate—or the House of Representatives . . . —has power . . . to compel a private individual to appear before it or one of its committees and give testimony needed to enable it efficiently to exercise a legislative function belonging to it under the Constitution.

The Constitution provides for a Congress consisting of a senate and House of Representatives and invests it with "all legislative powers" granted to the United States, and with power "to make all laws which shall be necessary and proper" for carrying into execution these powers and "all other powers" vested by the Constitution in the United States or in any department or officer thereof. . . . But there is no provision expressly investing either house with power to

make investigations and exact testimony to the end that it may exercise its legislative function advisedly and effectively. So the question arises whether this power is so far incidental to the legislative function as to be implied.

In actual legislative practice power to secure needed information by such means has long been treated as an attribute of the power to legislate. It was so regarded in the British Parliament and in the colonial legislatures before the American Revolution; and a like view has prevailed and been carried into effect in both houses of Congress and in most of the state legislatures. . . .

The state courts quite generally have held that the power to legislate carries with it by necessary implication ample authority to obtain information needed in the rightful exercise of that power, and to employ compulsory process for the purpose. . . .

[This Court has decided several cases that] are not decisive . . . [but] definitely settle two propositions . . .: One, that the two houses of Congress . . . possess not only such powers as are expressly granted to them by the Constitution, but such auxiliary powers as are necessary and appropriate to make the express powers effective; and, the other, that neither house is invested with "general" power to inquire into private affairs and compel disclosures, but only with such limited power of inquiry as is shown to exist when the rule of constitutional interpretation just stated is rightly applied. . . .

We are of opinion that the power of inquiry—with process to enforce it—is an essential and appropriate auxiliary to the legislative function. . . .

A legislative body cannot legislate wisely or effectively in the absence of information respecting the conditions which the legislation is intended to affect or change; and where the legislative body does not itself possess the requisite information . . . recourse must be had to others who do possess it. Experience has taught that mere requests for such information often are unavailing, and also that information which is volunteered is not always accurate or complete; so some means of compulsion are essential to obtain what is needed. All this was true before and when the Constitution was framed and adopted. In that period the power of inquiry—with enforcing process—was regarded and employed as a necessary and appropriate

38. *McGrain v. Daugherty*, 273 U.S. 403 (1896), Brief for the Appellee, 101.

39. Ibid., Brief for the Appellant, i.

attribute of the power to legislate—indeed, was treated as inhering in it. Thus there is ample warrant for thinking, as we do, that the constitutional provisions which commit the legislative function to the two houses are intended to include this attribute to the end that the function may be effectively exercised.

The contention is earnestly made on behalf of the witness that this power of inquiry, if sustained, may be abusively and oppressively exerted. If this be so, it affords no ground for denying the power. The same contention might be directed against the power to legislate, and of course would be unavailing. We must assume, for present purposes, that neither house will be disposed to exert the power beyond its proper bounds, or without due regard to the rights of witnesses. But if, contrary to this assumption, controlling limitations or restrictions are disregarded, the decision . . . in Kilbourn v. Thompson . . . point[s] to admissible measures of relief. And it is a necessary deduction from the decision . . . that a witness rightfully may refuse to answer where the bounds of the power are exceeded or the questions are not pertinent to the matter under inquiry.

We come now to the question whether it sufficiently appears that the purpose for which the witness's testimony was sought was to obtain information in aid of the legislative function. . . .

We are of opinion that . . . it sufficiently appears . . . that the object of the investigation and of the effort to secure the witness's testimony was to obtain information for legislative purposes.

It is quite true that the resolution directing the investigation does not in terms avow that it is intended to be in aid of legislation; but it does show that the subject to be investigated was . . . one on which legislation could be had and would be materially aided by the information which the investigation was calculated to elicit. This becomes manifest when it is reflected that the functions of the Department of Justice, the powers and duties of the Attorney General and the duties of his assistants, are all subject to regulation by congressional legislation, and that the department is maintained and its activities are carried on under such appropriations as in the judgment of Congress are needed from year to year.

The only legitimate object the Senate could have in ordering the investigation was to aid it in legislating; and we think the subject-matter was such that the presumption should be indulged that this was the real object. An express avowal of the object would have been better; but in view of the particular subject-matter was not indispensable. . . .

We conclude that the investigation was ordered for a legitimate object; that the witness wrongfully refused to appear and testify before the committee and was lawfully attached; [and] that the Senate is entitled to have him give testimony pertinent to the inquiry, either at its bar or before the committee.

McGrain is significant for two reasons. First, it firmly established Congress's power to inquire and to enforce that power with the ability to punish as an implied power. The Court said: "Experience has taught that mere requests for such information often are unavailing . . . so some means of compulsion are essential to obtain what is needed." But the justices were unwilling to allow a virtually limitless use of that power. Although they had backed away from the rigid stance of *Kilbourn,* they continued to assert its basic underpinning: Congress could not inquire, generally speaking, into private affairs. Second, and perhaps more important, *McGrain* provides some insight into another controversial area of congressional inquiries: the rights of witnesses. While it ruled against Daugherty, the Court held that witnesses may refuse to answer "where the bounds of the power are exceeded or the questions are not pertinent to the matter under inquiry."

This window of opportunity for witnesses to refuse to testify became quite important during World War II and in the postwar period when, out of fear of an influx of foreign ideologies into the United States, Congress embarked on a new type of investigation: the "inquisitorial panel."[40] In short, the "overriding purpose of the anti-sub-

40. *Guide to Congress,* 148.

Investigations of "Un-Americanism"

ONE OF THE most significant expansions of congressional investigative powers beyond direct legislative matters was the study of subversive movements after World War II. Instead of pursuing traditional lines of congressional inquiry—government operations and national social and economic problems—committees probed into the thoughts, actions, and associations of individuals and institutions.

The House Committee on Un-American Activities was the premier example of these investigative panels. The committee was abolished in January 1975, ending thirty years of controversy over its zealous pursuit of subversives. Its long survival surprised many observers. From the outset the panel, renamed the Internal Security Committee in 1969, was attacked by liberals and civil libertarians. Throughout the 1960s it withstood court suits challenging the constitutionality of its mandate and attempts in the House to end its funding. The death blow finally came when the House Democratic Caucus, by voice vote in January 1975, transferred its functions to the House Judiciary Committee.

Early History

The first congressional investigation of un-American activities was authorized September 19, 1918, toward the close of World War I. That original mandate was to investigate the activities of German brewing interests. The investigation, conducted by the Senate Judiciary Committee, was expanded in 1919 to cover "any efforts . . . to propagate in this country the principles of any party exercising . . . authority in Russia . . . and . . . to incite the overthrow" of the U.S. government.

The House on May 12, 1930, set up a Special Committee to Investigate Communist Activities in the United States—the Fish Committee, so called after its chairman, Rep. Hamilton Fish, Jr., R-N.Y. On March 20, 1934, the House created a Special Committee on Un-American Activities, under Chairman John W. McCormack, D-Mass. On May 26, 1938, three years after McCormack's committee submitted its report, which covered Nazi as well as communist activities in the United States, the House set up another Special Committee on Un-American Activities, under Chairman Martin Dies, Jr., D-Texas. The committee, whose chairman was avowedly anticommunist and anti-New Deal, was given a broad mandate to investigate subversion.

Dies focused his early investigations on organized labor groups, especially the Congress of Industrial Organizations, and set a tactical pattern that would guide the permanent Un-American Activities Committee, which was created in 1945.

Friendly witnesses, who often met in secret with Dies as a one-man subcommittee, accused hundreds of people of supporting communist activities, but few of the accused were permitted to testify in rebuttal. The press treated Dies's charges sensationally, a practice that was to continue after World War II.

The Dies Committee was reconstituted in succeeding Congresses until 1945. That January, at the beginning of the Seventy-ninth Congress, it was renamed the House Committee on Un-American Activities and made a standing committee.

The next five years marked the peak of the committee's influence. In 1947 it investigated communism in the motion picture industry, with repercussions that lasted almost a decade. Its hearings resulted in the Hollywood blacklist that kept many writers and actors suspected of communist leanings out of work.

The committee's investigation in 1948 of State Department official Alger Hiss, and Hiss's subsequent conviction for perjury, established communism as a leading political issue and the committee as an important political force. The case against Hiss was vigorously developed by a young member of the committee, Richard Nixon.

The committee's tactics during this period included extensive use of contempt citations against unfriendly witnesses, some of whom pleaded their Fifth Amendment right against self-incrimination. In 1950, for example, the House voted fifty-nine contempt citations, of which fifty-six had been recommended by the committee.

Senate Investigations

In the early 1950s the Un-American Activities Committee was overshadowed by Senate investigations conducted by Joseph R. McCarthy, R-Wis., chairman (1953–1954) of the Senate Government Operations Committee's Permanent Investigations Subcommittee. McCarthy's investigation into alleged subversion in the U.S. army—televised nationwide in 1954—intensified concern over the use by Congress of its investigating powers and led to his censure by the Senate in 1954.

During the same period, the Senate Judiciary Committee's Internal Security Subcommittee, established in 1951, also investigated subversive influences in various fields, including government, education, labor unions, the United Nations, and the press.

Source: *Guide to Congress,* 4th ed., ed. Mary Cohn (Washington, D.C.: Congressional Quarterly, 1991), 240.

The House Un-American Activities Committee holds a press conference December 3, 1948, after a closed session. Standing are two committee investigators. Seated are several reporters and, left to right, Richard Nixon, R-Calif., John Rankin, D-Miss., and John McDowell, R-Pa.

versive hearings was exposure,'' not necessarily ''information.'' [41]

As discussed in the box, opposite, this kind of ''investigation'' is similar to those held by the House Special Committee to Investigate Un-American Activities in the 1930s. However, the investigations carried on in the Senate by Joseph McCarthy and by the House Committee on Un-American Activities (HUAC) in the 1940s and 1950s produced the most controversy and criticism. At that time, the fear of communism was so pervasive that even being called to testify before McCarthy or HUAC created such suspicion that individuals lost their jobs, were placed on black-lists, and so forth. Moreover, many witnesses were sufficiently scared of being branded a communist sympathizer or supporter that they refused

to testify or asserted a constitutional protection against so doing, which resulted in an unusually high number of contempt citations. Between 1792 and 1942 Congress issued 108 citations; from 1945 to 1957, fourteen committees presented 226 contempt citations to their respective chambers.[42] HUAC alone held 144 ''uncooperative'' witnesses in contempt.[43]

In the late 1950s the Supreme Court decided two major cases involving the rights of witnesses to refuse to answer questions. While reading *Watkins v. United States* (1957) and *Barenblatt v. United States* (1959), think about this question: Did the Court treat the cases consistently? If not, what difference do you see?

41. Ibid., 151.

42. Ibid., 163.
43. Ralph A. Rossum and G. Alan Tarr, *American Constitutional Law*, 3d ed. (New York: St. Martin's Press, 1991), 94.

Watkins v. United States

354 U.S. 178 (1957)

Vote: 6 (Black, Brennan, Douglas, Frankfurter, Harlan,
*   Warren)*
*   1 (Clark)*
Opinion of the Court: Warren
Concurring opinion: Frankfurter
Dissenting opinion: Clark
Not participating: Burton, Whittaker

When the House Un-American Activities Committee was made a standing committee, Congress defined its charge as follows:

The Committee on Un-American Activities, as a whole or by subcommittee, is authorized to make from time to time investigations of (1) the extent, character, and objects of un-American propaganda activities in the United States, (2) the diffusion within the United States of subversive and un-American propaganda that is instigated from foreign countries or of a domestic origin and attacks the principle of the form of government as guaranteed by our Constitution, and (3) all other questions in relation thereto that would aid Congress in any necessary remedial legislation.

In the early 1950s HUAC took that mandate to mean that it could call witnesses to testify about Communist party infiltration into American society and their involvement in that organization.

Watkins v. United States crystallized when the committee invoked one of its favored modus operandi: asking a witness before it to "name names," to implicate others as Communist party members. Two witnesses told the committee that John T. Watkins, who had been involved in various labor organizations such as the United Electrical, Radio and Machine Workers and the United Auto Workers, was not only a Communist party member, but also a recruiter for the party.

When the committee subpoenaed Watkins in April 1954, he "answered these allegations freely and without reservation."[44] Among his responses was the following:

44. *Watkins v. United States,* 354 U.S. 178 at 183 (1957).

I would like to make it clear that for a period of time from approximately 1942 to 1947 I cooperated with the Communist Party and participated in Communist activities to such a degree that some persons may honestly believe that I was a member of the party. I have made contributions upon occasions to Communist causes. I have signed petitions for Communist causes. I attended caucuses at [a] . . . convention at which Communist Party officials were present. Since I freely cooperated with the Communist Party I have no motive for making the distinction between cooperation and membership except for the simple fact that it is the truth. I never carried a Communist Party card. I never accepted discipline and indeed on several occasions I opposed their position.

The government conceded that in addressing questions pertaining to his own activities, it could "hardly . . . imagine" a more "complete and candid statement."

But it alleged that Watkins went astray because he refused to answer questions about the activities of others. When the committee read a list of names, some of whom Watkins knew, and asked him to say whether they had been Communist party members, Watkins stated:

I refuse to answer certain questions that I believe are outside the proper scope of your committee's activities. I will answer any questions which this committee puts to me about myself. I will also answer questions about those persons whom I knew to be members of the Communist Party and whom I still believe are. I will not, however, answer any questions with respect to others with whom I associated in the past. I do not believe that any law in this country requires me to testify about persons who may in the past have been Communist Party members or otherwise engaged in Communist Party activity but who to my best knowledge and belief have long since removed themselves from the Communist movement.

As a result, the House held him in contempt and a U.S. attorney prosecuted him. He was found guilty.

In his brief to the Supreme Court, Watkins's lawyer made two interrelated arguments centering on the committee's authority. First, he complained that "the very idea of congressional committee exposure for the sake of exposure unrelated to a legislative purpose is incompatible with our constitutional system." Second, he suggested that the questions his client refused to answer fell beyond "the language of the Committee's authorization" in part because that "authorization is so vague and indefinitive of purpose" as to deprive Watkins of his rights.

Chief Justice Earl Warren delivered the opinion of the Court:

We start with several basic premises on which there is general agreement. The power of the Congress to conduct investigations is inherent in the legislative process. . . . No inquiry is an end in itself; it must be related to, and in furtherance of, a legitimate task of the Congress. Investigations conducted solely for the personal aggrandizement of the investigator or to "punish" those investigated are indefensible.

It is unquestionably the duty of all citizens to cooperate with the Congress in its efforts to obtain the facts needed for intelligent legislative action. . . . This, of course, assumes that the constitutional rights of witnesses will be respected by the Congress as they are in a court of justice. The Bill of Rights is applicable to investigations as to all forms of governmental action. . . .

Abuses of the investigative process may imperceptibly lead to abridgment of protected freedoms. The mere summoning of a witness and compelling him to testify, against his will, about his beliefs, expressions or associations is a measure of governmental interference. And when those forced revelations concern matters that are unorthodox, unpopular, or even hateful to the general public, the reaction in the life of the witness may be disastrous. This effect is even more harsh when it is past beliefs, expressions or associations that are disclosed and judged by current standards rather than those contemporary with the matters exposed. Nor does the witness alone suffer the consequences. Those who are identified by witnesses and thereby placed in the same glare of publicity are equally subject to public stigma, scorn and obloquy.

Beyond that, there is the more subtle and immeasurable effect upon those who tend to adhere to the most orthodox and uncontroversial views and associations in order to avoid a similar fate at some future time. That this impact is partly the result of nongovernmental activity by private persons cannot relieve the investigators of their responsibility for initiating the reaction. . . .

Accommodation of the congressional need for particular information with the individual and personal interest in privacy is an arduous and delicate task for any court. We do not underestimate the difficulties that would attend such an undertaking. It is manifest that despite the adverse effects which follow upon compelled disclosure of private matters, not all such inquiries are barred. Kilbourn v. Thompson teaches that such an investigation into individual affairs is invalid if unrelated to any legislative purpose. . . .

Petitioner has earnestly suggested that the difficult questions of protecting these rights from infringement by legislative inquiries can be surmounted in this case because there was no public purpose served in his interrogation. His conclusion is based upon the thesis that the Subcommittee was engaged in a program of exposure for the sake of exposure. . . .

The Government contends that the public interest at the core of the investigations of the Un-American Activities Committee is the need by the Congress to be informed of efforts to overthrow the Government by force and violence so that adequate legislative safeguards can be erected. From this core, however, the Committee can radiate outward infinitely to any topic thought to be related in some way to armed insurrection. The outer reaches of this domain are known only by the content of "un-American activities." . . .

An excessively broad charter, like that of the House Un-American Activities Committee, places the courts in an untenable position if they are to strike a balance between the public need for a particular interrogation and the right of citizens to carry on their affairs free from unnecessary governmental interference. It is impossible in such a situation to ascertain whether any legislative purpose justifies the disclosures sought and, if so, the importance of that information to the Congress in furtherance of its legislative function. The reason no court can make this critical judgment is that the House of Representatives itself has never made it. . . .

Absence of the qualitative consideration of petitioner's questioning by the House of Representatives aggravates a serious problem, revealed in this case, in the relationship of congressional investigating committees and the witnesses who appear before them. Plainly these committees are restricted to the missions delegated to them, i.e., to acquire certain data to be used by the House or the Senate in coping with a problem that falls within its legislative sphere. No witness can be compelled to make disclosures on matters outside that area. This is a jurisdictional concept of pertinency drawn from the nature of a congressional committee's source of authority. . . . When the definition of jurisdictional pertinency is as uncertain and wavering as in the case of the Un-American Activities Committee, it becomes extremely difficult for the Committee to limit its inquiries to statutory pertinency. . . .

The problem attains proportion when viewed from the standpoint of the witness who appears before a congressional committee. He must decide at the time the questions are propounded whether or not to answer. . . .

It is obvious that a person compelled to make this choice is entitled to have knowledge of the subject to which the interrogation is deemed pertinent. . . .

The statement of the Committee Chairman in this case, in response to petitioner's protest, was woefully inadequate to convey sufficient information as to the pertinency of the questions to the subject under inquiry. Petitioner was thus not accorded a fair opportunity to determine whether he was within his rights in refusing to answer, and his conviction is necessarily invalid under the Due Process Clause of the Fifth Amendment.

We are mindful of the complexities of modern government and the ample scope that must be left to the Congress as the sole constitutional depository of legislative power. Equally mindful are we of the indispensable function, in the exercise of that power, of congressional investigations. The conclusions we have reached in this case will not prevent the Congress, through its committees, from obtaining any information it needs for the proper fulfillment of its role in our scheme of government. . . . It is only those investigations that are conducted by use of compulsory process that give rise to a need to protect the rights of individuals against illegal encroachment. A measure of added care on the part of the House and the Senate in authorizing the use of compulsory process and by their committees in exercising that power would suffice. That is a small price to pay if it serves to uphold the principles of limited, constitutional government without constricting the power of the Congress to inform itself.

Barenblatt v. United States

360 U.S. 109 (1959)

Vote: 5 (Clark, Frankfurter, Harlan, Stewart, Whittaker)
4 (Black, Brennan, Douglas, Warren)
Opinion of the Court: Harlan
Dissenting opinions: Black, Brennan

On February 25, 1953, HUAC, operating under the same authority it had before the *Watkins* case, initiated a series of hearings called "Communist Methods of Infiltration (Education)." Before the hearings got under way, HUAC's chair stated that their purpose would be to "ascertain the character, extent and objects of Communist Party activities . . . carried on by [teachers] who are subject to the directives and discipline of the Communist Party." More generally, he observed that:

It has been fully established in testimony before congressional committees and before the courts of our land that the Communist Party of the United States is part of an international conspiracy which is being used as a tool or weapon by a foreign power to promote its own foreign policy and which has for its object the overthrow of the governments of all non-Communist countries, resorting to the use of force and violence, if necessary.

Among those testifying before the committee was Francis X. T. Crowley, who admitted that while he was a graduate student at the University of Michigan in 1950 he had belonged to a club with links to the Communist party. He also told the committee that Lloyd Barenblatt, with whom he had shared an apartment, also had been a member. Based on that information, in June 1954 the committee subpoenaed Barenblatt to testify before it. Since 1950 Barenblatt had been a psychology instructor at Vassar, but after he received the subpoena, the college refused to renew his contract. So it was an unemployed Barenblatt who appeared before HUAC.[45]

Barenblatt told the committee that he had been a teaching fellow at Michigan, as Crowley had testified. He also admitted that he knew Crowley. But he refused to answer five questions about his activities:

1. Are you now a member of the Communist Party?
2. Have you ever been a member of the Communist Party?
3. Now, you have stated you knew Francis Crowley. Did you know Francis Crowley as a member of the Communist Party?
4. Were you ever a member of the Haldane Club of the Communist Party while at the University of Michigan?
5. Were you a member while a student of the University of Michigan Council of Arts, Sciences, and Professions?

The House held him in contempt for unlawfully refusing to answer these questions, and a U.S. attorney sought and obtained a conviction against him.

On appeal to the Supreme Court, Barenblatt's American Civil Liberties Union lawyers raised two major claims. First, "on the basis of . . . *Watkins,* it is clear that the language of the legislation purportedly granting investigative authority to the House Committee was not sufficiently definite and specific to constitute a delegation of power, and thus there is a complete lack of authority in the Committee to investigate by compulsory process." In other words, they reiterated Warren's reasoning in *Watkins* that the authority of the committee was too vague and that the questions lacked pertinency. Second, they claimed that the questions infringed on Barenblatt's First Amendment right to expression and association.[46]

In response, the government argued that while the Court in *Watkins* "criticized the Committee's authorizing resolution," it did not invalidate it. And now the Court must wake up to the fact that Congress was quite serious about investigating communist infiltration, with the functions primarily falling to HUAC. As the government claimed:

Whatever justification there may be for criticism of [HUAC's] authorizing resolution on its face on grounds of vagueness and imprecision, the resolution comes before the Court, not in its bare terms alone, but with a "persuasive gloss of legislative history" . . . which shows beyond a doubt that there is one subject, above all others, which the House of Representatives has desired and does desire this Committee continuously to investigate and periodically to report on to it. That subject is Communism, in its various aspects and facets, and the menace posed by that system and ideology to American government and institutions.[47]

Justice John Marshall Harlan delivered the opinion of the Court:

Once more the Court is required to resolve the conflicting constitutional claims of congressional power and of an individual's right to resist its exercise. The congressional power in question concerns the internal process of Congress in moving within its legislative domain; it involves the utilization of its committees to secure "testimony needed to enable it efficiently to exercise a legislative function belonging to it under the Constitution." (McGrain v.

45. For more on Barenblatt, see Peter Irons, *The Courage of their Convictions* (New York: Free Press, 1988).

46. *Barenblatt v. United States,* 360 U.S. 109 (1959), Brief of Petitioner, 12-13.
47. Ibid., Brief for Respondent, 22-23.

Daugherty) . . . The scope of the power of inquiry, in short, is as penetrating and far-reaching as the potential power to enact and appropriate under the Constitution. . . .

At the outset it should be noted that Rule XI authorized this Subcommittee to compel testimony within the framework of the investigative authority conferred on the Un-American Activities Committee. Petitioner contends that Watkins v. United States nevertheless held the grant of this power in all circumstances ineffective because of the vagueness of Rule XI in delineating the Committee jurisdiction to which its exercise was to be appurtenant. . . .

The Watkins case cannot properly be read as standing for such a proposition. A principal contention in Watkins was that the refusals to answer were justified because the requirement . . . that the questions asked be ''pertinent to the question under inquiry'' had not been satisfied. This Court reversed the conviction solely on that ground, holding that Watkins had not been adequately apprised of the subject matter of the Subcommittee's investigation or the pertinency thereto of the questions he refused to answer. . . .

Petitioner also contends, independently of Watkins, that the vagueness of Rule XI deprived the Subcommittee of the right to compel testimony in this investigation into Communist activity. . . . Granting the vagueness of the Rule, we may not read it in isolation from its long history in the House of Representatives. Just as legislation is often given meaning by the gloss of legislative reports, administrative interpretation, and long usage, so the proper meaning of an authorization to a congressional committee is not to be derived alone from its abstract terms unrelated to the definite content furnished them by the course of congressional actions. The Rule comes to us with a ''persuasive gloss of legislative history,'' which shows beyond doubt that in pursuance of its legislative concerns in the domain of ''national security'' the House has clothed the Un-American Activities Committee with pervasive authority to investigate Communist activities in this country. . . .

In light of this . . . history it can hardly be seriously argued that the investigation of Communist activities generally, and the attendant use of compulsory process, was beyond the purview of the Committee's intended authority under Rule XI. . . .

Undeniably a conviction for contempt under 2 U.S.C. § 192, 2 U.S.C.A. § 192 cannot stand unless the questions asked are pertinent to the subject matter of the investigation. Watkins v. United States. But the factors which led us to rest decision on this ground in Watkins were very different from those involved here.

In Watkins the petitioner had made specific objection to the Subcommittee's questions on the ground of pertinency; the question under inquiry had not been disclosed in any illuminating manner; and the questions asked the petitioner were not only amorphous on their face, but in some instances clearly foreign to the alleged subject matter of the investigation—''Communism in labor.''

. . . What we deal with here is whether petitioner was sufficiently apprised of ''the topic under inquiry'' thus authorized ''and the connective reasoning whereby the precise questions asked relate[d] to it.'' In light of his prepared memorandum of constitutional objections there can be no doubt that this petitioner was well aware of the Subcommittee's authority and purpose to question him as it did. . . . The subject matter of the inquiry had been identified at the commencement of the investigation as Communist infiltration into the field of education. Just prior to petitioner's appearance before the Subcommittee, the scope of the day's hearings had been announced as ''in the main communism in education and the experiences and background in the party by Francis X. T. Crowley. It will deal with activities in Michigan, Boston, and in some small degree, New York.'' . . . [P]etitioner refused to answer questions as to his own Communist Party affiliations, whose pertinency of course was clear beyond doubt. . . .

Our function, at this point, is purely one of constitutional adjudication in the particular case and upon the particular record before us, not to pass judgment upon the general wisdom or efficacy of the activities of this Committee in a vexing and complicated field.

The precise constitutional issue confronting us is whether the Subcommittee's inquiry into petitioner's past or present membership in the Communist Party transgressed the provisions of the First Amendment, which of course reach and limit congressional investigations.

. . . [T]he protections of the First Amendment, unlike a proper claim of the privilege against self-incrimination under the Fifth Amendment, do not afford a witness the right to resist inquiry in all circumstances. Where First Amendment rights are asserted to bar governmental interrogation resolution of the issue always involves a balancing by the courts of the competing private and public interests at stake in the particular circumstances shown. These principles were recognized in the Watkins case. . . .

The first question is whether this investigation was related to a valid legislative purpose, for Congress may not constitutionally require an individual to disclose his political relationships or other private affairs except in relation to such a purpose.

That Congress has wide power to legislate in the field of Communist activity in this Country, and to conduct appropriate investigations in aid thereof, is hardly debatable. The existence of such power has never been questioned by this Court. . . . Justification for its exercise in turn rests on the long and widely accepted view that the tenets of the Communist Party include the ultimate overthrow of the Government of the United States by force and violence, a view which has been given formal expression by the Congress. . . .

Nor can we accept the further contention that this investigation should not be deemed to have been in furtherance of a legislative purpose because the true objective of the Committee and of the Congress was purely "exposure." So long as Congress acts in pursuance of its constitutional power, the Judiciary lacks authority to intervene on the basis of the motives which spurred the exercise of that power. . . . The constitutional legislative power of Congress in this instance is beyond question.

Finally, the record is barren of other factors which in themselves might sometimes lead to the conclusion that the individual interests at stake were not subordinate to those of the state. . . .

We conclude that the balance between the individual and the governmental interests here at stake must be struck in favor of the latter, and that therefore the provisions of the First Amendment have not been offended.

To return to our initial question: Did the Court treat the claims of Barenblatt and Watkins consistently? The majority in *Barenblatt* went to great lengths to indicate that it did, indeed, that *Barenblatt* amounted to nothing more or less that a "clarification" of *Watkins*. But many legal analysts suggest that at minimum the justices backed away from *Watkins,* and others say that *Barenblatt* signaled a reversal of the earlier ruling.

If it was a reversal, how can we explain the shift, which occurred within a two-year period? There are two possibilities. The first is that *Barenblatt* constituted "a strategic withdrawal" because at the time the Court was under "pressure of Congress and some sectors of public opinion."[48] In particular, *Watkins* and other "liberal" decisions on subversive activity and on discrimination such as *Brown v. Board of Education* (1954) made the Court the target of numerous congressional proposals. Some even sought to remove the Court's jurisdiction to hear cases involving subversive activities. According to some observers, the justices felt the heat and acceded to congressional pressure.

Another explanation is that personnel changes produced a more conservative Court, that *Barenblatt* represented a move "back toward a more conservative position" ushered in by President Dwight Eisenhower's appointments of Charles Whittaker and Potter Stewart.[49] By way of support, scholars point to the voting alignments in the two cases and to the general trend in the disposition of civil liberties cases. As Walter F. Murphy noted, during the 1956 term, which included *Watkins,* the Court ruled in favor of the civil liberties claim in 74 percent of the cases; that figure fell to 59 percent and 51 percent in the 1957 and 1958 terms, respectively.[50]

48. C. Herman Pritchett, *Congress versus the Supreme Court* (Minneapolis: University of Minnesota Press, 1961), 12.

49. Ibid.
50. Walter F. Murphy, *Congress and the Supreme Court* (Chicago: University of Chicago Press, 1962), 246.

Either way, the explanations indicate the susceptibility of the Court to political influences outside and inside its chambers. As the dangers associated with the cold war began to ebb, the justices again evinced a change of heart on the rights of witnesses. In case after case in the 1960s they reversed the convictions of many whom Congress had cited for contempt. But its most significant decision involved not Congress, but a state legislature. In *Gibson v. Florida Legislative Investigating Commission* (1963) the Court reversed the contempt conviction of a leader in the National Association for the Advancement of Colored People (NAACP) who refused to provide a committee with the organization's membership records. Theodore R. Gibson argued that doing so would abridge his First Amendment rights. The Supreme Court distinguished this dispute from *Barenblatt,* noting that the state had not sufficiently linked the NAACP to subversive activities and, therefore, had provided no compelling reason for wanting the membership lists. More generally, it held that:

[T]his Court's prior holdings demonstrate that there can be no question that the State has power adequately to inform itself—through legislative investigation, if it so desires—in order to act and protect its legitimate and vital interests. . . . It is no less obvious, however, that the legislative power to investigate, broad as it may be, is not without limit. . . . [W]e hold . . . that groups which themselves are neither engaged in subversive or other illegal or improper activities nor demonstrated to have any substantial connections with such activities are to be protected in their [First Amendment rights].

In essence, the Court sought to strike a balance between the rights of individuals and those of legislatures, no easy task largely because of the substantive nature of the power to investigate. Certainly, as HUAC's activities illustrate, plenty

of room for abuse exists. But, "responsibly used, the power to investigate is a vital safeguard against both governmental and private wrongdoing."[51] We have only to consider congressional hearings into the Watergate scandal, which we shall examine in Chapter 4, to see the truth in this.

Inherent Powers

As we have seen, Congress has enumerated powers and those powers that can be implied or inferred from, or are incidental to, its role as the lawmaking institution. In addition, as noted in Table 3-4, many analysts argue that Congress has certain inherent powers that are neither explicit nor even implied by the Constitution, but which somehow attach themselves to sovereign states. As Justice Story defined them, inherent powers are those that result "from the whole mass of the powers of the National Government, and from the nature of political society, [not as] a consequence or incident of the powers specifically enumerated.[52]

Although theorists have long espoused this concept, it found its way into constitutional law in *United States v. Curtiss-Wright Export Corp.* (1936). As you read this case, pay particular attention to Justice George Sutherland's explication of inherent powers. How does he define them? More important, how does he square the existence of inherent powers with the idea of a government based on enumeration? Before you read his opinion, note in his biography that he had international policy-making experience. How might this experience have affected his resolution of this dispute?

51. Pritchett, *Constitutional Law of the Federal System,* 195.
52. *Commentaries on the Constitution* (New York: Da Capa Press reprint of 1833 edition, 1970), vol. III, 124.

George Sutherland

(1922–1938)

George Sutherland was born March 25, 1862, in Buckinghamshire, England, and brought to the United States the following year by his parents. His father, a recent convert to the Church of Jesus Christ of Latter-day Saints, settled his family in Springville in the Utah Territory. The senior Sutherland soon deserted the Mormons, but the family remained in Utah. George Sutherland learned the value of thrift and hard work in his childhood—he left school at age twelve to help support the family. By the time he was sixteen, however, he had saved enough money to enroll at Brigham Young Academy in Provo. After three years there, he spent a year working for the company building the Rio Grande Western Railroad and in 1883 entered the University of Michigan Law School. He studied law for only one year before returning to Provo to start his law practice. He married Rosamund Lee of Beaver, Utah, on June 18, 1883. The couple had two daughters and one son.

After ten years in Provo, Sutherland in 1893 moved to Salt Lake City. The next year he helped found the Utah Bar Association. When the territory achieved statehood in 1896, Sutherland, running as a Republican, was elected to the first state Senate. In 1900 he was elected to the U.S. House of Representatives. He declined to run for a second term in the House but was elected in 1904 to the U.S. Senate, serving from 1905 to 1917.

During his first term in the Senate, Sutherland endorsed several reform measures, including the Pure Food and Drug Act (1906), the Postal Savings Act (1910), and a compensation bill for workers injured in interstate commerce (1911–1912). He also played a major role in the revision and codification of federal criminal statutes. Among legislative programs he opposed were statehood for Arizona and New Mexico (1912)—because their constitutions provided for recalls, initiatives, and referenda—the Federal Reserve Act (1913), the Sixteenth Amendment (1913), the Clayton Antitrust Act (1914), and the Federal Trade Commission Act (1914). He also opposed the nomination of Louis D. Brandeis to the Supreme Court.

In 1916 Sutherland failed in his attempt to be renominated by the Utah Republican party. He stayed in Washington, D.C., practiced law, and remained in touch with former Senate colleague Warren Harding. Sutherland developed into one of Harding's closest advisers and worked on his successful presidential campaign in 1920. Soon thereafter Sutherland represented the Harding administration as chairman of the advisory committee to the Washington Conference for the Limitation of Naval Armaments in 1921 and as counsel in arbitration between Norway and the United States over matters of shipping.

President Harding named Sutherland to the Supreme Court when Justice John H. Clarke unexpectedly resigned to work for the cause of world peace. He was confirmed by voice vote the same day he was nominated, September 5, 1922. Sutherland retired from the Court January 17, 1938, and died in Stockbridge, Massachusetts, July 18, 1942.

Source: Elder Witt, *Guide to the U.S. Supreme Court,* 2d ed. (Washington, D.C.: Congressional Quarterly, 1990), 855–856.

United States v. Curtiss-Wright Export Corp.

299 U.S. 304 (1936)

Vote: 7 (Brandeis, Butler, Cardozo, Hughes, Roberts, Sutherland, Van Devanter)
    1 (McReynolds)
Opinion of the Court: Sutherland
Not participating: Stone

After Charles Lindbergh's 1927 transatlantic flight, the aviation industry began to boom. Americans were convinced that "flying . . . would take its place as the new mode of transportation."[53] As a result, many new companies formed to build aircraft. Among them was Curtiss-Wright.

Although it started off on a strong footing, Curtiss-Wright soon fell prey to the Great Depression: between 1930 and 1931, it lost $13 million. To avoid going bankrupt, it looked beyond the United States into the foreign market, where money still could be made. However, Curtiss-Wright was not selling its wares to other private companies, but to foreign governments involved in military conflicts and in need of war planes.

The company found a ready buyer in Bolivia, which since 1932 had been at war with Paraguay over the Chaco, a region east of Bolivia. Land-locked Bolivia was determined to take control of the Chaco to gain access to the Atlantic Ocean. It became an excellent customer of Curtiss-Wright's, buying thirty-four planes in the early 1930s. The Chaco war, in turn, enabled the company to survive the depression.

Things began to turn sour in 1934. Books and articles appeared attacking companies like Curtiss-Wright as "merchants of death." More important, the League of Nations wanted to put an end to the Chaco war and asked the United States to help. Accordingly, President Roosevelt asked Congress to enact a resolution enabling him to

53. We adopt this and what follows from Robert A. Divine, "The Case of the Smuggled Bombers," in *Quarrels that Have Shaped the Constitution* by John A. Garraty (New York: Harper & Row, 1987).

prohibit the sale of arms to the warring countries. It did so on May 28, 1934.

[I]f the President finds that the prohibition of the sale of arms and munitions of war in the United States to those countries now engaged in armed conflict in the Chaco may contribute to the reestablishment of peace between those countries, and if after consultation with the governments of other American Republics and with their cooperation, as well as that of such other governments as he may deem necessary, he makes proclamation to that effect, it shall be unlawful to sell, except under such limitations and exceptions as the President prescribes, any arms or munitions of war in any place in the United States to the countries now engaged in that armed conflict, or to any person, company, or association acting in the interest of either country, until otherwise ordered by the President or by Congress.

Whoever sells any arms or munitions of war . . . shall . . . be punished by a fine not exceeding $10,000 or by imprisonment not exceeding two years, or both.

Shortly after the resolution was enacted, Roosevelt issued an order embargoing weapon sales to Bolivia and Paraguay. Curtiss-Wright refused to comply with the order and tried to get around it by disguising bombers as passenger planes. Eventually, it got caught and was charged with violating the order.

The company challenged the government's action. Among its arguments when the case reached the Court, the most pertinent was the contention that the 1934 resolution was invalid because it gave "uncontrolled" lawmaking "discretion" to the president. On this score, the company's reasoning appeared strong: in *Panama Refining Company v. Ryan* (1935) the Court had struck down a congressional act on the grounds that the legislature had delegated lawmaking authority to the president without sufficient guidelines *(see page 126)*. In the company's view, the 1934 resolution was no different from the law struck down in *Panama*.

The U.S. government tried to distinguish the facts in this case from those in the 1935 decision.

In its view, the congressional delegation of power in *Panama,* as we shall see, involved domestic, not international, affairs. This distinction was important, in the government's opinion, because "from the beginning of the government, in the conduct of foreign affairs, Congress has followed the practice of conferring upon the President power similar to that conferred by the present resolution." By way of example, U.S. attorneys indicated that as early as 1794, Congress had given the president the "duty of determining" when embargoes should be laid "upon vessels in ports of the United States bound for foreign ports."

Justice Sutherland delivered the opinion of the Court:

It is contended that by the Joint Resolution, the going into effect and continued operation of the resolution was conditioned (a) upon the President's judgment as to its beneficial effect upon the reestablishment of peace between the countries engaged in armed conflict in the Chaco; (b) upon the making of a proclamation, which was left to his unfettered discretion, thus constituting an attempted substitution of the President's will for that of Congress; (c) upon the making of a proclamation putting an end to the operation of the resolution, which again was left to the President's unfettered discretion; and (d) further, that the extent of its operation in particular cases was subject to limitation and exception by the President, controlled by no standard. In each of these particulars, appellees urge that Congress abdicated its essential functions and delegated them to the Executive.

Whether, if the Joint Resolution had related solely to internal affairs it would be open to the challenge that it constituted an unlawful delegation of legislative power to the Executive, we find it unnecessary to determine. The whole aim of the resolution is to affect a situation entirely external to the United States, and falling within the category of foreign affairs. The determination which we are called to make, therefore, is whether the Joint Resolution, as applied to that situation, is vulnerable to attack under the rule that forbids a delegation of the law-making power. In other words, assuming (but not deciding) that the challenged delegation, if it were confined to internal affairs, would be invalid, may it nevertheless be sustained on the ground that its exclusive aim is to afford a remedy for a hurtful condition within foreign territory?

It will contribute to the elucidation of the question if we first consider the differences between the powers of the Federal government in respect of foreign or external affairs and those in respect of domestic or internal affairs. That there are differences between them, and that these differences are fundamental, may not be doubted.

The two classes of powers are different, both in respect of their origin and their nature. The broad statement that the Federal government can exercise no powers except those specifically enumerated in the Constitution, and such implied powers as are necessary and proper to carry into effect the enumerated powers, is categorically true only in respect of our internal affairs. In that field, the primary purpose of the Constitution was to carve from the general mass of legislative powers *then possessed by the states* such portions as it was thought desirable to vest in the Federal government, leaving those not included in the enumeration still in the states. That this doctrine applies only to powers which the states had, is self-evident. And since the states severally never possessed international powers, such powers could not have been carved from the mass of state powers but obviously were transmitted to the United States from some other source. During the colonial period, those powers were possessed exclusively by and were entirely under the control of the Crown. By the Declaration of Independence, "the Representatives of the United States of America" declared the United [not the several] Colonies to be free and independent states, and as such to have "full Power to levy War, conclude Peace, contract Alliances, establish Commerce and to do all other Acts and Things which Independent States may of right do."

As a result of the separation from Great Britain by the colonies, acting as a unit, the powers of external sovereignty passed from the Crown not to the colonies severally, but to the colonies in their collective and corporate capacity as the United States of America. Even before the Declaration, the colonies were a unit in foreign affairs, acting through a common agency—namely the Continental Congress, composed of delegates from the thirteen colonies. That agency exercised the powers of war and peace, raised an army, created a navy, and finally adopted the Declaration of Independence. Rulers come and go; governments end and forms of government change; but sovereignty survives. A political society cannot endure without a supreme will somewhere. Sovereignty is never held in suspense. When, therefore, the external sovereignty of Great Britain in respect of the colonies ceased, it immediately passed to the Union. . . .

The Union existed before the Constitution, which was ordained and established among other things to form ''a more perfect Union.'' Prior to that event, it is clear that the Union, declared by the Articles of Confederation to be ''perpetual,'' was the sole possessor of external sovereignty, and in the Union it remained without change save in so far as the Constitution in express terms qualified its exercise. The Framers' Convention was called and exerted its powers upon the irrefutable postulate that though the states were several their people in respect of foreign affairs were one. . . .

It results that the investment of the Federal government with the powers of external sovereignty did not depend upon the affirmative grants of the Constitution. The powers to declare and wage war, to conclude peace, to make treaties, to maintain diplomatic relations with other sovereignties, if they had never been mentioned in the Constitution, would have vested in the Federal government as necessary concomitants of nationality. Neither the Constitution nor the laws passed in pursuance of it have any force in foreign territory unless in respect of our own citizens . . . and operations of the nation in such territory must be governed by treaties, international understandings and compacts, and the principles of international law. As a member of the family of nations, the right and power of the United States in that field are equal to the right and power of the other members of the international family. Otherwise, the United States is not completely sovereign. . . .

Practically every volume of the United States Statutes contains one or more acts or joint resolutions of Congress authorizing action by the President in respect of subjects affecting foreign relations, which either leave the exercise of the power to his unrestricted judgment, or provide a standard far more general than that which has always been considered requisite with regard to domestic affairs. . . .

The result of holding that the joint resolution here under attack is void and unenforceable as constituting an unlawful delegation of legislative power would be to stamp this multitude of comparable acts and resolutions as likewise invalid. And while this court may not, and should not, hesitate to declare acts of Congress, however many times repeated, to be unconstitutional if beyond all rational doubt it finds them to be so, an impressive array of legislation such as we have just set forth, enacted by nearly every Congress from the beginning of our national existence to the present day, must be given unusual weight in the process of reaching a correct determination of the problem. A legislative practice such as we have here, evidenced not by only occasional instances, but marked by the movement of a steady stream for a century and a half of time, goes a long way in the direction of proving the presence of unassailable ground for the constitutionality of the practice, to be found in the origin and history of the power involved, or in its nature, or in both combined. . . .

The uniform, long-continued and undisputed legislative practice just disclosed rests upon an admissible view of the Constitution which, even if the practice found far less support in principle than we think it does, we should not feel at liberty at this late day to disturb.

We deem it unnecessary to consider, seriatim, the several clauses which are said to evidence the unconstitutionality of the Joint Resolution as involving an unlawful delegation of legislative power. It is enough to summarize by saying that, both upon principle and in accordance with precedent, we conclude there is sufficient warrant for the broad discretion vested in the President to determine whether the enforcement of the statute will have a beneficial effect upon the reestablishment of peace in the affected countries; whether he shall make proclamation to bring the resolution into operation; whether and when the resolution shall cease to operate and to make proclamation accordingly; and to prescribe limitations and exceptions to which the enforcement of the resolution shall be subject.

Curtiss-Wright was a landmark ruling. As we shall see later in this chapter, the decision ran directly counter to what the Court was doing in other areas of the law. While it was striking down many segments of Roosevelt's New Deal, in part on the ground that the laws were unconstitutional delegations of power, here the Court upheld congressional authority to delegate power. Why it did so brings us to another important, and for present purposes more relevant, aspect of the decision: the distinction between foreign and domestic affairs. Sutherland justified the delegation here on the grounds that it involved external affairs, whereas the Court's rulings on the New Deal programs involved domestic programs.

In this dichotomy the majority found the concept of inherent powers. In its view, the U.S. Constitution transferred some domestic powers from the states to the federal government, leaving some with the states or the people. That is why Congress cannot exercise authority over internal affairs beyond that which is explicitly enumerated or can be implied from that document. In contrast, no such transfer occurred or could have occurred for authority over foreign affairs. Because the states never had such power to begin with, they could not have bestowed it on the federal government. Rather, "authority over foreign affairs is an inherent power, which attaches automatically to the federal government as a sovereign entity, and derives from the Constitution only as the Constitution is the creator of that sovereign entity."[54] It is not Congress specifically but the federal government that enjoys complete authority over foreign relations, which is an inherent power of sovereign nations, one that is derived not from their charters but from their status. Louis Henkin summarized:

Foreign affairs are national affairs. The United States is not a single nation-state, and it is the United States (not the States of the Union, singly or together) that has relations with other nations, and the United States Government that conducts these relations and makes foreign policy.[55]

What are we to make of the majority opinion? Some support certainly exists for its distinction between domestic and foreign affairs. We will explore this subject in greater detail in Chapter 4, but here we can say that some of the Framers would have approved of *Curtiss-Wright*. As Hamilton wrote in Federalist 23, "The circumstances that endanger the safety of nations are infinite, and for this reason no constitutional shackles can wisely be imposed on the power to which the care of it is committed." The idea, in short, was not novel, and Sutherland had espoused it during his Senate career.[56]

But *Curtiss-Wright* also has been the subject of some criticism. Historians and legal scholars assert that Sutherland's historical analysis was inaccurate: "There is evidence that, after independence, at least some of the erstwhile colonies . . . considered themselves sovereign, independent states."[57] More relevant here, however, is the argument that the entire notion of "inherent powers" cannot possibly conform with theories underlying the Constitution. The Tenth Amendment states: "The powers not delegated to the United States by the Constitution, nor prohibited by it to the States, are reserved to the States respectively, or to the people." Can it be that this language applies only to domestic powers and not foreign affairs? *Curtiss-Wright* seems to teach this lesson, and it makes some analysts squirm.

Even so, Sutherland's opinion remains authoritative doctrine. Its conceptualization of the federal government's inherent power over foreign affairs provides that entity with considerable leeway. And it is a doctrine to which the Court continues, generally speaking, to subscribe.

54. Pritchett, *Constitutional Law of the Federal System,* 305.

55. Louis Henkin, *Foreign Affairs and the Constitution* (New York: W. W. Norton, 1975), 15.
56. Fisher, *American Constitutional Law,* 302.
57. Henkin, *Foreign Affairs and the Constitution,* 23.

Amendment-Enforcing Power

Many discussions of congressional powers end with those powers inherent to sovereign nations. But it is important to understand, especially today, another source of legislative authority— amendment-enforcing power—because Congress makes frequent use of it as a basis for legislation.[58] Seven constitutional amendments contain some variant of the following language: Congress shall have power to enforce, by appropriate legislation, the provisions of this article. The first section of the Fifteenth Amendment says, "The right of citizens of the United States to vote shall not be denied . . . on account of race," and this statement is followed by an enforcement provision. Presumably, the writers of this Reconstruction amendment intended, at the very least, to implement its mandate; that is, Congress could pass legislation forbidding states to deny blacks the right to vote.

Many states, particularly in the South, however, continued to impose barriers such as literacy tests, poll taxes, grandfather clauses, and primary rules aimed at excluding blacks from voting. Throughout the 1950s Congress invoked its enforcement power under the Fifteenth Amendment to enact legislation to end these practices. The 1957 Civil Rights Act, for example, prohibited attempts to intimidate or prevent persons from voting in general or primary elections for federal offices; empowered the attorney general to seek an injunction when an individual was deprived or about to be deprived of the right to vote; gave the district courts jurisdiction over such proceedings, without requiring that administrative remedies be exhausted; and provided that any person cited for contempt should be defended by counsel and allowed to compel witnesses to appear.[59] Another act, passed three years later, "authorized judges to appoint referees to help [blacks] register and vote."[60]

Few analysts ever seriously questioned the constitutionality of these laws. Under the Fifteenth Amendment, Congress seemed to have the authority to ensure that states did not deny the right to vote, and, because these acts were aimed at accomplishing that end, they were deemed appropriate under the language of Section 2 of the amendment. But in the mid-1960s voting rights advocates clamored for even more drastic measures. They claimed that congressional legislation and the legal suits it authorized the attorney general to undertake were "expensive" and entirely too "piecemeal."[61] Moreover, the litigation was not all that successful "because in most localities the explicit voting requirements were perfectly constitutional but were administered in a highly discriminatory fashion."[62] The South, in other words, was following the letter, but not the spirit, of the laws. Voter registration figures for 1960 and 1964 support this observation: the percentage of voting-age nonwhites registered to vote remained dismally low *(see Table 3-5)*.

In 1965 Congress enacted the most comprehensive and, some say, drastic measure yet. Not only was it directed at eliminating every ingenious device designed to restrict suffrage racially, but also it gave the federal government extraordinary power to regulate elections. If a state or a political subdivision had used literacy tests prior to 1964, or if less than 50 percent of its voting-age population was registered to vote or had voted in the 1964 election—conditions known as the "triggering formula"—the government could send in federal examiners who, in turn, could order state officials to "register all persons found qualified to vote." Moreover, states under the

58. Craig R. Ducat and Harold W. Chase, *Constitutional Interpretation* 4th ed. (St. Paul, Minn.: West Publishing, 1988), 137-138.

59. *Revolution in Civil Rights,* 3d ed. (Washington, D.C.: Congressional Quarterly, 1967), 39.

60. Ibid., 42.

61. John R. Schmidhauser, *Constitutional Law in American Politics* (Monterey, Calif.: Brooks/Cole, 1984), 471.

62. Farber and Sherry, *A History of the American Constitution,* 342.

Table 3–5 White and Non-White Voting Registration Statistics, 1960, 1964

| | Percentage of Voting-Age Population Registered to Vote | | | |
| | 1960 | | 1964 | |
State	Whites	Non-Whites	Whites	Non-Whites
Alabama	63.6%	13.7%	70.7%	23.0%
Arkansas	60.9	37.7	71.7	54.4
Florida	69.5	39.0	84.0	54.4
Georgia	NA	NA	74.5	44.0
Louisiana	77.0	30.9	80.4	32.0
Mississippi	NA	6.1	70.7	6.7
North Carolina	92.8	38.2	92.5	46.8
South Carolina	NA	NA	78.5	38.8
Tennessee (63 counties)	83.5	64.1	72.9	69.4
Texas (213 counties)	50.9	33.7	53.2	57.7
Virginia	46.2	23.0	55.9	45.7
Totals	NA	NA	73.2	43.3

Source: *Revolution in Civil Rights* (Washington, D.C.: Congressional Quarterly, 1965), 43, 74.

triggering formula were required to receive "pre-clearance" from the attorney general or a district court before they could enact new voting laws.

The Voting Rights Act of 1965 marked a dramatic change from earlier laws. As we noted, in previous legislation "Congress simply provided enforcement mechanisms to implement the judicially declared rights." Now it was issuing sanctions against states (the preclearance requirements) and allowing the attorney general to take action against certain areas, "even though no court [had] found them" to be engaging in unconstitutional activity.[63]

63. Gunther, *Constitutional Law*, 930.

Did Congress's power to enforce amendments support such legislation? Was it appropriate under the amendment's language? Given that the act constituted a drastic intrusion of the federal government into state operations, it is not surprising that it was quickly challenged as an unconstitutional use of congressional power. As you read *South Carolina v. Katzenbach* (1966) consider the Court's response, and not just its reaction to the 1965 act. How did it resolve the larger issue of the scope of Congress's amendment-enforcing power?

South Carolina v. Katzenbach

383 U.S. 301 (1966)

Vote: 8 (Brennan, Clark, Douglas, Fortas, Harlan, Stewart, Warren, White)
1 (Black)
Opinion of the Court: Warren
Concurring/Dissenting opinion: Black

In accordance with the Voting Rights Act of 1965, the director of the Census Bureau sent the following notice to the attorney general in August 1965:

I have determined that in each of the following States less than 50 per centum of the persons of voting age residing therein voted in the presidential election of November 1964: Alabama, Alaska, Georgia, Louisiana, South Carolina, [and] Virginia.

These seven states, as well as parts of several others, met the criteria for coverage under the Voting Rights Act's remedial provisions.

Rather than accede to the federal government, South Carolina asked the U.S. Supreme Court, under its original jurisdiction, to find the act unconstitutional. In particular, South Carolina argued that the legislation was not appropriate to enforce the Fifteenth Amendment, that it infringed on states' rights, and that it had the effect of treating states in an unequal manner. Five of the other six states coming under the act's purview—Alaska did not participate—filed amicus curiae briefs in support of South Carolina.

In defense of the law, U.S. government attorneys, including Attorney General Nicholas Katzenbach and Solicitor General Thurgood Marshall, who would later serve on the Court, argued, "Section 2 of the Fifteenth Amendment confers upon Congress power to enact all legislation reasonably adapted to the objective of preventing abridgment of the right to vote on account of race or color."[64] Nineteen states, mostly in the East and Midwest, submitted an amicus curiae brief supporting the U.S. government.[65] In contrast to their southern counterparts, which supported South Carolina's states' rights position, they argued that "although a state has power to determine the qualifications for voting, such power may not be used to violate the Fourteenth and Fifteenth Amendments." The brief further stated, "Congress has power to enact appropriate legislation precluding the states from denying the right to vote on the basis of color."[66]

64. *South Carolina v. Katzenbach,* 383 U.S. 301 (1966), Brief for Defendant, I.
65. California and Illinois filed separate amicus curiae briefs in support of the act.
66. *South Carolina v. Katzenbach,* Brief for the Attorney General of Massachusetts et al., as amicus curiae, II.

Chief Justice Warren delivered the opinion of the Court:

The Voting Rights Act was designed by Congress to banish the blight of racial discrimination in voting, which has infected the electoral process in parts of our country for nearly a century. The Act creates stringent new remedies for voting discrimination where it persists on a pervasive scale, and in addition the statute strengthens existing remedies for pockets of voting discrimination elsewhere in the country. Congress assumed the power to prescribe these remedies from § 2 of the Fifteenth Amendment, which authorizes the National Legislature to effectuate by "appropriate" measures the constitutional prohibition against racial discrimination in voting. We hold that the sections of the Act which are properly before us are an appropriate means for carrying out Congress' constitutional responsibilities and are consonant with all other provisions of the Constitution. We therefore deny South Carolina's request that enforcement of these sections of the Act be enjoined.

The constitutional propriety of the Voting Rights Act of 1965 must be judged with reference to the historical experience which it reflects. Before enacting the measure, Congress explored with great care the problem of racial discrimination in voting. . . .

Two points emerge vividly from the voluminous legislative history of the Act contained in the committee hearings and floor debates. First: Congress felt itself confronted by an insidious and pervasive evil which had been perpetuated in certain parts of our country through unremitting and ingenious defiance of the Constitution. Second: Congress concluded that the unsuccessful remedies which it had prescribed in the past would have to be replaced by sterner and more elaborate measures in order to satisfy the clear commands of the Fifteenth Amendment. . . .

[P]rovisions of the Voting Rights Act of 1965 are challenged on the fundamental ground that they exceed the powers of Congress and encroach on an area reserved to the States by the Constitution. . . .

The objections to the Act which are raised under these provisions may therefore be considered only as additional aspects of the basic question presented by the case. Has Congress exercised its powers under the

Fifteenth Amendment in an appropriate manner with relation to the States?

The ground rules for resolving this question are clear. The language and purpose of the Fifteenth Amendment, the prior decisions construing its several provisions, and the general doctrines of constitutional interpretation, all point to one fundamental principle. As against the reserved powers of the States, Congress may use any rational means to effectuate the constitutional prohibition of racial discrimination in voting. . . . We turn now to a more detailed description of the standards which govern our review of the Act.

Section 1 of the Fifteenth Amendment declares that ''[t]he right of citizens of the United States to vote shall not be denied or abridged by the United States or by any State on account of race, color, or previous condition of servitude.'' This declaration has always been treated as self-executing and has repeatedly been construed, without further legislative specification, to invalidate state voting qualifications or procedures which are discriminatory on their face or in practice. See . . . Smith v. Allwright [1944]; Gomillion v. Lightfoot [1960]; Louisiana v. United States [1965]. Those decisions have been rendered with full respect for the general rule . . . that States ''have broad powers to determine the conditions under which the right of suffrage may be exercised.'' The gist of the matter is that the Fifteenth Amendment supersedes contrary exertions of state power. ''When a State exercises power wholly within the domain of state interest, it is insulated from federal judicial review. But such insulation is not carried over when state power is used as an instrument for circumventing a federally protected right.''

South Carolina contends that the cases cited above are precedents only for the authority of the judiciary to strike down state statutes and procedures—that to allow an exercise of this authority by Congress would be to rob the courts of their rightful constitutional role. On the contrary, § 2 of the Fifteenth Amendment expressly declares that ''Congress shall have power to enforce this article by appropriate legislation.'' By adding this authorization, the Framers indicated that Congress was to be chiefly responsible for implementing the rights created in § 1. ''It is the power of Congress which has been enlarged. Congress is autho-

rized to *enforce* the prohibitions by appropriate legislation. Some legislation is contemplated to make the [Civil War] amendments fully effective.'' Accordingly, in addition to the courts, Congress has full remedial powers to effectuate the constitutional prohibition against racial discrimination in voting.

Congress has repeatedly exercised these powers in the past, and its enactments have repeatedly been upheld. . . . On the rare occasions when the Court has found an unconstitutional exercise of these powers, in its opinion Congress had attacked evils not comprehended by the Fifteenth Amendment.

The basic test to be applied in a case involving § 2 of the Fifteenth Amendment is the same as in all cases concerning the express powers of Congress with relation to the reserved powers of the States. Chief Justice Marshall laid down the classic formulation, 50 years before the Fifteenth Amendment was ratified:

''Let the end be legitimate, let it be within the scope of the constitution, and all means which are appropriate, which are plainly adapted to that end, which are not prohibited, but consist with the letter and spirit of the constitution, are constitutional.'' McCulloch v. Maryland [1819].

The Court has subsequently echoed his language in describing each of the Civil War Amendments:

''Whatever legislation is appropriate, that is, adapted to carry out the objects the amendments have in view, whatever tends to enforce submission to the prohibitions they contain, and to secure to all persons the enjoyment of perfect equality of civil rights and the equal protection of the laws against State denial or invasion, if not prohibited, is brought within the domain of congressional power.'' Ex parte Virginia [1880].

This language was again employed, nearly 50 years later, with reference to Congress' related authority under § 2 of the Eighteenth Amendment.

We therefore reject South Carolina's argument that Congress may appropriately do no more than to forbid violations of the Fifteenth Amendment in general terms—that the task of fashioning specific remedies or of applying them to particular localities must necessarily be left entirely to the courts. Congress is not circumscribed by any such artificial rules under § 2 of the Fifteenth Amendment. In the oft-repeated words of Chief Justice Marshall, referring to another specific legislative authorization in the Constitution, "This power, like all others vested in Congress, is complete in itself, may be exercised to its utmost extent, and acknowledges no limitations, other than are prescribed in the constitution." Gibbons v. Ogden [1824]. . . .

After enduring nearly a century of widespread resistance to the Fifteenth Amendment, Congress has marshalled an array of potent weapons against the evil, with authority in the Attorney General to employ them effectively. Many of the areas directly affected by this development have indicated their willingness to abide by any restraints legitimately imposed upon them. We here hold that the portions of the Voting Rights Act properly before us are a valid means for carrying out the commands of the Fifteenth Amendment. Hopefully, millions of non-white Americans will now be able to participate for the first time on an equal basis in the government under which they live. We may finally look forward to the day when truly "[t]he right of citizens of the United States to vote shall not be denied or abridged by the United States or by any State on account of race, color, or previous condition of servitude."

The bill of complaint is dismissed.

Bill dismissed.

As we can see, the Court's standard for evaluating amendment-enforcing power, the words *appropriate legislation,* is not so different from "that employed to appraise the constitutionality of laws enacted under the Necessary and Proper Clause."[67] Indeed, not only does Warren cite *McCulloch v. Maryland* with approval, but also his logic reflects Marshall's. Compare Marshall's words, "Let the end be legitimate, let it be within the scope of the constitution, and all means which are appropriate . . . are constitutional," with Warren's: "Congress may use any rational means to effectuate the constitutional prohibition of racial discrimination in voting."

In the final analysis, *Katzenbach* greatly enhanced Congress's amendment-enforcing power, placing it on the same plane as implied powers. And, at least through the 1970s, the Court seemed content with this interpretation, applying it to legislation passed under the enforcing power of other constitutional amendments. In 1981, however, the Court indicated a willingness to move away from Warren's tour de force in *Katzenbach.* Ruling in a dispute that involved legislation a lower court had held constitutional under the Fourteenth Amendment's enforcement clause,

Justice William H. Rehnquist described the appropriate standard "for determining when Congress intends to enforce" Fourteenth Amendment guarantees:

Because such legislation [enforcing the amendment] imposes congressional policy on a State involuntarily, and because it often intrudes on traditional state authority, we should not quickly attribute to Congress an unstated intent to act under its authority to enforce the Fourteenth Amendment.[68]

This "intent" standard could potentially narrow congressional power to enforce constitutional amendments if Congress were vague about the law's underpinnings. But to date it remains unclear whether the Rehnquist Court will invoke that standard or something else as so far it has had no opportunity to consider further the scope of congressional enforcement power.

The Role of Congress in National Government

In our discussion so far, you may have noted a pattern in the Court's decisions dealing with the sources and scope of congressional power. On the

67. Ducat and Chase, *Constitutional Interpretation,* 137.

68. *Pennhurst State School and Hospital v. Halderman,* 451 U.S. 1 (1981).

whole, with a few scattered exceptions, the Court has allowed Congress a good deal of leeway in exercising enumerated and extraconstitutional power, especially in disputes involving that body's power to regulate its own affairs and to enact legislation, even if a law intrudes on state operations. Where the Court has wavered and, at times, has reined in Congress is over its authority vis-à-vis the other national institutions, particularly the executive. In other words, during certain periods of the nation's history, the Court has taken a hard line on the separation of powers doctrine, limiting both friendly and unfriendly relations between Congress and the president.

In this section, we explore Court rulings in both areas, beginning with a discussion of Congress's authority to interact with the president in a cooperative sense. Many times throughout the nation's history, Congress has sought to delegate some of its authority to a president who wants such power or has requested it. In the section on delegation of powers, we shall see whether the Court has agreed to such cooperation. Next, we look at congressional authority to oversee executive power, to act as an unwanted check on the president.

Although these sections deal with different substantive material, you may note some commonalities in Court rulings. Pay careful attention to how the Court delineates constitutional interactions from the unconstitutional. Has it acted in a consistent manner? Have the justices grounded their opinions in constitutional language or philosophy or have other factors had a greater impact?

The Delegation of Powers

Almost all discussions of the ability of Congress to delegate its lawmaking power begin with the old Latin maxim: *delegata potestas non potest delegari*, which means "a power once delegated cannot be redelegated." We could apply this to Congress in the following way: because the Constitution delegates to that institution all legislative powers—lawmaking authority—it cannot give such power to another body or person.

Why not? To answer that question, suppose that after you take the final examination in this course, your instructor delegates the responsibility of grading the test papers to a teaching assistant. Being busy with other work, the TA then delegates that task to a roommate who has never taken a constitutional law course. Who would be responsible—the professor, the TA, or the roommate—when your final grade did not fairly reflect your work?[69] The same argument could be applied to delegations of lawmaking power to a president in charge of executing laws who in turn hands authority over to a bureaucrat.

However, no political institution has accepted fully the language of the Latin maxim. From the First Congress on, the legislature has delegated its power to other branches or even to nongovernmental entities. But why would Congress want to give away some of its power? One reason is that, like the professor in the example, Congress is often busy with other matters and must delegate some authority if it is to fulfill all of its responsibilities. Another is that Congress might "succeed well enough in the task of formulating general policies, but [might] lack the time and expert information needed to prescribe specific methods for carrying out those policies."[70] As the job of governance grows increasingly technical and complex, this reason becomes even more valid. *Curtiss-Wright* provides yet another reason. Recall there that Congress had given the president authority to issue an arms embargo if that would help to bring peace to warring South American nations. What this illustrates is congressional recognition that once it enacts legislation it may

69. Ducat and Chase use a similar example, centering on a school principal delegating authority to a teacher, who delegates it to a groundskeeper, who in turn passes it off to a student.

70. Pritchett, *Constitutional Law of the Federal System*, 184.

be difficult to amend it, "whereas the problems with which legislation aims to deal," such as in the *Curtiss-Wright* example, "may be constantly changing."[71] Finally, there are political reasons why Congress might want to delegate. Sotirios Barber noted, "A Congress of buck passers is one of the results of the electorate's tendency to reward politicians who are responsive to its [the public's] immediate wants, not its [Congress's] considered constitutional duties."[72] In other words, to avoid dealing with certain "hot potato" issues, Congress might hand them off to others. The delegation of powers issue is tricky: it is accepted, theoretically, that Congress should not dole out its lawmaking authority, but it is a matter of practical and reasonable politics that it does so.

Not surprisingly, the Supreme Court has found itself enmeshed in this debate. As we saw in *Curtiss-Wright,* it has been asked to determine whether a particular delegation of power is appropriate, constitutionally speaking, and, as in that case, the Court generally has upheld such delegations, even if they involve domestic issues. *Wayman v. Southard* (1825) was the Court's first major ruling on the delegation of domestic powers. This dispute, unlike most in this area, involved a congressional grant of lawmaking authority to the *courts,* not to the executive. In particular, the case asked the justices to determine whether a section of the 1789 Judiciary Act, which gave the courts power to "make and establish all necessary laws" for the conduct of judicial business, constituted a violation of the separation of powers doctrine and, as such, an unconstitutional delegation of power.

Writing for the Court in *Wayman,* Chief Justice Marshall responded pragmatically. He sought to balance the letter of the Constitution with the practical concerns facing Congress when he formulated the following standard: The legislature must itself "entirely" regulate "important subjects"; but for "those of less interest," it can enact a general provision and authorize "those who are to act under such general provisions to fill up the details." Put simply, Marshall established a different set of rules for the delegation of power, varying by the importance of the subject under regulation.[73] Applying this standard to the delegation of power contained in the 1789 Judiciary Act, he found that Congress could grant courts authority to promulgate their own rules.

Wayman—in theory—created an important precedent for subsequent Courts to follow. We say "in theory" because, although for the next century or so the Supreme Court never struck down a congressional delegation of power, it did not quite follow Marshall's standard. Rather, it took an even broader approach to these kinds of cases. For example, in *Hampton & Company v. United States* (1928) it let stand a grant of authority to the president that some suggest failed Marshall's standard. The Court examined the Fordney-McComber Act in which Congress established a tariff commission within the executive branch and permitted the president to increase or decrease tariffs on imported goods by as much as 50 percent. Because Congress gave the president (and the commission) virtually unlimited discretion to adjust rates, an import company challenged the act as a violation of the separation of powers doctrine. The company argued that Congress had provided the president with what was essentially lawmaking power. Writing for a unanimous Court, Chief Justice William Howard Taft—a former president of the United States—disagreed: "In determining what [Congress] may do in seeking assistance from another branch, the extent and character of that assistance must be fixed according to common sense and the inherent necessities of the governmental coordination."

---

71. Ibid.

72. Sotirios A. Barber, *On What the Constitution Means* (Baltimore: Johns Hopkins University Press, 1984), 177.

73. Pritchett, *The American Constitution,* 175.

For nearly a decade, the Court seemed quite willing to accept the so-called "common sense and inherent necessities" approach to congressional delegations. But in 1935 and 1936 the Court dealt Congress and the president major blows when it struck down provisions of the National Industrial Recovery Act (NIRA) as excessive delegations of power. In the box *(page 126)* we describe the circumstances surrounding these cases—*Panama Refining Company v. Ryan* and *Schechter Poultry v. United States*—and the Court's rulings in them. *(For full details, see Chapter 6.)* The NIRA was a major piece of New Deal legislation designed to pull the nation out of the economic depression. In *Panama,* Congress had allowed the president to prohibit the shipment in interstate commerce of oil produced in excess of state quotas; in *Schechter,* Congress had authorized the president to approve fair competition codes and standards if representatives of a particular industry recommended he do so. In both instances, the Court struck down the delegations of power as unconstitutional.

Why did the Court decide these cases that way? Because Congress passed the NIRA under its power to regulate interstate commerce, we take up this question from a somewhat different angle in Chapter 6. For now, let us first consider it from a doctrinal perspective: Did earlier precedent, particularly *Wayman* and *Hampton,* necessarily lead to these outcomes? The Court undoubtedly thought so: it justified its opinions in *Panama* and *Schechter* as being firmly grounded in past decisions and it did so by wide margins. Eight of the nine justices agreed with the majority opinion in *Panama,* and the one dissenting justice, Benjamin Cardozo, joined the others in *Schechter,* noting that this law constituted "delegation running riot."

Was the Court on firm legal ground? One way to think about this is to compare its rulings here with those in *Wayman* and *Hampton.* Were the NIRA delegations of power more onerous than that in *Hampton?* Or did they not meet Marshall's standard in *Wayman?* Another is to consider the briefs and arguments in the 1935 and 1936 cases. Before the Supreme Court decided *Panama,* a federal court of appeals had upheld the law as a constitutional use of congressional commerce powers and, in so doing, gave "very casual treatment to the delegation issue," noting simply that it met previously set standards. When the oil company appealed the decision, U.S. attorneys responded with a 195-page brief filed with the Supreme Court. Apparently, "lulled . . . into a false sense of security" by the lower court ruling and believing that "precedent [was] uniformly on their side," the United States devoted only 3 of those 195 pages to the delegation of powers issue. Indeed, it probably would not have been seriously raised had it not been for oral arguments. There, the lawyers for the oil company hammered away at both issues, the delegation of powers and the commerce clause, arguing that Congress had "laid down no rule or criterion to guide or limit the President in the orders that he may promulgate." [74]

Based on this sort of analysis, many scholars suggest that the justices were merely using the delegation of powers as an excuse to strike down New Deal legislation that they fundamentally and ideologically opposed. Whether this is true we leave for you to decide. More important for now is that the rulings in *Panama* and *Schechter* represent anomalies. For reasons we offer later, by 1937 the Court had begun to uphold New Deal legislation, and by the end of the decade it was allowing for all sorts of congressional delegations of powers to a diverse range of executive agencies, some of which are listed in Table 3-6.

What can we conclude about congressional delegations of power? Some analysts suggest that

74. Peter H. Irons, *The New Deal Lawyers* (Princeton, N.J.: Princeton University Press, 1982), 69, 70, 71, 93.

Court's Decisions in *Panama* and *Schechter Poultry*

	Panama Refining Co. v. Ryan (January 7, 1935)	*Schechter Poultry v. United States* (May 27, 1935)
Problem	The oil industry, as a result of overproduction to meet the demand for oil in the 1920s, began to ship "hot oil" (that which had been produced in excess of state quotas) across state lines as a way of dealing with falling prices.	The depression indicated the need for greater regulation of various industries, particularly prohibitions on certain kinds of "unfair" competition.
Congressional solution	A provision of the National Industrial Recovery Act (NIRA), which permitted the president to prohibit the shipment of hot oil in interstate commerce.	The NIRA, which allowed the president, at the request of a representative of a particular industry, to approve codes for the entire industry.
FDR's action	Issued an order prohibiting the shipment of oil produced in excess of state established quotas.	Approved industry codes.
The specific dispute	Small oil companies challenged the quota system, alleging that it hurt independent, small producers.	The Schechter brothers challenged the Live Poultry Code, which established industry standards and set work hours.
Delegation of powers question	Did challenged sections of the NIRA constitute overly broad (and thus unconstitutional) congressional delegations of power to the president?	
Majority opinion	Struck down challenged section of the NIRA: "in every case in which the question has been raised, the Court has recognized that there are limits of delegation which there is no constitutional authority to transcend. We think [the challenged section of the NIRA] goes beyond those limits. As to the transportation of oil production in excess of state permission the Congress has declared no policy, has established no standard, has laid down no rule."	Struck down parts of the NIRA: "In view of the scope of [the] broad declaration and of the nature of the restrictions that are imposed, the discretion of the President in approving or prescribing codes, and thus enacting laws for the government of trade and industry throughout the country, is virtually unfettered. We think that the code-making authority . . . is an unconstitutional delegation of legislative power."
Cardozo's opinion	**In dissent:** "My point of difference with the majority is narrow. I concede that to uphold the delegation there is a need to discover in the terms of the act a standard reasonably clear whereby discretion must be governed. I deny that such a standard is lacking in respect of the prohibitions permitted by this section when the act . . . is considered as a whole."	**Concurring:** This is "delegation running riot."

Table 3–6   "Delegated" Powers Held by Major Federal Regulatory Commissions

Commission	Examples of the Scope of Power
Interstate Commerce Commission	Fixes rates for railroads and related carriers Sets standards for reasonable service Controls consolidations and mergers of carriers Regulates safety devices and services
Federal Trade Commission	Prevents practices leading to monopoly and restraint of trade such as unfair methods of competition and price discrimination Investigates and issues cease-and-desist orders
Federal Communications Commission	Regulates telegraph carriers Allocates radio frequencies Licenses radio and television stations Monitors broadcasts
National Labor Relations Board	Adjudicates charges of unfair labor practices on the part of employers or unions Enforces collective bargaining agreements

Source: *Guide to Congress,* 3d ed. (Washington, D.C.: Congressional Quarterly, 1982), 198.

the Court's rulings in 1935 had an effect on Congress, forcing it to be more specific in the guidelines it sets out. Is that accurate? As noted in Table 3-6, some executive agencies wield power just as enormous as that which the Court struck in the mid-1930s, but since 1936 the Supreme Court has not overturned a law on such grounds (although a few of the most suspect never have reached the Court). Many have concluded that

"Congress now as a matter of fact can delegate as it pleases." [75]

An interesting example is *Mistretta v. United States* (1989) in which the Supreme Court scrutinized an act of Congress designed to minimize judicial discretion in sentencing. The Court's opinion takes us back almost to our original starting point, *Wayman v. Southard.*

75. Ducat and Chase, *Constitutional Interpretation,* 140.

Mistretta v. United States
488 U.S. 361 (1989)

Vote: 8 (Blackmun, Brennan,[76] Kennedy, Marshall, O'Connor, Rehnquist, Stevens, White)
        1 (Scalia)
Opinion of the Court: Blackmun
Dissenting opinion: Scalia

Concerned about wide discrepancies in sentences imposed by federal court judges, Congress

76. Brennan joined the majority in all but note 11 of its opinion, which dealt with the death penalty.

enacted the Sentencing Reform Act of 1984, which created the U.S. Sentencing Commission as "an independent commission in the judicial branch of government." The commission was empowered to create sentencing guidelines for all federal offenses, to which lower court judges generally would be bound. It was to have seven members, nominated by the president and confirmed by the Senate. Three of its members, at minimum, were to be federal court judges, and no more than four members could be of the same political party.

The commission fulfilled its charge, promulgating sentencing guidelines for federal offenses, but the federal courts were not in agreement over their constitutionality. More than 150 lower court judges found the guidelines constitutionally defective, while more than 100 upheld them.[77]

In *Mistretta v. United States* the lower federal court judge had upheld the plan, but the arguments of John Mistretta, who had been convicted of three counts of selling cocaine, were similar to those proffered by judges who did not approve of the guidelines. Of particular relevance here was his charge that the act violated delegation of powers principles by giving the commission "excessive legislative authority."

Justice Harry A. Blackmun delivered the opinion of the Court:

Petitioner argues that in delegating the power to promulgate sentencing guidelines for every federal criminal offense to an independent Sentencing Commission, Congress has granted the Commission excessive legislative discretion in violation of the constitutionally based nondelegation doctrine. We do not agree.

The nondelegation doctrine is rooted in the principle of separation of powers that underlies our tripartite system of government. The Constitution provides that "[a]ll legislative Powers herein granted shall be vested in a Congress of the United States," and we long have insisted that "the integrity and maintenance of the system of government ordained by the Constitution," mandate that Congress generally cannot delegate its legislative power to another Branch. We also have recognized, however, that the separation-of-powers principle, and the nondelegation doctrine in particular, do not prevent Congress from obtaining the assistance of its coordinate Branches. In a passage now enshrined in our jurisprudence, Chief Justice Taft, writing for the Court, explained our approach to such cooperative ventures: "In determining what [Congress] may do in seeking assistance from another branch, the extent and

character of that assistance must be fixed according to common sense and the inherent necessities of the government co-ordination." *J. W. Hampton, Jr., & Co. v. United States* (1928). So long as Congress "shall lay down by legislative act an intelligible principle to which the person or body authorized to [exercise the delegated authority] is directed to conform, such legislative action is not a forbidden delegation of legislative power."

Applying this "intelligible principle" test to congressional delegations, our jurisprudence has been driven by a practical understanding that in our increasingly complex society, replete with ever changing and more technical problems, Congress simply cannot do its job absent an ability to delegate power under broad general directives. . . .

Until 1935, this Court never struck down a challenged statute on delegation grounds. . . . After invalidating in 1935 two statutes as excessive delegations, see *Schechter Poultry Corp. v. United States* (1935), and *Panama Refining Co. v. Ryan* [1935], we have upheld, again without deviation, Congress' ability to delegate power under broad standards.

In light of our approval of . . . broad delegations, we harbor no doubt that Congress' delegation of authority to the Sentencing Commission is sufficiently specific and detailed to meet constitutional requirements. Congress charged the Commission with three goals: to "assure the meeting of the purposes of sentencing as set forth" in the Act; to "provide certainty and fairness in meeting the purposes of sentencing, avoiding unwarranted sentencing disparities among defendants with similar records . . . while maintaining sufficient flexibility to permit individualized sentences," where appropriate; and to "reflect to the extent practicable, advancement in knowledge of human behavior as it relates to the criminal justice process." Congress further specified four "purposes" of sentencing that the Commission must pursue in carrying out its mandate: "to reflect the seriousness of the offense, to promote respect for the law, and to provide just punishment for the offense"; "to afford adequate deterrence to criminal conduct"; "to protect the public from further crimes of the defendant"; and "to provide the defendant with needed . . . correctional treatment."

In addition, Congress prescribed the specific tool—

77. See Rossum and Tarr, *American Constitutional Law,* 119.

the guidelines system—for the Commission to use in regulating sentencing. More particularly, Congress directed the Commission to develop a system of "sentencing ranges" applicable "for each category of offense involving each category of defendant." . . .

To guide the Commission in its formulation of offense categories, Congress directed it to consider seven factors: the grade of the offense; the aggravating and mitigating circumstances of the crime; the nature and degree of the harm caused by the crime; the community view of the gravity of the offense; the public concern generated by the crime; the deterrent effect that a particular sentence may have on others; and the current incidence of the offense. Congress set forth 11 factors for the Commission to consider in establishing categories of defendants. These include the offender's age, education, vocational skills, mental and emotional condition, physical condition (including drug dependence), previous employment record, family ties and responsibilities, community ties, role in the offense, criminal history, and degree of dependence upon crime for a livelihood. Congress also prohibited the Commission from considering the "race, sex, national origin, creed, and socio-economic status of offenders," and instructed that the guidelines should reflect the "general inappropriateness" of considering certain other factors, such as current unemployment, that might serve as proxies for forbidden factors.

In addition to these overarching constraints, Congress provided even more detailed guidance to the Commission about categories of offenses and offender characteristics. Congress directed that guidelines require a term of confinement at or near the statutory maximum for certain crimes of violence and for drug offenses, particularly when committed by recidivists. Congress further directed that the Commission assure a substantial term of imprisonment for an offense constituting a third felony conviction, for a career felon, for one convicted of a managerial role in a racketeering enterprise, for a crime of violence by an offender on release from a prior felony conviction, and for an offense involving a substantial quantity of narcotics. . . . In other words, although Congress granted the Commission substantial discretion in formulating guidelines, in actuality it legislated a full hierarchy of punishment—from near maximum imprisonment, to substantial imprisonment, to some imprisonment, to alternatives—and stipulated the most important offense and offender characteristics to place defendants within these categories.

We cannot dispute petitioner's contention that the Commission enjoys significant discretion in formulating guidelines. The Commission does have discretionary authority to determine the relative severity of federal crimes and to assess the relative weight of the offender characteristics that Congress listed for the Commission to consider. . . . The Commission also has significant discretion to determine which crimes have been punished too leniently, and which too severely. Congress has called upon the Commission to exercise its judgment about which types of crimes and which types of criminals are to be considered similar for the purposes of sentencing.

But our cases do not at all suggest that delegations of this type may not carry with them the need to exercise judgment on matters of policy. . . .

The Act sets forth more than merely an "intelligible principle" or minimal standards. One court has aptly put it: "The statute outlines the policies which prompted establishment of the Commission, explains what the Commission should do and how it should do it, and sets out specific directives to govern particular situations."

Developing proportionate penalties for hundreds of different crimes by a virtually limitless array of offenders is precisely the sort of intricate, labor-intensive task for which delegation to an expert body is especially appropriate. Although Congress has delegated significant discretion to the Commission to draw judgments from its analysis of existing sentencing practice and alternative sentencing models, "Congress is not confined to that method of executing its policy which involves the least possible delegation of discretion to administrative officers." We have no doubt that in the hands of the Commission "the criteria which Congress has supplied are wholly adequate for carrying out the general policy and purpose" of the Act.

Examples of Laws Containing Legislative Vetoes

International Development and Food Assistance Act of 1975. Foreign assistance to countries not meeting human rights standards may be terminated by concurrent resolution.

Nuclear Non-Proliferation Act of 1978. Cooperative agreements concerning storage and disposition of spent nuclear fuel, proposed export of nuclear facilities, materials, or technology, and proposed agreements for international cooperation in nuclear reactor development may be disapproved by concurrent resolution.

Civil Rights of Institutionalized Persons. Attorney General's proposed standards for resolution of grievances of adults confined in correctional facilities may be disapproved by resolution of either House.

Full Employment and Balanced Growth Act of 1978. Presidential timetable for reducing unemployment may be superseded by concurrent resolution.

War Powers Resolution. Absent a declaration of war, the president may be directed by concurrent resolution to remove United States armed forces engaged in foreign hostilities.

Unfriendly Relations: The Legislative Veto

The cases we discussed in the last section share a common thread: they involved cooperative relations between Congress and another branch of government, usually the executive. Congress was delegating some of its lawmaking authority—be it the establishment of tariff rates or the prohibition of the shipment of "hot oil"—to an executive desiring, perhaps even requesting, such authority. But Congress is not always so eager to give away its powers; indeed, on many occasions and through different devices, it has sought to exercise authority over the executive branch. One of those devices is the so-called legislative veto.

This kind of veto is a constitutional oddity because it flips the mandated lawmaking process. Rather than follow Article I procedures—both houses of Congress pass bills and the president signs or vetoes them—under this practice, the executive branch makes policies that Congress can veto by a vote of both houses, one house, or even a committee. It should come as no surprise that the legislative veto has been the source of contention between presidents and Congresses, with the former suggesting that they violate constitutional principles and the latter arguing that they represent a way to check all that lawmaking power Congress has delegated to the executive branch.

When it was first developed, the legislative veto was not all that contentious; to the contrary, it was part of a *quid pro quo* between Congress and President Herbert Hoover who wanted "authority to reorganize the executive branch without having to submit a bill to Congress." The legislature agreed to go along "only on the condition that either House could reject a reorganization plan by passing a resolution of disapproval." [78] When Congress passed the 1933 legislative ap-

78. Fisher, *American Constitutional Law*, 230.

propriations bill with that condition attached to it, the legislative veto was born.

Although Hoover had agreed to it, he was less than pleased when Congress used it the following year to veto part of the reorganization plan. In fact, his attorney general, William D. Mitchell, immediately decried it as a violation of the separation of powers doctrine. That sort of sparring over the legislative veto continued through the early 1980s, but the patterns of debate were somewhat contradictory and confusing. On the one hand, until 1972 Congress had used the device rather sparingly, attaching it to only fifty-one laws.[79] Moreover, it did not seem to be a matter that either the president or Congress took very seriously. Research by political scientist Dennis Simon indicates that presidents have rejected only a handful of laws solely because they contained legislative vetoes and that in those few instances Congress almost always repassed the bill without the veto provision.[80]

On the other hand, presidents have groused about the practice. Eisenhower, in particular,

loathed the legislative veto, claiming that it violated "fundamental constitutional principles." Complaints grew louder after the Nixon presidency, when Congress sought to reassert itself over the executive, and enacted sixty-two statutes with legislative vetoes between 1972 and 1979. In fact, in 1976 the House of Representatives "came within two votes of approving a proposal to make every rule and regulation of every executive agency subject to legislative review."[81]

This issue came to a head during the Carter administration. President Jimmy Carter, like Eisenhower, despised legislative vetoes. Suggesting that he did not consider them binding, he had the Justice Department initiate a case, *Immigration and Naturalization Service v. Chadha,* to test it. The result was the first U.S. Supreme Court ruling centering specifically on the constitutionality of the legislative veto. On what grounds did the Court strike down the practice? There were two strenuous dissents. Why did Justice Byron R. White believe that the Court had committed a grave error?

79. Urofsky, *A March of Liberty,* 945.
80. Dennis Simon, "Presidential Vetoes," research in progress.

81. Urofsky, *A March of Liberty,* 946.

Immigration and Naturalization Service v. Chadha

462 U.S. 919 (1983)

Vote: 7 (Blackmun, Brennan, Burger, Marshall,
  O'Connor, Powell, Stevens)
  2 (Rehnquist, White)
Opinion of the Court: Burger
Concurring opinion: Powell
Dissenting opinions: Rehnquist, White

Jagdish Rai Chadha, an East Indian born in Kenya and holder of a British passport, was admitted into the United States in 1966 on a six-year student visa. More than a year after his visa expired, in October 1973, the Immigration and

Naturalization Service ordered Chadha to attend a deportation hearing and show cause why he should not be deported. After two hearings, an immigration judge in June 1974 ordered a suspension of Chadha's deportation, which meant that Chadha could stay in the United States, because he was of "good moral character" and would "suffer extreme hardship" if deported.

Acting under a provision of the Immigration and Nationality Act, the U.S. attorney general recommended to Congress that Chadha be allowed to remain in the United States in accordance with the judge's opinion. The act states:

Upon application by any alien who is found by the Attorney General to meet the requirements of . . . this section the Attorney General may in his discretion suspend deportation of such alien. If the deportation of any alien is suspended . . . a complete and detailed statement of the facts and pertinent provisions of the law in the case shall be reported to the Congress with the reasons for such suspension. Such reports shall be submitted on the first day of each calendar month in which Congress is in session.

Congress, in turn, had the authority to veto—by a resolution passed in either house—the attorney general's decision. The act specifies:

[I]f during the session of the Congress at which a case is reported, or prior to the close of the session of the Congress next following the session at which a case is reported, either the Senate or the House of Representatives passes a resolution stating in substance that it does not factor the suspension of such deportation, the Attorney General shall thereupon deport such alien or authorize the alien's voluntary departure at his own expense under the order of deportation in the manner provided by law. If, within the time above specified, neither the Senate nor the House of Representatives shall pass such a resolution, the Attorney General shall cancel deportation proceedings.

For a while it appeared as if Chadha's suspension of deportation was secure, but at the last moment Congress asserted its veto power. Congress had until December 19, 1975, to take action, and on December 12 the chairman of a House committee introduced a resolution opposing the "granting of permanent residence in the United States to [six] aliens," including Chadha. Four days later the House of Representatives passed the motion. No debate or recorded vote occurred; indeed, it was never really clear why the chamber took the action.

That vote set the stage for a major showdown between Congress and the executive branch. Chadha filed a suit, first with the Immigration Court and then with a federal court of appeals, asking that they declare the legislative veto unconstitutional. The Carter administration joined

him to argue likewise. The president agreed with Chadha's basic position, and administration attorneys thought his suit provided a great test case because it "pointed up the worst features of the legislative veto—no debate, no recorded vote, no approval by the other chamber, and no chance for presidential review."[82] Given the importance of the dispute, the court of appeals asked both the House and the Senate to file amicus curiae briefs supporting the veto practice, but in 1980 it ruled against their position, finding that the device violated separation of powers principles.

By the time the case was first argued before the Supreme Court in February 1982, the Carter administration was out and Ronald Reagan was president. Reagan claimed he supported the legislative veto—at least that is what he said during his 1980 campaign. But, once in office, Reagan instructed the attorney general to go forward with the Chadha case. The Justice Department presented the Court with several reasons why the legislative veto violated the Constitution:

The Constitution explicitly requires that all congressional actions constituting the exercise of legislative power receive the concurrence of both Houses and be presented to the President for his approval or disapproval.

[The veto] violated the constitutional principle of separation of powers because it authorizes one House of Congress to participate in the execution of a previously enacted law.

The House and Senate, which had become parties to the suit, responded this way:

The Constitution provides separately for each of the three Branches, and describes each Branch as vested with the respective functions of legislating, executing, and judging. But the Constitution does not say that the three great functions shall at all times be kept separate and independent of each other, or that the three functions can never be blended or mixed or delegated as among the three Branches. The notion of total sep-

82. Ibid., 947.

aration of the powers "central or essential" to the operation of the three great departments is an illogical and impractical formulation of the separation doctrine, not a constitutional command.

They also noted that the legislative veto was a "pragmatic" and necessary device reflecting the realities of modern government.

The Court apparently had some difficulty ferreting through these claims. After the first round of orals, on the last day of the term, it ordered new arguments, which were held on the first day of the following term. But it took the Court until June 23—virtually all term—to issue its decision.

Chief Justice Warren E. Burger delivered the opinion of the Court:

We turn now to the question whether action of one House of Congress under § 244(c)(2) violates strictures of the Constitution. We begin, of course, with the presumption that the challenged statute is valid. Its wisdom is not the concern of the courts; if a challenged action does not violate the Constitution, it must be sustained. . . .

By the same token, the fact that a given law or procedure is efficient, convenient, and useful in facilitating functions of government, standing alone, will not save it if it is contrary to the Constitution. Convenience and efficiency are not the primary objectives— the hallmarks—of democratic government and our inquiry is sharpened rather than blunted by the fact that congressional veto provisions are appearing with increasing frequency in statutes which delegate authority to executive and independent agencies. . . .

Justice White undertakes to make a case for the proposition that the one-House veto is a useful "political invention," and we need not challenge that assertion. . . . But policy arguments supporting even useful "political inventions" are subject to the demands of the Constitution which defines powers and . . . sets out just how those powers are to be exercised.

Explicit and unambiguous provisions of the Constitution prescribe and define the respective functions of the Congress and of the Executive in the legislative process. . . .

Just as we relied on the textual provision of Art II, § 2, cl 2, to vindicate the principle of separation of powers in Buckley [v. Valeo, 1976], we see that the purposes underlying the Presentment Clauses, Art I, § 7, cls 2, 3, and the bicameral requirement of Art I, § 1, and § 7, cl 2, guide our resolution of the important question present in these cases. . . .

The records of the Constitutional Convention reveal that the requirement that all legislation be presented to the President before becoming law was uniformly accepted by the Framers. Presentment to the President and the Presidential veto were considered so imperative that the draftsmen took special pains to assure that these requirements could not be circumvented. . . .

The decision to provide the President with a limited and qualified power to nullify proposed legislation by veto was based on the profound conviction of the Framers that the powers conferred on Congress were the powers to be most carefully circumscribed. It is beyond doubt that lawmaking was a power to be shared by both Houses and the President. . . .

The bicameral requirement of Art I, §§ 1, 7, was of scarcely less concern to the Framers than was the Presidential veto and indeed the two concepts are interdependent. By providing that no law could take effect without the concurrence of the prescribed majority of the Members of both Houses, the Framers reemphasized their belief . . . that legislation should not be enacted unless it has been carefully and fully considered by the Nation's elected officials. . . .

We see therefore that the Framers were acutely conscious that the bicameral requirement and the Presentment Clauses would serve essential constitutional functions. The President's participation in the legislative process was to protect the Executive Branch from Congress and to protect the whole people from improvident laws. The division of the Congress into two distinctive bodies assures that the legislative power would be exercised only after opportunity for full study and debate in separate settings. The President's unilateral veto power, in turn, was limited by the power of two-thirds of both Houses of Congress to overrule a veto thereby precluding final arbitrary action of one person. It emerges clearly that the prescription for legislative action in Art I, §§ 1, 7, represents the

Framers' decision that the legislative power of the Federal Government be exercised in accord with a single, finely wrought and exhaustively considered, procedure. . . .

Examination of the action taken here by one House pursuant to § 244(c)(2) reveals that it was essentially legislative in purpose and effect. In purporting to exercise power defined in Art I, § 8, cl 4, to ''establish an uniform Rule of Naturalization,'' the House took action that had the purpose and effect of altering the legal rights, duties, and relations of persons, including the Attorney General, Executive Branch officials and Chadha, all outside the Legislative Branch. . . .

The legislative character of the one-House veto in these cases is confirmed by the character of the congressional action it supplants. Neither the House of Representatives nor the Senate contends that, absent the veto provision in § 244(c)(2), either one of them, or both of them acting together, could effectively require the Attorney General to deport an alien once the Attorney General, in the exercise of legislatively delegated authority, had determined the alien should remain in the United States. Without the challenged provision in § 244(c)(2), this could have been achieved, if at all, only by legislation requiring deportation. Similarly, a veto by one House of Congress . . . cannot be justified as an attempt at amending the standards set out in § 244(c)(2), or as a repeal of § 244 as applied to Chadha. Amendment and repeal of statutes, no less than enactment, must conform with Art I.

The nature of the decision implemented by the one-House veto in these cases further manifests its legislative character. . . . Congress made a deliberate choice to delegate to the Executive Branch . . . the authority to allow deportable aliens to remain in this country in certain specified circumstances. Congress must abide by its delegation of authority until that delegation is legislatively altered or revoked. . . .

Since it is clear that the action by the House . . . was an exercise of legislative power, that action was subject to the standards prescribed in Art I. . . . To accomplish what has been attempted by one House of Congress in this case requires action in conformity with the express procedures of the Constitution's prescription for legislative action: passage by a majority of both Houses and presentment to the President.

The veto authorized by § 244(c)(2) doubtless has been in many respects a convenient shortcut; the ''sharing'' with the Executive by Congress of its authority over aliens in this manner is, on its face, an appealing compromise. In purely practical terms, it is obviously easier for action to be taken by one House without submission to the President; but it is crystal clear from the records of the Convention, contemporaneous writings and debates, that the Framers ranked other values higher than efficiency. . . .

The choices we discern as having been made in the Constitutional Convention impose burdens on governmental processes that often seem clumsy, inefficient, even unworkable, but those hard choices were consciously made by men who had lived under a form of government that permitted arbitrary governmental acts to go unchecked. There is no support in the Constitution or decisions of this Court for the proposition that the cumbersomeness and delays often encountered in complying with explicit constitutional standards may be avoided, either by the Congress or by the President. With all the obvious flaws of delay, untidiness, and potential for abuse, we have not yet found a better way to preserve freedom than by making the exercise of power subject to the carefully crafted restraints spelled out in the Constitution.

We hold that the congressional veto provision . . . is severable from the Act and that it is unconstitutional.

Justice White, dissenting.

Today the Court not only invalidates § 244(c)(2) of the Immigration and Nationality Act, but also sounds the death knell for nearly 200 other statutory provisions in which Congress has reserved a ''legislative veto.'' For this reason, the Court's decision is of surpassing importance. And it is for this reason that the Court would have been well advised to decide the cases, if possible, on the narrower grounds of separation of powers, leaving for full consideration the constitutionality of other congressional review statutes operating on such varied matters as war powers and agency rulemaking, some of which concern the independent regulatory agencies.

The prominence of the legislative veto mechanism in our contemporary political system and its importance to Congress can hardly be overstated. It has become a central means by which Congress secures the accountability of executive and independent agencies. Without the legislative veto, Congress is faced with a Hobson's choice: either to refrain from delegating the necessary authority, leaving itself with a hopeless task of writing laws with the requisite specificity to cover endless special circumstances across the entire policy landscape, or in the alternative, to abdicate its lawmaking function to the Executive Branch and independent agencies. To choose the former leaves major national problems unresolved; to opt for the latter risks unaccountable policymaking by those not elected to fill that role. Accordingly, over the past five decades, the legislative veto has been placed in nearly 200 statutes. The device is known in every field of governmental concern: reorganization, budgets, foreign affairs, war powers, and regulation of trade, safety, energy, the environment, and the economy. . . .

I do not suggest that all legislative vetoes are necessarily consistent with separation-of-powers principles. A legislative check on an inherently executive function . . . poses an entirely different question. But the legislative veto device here—and in many other settings—is far from an instance of legislative tyranny over the Executive. It is a necessary check on the unavoidably expanding power of the agencies, both Executive and independent, as they engage in exercising authority delegated by Congress.

I regret that I am in disagreement with my colleagues on the fundamental questions that these cases present. But even more I regret the destructive scope of the Court's holding. It reflects a profoundly different conception of the Constitution than that held by the courts which sanctioned the modern administrative state. Today's decision strikes down in one fell swoop provisions in more laws enacted by Congress than the Court has cumulatively invalidated in its history. I fear it will now be more difficult to "insur[e] that the fundamental policy decisions in our society will be made not by an appointed official but by the body immediately responsible to the people," Arizona v California (1963) (Harlan, J., dissenting in part). I must dissent.

Separation of Powers Cases of the 1970s and 1980s

During the 1970s and 1980s the Supreme Court found itself unusually busy reviewing acts of Congress that were challenged as infringing on the separation of powers implicit in the Constitution. More often than not, the Court agreed with the challenge and struck down the law as infringing too far on the sphere of the executive or the courts.

The Court's decision in these cases included:

– *Buckley v. Valeo (424 U.S. 1, 1976)*. The 1974 Federal Election Campaign Act Amendments infringed executive power by giving Congress the power to appoint four of the five members of the Federal Election Commission, which would enforce the law.

– *Nixon v. General Services Administration (433 U.S. 425, 1977)*. The Presidential Recordings and Materials Preservation Act of 1974, placing the papers and tapes of the Nixon administration in federal custody, did not violate the separation of powers.

– *Bowsher v. Synar, United States Senate v. Synar, O'Neill v. Synar (478 U.S. 714, 1986)*. Congress infringed too far on the prerogatives of the president when it included in the 1985 Balanced Budget and Emergency Deficit Control Act a provision giving the comptroller general, an officer removable from office only at the initiative of Congress, the power to tell the president where to cut federal spending.

– *Morrison v. Olson (487 U.S. 654, 1988)*. The 1978 Ethics in Government Act did not usurp executive power when it authorized a panel of judges to appoint independent prosecutors to investigate charges of misconduct by high government officials.

Source: Excerpted from Elder Witt, *Guide to the U.S. Supreme Court*, 2d ed. (Washington, D.C.: Congressional Quarterly, 1990), 65.

In theory, the Court banished legislative vetoes from the government system because they undermined the spirit and letter of the Constitution. In practice, however, the Court's decision had a negligible effect on congressional-executive relations. Since *Chadha,* Congress has passed more than 140 laws containing legislative vetoes. But even more important is that the practice continues even in the absence of specific legislation—agencies and departments still pay heed to congressional rejections of policy.[83]

Why has the Court's opinion resulted in such blatant noncompliance? More to the point, why do executive agencies and departments continue to respect the wishes of Congress, even though they need not? One reason is purely pragmatic: because departments and agencies depend on Congress for fiscal support, they relent out of "fear of budgetary retaliation."[84] Another reason was implied by Justice White in his dissenting opinion: *Chadha* "did not, and could not, eliminate the conditions that gave rise to the legislative veto: the desire of executive officials for broad delegations of power, and the insistence of Congress that it control those delegations without having to pass another public law."[85]

In this particular instance, then, the president may have won the battle, but surely lost the war, as the legislative veto continues to operate. Perhaps the U.S. Supreme Court was the biggest loser: its decision offered a "solution" that was obviously "unacceptable to the political branches" and, as result, will continue to "be eroded by open defiance and subtle evasion."[86] But, as we shall see in the next chapter and as touched on in the box, page 135, in many other separation of powers cases in which the president has sought to assert his power over Congress, the Court has ruled for one side over the other, and has done so authoritatively. As you read the cases in Chapter 4, think about the difference between them and *Chadha.* Why is it that in some instances Congress and the president accept the authority of the Court, but in others—like *Chadha*—they pay no heed?

86. Ibid., 281.

83. Fisher, *American Constitutional Law,* 281.
84. Urofsky, *A March of Liberty,* 948.
85. Fisher, *American Constitutional Law,* 231.

READINGS

Barber, Sotirios A. *The Constitution and the Delegation of Congressional Power.* Chicago: University of Chicago Press, 1975.

Craig, Barbara H. *Chadha: The Story of an Epic Constitutional Struggle.* New York: Oxford University Press, 1988.

Elliott, Ward E. Y. *The Rise of Guardian Democracy: The Supreme Court's Role in Voting Rights Disputes, 1845-1969.* Cambridge, Mass.: Harvard University Press, 1974.

Goodman, Walter. *The Committee: The Extraordinary Career of the House Committee on Un-American Activites.* New York: Farrar, Straus, and Giroux, 1968.

Henkin, Louis. *Foreign Affairs and the Constitution.* New York: Norton, 1975.

Irons, Peter H. *The New Deal Lawyers.* Princeton, N.J.: Princeton University Press, 1982.

Murphy, Walter F. *Congress and the Court.* Chicago: University of Chicago Press, 1962.

Pritchett, C. Herman. *Congress versus the Supreme Court, 1957-1960.* Minneapolis: University of Minnesota Press, 1961.

CHAPTER 4

THE EXECUTIVE

The Framers would have great trouble recognizing today's presidency. The sentiment of the Philadelphia Convention was that the Articles of Confederation were flawed because they did not provide for an executive, but few delegates would have supported the far-reaching powers wielded by our modern presidents. After suffering under the British monarch, many delegates had serious reservations about awarding too much authority to the executive branch. Those who supported the New Jersey Plan even envisioned a plural executive in which two individuals would share the chief executive position as insurance against excessive power accruing to a single person. The Framers would be astonished at the vast military resources over which the president serves as commander in chief, to say nothing of the hundreds of departments, agencies, and bureaus that constitute the executive branch.

The rather loose wording of Article II has permitted this astonishing growth in the presidency. The article has neither the detail nor the precision of the Framers' Article I description of the legislature; instead, it is dominated by issues of selection and removal, and less attention is devoted to powers and limitations. The wording is often quite broad. For example, presidents are given the undefined "executive power" of the United States and are admonished to take care that the laws are "faithfully executed." Other grants of authority, such as the president's role as

"Commander in Chief of the Army and Navy" and the preferential position given the chief executive in matters of foreign policy, allow for significant expansion.

The presidency also has grown in response to the world's changing conditions. Over the years American society has increased in complexity, and the number of areas requiring government action has mushroomed. Because Congress has been overwhelmed by these demands, the legislature has delegated to the executive branch authority that was not anticipated by the Framers. In addition, the expanding importance of defense and foreign policy has demanded a more powerful presidency.

As these changes took place, the Supreme Court frequently was called upon to umpire disputes over the constitutional limits of executive authority. The Court's decisions have contributed significantly to the way the presidency has evolved, allowing considerable growth in authority and yet imposing necessary restraints.

Selection and Formal Powers

In Article II the Framers developed a novel way to select the chief executive. Until then the executives of most nations were chosen by bloodline, military power, or legislative selection. No other country had experimented with a system like the Electoral College apparatus created at the

Philadelphia Convention. Perhaps because it had never been tried, the system was plagued with defects that required correction over time.

Presidential Selection and Constitutional Change

The Framers designed the Electoral College system to allow the general electorate to have some influence on the selection of the chief executive without resorting to direct popular election. The original blueprint called for each state to select presidential electors equal in number to the state's delegates to the Senate and House of Representatives. The Constitution empowered the state legislatures to decide the method of choosing the electors. Popular election was always the most common method, but in the past some state legislatures voted for the electors. Article II disqualifies those who hold federal office, but otherwise there are no specified qualifications for being an elector. The Electoral College system was based on the theory that the states would select their most qualified citizens, who would exercise their best judgment in the selection of the president.

The Constitution mentions only three qualifications for presidential eligibility—citizenship, age, and residency. First, Article II requires that only individuals who are natural-born citizens may become president.[1] Naturalized citizens— those who attain citizenship after birth—may not hold the nation's highest office. Second, to be president a person must have reached the age of thirty-five. Third, the president must have been a resident of the United States for fourteen years. Although the original version of the Constitution made no mention of qualifications for vice president, this oversight was corrected with the 1804

1. The Constitution also allowed individuals who were citizens at the time the Constitution was adopted to be eligible to hold the presidency.

ratification of the Twelfth Amendment, which said that no person could serve as vice president who was not eligible to be president.

Under the original procedures detailed in Article II, the electors were to assemble in their respective state capitals on election day and cast votes for their presidential preferences. Each elector had two votes, no more than one of which could be cast for the candidate from the elector's home state. These votes were then sent to the federal capital where the president of the Senate opened them. The candidate receiving the most votes would be declared president, if the number of votes received was a majority of the number of electors. Article II anticipated two possible problems with this procedure. First, because the electors each cast two votes, it was possible for the balloting to result in a tie between two candidates. In this event, the Constitution stipulated that the House of Representatives should select one of the two. Second, if multiple candidates sought the presidency, it would be possible for no candidate to receive the required majority. In this case the House was to decide among the top five finishers in the Electoral College voting. In settling such disputed elections, each state delegation was to cast a single vote, rather than allowing the individual members to vote independently.

In the original scheme the vice president was selected right after the president. The formula for choosing the vice president was straightforward—the vice president was the presidential candidate who received the second highest number of electoral votes. If two or more candidates tied for second in the Electoral College voting, the Senate would select the vice president from among them.

The first two elections took place with no difficulty. In 1789 George Washington received one ballot from each of the 69 electors who participated and was elected president. John Adams became vice president because he got the next highest number of electoral votes (34). History repeated itself in the election of 1792, with Washington receiving one vote from each of the 132 electors. Adams again gathered the next highest number of votes (77) and returned to the vice presidency.

The first defects in the electoral system became apparent with the election of 1796. By this time political parties had begun to develop, and this election was a contest between the incumbent Federalists and the Democratic-Republicans. With Washington declining to run for a third term, John Adams became the candidate of the Federalists, and Thomas Jefferson was the choice of those who wanted political change. When the ballots were counted, Adams had won the presidency with seventy-one electoral votes, and Jefferson, with sixty-eight, became vice president. For the first time, the nation had a divided executive branch, with the president and vice president of different political parties.

Matters got even worse with the 1800 election. The Democratic-Republicans were now the more popular of the two major parties, and they backed Jefferson for president and Aaron Burr for vice president. The electors committed to the Democratic-Republican party candidates each cast one ballot for Jefferson and one for Burr. Although it was clear which man was running for which office, the method of selection did not allow for such distinctions. The result was that Jefferson and Burr each received seventy-three votes. According to the Constitution, the House of Representatives had to settle the election by breaking the tie. Each state had a single vote, and a majority of states was required for election. On February 11, 1801, the first vote in the House was taken. Jefferson received eight votes, and Burr six. Two states, Maryland and Vermont, were unable to express a preference because their state delegations were evenly divided. Votes continued to be taken over the next several days, until finally, on February 17, after thirty-six ballots, Jefferson received the support of ten state delegations and was named president, with Burr becoming vice president.

It was clear that the Constitution required changing to avoid such situations. Congress proposed the Twelfth Amendment in 1803, and the states ratified it the next year. The amendment altered the selection system by separating the offices of president and vice president. Rather than casting two votes for president, electors would vote for a presidential candidate and then vote separately for a vice presidential candidate. The House and Senate continued to settle presidential and vice presidential elections in which no candidate received a majority, although the procedures for such elections also were modified by the amendment.

Presidential and vice presidential elections are still governed by the Twelfth Amendment. However, the evolution of political parties and the reduction in the degree of independence exercised by presidential electors have made huge changes in the way the system operates. The Electoral College persists, although there has always been considerable support for replacing it with direct popular election. Proponents of this reform have never achieved enough strength to prompt Congress or the state legislatures to propose the necessary constitutional amendment. Historically, opposition to popular election has come from the smaller states, which enjoy more influence within the Electoral College system than they would under popular election reforms.

Tenure and Succession

The Constitution limits a presidential term to four years. Originally, it placed no restriction on the number of terms a president could serve; George Washington began the tradition of a two-term limit when he announced at the end of his second administration that he would not run again. This tradition was honored by every president until Franklin Roosevelt sought election to a third term in 1940 and further violated the custom by running for a fourth term in 1944. In reaction, Congress proposed the Twenty-second Amendment, which held that no person could run for president after having served more than six years in that office. The states ratified the amendment in 1951.

If an incumbent president or vice president abuses the office, the Constitution provides for impeachment as the method of removal. Impeachment is a two-stage process. First, the House of Representatives investigates the charges against the incumbent. The Constitution stipulates that impeachment can occur only upon charges of "Treason, Bribery, or other High Crimes and Misdemeanors." Once convinced that there is sufficient evidence of such misconduct, the House passes Articles of Impeachment specifying the crimes charged and authorizing a trial. The second stage, the trial, takes place in the Senate, but the chief justice of the United States presides. Conviction requires the agreement of two-thirds of the voting senators. Congress can impose no penalties on a convicted official other than removal from office. However, the officeholder may still be subject to a separate criminal prosecution in the courts. No president has been removed from office by Congress, although two barely escaped such a fate. Andrew Johnson was impeached by the House in 1868, but he survived by one vote; and Richard Nixon was well on his way to being impeached in 1974 when he resigned from office.

Eight other sitting presidents failed to complete their terms. Four (William Henry Harrison, Zachary Taylor, Warren G. Harding, and Franklin D. Roosevelt) died of natural causes, and four (Abraham Lincoln, James A. Garfield, William McKinley, and John F. Kennedy) were assassinated. The Framers provided in Article II that in

the event of the president's death or disability, the vice president assumes the powers and responsibilities of the office. The Constitution authorizes Congress to determine presidential succession if there is no sitting vice president when a vacancy occurs.

In 1965 Congress recommended additional changes in the Constitution to govern presidential succession. The need became apparent after Lyndon B. Johnson assumed the presidency following Kennedy's assassination in 1963. Johnson's ascension left the vice presidency vacant. If anything had happened to Johnson, next in line were Speaker of the House John McCormack, D-Mass., and the president pro tempore of the Senate, Carl Hayden, D-Ariz. In 1965 McCormack was seventy-four years old, and Hayden eighty-eight; neither was capable of handling the demands of the presidency. Congress proposed that the Constitution be amended to provide that when a vacancy occurs in the office of vice president, the president nominates a new vice president who takes office upon confirmation by both houses of Congress. The proposal also clarified procedures governing those times when a president is temporarily unable to carry out the duties of the office. The change was ratified by the states as the Twenty-fifth Amendment in 1967.

It was not long before the country needed the procedures outlined in the Twenty-fifth Amendment. In 1973 Vice President Spiro Agnew resigned when he was charged with income tax evasion stemming from alleged corruption during his years as governor of Maryland. Nixon nominated, and Congress confirmed, Rep. Gerald R. Ford of Michigan to become vice president. Just one year later, Nixon resigned the presidency, and Ford became the nation's first unelected chief executive. Ford selected Nelson Rockefeller, former governor of New York, to fill the new vacancy in the vice presidency.

Line of Succession

ON MARCH 30, 1981, President Ronald Reagan was shot by would-be assassin John Hinckley outside a Washington hotel and rushed to an area hospital for surgery. Vice President George Bush was on a plane returning to Washington from Texas. Presidential aides and cabinet members gathered at the White House, where questions arose among them and the press corps about who was "in charge."[1] Secretary of State Alexander M. Haig, Jr., rushed to the press briefing room and, before an audience of reporters and live television cameras, said, "As of now, I am in control here in the White House, pending the return of the vice president. . . . Constitutionally, gentlemen, you have the president, the vice president, and the secretary of state."

Haig was, as many gleeful critics subsequently pointed out, wrong. The Constitution says nothing about who follows the vice president in the line of succession. The Succession Act of 1947 (later modified to reflect the creation of new departments) establishes congressional leaders and the heads of the departments, in the order the departments were created, as filling the line of succession that follows the vice president.

The line of succession is:
vice president
Speaker of the House of Representatives
president pro tempore of the Senate
secretary of state
secretary of the Treasury
secretary of defense
attorney general
secretary of the interior
secretary of agriculture
secretary of commerce
secretary of labor
secretary of health and human services
secretary of housing and urban development
secretary of transportation
secretary of energy
secretary of education
secretary of veterans affairs

A different "line"—not of succession to the presidency, but of National Command Authority in situations of wartime emergency—was created according to the National Security Act of 1947. The command rules are detailed in secret presidential orders that each new president signs at the outset of the term. Among other things, the orders authorize the secretary of defense to act as commander in chief in certain specific, limited situations in which neither the president nor the vice president is available. Presumably, such situations would follow a nuclear attack on Washington.

1. "Confusion over Who Was in Charge Arose Following Reagan Shooting," *Wall Street Journal,* April 1, 1981.
Source: *Guide to the Presidency,* ed. Michael Nelson (Washington, D.C.: Congressional Quarterly, 1989), 339.

President Lyndon B. Johnson, surrounded by congressional leaders, signing the Twenty-fifth Amendment on February 23, 1967. The Amendment authorized the president to nominate a new vice president when a vacancy in that office occurred and also provided for an orderly transition of authority should the president become disabled. At the time, the vice presidency was vacant. If Johnson had died or become disabled, seventy-four-year-old Speaker John McCormack (far right) would have assumed the presidency. Next in line of succession was president pro tempore of the Senate, eighty-eight-year-old Carl Hayden (third from left, standing).

Constitutional Powers

Despite the constitutional changes dealing with presidential selection and succession, the president's formal powers are the same today as when they were drafted by the Philadelphia Convention. Those formal grants of authority fall into four categories.

General Executive Powers
To execute and enforce the laws
To appoint and remove executive branch officials

Military and Foreign Policy Powers
To be commander in chief of the armed forces

To appoint ambassadors
To receive foreign ambassadors
To make treaties

Powers Related to the Legislative Branch
To veto bills passed by Congress
To convene special sessions of Congress
To advise Congress on the state of the nation

Powers Related to the Judicial Branch
To appoint federal judges
To grant pardons to those convicted of federal crimes

These formal grants of authority form the constitutional basis of presidential power, but many of the specific provisions conferring executive power are vaguely worded and open to interpretation. In the course of American history, the struggle for political power among the three branches of government has led to many legal disputes over the nature and extent of presidential authority, and it has fallen to the Supreme Court to determine the contours of presidential power. This chapter examines the constitutional disputes that have shaped the presidency.

The Faithful Execution of the Laws

At the heart of executive power is the enforcement of the law; Article II, Section 3, states that the president shall be given the responsibility to "take Care that the Laws be faithfully executed." Undoubtedly, the Take Care Clause means that the provisions of the Constitution and the laws enacted by Congress are entrusted to the president for administration and enforcement. Presidents may use the substantial powers of the executive branch to see that the law is followed.

Initial Interpretations: Expanding Presidential Authority

The vague wording of Section 3 leaves open the question of how far the enforcement authority extends. Does the president have the power to protect the integrity of the laws only to the extent that Congress permits, or may the chief executive initiate enforcement actions in the absence of either congressional approval or judicial invitation? In one of the earliest disputes over the president's inherent powers to enforce the law, the Supreme Court approved a rather expansive interpretation of the chief executive's prerogatives. The appeal presenting this issue, *In re Neagle* (1890), was based on one of the more bizarre and twisted stories in constitutional history.[2] The dispute began some three decades before the case reached the Supreme Court. When the trial court reviewed the essential facts, the story took more than 500 pages. As you read this decision, consider the extent to which you think the Court's response was influenced by the fact that one of its own members had been threatened.

2. For a full account of the events surrounding this case, see Robert Kroninger, "The Justice and the Lady," in *1977 Yearbook of the Supreme Court Historical Society* (Washington, D.C.: Supreme Court Historical Society, 1977), 11–19.

In re Neagle

135 U.S. 1 (1890)

Vote: 6 (*Blatchford, Bradley, Brewer, Gray, Harlan, Miller*)
2 (*Fuller, Lamar*)
Opinion of the Court: Miller
Dissenting opinion: Lamar
Not participating: Field

Stephen J. Field and David S. Terry came to California during the 1849 gold rush, Field from New England and Terry from the South. Both became judges on the California Supreme Court, with Terry its chief justice. In 1859 a bitter dispute erupted between Judge Terry and David Broderick, a U.S. senator. Terry resigned his position, challenged Broderick to a duel, and killed him. Field was a close friend of Broderick, and he vowed never to forget the killing. Field was then elevated to the chief justiceship of the state court, and four years later President Lincoln appointed him to the U.S. Supreme Court.

Terry went into private practice and years later came to represent Sarah Althea Hill in a divorce action. Hill claimed to be the wife of William Sharon, a former U.S. senator from Nevada, who was a millionaire mine operator and hotel owner. Hill charged Sharon with adultery and sued for divorce, but Sharon denied ever having married her. Many believed that she was just one in a long series of mistresses Sharon had after his wife died. Sarah Hill claimed to have a document proving the marriage was valid, but during the divorce hearing the court ruled the document to be a forgery and dismissed her action.

In the meantime, William Sharon died, and his son Frederick took legal action to dismantle any claim Sarah Hill had to his father's estate. Attorney Terry by this time had fallen in love with his beautiful client (and perhaps also with her potentially large inheritance) and married her. As luck would have it, in September 1888 Justice Field was assigned to a three-judge circuit court to decide the suit brought by Frederick Sharon against Sarah Terry. When the judges announced their ruling in favor of Sharon, violence erupted in the courtroom. Sarah Terry shouted accusations that Field had been bribed to reach his decision. Field ordered the marshals to remove her, and David Terry, defending his wife, struck a marshal and knocked out a tooth. He also brandished a Bowie knife, and Sarah attempted to grab a revolver from her purse. The marshals subdued both of them. Sarah was sentenced to one month in jail for contempt, and David to six months in jail.

During his imprisonment, David Terry's hatred of his former colleague festered. On several occasions and before numerous witnesses, he pledged to horsewhip and then kill Field if the justice ever returned to California. Sarah Terry also threatened to kill Field. In response, President Benjamin Harrison and the U.S. attorney general decided to provide protection for Justice Field on his next judicial visit to California. The administration authorized a federal marshal, David Neagle, to act as Field's bodyguard when the justice was assigned circuit court duty in California.

Field returned to California in the summer of 1889. Neagle was with him at all times. Traveling from Los Angeles to San Francisco by train, Field disembarked at Lathrop to eat breakfast in the station dining room. The Terrys, who had been on the same train, entered the dining room and saw him. Sarah returned to the train to get her revolver, while David walked up behind Field, slapped him twice on the side of the face, and raised his fist for a third blow. Neagle immediately rose from his seat with his revolver drawn and ordered Terry to stop. Terry reached into his coat, and Neagle, fearing that he was going for a weapon, fired two shots, one to the chest and the other to the head. When Terry's body was searched, no weapons were found.

Sarah Terry, who was to spend her last forty-five years in a state mental institution, claimed that her husband had been murdered by Neagle in conspiracy with Field. She was sufficiently convincing that the bodyguard was arrested and charged with murder. Charges also were filed against Field as an accomplice, but they were later dropped.

A federal court granted a writ of habeas corpus ordering state authorities to release Neagle, and California appealed. The issue before the Supreme Court was Neagle's legal authority to act as he did. The central question was whether the president, without congressional action, could issue an executive order through the U.S. attorney general to authorize Neagle to protect Justice Field. The attorney general claimed that President Harrison's constitutional obligation to take care that the laws be faithfully executed was sufficient grounds for Neagle's appointment. The state contended that the president did not have such power.

Justice Samuel Miller delivered the opinion of the Court:

The justices of the Supreme Court have been members of the Circuit Courts of the United States ever since the organization of the government, and their attendance on the circuit and appearance at the places where the courts are held has always been thought to be

Justice Stephen J. Field, associate justice of the Supreme Court, 1863–1897.

Sarah Althea Hill Terry, wife of David Terry, and central figure in the dispute with Justice Stephen Field that led to the killing of her husband.

David S. Terry, former California state supreme court judge and husband of Sarah Terry. Killed by David Neagle, who was assigned to guard the life of Justice Stephen Field.

a matter of importance. In order to enable him to perform this duty, Mr. Justice Field had to travel each year from Washington City, near the Atlantic coast, to San Francisco, on the Pacific coast. In doing this he was as much in the discharge of a duty imposed upon him by law as he was while sitting in court and trying causes. There are many duties which the judge performs outside of the court-room where he sits to pronounce judgment or to preside over a trial. The statutes of the United States, and the established practice of the courts, require that the judge perform a very large share of his judicial labors at what is called "chambers." This chamber work is as important as necessary, as much a discharge of his official duty as that performed in the court-house. Important cases are often argued before the judge at any place convenient to the parties concerned, and a decision of the judge is arrived at by investigations made in his own room, wherever he may be, and it is idle to say that this is not as much the performance of judicial duty as the filing of the judgment with the clerk, and the announcement of the result in open court. . . .

Justice Field had not only left Washington and travelled the three thousand miles or more which were

necessary to reach his circuit, but he had entered upon the duties of that circuit, had held the court at San Francisco for some time; and, taking a short leave of that court, had gone down to Los Angeles, another place where a court was to be held, and sat as a judge there for several days, hearing cases and rendering decisions. It was in the necessary act of returning from Los Angeles to San Francisco, by the usual mode of travel between the two places, where his court was still in session, and where he was required to be, that he was assaulted by Terry. . . .

The occurrence which we are called upon to consider was of so extraordinary a character that it is not to be expected that many cases can be found to cite as authority upon the subject. . . .

We have no doubt that Mr. Justice Field when attacked by Terry was engaged in the discharge of his duties as Circuit Justice of the Ninth Circuit, and was entitled to all the protection under those circumstances which the law could give him.

It is urged, however, that there exists no statute authorizing any such protection as that which Neagle was instructed to give Judge Field in the present case, and indeed no protection whatever against a vindictive

An illustration of U.S. Deputy Marshal David Neagle, assigned to protect Justice Stephen Field, shooting David Terry in a railroad station restaurant at Lathrop, California, in 1889.

or malicious assault growing out of the faithful discharge of his official duties; and that the language of section 753 of the Revised Statutes, that the party seeking the benefit of the writ of *habeas corpus* must in this connection show that he is ''in custody for an act done or omitted in pursuance of a law of the United States,'' makes it necessary that upon this occasion it should be shown that the act for which Neagle is imprisoned was done by virtue of an act of Congress. It is not supposed that any special act of Congress exists which authorizes the marshals or deputy marshals of the United States in express terms to accompany the judges of the Supreme Court through their circuits, and act as a body-guard to them, to defend them against malicious assaults against their persons. But we are of opinion that this view of the statute is an unwarranted restriction of the meaning of a law designed to extend in a liberal manner the benefit of the writ of *habeas corpus* to persons imprisoned for the performance of

their duty. And we are satisfied that if it was the duty of Neagle, under the circumstances, a duty which could only arise under the laws of the United States, to defend Mr. Justice Field from a murderous attack upon him, he brings himself within the meaning of the section we have recited. This view of the subject is confirmed by the alternative provision, that he must be in custody ''for an act done or omitted in pursuance of a law of the United States or of an order, process, or decree of a court or judge thereof, or is in custody in violation of the Constitution or of a law or treaty of the United States.''

In the view we take of the Constitution of the United States, any obligation fairly and properly inferrible from that instrument, or any duty of the marshal to be derived from the general scope of his duties under the laws of the United States, is ''a law'' within the meaning of this phrase. It would be a great reproach to the system of government of the United States, declared to be within its sphere sovereign and supreme, if there is to be found within the domain of its powers no means of protecting the judges, in the conscientious and faithful discharge of their duties, from the malice and hatred of those upon whom their judgments may operate unfavorably. . . .

Where, then, are we to look for the protection which we have shown Judge Field was entitled to when engaged in the discharge of his official duties? Not to the courts of the United States; because, as has been more than once said in this court, in the division of the powers of government between the three great departments, executive, legislative and judicial, the judicial is the weakest for the purposes of self-protection and for the enforcement of the powers which it exercises. The ministerial officers through whom its commands must be executed are marshals of the United States, and belong emphatically to the executive department of the government. They are appointed by the President, with the advice and consent of the Senate. They are removable from office at his pleasure. They are subjected by act of Congress to the supervision and control of the Department of Justice, in the hands of one of the cabinet officers of the President, and their compensation is provided by acts of Congress. The same may be said of the district attorneys of the United States, who prosecute and defend the claims of the government in the courts.

The legislative branch of the government can only protect the judicial officers by the enactment of laws for that purpose, and the argument we are now combating assumes that no such law has been passed by Congress.

If we turn to the executive department of the government, we find a very different condition of affairs. The Constitution, section 3, Article 2, declares that the President "shall take care that the laws be faithfully executed," and he is provided with the means of fulfilling this obligation by his authority to commission all the officers of the United States, and, by and with the advice and consent of the Senate, to appoint the most important of them and to fill vacancies. He is declared to be commander-in-chief of the army and navy of the United States. The duties which are thus imposed upon him he is further enabled to perform by the recognition in the Constitution, and the creation by acts of Congress, of executive departments, which have varied in number from four or five to seven or eight, the heads of which are familiarly called cabinet ministers. These aid him in the performance of the great duties of his office, and represent him in a thousand acts to which it can hardly be supposed his personal attention is called, and thus he is enabled to fulfill the duty of his great department, expressed in the phrase that "he shall take care that the laws be faithfully executed."

Is this duty limited to the enforcement of acts of Congress or of treaties of the United States according to their *express terms,* or does it include the rights, duties and obligations growing out of the Constitution itself, our international relations, and all the protection implied by the nature of the government under the Constitution? . . .

We cannot doubt the power of the President to take measures for the protection of a judge of one of the courts of the United States, who, while in the discharge of the duties of his office, is threatened with a personal attack which may probably result in his death, and we think it clear that where this protection is to be afforded through the civil power, the Department of Justice is the proper one to set in motion the necessary means of protection. The correspondence already recited in this opinion between the marshal of the Northern District of California, and the Attorney General, and the district attorney of the United States for that district, although prescribing no very specific mode of affording this protection by the Attorney General, is sufficient, we think, to warrant the marshal in taking the steps which he did take, in making the provisions which he did make, for the protection and defence of Mr. Justice Field. . . .

But all these questions being conceded, it is urged against the relief sought by this writ of *habeas corpus,* that the question of the guilt of the prisoner of the crime of murder is a question to be determined by the laws of California, and to be decided by its courts, and that there exists no power in the government of the United States to take away the prisoner from the custody of the proper authorities of the State of California and carry him before a judge of the court of the United States, and release him without a trial by jury according to the laws of the State of California. That the statute of the

United States authorizes and directs such a proceeding and such a judgment in a case where the offence charged against the prisoner consists in an act done in pursuance of a law of the United States and by virtue of its authority, and where the imprisonment of the party is in violation of the Constitution and laws of the United States, is clear by its express language. . . .

It would seem as if the argument might close here. If the duty of the United States to protect its officers from violence, even to death, in discharge of the duties which its laws impose upon them, be established, and Congress has made the writ of *habeas corpus* one of the means by which this protection is made efficient, and if the facts of this case show that the prisoner was acting both under the authority of law, and the directions of his superior officers of the Department of Justice, we can see no reason why this writ should not be made to serve its purpose in the present case. . . .

The result at which we have arrived upon this examination is, that in the protection of the person and the life of Mr. Justice Field while in the discharge of his official duties, Neagle was authorized to resist the attack of Terry upon him; that Neagle was correct in the belief that without prompt action on his part the assault of Terry upon the judge would have ended in the death of the latter; that such being his well-founded belief, he was justified in taking the life of Terry, as the only means of preventing the death of the man who was intended to be his victim; that in taking the life of Terry, under the circumstances, he was acting under the authority of the law of the United States, and was justified in so doing; and that he is not liable to answer in the courts of California on account of his part in that transaction.

We therefore affirm the judgment of the Circuit Court authorizing his discharge from the custody of the sheriff of San Joaquin County.

The *Neagle* decision held that the president has the constitutional power to take those actions necessary to enforce the laws of the nation. The Court defined the term *laws* quite broadly and offered a rather expansive view of the options available to the president. Based on this authority, U.S. presidents have taken strong action to ensure that the nation's laws are not defied. For example, in May 1894 Grover Cleveland sent troops into Chicago to stop striking Pullman workers from obstructing the movement of the mails. In 1957, when opposition groups in Little Rock, Arkansas, blocked the court-ordered integration of Central High School, President Dwight Eisenhower dispatched paratroopers to encourage compliance with judicial orders.

Contemporary Conflicts with Congress

The Constitution obliges the president to enforce all the laws, not just those the administration supports. While a number of presidents have been criticized for failing to carry out certain laws with sufficient enthusiasm, it would be difficult to prove that the chief executive had not satisfied the constitutional mandate of faithful execution. On rare occasions, however, a president has openly refused to execute a law validly passed by Congress. In such cases court challenges are to be expected.

What happened when Congress passed the Federal Water Pollution Control Act Amendments of 1972 over President Nixon's veto is a good illustration. The act made federal money available to local governments for sewers and clean water projects. After losing the legislative battle, the president instructed the appropriate officials of his administration not to allot to local governments the full funds authorized by Congress.

New York City, which expected to be a recipient of these funds, filed suit against Russell Train, head of the Environmental Protection Agency, to force the administration to release the impounded money. In interpreting the legislation, the Supreme Court in *Train v. City of New York* (1975) found no congressional grant of discretion to the executive that would allow the president to decide how much of the appropriated money to allocate. In the absence of such a grant, the president's obligation was to carry out the terms of the statute. The Court held that the funds must be distributed according to the intent of Congress. Faithful execution of the laws requires the executive branch to enforce and administer the policies enacted by the legislature even if the president opposes them.

The Constitution unambiguously gives the president the responsibility and authority to enforce the laws. But is this power given exclusively to the president, or may the other branches also exercise enforcement? This question has been at the root of several important battles between Congress and the president.

One of the more important and controversial of these disputes evolved into the case of *Bowsher v. Synar* (1986). The suit involved a challenge to the constitutionality of certain provisions of the Balanced Budget and Emergency Deficit Control Act of 1985, better known as the Gramm-Rudman-Hollings Act. While reading this case, keep in mind the discussions of legislative power in Chapter 3. Did the Court make clear the distinction between legislative and executive functions? Was the Court's response to this statute reasonable, or was Justice Byron R. White correct when he argued in dissent that the majority invalidated an important piece of legislation on the basis of a trivial objection, placing formalism above substance?

Bowsher v. Synar

478 U.S. 714 (1986)

Vote: 7 *(Brennan, Burger, Marshall, O'Connor, Powell,*
Rehnquist, Stevens)
2 *(Blackmun, White)*
Opinion of the Court: Burger
Concurring opinion: Stevens
Dissenting opinions: Blackmun, White

President Reagan signed the Gramm-Rudman-Hollings bill into law December 12, 1985. The legislation attempted to control the federal budget deficit by imposing automatic budget cuts when members of Congress were unable or unwilling to exercise sufficient fiscal restraint. The law established maximum budget deficit levels for each year beginning in 1986. The size of the deficit was to decrease each year until fiscal 1991 when no deficit would be allowed. If the federal budget deficit in any year exceeded the maximum allowed, across-the-board budget cuts would automatically be imposed.

Triggering the cuts involved steps to be taken by several government officials. First, the director of the Office of Management and Budget (OMB) and the director of the Congressional Budget Office (CBO) would independently estimate the projected deficit, with program-by-program calculations. Second, these estimates would be jointly reported to the comptroller general of the United States. Third, the comptroller general would review the reports submitted by OMB and CBO and issue a final report with recommendations. Fourth, the comptroller general would send the report to the president who would issue an order mandating the automatic budget cuts recommended by the comptroller.

Just hours after the bill was signed, Rep. Mike Synar, D-Okla., who had voted against it, filed suit to have the law declared unconstitutional. At the same time, the National Treasury Employees Union took legal action to have the statute declared void. Among other issues, these parties claimed that Charles A. Bowsher, the comptroller general of the United States, fell under the authority of the legislative branch and had no constitutional authority to participate in a law enforcement process. A three-judge district court struck down the statutory provisions that permitted an enforcement role for the comptroller general. Bowsher, on behalf of Congress, appealed.

Chief Justice Warren Burger delivered the opinion of the Court:

The question presented by these appeals is whether the assignment by Congress to the Comptroller General of the United States of certain functions under the Balanced Budget and Emergency Deficit Control Act of 1985 violates the doctrine of separation of powers. . . .

Appellants urge that the Comptroller General performs his duties independently and is not subservient to Congress. We agree with the District Court that this contention does not bear close scrutiny.

The critical factor lies in the provisions of the statute defining the Comptroller General's office relating to removability. Although the Comptroller General is nominated by the President from a list of three individuals recommended by the Speaker of the House of Representatives and the President *pro tempore* of the Senate, and confirmed by the Senate, he is removable only at the initiative of Congress. He may be removed not only by impeachment but also by joint resolution of Congress "at any time" resting on any one of the following bases:

"(i) permanent disability;
"(ii) inefficiency;
"(iii) neglect of duty;
"(iv) malfeasance; or
"(v) a felony or conduct involving moral turpitude."

This provision was included, as one Congressman explained in urging passage of the Act, because Congress "felt that [the Comptroller General] should be brought under the sole control of Congress, so that Congress at any moment when it found he was inefficient and was not carrying on the duties of his office as he should and as the Congress expected, could remove him without the long, tedious process of a trial by impeachment." . . .

It is clear that Congress has consistently viewed the Comptroller General as an officer of the Legislative Branch. The Reorganization Acts of 1945 and 1949, for example, both stated that the Comptroller General and the GAO are "a part of the legislative branch of the Government." Similarly, in the Accounting and Auditing Act of 1950, Congress required the Comptroller General to conduct audits "as an agent of the Congress."

Over the years, the Comptrollers General have also viewed themselves as part of the Legislative Branch. In one of the early Annual Reports of Comptroller General, the official seal of his office was described as reflecting

"the independence of judgment to be exercised by the General Accounting Office, subject to the control of the legislative branch. . . . The combination represents an agency of the Congress independent of other authority auditing and checking the expenditures of the Government as required by law and subjecting any questions arising in that connection to quasi-judicial determination."

Later, Comptroller General Warren, who had been a Member of Congress for 15 years before being appointed Comptroller General, testified: "During most of my public life, . . . I have been a member of the legislative branch. Even now, although heading a great agency, it is an agency of the Congress, and *I am an agent of the Congress*." (Emphasis added.) And, in one conflict during Comptroller General McCarl's tenure, he asserted his independence of the Executive Branch, stating:

"Congress . . . is . . . the only authority to which there lies an appeal from the decision of this office. . . ."

Against this background, we see no escape from the conclusion that, because Congress has retained removal authority over the Comptroller General, he may not be entrusted with executive powers. The remaining question is whether the Comptroller General has been assigned such powers in the Balanced Budget and Emergency Deficit Control Act of 1985.

The primary responsibility of the Comptroller General under the instant Act is the preparation of a "report." This report must contain detailed estimates of projected federal revenues and expenditures. The report must also specify the reductions, if any, necessary to reduce the deficit to the target for the appropriate fiscal year. The reductions must be set forth on a program-by-program basis.

In preparing the report, the Comptroller General is to have "due regard" for the estimates and reductions set forth in a joint report submitted to him by the Director of CBO and the Director of OMB, the President's fiscal and budgetary adviser. However, the Act plainly contemplates that the Comptroller General will exercise his independent judgment and evaluation with respect to those estimates. The Act also provides that the Comptroller General's report "shall explain fully any differences between the contents of such report and the report of the Directors."

Appellants suggest that the duties assigned to the Comptroller General in the Act are essentially ministerial and mechanical so that their performance does not constitute "execution of the law" in a meaningful sense. On the contrary, we view these functions as plainly entailing execution of the law in constitutional terms. Interpreting a law enacted by Congress to implement the legislative mandate is the very essence of "execution" of the law. Under § 251, the Comptroller General must exercise judgment concerning facts that affect the application of the Act. He must also interpret the provisions of the Act to determine precisely what budgetary calculations are required. Decisions of that kind are typically made by officers charged with executing a statute.

The executive nature of the Comptroller General's functions under the Act is revealed in § 252(a)(3) which gives the Comptroller General the ultimate authority to determine the budget cuts to be made. Indeed, the Comptroller General commands the President himself to carry out, without the slightest variation (with exceptions not relevant to the constitutional issues presented), the directive of the Comptroller General as to the budget reductions:

"The [Presidential] order *must provide* for reductions in the manner specified in section 251(a)(3), *must incorporate* the provisions of the [Comptroller General's] report submitted under section 251(b), and *must be consistent with such report in all respects*. The President *may not modify or recalculate any of the estimates, determinations, specifications, bases, amounts, or percentages* set forth in the report submitted under section 251(b) in determining the reductions to be specified in the order with respect to

programs, projects, and activities, or with respect to budget activities, within an account. . . ." (Emphasis added.)

Congress of course initially determined the content of the Balanced Budget and Emergency Deficit Control Act; and undoubtedly the content of the Act determines the nature of the executive duty. However, as [INS v.] *Chadha* [1983] makes clear, once Congress makes its choice in enacting legislation, its participation ends. Congress can thereafter control the execution of its enactment only indirectly—by passing new legislation. By placing the responsibility for execution of the Balanced Budget and Emergency Deficit Control Act in the hands of an officer who is subject to removal only by itself, Congress in effect has retained control over the execution of the Act and has intruded into the executive function. The Constitution does not permit such intrusion. . . .

Justice WHITE, dissenting.

The Court, acting in the name of separation of powers, takes upon itself to strike down the Gramm-Rudman-Hollings Act, one of the most novel and far-reaching legislative responses to a national crisis since the New Deal. The basis of the Court's action is a solitary provision of another statute that was passed over 60 years ago and has lain dormant since that time. I cannot concur in the Court's action. Like the Court, I will not purport to speak to the wisdom of the policies incorporated in the legislation the Court invalidates; that is a matter for the Congress and the Executive, *both* of which expressed their assent to the statute barely half a year ago. I will, however, address the wisdom of the Court's willingness to interpose its distressingly formalistic view of separation of powers as a bar to the attainment of governmental objectives through the means chosen by the Congress and the President in the legislative process established by the Constitution. Twice in the past four years I have expressed my view that the Court's recent efforts to police the separation of powers have rested on untenable constitutional propositions leading to regrettable results. See *Northern Pipeline Construction Co. v. Marathon Pipe Line Co.* (1982) (WHITE, J., dissenting); *INS v. Chadha* (1983) (WHITE, J., dissenting). Today's result is even more misguided. . . . [T]he

Court's decision rests on a feature of the legislative scheme that is of minimal practical significance and that presents no substantial threat to the basic scheme of separation of powers. In attaching dispositive significance to what should be regarded as a triviality, the Court neglects what has in the past been recognized as a fundamental principle governing consideration of disputes over separation of powers:

"The actual art of governing under our Constitution does not and cannot conform to judicial definitions of the power of any of its branches based on isolated clauses or even single Articles torn from context. While the Constitution diffuses power the better to secure liberty, it also contemplates that practice will integrate the dispersed powers into a workable government." *Youngstown Sheet & Tube Co. v. Sawyer* (1952) (Jackson, J., concurring).

The *Bowsher* decision supplied an authoritative declaration of the boundaries between legislative and executive authority and, as such, provided guidelines for the future. The decision, however, had little impact on the legislation. Congress, anticipating the constitutional challenge, had written into the law certain "fallback" mechanisms to enforce the budget restrictions if any part of the original plan failed a constitutional challenge. This secondary plan removed the comptroller general from any enforcement activity, and the Supreme Court allowed this procedure to become operative.

Executive Immunity and Privilege

At the heart of the checks and balances philosophy is the debate over how far the other branches of government can intrude into executive affairs. The problems flowing from this issue fall into two related categories: immunity and privilege.

Protecting the President from Lawsuit

Immunity deals with the extent to which the president is protected from suit while in office, and the subject raises many interesting questions. May a president be ordered by a court to carry out certain executive actions, which are discretionary, or ministerial actions, which are performed as a matter of legal duty? Or, conversely, may a

president be restrained by a court from taking such actions? May a private party sue the president for damages that might have been suffered because of the president's actions or omissions? If so, may a court order the president to pay damages or provide some other restitution? These questions place us in quandary. To grant the president immunity from such legal actions may remove needed accountability. But to allow the chief executive to be subject to suit could make the execution of presidential duties impossible.

The Supreme Court's first significant venture into the area of executive immunity came in the aftermath of the Civil War. In this case, *Mississippi v. Johnson* (1867), the Court was asked to enjoin the president from executing laws passed by Congress on the grounds that the laws were unconstitutional. The justices concluded, unanimously, that the president was immune from such suits. Is this conclusion reasonable? Does the Court's distinction between executive and ministerial acts make sense? To what degree do you think the Court was responding to the political conditions of the times? Following the *Dred Scott* decision (1857) the Court's prestige was at an all-time low and congressional power was overwhelmingly dominant. Was the decision of the Court in *Mississippi v. Johnson* just a convenient way for the justices to avoid an unwinnable conflict with Congress?

Mississippi v. Johnson

4 Wall. 475 (1867)

Vote: 9 (Chase, Clifford, Davis, Field, Grier, Miller, Nelson, Swayne, Wayne)

0

Opinion of the Court: Chase

Following the Civil War, Congress passed a number of laws "for the more efficient government of the rebel states." More commonly known as the Reconstruction Acts, they imposed military rule over the southern states until such time as loyal republican governments could be established. President Andrew Johnson, a southerner from Tennessee, who had assumed the presidency after Lincoln's assassination, vetoed the legislation, but the Radical Republicans in Congress had sufficient votes to override him. Once the acts were part of federal law, the president had little choice but to enforce them, despite his belief that they were unconstitutional.

The state of Mississippi joined the fray. Applying directly to the Supreme Court, Mississippi sued President Johnson asking the justices to issue an order prohibiting him from enforcing the laws, which the state argued were unconstitutional.

Chief Justice Salmon P. Chase delivered the opinion of the Court.

A motion was made, some days since, in behalf of the State of Mississippi, for leave to file a bill in the name of the State, praying this court perpetually to enjoin and restrain Andrew Johnson, President of the United States, and E. O. C. Ord, general commanding in the District of Mississippi and Arkansas, from executing, or in any manner carrying out, certain acts of Congress therein named.

The acts referred to are those of March 2d and March 23d, 1867, commonly known as the Reconstruction Acts.

The Attorney-General objected to the leave asked for, upon the ground that no bill which makes a President a defendant, and seeks an injunction against him to restrain the performance of his duties as President, should be allowed to be filed in this court.

This point has been fully argued, and we will now dispose of it.

We shall limit our inquiry to the question presented by the objection, without expressing any opinion on the broader issues discussed in argument, whether, in any case, the President of the United States may be required, by the process of this court, to perform a purely ministerial act under a positive law, or may be held amenable, in any case, otherwise than by impeachment for crime.

The single point which requires consideration is this: Can the President be restrained by injunction from carrying into effect an act of Congress alleged to be unconstitutional?

It is assumed by the counsel for the State of Mississippi, that the President, in the execution of the Reconstruction Acts, is required to perform a mere ministerial duty. In this assumption there is, we think, a confounding of the terms ministerial and executive, which are by no means equivalent in import.

A ministerial duty, the performance of which may, in proper cases, be required of the head of a department, by judicial process, is one in respect to which nothing is left to discretion. It is a simple, definite duty, arising under conditions admitted or proved to exist, and imposed by law.

The case of *Marbury* v. *Madison, Secretary of State,* furnishes an illustration. A citizen had been nominated, confirmed, and appointed a justice of the peace for the District of Columbia, and his commission had been made out, signed, and sealed. Nothing remained to be done except delivery, and the duty of delivery was imposed by law on the Secretary of State. It was held that the performance of this duty might be enforced by *mandamus* issuing from a court having jurisdiction.

So, in the case of *Kendall, Postmaster-General,* v. *Stockton & Stokes,* an act of Congress had directed the Postmaster-General to credit Stockton & Stokes with such sums as the Solicitor of the Treasury should find due to them; and that officer refused to credit them with certain sums, so found due. It was held that the crediting of this money was a mere ministerial duty, the performance of which might be judicially enforced.

In each of these cases nothing was left to discretion.

There was no room for the exercise of judgment. The law required the performance of a single specific act; and that performance, it was held, might be required by *mandamus*.

Very different is the duty of the President in the exercise of the power to see that the laws are faithfully executed, and among these laws the acts named in the bill. By the first of these acts he is required to assign generals to command in the several military districts, and to detail sufficient military force to enable such officers to discharge their duties under the law. By the supplementary act, other duties are imposed on the several commanding generals, and these duties must necessarily be performed under the supervision of the President as commander-in-chief. The duty thus imposed on the President is in no just sense ministerial. It is purely executive and political.

An attempt on the part of the judicial department of the government to enforce the performance of such duties by the President might be justly characterized, in the language of Chief Justice Marshall, as ''an absurd and excessive extravagance.''

It is true that in the instance before us the interposition of the court is not sought to enforce action by the Executive under constitutional legislation, but to restrain such action under legislation alleged to be unconstitutional. But we are unable to perceive that this circumstance takes the case out of the general principles which forbid judicial interference with the exercise of Executive discretion.

It was admitted in the argument that the application now made to us is without a precedent; and this is of much weight against it. . . .

The fact that no such application was ever before made in any case indicates the general judgment of the profession that no such application should be entertained.

It will hardly be contended that Congress can interpose, in any case, to restrain the enactment of an unconstitutional law; and yet how can the right to judicial interposition to prevent such an enactment, when the purpose is evident and the execution of that purpose certain, be distinguished, in principle, from the right to such interposition against the execution of such a law by the President?

The Congress is the legislative department of the government; the President is the executive department. Neither can be restrained in its action by the judicial department; though the acts of both, when performed, are, in proper cases, subject to its cognizance.

The impropriety of such interference will be clearly seen upon consideration of its possible consequences.

Suppose the bill filed and the injunction prayed for allowed. If the President refuse obedience, it is needless to observe that the court is without power to enforce its process. If, on the other hand, the President complies with the order of the court and refuses to execute the acts of Congress, is it not clear that a collision may occur between the executive and legislative departments of the government? May not the House of Representatives impeach the President for such refusal? And in that case could this court interfere, in behalf of the President, thus endangered by compliance with its mandate, and restrain by injunction the Senate of the United States from sitting as a court of impeachment? Would the strange spectacle be offered to the public world of an attempt by this court to arrest proceedings in that court?

These questions answer themselves.

It is true that a State may file an original bill in this court. And it may be true, in some cases, that such a bill may be filed against the United States. But we are fully satisfied that this court has no jurisdiction of a bill to enjoin the President in the performance of his official duties; and that no such bill ought to be received by us.

It has been suggested that the bill contains a prayer that, if the relief sought cannot be had against Andrew Johnson, as President, it may be granted against Andrew Johnson as a citizen of Tennessee. But it is plain that relief as against the execution of an act of Congress by Andrew Johnson, is relief against its execution by the President. A bill praying an injunction against the execution of an act of Congress by the incumbent of the presidential office cannot be received, whether it describes him as President or as a citizen of a State.

The motion for leave to file the bill is, therefore,

DENIED.

The holding in this case is plain. The president of the United States cannot be sued to prevent the carrying out of executive responsibilities. But the Supreme Court has allowed suits against the actions of lower ranking executive officials. The very next year, for example, the Supreme Court heard *Georgia v. Stanton* (1868), in which an injunction was sought to stop the secretary of war from enforcing the Reconstruction Acts.

This suit also was unsuccessful, but it was decided on entirely different grounds—that it was a political question. The Court found no bar to suing an executive branch administrator, even at the cabinet level. Only suits against the president are prohibited by the doctrine of executive immunity.

While the decision in *Johnson* settles the issue of whether the president may be personally sued with the respect to executive functions, it does not answer the question of civil suits brought by private individuals who have been harmed by a president's actions. If an incumbent president engages in unlawful activities that cause damages to private individuals, can the president be held accountable in a court of law? Or is the president immune from such suits? President Nixon found himself the object of such a suit after he was involved in the dismissal of a federal employee.

Nixon v. Fitzgerald

457 U.S. 731 (1982)

Vote: 5 (Burger, O'Connor, Powell, Rehnquist, Stevens)
4 (Blackmun, Brennan, Marshall, White)
Opinion of the Court: Powell
Concurring opinion: Burger
Dissenting opinions: Blackmun, White

A. Ernest Fitzgerald was a civilian management analyst for the U.S. Air Force. In November 1968 Fitzgerald testified before a congressional committee chaired by Sen. William Proxmire, D-Wis. Fitzgerald reported that cost-overruns for the C-5A transport plane might reach as high as $2 billion. In addition, he spoke about the technical problems the manufacturer had encountered in producing the aircraft. Needless to say, Fitzgerald's testimony was not well received by the Defense Department or military contractors.

Thirteen months later, in January 1970, Fitzgerald was removed from his job on the grounds that a departmental reorganization had made a reduction in staff necessary. Fitzgerald believed he was fired in retaliation for his congressional appearance. The dismissal caused a great deal of concern among members of Congress, and Fitz-gerald's story was widely reported in the media. The question was whether the Nixon administration was just trying to get rid of a trouble-making whistle-blower. The president told a press conference that he would look into the matter, and there appeared to be some attempt to find Fitzgerald another government position. Those attempts failed, perhaps because of an internal memorandum circulated by presidential aide Alexander Butterfield concluding that "Fitzgerald is no doubt a top-notch cost expert, but he must be given very low marks in loyalty; and after all, loyalty is the name of the game . . . we should let him bleed, for a while at least."

Denied another government job, Fitzgerald began legal action, first complaining to the Civil Service Commission and then filing a suit for damages. When asked about the Fitzgerald matter, President Nixon responded, "I was totally aware that Mr. Fitzgerald would be fired or discharged or asked to resign. I approved it. . . . No, this was not a case of some person down the line deciding he should go. It was a decision that was submitted to me. I made it and I stick by it."

The next day the president's office retracted his statements, explaining that Nixon had confused Fitzgerald with another dismissal case.

Fitzgerald's lawsuit was against a number of federal executive branch officials, including Nixon, who had resigned during the early stages of the lower court proceedings. The former president's lawyers asserted that he should be removed from the suit on the grounds of absolute executive immunity from legal actions based on his official conduct as president. The lower courts rejected the absolute immunity claim, and Nixon appealed.

Justice Lewis F. Powell, Jr., delivered the opinion of the Court:

This case now presents the claim that the President of the United States is shielded by absolute immunity from civil damages liability. In the case of the President the inquiries into history and policy, though mandated independently by our cases, tend to converge. Because the Presidency did not exist through most of the development of common law, any historical analysis must draw its evidence primarily from our constitutional heritage and structure. Historical inquiry thus merges almost at its inception with the kind of "public policy" analysis appropriately undertaken by a federal court. This inquiry involves policies and principles that may be considered implicit in the nature of the President's office in a system structured to achieve effective government under a constitutionally mandated separation of powers.

Here a former President asserts his immunity from civil damages claims of two kinds. He stands named as a defendant in a direct action under the Constitution and in two statutory actions under federal laws of general applicability. In neither case has Congress taken express legislative action to subject the President to civil liability for his official acts.

Applying the principles of our cases to claims of this kind, we hold that petitioner, as a former President of the United States, is entitled to absolute immunity from damages liability predicated on his official acts. We consider this immunity a functionally mandated incident of the President's unique office, rooted in the constitutional tradition of the separation of powers and supported by our history. . . .

The President occupies a unique position in the constitutional scheme. Article II, § 1, of the Constitution provides that "[t]he executive Power shall be vested in a President of the United States. . . ." This grant of authority establishes the President as the chief constitutional officer of the Executive Branch, entrusted with supervisory and policy responsibilities of utmost discretion and sensitivity. These include the enforcement of federal law—it is the President who is charged constitutionally to "take Care that the Laws be faithfully executed"; the conduct of foreign affairs—a realm in which the Court has recognized that "[i]t would be intolerable that courts, without the relevant information, should review and perhaps nullify actions of the Executive taken on information properly held secret"; and management of the Executive Branch—a task for which "imperative reasons requir[e] an unrestricted power [in the President] to remove the most important of his subordinates in their most important duties."

In arguing that the President is entitled only to qualified immunity, the respondent relies on cases in which we have recognized immunity of this scope for governors and cabinet officers. We find these cases to be inapposite. The President's unique status under the Constitution distinguishes him from other executive officials.

Because of the singular importance of the President's duties, diversion of his energies by concern with private lawsuits would raise unique risks to the effective functioning of government. As is the case with prosecutors and judges—for whom absolute immunity now is established—a President must concern himself with matters likely to "arouse the most intense feelings." Yet, as our decisions have recognized, it is in precisely such cases that there exists the greatest public interest in providing an official "the maximum ability to deal fearlessly and impartially with" the duties of his office. This concern is compelling where the officeholder must make the most sensitive and far-reaching decisions entrusted to any official under our constitutional system. Nor can the sheer prominence of the President's office be ignored. In view of the visibility of his office and the effect of his actions on countless people, the President would be an easily identifiable target for suits for civil damages. Cognizance of this personal vulnerability frequently could distract a President from his public duties, to the detriment of not only the President and his office but also the Nation that the Presidency was designed to serve.

Courts traditionally have recognized the President's constitutional responsibilities and status as factors counseling judicial deference and restraint. For example, while courts generally have looked to the common law to determine the scope of an official's evidentiary privilege, we have recognized that the Presidential privilege is ''rooted in the separation of powers under the Constitution.'' *United States v. Nixon* [1974]. It is settled law that the separation-of-powers doctrine does not bar every exercise of jurisdiction over the President of the United States. But our cases also have established that a court, before exercising jurisdiction, must balance the constitutional weight of the interest to be served against the dangers of intrusion on the authority and functions of the Executive Branch. When judicial action is needed to serve broad public interests—as when the Court acts, not in derogation of the separation of powers, but to maintain their proper balance, or to vindicate the public interest in an ongoing criminal prosecution—the exercise of jurisdiction has been held warranted. In the case of this merely private suit for damages based on a President's official acts, we hold it is not.

In defining the scope of an official's absolute privilege, this Court has recognized that the sphere of protected action must be related closely to the immunity's justifying purposes. Frequently our decisions have held that an official's absolute immunity should extend only to acts in performance of particular functions of his office. But the Court also has refused to draw functional lines finer than history and reason would support. In view of the special nature of the President's constitutional office and functions, we think it appropriate to recognize absolute Presidential immunity from damages liability for acts within the ''outer perimeter'' of his official responsibility.

Under the Constitution and laws of the United States the President has discretionary responsibilities in a broad variety of areas, many of them highly sensitive. In many cases it would be difficult to determine which of the President's innumerable ''functions'' encompassed a particular action. In this case, for example, respondent argues that he was dismissed in retaliation for his testimony to Congress—a violation of 5 U.S.C. § 7211 (1976 ed., Supp. IV) and 18 U.S.C. § 1505. The Air Force, however, has claimed that the underlying reorganization was undertaken to promote efficiency. Assuming that petitioner Nixon ordered the reorganization in which respondent lost his job, an inquiry into the President's motives could not be avoided under the kind of ''functional'' theory asserted both by respondent and the dissent. Inquiries of this kind could be highly intrusive.

Here respondent argues that petitioner Nixon would have acted outside the outer perimeter of his duties by ordering the discharge of an employee who was lawfully entitled to retain his job in the absence of '' 'such cause as will promote the efficiency of the service.' '' Because Congress has granted this legislative protection, respondent argues, no federal official could, within the outer perimeter of his duties of office, cause Fitzgerald to be dismissed without satisfying this standard in prescribed statutory proceedings.

This construction would subject the President to trial on virtually every allegation that an action was unlawful, or was taken for a forbidden purpose. Adoption of this construction thus would deprive absolute immunity of its intended effect. It clearly is within the President's constitutional and statutory authority to prescribe the manner in which the Secretary will conduct the business of the Air Force. Because this mandate of office must include the authority to prescribe reorganizations and reductions in force, we conclude that petitioner's alleged wrongful acts lay well within the outer perimeter of his authority.

A rule of absolute immunity for the President will not leave the Nation without sufficient protection against misconduct on the part of the Chief Executive. There remains the constitutional remedy of impeachment. In addition, there are formal and informal checks on Presidential action that do not apply with equal force to other executive officials. The President is subjected to constant scrutiny by the press. Vigilant oversight by Congress also may serve to deter Presidential abuses of office, as well as to make credible the threat of impeachment. Other incentives to avoid misconduct may include a desire to earn reelection, the need to maintain prestige as an element of Presidential influence, and a President's traditional concern for his historical stature.

The existence of alternative remedies and deterrents establishes that absolute immunity will not place the President "above the law." For the President, as for judges and prosecutors, absolute immunity merely precludes a particular private remedy for alleged misconduct in order to advance compelling public ends.

For the reasons stated in this opinion, the decision of the Court of Appeals is reversed, and the case is remanded for action consistent with this opinion.

So ordered.

Protecting Presidential Confidentiality

Executive privilege is a variation on the notion that the president should be immune from liability for official acts. The privilege argument asserts that there are certain conversations, documents, and records that are so closely tied to the sensitive duties of the president that they should remain confidential. Neither the legislature nor the judiciary should be allowed access to these materials without presidential consent; nor should the other branches be empowered to compel the president to hand over such items. Matters concerning national security or foreign policy especially fall under this protection. Executive privilege, it is argued, is inherent to the office of the president.

Although infrequently invoked, the privilege doctrine has been part of American history since the beginning of the nation. In some early disputes between the president and Congress, chief executives refused to provide certain information to the legislature. George Washington balked at giving the House of Representatives certain documents pertaining to negotiations over the Jay Treaty. During the investigation and trial of Aaron Burr, Thomas Jefferson cooperated with congressional information requests, but only up to a point. He refused to produce some items and later declined to testify at the trial even though he was subpoenaed. Presidents through the years have refused to comply with congressional requests for testimony. It is generally accepted that Congress does not have the power to compel the president to come before it to answer questions. Other executive department officials generally are not covered by claims of privilege.

In most instances, disputes over executive privilege are handled through negotiation between the executive branch and the institution requesting information. Only rarely have such disputes blown up into major court cases. When pushed to the limit, executive privilege claims rarely prevail, but when sensitive military or diplomatic matters requiring secrecy are involved, a president can expect to be on relatively safe ground in asserting executive privilege.

No case involving executive privilege has been more important than *United States v. Nixon* (1974). It occurred at a time of great constitutional stress, with all three branches locked in a fight about fundamental separation of powers issues. The conflict ultimately was resolved when Nixon resigned. Much of the impetus for breaking the constitutional deadlock came from the unanimous decision of the justices in the *Nixon* case. Chief Justice Burger's opinion for the Court reviewed the issues surrounding the executive privilege controversy and then rejected Nixon's invocation of the doctrine.

United States v. Nixon

418 U.S. 683 (1974)

Vote: 8 (Blackmun, Brennan, Burger, Douglas,
*   Marshall, Powell, Stewart, White)*

o

Opinion of the Court: Burger
Not participating: Rehnquist

This case was one of many court actions spawned by the Watergate scandal. The controversy began on June 17, 1972, when seven men broke into the Democratic National Committee headquarters located in the Watergate complex in Washington, D.C. The seven were apprehended and charged with criminal offenses. All had ties either to the White House or to the Committee to Re-elect the President. Five of the seven pleaded guilty, and two were convicted. At the end of the trial, one of the defendants, James McCord, Jr., claimed that he had been pressured to plead guilty and that there were others involved in the break-in who had not been prosecuted. It was clear to many that the break-in was only the tip of a very large iceberg of shady dealings and cover-ups engaged in by influential persons closely tied to the Nixon administration.

In response to these events, the Senate began an investigation of the Watergate incident and the activities related to it. The star witness was John Dean III, special counsel to the president, who testified under a grant of immunity. Dean implicated high officials in the president's office, and he claimed that Nixon had known about the events and the subsequent cover-ups. As surprising as this testimony was, the most shocking revelation was made by Alexander Butterfield, who testified that the president had installed a secret taping system that automatically recorded all conversations in the Oval Office. Obviously, the tape recordings held information that would settle the dispute between the witnesses claiming White House involvement in the Watergate affair and the denial issued by administration officials.

In addition to the Senate investigation, a special prosecutor was appointed to look into the Watergate affair. The first person to hold this position, Archibald Cox, asked Nixon to turn over the tapes. When Nixon declined, Cox went to court to get an order compelling him to deliver the materials. The district and appeals courts ruled in favor of the prosecutor. Nixon then offered to release summaries of the recordings, but that did not satisfy Cox who continued to pursue the tapes. In response, Nixon ordered that Cox be fired. When the two highest officials in the Justice Department resigned rather than comply with the order, Solicitor General Robert Bork became the acting attorney general and dismissed Cox. The firing of the prosecutor, popularly known as the "Saturday Night Massacre," enraged the American people, and many began calling for the president's impeachment.

A new special prosecutor, Leon Jaworski, was appointed. The Houston attorney pursued the tapes with the same zeal as had Cox. Finally, Nixon relented and agreed to produce some of the the materials. But when he did so, the prosecutor found that the tapes had been heavily edited. One contained eighteen and one-half minutes of mysterious buzzing at a crucial point, indicating that conversation had been erased.

Jaworski obtained criminal indictments against several Nixon aides. Although no criminal charges were brought against the president, he was named in the indictment as a co-conspirator. At about the same time, the House Judiciary Committee began an investigation into whether the president should be impeached.

Both the Judiciary Committee and Jaworski sought more of the tapes to review. Nixon steadfastly refused to comply, claiming that it was his right under executive privilege to decide what would be released and what would remain secret. The district court issued a final subpoena *duces tecum,* an order to produce the tapes and other

This subpoena duces tecum *was issued July 23, 1973. It ordered President Richard Nixon or his representatives to appear before the federal grand jury on July 26 and to bring taped conversations relevant to the investigation of the Watergate affair.*

documents. Both the United States and Nixon requested that the Supreme Court review the case, and the justices accepted the case on an expedited basis, bypassing the court of appeals.

Chief Justice Burger delivered the opinion of the Court:

[W]e turn to the claim that the subpoena should be quashed because it demands "confidential conversations between a President and his close advisors that it would be inconsistent with the public interest to produce." The first contention is a broad claim that the separation of powers doctrine precludes judicial review of a President's claim of privilege. The second contention is that if he does not prevail on the claim of absolute privilege, the court should hold as a matter of constitutional law that the privilege prevails over the subpoena *duces tecum.*

In the performance of assigned constitutional duties each branch of the Government must initially interpret the Constitution, and the interpretation of its powers by

any branch is due great respect from the others. The President's counsel, as we have noted, reads the Constitution as providing an absolute privilege of confidentiality for all Presidential communications. Many decisions of this Court, however, have unequivocally reaffirmed the holding of *Marbury* v. *Madison* (1803) that "[i]t is emphatically the province and duty of the judicial department to say what the law is."

No holding of the Court has defined the scope of judicial power specifically relating to the enforcement of a subpoena for confidential Presidential communications for use in a criminal prosecution, but other exercises of power by the Executive Branch and the Legislative Branch have been found invalid as in conflict with the Constitution. *Powell* v. *McCormack* (1969); *Youngstown Sheet & Tube Co.* v. *Sawyer* (1952). . . .

Notwithstanding the deference each branch must accord the others, the "judicial Power of the United States" vested in the federal courts by Art. III, § 1, of the Constitution can no more be shared with the Executive Branch than the Chief Executive, for example, can share with the Judiciary the veto power, or the Congress share with the Judiciary the power to override a Presidential veto. Any other conclusion would be contrary to the basic concept of separation of powers and the checks and balances that flow from the scheme of a tripartite government. We therefore reaffirm that it is the province and duty of this Court "to say what the law is" with respect to the claim of privilege presented in this case.

In support of his claim of absolute privilege, the President's counsel urges two grounds, one of which is common to all governments and one of which is peculiar to our system of separation of powers. The first ground is the valid need for protection of communications between high Government officials and those who advise and assist them in the performance of their manifold duties; the importance of this confidentiality is too plain to require further discussion. Human experience teaches that those who expect public dissemination of their remarks may well temper candor with a concern for appearances and for their own interests to the detriment of the decisionmaking process. Whatever the nature of the privilege of confidentiality of Presidential communications in the exercise

This drawing illustrates Richard Nixon's attorney, James St. Clair, arguing the president's case before the Supreme Court in United States v. Nixon *(1974). The four justices are (left to right): Chief Justice Warren Burger, William J. Brennan, Jr., Byron R. White, and Harry A. Blackmun.*

of Art. II powers, the privilege can be said to derive from the supremacy of each branch within its own assigned area of constitutional duties. Certain powers and privileges flow from the nature of enumerated powers; the protection of the confidentiality of Presidential communications has similar constitutional underpinnings.

The second ground asserted by the President's counsel in support of the claim of absolute privilege rests on the doctrine of separation of powers. Here it is argued that the independence of the Executive Branch within its own sphere insulates a President from a judicial subpoena in an ongoing criminal prosecution, and thereby protects confidential Presidential communications.

However, neither the doctrine of separation of powers, nor the need for confidentiality of high-level communications, without more, can sustain an absolute, unqualified Presidential privilege of immunity from judicial process under all circumstances. The President's need for complete candor and objectivity from advisers calls for great deference from the courts. However, when the privilege depends solely on the broad, undifferentiated claim of public interest in the confidentiality of such conversations, a confrontation with other values arises. Absent a claim of need to

protect military, diplomatic, or sensitive national security secrets, we find it difficult to accept the argument that even the very important interest in confidentiality of Presidential communications is significantly diminished by production of such material for *in camera* inspection with all the protection that a district court will be obliged to provide.

The impediment that an absolute, unqualified privilege would place in the way of the primary constitutional duty of the Judicial Branch to do justice in criminal prosecutions would plainly conflict with the function of the courts under Art. III. In designing the structure of our Government and dividing and allocating the sovereign power among three co-equal branches, the Framers of the Constitution sought to provide a comprehensive system, but the separate powers were not intended to operate with absolute independence. . . . To read the Art. II powers of the President as providing an absolute privilege as against a subpoena essential to enforcement of criminal statutes on no more than a generalized claim of the public interest in confidentiality of nonmilitary and nondiplomatic discussions would upset the constitutional balance of "a workable government" and gravely impair the role of the courts under Art. III.

Since we conclude that the legitimate needs of the

judicial process may outweigh Presidential privilege, it is necessary to resolve those competing interests in a manner that preserves the essential functions of each branch. The right and indeed the duty to resolve that question does not free the Judiciary from according high respect to the representations made on behalf of the President.

The expectation of a President to the confidentiality of his conversations and correspondence, like the claim of confidentiality of judicial deliberations, for example, has all the values to which we accord deference for the privacy of all citizens and, added to those values, is the necessity for protection of the public interest in candid, objective, and even blunt or harsh opinions in Presidential decisionmaking. A President and those who assist him must be free to explore alternatives in the process of shaping policies and making decisions and to do so in a way many would be unwilling to express except privately. These are the considerations justifying a presumptive privilege for Presidential communications. The privilege is fundamental to the operation of Government and inextricably rooted in the separation of powers under the Constitution. . . .

But this presumptive privilege must be considered in light of our historic commitment to the rule of law. This is nowhere more profoundly manifest than in our view that "the twofold aim [of criminal justice] is that guilt shall not escape or innocence suffer." We have elected to employ an adversary system of criminal justice in which the parties contest all issues before a court of law. The need to develop all relevant facts in the adversary system is both fundamental and comprehensive. The ends of criminal justice would be defeated if judgments were to be founded on a partial or speculative presentation of the facts. The very integrity of the judicial system and public confidence in the system depend on full disclosure of all the facts, within the framework of the rules of evidence. To ensure that justice is done, it is imperative to the function of courts that compulsory process be available for the production of evidence needed either by the prosecution or by the defense. . . .

In this case the President challenges a subpoena served on him as a third party requiring the production of materials for use in a criminal prosecution; he does so on the claim that he has a privilege against disclosure of confidential communications. He does not place his claim of privilege on the ground they are military or diplomatic secrets. As to these areas of Art. II duties the courts have traditionally shown the utmost deference to Presidential responsibilities. . . . No case of the Court, however, has extended this high degree of deference to a President's generalized interest in confidentiality. Nowhere in the Constitution, as we have noted earlier, is there any explicit reference to a privilege of confidentiality, yet to the extent this interest relates to the effective discharge of a President's powers, it is constitutionally based.

The right to the production of all evidence at a criminal trial similarly has constitutional dimensions. The Sixth Amendment explicitly confers upon every defendant in a criminal trial the right "to be confronted with the witnesses against him" and "to have compulsory process for obtaining witnesses in his favor." Moreover, the Fifth Amendment also guarantees that no person shall be deprived of liberty without due process of law. It is the manifest duty of the courts to vindicate those guarantees, and to accomplish that it is essential that all relevant and admissible evidence be produced.

In this case we must weigh the importance of the general privilege of confidentiality of Presidential communications in performance of the President's responsibilities against the inroads of such a privilege on the fair administration of criminal justice. The interest in preserving confidentiality is weighty indeed and entitled to great respect. However, we cannot conclude that advisers will be moved to temper the candor of their remarks by the infrequent occasions of disclosure because of the possibility that such conversations will be called for in the context of a criminal prosecution.

On the other hand, the allowance of the privilege to withhold evidence that is demonstrably relevant in a criminal trial would cut deeply into the guarantee of due process of law and gravely impair the basic function of the courts. A President's acknowledged need for confidentiality in the communications of his office is general in nature, whereas the constitutional need for production of relevant evidence in a criminal proceeding is specific and central to the fair adjudication of a particular criminal case in the administration of justice. Without access to specific facts a criminal prosecution may be totally frustrated. The President's broad interest in confidentiality of communications will not be vitiated by disclosure of a limited number of conversations preliminarily shown to have some bearing on the pending criminal cases.

We conclude that when the ground for asserting privilege as to subpoenaed materials sought for use in a criminal trial is based only on the generalized interest in confidentiality, it cannot prevail over the fundamental demands of due process of law in the fair administration of criminal justice. The generalized assertion of privilege must yield to the demonstrated, specific need for evidence in a pending criminal trial.

The Court's ruling was clear. The peoples' interest in the fair administration of criminal justice outweighed the president's interest in confidentiality. Executive privilege was rejected as a justification for refusing to make the tapes available to the prosecutor.

Nixon complied with the Court's ruling, knowing full well that it meant the end of his presidency. In obeying the Court order, he avoided provoking what many feared would be the most serious of all constitutional confrontations. What if Nixon had refused to comply? What if he had destroyed the tapes rather than turn them over? Who could have enforced sanctions on the president for doing so? Remember that in *Mississippi v. Johnson* the Court cited these possible noncompliance and enforcement questions as reasons for not permitting the president personally to be sued for official conduct. Impeachment and conviction of the president probably would have been the only way to handle such a crisis. Whatever Nixon's culpability in Watergate and related matters, he spared the nation an unprecedented crisis by bowing to the Supreme Court's interpretation of the Constitution.

The Nixon tapes revealed substantial wrongdoing. It was obvious to all that if he had not voluntarily relinquished his position, the House of Representatives would have presented articles of impeachment, and a Senate trial would have taken place, resulting in Nixon's removal from office. Rather than put himself and the nation through such an ordeal, Nixon resigned.

AUGUST 9, 1974

Office of the White House Press Secretary

- -

THE WHITE HOUSE

The following letter was delivered by General Alexander M. Haig Jr. to the Secretary of State in his White House office at 11:35 a.m. today:

The White House
Washington

August 9, 1974

Dear Mr. Secretary:

I hereby resign the Office of President of the United States.

Sincerely,

/s/ Richard Nixon

The Honorable Henry A. Kissinger
The Secretary of State
Washington, D.C. 20520

With this one-sentence letter Richard Nixon became the first American president to resign from office.

Three years later the Supreme Court was once again called upon to consider these matters. At issue was the constitutionality of the act dealing with Nixon's tapes and papers. The majority rejected Nixon's executive privilege objections to the law, but Chief Justice Burger, who wrote the Court's opinion in *United States v. Nixon,* voted to uphold the former president's claim of executive confidentiality. The only other dissenting justice was William H. Rehnquist, who had not participated in the earlier decision.

Nixon v. Administrator of General Services

433 U.S. 425 (1977)

Vote: 7 (Blackmun, Brennan, Marshall, Powell, Stevens, Stewart, White)
2 (Burger, Rehnquist)
Opinion of the Court: Brennan
Concurring opinions: Blackmun, Powell, Stevens, White
Dissenting opinions: Burger, Rehnquist

Four months after Nixon's resignation, President Gerald Ford signed into law the Presidential Recordings and Materials Preservation Act. The statute authorized the administrator of the General Services Administration (GSA), an official of the executive branch, to take control of Nixon's White House papers and tapes and to establish a procedure to determine which of these materials were truly personal and private in nature. Personal and private papers were to be returned to Nixon, but the remaining documents were to be maintained by the GSA, which at that time was in charge of the National Archives. The administrator also was authorized to develop procedures for making the retained materials available to the public.

Congress passed the law because of the continuing significance of the Nixon papers and because the Watergate special prosecutor needed to have access to them. Historically, such papers, with few exceptions, were considered to be the property of former presidents. On the basis of historical precedent, Nixon wanted these materials, approximately 42 million pages of documents and 880 tape recordings of conversations, shipped to his home in California. After some negotiation Nixon and Arthur Sampson, the head of GSA, reached an agreement that called for both

to have access to the materials with significant qualifications and restrictions. Ten days after the announcement of this agreement, however, thirteen senators introduced a bill to supersede it and replace it with the act challenged in this case.

Nixon attacked the act's constitutionality on a number of grounds, claiming that it violated the separation of powers, presidential privilege, privacy rights, freedom of association, and the Bill of Attainder Clause. A special three-judge district court upheld the validity of the statute, and the former president appealed. We excerpt the portions of the Court's opinion dealing with the separation of powers and executive privilege claims.

Justice William J. Brennan, Jr., delivered the opinion of the Court:

We reject at the outset the appellant's argument that the Act's regulation of the disposition of Presidential materials within the Executive Branch constitutes, without more, a violation of the principle of separation of powers. Neither President Ford nor President Carter supports this claim. The Executive Branch became a party to the Act's regulation when President Ford signed the Act into law, and the administration of President Carter, acting through the Solicitor General, vigorously supports affirmance of the District Court's judgment sustaining its constitutionality. Moreover, the control over the materials remains in the Executive Branch. The Administrator of General Services, who must promulgate and administer the regulations that are the keystone of the statutory scheme, is himself an official of the Executive Branch, appointed by the President. The career archivists appointed to do the initial screening for the purpose of selecting out and returning to appellant his private and personal papers similarly are Executive Branch employees. . . .

It is therefore highly relevant that the Act provides for custody of the materials in officials of the Executive

Branch and that employees of that branch have access to the materials only "for lawful Government use, subject to the [Administrator's] regulations." For it is clearly less intrusive to place custody and screening of the materials within the Executive Branch itself than to have Congress or some outside agency perform the screening function. While the materials may also be made available for use in judicial proceedings, this provision is expressly qualified by any rights, defense, or privileges that any person may invoke including, of course, a valid claim of executive privilege. *United States v. Nixon* [1974]. Similarly, although some of the materials may eventually be made available for public access, the Act expressly recognizes the need both "to protect any party's opportunity to assert any legally or constitutionally based right or privilege," and to return purely private materials to appellant. These provisions plainly guard against disclosures barred by any defenses or privileges available to appellant or the Executive Branch. And appellant himself concedes that the Act "does not make the presidential materials available to the Congress—except insofar as Congressmen are members of the public and entitled to access when the public has it." The Executive Branch remains in full control of the Presidential materials, and the Act facially is designed to ensure that the materials can be released only when release is not barred by some applicable privilege inherent in that branch.

Thus, whatever are the future possibilities for constitutional conflict in the promulgation of regulations respecting public access to particular documents, nothing contained in the Act renders it unduly disruptive of the Executive Branch and, therefore, unconstitutional on its face. And, of course, there is abundant statutory precedent for the regulation and mandatory disclosure of documents in the possession of the Executive Branch. Such regulation of material generated in the Executive Branch has never been considered invalid as an invasion of its autonomy. Similar congressional power to regulate Executive Branch documents exists in this instance, a power that is augmented by the important interests that the Act seeks to attain.

Having concluded that the separation-of-powers principle is not necessarily violated by the Administrator's taking custody of and screening appellant's papers, we next consider appellant's more narrowly defined claim that the Presidential privilege shields these records from archival scrutiny. We start with what was established in *United States v. Nixon*—that the privilege is a qualified one. . . .

Unlike *United States v. Nixon*, in which appellant asserted a claim of absolute Presidential privilege against inquiry by the coordinate Judicial Branch, this case initially involves appellant's assertion of a privilege against the very Executive Branch in whose name the privilege is invoked. The nonfederal appellees rely on this apparent anomaly to contend that only an incumbent President can assert the privilege of the Presidency. Acceptance of that proposition would, of course, end this inquiry. . . .

It is true that only the incumbent is charged with performance of the executive duty under the Constitution. And an incumbent may be inhibited in disclosing confidences of a predecessor when he believes that the effect may be to discourage candid presentation of views by his contemporary advisers. Moreover, to the extent that the privilege serves as a shield for executive officials against burdensome requests for information which might interfere with the proper performance of their duties, a former President is in less need of it than an incumbent. In addition, there are obvious political checks against an incumbent's abuse of the privilege.

Nevertheless, we think that the Solicitor General states the sounder view, and we adopt it:

"This Court held in *United States v. Nixon* . . . that the privilege is necessary to provide the confidentiality required for the President's conduct of office. Unless he can give his advisers some assurance of confidentiality, a President could not expect to receive the full and frank submissions of facts and opinions upon which effective discharge of his duties depends. The confidentiality necessary to this exchange cannot be measured by the few months or years between the submission of the information and the end of the President's tenure; the privilege is not for the benefit of the President as an individual, but for the benefit of the Republic. Therefore the privilege survives the individual President's tenure."

. . . The appellant bases his claim of Presidential privilege in this case on the assertion that the potential disclosure of communications given to the appellant in confidence would adversely affect the ability of future Presidents to obtain the candid advice necessary for effective decisionmaking. We are called upon to adjudicate that claim, however, only with respect to the process by which the materials will be screened and catalogued by professional archivists. For any eventual public access will be governed by the guidelines of § 104, which direct the Administrator to take into account "the need to protect any party's opportunity to assert any . . . constitutionally based right or privilege" and the need to return purely private materials to the appellant.

In view of these specific directions, there is no reason to believe that the restriction on public access ultimately established by regulation will not be adequate to preserve executive confidentiality. An absolute barrier to all outside disclosure is not practically or constitutionally necessary. . . . All former Presidents from President Hoover to President Johnson have deposited their papers in Presidential libraries (an example appellant has said he intended to follow) for governmental preservation and eventual disclosure. The screening processes for sorting materials for lodgment in these libraries also involved comprehensive review by archivists, often involving materials upon which access restrictions ultimately have been imposed. The expectation of the confidentiality of executive communications thus has always been limited and subject to erosion over time after an administration leaves office.

We are thus left with the bare claim that the mere screening of the materials by the archivists will impermissibly interfere with candid communication of views by Presidential advisers. We agree with the District Court that, thus framed, the question is readily resolved. The screening constitutes a very limited intrusion by personnel in the Executive Branch sensitive to executive concerns. These very personnel have performed the identical task in each of the Presidential libraries without any suggestion that such activity has in any way interfered with executive confidentiality. Indeed, in light of this consistent historical practice, past and present executive officials must be well aware of the possibility that, at some time in the future, their communications may be reviewed on a confidential basis by professional archivists. Appellant has suggested no reason why review under the instant Act, rather than the Presidential Libraries Act, is significantly more likely to impair confidentiality, nor has he called into question the District Court's finding that the archivists' "record for discretion in handling confidential material is unblemished." . . .

The legislative history of the Act clearly reveals that, among other purposes, Congress acted to establish regular procedures to deal with the perceived need to preserve the materials for legitimate historical and governmental purposes. An incumbent President should not be dependent on happenstance or the whim of a prior President when he seeks access to records of past decisions that define or channel current governmental obligations. Nor should the American people's ability to reconstruct and come to terms with their history be truncated by an analysis of Presidential privilege that focuses only on the needs of the present. Congress can legitimately act to rectify the hit-or-miss approach that has characterized past attempts to protect these substantial interests by entrusting the materials to expert handling by trusted and disinterested professionals.

Other substantial public interests that led Congress to seek to preserve appellant's materials were the desire to restore public confidence in our political processes by preserving the materials as a source for facilitating a full airing of the events leading to appellant's resignation, and Congress' need to understand how those political processes had in fact operated in order to gauge the necessity for remedial legislation. Thus by preserving these materials, the Act may be thought to aid the legislative process and thus to be within the scope of Congress' broad investigative power. And, of course, the Congress repeatedly referred to the importance of the materials to the Judiciary in the event that they shed light upon issues in civil or criminal litigation, a social interest that cannot be doubted.

In light of these objectives, the scheme adopted by Congress for preservation of the appellant's Presidential materials cannot be said to be overbroad. It is true that among the voluminous materials to be screened by archivists are some materials that bear no relationship to any of these objectives (and whose prompt return to appellant is therefore mandated by § 104(a)(7). But these materials are commingled with other materials whose preservation the Act requires, for the appellant, like his predecessors, made no systematic attempt to segregate official, personal, and private materials. Even individual documents and tapes often intermingle communications relating to governmental duties, and of great interest to historians or future policymakers, with private and confidential communications.

Thus, as in the Presidential libraries, the intermingled state of the materials requires the comprehensive review and classification contemplated by the Act if Congress' important objectives are to be furthered. In the course of that process, the archivists will be required to view the small fraction of the materials that implicate Presidential confidentiality, as well as personal and private materials to be returned to appellant. But given the safeguards built into the Act to prevent disclosure of such materials and the minimal nature of the intrusion into the confidentiality of the Presidency, we believe that the claims of Presidential privilege clearly must yield to the important congressional purposes of preserving the materials and maintaining access to them for lawful governmental and historical purposes.

Mr. Justice REHNQUIST, dissenting.

Appellant resigned the Office of the Presidency nearly three years ago, and if the issue here were limited to the right of Congress to dispose of his particular Presidential papers, this case would not be of major constitutional significance. Unfortunately, however, today's decision countenances the power of any future Congress to seize the official papers of an outgoing President as he leaves the inaugural stand. In so doing, it poses a real threat to the ability of future Presidents to receive candid advice and to give candid instructions. This result, so at odds with our previous case law on the separation of powers, will daily stand as a veritable sword of Damocles over every succeeding President and his advisers. Believing as I do that the Act is a clear violation of the constitutional principle of separation of powers, I need not address the other issues considered by the Court.

My conclusion that the Act violates the principle of separation of powers is based upon three fundamental propositions. First, candid and open discourse among the President, his advisers, foreign heads of state and ambassadors, Members of Congress, and the others who deal with the White House on a sensitive basis is an absolute prerequisite to the effective discharge of the duties of that high office. Second, the effect of the Act, and of this Court's decision upholding its constitutionality, will undoubtedly restrain the necessary free flow of information to and from the present President and future Presidents. Third, any substantial intrusion upon the effective discharge of the duties of the President is sufficient to violate the principle of separation of powers, and our prior cases do not permit the sustaining of an Act such as this by "balancing" an intrusion of substantial magnitude against the interests assertedly fostered by the Act.

The Power of Appointment and Removal

For presidents to carry out the executive duties of the government effectively, they must be able to staff the various departments and offices with administrators who share their views and in whom they have confidence. This duty implies the power to appoint and the power to remove. The Constitution is relatively clear on the president's appointment power, but is silent on the right to remove.

Appointing Executive Officials

Article II, Section 2, contains what is known as the Appointments Clause. It details the president's authority to appoint major administrative and judicial officials, but also allows Congress to allocate that authority to other bodies for minor administrative positions:

[The President] shall nominate, and by and with the Advice and Consent of the Senate, shall appoint Ambassadors, other public Ministers and Consuls, Judges of the supreme Court, and all other Officers of the

United States, whose Appointments are not herein otherwise provided for, and which shall be established by Law: but the Congress may by Law vest the Appointment of such inferior Officers, as they think proper, in the President alone, in the Courts of Law, or in the Heads of Departments.

From time to time Congress has established government positions that, for various reasons, were to be filled by an appointing authority other than the president. When the executive has objected, legal disputes have arisen. In many cases the issue is whether the official holds a major position as an officer of the United States or is an inferior official. The former, according to the Appointments Clause, must be filled by presidential nomination and Senate confirmation, but the latter may be chosen by some other means as determined by Congress.

Buckley v. Valeo (1976) illustrates this point. The justices heard a challenge to the constitutionality of the 1974 amendments to the Federal Election Campaign Act. The appeal involved a complex set of issues regarding the regulations of federal election campaigns, including the question of who should enforce the law. The statute created the Federal Election Commission (FEC) to police the new regulations. In light of the just-concluded Watergate controversy, Congress did not want the eight members of the commission to be appointed exclusively by the president, so it devised a plan for choosing them. The secretary of the Senate and the clerk of the House were *ex officio* members without the right to vote. The president pro tempore of the Senate, the Speaker of the House, and the president each appointed two members, one Democrat and one Republican. The six voting members had to be confirmed by both houses of Congress.

This arrangement was challenged as being in violation of the Appointments Clause. The argument was that the commissioners were officers of the United States who should be appointed by the president only and confirmed by the Senate, with no House involvement. Furthermore, the commission's appointment procedures were attacked because as the body given responsibility to enforce the campaign laws (an executive function) the members should not be appointed by the legislature. To construct the commission this way was to violate the principle of separation of powers.

The Supreme Court, unanimously on this point, found the FEC to be unconstitutionally structured. The commissioners were not inferior officers; they were officers entrusted with major enforcement and administrative duties. As such, they belonged to the executive branch and should not be appointed by the legislature.

The Court reached a different conclusion in *Morrison v. Olson* (1988). This decision involved the creation of the office of special prosecutor. Given the kinds of cases special prosecutors are appointed to investigate, are you convinced by the Court's analysis that this official is an ''inferior officer'' under the meaning of the Appointments Clause? Or is the Court taking a pragmatic approach, recognizing that it would be unworkable for an official prosecuting crime and corruption in the executive branch to be appointed by the president?

Morrison v. Olson

487 U.S. 654 (1988)

Vote: 7 (Blackmun, Brennan, Marshall, O'Connor,
Rehnquist, Stevens, White)
1 (Scalia)
Opinion of the Court: Rehnquist
Dissenting opinion: Scalia
Not participating: Kennedy

Because of the problems encountered in prosecuting the Watergate case, Congress included a provision in the Ethics in Government Act of 1978 dealing with the position of special prosecutor. The law provided for an independent counsel to investigate and, when necessary, to prosecute high-ranking officials of the government for violations of federal criminal laws. The special prosecutor was to be chosen by a group of three federal judges, appointed by the chief justice for two years and known as the special division. The selection of special prosecutors and the description of the prosecutor's jurisdiction are the special division's only functions. It carries out these responsibilities only after a preliminary investigation by the attorney general indicates that a special prosecutor is necessary.

Once appointed, the special prosecutor may exercise all of the powers of the Justice Department. A prosecutor appointed under the act may be removed by the attorney general, but only for cause or disabilities that substantially impair the counsel from completing the required duties. Such dismissals may be reviewed by the federal district court. The special prosecutor's tenure otherwise ends when he or she declares the work to be completed, or the special division concludes that the independent counsel's assigned tasks have been accomplished.

In 1982 two House subcommittees investigated the activities of the Environmental Protection Agency and the Land and Natural Resources Division of the Justice Department. During that investigation the subcommittees asked the agencies to produce certain documents. A controversy flared up over whether the legislature could demand these documents from the executive branch, a dispute that was settled after contempt of Congress citations were made and lawsuits were filed. The following year the House Judiciary Committee began an investigation into the role of Justice Department officials in these events. Two years later, in 1985, the committee issued its report, which indicated that Theodore B. Olson, an assistant attorney general, had provided false and misleading statements when he testified before the committee. Two other Justice Department officials were implicated in obstructing the committee's investigation. The committee requested that the attorney general initiate action for the appointment of a special prosecutor to pursue these cases.

The special division appointed James McKay as special prosecutor, but when he resigned a month later, the judges selected Alexia Morrison. Olson and the other targets of the investigation refused to cooperate with orders to produce evidence on the grounds that the special prosecutor provision of the Ethics in Government Act violated the Constitution's Appointments Clause. They claimed that the special prosecutor was not an "inferior officer" and therefore had to be appointed by the president, not by a group of three judges. The federal district court upheld the validity of the Act, but the court of appeals reversed.

Chief Justice Rehnquist delivered the opinion of the Court:

The parties do not dispute that "[t]he Constitution for purposes of appointment . . . divides all its officers into two classes." As we stated in *Buckley v. Valeo* (1976), "[p]rincipal officers are selected by the President with the advice and consent of the Senate. Inferior officers Congress may allow to be appointed by the President alone, by the heads of departments, or by the Judiciary." The initial question is, accordingly, whether appellant is an "inferior" or a "principal" officer. If she is the latter, as the Court of Appeals concluded, then the Act is in violation of the Appointments Clause.

The line between "inferior" and "principal" officers is one that is far from clear, and the Framers provided little guidance into where it should be drawn. . . . We need not attempt here to decide exactly where the line falls between the two types of officers, because in our view appellant clearly falls on the "inferior officer" side of that line. Several factors lead to this conclusion.

First, appellant is subject to removal by a higher Executive Branch official. Although appellant may not be "subordinate" to the Attorney General (and the President) insofar as she possesses a degree of independent discretion to exercise the powers delegated to her under the Act, the fact that she can be removed by the Attorney General indicates that she is to some degree "inferior" in rank and authority. Second, appellant is empowered by the Act to perform only certain, limited duties. An independent counsel's role is restricted primarily to investigation and, if appropriate, prosecution for certain federal crimes. Admittedly, the Act delegates to appellant "full power and independent authority to exercise all investigative and prosecutorial functions and powers of the Department of Justice," § 594(a), but this grant of authority does not include any authority to formulate policy for the Government or the Executive Branch, nor does it give appellant any administrative duties outside of those necessary to operate her office. The Act specifically provides that in policy matters appellant is to comply to the extent possible with the policies of the Department.

Third, appellant's office is limited in jurisdiction. Not only is the Act itself restricted in applicability to certain federal officials suspected of certain serious federal crimes, but an independent counsel can only act within the scope of the jurisdiction that has been granted by the Special Division pursuant to a request by the Attorney General. Finally, appellant's office is limited in tenure. There is concededly no time limit on the appointment of a particular counsel. Nonetheless, the office of independent counsel is "temporary" in the sense that an independent counsel is appointed essentially to accomplish a single task, and when that task is over the office is terminated, either by the counsel herself or by action of the Special Division.

Unlike other prosecutors, appellant has no ongoing responsibilities that extend beyond the accomplishment of the mission that she was appointed for and authorized by the Special Division to undertake. In our view, these factors relating to the "ideas of tenure, duration . . . and duties" of the independent counsel are sufficient to establish that appellant is an "inferior" officer in the constitutional sense. . . .

This does not, however, end our inquiry under the Appointments Clause. Appellees argue that even if appellant is an "inferior" officer, the Clause does not empower Congress to place the power to appoint such an officer outside the Executive Branch. They contend that the Clause does not contemplate congressional authorization of "interbranch appointments," in which an officer of one branch is appointed by officers of another branch. The relevant language of the Appointments Clause is worth repeating. It reads: ". . . but the Congress may by Law vest the Appointment of such inferior Officers, as they think proper, in the President alone, in the courts of Law, or in the Heads of Departments." On its face, the language of this "excepting clause" admits of no limitation on interbranch appointments. Indeed, the inclusion of "as they think proper" seems clearly to give Congress significant discretion to determine whether it is "proper" to vest the appointment of, for example, executive officials in the "courts of Law." . . .

We also note that the history of the clause provides no support for appellees' position. Throughout most of the process of drafting the Constitution, the Convention concentrated on the problem of who should have the authority to appoint judges. At the suggestion of James Madison, the Convention adopted a proposal that the Senate should have this authority, and several attempts to transfer the appointment power to the president were rejected. The August 6, 1787, draft of the Constitution reported by the Committee of Detail retained Senate appointment of Supreme Court Judges, provided also for Senate appointment of ambassadors, and vested in the president the authority to "appoint officers in all cases not otherwise provided for by this Constitution." This scheme was maintained until September 4, when the Committee of Eleven reported its suggestions to the Convention. This Committee suggested that the Constitution be amended to state that the president "shall nominate and by and with the advice and consent of the Senate shall appoint ambassadors, and other public Ministers, Judges of the Supreme Court, and all other Officers of the [United States], whose appointments are not otherwise herein provided for." After the addition of "Consuls" to the list, the Committee's proposal was adopted, and was subsequently reported to the Convention by the Committee of Style. It was at this point, on September 15, that Gouverneur Morris moved to add the Excepting Clause to Art. II, § 2. The one comment made on this motion was by Madison, who felt that the Clause did not go far enough in that it did not allow Congress to vest appointment powers in "Superior Officers below Heads of Departments." The first vote on Morris's motion ended in tie. It was then put forward a second time, with the urging that "some such provision [was] too necessary, to be omitted." This time the proposal was adopted. As this discussion shows, there was little or no debate on the question of whether the Clause empowers Congress to provide for interbranch appointments, and there is nothing to suggest that the Framers intended to prevent Congress from having that power.

We do not mean to say that Congress' power to provide for interbranch appointments of "inferior officers" is unlimited. In addition to separation of powers concerns, which would arise if such provisions for appointment had the potential to impair the constitutional functions assigned to one of the branches, . . . Congress' decision to vest the appointment power in the courts would be improper if there was some "incongruity" between the functions normally performed by the courts and the performance of their duty to appoint. In this case, however, we do not think it impermissible for Congress to vest the power to appoint independent counsels in a specially created federal court. We thus disagree with the Court of Appeals' conclusion that there is an inherent incongruity about a court having the power to appoint prosecutorial officers. . . . Congress of course was concerned when it created the office of independent counsel with the conflicts of interest that could arise in situations when the Executive Branch is called upon to investigate its own high-ranking officers. If it were to remove the appointing authority from the Executive

Branch, the most logical place to put it was in the Judicial Branch. In the light of the Act's provision making the judges of the Special Division ineligible to participate in any matters relating to an independent counsel they have appointed, . . . we do not think that appointment of the independent counsels by the court runs afoul of the constitutional limitation on "incongruous" interbranch appointments.

Appellees next contend that the powers vested in the Special Division by the Act conflict with Article III of the Constitution. We have long recognized that by the express provision of Article III, the judicial power of the United States is limited to "Cases" and "Controversies." As a general rule, we have broadly stated that "executive or administrative duties of a nonjudicial nature may not be imposed on judges holding office under Art. III of the Constitution." The purpose of this limitation is to help ensure the independence of the Judicial Branch and to prevent the judiciary from encroaching into areas reserved for the other branches. With this in mind, we address in turn the various duties given to the Special Division by the Act.

Most importantly, the Act vests in the Special Division the power to choose who will serve as independent counsel and the power to define his or her jurisdiction. Clearly, once it is accepted that the Appointments Clause gives Congress the power to vest the appointment of officials such as the independent counsel in the "courts of Law," there can be no Article III objection to the Special Division's exercise of that power, as the power itself derives from the Appointments Clause, a source of authority for judicial action that is independent of Article III. . . .

We now turn to consider whether the Act is invalid under the constitutional principle of separation of powers. Two related issues must be addressed: The first is whether the provision of the Act restricting the Attorney General's power to remove the independent counsel to only those instances in which he can show "good cause," taken by itself, impermissibly interferes with the President's exercise of his constitutionally appointed functions. The second is whether, taken as a whole, the Act violates the separation of powers by reducing the President's ability to control the prosecutorial powers wielded by the independent counsel.

Two Terms ago we had occasion to consider whether it was consistent with the separation of powers for Congress to pass a statute that authorized a government official who is removable only by Congress to participate in what we found to be "executive powers." *Bowsher v. Synar* (1986). We held in *Bowsher* that "Congress cannot reserve for itself the power of removal of an officer charged with the execution of the laws except by impeachment." A primary antecedent for this ruling was our 1925 decision in *Myers v. United States* (1926). *Myers* had considered the propriety of a federal statute by which certain postmasters of the United States could be removed by the President only "by and with the advice and consent of the Senate." There too, Congress' attempt to involve itself in the removal of an executive official was found to be sufficient grounds to render the statute invalid. As we observed in *Bowsher*, the essence of the decision in *Myers* was the judgment that the Constitution prevents Congress from "draw[ing] to itself . . . the power to remove or the right to participate in the exercise of that power. To do this would be to go beyond the words and implications of the [Appointments Clause] and to infringe the constitutional principle of the separation of governmental powers."

Unlike both *Bowsher* and *Myers,* this case does not involve an attempt by Congress itself to gain a role in the removal of executive officials other than its established powers of impeachment and conviction. The Act instead puts the removal power squarely in the hands of the Executive Branch; an independent counsel may be removed from office, "only by the personal action of the Attorney General, and only for good cause." There is no requirement of congressional approval of the Attorney General's removal decision, though the decision is subject to judicial review. . . .

Considering for the moment the "good cause" removal provision in isolation from the other parts of the Act at issue in this case, we cannot say that the imposition of a "good cause" standard for removal by itself unduly trammels on executive authority. There is no real dispute that the functions performed by the independent counsel are "executive" in the sense that they are law enforcement functions that typically have been undertaken by officials within the Executive Branch. As we noted above, however, the independent counsel is an inferior officer under the Appointments Clause, with limited jurisdiction and tenure and lacking policymaking or significant administrative authority. Although the counsel exercises no small amount of discretion and judgment in deciding how to carry out her duties under the Act, we simply do not see how the President's need to control the exercise of that discretion is so central to the functioning of the Executive Branch as to require as a matter of constitutional law that the counsel be terminable at will by the President.

Nor do we think that the "good cause" removal provision at issue here impermissibly burdens the President's power to control or supervise the independent counsel, as an executive official, in the execution of her duties under the Act. This is not a case in which the power to remove an executive official has been completely stripped from the President, thus providing no means for the President to ensure the "faithful execution" of the laws. Rather, because the independent counsel may be terminated for "good cause," the Executive, through the Attorney General, retains ample authority to assure that the counsel is competently performing her statutory responsibilities in a manner that comports with the provisions of the Act. Although we need not decide in this case exactly what is encompassed within the term "good cause" under the Act, the legislative history of the removal provision also makes clear that the Attorney General may remove an independent counsel for "misconduct." Here, as with the provision of the Act conferring the appointment authority of the independent counsel on the special court, the congressional determination to limit the removal power of the Attorney General was essential, in the view of Congress, to establish the necessary independence of the office. We do not think that this limitation as it presently stands sufficiently deprives the President of control over the independent counsel to interfere impermissibly with his constitutional obligation to ensure the faithful execution of the laws.

The final question to be addressed is whether the Act, taken as a whole, violates the principle of separation of powers by unduly interfering with the role of the Executive Branch. Time and again we have reaffirmed the importance in our constitutional scheme of the separation of governmental powers into the three coordinate branches. As we stated in *Buckley v. Valeo* (1976), the system of separated powers and checks and balances established in the Constitution was regarded by the Framers as "a self-executing safeguard against the encroachment or aggrandizement of one branch at the expense of the other." We have not hesitated to invalidate provisions of law which violate this principle. On the other hand, we have never held that the Constitution requires that the three Branches of Government "operate with absolute independence." . . .

We observe first that this case does not involve an attempt by Congress to increase its own powers at the expense of the Executive Branch. Unlike some of our previous cases, most recently *Bowsher v. Synar,* this case simply does not pose a "dange[r] of congressional usurpation of Executive Branch functions." Indeed, with the exception of the power of impeachment—which applies to all officers of the United States—Congress retained for itself no powers of control or supervision over an independent counsel. The Act does empower certain members of Congress to request the Attorney General to apply for the appointment of an independent counsel, but the Attorney General has no duty to comply with the request, although he must respond within a certain time limit. Other than that, Congress' role under the Act is limited to receiving reports or other information and oversight of the independent counsel's activities, functions that we have recognized generally as being incidental to the legislative functions of Congress.

Similarly, we do not think that the Act works any *judicial* usurpation of properly executive functions. As should be apparent from our discussion of the Appointments Clause above, the power to appoint inferior officers such as independent counsels is not in itself an "executive" function in the constitutional sense, at least when Congress has exercised its power to vest the appointment of an inferior office in the "courts of Law." . . .

Finally, we do not think that the Act "impermissibly undermine[s]" the powers of the Executive Branch, or "disrupts the proper balance between the coordinate branches [by] prevent[ing] the Executive Branch from accomplishing its constitutionally assigned functions." It is undeniable that the Act reduces the amount of control or supervision that the Attorney General and, through him, the President exercises over the investigation and prosecution of a certain class of alleged criminal activity. The Attorney General is not allowed to appoint the individual of his choice; he does not determine the counsel's jurisdiction; and his power to remove a counsel is limited. Nonetheless, the Act does give the Attorney General several means of supervising or controlling the prosecutorial powers that may be wielded by an independent counsel. Most importantly, the Attorney General retains the power to remove the counsel for "good cause," a power that we have already concluded provides the Executive with substantial ability to ensure that the laws are "faithfully executed" by an independent counsel. No independent counsel may be appointed without a specific request by the Attorney General, and the Attorney General's decision not to request appointment if he finds "no reasonable grounds to believe that further investigation is warranted" is committed to his unreviewable discretion. The Act thus gives the Executive a degree of control over the power to initiate an investigation by the independent counsel. In addition, the jurisdiction of the independent counsel is defined with reference to the facts submitted by the Attorney General, and once a counsel is appointed, the Act requires that the counsel abide by Justice Department policy unless it is not "possible" to do so. Notwithstanding the fact that the counsel is to some degree "independent" and free from Executive supervision to a greater extent than other federal prosecutors, in our view these features of the Act give the Executive Branch sufficient control over the independent counsel to ensure that the President is able to perform his constitutionally assigned duties.

In sum, we conclude today that it does not violate the Appointments Clause for Congress to vest the appointment of independent counsels in the Special Division; that the powers exercised by the Special Division under the Act do not violate Article III; and that the Act does not violate the separation of powers principle by impermissibly interfering with the functions of the Executive Branch. The decision of the Court of Appeals is therefore

Reversed.

Dismissing Executive Officials

The president's need to have executive branch officials who support the administration's policy goals is only partially satisfied by the power to appoint. What also is required is the corollary—the discretionary right to remove administrative officials from office. This need may arise when a president's appointees do not carry out their duties the way the president wishes. It also applies when an official appointed by a previous administration will not voluntarily step aside to make way for a nominee of the new president's choosing.

Although an established removal procedure is oviously necessary, the Framers neglected to mention it in the Constitution. In the absence of constitutional guidelines, a lingering controversy has centered on whether administrative officials can be removed at the discretion of the president alone or whether Congress may play a role.

The argument supporting presidential discretion holds that the chief executive must be free to remove those subordinates who fail to meet the president's expectations or who are not loyal to the administration's policy objectives. It would be unreasonable to require the approval of Congress before such officials could be dismissed. Such a requirement might well paralyze the executive branch, particularly when the legislature and the presidency are under the control of different political parties.

The argument for legislative participation in the process holds that the Constitution anticipates Senate action. If the president can appoint major executive department officials only with senatorial approval, it is reasonable to infer that the chief executive can remove administrators only by going through the same process and obtaining the advice and consent of the Senate. This view was supported by Alexander Hamilton in *The Federalist Papers'* only reference to the removal powers. Hamilton flatly stated, ''The consent of that body [the Senate] would be necessary to displace as well as to appoint.''[3] Hamilton argued that if the president and the Senate agreed that an official should be removed the decision would be much better accepted than if the president acted alone. Furthermore, Hamilton asserted that a new president should be restrained from removing an experienced official who had conducted his duties satisfactorily just because the president preferred to have a different person in the position.

Historical practice generally has rejected Hamilton's position. From the very beginning, Congress allowed the chief executive to remove administrative officials without Senate consent. In the first Congress James Madison proposed that three executive departments be created: Foreign Affairs, Treasury, and War. The creation of the Foreign Affairs (later State) department received the most legislative attention. According to Madison's recommendation, the department was to have a secretary to be appointed by the president with the approval of the Senate who could be removed by the president alone. The House and the Senate held long comprehensive debates on the removal power at that time and passed legislation allowing the secretary of state to be removed at the president's discretion without Senate approval.

At times, however, the legislature has asserted a right to participate in the process. The most notable example occurred with the passage of the Tenure of Office Act in 1867. This statute was enacted to restrict the powers of Andrew Johnson, who became president following Lincoln's death in 1865. In the aftermath of the Civil War, the Radical Republicans dominated Congress and had little use for President Johnson, a Democrat from Tennessee. Congress did not want Johnson to be able to remove Lincoln's appointees. The Tenure of Office Act stipulated that the president could not remove high-ranking executive depart-

3. Alexander Hamilton, ''Federalist No. 77'' in *The Federalist Papers,* by Alexander Hamilton, James Madison, and John Jay (New York: New American Library, 1961) 459.

ment heads without first obtaining the approval of the Senate. Johnson blatantly defied the statute by dismissing Secretary of War Edwin M. Stanton in August 1867 and appointing Ulysses S. Grant as interim secretary. The Senate reacted by ordering Stanton reinstated. Grant left office and Stanton returned in January 1868. The next month Johnson fired Stanton again. President Johnson's failure to comply with the Tenure of Office Act constituted one of the grounds upon which the House based its Articles of Impeachment against him.

The Tenure of Office Act never had a judicial test. Once Johnson's term expired, the statute was weakened by amendment and then repealed in 1887. Consequently, as the nation entered the twentieth century there had yet to be an authoritative declaration of the constitutional parameters of the removal power, although some statutes remained on the books asserting a role for the Senate in the dismissal of administrative officials.

The Supreme Court finally faced this issue in 1926 when presented with an appeal from a fired postmaster. The Court's opinion was written by Chief Justice William Howard Taft, who had one of the nation's most spectacular résumés. Among his positions were solicitor general, governor of the Philippines, secretary of war, president of the United States, and chief justice of the Supreme Court. Given Taft's rich experience in the executive branch and the fact that he had not served in the legislature, we would expect, correctly, that he would support a broad interpretation of the president's removal powers and reject the notion that the Senate had the right to limit that discretion. His long, detailed opinion, combined with the dissenting opinions it provoked, filled 243 pages.

Myers v. United States

272 U.S. 52 (1926)

Vote: 6 (Butler, Sanford, Stone, Sutherland, Taft,
Van Devanter)
3 (Brandeis, Holmes, McReynolds)
Opinion of the Court: Taft
Dissenting opinions: Brandeis, Holmes, McReynolds

Prior to its replacement by the United States Postal Service in 1970, the post office department was considered a patronage agency. Postal officials, beginning with the postmaster general and continuing down to the local postmasters, were political appointees rewarded for loyal party service. In July 1917 President Woodrow Wilson, with the advice and consent of the Senate, appointed Frank Myers to be a first class postmaster in Portland, Oregon, for a four-year term. Wilson strongly believed that his right to remove individuals from appointed office was not to be shared with Congress. In fact, Wilson had engaged in some bitter fights with Congress over this point.

In January 1920 Wilson asked for Myers's resignation. When Myers ignored tradition and refused Wilson's request, the president ordered the postmaster general to fire him, an act that was carried out in February. Myers complained that his removal was illegal. The basis for his argument was a law passed by Congress in 1876 stipulating that "Postmasters of the first, second and third classes shall be appointed and may be removed by the President by and with the advice and consent of the Senate and shall hold their offices for four years unless sooner removed or suspended according to law." Because Wilson had not received the approval of the Senate for the dismissal, Myers claimed to have been unlawfully fired. He sued for his unpaid salary from the date of his removal to the expiration of his four-year term, a claim of $8,838.71. During the period under question Myers accepted no other employment, and the Senate confirmed no other

William Howard Taft

(1921–1930)

PUBLIC SERVICE was a tradition in the Taft family; William Howard Taft extended it to its limit during his lifetime. His grandfather, Peter Rawson Taft, was a judge on the probate and county courts in Windham County, Vermont; Alphonso Taft, William's father, served two terms on the Ohio Superior Court before he was named secretary of war in the last months of the Grant administration. He also briefly served President Ulysses S. Grant as attorney general, and later was ambassador to Austria-Hungary and Russia during the Arthur administration. William's brother, Charles Phelps Taft, R-Ohio, served a term in the U.S. House of Representatives, 1895–1897.

Born in Cincinnati September 15, 1857, Taft received an A.B. in 1878 from Yale University, where he was the salutatorian of his graduating class. He entered Cincinnati Law School and took a job as a law reporter for the *Cincinnati Commercial.* He continued to report for the newspaper through 1880, the year in which he received his LL.B. and was admitted to the bar.

On June 19, 1886, he married Helen Herron. They had one daughter and two sons, one of whom, Robert Alphonso Taft, R-Ohio, served in the U.S. Senate, 1939–1953. Taft's grandson, Robert Taft, Jr., R-Ohio, served in the House of Representatives, 1963–1965, 1967–1971, and the Senate, 1971–1976.

In 1881 Taft plunged into Republican politics and gave his support to a candidate for county prosecutor in Hamilton County, Ohio. After his candidate won, Taft was selected to be an assistant county prosecutor. He went back to private practice in 1883.

Taft was named to a two-year term as assistant county solicitor for Hamilton County in 1885 and, in 1887, when he was barely thirty years old, was appointed to the Ohio Superior Court.

He sat on the superior court bench until President Benjamin Harrison in 1890 named him U.S. solicitor general. In 1892, after Congress created additional judgeships for the federal circuit courts, Taft sought and received appointment to the Sixth Circuit.

Taft remained on the circuit court for eight years. He left reluctantly in 1900 when President William McKinley asked him to head a commission established to ensure the smooth transition from military to civilian government in the Philippines in the aftermath of the Spanish-American War. In 1901 he was made civilian governor of the Philippines, a position he held until President Theodore Roosevelt named him secretary of war to replace Elihu Root in 1904.

Once in the cabinet, Taft became one of Roosevelt's closest advisers; the president increasingly relied on Taft to handle important matters for the administration. As secretary of war Taft was in command of the Panama Canal project and made a goodwill tour of the site. He also was dispatched in 1906 to Cuba to investigate reports of revolutionary activity.

As Taft's prestige grew, so did his influence in the Republican party. With Roosevelt's backing he won the party's nomination for president and the subsequent election in 1908. He was sworn in as the twenty-ninth president of the United States March 4, 1909.

The presidency was a post that Taft did not particularly covet—he would have preferred a seat on the Supreme Court as chief justice—but he sought the presidency at the urging of his wife and Republican party regulars. His single term in office was not controversial. It saw the institution of the postal savings system and the Tariff Board, the intervention of American troops in the affairs of the Dominican Republic, the ratification of the Sixteenth Amendment to the

Constitution, and a continuation of the trustbusting begun under Theodore Roosevelt.

Taft also named six men to the Supreme Court, including a chief justice, Edward D. White. The others were Horace A. Lurton, Charles Evans Hughes (who resigned from the Court to run for president in 1916, lost, and was named chief justice in 1930 by President Herbert Hoover to replace Taft), Willis Van Devanter, Joseph R. Lamar, and Mahlon Pitney. When Taft was named chief justice in 1921 only two of his appointees, Van Devanter and Pitney, were still on the bench.

Soon after he was elected president, Taft began to fall out of favor with former president Roosevelt. The two men came to represent opposing sides of a division within the Republican party; when Taft was renominated in 1912, Roosevelt ran for president under the banner of his Bull Moose party and effectively splintered the Republican vote. After the election, which was won by Democrat Woodrow Wilson, Taft described Roosevelt as "the most dangerous man that we have had in the country since its origin."

After leaving the White House, Taft taught constitutional law at Yale University, served a year as president of the American Bar Association, wrote magazine articles and was a frequent participant on the lecture circuit. He was elected president of the League to Enforce Peace in 1915. In 1916 he and four other former presidents of the American Bar Association joined with current president Elihu Root in writing to the U.S. Senate to register their disapproval of President Wilson's nomination of Louis D. Brandeis to the Supreme Court. During this period Taft also continued discreetly to publicize his desire to be named to the Court, especially as chief justice.

Taft served as the joint chairman of the National War Labor Board, 1918–1919. An enthusiastic advocate of the League of Nations, he embarked on a fifteen-state tour in an attempt to rally support for it.

His greatest ambition was achieved when President Harding named him chief justice June 30, 1921, to replace Chief Justice White. The Senate confirmed him by voice vote the same day. Taft is the only person in U.S. history to hold both the presidency and the chief justiceship. He retired from the Court February 3, 1930, and died a month later on March 8 in Washington, D.C.

Source: Elder Witt, *Guide to the U.S. Supreme Court*, 2d ed. (Washington, D.C.: Congressional Quarterly, 1990), 854–855.

nominee for the position. After Myers died, his executor continued the legal action on behalf of his estate. The court of claims rejected Myers's suit, and an appeal was made to the Supreme Court. After a detailed discussion of the events surrounding Madison's proposals during the First Congress (the decision of 1789) and the controversy over the Tenure of Office Act, Chief Justice Taft explained the Court's decision in favor of presidential discretion in exercising the removal power.

Chief Justice Taft delivered the opinion of the Court:

This case presents the question whether under the Constitution the President has the exclusive power of removing executive officers of the United States whom he has appointed by and with the advice and consent of the Senate. . . .

A veto by the Senate—a part of the legislative branch of the Government—upon removals is a much greater limitation upon the executive branch and a much more serious blending of the legislative with the executive than a rejection of a proposed appointment. It is not to be implied. The rejection of a nominee of the President for a particular office does not greatly embarrass him in the conscientious discharge of his high duties in the selection of those who are to aid him, because the President usually has an ample field from which to select for office, according to his preference, competent and capable men. The Senate has full power to reject newly proposed appointees whenever the President shall remove the incumbents. Such a check enables the Senate to prevent the filling of offices with bad or incompetent men or with those against whom there is tenable objection.

The power to prevent the removal of an officer who has served under the President is different from the authority to consent to or reject his appointment. When a nomination is made, it may be presumed that the Senate is, or may become, as well advised as to the fitness of the nominee as the President, but in the nature of things the defects in ability or intelligence or loyalty in the administration of the laws of one who has served as an officer under the President, are facts as to which the President, or his trusted subordinates, must be better informed than the Senate, and the power to remove him may, therefore, be regarded as confined, for very sound and practical reasons, to the governmental authority which has administrative control. The power of removal is incident to the power of appointment, not to the power of advising and consenting to appointment, and when the grant of the executive power is enforced by the express mandate to take care that the laws be faithfully executed, it emphasizes the necessity for including within the executive power as conferred the exclusive power of removal. . . .

The constitutional construction that excludes Congress from legislative power to provide for the removal of superior officers finds support in the second section of Article II. By it the appointment of all officers, whether superior or inferior, by the President is declared to be subject to the advice and consent of the Senate. In the absence of any specific provision to the contrary, the power of appointment to executive office carries with it, as a necessary incident, the power of removal. Whether the Senate must concur in the removal is aside from the point we now are considering. That point is, that by the specific constitutional provision for appointment of executive officers with its necessary incident of removal, the power of appointment and removal is clearly provided for by the Constitution, and the legislative power of Congress in respect to both is excluded save by the specific exception as to inferior offices. . . .

A reference of the whole power of removal to general legislation by Congress is quite out of keeping with the plan of government devised by the framers of the Constitution. It could never have been intended to leave to Congress unlimited discretion to vary fundamentally the operation of the great independent executive branch of government and thus most seriously to weaken it. It would be a delegation by the Convention to Congress of the function of defining the primary boundaries of another of the three great divisions of government. The inclusion of removals of executive officers in the executive power vested in the President by Article II, according to its usual definition, and the implication of his power of removal of such officers from the provision of section 2 expressly recognizing in him the power of their appointment, are a much

more natural and appropriate source of the removing power.

It is reasonable to suppose also that, had it been intended to give to Congress power to regulate or control removals in the manner suggested, it would have been included among the specifically enumerated legislative powers in Article I, or in the specified limitations on the executive power in Article II. The difference between the grant of legislative power under Article I to Congress, which is limited to powers therein enumerated, and the more general grant of the executive power to the President under Article II, is significant. The fact that the executive power is given in general terms strengthened by specific terms where emphasis is appropriate, and limited by direct expressions where limitation is needed and that no express limit is placed on the power of removal by the executive, is a convincing indication that none was intended. . . .

Made responsible under the Constitution for the effective enforcement of the law, the President needs as an indispensable aid to meet it the disciplinary influence upon those who act under him of a reserve power of removal. But it is contended that executive officers appointed by the President with the consent of the Senate are bound by the statutory law and are not his servants to do his will, and that his obligation to care for the faithful execution of the laws does not authorize him to treat them as such. The degree of guidance in the discharge of their duties that the President may exercise over executive officers varies with the character of their service as prescribed in the law under which they act. The highest and most important duties which his subordinates perform are those in which they act for him. In such cases they are exercising not their own but his discretion. This field is a very large one. It is sometimes described as political. Each head of a department is and must be the President's *alter ego* in the matters of that department where the President is required by law to exercise authority. . . .

In all such cases, the discretion to be exercised is that of the President in determining the national public interest and in directing the action to be taken by his executive subordinates to protect it. In this field his cabinet officers must do his will. He must place in each member of his official family, and his chief executive subordinates, implicit faith. The moment that he loses confidence in the intelligence, ability, judgment or loyalty of any one of them, he must have the power to remove him without delay. To require him to file charges and submit them to the consideration of the Senate might make impossible that unity and co-ordination in executive administration essential to effective action.

The duties of the heads of departments and bureaus in which the discretion of the President is exercised and which we have described, are the most important in the whole field of executive action of the Government. There is nothing in the Constitution which permits a distinction between the removal of the head of a department or a bureau, when he discharges a political duty of the President or exercises his discretion, and the removal of executive officers engaged in the discharge of their other normal duties. The imperative reasons requiring an unrestricted power to remove the most important of his subordinates in their most important duties must, therefore, control the interpretation of the Constitution as to all appointed by him.

But this is not to say that there are not strong reasons why the President should have a like power to remove his appointees charged with other duties than those above described. The ordinary duties of officers prescribed by statute come under the general administrative control of the President by virtue of the general grant to him of the executive power, and he may properly supervise and guide their construction of the statutes under which they act in order to secure that unitary and uniform execution of the laws which Article II of the Constitution evidently contemplated in vesting general executive power in the President alone. Laws are often passed with specific provision for the adoption of regulations by a department or bureau head to make the law workable and effective. The ability and judgment manifested by the official thus empowered, as well as his energy and stimulation of his subordinates, are subjects which the President must consider and supervise in his administrative control. Finding such officers to be negligent and inefficient, the President should have the power to remove them. Of course there may be duties so peculiarly and specifically committed to the discretion of a particular officer

as to raise a question whether the President may overrule or revise the officer's interpretation of his statutory duty in a particular instance. Then there may be duties of a quasi-judicial character imposed on executive officers and members of executive tribunals whose decisions after hearing affect interests of individuals, the discharge of which the President can not in a particular case properly influence or control. But even in such a case he may consider the decision after its rendition as a reason for removing the officer, on the ground that the discretion regularly entrusted to that officer by statute has not been on the whole intelligently or wisely exercised. Otherwise he does not discharge his own constitutional duty of seeing that the laws be faithfully executed.

We have devoted much space to this discussion and decision of the question of the Presidential power of removal in the First Congress, not because a Congressional conclusion on a constitutional issue is conclusive, but, first, because of our agreement with the reasons upon which it was avowedly based; second, because this was the decision of the First Congress, on a question of primary importance in the organization of the Government, made within two years after the Constitutional Convention and within a much shorter time after its ratification; and, third, because that Congress numbered among its leaders those who had been members of the Convention. . . .

We come now to consider an argument advanced and strongly pressed on behalf of the complainant, that this case concerns only the removal of a postmaster; that a postmaster is an inferior officer; that such an office was not included within the legislative decision of 1789, which related only to superior officers to be appointed by the President by and with the advice and consent of the Senate. . . .

The power to remove inferior executive officers, like that to remove superior executive officers, is an incident of the power to appoint them, and is in its nature an executive power. The authority of Congress given by the excepting clause to vest the appointment of such inferior officers in the heads of departments carries with it authority incidentally to invest the heads of departments with power to remove. It has been the practice of Congress to do so and this Court has recognized that power. . . . But the Court never has held, nor reasonably could hold, although it is argued to the contrary on behalf of the appellant, that the excepting clause enables Congress to draw to itself, or to either branch of it, the power to remove or the right to participate in the exercise of that power. To do this would be to go beyond the words and implications of that clause and to infringe the constitutional principle of the separation of governmental powers.

Assuming then the power of Congress to regulate removals as incidental to the exercise of its constitutional power to vest appointments of inferior officers in the heads of departments, certainly so long as Congress does not exercise that power, the power of removal must remain where the Constitution places it, with the President, as part of the executive power, in accordance with the legislative decision of 1789 which we have been considering. . . .

Our conclusion on the merits, sustained by the arguments before stated, is that Article II grants to the President the executive power of Government, i.e., the general administrative control of those executing the laws, including the power of appointment and removal of executive officers—a conclusion confirmed by his obligation to take care that the laws be faithfully executed; that Article II excludes the exercise of legislative power by Congress to provide for appointments and removals, except only as granted therein to Congress in the matter of inferior offices; that Congress is only given power to provide for appointments and removals of inferior officers after it has vested, and on condition that it does vest, their appointment in other authority than the President with the Senate's consent; that the provisions of the second section of Article II, which blend action by the legislative branch, or by part of it, in the work of the executive, are limitations to be strictly construed and not to be extended by implication; that the President's power of removal is further established as an incident to his specifically enumerated function of appointment by and with the advice of the Senate, but that such incident does not by implication extend to removals the Senate's power of checking appointments; and finally that to hold otherwise would make it impossible for the President, in case of political or other differences with the Senate or Congress, to take care that the laws be faithfully executed. . . .

When, on the merits, we find our conclusion strongly favoring the view which prevailed in the First Congress, we have no hesitation in holding that conclusion to be correct; and it therefore follows that the Tenure of Office Act of 1867, in so far as it attempted to prevent the President from removing executive officers who had been appointed by him by and with the advice and consent of the Senate, was invalid, and that subsequent legislation of the same effect was equally so.

For the reasons given, we must therefore hold that the provision of the law of 1876, by which the unrestricted power of removal of first class postmasters is denied to the President, is in violation of the Constitution, and invalid. This leads to an affirmance of the judgment of the Court of Claims.

Nine years later the president's discretionary power to remove administrators was challenged again. This time the stakes were somewhat greater because the office involved had much more policy-making power than did the local postmaster position at issue in *Myers*. Here the fired officer was not a member of the regular executive branch departments, but a member of the Federal Trade Commission, an independent regulatory board. Did these differences prompt the justices to rule differently on the president's removal power, or did the *Myers* precedent apply here as well?

Humphrey's Executor v. United States

295 U.S. 602 (1935)

*Vote: 9 (Brandeis, Butler, Cardozo, Hughes,
        McReynolds, Roberts, Stone, Sutherland,
        Van Devanter)*

0

Opinion of the Court: Sutherland

In 1914 Congress created the Federal Trade Commission as an independent regulatory agency to enforce antitrust laws and prevent unfair methods of commercial competition. The statute called for the FTC to be staffed by five commissioners appointed by the president and confirmed by the Senate. Not more than three members could be of the same political party, and members were to serve staggered seven-year terms. These provisions were intended to increase the independence of the board and prevent its domination by the incumbent chief executive. The president could remove commissioners, but only for inefficiency, neglect of duty, or malfeasance in office. The commission had the powers of rule making, investigation, and enforcement.

In 1931 FTC commissioner William E. Humphrey was named by President Herbert Hoover to a second seven-year term, which would expire in 1938. Following his election in 1932, Franklin Roosevelt made every effort to staff the executive branch with people who were committed to his New Deal programs for combating the depression. The president wrote to Humphrey July 25, 1933, asking him to resign from his post on the grounds that "the aims and purposes of the Administration with respect to the work of the Commission can be carried out most effectively with personnel of my own selection." When Humphrey did not reply, the president wrote to him August 31: "You will, I know, realize that I do not feel that your mind and my mind go along together on either the policies or the administering of the Federal Trade Commission, and, frankly, I think it best for the people of this country that I

should have a full confidence." Humphrey then told the president that he would not resign. In his third letter, dated October 7, Roosevelt wrote to Humphrey: "Effective as of this date you are hereby removed from the office of Commissioner of the Federal Trade Commission." The president did not rest his action on any of the statutory grounds for removing a commissioner; rather, he fired Humphrey because he did not approve of his positions on policy matters related to the jurisdiction of the FTC. Humphrey claimed he had been illegally removed.

Humphrey died in February 1934. His executor filed suit in the court of claims on behalf of Humphrey's estate to recover the salary lost between the date of his dismissal and his death. The administration argued on the basis of *Myers* that the president was free to remove executive officials at will. Humphrey's executor claimed that the law establishing the FTC placed constitutionally valid restraints on the president's discretion to remove officeholders. The court of claims requested the Supreme Court to answer two questions: Did the Federal Trade Commission Act restrict the president's removal power to those grounds cited in the statute? And, if so, is such a restriction constitutional?

Justice George Sutherland delivered the opinion of the Court:

First. The question first to be considered is whether, by the provisions of § 1 of the Federal Trade Commission Act already quoted, the President's power is limited to removal for the specific causes enumerated therein. . . .

The commission is to be non-partisan; and it must, from the very nature of its duties, act with entire impartiality. It is charged with the enforcement of no policy except the policy of the law. Its duties are neither political nor executive, but predominantly quasi-judicial and quasi-legislative. Like the Interstate Commerce Commission, its members are called upon to exercise the trained judgment of a body of experts "appointed by law and informed by experience."

The legislative reports in both houses of Congress clearly reflect the view that a fixed term was necessary to the effective and fair administration of the law. In the report to the Senate the Senate Committee on Interstate Commerce, in support of the bill which afterwards became the act in question, after referring to the provision fixing the term of office at seven years, so arranged that the membership would not be subject to complete change at any one time. . . .

The debates in both houses demonstrate that the prevailing view was that the commission was not to be "subject to anybody in the government but . . . only to the people of the United States"; free from "political domination or control" or the "probability or possibility of such a thing"; to be "separate and apart from any existing department of the government—not subject to the orders of the President."

More to the same effect appears in the debates, which were long and thorough and contain nothing to the contrary. While the general rule precludes the use of these debates to explain the meaning of the words of the statute, they may be considered as reflecting light upon its general purposes and the evils which it sought to remedy.

Thus, the language of the act, the legislative reports, and the general purposes of the legislation as reflected by the debates, all combine to demonstrate the Congressional intent to create a body of experts who shall gain experience by length of service—a body which shall be independent of executive authority, *except in its selection,* and free to exercise its judgment without the leave or hindrance of any other official or department of the government. To the accomplishment of these purposes, it is clear that Congress was of opinion that length and certainty of tenure would vitally contribute. And to hold that, nevertheless, the members of the commission continue in office at the mere will of the President, might be to thwart, in large measure, the very ends which Congress sought to realize by definitely fixing the term of office.

We conclude that the intent of the act is to limit the executive power of removal to the causes enumerated, the existence of none of which is claimed here; and we pass to the second question.

Second. To support its contention that the removal provision of § 1, as we have just construed it, is an unconstitutional interference with the executive power of the President, the government's chief reliance is *Myers* v. *United States.* That case has been so recently decided, and the prevailing and dissenting opinions so fully review the general subject of the power of executive removal, that further discussion would add little to the value of the wealth of material there collected. These opinions examine at length the historical, legislative and judicial data bearing upon the question, beginning with what is called "the decision of 1789" in the first Congress and coming down almost to the day when the opinions were delivered. . . . Nevertheless, the narrow point actually decided was only that the President had power to remove a postmaster of the first class, without the advice and consent of the Senate as required by act of Congress. In the course of the opinion of the court, expressions occur which tend to sustain the government's contention, but these are beyond the point involved and, therefore, do not come within the rule of *stare decisis.* In so far as they are out of harmony with the views here set forth, these expressions are disapproved. . . .

The office of a postmaster is so essentially unlike the office now involved that the decision in the *Myers* case cannot be accepted as controlling our decision here. A postmaster is an executive officer restricted to the performance of executive functions. He is charged with no duty at all related to either the legislative or judicial power. The actual decision in the *Myers* case finds support in the theory that such an officer is merely one of the units in the executive department and, hence, inherently subject to the exclusive and illimitable power of removal by the Chief Executive, whose subordinate and aid he is. Putting aside *dicta,* which may be followed if sufficiently persuasive but which are not controlling, the necessary reach of the decision goes far enough to include all purely executive officers. It goes no farther;—much less does it include an officer who occupies no place in the executive department and who exercises no part of the executive power vested by the Constitution in the President.

The Federal Trade Commission is an administrative body created by Congress to carry into effect legislative policies embodied in the statute in accordance with the legislative standard therein prescribed, and to perform other specified duties as a legislative or as a judicial aid. Such a body cannot in any proper sense be characterized as an arm or an eye of the executive. Its duties are performed without executive leave and, in the contemplation of the statute, must be free from executive control. In administering the provisions of the statute in respect of "unfair methods of competition"—that is to say in filling in and administering the details embodied by that general standard—the commission acts in part quasi-legislatively and in part quasi-judicially. In making investigations and reports thereon for the information of Congress under § 6, in aid of the legislative power, it acts as a legislative agency. Under § 7, which authorizes the commission to act as a master in chancery under rules prescribed by the court, it acts as an agency of the judiciary. To the extent that it exercises any executive function—as distinguished from executive power in the constitutional sense—it does so in the discharge and effectuation of its quasi-legislative or quasi-judicial powers, or as an agency of the legislative or judicial departments of the government. . . .

We think it plain under the Constitution that illimitable power of removal is not possessed by the President in respect of officers of the character of those just named. The authority of Congress, in creating quasi-legislative or quasi-judicial agencies, to require them to act in discharge of their duties independently of executive control cannot well be doubted; and that authority includes, as an appropriate incident, power to fix the period during which they shall continue in office, and to forbid their removal except for cause in the meantime. For it is quite evident that one who holds his office only during the pleasure of another, cannot be depended upon to maintain an attitude of independence against the latter's will.

The fundamental necessity of maintaining each of the three general departments of government entirely free from the control or coercive influence, direct or indirect, of either of the others, has often been stressed and is hardly open to serious question. So much is implied in the very fact of the separation of the powers of these departments by the Constitution; and in the rule which recognizes their essential co-equality. The sound application of a principle that makes one master in his own house precludes him from imposing his control in the house of another who is master there. . . .

The power of removal here claimed for the President falls within this principle, since its coercive influence threatens the independence of a commission, which is not only wholly disconnected from the executive department, but which, as already fully appears, was created by Congress as a means of carrying into operation legislative and judicial powers, and as an agency of the legislative and judicial departments. . . .

The result of what we now have said is this: Whether the power of the President to remove an officer shall prevail over the authority of Congress to condition the power by fixing a definite term and precluding a removal except for cause, will depend upon the character of the office; the *Myers* decision, affirming the power of the President alone to make the removal, is confined to purely executive officers; and as to officers of the kind here under consideration, we hold that no removal can be made during the prescribed term for which the officer is appointed, except for one or more of the causes named in the applicable statute.

To the extent that, between the decision in the *Myers* case, which sustains the unrestrictable power of the President to remove purely executive officers, and our present decision that such power does not extend to an office such as that here involved, there shall remain a field of doubt, we leave such cases as may fall within it for future consideration and determination as they may arise.

In *Humphrey's Executor* the Court distinguished between officials who exercise purely executive powers and those who carry out quasi-legislative and quasi-judicial functions. The former serve at the pleasure of the president and may be removed at his discretion. The latter may be removed only with procedures consistent with statutory conditions enacted by Congress.

This classification scheme was reaffirmed in *Wiener v. United States* (1958). The case involved a member of the War Claims Commission, a body established by Congress in 1948 to receive and adjudicate claims for compensating certain parties who suffered damages at the hands of the enemy in World War II. The statute created a three-member commission appointed by the president and confirmed by the Senate. The commission was scheduled to go out of existence two years after the deadline for filing claims, but, after some legislative extensions, the expiration date was changed to 1954. The statute contained no provisions for terms of office or procedures for removal.

Myron Wiener was appointed to the commission by President Harry S. Truman in 1950. Dwight Eisenhower was elected in 1952, and he wanted to replace the commission members with Republicans; he requested the resignations of the incumbents. Eisenhower wrote to Wiener, ''I regard it as in the national interest to complete the administration of the War Claims Act of 1948, as amended, with personnel of my own selection.'' When the incumbents refused to resign, Eisenhower ordered Wiener and the others dismissed and appointed their replacements. The Eisenhower appointees served in office as recess appointments. The Senate had not yet confirmed them when the commission ceased to exist. Wiener sued for the salary denied him from the date of his removal to the expiration of the commission. The court of claims ruled in favor of the government, and Wiener appealed to the Supreme Court.

Justice Felix Frankfurter, writing for a unanimous bench, reversed. The justices concluded that Wiener had been fired illegally. The war claims commissioners exercised quasi-judicial functions, and therefore the position was governed by the decision in *Humphrey's Executor* rather than *Myers*. Because Wiener did not exercise purely executive powers, Eisenhower had no power under the Constitution or the statute creating the commission to remove him. The *Wiener* decision is important because, by reaffirming *Humphrey's Executor*, it brought an authoritative

end to questions regarding the extent of the president's power to remove officeholders at his discretion alone.

The Power to Pardon

Executive power historically has included the authority to reduce or rescind criminal punishments in individual cases. The executive stands as the last source of mercy, capable of sparing a person when extraordinary circumstances warrant such action. This power was exercised by monarchs in Europe long before the creation of the United States, so it was not surprising that the Constitutional Convention also gave it to the president. The wording of the Pardon Clause is straightforward: the president ''shall have Power to grant Reprieves and Pardons for Offenses against the United States, except in Cases of Impeachment.''

A pardon erases all penalties and other legal effects of a criminal conviction. It is, as described by Chief Justice John Marshall, an act of grace. A person receiving a complete pardon is released from serving any remaining sentence and has full civil rights restored. Legally, it is as if the individual had never committed the crime.[4] A reprieve, in contrast, is a presidential act that merely postpones the serving of a criminal penalty.

There are only a few limitations on the president's power to grant pardons and reprieves. The words of Article II restrict the president's authority to crimes against the United States, which means that the president may pardon only individuals charged with federal offenses, not those in violation of state criminal laws. The governors of the various states have similar pardoning or clemency authority. Article II also prohibits the use of the pardoning power to nullify the effects of impeachment. And finally, the president may not

4. See *Ex parte Garland*, 71 U.S. 333 (1867).

impose a pardon on someone who refuses to accept it.[5]

Aside from these limitations, the president is free to exercise the pardoning authority with full discretion, and some presidents have been quite generous in granting pardons. A pardon may completely void all criminal penalties for a crime or eliminate only a portion of the sentence. The president even may place conditions on a pardon. For instance, in 1960 President Eisenhower spared army master sergeant Maurice Schick, a convicted murderer, from the death penalty on the condition that he be imprisoned for life without the possibility of parole.[6] A president may pardon individuals before or after they are tried for an offense or even before the filing of formal crimi-

5. See *United States v. Wilson*, 7 Pet. 150 (1833); *Burdick v. United States*, 236 U.S. 79 (1915). In 1927, however, the Court held that acceptance was not required when the president commuted a death sentence to life in prison (*Biddle v. Perovich*, 274 U.S. 480).
6. See *Schick v. Reed*, 419 U.S. 256 (1974).

nal charges. Pardons may be granted to a single person or an entire class of individuals. For example, in 1795 George Washington granted amnesty to those who had participated in the Whiskey Rebellion, and in 1977 Jimmy Carter pardoned all Vietnam War draft evaders, an action applying to an estimated 100,000 men.

For the most part, the Supreme Court has granted the chief executive great leeway in the exercise of the pardon power. *Ex parte Grossman* (1925) provides an example. The issue in this case was whether the president's pardon power extended to criminal contempt penalties imposed by a federal judge. Chief Justice Taft wrote the opinion of the Court. Consistent with his philosophy favoring executive power that we saw in *Myers v. United States*, the chief justice expressed strong support for a broad interpretation of the pardoning authority. In *Grossman* note Taft's use of history as a means of interpreting the Constitution.

Ex parte Grossman

267 U.S. 87 (1925)

Vote: 8 (Brandeis, Butler, Holmes, McReynolds, Sanford, Sutherland, Taft, Van Devanter)

0

Opinion of the Court: Taft

On November 24, 1920, the United States took legal action against Philip Grossman in the federal court for the northern district of Illinois. He was charged with selling liquor at his place of business in violation of the National Prohibition Act. Government attorneys requested that the court issue an injunction prohibiting Grossman from any further violations, and two days later a judge issued the injunction. On January 11, 1921, the government filed charges against Grossman for violating the judge's order, claiming that he had continued to sell alcoholic beverages at his estab-

lishment. The district court tried Grossman and found him guilty of criminal contempt of court for disobeying the order. The judged sentenced him to one year in prison and a fine of $1,000, and the sentence was upheld by the court of appeals.

In December 1923 President Calvin Coolidge issued a pardon in which he reduced Grossman's sentence to payment of the fine. Grossman accepted the pardon, paid the fine, and was released from prison. The district judge, however, refused to acknowledge the pardon on the grounds that the president had no authority to commute a sentence for criminal contempt of court. He ordered Grossman to serve the remainder of his sentence. Grossman objected and filed a habeas corpus action against prison superintendent Ritchie Graham demanding to be released.

Chief Justice Taft delivered the opinion of the Court:

The argument for the respondent is that the President's power extends only to offenses against the United States and a contempt of Court is not such an offense, that offenses against the United States are not common law offenses but can only be created by legislative act, that the President's pardoning power is more limited than that of the King of England at common law, which was a broad prerogative and included contempts against his courts chiefly because the judges thereof were his agents and acted in his name; that the context of the Constitution shows that the word "offences" is used in that instrument only to include crimes and misdemeanors triable by jury and not contempts of the dignity and authority of the federal courts, and that to construe the pardon clause to include contempts of court would be to violate the fundamental principle of the Constitution in the division of powers between the Legislative, Executive and Judicial branches, and to take from the federal courts their independence and the essential means of protecting their dignity and authority.

The language of the Constitution cannot be interpreted safely except by reference to the common law and to British institutions as they were when the instrument was framed and adopted. The statesmen and lawyers of the Convention who submitted it to the ratification of the Conventions of the thirteen States, were born and brought up in the atmosphere of the common law, and thought and spoke in its vocabulary. They were familiar with other forms of government, recent and ancient, and indicated in their discussions earnest study and consideration of many of them, but when they came to put their conclusions into the form of fundamental law in a compact draft, they expressed them in terms of the common law, confident that they could be shortly and easily understood. . . .

The King of England before our Revolution, in the exercise of his prerogative, had always exercised the power to pardon contempts of court, just as he did ordinary crimes and misdemeanors and as he has done to the present day. In the mind of a common law lawyer of the eighteenth century the word pardon included within its scope the ending by the King's grace of the punishment of such derelictions, whether it was im-

posed by the court without a jury or upon indictment, for both forms of trial for contempts were had. . . .

Nor is there any substance in the contention that there is any substantial difference in this matter between the executive power of pardon in our Government and the King's prerogative. The courts of Great Britain were called the King's Courts, as indeed they were; but for years before our Constitution they were as independent of the King's interference as they are today. The extent of the King's pardon was clearly circumscribed by law and the British Constitution, as the cases cited above show. The framers of our Constitution had in mind no necessity for curtailing this feature of the King's prerogative in transplanting it into the American governmental structures, save by excepting cases of impeachment; and even in that regard, as already pointed out, the common law forbade the pleading a pardon in bar to an impeachment. The suggestion that the President's power of pardon should be regarded as necessarily less than that of the King was pressed upon this Court . . . in *Ex parte William Wells,* but it did not prevail with the majority. . . .

Nothing in the ordinary meaning of the words "offences against the United States" excludes criminal contempts. That which violates the dignity and authority of federal courts such as an intentional effort to defeat their decrees justifying punishment violates a law of the United States, and so must be an offense against the United States. Moreover, this Court has held that the general statute of limitation which forbids prosecutions "for any offense unless instituted within three years next after such offense shall have been committed," applies to criminal contempts. . . .

[C]riminal contempts of a federal court have been pardoned for eighty-five years. In that time the power has been exercised twenty-seven times. . . .

Executive clemency exists to afford relief from undue harshness or evident mistake in the operation or enforcement of the criminal law. The administration of justice by the courts is not necessarily always wise or certainly considerate of circumstances which may properly mitigate guilt. To afford a remedy, it has always been thought essential in popular governments, as well as in monarchies, to vest in some other authority than the courts power to ameliorate or avoid particular criminal judgments. It is a check entrusted to the executive for special cases. To exercise it to the extent of destroying the deterrent effect of judicial punishment would be to pervert it; but whoever is to make it useful must have full discretion to exercise it. Our Constitution confers this discretion on the highest officer in the nation in confidence that he will not abuse it. An abuse in pardoning contempts would certainly embarrass courts, but it is questionable how much more it would lessen their effectiveness than a wholesale pardon of other offenses. If we could conjure up in our minds a President willing to paralyze courts by pardoning all criminal contempts, why not a President ordering a general jail delivery? A pardon can only be granted for a contempt fully completed. Neither in this country nor in England can it interfere with the use of coercive measures to enforce a suitor's right. The detrimental effect of excessive pardons of completed contempts would be in the loss of the deterrent influence upon future contempts. It is of the same character as that of the excessive pardons of other offenses. The difference does not justify our reading criminal contempts out of the pardon clause by departing from its ordinary meaning confirmed by its common law origin and long years of practice and acquiescence.

If it be said that the President, by successive pardons of constantly recurring contempts in particular litigation, might deprive a court of power to enforce its orders in a recalcitrant neighborhood, it is enough to observe that such a course is so improbable as to furnish but little basis for argument. Exceptional cases like this, if to be imagined at all, would suggest a resort to impeachment rather than to a narrow and strained construction of the general powers of the President.

The power of a court to protect itself and its usefulness by punishing contemnors is of course necessary, but it is one exercised without the restraining influence of a jury and without many of the guaranties which the bill of rights offers to protect the individual against unjust conviction. Is it unreasonable to provide for the possibility that the personal element may sometimes enter into a summary judgment pronounced by a judge who thinks his authority is flouted or denied? May it not be fairly said that in order to avoid possible mistake, undue prejudice or needless severity, the chance of pardon should exist at least as much in favor of a person convicted by a judge without a jury as in favor of one convicted in a jury trial? The pardoning by the President of criminal contempts has been practiced more than three-quarters of a century, and no abuses during all that time developed sufficiently to invoke a test in the federal courts of its validity.

It goes without saying that nowhere is there a more earnest will to maintain the independence of federal courts and the preservation of every legitimate safeguard of their effectiveness afforded by the Constitution than in this Court. But the qualified independence which they fortunately enjoy is not likely to be permanently strengthened by ignoring precedent and practice and minimizing the importance of the coordinating checks and balances of the Constitution.

The rule is made absolute and the petitioner is discharged.

Undoubtedly, the most controversial exercise of the power was Gerald Ford's pardon of former president Nixon in 1974. By resigning, Nixon kept all of the benefits the nation provides its former chief executives, but the resignation did not make him immune from a trial for any crimes related to Watergate. The pardon covered any crimes Nixon may have committed during his entire tenure as chief executive, from January 20, 1969, through August 9, 1974. It was an extraordinary act: not only was Nixon the first president to be pardoned for possible wrongdoing, but the pardon was a blanket one, covering almost six years and not restricted to any specific crimes or incidents. Furthermore, the pardon came before any formal criminal charges were brought against Nixon. Ford's stated intent was to begin to heal the nation by putting Watergate to rest.

Many people were appalled at the pardon, believing that if Nixon committed criminal acts he should be put on trial like any other citizen. They thought it was necessary for the former president to stand trial because his alleged wrongdoing compromised the very foundation of the Ameri-

Nixon Pardon Proclamation

Following is the text of the proclamation by which President Gerald R. Ford, September 8, 1974, pardoned former president Richard Nixon:

Richard Nixon became the thirty-seventh President of the United States on January 20, 1969, and was re-elected in 1972 for a second term by the electors of forty-nine of the fifty states. His term in office continued until his resignation on August 9, 1974.

Pursuant to resolutions of the House of Representatives, its Committee on the Judiciary conducted an inquiry and investigation on the impeachment of the President extending over more than eight months. The hearings of the committee and its deliberations, which received wide national publicity over television, radio, and in printed media, resulted in votes adverse to Richard Nixon on recommended articles of impeachment.

As a result of certain acts or omissions occurring before his resignation from the office of President, Richard Nixon has become liable to possible indictment and trial for offenses against the United States. Whether or not he shall be so prosecuted depends on findings of the appropriate grand jury and on the discretion of the authorized prosecutor. Should an indictment ensue, the accused shall then be entitled to a fair trial by an impartial jury, as guaranteed to every individual by the Constitution.

It is believed that a trial of Richard Nixon, if it became necessary, could not fairly begin until a year or more has elapsed. In the meantime, the tranquility to which this nation has been restored by the events of recent weeks could be irreparably lost by the prospects of bringing to trial a former President of the United States. The prospects of such trial will cause prolonged and divisive debate over the propriety of exposing to further punishment and degradation a man who has already paid the unprecedented penalty of relinquishing the highest elective office in the United States.

Now, therefore, I, Gerald R. Ford, President of the United States, pursuant to the pardon power conferred upon me by Article II, Section 2, of the Constitution, have granted and by these presents do grant a full, free, and absolute pardon unto Richard Nixon for all offenses against the United States which he, Richard Nixon, has committed or may have committed or taken part in during the period from January 20, 1969, through August 9, 1974.

In witness whereof, I have hereunto set my hand this 8th day of September in the year of Our Lord Nineteen Hundred Seventy-Four, and of the Independence of the United States of America the 199th.

---

can government and violated the sacred trust of the people. Ford's granting of this blanket protection to Nixon was widely criticized, and some analysts cite it as one reason why Ford lost the 1976 election to Carter.

Given the Supreme Court's interpretations of the pardon power, there was little doubt that Ford was acting constitutionally. Few legal scholars thought a court challenge had any chance of success. Prevailing legal opinion, however, did not deter a Michigan attorney from filing suit against Ford to have the pardon declared unconstitutional. The dispute did not reach the Supreme Court, but was heard and decided in federal district court. As you read the opinion of the judge in *Murphy v. Ford,* notice how closely he ties his decision to the intention of the Framers and to the precedents handed down by the Supreme Court.

Murphy v. Ford

390 F. Supp. 1372 (1975)

*Decision of the U.S. District Court for the Western District
   of Michigan*
Noel P. Fox, Chief Judge

F. Gregory Murphy, an attorney from Mar-
quette, Michigan, filed suit against President
Ford, asking the court to declare his unconditional
pardon of Richard Nixon void. Murphy contended that a pardon cannot constitutionally be
granted to a person who has not been indicted or
convicted and who has not been formally charged
with any crime against the United States. The suit
was heard by Judge Noel Fox, a Democrat appointed to the district court by President John F.
Kennedy.

Chief Judge Fox delivered the opinion of the
court:

The main issue is, did President Ford have the
constitutional power to pardon former President Nixon
for the latter's offenses against the United States?

In The Federalist No. 74, written in 1788 in support
of the proposed Constitution, Alexander Hamilton
explained why the Founding Fathers gave the President a discretionary power to pardon: "The principal
argument for reposing the power of pardoning
. . . [in] the Chief Magistrate," Hamilton wrote, "is
this: in seasons of insurrection or rebellion, there are
often critical moments, when a well-timed offer of
pardon to the insurgents or rebels may restore the
tranquillity of the commonwealth; and which, if suffered to pass unimproved, it may never be possible
afterwards to recall."

Few would today deny that the period from the
break-in at the Watergate in June 1972, until the
resignation of President Nixon in August 1974, was a
"season of insurrection or rebellion" by many actually
in the Government. Since the end of 1970, various top
officials of the Nixon Administration at times during
this period deliberately and flagrantly violated the civil
liberties of individual citizens and engaged in criminal
violations of the campaign laws in order to preserve
and expand their own and Nixon's personal power

beyond constitutional limitations. When many illegal
activities were threatened with exposure, some Nixon
Administration officials formed and executed a criminal conspiracy to obstruct justice. Evidence now available suggests a strong probability that the Nixon Administration was conducting a covert assault on
American liberty and an insurrection and rebellion
against constitutional government itself, an insurrection and rebellion which might have succeeded but for
timely intervention by a courageous free press, an
enlightened Congress, and a diligent Judiciary dedi-
cated to preserving the rule of law.

Certainly the summer and early fall of 1974 were a
period of popular discontent, as the full extent of the
Nixon Administration's misdeeds became known, and
public trust in government virtually collapsed. After
Mr. Nixon's resignation in August, the public clamor
over the whole Watergate episode did not immediately
subside; attention continued to focus on Mr. Nixon and
his fate. When Mr. Ford became President, the executive branch was foundering in the wreckage of Watergate, and the country was in the grips of an apparently
uncontrollable inflationary spiral and an energy crisis
of unprecedented proportions.

Under these circumstances, President Ford concluded that the public interest required *positive steps to
end the divisions caused by Watergate and to shift the
focus of attention from the immediate problem of Mr.
Nixon to the hard social and economic problems which
were of more lasting significance.*

By pardoning Richard Nixon, who many believed
was the leader of a conspiratorial insurrection and
rebellion against American liberty and constitutional
government, President Ford was taking steps, in the
words of Alexander Hamilton in The Federalist, to
*"restore the tranquillity of the commonwealth" by a
"well-timed offer of pardon"* to the putative rebel
leader. President Ford's pardon of Richard M. Nixon
was thus within the letter and the spirit of the Presidential Pardoning Power granted by the Constitution. It
was a prudent public policy judgment.

The fact that Mr. Nixon had been neither indicted
nor convicted of an offense against the United States
does not affect the validity of the pardon. Ex parte
Garland (1867). In that case the Supreme Court considered the nature of the President's Pardoning Power,

and the effect of a Presidential pardon. Mr. Justice Field, speaking for the court, said that the Pardoning Power is *"unlimited,"* except in cases of impeachment. "[The Power] extends to every offense known to the law, and may be exercised *at any time after its commission, either before legal proceedings are taken*, or during their pendency, or after conviction and judgment. . . . The benign prerogative of mercy reposed in [the President] cannot be fettered by any legislative restrictions.

"Such being the case, the inquiry arises as to the effect and operation of a pardon, and on this point all the authorities concur. A pardon reaches both the punishment prescribed for the offense and the guilt of the offender; and when the pardon is full, it releases the punishment and blots out of existence the guilt,

. . . If granted before conviction, it prevents any of the penalties and disabilities consequent from conviction from attaching; . . .

"There is only this limitation to its operation: it does not restore offices forfeited, or property or interests vested in others in consequence of the conviction and judgment." (Emphasis supplied.)

However, ". . . as the very essence of a pardon is forgiveness or remission of penalty, a pardon implies guilt; *it does not obliterate the fact of the commission of the crime and the conviction thereof; it does not wash out the moral stain; as has been tersely said; it involves forgiveness and not forgetfulness."* Page v. Watson [Florida Supreme Court, 1938]. (Emphasis supplied.)

The . . . motion to dismiss this action is hereby granted.

The President and Foreign Policy

There can be no doubt that the Constitution confers on the president special authority over matters of foreign policy. A review of the powers granted to the chief executive by the Constitution demonstrates why this is the case.

First, Article II, Section 2, assigns to the president the role of commander in chief of the army and navy. The military capability of a nation clearly is tied to its foreign policy. Military power not only enables a nation to deter hostile actions from other countries, but also it can be used as a credible threat to persuade other nations to follow certain preferred courses of action. Armed interventions and full-scale wars can be major elements in executing a nation's foreign policy. Recent military actions, both small and large, taken by the United States in Grenada, Panama, and the Persian Gulf, demonstrate the use of this power.

Second, Article II gives the president the sole authority to make treaties on behalf of the United States. These international agreements may cover almost any area of interaction among nations, including defense pacts, economic understandings, and human rights accords.

Third, the president selects the individuals to represent the United States in contacts with other nations. The power to appoint ambassadors and ministers influences our relations with the leaders of other states.

Fourth, Article II, Section 3, provides that the president is the appropriate official to receive ambassadors and ministers from foreign nations. When the president accepts the credentials of foreign emissaries, the act confers U.S. recognition on the governments they represent. This provision also means that when foreign diplomats communicate with the United States they must do so through the president.

The Supreme Court has endorsed the notion that by the sum of these powers the Constitution has entrusted the president with the primary responsibility for creating and implementing foreign policy. For the most comprehensive statement of this position we need to refer once again to the Court's decision in *United States v. Curtiss-Wright Export Corp.* (1936). As you recall, we discussed this case in Chapter 3 for what it demonstrated about the constitutional limits on the delegation of legislative power to the executive branch. But Justice Sutherland's opinion for the Court also develops nicely the president's constitutional position in matters of foreign policy. A brief review of the essential facts appears below to remind you of the issues involved in this dispute.

United States v. Curtiss-Wright Export Corp.

299 U.S. 304 (1936)

Vote: 7 (Brandeis, Butler, Cardozo, Hughes, Roberts, Sutherland, Van Devanter)
1 (McReynolds)
Opinion of the Court: Sutherland
Not participating: Stone

On May 28, 1934, Congress passed a joint resolution aimed at quelling the war between Bolivia and Paraguay over the Chaco region. The resolution gave the president the power to prohibit arms sales to the warring parties if that would help to reestablish peace. Once the president issued a proclamation to that effect, the sale of any arms and ammunitions to the hostile nations would constitute a crime punishable by a fine and/or imprisonment. The day after passage of the joint resolution, President Roosevelt announced the arms sale proclamation and the criminal sanctions immediately went into effect. On November 14, 1935, Roosevelt issued a second proclamation revoking the first.

On January 27, 1936, a grand jury returned an indictment against Curtiss-Wright Export Corporation charging that the company conspired to sell military equipment to Bolivia during the period covered by the first proclamation. Curtiss-Wright moved to quash the indictment and received a favorable ruling from the federal district court on one of the three points it asserted. The United States appealed. After explaining that Congress had not engaged in an unconstitutional delegation of powers to the executive branch, Justice Sutherland described the role the Constitution prescribes for the president in the area of foreign policy.

Justice Sutherland delivered the opinion of the Court:

Not only, as we have shown, is the federal power over external affairs in origin and essential character different from that over internal affairs, but participation in the exercise of the power is significantly limited. In this vast external realm, with its important, complicated, delicate and manifold problems, the President alone has the power to speak or listen as a representative of the nation. He *makes* treaties with the advice and consent of the Senate; but he alone negotiates. Into the field of negotiation the Senate cannot intrude; and Congress itself is powerless to invade it. As Marshall said in his great argument of March 7, 1800, in the House of Representatives, "The President is the sole organ of the nation in its external relations, and its sole representative with foreign nations." The Senate Committee on Foreign Relations at a very early day in our history (February 15, 1816), reported to the Senate, among other things, as follows:

"The President is the constitutional representative of the United States with regard to foreign nations. He manages our concerns with foreign nations and must necessarily be most competent to determine when, how, and upon what subjects negotiation may be urged with the greatest prospect of success. For his conduct he is responsible to the Constitution. The committee consider this responsibility the surest pledge for the faithful discharge of his duty. They think the interference of the Senate in the direction of foreign negotiations calculated to diminish that responsibility and thereby to impair the best security for the national safety. The nature of transactions with foreign nations, moreover, requires caution and unity of design, and their success frequently depends on secrecy and dispatch.''

It is important to bear in mind that we are here dealing not alone with an authority vested in the President by an exertion of legislative power, but with such an authority plus the very delicate, plenary and exclusive power of the President as the sole organ of the federal government in the field of international relations—a power which does not require as a basis for its exercise an act of Congress, but which, of course, like every other governmental power, must be exercised in subordination to the applicable provisions of the Constitution. It is quite apparent that if, in the maintenance of our international relations, embarrassment—perhaps serious embarrassment—is to be avoided and success for our aims achieved, congressional legislation which is to be made effective through negotiation and inquiry within the international field must often accord to the President a degree of discretion and freedom from statutory restriction which would not be admissible were domestic affairs alone involved. Moreover, he, not Congress, has the better opportunity of knowing the conditions which prevail in foreign countries, and especially is this true in time of war. He has his confidential sources of information. He has his agents in the form of diplomatic, consular and other officials. Secrecy in respect of information gathered by them may be highly necessary, and the premature disclosure of it productive of harmful results. Indeed, so clearly is this true that the first President refused to accede to a request to lay before the House of Representatives the instructions, correspondence and documents relating to the negotiation of the Jay Treaty—a refusal the wisdom of which was recognized by the House itself and has never since been doubted. In his reply to the request, President Washington said:

''The nature of foreign negotiations requires caution, and their success must often depend on secrecy; and even when brought to a conclusion a full disclosure of all the measures, demands, or eventual concessions which may have been proposed or contemplated would be extremely impolitic: for this might have a pernicious influence on future negotiations, or produce immediate inconveniences, perhaps danger and mischief, in relation to other powers. The necessity of such caution and secrecy was one cogent reason for vesting the power of making treaties in the President, with the advice and consent of the Senate, the principle on which that body was formed confining it to a small number of members. To admit, then, a right in the House of Representatives to demand and to have as a matter of course all the papers respecting a negotiation with a foreign power would be to establish a dangerous precedent.''

The marked difference between foreign affairs and domestic affairs in this respect is recognized by both houses of Congress in the very form of their requisitions for information from the executive departments. In the case of every department except the Department of State, the resolution *directs* the official to furnish the information. In the case of the State Department, dealing with foreign affairs, the President is *requested* to furnish the information ''if not incompatible with the public interest.'' A statement that to furnish the information is not compatible with the public interest rarely, if ever, is questioned.

When the President is to be authorized by legislation to act in respect of a matter intended to affect a situation in foreign territory, the legislator properly bears in mind the important consideration that the form of the President's action—or, indeed, whether he shall act at all—may well depend, among other things, upon the nature of the confidential information which he has or may thereafter receive, or upon the effect which his action may have upon our foreign relations. This consideration, in connection with what we have already said on the subject, discloses the unwisdom of requiring Congress in this field of governmental power to lay down narrowly definite standards by which the President is to be governed. As this court said in *Mackenzie* v. *Hare* [1915], ''As a government, the United States is invested with all the attributes of sovereignty. As it has the character of nationality it has the powers of nationality, especially those which concern its relations and intercourse with other countries. *We should hesitate long before limiting or embarrassing such powers.*'' (Italics supplied.)

In the light of the foregoing observations, it is evident that this court should not be in haste to apply a general rule which will have the effect of condemning legislation like that under review as constituting an unlawful delegation of legislative power. The principles which justify such legislation find overwhelming support in the unbroken legislative practice which has prevailed almost from the inception of the national government to the present day.

The Constitution does not leave the president completely unfettered in the pursuit of the nation's foreign policy. In fact, the Framers were sufficiently concerned about the distribution of these foreign policy prerogatives that they gave the legislative branch certain powers to counterbalance those of the executive.

Although the president is commander in chief of the military, Congress has the power to raise and support the army and the navy, to make rules for the military, and to call up the militia. According to Article I, only Congress may declare war. The president has the constitutional authority to make treaties, but a treaty cannot take effect unless the Senate ratifies it by a two-thirds vote. The president's appointments of ambassadors and other foreign policy ministers must be confirmed by the Senate.

The Supreme Court generally has been sympathetic to the executive branch when deciding disputes over the president's foreign policy role. The justices, for example, have been quite lenient in the handling of the president's power to make treaties. For example, in *Goldwater v. Carter* (1979) Sen. Barry Goldwater, R-Ariz., challenged President Carter's authority to terminate a defense treaty with Taiwan without the consent of the Senate. The justices were badly divided as to reasons, but seven refused to intervene on political question or justiciability grounds.

The Court also has supported the growing tendency of presidents to enter into executive agreements with other nations. Unlike treaties, these arrangements do not require Senate ratification. Consequently, they are often used when the president wants to avoid the time-consuming and very public ratification process. But executive agreements have their limitations; federal law requires that the president inform Congress whenever such agreements are made, and they can be nullified by acts of Congress. Moreover, executive agreements are not binding on future presidents without their consent.

As early as 1937, in *United States v. Belmont,* the Court not only endorsed the use of executive agreements but also blurred the distinction between such arrangements and fully ratified treaties. The Court held that the international agreements entered into by the president as part of the recognition of the Soviet Union had the force of law within the United States. The same set of agreements later was held to have sufficient force to supersede state law, just as treaties do.[7] Because of the advantages of executive agreements and their approval by the Court, presidents have grown to favor them over treaties. During its first century the United States entered into 275 treaties and 265 executive agreements, but between 1945 and 1990 the nation concluded 673 treaties and 12,107 executive agreements. President Ronald Reagan alone entered into 2,837 executive agreements, but only 117 treaties.[8]

In other areas, too, the justices have allowed the president to take actions in pursuit of American foreign policy that would be highly suspect in domestic affairs. *Haig v. Agee* (1981) provides illustration. Philip Agee was an American citizen living in what was then West Germany. Between 1957 and 1968 he worked for the Central Intel-

---

7. *United States v. Pink,* 315 U.S. 203 (1942). See also, *Dames & Moore v. Regan,* 453 U.S. 654 (1981).

8. Harold W. Stanley and Richard G. Niemi, *Vital Statistics on American Politics,* 3d ed. (Washington, D.C.: CQ Press, 1992), 278.

ligence Agency and was involved in covert intelligence-gathering in foreign countries. During this period he acquired a vast knowledge of CIA operations and of agents in the field. After he left government service, Agee called a press conference to declare a personal war against the CIA. He said he would do everything he could to expose CIA agents and drive them out of the countries where they worked. Agee pursued this goal by traveling to various countries, using his contacts to identify CIA agents, and then exposing them. He published two books that revealed secret information about the activities of the agency and made public the identities of undercover CIA operatives. In reaction, President Carter, through his secretary of state, revoked Agee's passport, thereby making it impossible for him to travel abroad legally. Agee claimed that the executive branch did not have the authority to revoke his passport. The Supreme Court, however, interpreted the powers of the president quite broadly and by a 7-2 vote rejected Agee's objections. The Court essentially agreed that the executive branch could use its power to issue passports—or not issue them—as a way of protecting the nation's foreign policy efforts.

Presidential Power During War and National Emergencies

Questions concerning the constitutional authority to make and wage war have plagued the nation from the very beginning. Even today many questions remain unresolved. Because war and conditions of national emergency customarily demand quick action, there is rarely sufficient time for the dispassionate consideration of legal questions. When national survival is at risk, the country is usually in an emotionally heightened state and may be willing to ignore the limitations on government power that would be insisted upon in peacetime.[9] Once the crisis has passed, the country turns to other matters and questions of war do not again capture the nation's attention until the next threat occurs.

The Constitutional War Powers

The constitutional authority to send troops into combat has always sparked controversy. The root of the problem is that both the legislative and the executive branches have powers that can be interpreted as controlling the commitment of military forces to combat.[10] The case for presidential control is based on the following passage: "The President shall be Commander in Chief of the Army and Navy of the United States, and of the Militia of the several States, when called into actual Service of the United States." (Article II, Section 2.) Proponents of congressional dominance over the making of war rest their case on these words:

The Congress shall have Power . . . to declare War, grant Letters of Marque and Reprisal, and make Rules concerning Captures on Land and Water; To raise and support Armies, but no Appropriation of Money to that Use shall be for a longer Term than two Years; To provide and maintain a Navy; To make Rules for the Government and Regulation of the land and naval Forces; To provide for calling forth the Militia to execute the Laws of the Union, suppress Insurrections, and repel Invasions. (Article I, Section 8.)

The distribution of war-making powers as determined by the Framers envisioned a situation in which Congress would raise and support military forces when necessary and provide the general rules governing them. By granting Congress the

9. Clinton L. Rossiter, *Constitutional Dictatorship: Crisis Government in the Modern Democracies* (Princeton, N.J.: Princeton University Press, 1948).

10. See Joan Biskupic, "Constitution's Conflicting Clauses Underscored by Iraq Crisis," *Congressional Quarterly Weekly Report,* Jan. 5, 1991, 33-36.

power to declare war, the Constitution anticipates that the legislature should determine when military force is to be used. Once the military is raised and war is declared, executive power then would be dominant, consistent with the philosophy that to wage war successfully requires a single official to be in charge.

This allocation of powers was more realistic at the end of the eighteenth century than it is today. At the time the Framers considered these issues, the United States was a remote nation far removed from the frequent wars taking place in Europe. It took weeks for vessels to cross the Atlantic, allowing plenty of time for Congress to debate the question of initiating hostilities. Most delegates at the Constitutional Convention did not even anticipate the establishment of a standing military.

Today, with the rapid deployment of troops, air power, and intercontinental missiles, hostile conditions demand quick and decisive actions. The nation expects the president to act immediately to repel a hostile attack and to worry about congressional approval later.

The vast majority of United States military actions have occurred without a declaration of war. The first such declared action was taken by President John Adams when he authorized military strikes against French privateers.[11] Since then literally hundreds of U.S. military actions have been initiated without a declaration of war. Most have been quick actions rather than prolonged conflicts. However, both the Korean War and the Vietnam War were major long-term military efforts that were conducted without the benefit of Congress declaring war. In fact, Congress has taken the positive action of declaring

a state of war only five times in the nation's history.[12]

1. The War of 1812 against Great Britain
2. The Mexican War in 1846
3. The Spanish American War in 1898
4. The First World War in 1917
5. The Second World War in 1941

Occasionally, military force is begun and ended so quickly that the president's actions permit no opportunity for congressional approval, such as President Reagan's overnight air strike against Libya. When military actions extend over greater periods of time, Congress often has given approval through means other than a formal declaration of war. This approval may come in the form of a resolution authorizing the president to conduct some form of military action, such as the 1964 Tonkin Gulf Resolution that granted President Johnson authority to use force to repel attacks on U.S. forces and to prevent any future aggression. Similarly, on January 12, 1991, Congress passed a joint resolution authorizing President George Bush to use force against Iraq; Congress gave its approval to the Persian Gulf conflict in words just short of a formal declaration of war. Indirect approval also may take the form of continuing congressional appropriations to support the military action.

But Congress has not abdicated its constitutional authority to approve war; in fact, the legislature has been adamant about the president consulting it on all military actions. In 1973 Congress passed the War Powers Act over Richard Nixon's veto. This legislation acknowledges the right of the president to undertake limited military action without first obtaining formal approval from Congress. However, the statute requires the president

---

11. For a good review of the history of undeclared military engagements, see Ronald D. Elving, ''America's Most Frequent Fight Has Been the Undeclared War,'' *Congressional Quarterly Weekly Report,* Jan. 5, 1991, 37-40.

12. Congress also declared a state of war during the Civil War, but this conflict is technically classified as an internal rebellion rather than a true war between independent nations.

to file a formal report with Congress within forty-eight hours of initiating hostilities. Military action under this act is limited to sixty days with a possible thirty-day extension. If the president wishes to pursue military activity beyond these limits, prior congressional consent is required. While the legislature intended to impose restrictions on the president with the passage of the War Powers Act, most experts believe the law actually expands the chief executive's right to employ military force.

Because it must wait for an appropriate case to be filed before it can act, and because of its slow, deliberative procedures, the judicial branch is least capable of taking a role in matters of war and national emergency. Furthermore, the Constitution gives the courts no specified authority in these areas. However, the judiciary is sometimes called upon to decide when government power is used legitimately and when constitutional limits have been exceeded. In times of war and national emergency the executive branch may find it necessary to take actions that would be unlawful at other times. The limits of the Constitution may be stretched to respond to the crisis. When legal disputes arise from such situations, the courts become active participants in determining the government's legitimate authority.

Civil War Disputes

If it is a generally recognized constitutional doctrine that government may exercise more power during times of war and national emergency than during times of peace and security, what is not evident from this rather vague statement is at what point the extraordinary powers of the government are activated. This question came to the Supreme Court in the *Prize Cases* in 1863. The disputes giving rise to these cases present the most fundamental questions of the constitutional allocation of the war powers. When does war begin? Who has power to initiate war? What war powers may the president pursue without a formal declaration from Congress?

The Prize Cases

2 Black 635 (1863)

Vote: 5 (Davis, Grier, Miller, Swayne, Wayne)
*   4 (Catron, Clifford, Nelson, Taney)*
Opinion of the Court: Grier
Dissenting opinion: Nelson

Abraham Lincoln was elected president in November 1860. Before his inauguration on March 4, 1861, seven southern states seceded from the Union, and Lincoln knew that he had to act quickly and decisively to restore the nation. Beginning in mid-April, shortly after the first shots were fired at Fort Sumter, Lincoln imposed a naval blockade of southern ports. He took this action unilaterally without seeking the prior approval of Congress, which did not enact a formal declaration of hostilities until July 13. Before Congress could act, Union war vessels seized a number of ships trading with the Confederate states. The owners of the captured ships brought suit to recover their property, claiming that Lincoln had no authority to institute a blockade in the absence of a congressional declaration of war and that the seizures were illegal. Among other matters, the justices confronted this important constitutional issue: Did the president have the right to institute a blockade of ports under the control of persons in armed rebellion against the government?

Justice Robert C. Grier delivered the opinion of the Court:

Neutrals have a right to challenge the existence of a blockade *de facto,* and also the authority of the party exercising the right to institute it. They have a right to enter the ports of a friendly nation for the purposes of trade and commerce, but are bound to recognize the rights of a belligerent engaged in actual war, to use this mode of coercion, for the purpose of subduing the enemy.

That a blockade *de facto* actually existed, and was formally declared and notified by the President on the 27th and 30th of April, 1861, is an admitted fact in these cases.

That the President, as the Executive Chief of the Government and Commander-in-chief of the Army and Navy, was the proper person to make such notification, has not been, and cannot be disputed.

The right of prize and capture has its origin in the "*jus belli,*" [laws of war] and is governed and adjudged under the law of nations. To legitimate the capture of a neutral vessel or property on the high seas, a war must exist *de facto,* and the neutral must have a knowledge or notice of the intention of one of the parties belligerent to use this mode of coercion against a port, city, or territory, in possession of the other.

Let us enquire whether, at the time this blockade was instituted, a state of war existed which would justify a resort to these means of subduing the hostile force.

War has been well defined to be, "That state in which a nation prosecutes its right by force."

The parties belligerent in a public war are independent nations. But it is not necessary to constitute war, that both parties should be acknowledged as independent nations or sovereign States. A war may exist where one of the belligerents, claims sovereign rights as against the other.

Insurrection against a government may or may not culminate in an organized rebellion, but a civil war always begins by insurrection against the lawful authority of the Government. A civil war is never solemnly declared; it becomes such by its accidents—the number, power, and organization of the persons who originate and carry it on. When the party in rebellion occupy and hold in a hostile manner a certain portion of territory; have declared their independence; have cast off their allegiance; have organized armies; have commenced hostilities against their former sovereign, the world acknowledges them as belligerents, and the contest a *war. They* claim to be in arms to establish their liberty and independence, in order to become a sovereign State, while the sovereign party treats them as insurgents and rebels who owe allegiance, and who should be punished with death for their treason. . . .

As a civil war is never publicly proclaimed, *eo nomine* [under that name] against insurgents, its actual existence is a fact in our domestic history which the Court is bound to notice and to know.

The true test of its existence, as found in the writing of the sages of the common law, may be thus summarily stated: "When the regular course of justice is interrupted by revolt, rebellion, or insurrection, so that the Courts of Justice cannot be kept open, *civil war exists* and hostilities may be prosecuted on the same footing as if those opposing the Government were foreign enemies invading the land."

By the Constitution, Congress alone has the power to declare a national or foreign war. It cannot declare war against a State, or any number of States, by virtue of any clause in the Constitution. The Constitution confers on the President the whole Executive power. He is bound to take care that the laws be faithfully executed. He is Commander-in-chief of the Army and Navy of the United States, and of the militia of the several States when called into the actual service of the United States. He has no power to initiate or declare a war either against a foreign nation or a domestic State. But by the Acts of Congress of February 28th, 1795, and 3d of March, 1807, he is authorized to call out the militia and use the military and naval forces of the United States in case of invasion by foreign nations, and to suppress insurrection against the government of a State or of the United States.

If a war be made by invasion of a foreign nation, the President is not only authorized but bound to resist force by force. He does not initiate the war, but is bound to accept the challenge without waiting for any special legislative authority. And whether the hostile party be a foreign invader, or States organized in rebellion, it is none the less a war, although the declaration of it be "*unilateral.*" Lord Stowell observes, "It is not the less a war on *that account,* for war may exist without a declaration on either side. It is so laid down by the best writers on the law of nations. A declaration of war by one country only, is not a mere challenge to be accepted or refused at pleasure by the other.'' . . .

This greatest of civil wars was not gradually developed by popular commotion, tumultuous assemblies, or local unorganized insurrections. However long may have been its previous conception, it nevertheless sprung forth suddenly from the parent brain, a Minerva in the full panoply of *war*. The President was bound to meet it in the shape it presented itself, without waiting for Congress to baptize it with a name; and no name given to it by him or them could change the fact.

It is not the less a civil war, with belligerent parties in hostile array, because it may be called an ''insurrection'' by one side, and the insurgents be considered as rebels or traitors. It is not necessary that the independence of the revolted province or State be acknowledged in order to constitute it a party belligerent in a war according to the law of nations. Foreign nations acknowledge it as war by a declaration of neutrality. The condition of neutrality cannot exist unless there be two belligerent parties. . . .

The law of nations is also called the law of nature; it is founded on the common consent as well as the common sense of the world. It contains no such anomalous doctrine as that which this Court are now for the first time desired to pronounce, to wit: That insurgents who have risen in rebellion against their sovereign, expelled her Courts, established a revolutionary government, organized armies, and commenced hostilities, are not *enemies* because they are *traitors;* and a war levied on the Government by traitors, in order to dismember and destroy it, is not a *war* because it is an ''insurrection.''

Whether the President in fulfilling his duties, as Commander-in-chief, in suppressing an insurrection, has met with such armed hostile resistance, and a civil war of such alarming proportions as will compel him to accord to them the character of belligerents, is a question to be decided *by him,* and this Court must be governed by the decisions and acts of the political department of the Government to which this power was entrusted. ''He must determine what degree of force the crisis demands.'' The proclamation of blockade is itself official and conclusive evidence to the Court that a state of war existed which demanded and authorized a recourse to such a measure, under the circumstances peculiar to the case. . . .

[T]herefore we are of the opinion that the President had a right, *jure belli,* to institute a blockade of ports in possession of the States in rebellion, which neutrals are bound to regard.

Mr. Justice NELSON, dissenting.

Upon the whole, after the most careful consideration of this case which the pressure of other duties has admitted, I am compelled to the conclusion that no civil war existed between this Government and the States in insurrection till recognized by the Act of Congress 13th of July, 1861; that the President does not possess the power under the Constitution to declare war or recognize its existence within the meaning of the law of nations, which carries with it belligerent rights, and thus change the country and all its citizens from a state of peace to a state of war; that this power belongs exclusively to the Congress of the United States, and, consequently, that the President had no power to set on foot a blockade under the law of nations, and that the capture of the vessel and cargo in this case, and in all cases before us in which the capture occurred before the 13th of July, 1861, for breach of blockade, or as enemies' property, are illegal and void, and that the decrees of condemnation should be reversed and the vessel and cargo restored.

Lincoln's actions were supported by the barest of majorities. Three of the justices who voted to endorse the validity of the blockade were his own appointees, Samuel Miller, Noah Swayne, and David Davis. They were joined by two Democrats, Robert Grier of Pennsylvania and James Wayne, a Georgian who remained loyal to the Union. The decision is significant for expanding the right of the president to take military action without waiting for congressional approval. It further established that a state of war comes into existence when certain conditions are present, not when the legislature declares that it exists. The decision, however, did not fully settle the issue. The arguments raised in the majority and dissenting opinions in this case seem to reappear whenever a controversy over the power to conduct war arises.

The blockade was only the first of Lincoln's acts that were of questionable constitutionality. More severely criticized were his actions suppressing civil liberties. The Civil War was unlike other wars Americans had faced. In this war the enemies were fellow Americans, not foreigners. The conflict touched every part of the nation. Lincoln particularly worried about the presence of Confederate supporters in the northern and border states. These individuals were capable of aiding the southern forces without joining the Confederate Army. Of special concern were the large numbers of southern sympathizers, known as Copperheads, active in Indiana, Illinois, Ohio, and Missouri. Combating these civilian enemies posed a difficult problem for the president. He decided that the Union was more important than the procedural rights of individuals. Consequently, Lincoln gave his military commanders broad powers to arrest civilians suspected of engaging in traitorous activities. These suspects were to be tried in military courts.

In those areas of the country where hostilities were not occurring, however, the army had no legal authority to arrest and try civilians. The regular state and federal courts were in full operation and were capable of trying civilians charged with treason or any other crime. To allow arrests and military trials for civilians a state of martial law had to be declared, and to do that, the right of habeas corpus had to be suspended. Habeas corpus is a legal procedure with roots extending far back into English legal history; it permits an arrested person to have a judge determine whether the detention is legal. If the court determines that there are no legal grounds for the arrest, it may order the release of the detained individual. Habeas corpus is essential to the doctrine of checks and balances because it gives the judiciary the right to intervene if the executive branch abuses the law enforcement power.

Article I, Section 9, of the Constitution provides for the suspension of habeas corpus in the following words: "The Privilege of the Writ of Habeas Corpus shall not be suspended, unless when in Cases of Rebellion or Invasion the public Safety may require it." This provision posed two problems for Lincoln. First, the suspension provision is found in Article I, which outlines legislative, not executive, powers. And second, if the civilian courts are in full operation and no armed hostilities are taking place in the area, the public safety probably does not demand a suspension of habeas corpus procedures.

These obstacles did not stop the president. Several times during the war he issued orders expanding military control over civilian areas, permitting military arrests and trials of civilians, and suspending habeas corpus. Congress later endorsed some of these actions. Arrests of suspected traitors and conspirators were common and often based on little evidence. Were such actions constitutional under the war powers doctrine? The Court addressed this question in *Ex parte Milligan* (1866), a decision of great importance in defining the wartime powers of the chief executive.[13] The ruling came after Lincoln's death and the war's conclusion. Do you think the Court's decision would have been different had the case been heard when hostilities were at their peak and Confederate troops were scoring successes on the battlefield?

13. For a description of the events leading up to the Court's decision, see Allan Nevins, "The Case of the Copperhead Conspirator," in *Quarrels That Have Shaped the Constitution*, ed. John A. Garraty (New York: Harper Colophon Books, 1964).

Ex parte Milligan

4 Wall. 2 (1866)

Vote: 9 (Chase, Clifford, Davis, Field, Grier, Miller, Nelson, Swayne, Wayne)

0

Opinion of the Court: Davis
Concurring opinion: Chase

Lambdin P. Milligan was an attorney residing in southern Indiana. As a member of the Democratic party, with strong states' rights beliefs, his sympathies lay with the Confederate cause during the war. He openly organized groups and gave speeches in support of the South. He also was involved in efforts to persuade men not to join the Union army. At one point Milligan and his fellow Copperheads were suspected of hatching a plan to raid prisoner of war camps in Illinois, Indiana, and Ohio and release the imprisoned Confederate soldiers, who would then take control of the three states. Federal military investigators followed Milligan closely and kept records of his activities and contacts.

On October 5, 1864, under orders from Gen. Alvin Hovey, commander of the Union armies in Indiana, federal agents arrested Milligan at his home. They also arrested four of Milligan's fellow Confederate sympathizers. Sixteen days later Hovey placed Milligan on trial before a military tribunal in Indianapolis. He was found guilty and sentenced to be hanged on May 19, 1865. Just after the war ended with Lee's surrender at Appomattox, Milligan filed for a writ of habeas corpus claiming that he had been illegally arrested and tried.

Justice Davis delivered the opinion of the Court:

Milligan insists that said military commission had no jurisdiction to try him upon the charges preferred, or upon any charges whatever; because he was a citizen of the United States and the State of Indiana, and had not been, since the commencement of the late Rebellion, a resident of any of the States whose citizens were arrayed against the government, and that the right of trial by jury was guaranteed to him by the Constitution of the United States. . . .

The importance of the main question presented by this record cannot be overstated; for it involves the very framework of the government and the fundamental principles of American liberty.

During the late wicked Rebellion, the temper of the times did not allow that calmness in deliberation and discussion so necessary to a correct conclusion of a purely judicial question. *Then*, considerations of safety were mingled with the exercise of power; and feelings and interests prevailed which are happily terminated. *Now* that the public safety is assured, this question, as well as all others, can be discussed and decided without passion or the admixture of any element not required to form a legal judgment. We approach the investigation of this case, fully sensible of the magnitude of the inquiry and the necessity of full and cautious deliberation. . . .

The controlling question in the case is this: Upon the *facts* stated in Milligan's petition, and the exhibits filed, had the military commission mentioned in it *jurisdiction*, legally, to try and sentence him? Milligan, not a resident of one of the rebellious states, or a prisoner of war, but a citizen of Indiana for twenty years past, and never in the military or naval service, is, while at his home, arrested by the military power of the United States, imprisoned, and, on certain criminal charges preferred against him, tried, convicted, and sentenced to be hanged by a military commission, organized under the direction of the military commander of the military district of Indiana. Had this tribunal the *legal* power and authority to try and punish this man?

No graver question was ever considered by this court, nor one which more nearly concerns the rights of the whole people; for it is the birthright of every American citizen when charged with crime, to be tried and punished according to law. The power of punishment is, alone through the means which the laws have provided for that purpose, and if they are ineffectual, there is an immunity from punishment, no matter how great an offender the individual may be, or how much his crimes may have shocked the sense of justice of the country, or endangered its safety. By the protection of

The Union Army military commission that tried Lambdin P. Milligan and his fellow conspirators in October 1864.

the law human rights are secured; withdraw that protection, and they are at the mercy of wicked rulers, or the clamor of an excited people. If there was law to justify this military trial, it is not our province to interfere; if there was not, it is our duty to declare the nullity of the whole proceedings. The decision of this question does not depend on argument or judicial precedents, numerous and highly illustrative as they are. These precedents inform us of the extent of the struggle to preserve liberty and to relieve those in civil life from military trials. The founders of our government were familiar with the history of that struggle; and secured in a written constitution every right which the people had wrested from power during a contest of ages. By that Constitution and the laws authorized by it this question must be determined. The provisions of that instrument on the administration of criminal justice are too plain and direct, to leave room for misconstruction or doubt of their true meaning. Those

applicable to this case are found in that clause of the original Constitution which says, ''That the trial of all crimes, except in case of impeachment, shall be by jury;'' . . .

Time has proven the discernment of our ancestors; for even these provisions, expressed in such plain English words, that it would seem the ingenuity of man could not evade them, are *now*, after the lapse of more than seventy years, sought to be avoided. Those great and good men foresaw that troublous times would arise, when rulers and people would become restive under restraint, and seek by sharp and decisive measures to accomplish ends deemed just and proper; and that the principles of constitutional liberty would be in peril, unless established by irrepealable law. The history of the world had taught them that what was done in the past might be attempted in the future. The Constitution of the United States is a law for rulers and people, equally in war and in peace, and covers with the shield

Five southern sympathizers were charged with treason by military authorities. The question of the constitutionality of their arrests and trials before a military commission was settled by the Supreme Court in Ex parte Milligan *(1866). Clockwise from top: William A. Bowles, Andrew Humphreys, Stephen Horsey, H. Heffren, and Lambdin P. Milligan.*

of its protection all classes of men, at all times, and under all circumstances. No doctrine, involving more pernicious consequences, was ever invented by the wit of man than that any of its provisions can be suspended during any of the great exigencies of government. Such a doctrine leads directly to anarchy or despotism, but the theory of necessity on which it is based is false; for the government, within the Constitution, has all the powers granted to it, which are necessary to preserve its existence; as has been happily proved by the result of the great effort to throw off its just authority.

Have any of the rights guaranteed by the Constitution been violated in the case of Milligan? and if so, what are they?

Every trial involves the exercise of judicial power; and from what source did the military commission that tried him derive their authority? Certainly no part of the judicial power of the country was conferred on them; because the Constitution expressly vests it "in one supreme court and such inferior courts as the Congress may from time to time ordain and establish," and it is not pretended that the commission was a court ordained and established by Congress. They cannot justify on the mandate of the President; because he is controlled by law, and has his appropriate sphere of duty, which is to execute, not to make, the laws; and there is "no unwritten criminal code to which resort can be had as a source of jurisdiction."

But it is said that the jurisdiction is complete under the "laws and usages of war."

It can serve no useful purpose to inquire what those laws and usages are, whence they originated, where found, and on whom they operate; they can never be applied to citizens in states which have upheld the authority of the government, and where the courts are open and their process unobstructed. This court has judicial knowledge that in Indiana the Federal authority was always unopposed, and its courts always open to hear criminal accusations and redress grievances; and no usage of war could sanction a military trial there for any offence whatever of a citizen in civil life, in nowise connected with the military service. Congress could grant no such power; and to the honor of our national legislature be it said, it has never been provoked by the state of the country even to attempt its exercise. One of the plainest constitutional provisions was, therefore, infringed when Milligan was tried by a court not ordained and established by Congress, and not composed of judges appointed during good behavior.

Why was he not delivered to the Circuit Court of Indiana to be proceeded against according to law? No reason of necessity could be urged against it; because Congress had declared penalties against the offences charged, provided for their punishment, and directed that court to hear and determine them. And soon after this military tribunal was ended, the Circuit Court met, peacefully transacted its business, and adjourned. It needed no bayonets to protect it, and required no military aid to execute its judgments. It was held in a state, eminently distinguished for patriotism, by judges commissioned during the Rebellion, who were

provided with juries, upright, intelligent, and selected by a marshal appointed by the President. The government had no right to conclude that Milligan, if guilty, would not receive in that court merited punishment; for its records disclose that it was constantly engaged in the trial of similar offences, and was never interrupted in its administration of criminal justice. If it was dangerous, in the distracted condition of affairs, to leave Milligan unrestrained of his liberty, because he "conspired against the government, afforded aid and comfort to rebels, and incited the people to insurrection," the *law* said arrest him, confine him closely, render him powerless to do further mischief; and then present his case to the grand jury of the district, with proofs of his guilt, and, if indicted, try him according to the course of the common law. If this had been done, the Constitution would have been vindicated, the law of 1863 enforced, and the securities for personal liberty preserved and defended.

Another guarantee of freedom was broken when Milligan was denied a trial by jury. The great minds of the country have differed on the correct interpretation to be given to various provisions of the Federal Constitution; and judicial decision has been often invoked to settle their true meaning; but until recently no one ever doubted that the right of trial by jury was fortified in the organic law against the power of attack. It is *now* assailed; but if ideas can be expressed in words, and language has any meaning, *this right*—one of the most valuable in a free country—is preserved to every one accused of crime who is not attached to the army, or navy, or militia in actual service. The sixth amendment affirms that "in all criminal prosecutions the accused shall enjoy the right to a speedy and public trial by an impartial jury," language broad enough to embrace all persons and cases; but the fifth, recognizing the necessity of an indictment, or presentment, before any one can be held to answer for high crimes, "*excepts* cases arising in the land or naval forces, or in the militia, when in actual service, in time of war or public danger;" and the framers of the Constitution, doubtless, meant to limit the right of trial by jury, in the sixth amendment, to those persons who were subject to indictment or presentment in the fifth.

The discipline necessary to the efficiency of the army and navy, required other and swifter modes of trial than are furnished by the common law courts; and, in pursuance of the power conferred by the Constitution, Congress has declared the kinds of trial, and the manner in which they shall be conducted, for offences committed while the party is in the military or naval service. Every one connected with these branches of the public service is amenable to the jurisdiction which Congress has created for their government, and, while thus serving, surrenders his right to be tried by the civil courts. *All other persons,* citizens of states where the courts are open, if charged with crime, are guaranteed the inestimable privilege of trial by jury. This privilege is a vital principle, underlying the whole administration of criminal justice; it is not held by sufferance, and cannot be frittered away on any plea of state or political necessity. When peace prevails, and the authority of the government is undisputed, there is no difficulty of preserving the safeguards of liberty; for the ordinary modes of trial are never neglected, and no one wishes it otherwise; but if society is disturbed by civil commotion—if the passions of men are aroused and the restraints of law weakened, if not disregarded—these safeguards need, and should receive, the watchful care of those intrusted with the guardianship of the Constitution and laws. In no other way can we transmit to posterity unimpaired the blessings of liberty, consecrated by the sacrifices of the Revolution.

It is claimed that martial law covers with its broad mantle the proceedings of this military commission. The proposition is this: that in a time of war the commander of an armed force (if in his opinion the exigencies of the country demand it, and of which he is to judge), has the power, within the lines of his military district, to suspend all civil rights and their remedies, and subject citizens as well as soldiers to the rule of *his will;* and in the exercise of his lawful authority cannot be restrained, except by his superior officer or the President of the United States.

If this position is sound to the extent claimed, then when war exists, foreign or domestic, and the country is subdivided into military departments for mere convenience, the commander of one of them can, if he chooses, within his limits, on the plea of necessity, with the approval of the Executive, substitute military force for and to the exclusion of the laws, and punish all persons, as he thinks right and proper, without fixed or certain rules.

The statement of this proposition shows its importance; for, if true, republican government is a failure, and there is an end of liberty regulated by law. Martial law, established on such a basis, destroys every guarantee of the Constitution, and effectually renders the "military independent of and superior to the civil power"—the attempt to do which by the King of Great Britain was deemed by our fathers such an offence, that they assigned it to the world as one of the causes which impelled them to declare their independence. Civil liberty and this kind of martial law cannot endure together; the antagonism is irreconcilable; and, in the conflict, one or the other must perish.

This nation, as experience has proved, cannot always remain at peace, and has no right to expect that it will always have wise and humane rulers, sincerely attached to the principles of the Constitution. Wicked men, ambitious of power, with hatred of liberty and contempt of law, may fill the place once occupied by Washington and Lincoln; and if this right is conceded, and the calamities of war again befall us, the dangers to human liberty are frightful to contemplate. If our fathers had failed to provide for just such a contingency, they would have been false to the trust reposed in them. They knew—the history of the world told them—the nation they were founding, be its existence short or long, would be involved in war; how often or how long continued, human foresight could not tell; and that unlimited power, wherever lodged at such a time, was especially hazardous to freemen. For this, and other equally weighty reasons, they secured the inheritance they had fought to maintain, by incorporating in a written constitution the safeguards which *time* had proved were essential to its preservation. Not one of these safeguards can the President, or Congress, or the Judiciary disturb, except the one concerning the writ of *habeas corpus.*

It is essential to the safety of every government that, in a great crisis, like the one we have just passed through, there should be a power somewhere of suspending the writ of *habeas corpus.* In every war, there are men of previously good character, wicked enough to counsel their fellow-citizens to resist the measures deemed necessary by a good government to sustain its just authority and overthrow its enemies; and their influence may lead to dangerous combinations. In the emergency of the times, an immediate public investigation according to law may not be possible; and yet, the peril to the country may be too imminent to suffer such persons to go at large. Unquestionably, there is then an exigency which demands that the government, if it should see fit in the exercise of a proper discretion to make arrests, should not be required to produce the persons arrested in answer to a writ of *habeas corpus*. The Constitution goes no further. It does not say after a writ of *habeas corpus* is denied a citizen, that he shall be tried otherwise than by the course of the common law; if it had intended this result, it was easy by the use of direct words to have accomplished it. The illustrious men who framed that instrument were guarding the foundations of civil liberty against the abuses of unlimited power; they were full of wisdom, and the lessons of history informed them that a trial by an established court, assisted by an impartial jury, was the only sure way of protecting the citizen against oppression and wrong. Knowing this, they limited the suspension to one great right, and left the rest to remain forever inviolable. But, it is insisted that the safety of the country in time of war demands that this broad claim for martial law shall be sustained. If this were true, it could be well said that a country, preserved at the sacrifice of all the cardinal principles of liberty, is not worth the cost of preservation. Happily, it is not so.

It will be borne in mind that this is not a question of the power to proclaim martial law, when war exists in a community and the courts and civil authorities are overthrown. Nor is it a question what rule a military commander, at the head of his army, can impose on states in rebellion to cripple their resources and quell the insurrection. The jurisdiction claimed is much more extensive. The necessities of the service, during the late Rebellion, required that the loyal states should be placed within the limits of certain military districts and commanders appointed in them; and, it is urged, that this, in a military sense, constituted them the theatre of military operations; and, as in this case, Indiana had been and was again threatened with invasion by the enemy, the occasion was furnished to establish martial law. The conclusion does not follow from the premises. If armies were collected in Indiana, they were to be employed in another locality, where the laws were obstructed and the national authority disputed. On *her* soil there was no hostile foot; if once invaded, that invasion was at an end, and with it all pretext for martial law. Martial law cannot arise from a *threatened* invasion. The necessity must be actual and present; the invasion real, such as effectually closes the courts and deposes the civil administration.

It is difficult to see how the *safety* of the country required martial law in Indiana. If any of her citizens were plotting treason, the power of arrest could secure them, until the government was prepared for their trial, when the courts were open and ready to try them. It was as easy to protect witnesses before a civil as a military tribunal; and as there could be no wish to convict, except on sufficient legal evidence, surely an ordained and established court was better able to judge of this than a military tribunal composed of gentlemen not trained to the profession of the law.

Although the Court's decision was unanimous as to Milligan's claim of illegal imprisonment, the justices split on the power of the government to suspend habeas corpus under conditions presented in the case. A majority of five (Clifford, Davis, Field, Grier, and Nelson) held that neither the president nor Congress, acting separately or in agreement, could suspend the writ of habeas corpus as long as the civilian courts were in full operation and the area was not a combat zone. In a concurring opinion joined by Miller, Swayne, and Wayne, Chief Justice Chase argued that, while the president did not have the power to establish these military tribunals, Congress did.

Before the Court handed down its ruling in this case, President Johnson commuted Milligan's sentence to life in prison, a sentence he was serving under General Hovey in an Ohio prison when the case was decided. Milligan was released from custody in April 1866.

Japanese-Americans at the federal detention center in Owens Valley, California. In 1890, more than four decades after the war, Congress appropriated $20,000 in compensation for each of the 75,000 relocation camp survivors.

World War II and the Korean Conflict

The restriction of civil liberties during time of war is not uncommon. Nations pressed for their very survival may feel compelled to deny basic liberties to insure against the efforts of traitors and saboteurs. The most infamous of such actions in the United States was the World War II internment of Japanese-Americans.

The Japanese bombing of Pearl Harbor on December 7, 1941, touched off a wave of anti-Japanese hysteria. In the early weeks of the Pacific War the Japanese fleet showed remarkable strength and power, and the United States feared that Japanese forces were planning an invasion of the West Coast. There was also a great deal of concern about the large numbers of people of Japanese ancestry who lived on the coast. Many thought that among the Japanese-American population were significant numbers of people sympathetic to the Japanese war effort, people who might aid the enemy in an invasion of the United States.

To prevent such an occurrence President Roosevelt on February 19, 1942, issued the first of several orders affecting all people of Japanese background residing on the West Coast. His initial command placed all Japanese-Americans under a tight curfew that required them to stay in their homes between 8:00 p.m. and 6:00 a.m. and to register for future relocation. This act was followed by the much harsher orders to evacuate Japanese-Americans from the Pacific Coast area and move them to inland detention centers. Congress later enacted these orders into law. The program made no attempt to distinguish the loyal from the disloyal or the citizen from the noncitizen. The orders affected all persons of Japanese ancestry. The government interned an estimated 110,000 Japanese-American citizens and resident aliens, some for as long as four years.[14] These programs spawned a number of important lawsuits.

In 1943 the Supreme Court heard a challenge to the curfew regulations that was brought by Gordon Hirabayashi, an American citizen of Japanese descent. He was a native of Washington State and a pacifist of the Quaker faith. At the time he challenged the government actions, he was a

14. See Peter H. Irons, *Justice at War: The Story of the Japanese-American Internment Cases* (New York: Oxford University Press, 1983).

senior at the University of Washington. In *Hirabayashi v. United States* (1943) the Supreme Court unanimously upheld the constitutionality of the curfew program. For the Court, Chief Justice Harlan F. Stone explained that the war powers doctrine gave the government ample authority to impose the restrictions. The grave and threatening conditions of war made the racially based program constitutionally acceptable.

The following year the Court heard *Korematsu v. United States* (1944), an appeal attacking the most serious denial of the civil liberties of Japanese-Americans—the orders removing the Japanese-Americans to detention camps. Read Justice Hugo L. Black's decision carefully. Does he make a convincing case that war conditions stretch the Constitution to the point that exclusion orders based on race or national origin are permissible? How can you explain the fact that some of the justices most sympathetic to civil liberties causes—Black, Stone, William O. Douglas, and Wiley Rutledge—voted to approve the military orders? Compare Black's opinion with the dissent of Justice Robert H. Jackson, who states the case for preserving civil liberties guarantees even in times of war or national emergency.

Korematsu v. United States

323 U.S. 214 (1944)

Vote: 6 (Black, Douglas, Frankfurter, Reed, Rutledge, Stone)
3 (Jackson, Murphy, Roberts)
Opinion of the Court: Black
Concurring opinion: Frankfurter
Dissenting opinions: Jackson, Murphy, Roberts

On May 30, 1942, Fred Korematsu was arrested by San Leandro, California, police for being on the public streets in violation of the government's evacuation orders. Korematsu was a young welder who had been born in the United States of Japanese-American parents. At first he

tried to convince police that he was of Spanish-Hawaiian origin. He had undergone plastic surgery to make his racial characteristics less pronounced in an effort to avoid the anti-Japanese discrimination he feared because of his engagement to an Italian-American woman.[15] After the arrest, representatives of the American Civil Liberties Union approached Korematsu and offered to defend him and challenge the validity of the evacuation program. The Japanese-American Citizens League also lent support.

15. Ibid., 93–99.

Justice Black delivered the opinion of the Court:

It should be noted, to begin with, that all legal restrictions which curtail the civil rights of a single racial group are immediately suspect. That is not to say that all such restrictions are unconstitutional. It is to say that courts must subject them to the most rigid scrutiny. Pressing public necessity may sometimes justify the existence of such restrictions; racial antagonism never can. . . .

In the light of the principles we announced in the *Hirabayashi* case, we are unable to conclude that it was beyond the war power of Congress and the Executive to exclude those of Japanese ancestry from the West Coast war area at the time they did. True, exclusion from the area in which one's home is located is a far greater deprivation than constant confinement to the home from 8 p. m. to 6 a. m. Nothing short of apprehension by the proper military authorities of the gravest imminent danger to the public safety can constitutionally justify either. But exclusion from a threatened area, no less than curfew, has a definite and close relationship to the prevention of espionage and sabotage. The military authorities, charged with the primary responsibility of defending our shores, concluded that curfew provided inadequate protection and ordered exclusion. They did so, as pointed out in our *Hirabayashi* opinion, in accordance with Congressional authority to the military to say who should, and who should not, remain in the threatened areas.

In this case the petitioner challenges the assumptions upon which we rested our conclusions in the *Hirabayashi* case. He also urges that by May 1942, when Order No. 34 was promulgated, all danger of Japanese invasion of the West Coast had disappeared. After careful consideration of these contentions we are compelled to reject them.

Here, as in the *Hirabayashi* case, ". . . we cannot reject as unfounded the judgment of the military authorities and of Congress that there were disloyal members of that population, whose number and strength could not be precisely and quickly ascertained. We cannot say that the war-making branches of the Government did not have ground for believing that in a critical hour such persons could not readily be isolated and separately dealt with, and constituted a menace to the national defense and safety, which demanded that prompt and adequate measures be taken to guard against it.''

Like curfew, exclusion of those of Japanese origin was deemed necessary because of the presence of an unascertained number of disloyal members of the group, most of whom we have no doubt were loyal to this country. It was because we could not reject the finding of the military authorities that it was impossible to bring about an immediate segregation of the disloyal from the loyal that we sustained the validity of the curfew order as applying to the whole group. In the instant case, temporary exclusion of the entire group was rested by the military on the same ground. The judgment that exclusion of the whole group was for the same reason a military imperative answers the contention that the exclusion was in the nature of group punishment based on antagonism to those of Japanese origin. That there were members of the group who retained loyalties to Japan has been confirmed by investigations made subsequent to the exclusion. Approximately five thousand American citizens of Japanese ancestry refused to swear unqualified allegiance to the United States and to renounce allegiance to the Japanese Emperor, and several thousand evacuees requested repatriation to Japan.

We uphold the exclusion order as of the time it was made and when the petitioner violated it. In doing so, we are not unmindful of the hardships imposed by it upon a large group of American citizens. But hardships are part of war, and war is an aggregation of hardships. All citizens alike, both in and out of uniform, feel the impact of war in greater or lesser measure. Citizenship has its responsibilities as well as its privileges, and in time of war the burden is always heavier. Compulsory exclusion of large groups of citizens from their homes, except under circumstances of direst emergency and peril, is inconsistent with our basic governmental institutions. But when under conditions of modern warfare our shores are threatened by hostile forces, the power to protect must be commensurate with the threatened danger. . . .

It is said that we are dealing here with the case of imprisonment of a citizen in a concentration camp solely because of his ancestry, without evidence or inquiry concerning his loyalty and good disposition towards the United States. Our task would be simple, our duty clear, were this a case involving the imprisonment of a loyal citizen in a concentration camp because of racial prejudice. Regardless of the true nature of the assembly and relocation centers—and we deem it unjustifiable to call them concentration camps with all the ugly connotations that term implies—we are dealing specifically with nothing but an exclusion order. To cast this case into outlines of racial prejudice, without reference to the real military dangers which were presented, merely confuses the issue. Korematsu was not excluded from the Military Area because of hostility to him or his race. He *was* excluded because we are at war with the Japanese Empire, because the properly constituted military authorities feared an invasion of our West Coast and felt constrained to take proper security measures, because they decided that the military urgency of the situation demanded that all citizens of Japanese ancestry be segregated from the West Coast temporarily, and finally, because Congress, reposing its confidence in this time of war in our military leaders—as inevitably it must—determined that they should have the power to do just this. There was evidence of disloyalty on the part of some, the military authorities considered that the need for action was great, and time was short. We cannot—by availing ourselves of the calm perspective of hindsight—now say that at that time these actions were unjustified.

Affirmed.

Mr. Justice JACKSON, dissenting.

Korematsu was born on our soil, of parents born in Japan. The Constitution makes him a citizen of the United States by nativity and a citizen of California by residence. No claim is made that he is not loyal to this country. There is no suggestion that apart from the matter involved here he is not law-abiding and well disposed. Korematsu, however, has been convicted of an act not commonly a crime. It consists merely of being present in the state whereof he is a citizen, near the place where he was born, and where all his life he has lived.

Even more unusual is the series of military orders which made this conduct a crime. They forbid such a one to remain, and they also forbid him to leave. They were so drawn that the only way Korematsu could

avoid violation was to give himself up to the military authority. This meant submission to custody, examination, and transportation out of the territory, to be followed by indeterminate confinement in detention camps.

A citizen's presence in the locality, however, was made a crime only if his parents were of Japanese birth. Had Korematsu been one of four—the others being, say, a German alien enemy, an Italian alien enemy, and a citizen of American-born ancestors, convicted of treason but out on parole—only Korematsu's presence would have violated the order. The difference between their innocence and his crime would result, not from anything he did, said, or thought, different than they, but only in that he was born of different racial stock.

Now, if any fundamental assumption underlies our system, it is that guilt is personal and not inheritable. Even if all of one's antecedents had been convicted of treason, the Constitution forbids its penalties to be visited upon him, for it provides that "no attainder of treason shall work corruption of blood, or forfeiture except during the life of the person attainted." But here is an attempt to make an otherwise innocent act a crime merely because this prisoner is the son of parents as to whom he had no choice, and belongs to a race from which there is no way to resign. If Congress in peace-time legislation should enact such a criminal law, I should suppose this Court would refuse to enforce it.

But the "law" which this prisoner is convicted of disregarding is not found in an act of Congress, but in a military order. Neither the Act of Congress nor the Executive Order of the President, nor both together, would afford a basis for this conviction. It rests on the orders of General DeWitt. And it is said that if the military commander had reasonable military grounds for promulgating the orders, they are constitutional and become law, and the Court is required to enforce them. There are several reasons why I cannot subscribe to this doctrine. . . .

Much is said of the danger to liberty from the Army program for deporting and detaining these citizens of Japanese extraction. But a judicial construction of the due process clause that will sustain this order is a far more subtle blow to liberty than the promulgation of the order itself. A military order, however unconstitutional, is not apt to last longer than the military emergency. Even during that period a succeeding commander may revoke it all. But once a judicial opinion rationalizes such an order to show that it conforms to the Constitution, or rather rationalizes the Constitution to show that the Constitution sanctions such an order, the Court for all time has validated the principle of racial discrimination in criminal procedure and of transplanting American citizens. The principle then lies about like a loaded weapon ready for the hand of any authority that can bring forward a plausible claim of an urgent need. . . .

I should hold that a civil court cannot be made to enforce an order which violates constitutional limita-tions even if it is a reasonable exercise of military authority. The courts can exercise only the judicial power, can apply only law, and must abide by the Constitution, or they cease to be civil courts and become instruments of military policy. . . .

My duties as a justice as I see them do not require me to make a military judgment as to whether General DeWitt's evacuation and detention program was a reasonable military necessity. I do not suggest that the courts should have attempted to interfere with the Army in carrying out its task. But I do not think they may be asked to execute a military expedient that has no place in law under the Constitution. I would reverse the judgment and discharge the prisoner.

The *Korematsu* decision was softened, but only slightly, by *Ex parte Endo* (1944), a decision handed down the same day. In this case Mitsuye Endo had been caught escaping from a detention center. However, she had gone through the appro-priate government procedures and had been clas-sified as loyal to the United States. The justices ruled in her favor, holding that the government does not have the authority to detain persons whose loyalty has been established.

During the Korean conflict the justices were called upon to decide the constitutional validity of another executive action taken in the name of the war powers doctrine. This case involved prop-erty rights rather than civil liberties. As you read Justice Black's opinion for the Court in *Youngs-town Sheet and Tube Company v. Sawyer* (1952), compare it to his opinion in *Korematsu*. Both involved the president taking actions to strengthen war efforts. Does it make sense to you that the Court approved the detention of more than 110,000 individuals on the basis of national ori-gin, but ruled that the government could not take nominal possession of the steel mills? Note the analysis provided in Justice Jackson's concurring opinion, in which he lays out a formula for deciding questions of presidential power in rela-tion to congressional action.

Youngstown Sheet and Tube Company v. Sawyer

343 U.S. 579 (1952)

Vote: 6 (Black, Burton, Clark, Douglas, Frankfurter, Jackson)
3 (Minton, Reed, Vinson)
Opinion of the Court: Black
Concurring opinions: Burton, Clark, Douglas, Frankfurter, Jackson
Dissenting opinion: Vinson

In 1951 a labor dispute began in the steel industry. In December the United Steelworkers Union announced that it would call a strike at the end of that month, when its contract with the steel companies expired. For the next several months the Federal Mediation and Conciliation Service and the Federal Wage Stabilization Board tried to work out a settlement, but the efforts were unsuc-cessful. On April 4, 1952, the union said that its strike would begin on April 9.

The attorney representing the steel industry, John W. Davis, Jr., (left) arriving at the Supreme Court May 13, 1952, with acting attorney general Philip B. Perlman. Davis was the Democratic nominee for the presidency in 1924, capturing 29 percent of the popular vote in a loss to Calvin Coolidge. He later represented the school board defendants in the 1954 school desegregation cases.

President Truman was not about to let a strike hit the steel industry. The nation was engaged in the Korean War, and steel production was necessary to produce the arms and equipment needed by American troops in battle. Only hours before the strike was to begin, Truman issued an executive order commanding Secretary of Commerce Charles Sawyer to seize the nation's steel mills and keep them in operation. Sawyer in turn ordered the mill owners to continue to run their facilities as operators for the United States.

Truman's seizure order cited no statutory authority for his action because there was none. There were federal statutes permitting the seizure of industrial plants for certain specified reasons, but the settlement of a labor dispute was not one of them. In fact, the Taft-Hartley Act of 1946 rejected the idea that labor disputes could be resolved by such means. Instead, the act authorized the president to impose an eighty-day cooling-off period as a way to postpone any strike that seriously threatened the public interest. Truman, however, had little regard for the Taft-Hartley Act, which Congress had passed over his veto. The president ignored the cooling-off period alternative and took the direct action of seizing the mills. The inherent powers of the chief executive, he maintained, were enough to authorize the action.

Congress might have improved the president's legal ground by immediately passing legislation authorizing such seizures retroactively, but it did not. The mill owners complied with the seizure orders under protest and filed suit in federal court to have Truman's action declared unconstitutional. The district court ruled in favor of the steel industry enjoining the secretary from seizing the plants, but the same day the court of appeals stayed the injunction.

Justice Black delivered the opinion of the Court:

We are asked to decide whether the President was acting within his constitutional power when he issued an order directing the Secretary of Commerce to take possession of and operate most of the Nation's steel mills. The mill owners argue that the President's order amounts to lawmaking, a legislative function which the Constitution has expressly confided to the Congress and not to the President. The Government's position is that the order was made on findings of the President that his action was necessary to avert a national catastrophe which would inevitably result from a stoppage of steel production, and that in meeting this grave emergency the President was acting within the aggregate of his constitutional powers as the Nation's Chief Executive and the Commander in Chief of the Armed Forces of the United States. . . .

The President's power, if any, to issue the order must stem either from an act of Congress or from the Constitution itself. There is no statute that expressly authorizes the President to take possession of property as he did here. Nor is there any act of Congress to which our attention has been directed from which such a power can fairly be implied. Indeed, we do not understand the Government to rely on statutory authorization for this seizure. . . .

It is clear that if the President had authority to issue the order he did, it must be found in some provision of the Constitution. And it is not claimed that express constitutional language grants this power to the President. The contention is that presidential power should be implied from the aggregate of his powers under the Constitution. Particular reliance is placed on provisions in Article II which say that "The executive Power shall be vested in a President . . ."; that "he shall take Care that the Laws be faithfully executed"; and that he "shall be Commander in Chief of the Army and Navy of the United States."

The order cannot properly be sustained as an exercise of the President's military power as Commander in Chief of the Armed Forces. The Government attempts to do so by citing a number of cases upholding broad powers in military commanders engaged in day-to-day fighting in a theater of war. Such cases need not concern us here. Even though "theater of war" be an expanding concept, we cannot with faithfulness to our constitutional system hold that the Commander in Chief of the Armed Forces has the ultimate power as such to take possession of private property in order to keep labor disputes from stopping production. This is a job for the Nation's lawmakers, not for its military authorities.

Nor can the seizure order be sustained because of the several constitutional provisions that grant executive power to the President. In the framework of our Constitution, the President's power to see that the laws are faithfully executed refutes the idea that he is to be a lawmaker. The Constitution limits his functions in the lawmaking process to the recommending of laws he thinks wise and the vetoing of laws he thinks bad. And the Constitution is neither silent nor equivocal about who shall make laws which the President is to execute. The first section of the first article says that "All legislative Powers herein granted shall be vested in a Congress of the United States. . . ." After granting many powers to the Congress, Article I goes on to provide that Congress may "make all Laws which shall be necessary and proper for carrying into Execution the foregoing Powers, and all other Powers vested by this Constitution in the Government of the United States, or in any Department or Officer thereof."

The President's order does not direct that a congressional policy be executed in a manner prescribed by Congress—it directs that a presidential policy be executed in a manner prescribed by the President. The preamble of the order itself, like that of many statutes, sets out reasons why the President believes certain policies should be adopted, proclaims these policies as rules of conduct to be followed, and again, like a statute, authorizes a government official to promulgate additional rules and regulations consistent with the policy proclaimed and needed to carry that policy into execution. The power of Congress to adopt such public policies as those proclaimed by the order is beyond question. It can authorize the taking of private property for public use. It can make laws regulating the relationships between employers and employees, prescribing rules designed to settle labor disputes, and fixing wages and working conditions in certain fields of our economy. The Constitution does not subject this lawmaking power of Congress to presidential or military supervision or control.

It is said that other Presidents without congressional authority have taken possession of private business enterprises in order to settle labor disputes. But even if this be true, Congress has not thereby lost its exclusive constitutional authority to make laws necessary and proper to carry out the powers vested by the Constitution "in the Government of the United States, or any Department or Officer thereof."

The Founders of this Nation entrusted the lawmaking power to the Congress alone in both good and bad times. It would do no good to recall the historical events, the fears of power and the hopes for freedom that lay behind their choice. Such a review would but confirm our holding that this seizure order cannot stand.

The judgment of the District Court is

Affirmed.

Mr. Justice JACKSON, concurring in the judgment and opinion of the Court. . . .

A judge, like an executive adviser, may be surprised at the poverty of really useful and unambiguous authority applicable to concrete problems of executive power as they actually present themselves. Just what our forefathers did envision, or would have envisioned had they foreseen modern conditions, must be divined from materials almost as enigmatic as the dreams Joseph was called upon to interpret for Pharaoh. A century and a half of partisan debate and scholarly speculation yields no net result but only supplies more or less apt quotations from respected sources on each side of any question. They largely cancel each other. And court decisions are indecisive because of the judicial practice of dealing with the largest questions in the most narrow way.

. . . We may well begin by a somewhat oversimplified grouping of practical situations in which a President may doubt, or others may challenge, his powers, and by distinguishing roughly the legal consequences of this factor of relativity.

1. When the President acts pursuant to an express or implied authorization of Congress, his authority is at its maximum, for it includes all that he possesses in his own right plus all that Congress can delegate. . . .

2. When the President acts in absence of either a congressional grant or denial of authority, he can only rely upon his own independent powers, but there is a zone of twilight in which he and Congress may have concurrent authority, or in which its distribution is uncertain. Therefore, congressional inertia, indifference or quiescence may sometimes, at least as a practical matter, enable, if not invite, measures on independent presidential responsibility. In this area, any actual test of power is likely to depend on the imperatives of events and contemporary imponderables rather than on abstract theories of law.

3. When the President takes measures incompatible with the expressed or implied will of Congress, his power is at its lowest ebb, for then he can rely only upon his own constitutional powers minus any constitutional powers of Congress over the matter. . . .

Into which of these classifications does this executive seizure of the steel industry fit? It is eliminated from the first by admission, for it is conceded that no congressional authorization exists for this seizure. That takes away also the support of the many precedents and declarations which were made in relation, and must be confined, to this category.

Can it then be defended under flexible tests available to the second category? It seems clearly eliminated from that class because Congress has not left seizure of private property an open field but has covered it by three statutory policies inconsistent with this seizure. . . .

This leaves the current seizure to be justified only by the severe tests under the third grouping, where it can be supported only by any remainder of executive power after subtraction of such powers as Congress may have over the subject. In short, we can sustain the President only by holding that seizure of such strike-bound industries is within his domain and beyond control by Congress. Thus, this Court's first review of such seizures occurs under circumstances which leave presidential power most vulnerable to attack and in the least favorable of possible constitutional postures. . . .

The Solicitor General, acknowledging that Congress has never authorized the seizure here, says practice of prior Presidents has authorized it. He seeks color of legality from claimed executive precedents, chief of which is President Roosevelt's seizure on June 9, 1941, of the California plant of the North American Aviation Company. Its superficial similarities with the present case, upon analysis, yield to distinctions so decisive that it cannot be regarded as even a precedent, much less an authority for the present seizure.

The appeal, however, that we declare the existence of inherent powers *ex necessitate* to meet an emergency asks us to do what many think would be wise, although it is something the forefathers omitted. They knew what emergencies were, knew the pressures they engender for authoritative action, knew, too, how they afford a ready pretext for usurpation. We may also suspect that they suspected that emergency powers would tend to kindle emergencies. Aside from suspension of the privilege of the writ of habeas corpus in time of rebellion or invasion, when the public safety may require it, they made no express provision for exercise of extraordinary authority because of a crisis. I do not think we rightfully may so amend their work, and, if we could, I am not convinced it would be wise to do so, although many modern nations have forthrightly recognized that war and economic crises may upset the normal balance between liberty and authority. . . .

The essence of our free Government is "leave to live by no man's leave, underneath the law"—to be governed by those impersonal forces which we call law. Our Government is fashioned to fulfill this concept so far as humanly possible. The Executive, except for recommendation and veto, has no legislative power. The executive action we have here originates in the individual will of the President and represents an exercise of authority without law. No one, perhaps not even the President, knows the limits of the power he may seek to exert in this instance and the parties affected cannot learn the limit of their rights. We do not know today what powers over labor or property would be claimed to flow from Government possession if we should legalize it, what rights to compensation would be claimed or recognized, or on what contingency it would end. With all its defects, delays and inconveniences, men have discovered no technique for long preserving free government except that the Executive be under the law, and that the law be made by parliamentary deliberations.

Such institutions may be destined to pass away. But it is the duty of the Court to be last, not first, to give them up.

Contemporary Crises

The majority and concurring opinions in *Youngstown Sheet and Tube* have provided the Court with useful guides for dealing with similar cases in times of national emergency. In 1981, for example, the justices considered an appeal based on one of the more serious foreign policy problems the United States faced in recent years—the Iran hostage crisis. The case of *Dames & Moore v. Regan* involved the power of the president to seize the assets of Iran and use them as a bargaining chip to help settle an international stalemate. To preserve the assets under his control, the president disallowed any lawsuits by U.S. citizens and corporations requesting that the assets be used to pay off judgments against Iran. Was the president acting within his legitimate foreign policy powers? Or was Dames & Moore Company correct in arguing that he had gone too far? As you read the opinion, compare it to the views expressed in the *Steel Seizure* case. See how closely Rehnquist ties his opinion to Black's majority views and Jackson's concurrence in *Youngstown*.

Dames & Moore v. Regan

453 U.S. 654 (1981)

Vote: 9 (Blackmun, Brennan, Burger, Marshall, Powell, Rehnquist, Stevens, Stewart, White)
    0
Opinion of the Court: Rehnquist
Opinion concurring in part: Stevens
Opinion concurring in part and dissenting in part: Powell

On November 4, 1979, Iranians seized the American Embassy in Tehran, captured its diplomatic personnel, and held them hostage. In response, President Carter invoked the International Economic Emergency Powers Act (IEEPA) and froze all assets of the Iranian government or its agencies within the jurisdiction of the United States. As part of the regulations enforcing that order, the Department of the Treasury ruled that, unless otherwise stipulated, the seized Iranian assets were protected against judgments, decrees, or attachments by United States courts.

On December 19 Dames & Moore Company filed suit in federal district court against the government of Iran, the Atomic Energy Organization of Iran, and a number of Iranian banks. The suit claimed that the company had been under contract with the Iranian Atomic Energy Organization to conduct site inspections for a proposed nuclear power facility and had not been fully paid for its services. Dames & Moore contended that the Iranians still owed the company almost $3.5 million and asked the court to grant it the back payments plus interest. Furthermore, Dames & Moore wanted the district court to attach Iranian assets in the United States to ensure payment of the judgment.

The crisis ended in January 1981 when the United States and Iran reached an agreement and the hostages were released. As part of the settlement the United States agreed to terminate all American lawsuits involving the frozen Iranian assets. A special Iran-United States Claims Tribunal was established to settle disputes over the Iranian assets; the tribunal's judgments were to be final and enforceable in the courts of any nation. To implement these arrangements, President Carter ordered that all frozen Iranian assets be moved to the Federal Reserve Bank in New York for ultimate transfer back to Iran, with a portion set aside for payment of Claims Tribunal judgments. In February 1981, shortly after assuming office, President Reagan issued executive orders reaffirming Carter's actions.

With these orders in effect, the district court denied attachments against the Iranian assets to pay Dames & Moore. The company then filed a suit against Secretary of the Treasury Donald Regan, arguing that the president had exceeded his constitutional and statutory power by removing Iranian assets from possible attachment by the federal courts. Furthermore, the company protested that the president did not have authority to impose claims settlement procedures by executive agreement. The district court ruled in favor of

the government, and the Supreme Court accepted the company's appeal using expedited procedures to bring the case immediately before the justices.

Justice William Rehnquist delivered the opinion of the Court:

[W]e freely confess that we are obviously deciding only one more episode in the never-ending tension between the President exercising the executive authority in a world that presents each day some new challenge with which he must deal and the Constitution under which we all live and which no one disputes embodies some sort of system of checks and balances. . . .

The parties and the lower courts . . . have all agreed that much relevant analysis is contained in *Youngstown Sheet & Tube Co. v. Sawyer* (1952). Justice Black's opinion for the Court in that case, involving the validity of President Truman's effort to seize the country's steel mills in the wake of a nationwide strike, recognized that "[t]he President's power, if any, to issue the order must stem either from an act of Congress or from the Constitution itself." Justice Jackson's concurring opinion elaborated in a general way the consequences of different types of interaction between the two democratic branches in assessing Presidential authority to act in any given case. When the President acts pursuant to an express or implied authorization from Congress, he exercises not only his powers but also those delegated by Congress. In such a case the executive action "would be supported by the strongest of presumptions and the widest latitude of judicial interpretation, and the burden of persuasion would rest heavily upon any who might attack it." When the President acts in the absence of congressional authorization he may enter "a zone of twilight in which he and Congress may have concurrent authority, or in which its distribution is uncertain." In such a case the analysis becomes more complicated, and the validity of the President's action, at least so far as separation-of-powers principles are concerned, hinges on a consideration of all the circumstances which might shed light on the views of the Legislative Branch toward such action, including "congressional inertia, indifference or quiescence." Finally, when the President acts in contravention of the will of Congress, "his power is at its lowest ebb,'' and the Court can sustain his actions ''only by disabling the Congress from acting upon the subject.''

Although we have in the past found and do today find Justice Jackson's classification of executive actions into three general categories analytically useful, we should be mindful of Justice Holmes' admonition, . . . that ''[t]he great ordinances of the Constitution do not establish and divide fields of black and white.'' *Springer* v. *Philippine Islands* (1928) (dissenting opinion). Justice Jackson himself recognized that his three categories represented ''a somewhat over-simplified grouping,'' and it is doubtless the case that executive action in any particular instance falls, not neatly in one of three pigeonholes, but rather at some point along a spectrum running from explicit congressional authorization to explicit congressional prohibition. This is particularly true as respects cases such as the one before us, involving responses to international crises the nature of which Congress can hardly have been expected to anticipate in any detail. . . .

This Court has previously recognized that the congressional purpose in authorizing blocking orders is ''to put control of foreign assets in the hands of the President. . . .'' *Propper* v. *Clark* (1949). Such orders permit the President to maintain the foreign assets at his disposal for use in negotiating the resolution of a declared national emergency. The frozen assets serve as a ''bargaining chip'' to be used by the President when dealing with a hostile country. Accordingly, it is difficult to accept petitioner's argument because the practical effect of it is to allow individual claimants throughout the country to minimize or wholly eliminate this ''bargaining chip'' through attachments, garnishments, or similar encumbrances on property. Neither the purpose the statute was enacted to serve nor its plain language supports such a result.

Because the President's action in nullifying the attachments and ordering the transfer of the assets was taken pursuant to specific congressional authorization, it is ''supported by the strongest of presumptions and the widest latitude of judicial interpretation, and the burden of persuasion would rest heavily upon any who might attack it.'' *Youngstown* (Jackson, J., concurring). Under the circumstances of this case, we cannot

say that petitioner has sustained that heavy burden. A contrary ruling would mean that the Federal Government as a whole lacked the power exercised by the President, and that we are not prepared to say. . . .

Although we have declined to conclude that the IEEPA or the Hostage Act directly authorizes the President's suspension of claims for the reasons noted, we cannot ignore the general tenor of Congress' legislation in this area in trying to determine whether the President is acting alone or at least with the acceptance of Congress. As we have noted, Congress cannot anticipate and legislate with regard to every possible action the President may find it necessary to take or every possible situation in which he might act. Such failure of Congress specifically to delegate authority does not, ''especially . . . in the areas of foreign policy and national security,'' imply ''congressional disapproval'' of action taken by the Executive. On the contrary, the enactment of legislation closely related to the question of the President's authority in a particular case which evinces legislative intent to accord the President broad discretion may be considered to ''invite'' ''measures on independent presidential responsibility,'' *Youngstown* (Jackson, J., concurring). At least this is so where there is no contrary indication of legislative intent and when, as here, there is a history of congressional acquiescence in conduct of the sort engaged in by the President. It is to that history which we now turn.

Not infrequently in affairs between nations, outstanding claims by nationals of one country against the government of another country are ''sources of friction'' between the two sovereigns. *United States* v. *Pink* (1942). To resolve these difficulties, nations have often entered into agreements settling the claims of their respective nationals. . . . Consistent with that principle, the United States has repeatedly exercised its sovereign authority to settle the claims of its nationals against foreign countries. Though those settlements have sometimes been made by treaty, there has also been a longstanding practice of settling such claims by executive agreement without the advice and consent of the Senate. Under such agreements, the President has agreed to renounce or extinguish claims of United States nationals against foreign governments in return for lump-sum payments or the establishment of arbitration procedures. To be sure, many of these settlements were encouraged by the United States claimants themselves, since a claimant's only hope of obtaining any payment at all might lie in having his Government negotiate a diplomatic settlement on his behalf. . . . Since 1952, the President has entered into at least 10 binding settlements with foreign nations, including an $80 million settlement with the People's Republic of China.

Crucial to our decision today is the conclusion that Congress has implicitly approved the practice of claim settlement by executive agreement. This is best demonstrated by Congress' enactment of the International Claims Settlement Act of 1949. The Act had two purposes: (1) to allocate to United States nationals funds received in the course of an executive claims settlement with Yugoslavia, and (2) to provide a procedure whereby funds resulting from future settlements could be distributed. To achieve these ends Congress created the International Claims Commission, now the Foreign Claims Settlement Commission, and gave it jurisdiction to make final and binding decisions with respect to claims by United States nationals against settlement funds. By creating a procedure to implement future settlement agreements, Congress placed its stamp of approval on such agreements. Indeed, the legislative history of the Act observed that the United States was seeking settlements with countries other than Yugoslavia and that the bill contemplated settlements of a similar nature in the future. . . .

In addition to congressional acquiescence in the President's power to settle claims, prior cases of this Court have also recognized that the President does have some measure of power to enter into executive agreements without obtaining the advice and consent of the Senate. In *United States v. Pink,* for example, the Court upheld the validity of the Litvinov Assignment, which was part of an Executive Agreement whereby the Soviet Union assigned to the United States amounts owed to it by American nationals so that outstanding claims of other American nationals could be paid. . . .

In light of all the foregoing—the inferences to be drawn from the character of the legislation Congress has enacted in the area, such as the IEEPA and the Hostage Act, and from the history of acquiescence in executive claims settlement—we conclude that the President was authorized to suspend pending claims pursuant to Executive Order No. 12294. . . .

Just as importantly, Congress has not disapproved of the action taken here. Though Congress has held hearings on the Iranian Agreement itself, Congress has not enacted legislation or even passed a resolution, indicating its displeasure with the Agreement. Quite the contrary, the relevant Senate Committee has stated that the establishment of the Tribunal is "of vital importance to the United States." We are thus clearly not confronted with a situation in which Congress has in some way resisted the exercise of Presidential authority.

Finally, we re-emphasize the narrowness of our decision. We do not decide that the President possesses plenary power to settle claims, even as against foreign governmental entities. . . . But where, as here, the settlement of claims has been determined to be a necessary incident to the resolution of a major foreign policy dispute between our country and another, and where, as here, we can conclude that Congress acquiesced in the President's action, we are not prepared to say that the President lacks the power to settle such claims.

The *Dames & Moore* decision underscores the same principle that the Court articulated almost a half-century earlier in *Curtiss-Wright*—the president is the primary government authority over matters of foreign policy. The decision also recognizes that in times of emergency the president's powers expand. Yet those powers are not unlimited, and undoubtedly the Court will continue to be faced with claims that the president has exceeded his constitutional authority. As emphasized in the *Steel Seizure* case as well as in *Dames & Moore,* the president stands on much firmer constitutional ground when acting with the assent of Congress.

READINGS

Berger, Raoul. *Executive Privilege: A Constitutional Myth.* Cambridge, Mass.: Harvard University Press, 1974.

Bessette, Joseph, and Jeffrey Tulis. *The Presidency in the Constitutional Order.* Baton Rouge: Louisiana State University Press, 1981.

Corwin, Edward S. *The President: Office and Powers,* 5th rev. ed. New York: New York University Press, 1984.

Crovitz, L. Gordon, and Jeremy A. Rabkin, eds. *The Fettered Presidency: Legal Constraints on the Executive Branch.* Washington, D.C.: American Enterprise Institute for Public Policy Research, 1989.

Henkin, Louis. *Foreign Affairs and the Constitution.* Mineola, N.Y.: Foundation Press, 1972.

Irons, Peter. *Justice at War: The Story of the Japanese-American Internment Cases.* New York: Oxford University Press, 1983.

Koenig, Louis. *The Chief Executive,* 3d ed. New York: Harcourt Brace Jovanovich, 1975.

Marcus, Maeva. *Truman and the Steel Seizure Case: The Limits of Presidential Power.* New York: Columbia University Press, 1987.

May, Christopher. *In the Name of War: Judicial Review and the War Powers Since 1918.* Cambridge, Mass.: Harvard University Press, 1989.

McKenzie, G. Calvin. *The Politics of Presidential Appointments.* New York: Free Press, 1981.

Randall, James. *Constitutional Problems under Lincoln.* Urbana: University of Illinois Press, 1964.

Reveley, W. Taylor III. *War Powers of the President and Congress.* Charlottesville: University Press of Virginia, 1981.

Rossiter, Clinton L. *Constitutional Dictatorship: Crisis Government in the Modern Democracies.* Princeton, N.J.: Princeton University Press, 1948.

Westin, Alan F. *Anatomy of a Constitutional Law Case.* New York: Macmillan, 1958.

PART III

NATION-STATE RELATIONS

FEDERALISM

FEDERALISM

If we catalogued the types of governments existing in the world today, we would have a fairly diverse list. Some are unitary systems in which power is located in a central authority that may or may not mete out some power to its subdivisions. Others are virtually the opposite: authority rests largely with local governments with only certain powers reserved to national authority. When the Framers drafted the Constitution, they had to make some basic decisions about the balance between the states and the national government they were creating. Their choice, generally speaking, was federalism: a system in which "a constitution divides governmental power between a central government and one or more subdivisional governments, giving each substantial functions."[1]

That decision turned out to be a good one, and we reap the advantages of it today. For example, because the government is multitiered and layered, Americans have many points of access to influence the system.[2] If your state enacts legislation you do not like, you might be able to challenge it in a federal court or to lobby your representative in Congress. Moreover, the system provides for further checks on the exercise of government power because federal, state, and even local systems are all involved in policy making. Finally, it encourages experimentation and provides for flexibility. Justice Louis D. Brandeis once wrote, "It is one of the happy incidents of the federal system that a single courageous State may, if its citizens choose, serve as a laboratory; and try novel social and economic experiments without risk to the rest of the country."[3] While "experimenting with policy on the national level poses great risks," states are uniquely poised to fashion solutions for their own localized problems, some of which may be applicable to the nation.[4] The states were first to implement tougher drinking and driving laws, policies protecting workers' rights, and so forth.

But federalism is not perfect. It can be costly. In some countries citizens pay a single tax; Americans pay many: local property taxes, state sales and income taxes, and federal assessments. In addition, the system lacks efficiency. The implementation of certain kinds of policies might require the coordination of the national government, fifty states, and numerous subdivisions, which inevitably slows down the process.

For our purposes, the most relevant concern about federalism is its complexity. The system "makes it difficult for citizens to keep informed

1. J. W. Peltason, *Understanding the Constitution*, 11th ed. (New York: Holt, Rinehart and Winston, 1988), 16.

2. We derive this and what follows from Paul Johnson et al., *American Government* (Boston: Houghton Mifflin, 1990), 75-79.

3. Dissent in *New State Ice Co. v. Liebmann*, 285 U.S. 262 at 311 (1932).

4. Johnson et al., *American Government*, 77.

about their government.''[5] People may not understand which level of government makes specific policies, and some citizens may have so little interest that they do not know the names of their state representatives. At the other end of the spectrum, governments sometimes do not well understand the boundaries of their own power. American history is full of examples of states alleging that the federal government has gone too far in regulating ''their'' business; indeed, this was one issue over which the Civil War, the most extreme disagreement, was fought.

Yet, in most circumstances, it is neither war that has resolved these disputes nor the entities themselves that have shed light on their complexities. Rather, since the nation's founding, the U.S. Supreme Court has played the major role in delineating and defining the contours of American federalism. Why and how it has done so are the subjects of the chapters that follow. Chapter 5 focuses on the various and general theories of federal-state relations with which the Court has dealt. Chapters 6 and 7 consider the exercise of government power over the most contentious of issues: commerce and taxing and spending.

But first, let us explore several issues emanating from our discussion so far: the kind of system the Framers adopted, the amending of that system, and its complexity, which often requires the involvement of ''neutral'' arbiters—judges and Supreme Court justices.

The Framers and Federalism

We have already mentioned that the Framers selected federalism among several alternative forms of government, although the word *federalism* does not appear in the Constitution. The Founders had some general vision of the sort of government they wanted or, more aptly, of those they did not want. They rejected a unitary system

as wholly incompatible with basic values and traditions already existing within the states. Nor did they favor a confederation of nations in which power would reside with the states; after all, that is what they had under the Articles of Confederation, the charter they came to Philadelphia to revise.

How to divide power, then, became the delegates' central concern. In the end, they wrote into the document a rather elaborate ''pattern of allocation,'' but its ambiguity ultimately failed to satisfy them.[6] The ambiguity stemmed from several sources. First, there was the question of constitutional relationships; that is, in the parlance of the eighteenth century, the Framers looked at the Constitution as a contract, but a contract between whom? Some commentators argue that it specifies the relationship between the people and the national government and that the former empower the latter. Justice Joseph Story wrote:

The constitution of the United States was ordained and established, not by the states in their sovereign capacities, but emphatically, as the preamble of the constitution declares, by ''the people of the United States.'' . . . The constitution was not, therefore, necessarily carved out of existing state sovereignties, nor a surrender of powers already existing in state institutions.[7]

Others suggest that the contract is between the states and the nation. In a 1798 resolution of the Virginia Assembly, James Madison wrote:

That this Assembly doth explicitly and peremptorily declare that it views the powers of the Federal Government as resulting from the compact, to which the States are parties, as limited by the plain sense and intention of the instrument constituting that compact; as no further valid than they are authorized by the grants enumerated in that compact; and that in case of deliberate,

5. Ibid., 75.

6. C. Herman Pritchett, *Constitutional Law of the Federal System* (Englewood Cliffs, N.J.: Prentice-Hall, 1984), 58.
7. *Martin v. Hunter's Lessee,* 1 Wheat. 304 at 324-325 (1816).

palpable, and dangerous exercise of other powers not granted by the said compact, the States, who are the parties thereto, have the right, and are in duty bound, to interpose for arresting the progress of the evil, and for maintaining within their respective limits, the authorities, rights, and liberties appertaining to them.[8]

This is not merely an abstract debate, but one with real consequences. In its most violent incarnation, the Civil War, southern leaders took Madison's logic to its limit. They argued that because the Constitution represented a contract between the states and the federal government, with the states creating the national government, when the latter—the North—abrogated its end of the contract, it was no longer valid. The Civil War ended that particular dispute, but the principal continued to flare up in less extreme, but no less important, forms. The refusal of some southern states to abide by federal civil rights laws is one example.

This problem continues to manifest itself largely because the Constitution supports both sides and therefore neither. Those who favor the national government-people approach point to the document's preamble: *"We the people of the United States . . . do ordain and establish this Constitution."* To support the national government-state argument, proponents turn to Article VII's language, that the ratification of nine states "shall be sufficient for the Establishment of this Constitution *between the States* so ratifying." When the issue of the contractual nature of the Constitution arises, therefore, many look to the Supreme Court to resolve it. As we shall see in the next chapter, different Courts have approached this debate in varying ways, adopting one view over the other at distinct points in American history.

8. Reprinted in *Documents of American Constitutional and Legal History,* vol. 1, ed. Melvin I. Urofsky (New York: Knopf, 1989), 159.

Amending the Constitution: The Tenth Amendment

Arguments over the parties to the contract, the U.S. Constitution, may never be fully resolved. Another point of ambiguity was thought so onerous that it could not be left up to mere interpretation. That area is the balance of power between the states and the federal government. The original charter, in the view of many, placed too much authority with the federal government. In particular, states' rights advocates pointed to two sections of the Constitution as working against their interests. The first is the Necessary and Proper Clause: "Congress has the power To make all Laws which shall be necessary and proper for carrying into Execution [its] Powers, and all other Powers vested by this Constitution in the Government of the United States, or in any Department or Officer thereof." The other is the Supremacy Clause: "This Constitution, and the Laws of the United States which shall be made in Pursuance thereof; and all Treaties made, or which shall be made, under the Authority of the United States, shall be the supreme Law of the Land; and the Judges in every state shall be bound thereby, any Thing in the Constitution or Laws of any State to the Contrary notwithstanding." These clauses seem to allocate a great deal of power to the national government. Yet, as Madison wrote in Federalist 45:

The powers delegated by the proposed Constitution to the federal government are few and defined. Those which are to remain in the State governments are numerous and indefinite. The former will be exercised principally on external objects, as war, peace, negotiation, and foreign commerce; with which last the power of taxation will, for the most part, be connected. The powers reserved to the several States will extend to all the objects which, in the ordinary course of affairs, concern the lives, liberties, and properties of the people, and the internal order, improvement, and prosperity of the State.

Nevertheless, states remained concerned that the national government would attempt to cut into their power and sovereignty, and the language of the Constitution did little to allay their fears. At worst, it suggested that the federal institutions always would be supreme; at best, it was highly ambiguous. Even Madison recognized its lack of clarity when he wrote in Federalist 39:

The proposed Constitution, therefore . . . is, in strictness, neither a national nor a federal Constitution, but a composition of both. In its foundation it is federal, not national; in the sources from which the ordinary powers of the government are drawn, it is partly federal and partly national; in the operation of these powers, it is national, not federal; in the extent to them, again, it is federal, not national; and, finally in the authoritative mode of introducing amendments, it is neither wholly federal nor wholly national.

Madison clearly thought this ambiguity an asset of the new system of government, an advantage that made it fit compatibly into the overall philosophies of separation of powers and checks and balances. But this argument proved insufficient; when the perceived unfair balance of power proved to be an obstacle to the ratification of the Constitution, those favoring its adoption promised to remedy it.

This remedy took the form of the Tenth Amendment, which—in terms of the rest of the Bill of Rights—is a constitutional oddity. While the first nine amendments deal mainly with the rights of the people vis-à-vis the federal government (for example, the First Amendment: ''Congress shall make no law respecting an establishment of religion,'' and so forth), the Tenth Amendment states: ''The powers not delegated to the United States by the Constitution, nor prohibited by it to the States, are reserved to the States respectively, or to the people.'' With these words in place, states' rights advocates were mollified, at least temporarily, and our system of government—that unique brand of federalism—was established.

In the final analysis, what does the system look like? In other words, who gets what? Table III-1 depicts the allocation of powers emanating from the Constitution and the Tenth Amendment. As we can see, the levels of government have some exclusive and some concurrent powers, but also they are prohibited from operating in certain spheres.

The elaborate system of American federalism depicted in Table III-1 seems to belie what we noted at the beginning of this chapter. At this point, you may be wondering how such a well-articulated division of power could be the center of so much controversy? In part, the answer takes us back to the contractual nature of the Constitution. As we shall see in the following chapter, in which we explore general theoretical approaches to federalism, the Court has had some difficulty determining the parties to the contract, and its confusion encouraged litigation. In more concrete terms, no matter how elaborate the design, it does not (and perhaps cannot) address the range of real disputes that arise between nation and state. Indeed, the irony here is that the complexity of the system coupled with the language of the Constitution is what fosters the need for interpretation. Take another look at Table III-1, particularly the last column illustrating concurrent powers. Where do state powers begin and federal powers end or vice versa? For example, states have the authority to regulate intrastate commerce, and the federal government regulates interstate commerce, but is it so easy to delineate those boundaries? Which entity controls the manufacturing of goods in a given state that are shipped to another? And, more to the point, what happens when they have different ideas over how to regulate the manufacturing?

If that problem is not enough, compare the constitutional language of the Tenth Amendment with that of the Necessary and Proper and Supremacy Clauses. The last prohibits states from passing laws that directly conflict with the Consti-

Table III-1   The Constitutional Allocation of Government Power

Powers Specified Within the Constitution or by Court Interpretation

Powers Exclusive to the National Government	*Powers Exclusive to State Governments*	*Concurrent Powers to both Federal and State Governments*
Coin money	Run elections	Tax
Regulate interstate and foreign commerce	Regulate intrastate commerce	Borrow money
Tax imports and exports	Establish republican forms of state and local governments	Establish courts
Make treaties	Protect public health, safety, and morals	Charter banks and corporations
Make all laws "necessary and proper"		Make and enforce laws
Make war	All powers not delegated to the national government or denied to the states by the Constitution	Take property (power of eminent domain)
Regulate postal system		

Powers Denied by the Constitution or by Court Interpretation

Expressly Prohibited to the National Government	*Expressly Prohibited to State Government*	*Expressly Prohibited to Both*
Tax state exports	Tax imports and exports	Pass bills of attainder
Change state boundaries	Coin money	Pass ex post facto laws
	Enter into treaties	Grant titles of nobility
	Impair obligation of contracts	Impose religious tests
		Pass laws in conflict with the Bill of Rights and subsequent amendments

Source: Adapted from Paul E. Johnson et al., *American Government* (Boston: Houghton Mifflin, 1990), 84; J. W. Peltason, *Corwin & Peltason's Understanding the Constitution* (New York: Holt, Rinehart and Winston, 1988), 19; C. Herman Prichett, *Constitutional Law of the Federal System* (Englewood Cliffs, N.J.: Prentice-Hall, 1984), 58.

tution, federal laws, and so forth. But so often it is simply not that clear. For example, is the federal authority supreme only in its sphere of operations (those activities where it has clear constitutional mandates) as some argue the Tenth Amendment states? Or is it the case that every time the federal government enters into a particular realm, it automatically preempts states from acting? Or does the answer depend on the intent of Congress, that is, whether it intended to preempt state action?

It should be clear that American federalism is something of a double-edged sword. On the one hand, the balance of power it created not only pacified those who were opposed to ratifying the Constitution, but also it continues to define the contours of our system of government. On the other, its complexity has given rise to tensions

between the levels of government, tensions that often require settlement by the courts. It may be that the system has been so resilient because of the interpretation it constantly requires. But we will leave that up to you to decide as we now turn to the way the Supreme Court has formulated theories and specific rulings in response to two distinct but interrelated issues: the general contours of state-federal relations and the important powers of commerce and taxing and spending.

READINGS

Berger, Raoul. *Federalism: The Founders' Design.* Norman: University of Oklahoma Press, 1987.
Davis, S. R. *The Federal Principle.* Berkeley: University of California Press, 1978.
Mason, Alpheus. *The States Rights Debate: Anti-Federalism*

and the Constitution. Englewood Cliffs, N.J.: Prentice-Hall, 1964.

Rutland, Robert. *The Ordeal of the Constitution: The Antifederalists and the Ratification Struggle of 1787-1788.* Norman: University of Oklahoma Press, 1966.

Schmidhauser, John R. *The Supreme Court as Final Arbiter in Federal-State Relations, 1789-1957.* Chapel Hill: University of North Carolina Press, 1958.

Sprague, John D. *Voting Patterns of the U.S. Supreme Court: Cases in Federalism, 1889-1959.* Indianapolis: Bobbs-Merrill, 1968.

Vile, M. J. C. *The Structure of American Federalism.* London: Oxford University Press, 1961.

CHAPTER 5

NATION-STATE RELATIONS

During the 1960s Congress amended a labor standards act and required state governments to pay virtually all their employees a specified minimum wage and to compensate them for overtime work. Were these amendments constitutional or did they interfere with state authority and autonomy? The answer depends on how we view the letter and spirit of the Constitution; we would reach very different conclusions depending on whether we subscribed to the dual approach or the cooperative approach to nation-state relations *(see Table 5-1, page 228).*

Proponents of dual federalism would want the Court to strike down the law. As advocates of states' rights, they would argue that the Constitution represents an agreement between the states and the federal government in which the states empower the central government; states, therefore, are not subservient to the federal government. In other words, because each is supreme within its own sphere, the federal government could no more impose minimum wage requirements on states than the states could on the federal government. To back their theory, dual federalists invoke the Tenth Amendment, arguing that Congress cannot ''invade'' power reserved to the states and, if Congress does enact legislation touching traditional state functions, courts should void the federal act.

Cooperative federalism takes precisely the opposite view. It argues that the people, not the

states, created and animated the federal government. Moreover, it holds that the Supremacy Clause and the Necessary and Proper Clause would control the outcome here, not the Tenth Amendment. That amendment, under cooperative federalism, grants no express power to the states. As a result, the law regulating wages would pass constitutional muster.

At present, the Supreme Court seems to subscribe to cooperative federalism, but that has not always been the case. The amendments to the labor standards act, in fact, were struck down by the Court in 1976 in *National League of Cities v. Usery,* only to be upheld in 1985 in *Garcia v. San Antonio Metropolitan Transit Authority,* which effectively overruled the 1976 decision.

Nation-State Relations: The Doctrinal Cycle

The Court's about-face from *National League* to *Garcia* is not an anomaly in this area of the law; rather, it is a symptom of the general confusion that has surrounded American federalism since the eighteenth century. As depicted in Table 5-2, page 228, throughout U.S. history different Courts have subscribed to dual or cooperative federalism or one of their variants. Even more intriguing is that something of a doctrinal cycle has developed with the justices moving between states' rights and national supremacy positions

Table 5-1   A Comparison of Dual and Cooperative Federalism

	Dual Federalism	Cooperative Federalism
General View	Operates under the assumption that the two levels of government are co-equal sovereigns, each supreme within its own sphere.	Operates under the assumption that the national government is supreme even if its actions touch state functions. States and the federal government are ''partners,'' but the latter largely sets policy for the nation.
View of the Constitution	It is a compact among the states and a contract between the states and the federal government.	Rejects view of it as a ''compact''; the people, not the states, empower the national government.
Constitutional Support	Tenth Amendment reserves certain powers to the states and, thus, limits the national government to those powers specifically delegated to it.	Tenth Amendment does not provide additional powers to the states.
	Necessary and Proper Clause is to be read literally and narrowly.	Necessary and Proper Clause is to be read expansively and loosely.
		Supremacy Clause means that the national government is supreme within its own sphere, even if its actions touch on state functions.

Table 5-2   Doctrinal Cycles of Nation-State Relations

Court Era	General Approach Adopted
Marshall Court (1801–1835)	Cooperative Federalism (National Supremacy)
Taney Court (1835–1864)	Dual Federalism
Civil War/Reconstruction Courts (1865–1895)	Cooperative Federalism (National Supremacy)
Laissez-Faire Courts (1896–1936)	Dual Federalism (grounded in a laissez-faire philosophy)
Post-New Deal Courts (1937–1975)	Cooperative Federalism
Burger Court: *National League of Cities v. Usery* (1976)	Dual Federalism (Traditional State Functions)
Burger Court: *Garcia v. SAMTA* (1985)	Cooperative Federalism

positions over time. This chapter examines the components of the cycle. As you read the cases, consider not only which doctrine governed each decision, but also why the philosophies have grown stronger or weaker. What forces—legal, political, and historical—have led the justices to choose one approach over the other? This issue, always important, is perhaps critical today because it is quite possible that the Rehnquist Court might return to a dualist approach to nation-state questions. What impact would this approach have on the Court's decisions?

The Marshall Court and the Rise of National Supremacy

An ardent Federalist, Chief Justice John Marshall was true to his party's tenets over the course of his long career on the Supreme Court. In case after case *(see, in particular, Cohens v. Virginia, page 47),* he was more than willing to elevate the powers of the federal government above the states. Perhaps his most significant statement on national supremacy came in *McCulloch v. Maryland* (1819). In Chapter 3 we saw how he used this case to assert firmly that Congress has implied powers. Here, we shall see that *McCulloch* also served as his vehicle to expound the notion of national supremacy. A brief review of the essential facts is offered to remind you of the issues in this case.

McCulloch v. Maryland
4 Wheat. 316 (1819)

Vote: 6 (Duvall, Johnson, Livingston, Marshall, Story, Washington)

o

Opinion of the Court: Marshall
Not participating: Todd

Congress established the second Bank of the United States in 1816. Because of inefficiency and corruption, the bank was very unpopular; many went so far as to blame it for the nation's economic problems. To show its displeasure, the Maryland legislature passed a law saying that banks operating in the state that were not chartered by the state—in other words, the national bank—could issue bank notes only on special paper, which the state taxed. When James McCulloch, the cashier of the Baltimore branch of the Bank of the United States, refused to pay, Maryland took legal action to enforce its law. The United States challenged the constitutionality of the Maryland tax, and in return Maryland disputed the constitutionality of the bank.

Chief Justice Marshall delivered the opinion of the Court:

The constitution of our country, in its most interesting and vital parts, is to be considered; the conflicting powers of the government of the Union and of its members, as marked in that constitution, are to be discussed; and an opinion given, which may essentially influence the great operations of the government. . . .

In discussing this . . . the counsel for the state of Maryland have deemed it of some importance, in the construction of the constitution, to consider that instrument not as emanating from the people, but as the act of sovereign and independent states. The powers of the general government, it has been said, are delegated by the states, who alone are truly sovereign; and must be exercised in subordination to the states, who alone possess supreme dominion.

It would be difficult to sustain this proposition. The convention which framed the constitution was indeed elected by the state legislatures. But the instrument, when it came from their hands, was a mere proposal, without obligation, or pretensions to it. It was reported to the then existing Congress of the United States, with a request that it might "be submitted to a convention of delegates, chosen in each state by the people thereof, under the recommendation of its legislature, for their assent and ratification." This mode of proceeding was adopted; and by the convention, by Congress, and by the state legislatures, the instrument was submitted to the people. They acted upon it in the only manner in which they can act safely, effectively, and wisely, on such a subject, by assembling in convention. It is true, they assembled in their several states—and where else should they have assembled? No political dreamer was ever wild enough to think of breaking down the lines which separate the states, and of compounding the American people into one common mass. Of consequence, when they act, they act in their states. But the measures they adopt do not, on that account, cease to be the measures of the people themselves, or become the measures of the state governments. . . .

The government of the Union, then . . . is, emphatically, and truly, a government of the people. . . .

It is the government of all; its powers are delegated by all; it represents all, and acts for all. Though any one state may be willing to control its operations, no state is willing to allow others to control them. The nation, on those subjects on which it can act, must necessarily bind its component parts. But this question is not left to mere reason; the people have, in express terms, decided it by saying, "this constitution, and the laws of the United States, which shall be made in pursuance thereof," "shall be the supreme law of the land," and by requiring that the members of the state legislatures, and the officers of the executive and judicial departments of the states shall take the oath of fidelity to it. . . .

Among the enumerated powers, we do not find that of establishing a bank or creating a corporation. But there is no phrase in the instrument which, like the articles of confederation, excludes incidental or implied powers; and which requires that everything granted shall be expressly and minutely described. Even the 10th amendment, which was framed for the purpose of quieting the excessive jealousies which had been excited, omits the word "expressly," and declares only that the powers "not delegated to the United States, nor prohibited to the states, are reserved to the states or to the people;" thus leaving the question, whether the particular power which may become the subject of contest has been delegated to the one government, or prohibited to the other, to depend on a fair construction of the whole instrument. The men who drew and adopted this amendment had experienced the embarrassments resulting from the insertion of this word in the articles of confederation, and probably omitted it to avoid those embarrassments. A constitution, to contain an accurate detail of all the subdivisions of which its great powers will admit, and of all the means by which they may be carried into execution, would partake of a prolixity of a legal code, and could scarcely be embraced by the human mind. It would probably never be understood by the public. Its nature, therefore, requires, that only its great outlines should be marked, its important objects designated, and the minor ingredients which compose those objects be deduced from the nature of the objects themselves. That this idea was entertained by the framers of the American constitution, is not only to be inferred from the nature of the instrument, but from the language. . . .

After this declaration, it can scarcely be necessary to say that the existence of state banks can have no possible influence on the question. No trace is to be found in the constitution of an intention to create a dependence of the government of the Union on those of the states, for the execution of the great powers assigned to it. Its means are adequate to its ends; and on those means alone was it expected to rely for the accomplishment of its ends. To impose on it the necessity of resorting to means which it cannot control, which another government may furnish or withhold, would render its course precarious; the result of its measures uncertain, and create a dependence on other governments, which might disappoint its most important designs and is incompatible with the language of the constitution. But were it otherwise, the choice of means implies a right to choose a national bank in preference to state banks, and Congress alone can make the election.

After the most deliberate consideration, it is the unanimous and decided opinion of this court that the act to incorporate the bank of the United States is a law made in pursuance of the constitution, and is part of the supreme law of the land. . . .

This great principle is, that the constitution and the laws made in pursuance thereof are supreme; that they control the constitution and laws of the respective states, and cannot be controlled by them. From this, which may be almost termed as axiom, other propositions are deduced as corollaries, on the truth or error of which, and on their application to this case, the cause has been supposed to depend. These are, 1st. that a power to create implies a power to preserve. 2d. That a power to destroy, if wielded by a different hand, is hostile to, and incompatible with these powers to create and to preserve. 3d. That where this repugnancy exists, that authority which is supreme must control, not yield to that over which it is supreme. . . .

That the power to tax involves the power to destroy; that the power to destroy may defeat and render useless the power to create; that there is a plain repugnance, in conferring on one government a power to control the constitutional measures of another, which other, with respect to those very measures, is declared to be supreme over that which exerts the control, are propositions not to be denied. . . .

The court has bestowed on this subject its most

deliberate consideration. The result is a conviction that the states have no power, by taxation or otherwise, to retard, impede, burden, or in any manner control the operations of the constitutional laws enacted by Congress to carry into execution the powers vested in the general government. This is, we think, the unavoid-

able consequence of that supremacy which the constitution has declared.

We are unanimously of opinion that the law passed by the legislature of Maryland, imposing a tax on the Bank of the United States, is unconstitutional and void.

Constitutional scholars regard *McCulloch* as an awesome statement of national power over the states. Its strength lies in Marshall's treatment of the three relevant constitutional provisions: the Necessary and Proper Clause, the Tenth Amendment, and the Supremacy Clause.

First, the Necessary and Proper Clause permits Congress to pass legislation implied by its enumerated functions, bounded only in this way:

Let the end be legitimate, let it be within the scope of the constitution, and all means which are appropriate, which are plainly adapted to that end, which are not prohibited, but consist with the letter and spirit of the constitution, are constitutional.[1]

Second, because the Tenth Amendment only reserves to the states or to the people power that has not been delegated to Congress (and not *expressly* delegated), it stands as no significant bar to congressional exercise of its powers, including those that are implied. Given Marshall's treatment of the Necessary and Proper Clause, implied powers are quite broad. Third, the Supremacy Clause places the national government at the top within its sphere of operation, a sphere that again, according to Marshall's interpretation of the Necessary and Proper Clause, is expansive. If the Supremacy Clause means anything, it means that no state may "retard, impede, burden, or in any manner control, the operations of the constitutional laws enacted by Congress." Note, too, Marshall's view of the constitutional arrange-

ment; as one would expect, he fully endorsed the position that the charter represents a contract between the people—not the states—and the federal government.

McCulloch's holdings—supporting congressional creation of the bank and negating state taxation of it—were not particularly surprising. Most observers thought the Marshall Court would rule the way it did.[2] It was the chief justice's language and the constitutional theories he offered that sparked a "fierce ideological debate" in a states' rights newspaper, the *Richmond Enquirer*.[3] It began just weeks after *McCulloch* was decided with a barrage of state rights' advocates writing in to condemn the ruling. Apparently concerned that if their views took hold "the constitution would be converted into the old confederation," Marshall took an unusual step for a Supreme Court justice; he responded to his critics.[4] Initially, he wrote two articles, carried by a Philadelphia newspaper, defending *McCulloch*. But when an old enemy, Spence Roane, the Virginia Supreme Court judge who was the target of the Court's decision in *Martin v. Hunter's Lessee,* launched an unbridled attack, Marshall responded with nine "elaborate essays," published under the pseudonym, "A Friend of the Constitution."[5]

---

1. *McCulloch v. Maryland,* 4 Wheat. 316 at 421 (1819).

2. See Gerald Gunther, *Constitutional Law,* 11th ed. (Mineola, N.Y.: Foundation Press, 1985), 91.
3. Ibid.
4. Ibid.
5. Ibid. For records of these essays, see Gerald Gunther, ed., *John Marshall's Defense of McCulloch v. Maryland* (Stanford, Calif.: Stanford University Press, 1969).

The Taney Court and the (Re)Emergence of States' Rights

The debate between Marshall and Roane was just that—a debate of words. While Marshall was chief justice of the United States, it was his view of nation-state relations, not Roane's, that prevailed. But their argument foreshadowed changes that occurred upon Marshall's death in 1835 and Roger B. Taney's ascension to the chief justiceship.

In some ways, Marshall and Taney were alike. Both began their political careers in their respective states—Virginia and Maryland—and then held major positions within the executive branch of the national government. Both were committed partisan activists. The difference was that they were committed to completely opposite conceptions of government structure, particularly of nation-state relations. In contrast to Marshall's Federalist sentiments, Taney was a Jacksonian Democrat, a full believer in those ideas espoused by President Andrew Jackson, under whom he had served as attorney general, secretary of war, and secretary of the Treasury, and who had appointed him chief justice. Marshall viewed the federal government as supreme, but Taney (and Jackson) thought states' rights were not incompatible with those possessed by the national government. The two chief justices' views on the Bank of the United States provide a wonderful juxtaposition. In *McCulloch* Marshall lent his full support to the bank; in 1832 Taney helped write President Jackson's veto message in which he "condemned the Second Bank of the United States," and refused to recharter it.[6]

Had Taney been President Jackson's only appointment to the Court, he might not have been able to change the course of federalism doctrine. But that was not the case. Table 5-3 shows that by

Table 5-3   From the Marshall Court to the Taney Court

Marshall Court (1819)	Taney Court (1841)
Marshall	Taney
Livingston	Thompson
Story	Story
Washington	Baldwin
Duval	Daniel
Johnson	Wayne
Todd	McLean
	Catron
	McKinley

1841 Joseph Story was the only justice remaining from the Marshall Court that decided *McCulloch*. The others, like Taney, were schooled in Jacksonian Democracy. It was, R. Kent Newmyer noted, no longer "the Marshall Court. But, then again it was not the age of Marshall."[7] This observation holds on two levels: doctrinally and politically. The Taney Court ushered in substantial legal changes, especially in federal-state relations. Although there is no true Taney corollary to Marshall's opinion in *McCulloch*, examples of his views abound: in many opinions he explicated the doctrine of dual federalism, that national and state government are equivalent sovereigns within their own spheres of operation. Unlike Marshall, he read the Tenth Amendment in a broad sense: that it did, in fact, reserve to the states certain powers and limited the power of the federal government over them. In the *License Cases* (1847), Taney wrote:

Every power delegated to the federal government must be in coincidence with a perfect right in the states to all that they have not been delegated; in coincidence, too, with the possessing of every power and right necessary for their existence and preservation.

Early Taney Court decisions, such as the *License Cases,* were not controversial. They may have represented a break from previous doctrine, but they matched the tenor of the times. Although

6. R. Kent Newmyer, *The Supreme Court under Marshall and Taney* (New York: Crowell, 1968), 93.

7. Ibid., 94.

Roger Brooke Taney
(1836–1864)

Roger Taney was descended on both sides from prominent Maryland families. His mother's family, named Brooke, first arrived in the state in 1650, complete with fox hounds and other trappings of aristocracy. The first Taney arrived about 1660 as an indentured servant but was able to acquire a large amount of property and became a member of the landed Maryland tidewater gentry.

Taney was born March 17, 1777, on his father's tobacco plantation in Calvert County. He was educated in local rural schools and privately tutored by a Princeton student. In 1795, at the age of eighteen, he graduated first in his class from Dickinson College in Pennsylvania.

As his father's second son, Taney was not in line to inherit the family property and so decided on a career in law and politics. For three years, he was an apprentice lawyer in the office of Judge Jeremiah Chase of the Maryland General Court in Annapolis. He was admitted to the bar in 1799.

Taney married Anne Key, daughter of a prominent farmer and the sister of Francis Scott Key, on January 7, 1806. Since Taney was a devout Roman Catholic and his wife an Episcopalian, they agreed to raise their sons as Catholics and their daughters as Episcopalians. The couple had six daughters and a son who died in infancy. In 1855, the year *Scott v. Sandford* came before the Supreme Court, Taney's wife and youngest daughter died of yellow fever.

Taney began his political career as a member of the Federalist party, serving one term in the Maryland legislature from 1799 to 1800. After being defeated for reelection, he moved from Calvert County to Frederick, where he began to develop a profitable law practice. In 1803 Taney was beaten again in an attempt to return to the House of Delegates. Despite this setback, he began to achieve prominence in the Frederick community as a lawyer and politician. He lived there for twenty years.

In supporting the War of 1812, Taney split with the majority of Maryland Federalists. But in 1816, as a result of shifting political loyalties, he was elected to the state senate and became a dominant figure in party politics. Taney's term expired in 1821. In 1823 he settled in Baltimore, where he continued his successful law practice and political activities. By this time, the Federalist party had virtually disintegrated, and Taney threw his support to the Jackson Democrats. He led Jackson's 1828 presidential campaign in Maryland and served as the state's attorney general from 1827 until 1831. At that time, he was named U.S. attorney general for the Jackson administration and left Baltimore for Washington.

It was at this stage in his career that Taney played a leading role in the controversy over the second Bank of the United States, helping to write President Andrew Jackson's message in 1832 vetoing the bank's recharter. The next year, when Treasury Secretary William Duane refused to withdraw federal deposits from the national bank, Duane was dismissed and replaced by Taney, who promptly carried out the action.

Taney held the Treasury job for nine months, presiding over a new system of state bank depositories called "pet banks." Jackson, who had delayed as long as he could, was eventually forced to submit Taney's nomination as Treasury secretary to the Senate, which rejected it. Taney was forced to resign.

In 1835 Jackson named Taney to replace aging Supreme Court justice Gabriel Duvall, but the nomination was indefinitely postponed by a close Senate vote. Ten months later, on December 28, Jackson proposed Taney's name again, this time to fill the seat left vacant by the death of Chief Justice John Marshall. To the horror of the Whigs, who considered him much too radical, Taney was confirmed as chief justice on March 15, 1836. He served until his death in Washington, October 12, 1864.

Source: Elder Witt, *Guide to the U.S. Supreme Court*, 2d ed. (Washington, D.C.: Congressional Quarterly, 1990), 819–820.

President Jackson had his own feuds with the states, his general philosophical approach to federalism and to governance were those popularly held. But when the Court interceded in the slavery dispute, firmly planting its feet in the states' rights camp of the South, things started to heat up. As you read Taney's opinion in the infamous *Dred Scott* case, note his theory of the nature of the constitutional contract. How do his views differ from those of Marshall's in *McCulloch?*

Dred Scott v. Sandford

19 How. 393 (1857)

Vote: 7 (Campbell, Catron, Daniel, Grier, Nelson, Taney, Wayne)
*   2 (Curtis, McLean)*
Opinion of the Court: Taney
Concurring opinions: Campbell, Catron, Daniel, Grier, Nelson, Wayne
Dissenting opinions: Curtis, McLean

Dred Scott, a slave purchased in Missouri, was the "property" of Dr. John Emerson, an army surgeon. In 1834 Emerson took Scott to the free state of Illinois and in 1836, to the Upper Louisiana territory, which was to remain free of slavery under the Missouri Compromise of 1820. Eventually, Scott and Emerson returned to Missouri, but the doctor died shortly thereafter, leaving title to Scott to his brother-in-law, John Sanford, who was a citizen of New York.[8] Believing that he no longer had slave status because he had lived on free soil, Scott sued for his freedom in a Missouri state court in 1846. He received a favorable decision at the trial court level but lost in the Missouri Supreme Court. Several years later, Scott and his lawyer decided to try again. This time, however, they brought the case to a federal district court, contending that they had a diversity suit—Scott was a citizen of Missouri and Sanford of New York. Sanford argued that the suit should be dismissed because blacks could not be citizens. The federal courts seemed perplexed by the issue. In the end, they ruled in favor of Sanford but

8. The party's name, Sanford, was misspelled Sandford in the official records.

Dred Scott

suggested that for legal purposes Scott may be a citizen.

By the time the case arrived at the U.S. Supreme Court for final judgment in 1856, the facts and the political situation had grown increasingly complex. In 1854, under mounting pressure, Congress had repealed the Missouri Compromise, replacing it with legislation declaring congressional neutrality on the issue of slavery. Given this new law and the growing tensions between the North and the South and the free and slave states, some observers speculated that the Court would decline to decide the case: it had become highly controversial and overtly political.

For at least a year, the Court chose that route. Historians, in fact, have suggested that after hearing the case the majority of the Court wanted to dismiss it because of the tremendous effect its decision might have on relations between the North and South. But when several of the justices began to write dissenting opinions, the Court, under the leadership of Chief Justice Taney, a former slaveholder, realized it had to deal with the issue. Waiting until after the presidential election, a very divided Court (nine separate opinions were written), announced its decision.

Chief Justice Taney delivered the opinion of the Court:

The question is simply this: can a negro, whose ancestors were imported into this country and sold as slaves, become a member of the political community formed and brought into existence by the Constitution of the United States, and as such become entitled to all the rights, and privileges, and immunities, guarantied by that instrument to the citizen. One of these rights is the privilege of suing in a court of the United States in the cases specified in the Constitution.

It will be observed, that the plea applies to that class of persons only whose ancestors were negroes of the African race, and imported into this country, and sold and held as slaves. The only matter in issue before the court, therefore, is, whether the descendants of such slaves, when they shall be emancipated, or who are born of parents who had become free before their birth, are citizens of a state, in the sense in which the word "citizen" is used in the Constitution of the United States. And this being the only matter in dispute on the pleadings, the court must be understood as speaking in this opinion of that class only; that is, of those persons who are the descendants of Africans who were imported into this country and sold as slaves. . . .

We proceed to examine the case as presented by the pleadings.

The words "people of the United States" and "citizens" are synonymous terms, and mean the same thing. They both describe the political body, who, according to our republican institutions, form the sovereignty, and who hold the power and conduct the government through their representatives. They are what we familiarly call the "sovereign people," and every citizen is one of this people, and a constituent member of this sovereignty. The question before us is, whether the class of persons described in the plea in abatement compose a portion of this people, and are constituent members of this sovereignty. We think they are not, and that they are not included, and were not intended to be included, under the word "citizens" in the Constitution, and can, therefore, claim none of the rights and privileges which that instrument provides for and secures to citizens of the United States. On the contrary, they were at that time considered as a subordinate and inferior class of beings, who had been subjugated by the dominant race, and whether emancipated or not, yet remained subject to their authority, and had no rights or privileges but such as those who held the power and the government might choose to grant them.

It is not the province of the court to decide upon the justice or injustice, the policy or impolicy of these laws. The decision of that question belonged to the political or law-making power; to those who formed the sovereignty and framed the Constitution. The duty of the court is to interpret the instrument they have framed, with the best lights we can obtain on the subject, and to administer it as we find it, according to its true intent and meaning when it was adopted.

In discussing this question, we must not confound the rights of citizenship which a state may confer within its own limits, and the rights of citizenship as a member of the Union. It does not by any means follow, because he has all the rights and privileges of a citizen of a State, that he must be a citizen of the United States. He may have all the rights and privileges of the citizen of a State, and yet not be entitled to the rights and privileges of a citizen in any other State. For, previous to the adoption of the Constitution of the United States, every State had the undoubted right to confer on whomsoever it pleased the character of a citizen, and to endow him with all its rights. But this character, of course, was confined to the boundaries of the State, and gave him no rights or privileges in other States beyond those secured to him by the laws of nations and the comity of States. Nor have the several States surrendered the power of conferring these rights and privileges by adopting the Constitution of the United States. Each State may still confer them upon an alien, or any one it thinks proper, or upon any class or description of persons; yet he would not be a citizen in the sense in which that word is used in the Constitution of the United States, nor entitled to sue as such in one of its courts, nor to the privileges and immunities of a citizen in the other States. The rights which he would acquire would be restricted to the State which gave them. The Constitution has conferred on Congress the right to establish an uniform rule of naturalization, and this right is evidently exclusive, and has always been held by this court to be so. Consequently, no State, since the adoption of the Constitution, can, by naturalizing an alien, invest him with the rights and privileges secured to a citizen of a State under the federal government, although, so far as the State alone was concerned, he would undoubtedly be entitled to the rights of a citizen, and clothed with all the rights and immunities which the Constitution and laws of the State attached to that character.

It is very clear, therefore, that no State can, by any Act or law of its own, passed, since the adoption of the Constitution, introduce a new member into the political community created by the Constitution of the United States. It cannot make him a member of this community by making him a member of its own. And for the same reason it cannot introduce any person, or description of persons, who were not intended to be embraced in this new political family, which the Constitution brought into existence, but were intended to be excluded from it.

The question then arises, whether the provisions of the Constitution, in relation to the personal rights and privileges to which the citizen of a state should be entitled, embraced the negro African race, at that time in this country, or who might afterwards be imported, who had then or should afterwards be made free in any State; and to put it in the power of a single State to make him a citizen of the United States, and endue him with the full rights of citizenship in every other State without their consent. Does the Constitution of the United States act upon him whenever he shall be made free under the laws of a State, and raised there to the rank of a citizen, and immediately clothe him with all the privileges of a citizen in every other State, and in its own courts?

The court think the affirmative of these propositions cannot be maintained. And if it cannot, the plaintiff in error could not be a citizen of the State of Missouri, within the meaning of the Constitution of the United States, and, consequently, was not entitled to sue in its courts.

It is true, every person, and every class and description of persons, who were at the time of the adoption of the Constitution recognized as citizens in the several States, became also citizens of this new political body; but none other; it was formed by them, and for them and their posterity, but for no one else. And the personal rights and privileges guarantied to citizens of this new sovereignty were intended to embrace those only who were then members of the several state communities, or who should afterwards, by birthright or otherwise, become members, according to the provisions of the Constitution and the principles on which it was founded. It was the union of those who were at that time members of distinct and separate political communities into one political family, whose power, for certain specified purposes, was to extend over the whole territory of the United States. And it gave to each citizen rights and privileges outside of his State which he did not before possess, and placed him in every other State upon a perfect equality with its own citizens as to rights of person and rights of property; it made him a citizen of the United States.

It becomes necessary, therefore, to determine who were citizens of the several States when the Constitution was adopted. . . .

In the opinion of the court, the legislation and histories of the times, and the language used in the Declaration of Independence, show, that neither the class of persons who had been imported as slaves, nor their descendants, whether they had become free or not, were then acknowledged as a part of the people, nor intended to be included in the general words used in that memorable instrument. . . .

The legislation of the States . . . shows, in a manner not to be mistaken, the inferior and subject condition of that race at the time the Constitution was adopted, and long afterwards, throughout the thirteen States by which that instrument was framed; and it is hardly consistent with the respect due to these States, to suppose that they regarded at that time, as fellow citizens and members of the sovereignty, a class of beings whom they had thus stigmatized; whom, as we are bound, out of respect to the State sovereignties, to assume they had deemed it just and necessary thus to stigmatize, and upon whom they had impressed such deep and enduring marks of inferiority and degradation; or that when they met in convention to form the Constitution, they looked upon them as a portion of their constituents, or designed to include them in the provisions so carefully inserted for the security and protection of the liberties and rights of their citizens. It cannot be supposed that they intended to secure to them rights, and privileges, and rank, in the new political body throughout the Union, which every one of them denied within the limits of its own dominion. More especially, it cannot be believed that the large slaveholding States regarded them as included in the word ''citizens,'' or would have consented to a constitution which might compel them to receive them in that character from another State. For if they were so received, and entitled to the privileges and immunities of citizens, it would exempt them from the operation of the special laws and from the police regulations which they considered to be necessary for their own safety. It would give to persons of the negro race, who were recognized as citizens in any one State of the Union, the right to enter every other State whenever they pleased, singly or in companies, without pass or passport, and without obstruction, to sojourn there as long as they pleased, to go where they pleased at every hour of the day or night without molestation, unless they committed some violation of law for which a white man would be punished; and it would give them the full liberty of speech in public and in private upon all subjects upon which its own citizens might speak; to hold public meetings upon political affairs, and to keep and carry arms wherever they went. And all of this would be done in the face of the subject race of the same color, both free and slaves, inevitably producing discontent and insubordination among them, and endangering the peace and safety of the State.

It is impossible, it would seem, to believe that the great men of the slaveholding States, who took so large a share in framing the Constitution of the United States, and exercised so much influence in procuring its adoption, could have been so forgetful or regardless of their own safety and the safety of those who trusted and confided in them. . . .

What the construction was at that time, we think can hardly admit of doubt. We have the language of the Declaration of Independence and of the Articles of Confederation, in addition to the plain words of the Constitution itself; we have the legislation of the different States, before, about the time, and since the Constitution was adopted; we have the legislation of Congress, from the time of its adoption to a recent period; and we have the constant and uniform action of the Executive Department, all concurring together, and leading to the same result. And if anything in relation to the construction of the Constitution can be regarded as settled, it is that which we now give to the word ''citizen'' and the word ''people.''

And upon a full and careful consideration of the subject, the court is of opinion that, upon the facts stated in the plea in abatement, Dred Scott was not a citizen of Missouri within the meaning of the Constitution of the United States, and not entitled as such to sue in its courts; and, consequently, that the Circuit Court had no jurisdiction of the case, and that the judgment on the plea in abatement is erroneous. . . .

The case before us still more strongly imposes upon this court the duty of examining whether the court below has not committed an error, in taking jurisdiction and giving a judgment for costs in favor of the defendant. . . . [I]n this case it does appear that the plaintiff was born a slave; and if the facts upon which he relies have not made him free, then it appears affirmatively on the record that he is not a citizen, and consequently his suit against Sandford was not a suit between citizens of different States, and the court had no authority to pass any judgment between the parties. The suit ought, in this view of it, to have been dismissed by the Circuit Court, and its judgment in favor of Sandford is erroneous, and must be reversed.

It is true that the result either way, by dismissal or by a judgment for the defendant, makes very little, if any difference in a pecuniary or personal point of view to either party. But the fact that the result would be very nearly the same to the parties in either form of judgment, would not justify this court in sanctioning an error in the judgment which is patent on the record, and which, if sanctioned, might be drawn into precedent, and lead to serious mischief and injustice in some future suit.

We proceed, therefore, to inquire whether the facts relied on by the plaintiff entitled him to his freedom. . . .

The counsel for the plaintiff has laid much stress upon that article in the Constitution which confers on Congress the power ''to dispose of and make all needful rules and regulations respecting the territory or other property belonging to the United States;'' but, in the judgment of the court, that provision has no bearing on the present controversy, and the power there given, whatever it may be, is confined, and was intended to be confined, to the territory which at that time belonged to, or was claimed by, the United States, and was within their boundaries as settled by the Treaty with Great Britain, and can have no influence upon a territory afterwards acquired from a foreign government. It was a special provision for a known and particular Territory, and to meet a present emergency, and nothing more. . . .

It was intended for a specific purpose. . . . It was to transfer to the new government the property then held in common by the States, and to give to that government power to apply it to the objects for which it had been destined by mutual agreement among the States before their league was dissolved. It applied only to the property which the States held in common at that time, and has no reference whatever to any territory or other property which the new sovereignty might afterwards itself acquire.

. . . And whatever construction may now be given to these words, everyone, we think, must admit that they are not the words usually employed by statesmen in giving supreme power of legislation. They are certainly very unlike the words used in the power granted to legislate over territory which the new government might afterwards itself obtain by cession from a state, either for its seat of government, or for forts, magazines, arsenals, dockyards, and other needful buildings. . . .

No one, it is believed, would think a moment of deriving the power of Congress to make needful rules and regulations in relation to property of this kind from this clause of the Constitution. Nor can it, upon any fair construction, be applied to any property but that which the new government was about to receive from the confederated States. And if this be true as to this property, it must be equally true and limited as to the territory, which is so carefully and precisely coupled with it—and like it referred to as property in the power granted. The concluding words of the clause appear to render this construction irresistible; for, after the provisions we have mentioned, it proceeds to say, ''that nothing in the Constitution shall be so construed as to prejudice any claims of the United States, or of any particular State.'' . . .

This brings us to examine by what provision of the Constitution the present Federal Government under its delegated and restricted powers, is authorized to acquire territory outside of the original limits of the United States, and what powers it may exercise therein over the person or property of a citizen of the United States, while it remains a territory, and until it shall be admitted as one of the States of the Union.

There is certainly no power given by the Constitution to the Federal Government to establish or maintain Colonies bordering on the United States or at a distance, to be ruled and governed at its own pleasure; nor to enlarge its territorial limits in any way, except by the admission of new States. That power is plainly given; and if a new State is admitted it needs no further legislation by Congress, because the Constitution itself defines the relative rights and powers and duties of the State, and the citizens of the State, and the Federal Government. But no power is given to acquire a Territory to be held and governed permanently in that character. . . .

We do not mean, however, to question the power of Congress in this respect. The power to expand the territory of the United States by the admission of new States is plainly given; and in the construction of this power by all the departments of the government, it has been held to authorize the acquisition of territory, not fit for admission at the time, but to be admitted as soon as its population and situation would entitle it to admission. It is acquired to become a State, and not to be held as a colony and governed by Congress with absolute authority; and as the propriety of admitting a new State is committed to the sound discretion of Congress, the power to acquire territory for that purpose, to be held by the United States until it is in a suitable condition to become a state upon an equal footing with the other States, must rest upon the same discretion. . . . All we mean to say on this point is, that, as there is no express regulation in the Constitution defining the power which the general government may exercise over the person or property of a citizen in a territory thus acquired, the court must necessarily look to the provisions and principles of the Constitution, and its distribution of powers, for the rules and principles by which its decision must be governed.

Taking this rule to guide us, it may be safely assumed that citizens of the United States who migrate to a territory belonging to the people of the United States, cannot be ruled as mere colonists, dependent upon the will of the general government, and to be governed by any laws it may think proper to impose. The principle upon which our governments rest, and upon which alone they continue to exist, is the union of States, sovereign and independent within their own limits in their internal and domestic concerns, and bound together as one people by a general government, possessing certain enumerated and restricted powers, delegated to it by the people of the several States, and exercising supreme authority within the scope of the powers granted to it, throughout the dominion of the United States. A power, therefore, in the general government to obtain and hold Colonies and dependent Territories, over which they might legislate without restriction, would be inconsistent with its own existence in its present form. Whatever it acquires, it acquires for the benefit of the people of the several States who created it. It is their trustee acting for them, and charged with the duty of promoting the interests of the whole people of the Union in the exercise of the powers specifically granted.

At the time when the Territory in question was obtained by cession from France, it contained no population fit to be associated together and admitted as a State; and it therefore was absolutely necessary to hold possession of it as a Territory belonging to the United States until it was settled and inhabited by a civilized community capable of self-government, and in a condition to be admitted on equal terms with the other States as a member of the Union. But, as we have before said, it was acquired by the general government as the representative and trustee of the people of the United States, and it must, therefore, be held in that character for their common and equal benefit; for it was the people of the several States, acting through the agent and representative, the Federal Government, who in fact acquired the territory in question, and the government holds it for their common use until it shall be associated with the other States as a member of the Union.

But until that time arrives, it is undoubtedly necessary that some government should be established, in order to organize society, and to protect the inhabitants in their persons and property; and as the people of the United States could act in this matter only through the government which represented them, and through which they spoke and acted when the territory was obtained, it was not only within the scope of its powers, but it was its duty to pass such laws and establish such a government as would enable those by whose authority they acted to reap the advantages anticipated from its acquisition, and to gather there a population which would enable it to assume the position to which it was destined among the States of the Union. The power to acquire, necessarily carries with it the power to preserve and apply to the purposes for which it was acquired. The form of government to be established necessarily rested in the discretion of Congress. It was their duty to establish the one that would be best suited for the protection and security of the citizens of the United States and other inhabitants who might be authorized to take up their abode there, and that must always depend upon the existing condition of the Territory, as to the number and character of its inhabitants, and the situation in the Territory. In some cases a government, consisting of persons appointed by the Federal Government, would best subserve the interests of the Territory, when the inhabitants were few and scattered, and new to one another. In other instances, it would be more advisable to commit the powers of self-government to the people who had settled in the territory, as being the most competent to determine what was best for their own interests. But some form of civil authority would be absolutely necessary to organize and preserve civilized society, and prepare it to become a state; and what is the best form must always depend on the condition of the territory at the time, and the choice of the mode must depend upon the exercise of a discretionary power by Congress acting within the scope of its constitutional authority, and not infringing upon the legal rights of person or rights of property of the citizen who might go there to reside or for any other lawful purpose. It was acquired by the exercise of this discretion and it must be held and governed in like manner, until it is fitted to be a state.

But the power of Congress over the person or property of a citizen can never be a mere discretionary power under our Constitution and form of government. The powers of the government and the rights and privileges of the citizen are regulated and plainly defined by the Constitution itself. And when the territory becomes a part of the United States, the Federal Government enters into possession in the character impressed upon it by those who created it. It enters upon it with its powers over the citizen strictly defined, and limited by the Constitution, from which it derives its own existence, and by virtue of which alone it continues to exist and act as a government and sovereignty. It has no power of any kind beyond it; and it cannot, when it enters a territory of the United States, put off its character, and assume discretionary or despotic powers which the Constitution has denied to it. It cannot create for itself a new character separated from the citizens of the United States, and the duties it owes them under the provisions of the Constitution. The territory being a part of the United States, the government and the citizen both enter it under the authority of the Constitution, with their respective rights defined and marked out; and the Federal Government can exercise no power over his person or property, beyond what that instrument confers, nor lawfully deny any right which it has reserved. . . .

The powers over person and property of which we speak are not only not granted to Congress, but are in express terms denied, and they are forbidden to exercise them. And this prohibition is not confined to the States, but the words are general, and extend to the whole territory over which the Constitution gives it power to legislate, including those portions of it remaining under territorial government, as well as that covered by States. It is a total absence of power everywhere within the dominion of the United States, and places the citizens of a territory, so far as these rights are concerned, on the same footing with citizens of the States, and guards them as firmly and plainly against any inroads which the general government might attempt, under the plea of implied or incidental powers. And if Congress itself cannot do this—if it is beyond the powers conferred on the Federal Government—it will be admitted, we presume, that it could not authorize a territorial government to exercise them. It could confer no power on any local government, established by its authority, to violate the provisions of the Constitution.

It seems, however, to be supposed, that there is a difference between property in a slave and other property, and that different rules may be applied to it in expounding the Constitution of the United States. And the laws and usages of nations, and the writings of eminent jurists upon the relation of master and slave and their mutual rights and duties, and the powers which governments may exercise over it, have been dwelt upon in the argument.

But in considering the question before us, it must be borne in mind that there is no law of nations standing between the people of the United States and their government and interfering with their relation to each other. The powers of the government, and the rights of the citizen under it, are positive and practical regulations plainly written down. The people of the United States have delegated to it certain enumerated powers, and forbidden it to exercise others. It has no power over the person or property of a citizen but what the citizens of the United States have granted. And no laws or usages of other nations, or reasoning of statesmen or jurists upon the relations of master and slave, can enlarge the powers of the government, or take from the citizens the rights they have reserved. And if the Constitution recognizes the right of property of the master in a slave, and makes no distinction between that description of property and other property owned by a citizen, no tribunal, acting under the authority of the United States, whether it be legislative, executive, or judicial, has a right to draw such a distinction, or deny to it the benefit of the provisions and guarantees which have been provided for the protection of private property against the encroachments of the governments.

Now, as we have already said in an earlier part of this opinion, upon a different point, the right of property in a slave is distinctly and expressly affirmed in the Constitution. The right to traffic in it, like an ordinary article of merchandise and property, was guaranteed to the citizens of the United States, in every State that might desire it, for twenty years. And the government in express terms is pledged to protect it in all future time, if the slave escapes from his owner. This is done in plain words—too plain to be misunderstood. And no word can be found in the Constitution which gives Congress a greater power over slave property, or which entitles property of that kind to less protection than property of any other description. The only power conferred is the power coupled with the duty of guarding and protecting the owner in his rights.

Upon these considerations, it is the opinion of the court that the Act of Congress which prohibited a citizen from holding and owning property of this kind in the territory of the United States north of the line therein mentioned, is not warranted by the Constitution, and is therefore void; and that neither Dred Scott himself, nor any of his family, were made free by being carried into this territory; even if they had been carried there by the owner, with the intention of becoming a permanent resident.

Dred Scott could not have come at a worse time for nationalists or a better one for states' rights advocates. The nation was on the verge of collapse *(see Table 5-4)*. Taney's holding, coupled with his vision of the nature of the federal-state relationship, rather than calming matters, proba-

Table 5–4   Selected Events Leading to the Civil War

Year	Event	Significance
1832	South Carolina Ordinance of Nullification	Suggests that states can nullify acts of the federal government.
1833	Webster-Calhoun debates over Jackson administration's proposal to compel states to enforce tariff laws	Calhoun offers a view of state sovereignty in which states can resist federal acts. Sometimes called the "doctrine of concurrent majorities," it would permit states a veto over federal policies.
1835	Jackson nominates Taney to the Court.	The Senate delays confirming Taney, a former slaveholder, until 1836.
1854	Congress repeals the Missouri Compromise.	Allows territories to enter into the union with or without slavery.
1857	*Dred Scott v. Sandford*	Provides fodder for increasing tension between the North and the South, as the former loudly denounces the decision.
1860 (Nov.)	Lincoln is elected president	South proclaims that secession is inevitable.
1860 (Dec.)	South Carolina Ordinance of Secession	South Carolina votes to secede from the union. Within a few weeks, six other states follow suit.

bly added fuel to the fire. Indeed, several years later, his dual federalism appeared in an even more energized form, when South Carolina issued its Declaration of the Causes of Secession. President Abraham Lincoln presented precisely the opposite view—the Marshall approach—in his 1861 inaugural address, but his words were insufficient to stop the outbreak of war.

At its core, the Civil War was about not only slavery but also the supremacy of the national government over the states. It was the culmination of the debates between the Federalists and Anti-Federalists, between Marshall and Roane, and so forth. When the Union won the war, it seemed to have also won the debate over the nature of federal-state relations. In the immediate aftermath of the battle, the Court acceded, although not willingly, to congressional power over the defeated region.

Dual Federalism and Laissez-Faire Economics

Did the end of the war and the rise of national supremacy mean that Taney's dual federalism had seen its last days? Indeed, it remained under wraps for several decades but then resurfaced in a somewhat different form in the courts from the 1890s to the 1930s. The most vivid example of its revival came in *Hammer v. Dagenhart* (1918). Some analysts think that this Court's version of dual federalism differed from Taney's in *Dred Scott*. Do you see the distinction? Or do the words of the *Hammer* Court echo its predecessor's sentiment?

Hammer v. Dagenhart

247 U.S. 251 (1918)

Vote: 5 (Day, McReynolds, Pitney, Van Devanter, White)
*   4 (Brandeis, Clarke, Holmes, McKenna)*
Opinion of the Court: Day
Dissenting opinion: Holmes

In the 1880s America entered the industrial age, which was characterized by the unfettered growth of the private-sector economy. Although the industrial revolution forever changed the United States for the better in countless ways, it also had many negative effects. Lacking any significant government controls, many businesses engaged in less than benevolent relations with their workers. Some forced employees to work more than fourteen hours a day at absurdly low wages and under awful conditions. They also had no qualms about employing children under the age of sixteen.

Americans were divided over these practices. On one side were the entrepreneurs, stockholders, and others who gained from worker exploitation. By employing children, paying low wages, and providing no benefits, they were able to minimize expenses and maximize profits. On the other side were the Progressives, reformist groups, and individuals who sought to convince the states and the federal government to enact laws to protect workers. These two camps repeatedly clashed in their struggle to attain diametrically opposed policy ends.[9]

One of the first battles came in 1915 when Congress was considering the Federal Child Labor Act. The bill prohibited shipment in interstate commerce of factory products made by children under the age of fourteen or by children aged fourteen to sixteen who worked more than eight hours a day. Supported by numerous progressive groups, the legislation faced substantial opposi-

9. We derive what follows from Lee Epstein, *Conservatives in Court* (Knoxville: University of Tennessee Press, 1985); and Stephen B. Wood, *Constitutional Politics in the Progressive Era* (Chicago: University of Chicago Press, 1968).

tion from employer associations, including the Executive Committee of Southern Cotton Manufacturers. The committee was made up of militant mill owners who organized in 1915 solely to counter federal child labor legislation. But its first attempt failed, and in 1916 Congress passed the Federal Child Labor Act. The committee's leader, David Clark, vowed that his group would challenge the constitutionality of the act in court. He retained the services of a corporate law firm that held a laissez-faire philosophy and had successfully placed this argument before the Supreme Court. He then sought the right test case to challenge the law. Eventually, he decided on a suit against the Fidelity Manufacturing Company.

The case he brought was perfect for the committee's needs. Roland Dagenhart and his two minor sons were employed by Fidelity, a cotton mill in North Carolina. Under state law, both of Dagenhart's sons were permitted to work up to eleven hours a day. Under the new federal act, however, the older boy could work only eight hours, and the younger one could not work at all. Not only were the facts relating to the Dagenharts advantageous, but also Clark secured the cooperation of the company, which had equal disdain for the law, in planning the litigation. One month before the effective date of the law, the company posted the new federal regulations on its door, and "explained" to affected employees that they would be unable to continue to work. A week later, having already secured the consent of the Dagenharts and of the factory, the committee's attorneys filed an injunction against the company and William C. Hammer, a U.S. attorney, to prevent enforcement of the law.

Within a month, the district court heard arguments and ruled the act unconstitutional. The judge did not write an opinion, but when he handed down his decision, he fully agreed with the Executive Committee's arguments, suggesting that the federal government had usurped state power.

Once the district court stayed enforcement of the act, both the committee and the U.S. Justice Department began to plan the strategies they would use before the U.S. Supreme Court. The committee argued that Congress had no authority to impose its policies on the states. The government's defense was led by Solicitor General John W. Davis. One of the great attorneys of the day, he made a strong case for the law, although he probably opposed it. Not only did he argue that the regulation of child labor fell squarely within Congress's purview, but he also supplied the Court with data indicating that the states themselves had sought to eliminate such practices. His brief pointed out that only three states placed no age limit on factory employees, and only ten allowed those between the ages of fourteen and sixteen to work.

Justice William R. Day delivered the opinion of the Court:

It is . . . contended that the authority of Congress may be exerted to control interstate commerce in the shipment of child-made goods because of the effect of the circulation of such goods in other states where the evil of this class of labor has been recognized by local legislation, and the right to thus employ child labor has been more rigorously restrained than in the state of production. In other words, that the unfair competition thus engendered may be controlled by closing the channels of interstate commerce to manufacturers in those states where the local laws do not meet what Congress deems to be the more just standard of other states.

There is no power vested in Congress to require the states to exercise their police power so as to prevent possible unfair competition. Many causes may cooperate to give one state, by reason of local laws or conditions, an economic advantage over others. The commerce clause was not intended to give to Congress a general authority to equalize such conditions. In some of the states laws have been passed fixing minimum wages for women; in others the local law regulates the hours of labor of women in various employments. Business done in such states may be at an economic disadvantage when compared with states which have no such regulations; surely, this fact does not give Congress the power to deny transportation in interstate commerce to those who carry on business where the hours of labor and the rate of compensation for women have not been fixed by a standard in the use in other states and approved by Congress.

The grant of power to Congress over the subject of interstate commerce was to enable it to regulate such commerce, and not to give it authority to control the states in their exercise of the police power over local trade and manufacture.

The grant of authority over a purely Federal matter was not intended to destroy the local power always existing and carefully reserved to the states in the 10th Amendment to the Constitution. . . .

That there should be limitations upon the right to employ children in mines and factories in the interest of their own and the public welfare, all will admit. That such employment is generally deemed to require regulation is shown by the fact that the brief of counsel states that every state in the Union has a law upon the subject, limiting the right to thus employ children. In North Carolina, the state wherein is located the factory in which the employment was had in the present case, no child under twelve years of age is permitted to work.

. . . The maintenance of the authority of the states over matters purely local is as essential to the preservation of our institutions as is the conservation of the supremacy of the Federal power in all matters intrusted to the nation by the Federal Constitution.

In interpreting the Constitution it must never be forgotten that the nation is made up of states, to which are intrusted the powers of local government. And to them and to the people the powers not expressly delegated to the national government are reserved. The power of the states to regulate their purely internal affairs by such laws as seem wise to the local authority is inherent, and has never been surrendered to the general government. To sustain this statute would not be, in our judgment, a recognition of the lawful exertion of congressional authority over interstate commerce, but would sanction an invasion by the Federal power of the control of a matter purely local in its character, and over which no authority has been dele-

gated to Congress in conferring the power to regulate commerce among the states.

We have neither authority nor disposition to question the motives of Congress in enacting this legislation. The purposes intended must be attained consistently with constitutional limitations, and not by an invasion of the powers of the states. This court has no more important function than that which devolves upon it the obligation to preserve inviolate the constitutional limitations upon the exercise of authority, Federal and state, to the end that each may continue to discharge, harmoniously with the other, the duties intrusted to it by the Constitution.

In our view the necessary effect of this act is, by means of a prohibition against the movement in interstate commerce of ordinary commercial commodities, to regulate the hours of labor of children in factories and mines within the states,—a purely state authority. Thus the act in a twofold sense is repugnant to the Constitution. It not only transcends the authority delegated to Congress over commerce, but also exerts a power as to a purely local matter to which the Federal authority does not extend. The far-reaching result of upholding the act cannot be more plainly indicated than by pointing out that if Congress can thus regulate matters intrusted to local authority by prohibition of the movement of commodities in interstate commerce, all freedom of commerce will be at an end, and the power of the states over local matters may be eliminated, and thus our system of government be practically destroyed.

For these reasons we hold that this law exceeds the constitutional authority of Congress. It follows that the decree of the District Court must be affirmed.

Mr. Justice Holmes, dissenting:

The act does not meddle with anything belonging to the states. They may regulate their internal affairs and their domestic commerce as they like. But when they seek to send their products across the state line they are no longer within their rights. If there were no Constitution and no Congress their power to cross the line would depend upon their neighbors. Under the Constitution such commerce belongs not to the states, but to Congress to regulate. It may carry out its views of public policy whatever indirect effect they may have upon the activities of the states. Instead of being encountered by a prohibitive tariff at her boundaries, the state encounters the public policy of the United States which it is for Congress to express. The public policy of the United States is shaped with a view to the benefit of the nation as a whole. . . . The national

welfare as understood by Congress may require a different attitude within its sphere from that of some self-seeking state. It seems to me entirely constitutional for Congress to enforce its understanding by all the means at its command.

Day's decision was a total victory for the Executive Committee; in fact, C. Herman Pritchett has called *Hammer* the Court's "clearest statement" of dual federalism.[10] But the opinion rested on tenuous grounds. Pritchett points out that Justice Day misquoted the Tenth Amendment: it does not contain the word "expressly."[11] In so doing, he ignored Marshall's reasoning in *McCulloch*. It was critical to Marshall's interpretation of congressional powers that the word *expressly* did not appear. So Day assumed "a position that was historically inaccurate."[12] When Congress considered the Tenth Amendment, one representative proposed to "add the word 'expressly' so as to read 'the powers not expressly delegated by this Constitution.'" James Madison and others objected and the motion was defeated.[13]

Although this error seemed to undermine Day's logic, a more important question may be this: Was Day's explication of dual federalism the same as Taney's? Many scholars think not; in fact, they argue that *Hammer*—taken in conjunction with other opinions of that Court era— diverges from Taney's philosophy. While Taney viewed dual federalism as a way to equalize state and federal power, it may be that the Supreme Court between 1890 and 1930 was not concerned with the rights of states as states. Rather, the justices were bent on prohibiting any state *or*

federal interference with the growth of the nation's booming private-sector economy. They "turned to dual federalism as a weapon against federal regulation" of the sort at issue in *Hammer*.[14] At the same time, the Court limited the ability of states to pass similar legislation under the guise that it would restrict individual liberties. *(See Chapter 9 for a discussion of limits on state regulatory efforts during this time.)* The Court's approach was quite distinct from Taney's. For the Courts from the 1890s through the 1930s, dual federalism and the Tenth Amendment were masks to hide their laissez-faire philosophy.

The justices' frame of reference, their wholehearted support of business, was as well suited to the context of their day as Taney's was to his, or so some have argued. At the very least, the Court's willingness to embrace a free enterprise philosophy reflected the general mood of Americans, some of whom were benefiting financially from the growth of the economy. When the economic boom of the 1920s turned into the Great Depression of the 1930s, however, citizens and their newly elected leaders clamored for the sort of regulation struck down in *Hammer*. Yet, as we saw in the delegation of powers section of Chapter 3, the Court was set in a 1920s mold. It struck down one New Deal program after another on various grounds that included the unconstitutional delegation of power and the impermissible congressional use of its authority to regulate commerce *(see Chapter 6)*. It also invoked the Tenth Amendment. In *Schechter Poultry Corporation*

10. C. Herman Pritchett, *Constitutional Law of the Federal System* (Englewood Cliffs, N.J.: Prentice-Hall, 1984), 60.

11. Ibid.

12. Ibid., 60-61.

13. Daniel A. Farber and Suzanna Sherry, *A History of the American Constitution* (St. Paul, Minn.: West Publishing, 1990), 239.

14. Walter F. Murphy, James E. Fleming, and William F. Harris II, *American Constitutional Interpretation* (Mineola, N.Y.: Foundation Press, 1986), 403.

v. United States (1935), involving the constitutionality of the National Industrial Recovery Act—a major piece of New Deal legislation—the Court noted:

We are told that the provision of the statute authorizing the adoption of codes must be viewed in the light of the grave national crisis with which Congress was confronted. Undoubtedly, the conditions to which power is addressed are always to be considered when the exercise of power is challenged. Extraordinary conditions may call for extraordinary remedies. But the argument necessarily stops short of an attempt to justify action which lies outside the sphere of constitutional authority. Extraordinary conditions do not create or enlarge constitutional power. The Constitution established a national government with powers deemed to be adequate, as they have proved to be both in war and peace, but these powers of the national government are limited by the constitutional grants. Those who act under these grants are not at liberty to transcend the imposed limits because they believe that more or different power is necessary. *Such assertions of extra-constitutional authority were anticipated and precluded by the explicit terms of the Tenth Amendment* (emphasis added).

The (Re)Emergence of National Supremacy: Cooperative Federalism

Despite the Court's language, the heyday of dual federalism was numbered. Amid increasing pressure for change, including President Franklin D. Roosevelt's Court-packing scheme, came the famous "switch-in-time-that-saved nine" and with it the demise of broad interpretations of the Tenth Amendment. Although this process began in 1937, the death knell rang most loudly with the decision in *United States v. Darby Lumber* (1941).[15] As you read Chief Justice Harlan F. Stone's opinion, think about John Marshall's in *McCulloch.* Are they making similar claims or can you detect distinctions?

15. See Joseph F. Kobylka, "The Court, Justice Blackmun, and Federalism," *Creighton Law Review* 19 (1985-1986): 21.

United States v. Darby Lumber

312 U.S. 100 (1941)

Vote: 8 (Black, Douglas, Frankfurter, Hughes, Murphy, Reed, Roberts, Stone)

o

Opinion of the Court: Stone

In 1938 Congress, under its power to regulate interstate commerce, enacted an important piece of New Deal legislation, the Fair Labor Standards Act (FLSA). It provided that all employers "engaged in interstate commerce, or in the production of goods for that commerce" must pay all their employees a minimum wage of twenty-five cents per hour and not permit employees to work longer than forty-four hours per week without paying them one and one-half times their regular pay. In November 1939 the federal government sought and obtained an indictment against Fred W. Darby for violating the FLSA. The indictment alleged that Darby, the owner of a lumber company, was engaged in the production and manufacturing of goods shipped out of state, but that he had not abided by either of FLSA's major pay requirements.

Darby did not dispute the charges. Rather, invoking the logic of *Hammer,* his brief argued:

The Fair Labor Standards Act . . . is an unconstitutional attempt to regulate conditions in production of goods and commodities and it can not be sustained as a regulation of interstate commerce within the delegated power of Congress under the commerce clause. It violated the Tenth Amendment.

The government responded more pragmatically than legally, stating:

State legislators, Congressional committees, federal commissions, and businessmen over a period of time have realized that no state, acting alone, could require labor standards substantially higher than those obtained in other states whose producers and manufacturers competed in the interstate market.

The reiterated conclusion that the individual states were helpless gained added force during the prolonged economic depression of the 1930's. The . . . National Industrial Recovery Act . . . and the Fair Labor Standards Act itself each reflect a great volume of testimony adduced at congressional hearings and elsewhere to the effect that employers with lower labor standards possess an unfair advantage in interstate competition, and that only the national government could deal with the problem.

The lumber industry, the government asserted, well illustrated ''the inability of the particular states to ensure adequate labor standards; over 57 percent of the lumber produced enters into interstate or foreign commerce from 45 of the states.''

Justice Stone delivered the opinion of the Court:

The motive and purpose of the present regulation are plainly to make effective the Congressional conception of public policy that interstate commerce should not be made the instrument of competition in the distribution of goods produced under substandard labor conditions, which competition is injurious to the commerce and to the states from and to which the commerce flows. The motive and purpose of a regulation of interstate commerce are matters for the legisla-

tive judgment upon the exercise of which the Constitution places no restriction and over which the courts are given no control. . . . Whatever their motive and purpose, regulations of commerce which do not infringe some constitutional prohibition are within the plenary power conferred on Congress by the Commerce Clause. Subject only to that limitation, presently to be considered, we conclude that the prohibition of the shipment interstate of goods produced under the forbidden substandard labor conditions is within the constitutional authority of Congress. . . .

Our conclusion is unaffected by the Tenth Amendment which provides: ''The powers not delegated to the United States by the Constitution nor prohibited by it to the states are reserved to the states respectively or to the people.'' The amendment states but a truism that all is retained which has not been surrendered. There is nothing in the history of its adoption to suggest that it was more than declaratory of the relationship between the national and state governments as it had been established by the Constitution before the amendment or that its purpose was other than to allay fears that the new national government might seek to exercise powers not granted, and that the states might not be able to exercise fully their reserved powers.

From the beginning and for many years the amendment has been construed as not depriving the national government of authority to resort to all means for the exercise of a granted power which are appropriate and plainly adapted to the permitted end. . . .

Reversed.

Justice Stone's opinion in *Darby Lumber* brought the Court full circle, from Marshall's nationalism to Taney's dual federalism and back. Not only did *Darby Lumber* explicitly overrule *Hammer* and uphold the FLSA, but also it gutted the Tenth Amendment: it denied that the amendment constituted an ''affirmative base of power from which states may challenge the wide-ranging effects of national legislation.''[16]

16. Craig R. Ducat and Harold W. Chase, *Constitutional Interpretation*, 4th ed. (St. Paul, Minn.: West Publishing, 1988), 360.

For the next thirty-five years dual federalism was out and Stone's cooperative federalism was in. Under this doctrine, at least theoretically, the various levels of government shared policy-making responsibilities. In practice, it meant, as Stone's opinion implies, that the national government took the lead in formulating policy goals, which it expected state and local officials to implement. Tremendous changes in government followed, not the least of which was that, as depicted in Figure 5-1, a huge shift occurred

Figure 5-1. *Government Spending as a Percentage of GNP, 1929–1989*

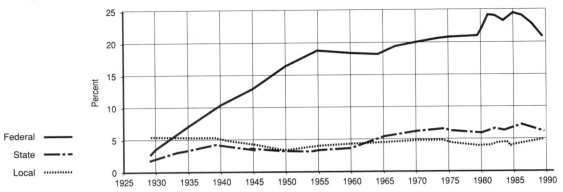

Note: State and local figures unavailable for 1989. Shown is "own source" spencing, i.e., before intergovernmental transfers.
Source: Harold W. Stanley and Richard G. Niemi, *Vital Statistics on American Politics,* 3d ed. (Washington, D.C.; CQ Press, 1992), 331.

in the balance between national and state spending. As the federal government took advantage of its new constitutional freedom—creating more and more programs and projects covering all aspects of American life—it began to account for greater and greater percentages of government spending. By the 1960s the federal government reigned supreme.

Although federal supremacy was a fact of American life, it was not universally applauded or even accepted. Some opposition came from familiar sources: politicians in southern states, who vehemently opposed congressional (and Court) efforts to force integration of schools and other public facilities. Governors, like Alabama's George Wallace, simply refused to relent, making similar kinds of arguments their counterparts had made in the 1860s. He and others even formed their own political party to advocate states' rights.

Other opposition was more national in scope. President Richard Nixon lamented the tremendous growth of the federal government and the concomitant demise of states' authority over their own affairs. To restore some balance he proposed a "new federalism" plan. Under it, states and

localities would have increased authority to determine how they spent their money because they would participate in a revenue-sharing arrangement with the federal government, which would allocate money to them to spend as they saw fit.

New federalism, however, was not dual federalism. Nixon may have wanted to give the states and localities greater authority in certain policy arenas, but he was not one to argue that the federal government, particularly the executive branch, and the states were "co-equal sovereigns." Moreover, issues of federalism were never the most important items on the president's agenda, particularly when it came to nominations to the Supreme Court. Nixon looked for jurists who would be inclined toward judicial restraint generally and to a law and order posture, in particular.

When "Nixon's" Supreme Court handed down its decision in *National League of Cities v. Usery* (1976), therefore, it took many legal scholars by surprise. A greater concern with states' rights was certainly within the realm of the politics of the day, but the Court took that concern to a rather extreme level. What did the justices rule in *National League,* and why was their ruling so controversial?

National League of Cities v. Usery

426 U.S. 833 (1976)

Vote: 5 (Blackmun, Burger, Powell, Rehnquist, Stewart)
4 (Brennan, Marshall, Stevens, White)
Opinion of the Court: Rehnquist
Concurring opinion: Blackmun
Dissenting opinions: Brennan, Stevens

At issue in this case was the Federal Labor Standards Act, which the Court had upheld in *United States v. Darby Lumber.* Since the decision in 1941, Congress had amended the Act to cover public employees, and those amendments, along with other attempts to regulate state employment, were themselves the subject of several major Supreme Court rulings. As noted in the box, opposite, the Court had upheld those regulations.

This case crystallized when Congress in 1974 once again expanded the scope of the FLSA, this time bringing virtually all state public employees, who were excluded in the original legislation, under its reach. As a result, various cities and states and two organizations representing their collective interests, the National League of Cities and the National Governors' Conference, challenged the constitutionality of the new amendments. In particular, they argued that the amendments represented a "collision" between federal expansion and states' rights in violation of the Tenth Amendment. As one litigant claimed, the Tenth Amendment should protect the powers states already possessed, including authority over public workers. It is interesting to note that in representing the federal government Solicitor General Robert Bork did not take issue with this analysis. Rather, he argued that the Tenth Amendment was inapplicable because Congress had passed the 1974 amendments under its power to regulate commerce.

Justice William H. Rehnquist delivered the opinion of the Court:

Appellants' essential contention is that the 1974 amendments to the Act, while undoubtedly within the scope of the Commerce Clause, encounter a similar constitutional barrier because they are to be applied directly to the States and subdivisions of States as employers. . . .

Appellee Secretary argues that the cases in which this Court has upheld sweeping exercises of authority by Congress, even though those exercises pre-empted state regulation of the private sector, have already curtailed the sovereignty of the States quite as much as the 1974 amendments to the Fair Labor Standards Act. We do not agree. It is one thing to recognize the authority of Congress to enact laws regulating individual businesses necessarily subject to the dual sovereignty of the government of the Nation and of the State in which they reside. It is quite another to uphold a similar exercise of congressional authority directed, not to private citizens, but to the States as States. We have repeatedly recognized that there are attributes of sovereignty attaching to every state government which may not be impaired by Congress, not because Congress may lack an affirmative grant of legislative authority to reach the matter, but because the Constitution prohibits it from exercising the authority in that manner. . . .

One undoubted attribute of state sovereignty is the States' power to determine the wages which shall be paid to those whom they employ in order to carry out their governmental functions, what hours those persons will work, and what compensation will be provided where these employees may be called upon to work overtime. The question we must resolve here, then, is whether these determinations are "'functions essential to separate and independent existence'" so that Congress may not abrogate the States' otherwise plenary authority to make them.

In their complaint appellants advanced estimates of substantial costs which will be imposed upon them by the 1974 amendments. Since the District Court dismissed their complaint, we take its well-pleaded allegations as true, although it appears from appellee's submissions in the District Court and in this Court that resolution of the factual disputes as to the effect of the amendments is not critical to our disposition of the case.

Judged solely in terms of increased costs in dollars, these allegations show a significant impact on the

History of the Wage Regulation Leading to *National League of Cities v. Usery*

Congressional Action	*Court Response*
Fair Labor Standards Act of 1938 (FLSA): requires employers to pay employees a minimum wage and one and one-half times their regular pay for overtime work. States and localities are excluded from the act.	Upheld in *United States v. Darby Lumber* (1941).
1966 Extension of the FLSA: extended the law to workers in publicly operated schools, hospitals, and institutions. The extension covered employees of transit companies insofar as their public employers had to pay them minimum wage. But the 1966 extension did not provide overtime pay protection.	Upheld in *Maryland v. Wirtz* (1968). Congress can prescribe wage regulations for employees, even if their employer is a state.
Economic Stabilization Act of 1970: limited wage increases for state employees.	Upheld in *Fry v. United States* (1975). This act falls under Congress's commerce power. However, Congress cannot use its "power in a fashion that impairs the States' integrity or their ability to function effectively in a federal system."

Source: Adapted from Joseph F. Kobylka, "The Court, Justice Blackmun, and Federalism," *Creighton Law Review* 19 (1985–1986): 22–23.

functioning of the governmental bodies involved. The Metropolitan Government of Nashville and Davidson County, Tenn., for example, asserted that the Act will increase its costs of providing essential police and fire protection, without any increase in service or in current salary levels, by $938,000 per year. . . .

Increased costs are not, of course, the only adverse effects which compliance with the Act will visit upon state and local governments, and in turn upon the citizens who depend upon those governments. In its complaint in intervention, for example, California asserted that it could not comply with the overtime costs (approximately $750,000 per year) which the Act required to be paid to California Highway Patrol cadets during their academy training program. California reported that it had thus been forced to reduce its academy training program from 2,080 hours to only 960 hours, a compromise undoubtedly of substantial importance to those whose safety and welfare may depend upon the preparedness of the California Highway Patrol. . . .

Quite apart from the substantial costs imposed upon the States and their political subdivisions, the Act displaces state policies regarding the manner in which they will structure delivery of those governmental services which their citizens require. The Act, speaking directly to the States qua States, requires that they shall pay all but an extremely limited minority of their employees the minimum wage rates currently chosen by Congress. It may well be that as a matter of economic policy it would be desirable that States, just as private employers, comply with these minimum wage requirements. But it cannot be gainsaid that the federal requirement directly supplants the considered policy choices of the States' elected officials and administrators as to how they wish to structure pay scales in state employment. The State might wish to employ persons with little or no training, or those who wish to work on a casual basis, or those who for some other reason do not possess minimum employment requirements, and pay them less than the federally prescribed minimum wage. It may wish to offer part-time or summer employment to teenagers at a figure less than the minimum wage, and if unable to do so may decline to offer such employment at all. But the Act would forbid such choices by the States. The only "discretion" left to them under the Act is either to attempt to increase their revenue to meet the additional financial burden imposed upon them by paying congressionally prescribed wages to their existing complement of employees, or to reduce that complement to a number which can be paid the federal minimum wage without increasing revenue.

This dilemma presented by the minimum wage restrictions may seem not immediately different from that faced by private employers, who have long been covered by the Act and who must find ways to increase their gross income if they are to pay higher wages while maintaining current earnings. The difference, however, is that a State is not merely a factor in the "shifting economic arrangements" of the private sector of the economy, but is itself a coordinate element in the system established by the Framers for governing our Federal Union.

The degree to which FLSA amendments would interfere with traditional aspects of state sovereignty can be seen even more clearly upon examining the overtime requirements of the Act. The general effect of these provisions is to require the States to pay their employees at premium rates whenever their work exceeds a specified number of hours in a given period. . . . [T]he vice of the Act as sought to be applied here is that it directly penalizes the States for choosing to hire governmental employees on terms different from those which Congress has sought to impose.

This congressionally imposed displacement of state decisions may substantially restructure traditional ways in which the local governments have arranged their affairs. Although at this point many of the actual effects under the proposed amendments remain a matter of some dispute among the parties, enough can be satisfactorily anticipated for an outline discussion of their general import. The requirement imposing premium rates upon any employment in excess of what Congress has decided is appropriate for a governmental employee's workweek, for example, appears likely to have the effect of coercing the States to structure work periods in some employment areas, such as police and fire protection, in a manner substantially different from practices which have long been commonly accepted among local governments of this Nation. In addition, appellee represents that the Act will require that the premium compensation for overtime worked must be paid in cash, rather than with compensatory time off, unless such compensatory time is taken in the same pay period. This too appears likely to be highly disruptive of accepted employment practices in many governmental areas where the demand for a number of employees to perform important jobs for extended periods on short notice can be both unpredictable and critical. . . .

Our examination of the effect of the 1974 amendments, as sought to be extended to the States and their political subdivisions, satisfies us that both the minimum wage and the maximum hour provisions will impermissibly interfere with the integral governmental functions of these bodies. We earlier noted some disagreement between the parties regarding the precise effect the amendments will have in application. We do not believe particularized assessments of actual impact are crucial to resolution of the issue presented, however. For even if we accept appellee's assessments concerning the impact of the amendments, their application will nonetheless significantly alter or displace the States' abilities to structure employer-employee relationships in such areas as fire prevention, police protection, sanitation, public health, and parks and recreation. These activities are typical of those performed by state and local governments in discharging their dual functions of administering the public law and furnishing public services. Indeed, it is functions such as these which governments are created to provide, services such as these which the States have traditionally afforded their citizens. If Congress may withdraw from the States the authority to make those fundamental employment decisions upon which their systems for performance of these functions must rest, we think there would be little left of the States' "'separate and independent existence.'" Thus, even if appellants may have overestimated the effect which the Act will have upon their current levels and patterns of governmental activity, the dispositive factor is that Congress has attempted to exercise its Commerce Clause authority to prescribe minimum wages and maximum hours to be paid by the States in their capacities as sovereign governments. In so doing, Congress has sought to wield its power in a fashion that would impair the States' "ability to function effectively in a federal system." This exercise of congressional authority does not comport with the federal system of government embodied in the Constitution. We hold that insofar as the challenged amendments operate to directly displace the States' freedom to structure integral operations in areas of traditional governmental functions, they are not within the authority granted Congress by Art I, § 8, cl 3.

One final matter requires our attention. Appellee has vigorously urged that we cannot, consistently with the Court's decisions in Maryland v Wirtz (1968) and Fry [v. United States, 1975], rule against him here. It is important to examine this contention so that it will be clear what we hold today, and what we do not. . . .

We think our holding today quite consistent with Fry. The enactment at issue there was occasioned by an extremely serious problem which endangered the well-being of all the component parts of our federal system and which only collective action by the National Government might forestall. The means selected were carefully drafted so as not to interfere with the States' freedom beyond a very limited, specific period of time. . . .

With respect to the Court's decision in Wirtz, we reach a different conclusion. Both appellee and the District Court thought that decision required rejection of appellants' claims. Appellants, in turn, advance several arguments by which they seek to distinguish the facts before the Court in Wirtz from those presented by the 1974 amendments to the Act. There are undoubtedly factual distinctions between the two situations, but in view of the conclusions expressed earlier in this opinion we do not believe the reasoning in Wirtz may any longer be regarded as authoritative. . . .

[W]e have reaffirmed today that the States as States stand on a quite different footing from an individual or a corporation when challenging the exercise of Congress' power to regulate commerce. . . . Congress may not exercise that power so as to force directly upon the States its choices as to how essential decisions regarding the conduct of integral governmental functions are to be made. We agree that such assertions of power, if unchecked, would indeed, as Mr. Justice Douglas cautioned in his dissent in Wirtz, allow "the National Government [to] devour the essentials of state sovereignty," and would therefore transgress the bounds of the authority granted Congress under the Commerce Clause. While there are obvious differences between the schools and hospitals involved in Wirtz, and the fire and police departments affected here, each provides an integral portion of those governmental services which the States and their political subdivisions have traditionally afforded their citizens. We are therefore persuaded that Wirtz must be overruled.

In their scrutiny of the FLSA, the Nixon appointees plus Justice Potter Stewart "transmitted strong hints that dual federalism was beginning a new incarnation."[17] As you undoubtedly noted, the decision echoed the underlying federalism logic seen in cases like *Dred Scott* and *Hammer,* when it suggested that the Court had "repeatedly recognized that there are attributes of sovereignty attaching to every state government which may not be impaired by Congress, not because Congress may lack an affirmative grant of legislative authority to reach the matter, but because the

17. Murphy, Fleming, and Harris, *American Constitutional Interpretation,* 405.

Constitution prohibits it from exercising the authority in that manner.''

Where is the line separating constitutional from unconstitutional federal intrusions into state business? Rehnquist provided one answer when he wrote in *Usery:*

Congress may not exercise that power so as to force directly upon the States its choices as to how essential decisions regarding the conduct of integral governmental functions are to be made.

''While clearly not delineating these functions,'' Joseph Kobylka wrote, ''the Court did say that they must be 'essential to [the] separate and independent existence of the states.' '' [18] Examples of activities outside congressional authority and ''well within the area of traditional operations of state and local governments'' included fire

18. Kobylka, ''The Court,'' 24-25.

Table 5-5   Supreme Court Cases Between *National League of Cities* and *Garcia*

Case	Question	Holding (Vote)
Hodel v. Virginia Surface Mining & Reclamation Assn. (1981)	Is the Surface Mining and Reclamation Act of 1977, which sets minimum federal standards with which states had to comply and imposed federal standards on those that did not, an impermissible regulation of interstate commerce under *National League of Cities?*	No. (9–0) Marshall, for the majority, read *National League* to provide a three-prong test (now the *Hodel* test): ''First, there must be a showing that the challenged statute regulates the 'States as States.' . . . Second, the federal regulation must address matters that are indisputably 'attribute[s] of state sovereignty.' . . . And third, it must be apparent that the States' compliance with the federal law would directly impair their ability 'to structure integral operations in areas of traditional governmental functions.' '' Since this Act fails to meet the first prong, it is a permissible regulation.
United Transportation Union v. Long Island Rail Road (1982)	Does the Federal Railway Act, as applied to employees of a state-operated railroad, transgress the limitations of national power?	No. (9–0) The Court held that the act did not ''directly impair [the state's] ability 'to structure integral operations in areas of traditional governmental functions''' and therefore was within the bounds of national power.
FERC v. Mississippi (1982)	Is the Public Utility Regulatory Policies Act, which provided for the guidance and regulation of state utility regulatory commissions by the FERC and the states, beyond the limits on federal power enunciated in *National League?*	No. (5–4) Since *National League* did not hold that ''all aspects of a State's sovereign authority are immune from federal control,'' the nature of the federal interest can overcome state sovereignty, and the interest here does not act to ''impair the ability of the States.''
EEOC v. Wyoming (1983)	Is the Age Discrimination Act, which sets the mandatory retirement age of state game wardens at 55, unconstitutional under *National League?*	No. (5–4) Although the act did regulate the ''States as States,'' it did not '' 'directly impair' the State's ability to 'structure integral operations in areas of traditional governmental functions.' ''

Source: Adapted from Joseph F. Kobylka, ''The Court, Justice Blackmun, and Federalism,'' *Creighton Law Review* 19 (1985–1986): 26–31.

fighting, police protection, sanitation, public health, and parks and recreation.

In his concurrence, Justice Harry A. Blackmun argued that the Court was adopting a "balancing approach" to federal-state relations. But many saw it quite differently. *National League,* in fact, "generated a tremendous volume of constitutional commentary, much of it unfavorable."[19] Some scholars criticized the Court for elevating the Tenth Amendment and for reasserting the "discredited" doctrine of dual federalism. Others focused on the "uncertainties raised by the ruling." In particular, what would the justices define as "essential to the separate and independent existence of the state"?[20] This was not a question of mere academic interest: between 1976 and

19. Pritchett, *Constitutional Law of the Federal System,* 235.
20. Ibid.

1978 litigants filed some 45 cases asking the Court to address it.

As noted in Table 5-5, the Court issued several decisions designed to clarify its 1976 ruling. But almost from the start the justices began to chip away at its core. In *Hodel v. Virginia Surface Mining & Reclamation Assn.* (1981) and *United Transportation Union v. Long Island Rail Road* (1982) a unanimous Court rejected invitations to apply and thus expand the 1976 ruling. Major breaks with the decision, however, came in 1982 and 1983 when sharply divided Courts so whittled down *National League* as to make it almost invisible.

In theory, *National League* remained "on the books" as good law, at least until 1985. In *Garcia v. San Antonio Metropolitan Transit Authority,* the justices made it official and overruled *National League.*

Garcia v. San Antonio Metropolitan Transit Authority

469 U.S. 528 (1985)

Vote: 5 (Blackmun, Brennan, Marshall, Stevens, White)
     4 (Burger, O'Connor, Powell, Rehnquist)
Opinion of the Court: Blackmun
Dissenting opinions: Powell, O'Connor, Rehnquist

Garcia was virtually a carbon copy of *National League.* Once again litigation centered on amendments to the FLSA that required states to pay virtually all public employees minimum wages and overtime. The facts, however, were a bit more complicated.

In 1959 San Antonio created a mass transit system called SATS (San Antonio Transit System). For almost a decade SATS was a money-making venture, but by 1969 it was operating at a loss and turned to the federal government for assistance. The federal Urban Mass Transit Administration provided it with a $4 million grant.

When the city replaced SATS with SAMTA (San Antonio Metropolitan Transit Authority) in 1978, federal grants continued to subsidize its operations. Between 1970 and 1980, the transit system received more than $51 million or 40 percent of its costs from the federal government. The case started in 1979 when, "in response to a specific inquiry about the applicability of the FLSA to employees of SAMTA," the Department of Labor issued an opinion holding that SAMTA must abide by the act's wage provisions. SAMTA filed a challenge to the department's holding, and Joe G. Garcia and other SAMTA employees, in turn, initiated a suit against their employer for overtime pay.

When the case reached the U.S. Supreme Court, SAMTA relied heavily on *National League.* It argued, for example, that "transit is a traditional [city] function" and that, as the operator of that function, it was not covered by FLSA amendments. The U.S. government and Garcia countered by arguing that *National League* was not necessarily applicable. In their view, application of the FLSA to public transit did not violate the Tenth Amendment because (1) operation of a transit system is not a traditional government function, and (2) operation of a transit system is not a core government function that must be exempted from federal commerce power legislation to preserve the states' independence. To demonstrate these points, attorneys emphasized the fact that SAMTA received significant funding from the federal government. This, in their view, indicated that "the growth of public transit service reflects cooperative federalism, not independent state initiatives."

Justice Blackmun delivered the opinion of the Court:

We revisit in these cases an issue raised in National League of Cities v Usery (1976). In that litigation, this Court, by a sharply divided vote, ruled that the Commerce Clause does not empower Congress to enforce the minimum-wage and overtime provisions of the Fair Labor Standards Act (FLSA) against the States "in areas of traditional government functions." Although National League of Cities supplied some examples of "traditional governmental functions," it did not offer a general explanation of how a "traditional" function is to be distinguished from a "nontraditional" one. Since then, federal and state courts have struggled with the task, thus imposed, of identifying a traditional function for purposes of state immunity under the Commerce Clause.

In the present cases, a Federal District Court concluded that municipal ownership and operation of a mass-transit system is a traditional governmental function and thus, under National League of Cities, is exempt from the obligations imposed by the FLSA. Faced with the identical question, three Federal Courts of Appeals and one state appellate court have reached the opposite conclusion.

Our examination of this "function" standard applied in these and other cases over the last eight years

now persuades us that the attempt to draw the boundaries of state regulatory immunity in terms of "traditional governmental function" is not only unworkable but is also inconsistent with established principles of federalism and, indeed, with those very federalism principles on which National League of Cities purported to rest. That case, accordingly, is overruled. . . .

The central theme of National League of Cities was that the States occupy a special position in our constitutional system and that the scope of Congress' authority under the Commerce Clause must reflect that position. Of course, the Commerce Clause by its specific language does not provide any special limitation on Congress' actions with respect to the States. It is equally true, however, that the text of the Constitution provides the beginning rather than the final answer to every inquiry into questions of federalism, for "[b]ehind the words of the constitutional provisions are postulates which limit and control." National League of Cities reflected the general conviction that the Constitution precludes "the National Government [from] devour[ing] the essentials of state sovereignty." In order to be faithful to the underlying federal premises of the Constitution, courts must look for the "postulates which limit and control."

What has proved problematic is not the perception that the Constitution's federal structure imposes limitations on the Commerce Clause, but rather the nature and content of those limitations. One approach to defining the limits on Congress' authority to regulate the States under the Commerce Clause is to identify certain underlying elements of political sovereignty that are deemed essential to the States' "separate and independent existence." This approach obviously underlay the Court's use of the "traditional governmental function" concept in National League of Cities. It also has led to the separate requirement that the challenged federal statute "address matters that are indisputably 'attribute[s]' of state sovereignty.'" In National League of Cities itself, for example, the Court concluded that decisions by a State concerning the wages and hours of its employees are an "undoubted attribute of state sovereignty." The opinion did not explain what aspects of such decisions made them such an "undoubted attribute," and the Court since then has remarked on the uncertain scope of the concept. The point of the inquiry, however, has remained to single out particular features of a State's internal governance that are deemed to be intrinsic parts of state sovereignty.

We doubt that courts ultimately can identify principled constitutional limitations on the scope of Congress' Commerce Clause powers over the States merely by relying on a priori definitions of state sovereignty. In part, this is because of the elusiveness of objective criteria for "fundamental" elements of state sovereignty, a problem we have witnessed in the search for "traditional governmental functions." There is, however, a more fundamental reason: the sovereignty of the States is limited by the Constitution itself. A variety of sovereign powers, for example, are withdrawn from the States by Article I, § 10. Section 8 of the same Article works an equally sharp contraction of state sovereignty by authorizing Congress to exercise a wide range of legislative powers and (in conjunction with the Supremacy Clause of Article VI) to displace contrary state legislation. . . .

The States unquestionably do "retai[n] a significant measure of sovereign authority." They do so, however, only to the extent that the Constitution has not divested them of their original powers and transferred those powers to the Federal Government. In the words of James Madison to the Members of the First Congress: "Interference with the power of the States was no constitutional criterion of the power of Congress. If the power was not given, Congress could not exercise it; if given, they might exercise it, although it should interfere with the laws, or even the Constitution of the states." . . .

As a result, to say that the Constitution assumes the continued role of the States is to say little about the nature of that role. Only recently, this Court recognized that the purpose of the constitutional immunity recognized in National League of Cities is not to preserve "a sacred province of state autonomy." With rare exceptions, like the guarantee, in Article IV, § 3, of state territorial integrity, the Constitution does not carve out express elements of state sovereignty that Congress may not employ its delegated powers to displace. . . . The power of the Federal Government is a "power to be respected" as well, and the fact that

the States remain sovereign as to all powers not vested in Congress or denied them by the Constitution offers no guidance about where the frontier between state and federal power lies. In short, we have no license to employ freestanding conceptions of state sovereignty when measuring congressional authority under the Commerce Clause. . . .

Insofar as the present cases are concerned, then, we need go no further than to state that we perceive nothing in the overtime and minimum-wage requirements of the FLSA, as applied to SAMTA, that is destructive of state sovereignty or violative of any constitutional provision. SAMTA faces nothing more than the same minimum-wage and overtime obligations that hundreds of thousands of other employers, public as well as private, have to meet.

In these cases, the status of public mass transit simply underscores the extent to which the structural protections of the Constitution insulate the States from federally imposed burdens. When Congress first subjected state mass-transit systems to FLSA obligations in 1966, and when it expanded those obligations in 1974, it simultaneously provided extensive funding for state and local mass transit through UMTA. In the two decades since its enactment, UMTA has provided over $22 billion in mass-transit aid to States and localities. In 1983 alone, UMTA funding amounted to $3.7 billion. . . . In short, Congress has not simply placed a financial burden on the shoulders of States and localities that operate mass-transit systems, but has provided substantial countervailing financial assistance as well, assistance that may leave individual mass-transit systems better off than they would have been had Congress never intervened at all in the area. Congress' treatment of public mass transit reinforces our conviction that the national political process systematically protects States from the risk of having their functions in that area handicapped by Commerce Clause regulation.

This analysis makes clear that Congress' action in affording SAMTA employees the protections of the wage and hour provisions of the FLSA contravened no affirmative limit on Congress' power under the Commerce Clause. The judgment of the District Court therefore must be reversed.

Of course, we continue to recognize that the States

occupy a special and specific position in our constitutional system and that the scope of Congress' authority under the Commerce Clause must reflect that position. But the principal and basic limit on the federal commerce power is that inherent in all congressional action—the built-in restraints that our system provides through state participation in federal governmental action. The political process ensures that laws that unduly burden the States will not be promulgated. In the factual setting of these cases the internal safeguards of the political process have performed as intended.

These cases do not require us to identify or define what affirmative limits the constitutional structure might impose on federal action affecting the States under the Commerce Clause. . . .

Though the separate concurrence providing the fifth vote in National League of Cities was "not untroubled by certain possible implications" of the decision, the Court in that case attempted to articulate affirmative limits on the Commerce Clause power in terms of core governmental functions and fundamental attributes of state sovereignty. But the model of democratic decisionmaking the Court there identified underestimated, in our view, the solicitude of the national political process for the continued vitality of the States. Attempts by other courts since then to draw guidance from this model have proved it both impracticable and doctrinally barren. In sum, in National League of Cities the Court tried to repair what did not need repair.

We do not lightly overrule recent precedent. We have not hesitated, however, when it has become apparent that a prior decision has departed from a proper understanding of congressional power under the Commerce Clause. Due respect for the reach of congressional power within the federal system mandates that we do so now.

National League of Cities v Usery (1976) is overruled. The judgment of the District Court is reversed, and these cases are remanded to that court for further proceedings consistent with this opinion.

It is so ordered.

Justice O'Connor, with whom Justice Powell and Justice Rehnquist join, dissenting.

The Court today surveys the battle scene of federalism and sounds a retreat. . . . I would prefer to hold the field and, at the very least, render a little aid to the wounded. . . . I . . . write separately to note my fundamental disagreement with the majority's views of federalism and the duty of this Court.

The Court overrules National League of Cities v Usery (1976) on the grounds that it is not "faithful to the role of federalism in a democratic society." National League of Cities is held to be inconsistent with this narrow view of federalism because it attempts to protect only those fundamental aspects of state sovereignty that are essential to the States' separate and independent existence, rather than protecting all state activities "equally."

In my view, federalism cannot be reduced to the weak "essence" distilled by the majority today. There is more to federalism than the nature of the constraints that can be imposed on the States in "the realm of authority left open to them by the Constitution." The central issue of federalism, of course, is whether any realm is left open to the States by the Constitution—whether any area remains in which a State may act free of federal interference. "The issue . . . is whether the federal system has any *legal* substance, any core of constitutional right that courts will enforce." The true "essence" of federalism is that the States *as* States have legitimate interests which the National Government is bound to respect even though its laws are supreme. If federalism so conceived and so carefully cultivated by the Framers of our Constitution is to remain meaningful, this Court cannot abdicate its constitutional responsibility to oversee the Federal Government's compliance with its duty to respect the legitimate interests of the States.

Due to the emergence of an integrated and industrialized national economy, this Court has been required to examine and review a breathtaking expansion of the powers of Congress. In doing so the Court correctly perceived that the Framers of our Constitution intended Congress to have sufficient power to address national problems. . . .

It would be erroneous, however, to conclude that the Supreme Court was blind to the threat to federalism when it expanded the commerce power. The Court based the expansion on the authority of Congress, through the Necessary and Proper Clause, "to resort to all means for the exercise of a granted power which are appropriate and plainly adapted to the permitted end.'' It is through this reasoning that an interstate activity ''affecting'' interstate commerce can be reached through the commerce power. . . .

It is worth recalling the cited passage in McCulloch v Maryland (1819) that lies at the source of the recent expansion of the commerce power. ''Let the end be legitimate, let it be within the scope of the constitution,'' Chief Justice Marshall said, ''and all means which are appropriate, which are plainly adapted to that end, which are not prohibited, but consist with the letter *and spirit* of the constitution, are constitutional'' (emphasis added). The *spirit* of the Tenth Amendment, of course, is that the States will retain their integrity in a system in which the laws of the United States are nevertheless supreme.

It is not enough that the ''end be legitimate''; the means to that end chosen by Congress must not contravene the spirit of the Constitution. Thus many of this Court's decision acknowledge that the means by which national power is exercised must take into account concerns for state autonomy. . . . The operative language of these cases varies, but the underlying principle is consistent: state autonomy is a relevant factor in assessing the means by which Congress exercises its powers.

This principle requires the Court to enforce affirmative limits on federal regulation of the States to complement the judicially crafted expansion of the interstate commerce power. National League of Cities v Usery represented an attempt to define such limits. The Court today rejects National League of Cities and washes its hands of all efforts to protect the States. In the process, the Court opines that unwarranted federal encroachments on state authority are and will remain '' 'horrible possibilities that never happen in the real world.' '' There is ample reason to believe to the contrary.

The last two decades have seen an unprecedented growth of federal regulatory activity, as the majority itself acknowledges. . . . Today, as federal legislation and coercive grant programs have expanded to embrace innumerable activities that were once viewed as local, the burden of persuasion has surely shifted, and the extraordinary has become ordinary. For example, recently the Federal Government has, with this

Court's blessing, undertaken to tell the States the age at which they can retire their law enforcement officers, and the regulatory standards, procedures, and even the agenda which their utilities commissions must consider and follow. See EEOC v. Wyoming. The political process has not protected against these encroachments on state activities, even though they directly impinge on a State's ability to make and enforce its laws. With the abandonment of National League of Cities, all that stands between the remaining essentials of state sovereignty and Congress is the latter's underdeveloped capacity for self-restraint.

The problems of federalism in an integrated national economy are capable of more responsible resolution than holding that the States as States retain no status apart from that which Congress chooses to let them retain. The proper resolution, I suggest, lies in weighing state autonomy as a factor in the balance when interpreting the means by which Congress can exercise its authority on the States as States. It is insufficient, in assessing the validity of congressional regulation of a State pursuant to the commerce power, to ask only whether the same regulation would be valid if enforced against a private party. That reasoning, embodied in the majority opinion, is inconsistent with the spirit of our Constitution. It remains relevant that a State is being regulated, as National League of Cities and every recent case have recognized. . . .

It has been difficult for this Court to craft bright lines defining the scope of the state autonomy protected by National League of Cities. Such difficulty is to be expected whenever constitutional concerns as important as federalism and the effectiveness of the commerce power come into conflict. Regardless of the difficulty, it is and will remain the duty of this Court to reconcile these concerns in the final instance. That the Court shuns the task today by appealing to the ''essence of federalism'' can provide scant comfort to those who believe our federal system requires something more than a unitary, centralized government. I would not shirk the duty acknowledged by National League of Cities and its progeny, and I share Justice Rehnquist's belief that this Court will in time again assume its constitutional responsibility.

I respectfully dissent.

With his opinion in *Garcia,* Justice Blackmun once again buried dual federalism and returned the Court to its posture in *Darby Lumber.* The timing of the decision also was interesting. Stephen L. Wasby wrote:

If *National League of Cities* came at the end of eight years of a Republican administration that made some efforts to return matters to the states, *Garcia* came during a subsequent Republican administration far more committed not merely to limiting, but to reducing the national government's power. By sustaining national authority, Blackmun helped lead the Court's majority on a path counter to the thrust of contemporary political developments.[21]

President Ronald Reagan was, in fact, far more determined to return power to the states than any of his immediate predecessors; *Garcia* put a damper on his plans.[22] J. W. Peltason noted, "It is accurate, even if technically incorrect, to make the generalization that Congress has the power to do whatever it believes necessary and proper to promote the general welfare." And that the most significant constraints on the exercise of national power today are not those "designed to preserve the powers of the individual state governments," but those that emanate from specific liberties and rights guaranteed to the people, such as the freedoms of speech and press.[23] As for the Tenth Amendment, Justice Rehnquist said:

It is illuminating for purposes of reflection, if not for argument, to note that one of the greatest "fictions" of our federal system is that the Congress exercises only those powers delegated to it, while the remainder are reserved to the States or to the people.[24]

An even more important question emanating from this decision, however, may be how long it survives. As we show in Table 5-6, the ground it

21. Stephen L. Wasby, "Justice Harry A. Blackmun in the Burger Court," *Hamline Law Review* 11 (1988): 214.
22. Congress softened its impact by enacting legislation in 1985 that allowed states to provide employees with compensation time instead of pay.

23. J. W. Peltason, *Understanding the Constitution,* 11th ed. (New York: Holt, Rinehart and Winston, 1989), 21.
24. *Hodel v. Virginia Surface Mining,* 452 U.S. 264 (1981).

Table 5-6   Changes in Court Personnel and Nation-State Relations

Justice	Vote in National League	Vote in Garcia	Current View
Blackmun	Majority	Majority	Cooperative federalism
Brennan	Minority	Majority	Not on Court
Burger	Majority	Minority	Not on Court
Kennedy	Not on Court	Not on Court	?
Marshall	Minority	Majority	Not on Court
O'Connor	Not on Court	Minority	Dual federalism
Powell	Majority	Minority	Not on Court
Rehnquist	Majority	Minority	Dual federalism
Scalia	Not on Court	Not on Court	?
Souter	Not on Court	Not on Court	?
Stevens	Minority	Majority	Cooperative federalism
Stewart	Majority	Not on Court	Not on Court
Thomas	Not on Court	Not on Court	?
White	Minority	Majority	Cooperative federalism

rests on is tenuous. Justice Blackmun's defection from the *National League* majority made *Garcia* possible, but with the retirements of Justice William J. Brennan, Jr., and Justice Thurgood Marshall, *Garcia* may be short-lived. Many argue that it is only a matter of time before the Court restarts the cycle of nation-state relations and adopts the logic of Justice O'Connor's dissent. Given the fluctuations of doctrine in this area, would that surprise you?

National Preemption of State Laws

The Court's adoption of "cooperative federalism" tells us a good deal about how it should decide certain federalism cases, if in fact it follows *Garcia*. In particular, we know that federal institutions—especially Congress—wield significant power to promote and enforce their policy preferences when states have not voluntarily complied. Even so, many of the cases we have considered center on disputes in which a private party—not a state—challenged the authority of Congress to promote regulation that may or may not touch on state power. *Hammer v. Dagenhart* and *United States v. Darby Lumber* are good examples.

Such litigation, however, does not address at least two other issues of nation-state relations. First, what happens when states enact laws involving an issue over which Congress has not acted but also has some authority? Because many of the cases addressing this question involve concurrent powers, such as the regulation of commerce, and taxing and spending, we take them up in the next two chapters. For now, let us consider the second and equally important question: What happens when Congress and a state both lay claim to the same general subject? The Supremacy Clause seems to offer an easy answer: if Congress passes legislation with the intent of occupying a certain issue area and precluding state involvement in that area, then any state legislation that "stands as an obstacle" must fall. The federal statute would preempt state involvement, even if Congress and the states exercise concurrent authority over the subject in question. The problem is that federal laws usually do not specify whether they are intended to preclude state action. In such instances, it is up to the Supreme Court to determine whether Congress "has chosen, explicitly or implicitly, to exercise exclusive or concurrent supervision." [25]

For certain subjects, the Court has found the task easy. There is little question, in the Court's view, that when Congress acts in the area of foreign affairs, it does so exclusively even if its actions touch on areas over which states have some authority. The Court made this point quite clear in *Missouri v. Holland* (1920).

25. Ducat and Chase, *Constitutional Interpretation*, 362.

Missouri v. Holland

252 U.S. 416 (1920)

Vote: 7 (Brandeis, Clark, Day, Holmes, McKenna, McReynolds, White)
2 (Pitney, Van Devanter)
Opinion of the Court: Holmes

In 1913 Congress enacted legislation to protect certain species of migratory birds in danger of extinction, but the act was struck down as an unconstitutional use of congressional commerce power. Three years later, the United States and Great Britain entered into a treaty that addressed a similar concern. The treaty noted that many species of migratory birds "traversed certain parts of the United States and of Canada, that they were of great value as a source of food and in destroying insects injurious to vegetation, but were in danger of extermination through lack of adequate protection.''[26] Britain and the United States agreed that their ''law-making bodies'' should take steps to prevent the extinction of these birds. To give effect to this agreement, Congress in 1918 enacted another law, the Migratory Bird Treaty Act, which prohibited anyone from ''killing, capturing, or selling'' any species of birds cited in the treaty.

The State of Missouri challenged the act, bringing suit against a U.S. game warden to prevent him from enforcing it. The state alleged, in accord with dual federalism, that the act was just like the earlier law that had been struck down; Congress was merely using its treaty power as a vehicle to interfere with rights reserved to the states under the Tenth Amendment. In other words, Missouri argued that the law infringed on states' rights regardless of whether it is based in congressional commerce power or in treaty-making authority.

Justice Oliver Wendell Holmes, Jr., delivered the opinion of the Court:

[T]he question raised is the general one whether the treaty and statute are void as an interference with the rights reserved to the states.

To answer this question it is not enough to refer to the 10th Amendment, reserving the powers not delegated to the United States, because by article 2, § 2, the power to make treaties is delegated expressly, and by article 6, treaties made under the authority of the United States, along with the Constitution and laws of the United States, made in pursuance thereof, are declared the supreme law of the land. If the treaty is valid, there can be no dispute about the validity of the statute under article 1, § 8, as a necessary and proper means to execute the powers of the government. The language of the Constitution as to the supremacy of treaties being general, the question before us is narrowed to an inquiry into the ground upon which the present supposed exception is placed.

It is said that a treaty cannot be valid if it infringes

26. *Missouri v. Holland,* 252 U.S. 416 (1920).

the Constitution; that there are limits, therefore, to the treaty-making power; and that one such limit is that what an act of Congress could not do unaided, in derogation of the powers reserved to the states, a treaty cannot do. An earlier act of Congress that attempted by itself, and not in pursuance of a treaty, to regulate the killing of migratory birds within the states, had been held bad in the district court. United States v. Shauver; United States v. McCullagh. Those decisions were supported by arguments that migratory birds were owned by the states in their sovereign capacity, for the benefit of their people, and that . . . this control was one that Congress had no power to displace. The same argument is supposed to apply now with equal force.

Whether the two cases cited were decided rightly or not, they cannot be accepted as a test of the treaty power. Acts of Congress are the supreme law of the land only when made in pursuance of the Constitution, while treaties are declared to be so when made under the authority of the United States. It is open to question whether the authority of the United States means more than the formal acts prescribed to make the convention. We do not mean to imply that there are no qualifications to the treaty-making power; but they must be ascertained in a different way. It is obvious that there may be matters of the sharpest exigency for the national well-being that an act of Congress could not deal with, but that a treaty followed by such an act could, and it is not lightly to be assumed that, in matters requiring national action, ''a power which must belong to and somewhere reside in every civilized government'' is not to be found. What was said in that case with regard to the powers of the states applies with equal force to the powers of the nation in cases where the states individually are incompetent to act. We are not yet discussing the particular case before us, but only are considering the validity of the test proposed. With regard to that, we may add that when we are dealing with words that also are a constituent act, like the Constitution of the United States, we must realize that they have called into life a being the development of which could not have been foreseen completely by the most gifted of its begetters. It was enough for them to realize or to hope that they had created an organism; it has taken a century and has cost their successors much sweat and blood to prove that they created a nation. The case before us must be considered in the light of our whole experience, and not merely in that of what was said a hundred years ago. The treaty in question does not contravene any prohibitory words to be found in the Constitution. The only question is whether it is forbidden by some invisible radiation from the general terms of the 10th Amendment. We must consider what this country has become in deciding what that amendment has reserved.

The state, as we have intimated, founds its claim of exclusive authority upon an assertion of title to migratory birds,—an assertion that is embodied in statute. No doubt it is true that, as between a state and its inhabitants, the state may regulate the killing and sale of such birds, but it does not follow that its authority is exclusive of paramount powers. To put the claim of the state upon title is to lean upon a slender reed. Wild birds are not in the possession of anyone; and possession is the beginning of ownership. The whole foundation of the state's rights is the presence within their jurisdiction of birds that yesterday had not arrived, tomorrow may be in another state, and in a week a thousand miles away. If we are to be accurate, we cannot put the case of the state upon higher ground than that the treaty deals with creatures that for the moment are within the state borders, that it must be carried out by officers of the United States within the same territory, and that, but for the treaty, the state would be free to regulate this subject itself.

As most of the laws of the United States are carried out within the states, and as many of them deal with matters which, in the silence of such laws, the state might regulate, such general grounds are not enough to support Missouri's claim. Valid treaties, of course, "are as binding within the territorial limits of the states as they are effective throughout the dominion of the United States." No doubt the great body of private relations usually falls within the control of the state, but a treaty may override its power. . . .

Here a national interest of very nearly the first magnitude is involved. It can be protected only by national action in concert with that of another power. The subject-matter is only transitorily within the state, and has no permanent habitat therein. But for the treaty and the statute, there soon might be no birds for any powers to deal with. We see nothing in the Constitution that compels the government to sit by while a food supply is cut off and the protectors of our forests and of our crops are destroyed. It is not sufficient to rely upon the states. The reliance is vain, and were it otherwise, the question is whether the United States is forbidden to act. We are of opinion that the treaty and statute must be upheld.

Decree affirmed.

Justice Holmes's opinion was narrowly drawn; he focused on the matter at hand. Even so, his message was clear. Where the Court had greater difficulty explicating a coherent preemption doctrine was in cases involving domestic power—but not for lack of effort. In *Pennsylvania v. Nelson,* the justices sought to lay out a standard for adjudicating these sorts of disputes. What was that test? Is it sufficiently specific or does it leave room for interpretation?

Pennsylvania v. Nelson

350 U.S. 497 (1956)

Vote: 6 (Black, Clark, Douglas, Frankfurter, Harlan, Warren)
     3 (Burton, Minton, Reed)
Opinion of the Court: Warren
Dissenting opinion: Reed

During the 1940s and 1950s Congress passed a host of legislation designed to combat subversive activities in the United States. Among these was the Smith Act of 1940, which prohibited the willful advocacy of the overthrow of the United States by force and violence. Those found guilty could face a maximum penalty of a $10,000 fine and/or a ten-year prison sentence.

Congress, however, was not the only legislature concerned with subversive activities. Several states, including Pennsylvania, had enacted laws similar to the Smith Act. They made it a crime to advocate the violent overthrow of both state and federal governments, and some carried harsher penalties than the federal statute. Under Pennsylvania's law, for example, violators could receive twenty or more years in jail.

Steve Nelson, a Communist party member convicted of violating Pennsylvania's law, challenged the constitutionality of the act. In his view, the federal law preempted the state's: Congress had passed antisubversive legislation, and it now occupied that field. Had Congress wanted state action as well, it would have said so in the Smith Act. The state's response was not surprising: because the law represented a perfectly legitimate exercise of its police powers—states have a paramount interest in their self-preservation—and because it was compatible with Congress's law, the "dual form of government" would be devastated by such a reading of the Smith Act.

Chief Justice Earl Warren delivered the opinion of the Court:

Many State Attorneys General and the Solicitor General of the United States appeared as amici curiae for petitioner, and several briefs were filed on behalf of the respondent. Because of the important question of federal-state relationship involved, we granted certiorari.

It should be said at the outset that the decision in this case does not affect the right of States to enforce their sedition laws at times when the Federal Government has not occupied the field and is not protecting the entire country from seditious conduct. The distinction between the two situations was clearly recognized by the court below. Nor does it limit the jurisdiction of the States where the Constitution and Congress have specifically given them concurrent jurisdiction. . . . Neither does it limit the right of the State to protect itself at any time against sabotage or attempted violence of all kinds. Nor does it prevent the State from prosecuting where the same act constitutes both a federal offense and a state offense under the police power. . . .

Where, as in the instant case, Congress has not stated specifically whether a federal statute has occupied a field in which the States are otherwise free to legislate, different criteria have furnished touchstones for decision. Thus,

"[t]his Court, in considering the validity of state laws in the light of . . . federal laws touching the same subject, has made use of the following expressions: conflicting; contrary to; occupying the field; repugnance; difference; irreconcilability; inconsistency; violation; curtailment; and interference. But none of these expressions provides an infallible constitutional test or an exclusive constitutional yardstick. In the final analysis, there can be no one crystal clear distinctly marked formula."

In this case, we think that each of several tests of supersession is met.

First, "[t]he scheme of federal regulation [is] so pervasive as to make reasonable the inference that Congress left no room for the States to supplement it." The Congress determined in 1940 that it was necessary for it to re-enter the field of antisubversive legislation, which had been abandoned by it in 1921. In that year, it enacted the Smith Act which proscribes advocacy of the overthrow of any government—federal, state or local—by force and violence and organization of and knowing membership in a group which so advocates. . . . The Internal Security Act of 1950 is aimed more directly at Communist organizations. . . . The Communist Control Act of 1954 declares "that the Communist Party of the United States, although purportedly a political party, is in fact an instrumentality of a conspiracy to overthrow the Government of the United States" and that "its role as the agency of a hostile foreign power renders its existence a clear present and continuing danger to the security of the United States." . . .

We examine these Acts only to determine the congressional plan. Looking to all of them in the aggregate, the conclusion is inescapable that Congress has intended to occupy the field of sedition. Taken as a whole, they evince a congressional plan which makes it reasonable to determine that no room has been left for the States to supplement it. Therefore, a state sedition statute is superseded regardless of whether it purports to supplement the federal law. . . .

Second, the federal statutes "touch a field in which the federal interest is so dominant that the federal system [must] be assumed to preclude enforcement of state laws on the same subject." Congress has devised an all-embracing program for resistance to the various forms of totalitarian aggression. Our external defenses have been strengthened, and a plan to protect against internal subversion has been made by it. It has appropriated vast sums, not only for our own protection, but also to strengthen freedom throughout the world. It has charged the Federal Bureau of Investigation and the Central Intelligence Agency with responsibility for intelligence concerning Communist seditious activities against our Government, and has denominated such activities as part of a world conspiracy. It accordingly proscribed sedition against all government in the nation—national, state and local. . . . Congress having thus treated seditious conduct as a matter of vital national concern, it is in no sense a local enforcement problem. . . .

Third, enforcement of state sedition acts presents a serious danger of conflict with the administration of the federal program. Since 1939, in order to avoid a hampering of uniform enforcement of its program by sporadic local prosecutions, the Federal Government has urged local authorities not to intervene in such matters, but to turn over to the federal authorities immediately and unevaluated all information concerning subversive activities. . . .

Since we find that Congress has occupied the field to the exclusion of parallel state legislation, that the dominant interest of the Federal Government precludes state intervention, and that administration of state Acts would conflict with the operation of the federal plan, we are convinced that the decision of the Supreme Court of Pennsylvania is unassailable.

We are not unmindful of the risk of compounding punishments which would be created by finding concurrent state power. In our view of the case, we do not reach the question whether double or multiple punishment for the same overt acts directed against the United States has constitutional sanction. Without compelling indication to the contrary, we will not assume that Congress intended to permit the possibility of double punishment.

The judgment of the Supreme Court of Pennsylvania is

Affirmed.

Although the Court clearly set out a preemption standard, many argue that it has led to an ad hoc balancing of state-federal interests, turning more or less on the particular facts of disputes. As noted in Table 5-7, which lists some of the Court's preemption rulings, this observation may be true. Given Warren's opinion in *Nelson*, is that not to be expected?

Table 5-7   Preemption Cases After *Pennsylvania v. Nelson*

Case	Question	Holding (Vote)
Campbell v. Hussey (1961)	Is Georgia's Tobacco Identification Act, which requires that a certain type of tobacco be marked with a white tag, barred by the 1935 Federal Tobacco Inspection Act?	Yes. (6–3) Douglas, for a plurality, held that "[w]e do not have here the question whether Georgia's law conflicts with the federal law. Rather we have the question of preemption. . . . Congress, in legislating concerning types of tobacco . . . preempted the field."
Florida Lime & Avocado Growers, Inc. v. Paul (1963)	Is California's requirement of minimum oil content for avocados preempted by federal regulations that certify as mature avocados that have a lower level of oil?	No. (5–4) Brennan, for the majority, concluded that "there is neither such actual conflict between the two schemes of regulation that both cannot stand in the same area, nor evidence of a congressional design to pre-empt the field."
City of Burbank v. Lockheed Air Terminal (1973)	Is a City of Burbank ordinance that prohibits the take-off of aircraft between 11 p.m. and 7 a.m. preempted by federal laws regulating the aviation industry?	Yes. (5–4) The pervasively national nature of the airline industry requires preemption of local regulations by federal law.
Pacific Gas & Electric Co. v. State Energy Commission (1983)	Does the federal Atomic Energy Act preempt a California law imposing a statewide moratorium on the certification of nuclear energy plants for reasons other than safety?	No. (9–0) While "the Federal Government has occupied the entire field of nuclear safety concerns," such preemption would only prevent state moratoriums that had as their rationale safety concerns. Since California provided other, non-safety reasons for its action, the law is valid.
Silkwood v. Kerr-McGee (1984)	Does the Atomic Energy Act preempt a state tort law system that allows for the award of punitive damages for harm caused by the escape of plutonium from a federally licensed nuclear facility?	No. (5–4) Although such awards may influence the safety decisions that are at the heart of the AEA, there is no evidence that Congress intended to preempt state tort law remedies. Absent such a congressional intent, the state tort remedy is valid.

READINGS

Corwin, Edward S. "The Passing of Dual Federalism." *Virginia Law Review* 36 (1950): 1-24.

Gunther, Gerald, ed. *John Marshall's Defense of McCulloch v. Maryland.* Stanford, Calif.: Stanford University Press, 1969.

Howard, A. E. Dick. "The States and the Supreme Court." *Catholic University Law Review* 31 (1982): 375-438.

Kobylka, Joseph F. "The Court, Justice Blackmun, and Federalism." *Creighton Law Review* 19 (1985-1986): 9-49.

Mason, Alpheus. *The States' Rights Debate: Anti-Federalism and the Constitution.* New York: Oxford University Press, 1972.

Newmyer, R. Kent *The Supreme Court under Marshall and Taney.* New York: Crowell, 1968.

Porter, M. C. "State Supreme Courts and the Legacy of the Warren Court: Some Old Inquiries for a New Situation." *Publius* 8 (1978): 55-74.

Schmidhauser, John. *The Supreme Court as a Final Arbitrator of Federal-State Relations.* Chapel Hill: University of North Carolina Press, 1958.

Semonche, John E. *Charting the Future: The Supreme Court Responds to a Changing Society, 1890-1920.* Westport, Conn.: Greenwood Press, 1978.

Schecter, Stephen. "The State of American Federalism." *Publius* 10 (1980): 3-11.

Wasby, Stephen L. "Justice Harry Blackmun in the Burger Court." *Hamline Law Review* 11 (1988): 183-245.

Wood, Stephen B. *Constitutional Politics in the Progressive Era: Child Labor and the Law.* Chicago: University of Chicago Press, 1968.

CHAPTER 6

THE COMMERCE POWER

Of all the powers granted to government perhaps none has caused more important controversies and litigation than the power to regulate commerce. Concern over the exercise of this power was present at the Constitution's birth and continues today. At each stage of the nation's development from a former colony isolated from the world's commercial centers to a country wielding vast economic power, legal disputes of great significance tested the powers of government to regulate the economy. During certain periods, such as John Marshall's chief justiceship, the decisions of the Supreme Court enhanced the role of the federal government in promoting economic development. At other times, however, such as the period immediately following the Great Depression, the Court's interpretations thwarted the government's attempts to overcome economic collapse. From the earliest days of the nation, battles over the commerce power have raised basic questions. What is commerce? What is interstate commerce? What powers of commercial regulation did the Constitution grant to the federal government and what role remains to be played by the states?

The Constitutional Foundations of the Commerce Power

A primary reason for calling the Constitutional Convention was the inability of the government under the Articles of Confederation to control the country's commercial activity effectively. Economic conditions following the Revolutionary War were dismal. The national and state governments were deeply in debt. The tax base of the newly independent nation was minimal, and commerce was undeveloped, leaving property taxes and customs duties the primary sources of government funds.

The states were almost exclusively in charge of economic regulation. To raise enough revenue to pay their debts, the states imposed substantial taxes on land, placing farmers in an economically precarious condition. The states also erected trade barriers and imposed duties on the importation of foreign goods. While such policies were enacted in part to promote the states' domestic businesses, the result was a general strangulation of commercial activity. Several states printed their own money and passed statutes canceling debts. With each of the states working independently, the national economy continued to slide into stagnation, and, for all practical purposes, the central government was powerless to respond effectively.

When agrarian interests reached their economic breaking point, culminating in a makeshift army of farmers led by Daniel Shays marching on the Massachusetts state capital in 1787, it was the final indicator that something had to be done. Congress called for a convention to reconsider the status of the Articles, a convention that ultimately resulted in the drafting of the United States Constitution.

Commerce and the Constitutional Convention

The delegates to the Constitutional Convention realized the necessity of giving the power to regulate the economy to the central government. The state of the nation could no longer tolerate the individual states pursuing independent policies, each having a different impact on the country's economic health. To that end Article I of the Constitution removed certain powers from the states and gave the federal government powers it did not have under the Articles. States were stripped of any ability to print money, to impair the obligation of contracts, or to levy import duties. The federal government obtained the authority necessary to impose uniform regulations for the national economy. Among the powers granted to the central government were the authority to tax and impose customs duties, to spend and borrow, to develop and protect a single monetary system, and to regulate bankruptcies. Most important was the authority to regulate interstate and foreign commerce. Article I, Section 8, states: "The Congress shall have the power . . . to regulate Commerce with foreign Nations, and among the several States, and with the Indian Tribes."

The need for Congress to speak for the nation with a single voice on these matters was clear to the Framers. Even Alexander Hamilton and James Madison, who disagreed on many questions of federalism, were in accord on the necessity of the central government to control interstate and foreign commerce. Hamilton wrote in *The Federalist Papers:*

In addition to the defects already enumerated in the existing federal system, there are others of not less importance which concur in rendering it altogether unfit for the administration of the affairs of the Union. The want of a power to regulate commerce is by all parties allowed to be of the number.[1]

Madison took a similar position, arguing that the experience under the Articles, as well as that of the European nations, demonstrated that a central government without broad powers over the nation's commerce was destined to fail.[2]

Congress quickly seized upon the authority to regulate commerce with other nations. Almost immediately, it imposed import duties as a means of raising revenue. The constitutional grant in this area was clear: the power to regulate foreign commerce, as well as other matters of foreign policy, was given unambiguously to the national government, and the role of the states was eliminated. Since ratification the states have challenged congressional supremacy over foreign commerce only on rare occasions.

The power to regulate interstate commerce, however, was a different story. Congress was slow in responding to this grant of authority, despite its constitutional power to regulate commerce among the states. For the first several decades, federal officials continued to view business as an activity occurring within the borders of the individual states. In fact, Congress did not pass comprehensive legislation governing commerce among the states until the Interstate Commerce Act of 1887.

Marshall Defines Commerce

Disputes over the meaning of the Commerce Clause came before the Supreme Court even during the early years of nationhood. The justices

1. Alexander Hamilton, "Federalist No. 22," in *The Federalist Papers,* ed. Clinton Rossiter (New York: New American Library, 1961).
2. James Madison, "Federalist No. 42,"in *The Federalist Papers,* ed. Clinton Rossiter (New York: New American Library, 1961).

probed the constitutional definition of commerce and the proper division of federal and state power to regulate it. Of the commerce cases decided by the Supreme Court in those early decades, none was more important than *Gibbons v. Ogden* (1824). This dispute involved some of the nation's most prominent and powerful businessmen and attorneys. A great deal was at stake both economically and politically. In his opinion for the Court, Chief Justice John Marshall responded to the fundamental problems of defining commerce and allocating the power to control it. His answers to the questions presented in this case are still very much a part of our constitutional fabric.

Gibbons v. Ogden
9 Wheat. 1 (1824)

Vote: 6 (Duvall, Johnson, Marshall, Story, Todd, Washington)

0

Opinion of the Court: Marshall
Concurring opinion: Johnson
Not participating: Thompson

This complicated litigation can be traced back to 1798 when the New York legislature granted the wealthy and prominent Robert R. Livingston a monopoly to operate steamboats on all waters within the state, including the two most important commercial waterways, New York Harbor and the Hudson River. New York officials did not see the monopoly grant as particularly important because no one had yet developed a steamship that could operate reliably and profitably. Livingston, however, joined forces with Robert Fulton, and together they produced a commercially viable steamship. This mode of transportation became extremely popular and very profitable for the partners. When they obtained a similar monopoly over the port of New Orleans in 1811, they had significant control over the nation's two most important harbors.

The rapid westward expansion taking place at that time fueled the need for modern transportation systems. The Livingston-Fulton monopoly, however, put a damper on the use of steam in the evolution of that system. The New York monopoly was so strong and so vigorously enforced that retaliatory laws were enacted by other states, which refused to let steam-powered vessels from New York use their waters. Especially hostile relations developed between New York and New Jersey, with violence between the crews of rival companies a common occurrence. Livingston died in 1813, followed two years later by Fulton, but their monopoly lived on.

Aaron Ogden, a former governor of New Jersey, and Thomas Gibbons, a successful Georgia lawyer, entered into a partnership to carry passengers between New York City and Elizabethtown, New Jersey. Ogden had purchased the right to operate in New York waters from the Livingston-Fulton monopoly, and Gibbons had a federal permit issued under the 1793 Coastal Licensing Act to operate steamships along the coast. With these grants of authority the two partners could carry passengers between New York and New Jersey. The New York monopoly, however, pressured Ogden to terminate his relationship with Gibbons. As a result the partnership dissolved.

Gibbons then joined forces with Cornelius Vanderbilt, and they became fierce competitors with Ogden and the New York monopoly interests. Gibbons and Vanderbilt entered New York waters in violation of the monopoly whenever they could, picking up as much New York business as possible. In response, Ogden successfully convinced the New York courts to enjoin Gibbons from entering New York waters. Gibbons appealed this ruling to the United States Supreme Court.

To press their case, Gibbons and Vanderbilt acquired the services of two of the best lawyers of the day, Daniel Webster and William Wirt, who later served as attorney general of the United States. Wirt argued that the federal permit issued to Gibbons took precedence over any state-issued monopoly and therefore Gibbons had the right to enter New York waters. Webster took a more radical position, explicitly stating that the Commerce Clause of the Constitution gave Congress exclusive power over commerce and that the state-granted monopoly was a violation of that clause. Ogden's lawyer responded that navigation was not commerce under the meaning of the Constitution, but instead was an intrastate enterprise left to the states to regulate. The arguments in the case lasted four and a half days.

Chief Justice Marshall delivered the opinion of the Court:

The appellant contends that this decree is erroneous, because the laws which purport to give the exclusive privilege it sustains, are repugnant to the constitution and laws of the United States.

' They are said to be repugnant—

To that clause in the constitution which authorizes Congress to regulate commerce. . . .

The words are, "Congress shall have power to regulate commerce with foreign nations, and among the several States, and with the Indian tribes."

The subject to be regulated is commerce; and our constitution being . . . one of enumeration, and not of definition, to ascertain the extent of the power, it becomes necessary to settle the meaning of the word. The counsel for the appellee would limit it to traffic, to buying and selling, or the interchange of commodities, and do not admit that it comprehends navigation. This would restrict a general term, applicable to many objects, to one of its significations. Commerce, undoubtedly, is traffic, but it is something more: it is intercourse. It describes the commercial intercourse between nations, and parts of nations, in all its branches, and is regulated by prescribing rules for carrying on that intercourse. The mind can scarcely conceive a system for regulating commerce between nations, which shall exclude all laws concerning navi-

Aaron Ogden

Thomas Gibbons

Daniel Webster's 1821 handwritten note to Cornelius Vanderbilt acknowledging receipt of a $500 retainer to represent Thomas Gibbons in the case of Gibbons v. Ogden.

gation, which shall be silent on the admission of the vessels of the one nation into the ports of the other, and be confined to prescribing rules for the conduct of individuals, in the actual employment of buying and selling, or of barter.

If commerce does not include navigation, the government of the Union has no direct power over that subject, and can make no law prescribing what shall constitute American vessels, or requiring that they shall be navigated by American seamen. Yet this power has been exercised from the commencement of the government, has been exercised with the consent of all, and has been understood by all to be a commercial regulation. All America understands, and has uniformly understood, the word "commerce," to comprehend navigation. It was so understood, and must have been so understood, when the constitution was framed. The power over commerce, including navigation, was one of the primary objects for which the people of America adopted their government, and must have been contemplated in forming it. The convention must have used the word in that sense, because all have understood it in that sense; and the attempt to restrict it comes too late. . . .

The word used in the constitution, then, comprehends, and has been always understood to comprehend, navigation within its meaning; and a power to regulate navigation, is as expressly granted, as if that term had been added to the word "commerce."

To what commerce does this power extend? The constitution informs us, to commerce "with foreign nations, and among the several States, and with the Indian tribes."

It has, we believe, been universally admitted, that these words comprehend every species of commercial intercourse between the United States and foreign nations. No sort of trade can be carried on between this country and any other, to which this power does not extend. It has been truly said, that commerce, as the word is used in the constitution, is a unit, every part of which is indicated by the term.

If this be the admitted meaning of the word, in its application to foreign nations, it must carry the same meaning throughout the sentence, and remain a unit, unless there be some plain intelligible cause which alters it.

The subject to which the power is next applied, is to commerce "among the several States." The word "among" means intermingled with. A thing which is among others, is intermingled with them. Commerce among the States, cannot stop at the external boundary line of each State, but may be introduced into the interior.

It is not intended to say that these words comprehend that commerce, which is completely internal, which is carried on between man and man in a State, or between different parts of the same State, and which does not extend to or affect other States. Such a power would be inconvenient, and is certainly unnecessary.

Comprehensive as the word "among" is, it may

very properly be restricted to that commerce which concerns more States than one. The phrase is not one which would probably have been selected to indicate the completely interior traffic of a State, because it is not an apt phrase for that purpose; and the enumeration of the particular classes of commerce, to which the power was to be extended, would not have been made, had the intention been to extend the power to every description. The enumeration presupposes something not enumerated; and that something, if we regard the language or the subject of the sentence, must be the exclusively internal commerce of a State. The genius and character of the whole government seem to be, that its action is to be applied to all the external concerns of the nation, and to those internal concerns which affect the States generally; but not to those which are completely within a particular State, which do not affect other States, and with which it is not necessary to interfere, for the purpose of executing some of the general powers of the government. The completely internal commerce of a State, then, may be considered as reserved for the State itself.

But, in regulating commerce with foreign nations, the power of Congress does not stop at the jurisdictional lines of the several States. It would be a very useless power, if it could not pass those lines. The commerce of the United States with foreign nations, is that of the whole United States. Every district has a right to participate in it. The deep streams which penetrate our country in every direction, pass through the interior of almost every State in the Union, and furnish the means of exercising this right. If Congress has the power to regulate it, that power must be exercised whenever the subject exists. If it exists within the States, if a foreign voyage may commence or terminate at a port within a State, then the power of Congress may be exercised within a State.

This principle is, if possible, still more clear, when applied to commerce "among the several States." They either join each other, in which case they are separated by a mathematical line, or they are remote from each other, in which case other States lie between them. What is commerce "among" them; and how is it to be conducted? Can a trading expedition between two adjoining States, commence and terminate outside of each? And if the trading intercourse be between two States remote from each other, must it not commence in one, terminate in the other, and probably pass through a third? Commerce among the States must, of necessity, be commerce with the States. . . .

We are now arrived at the inquiry—What is this power?

It is the power to regulate; that is, to prescribe the rule by which commerce is to be governed. This power, like all others vested in Congress, is complete in itself, may be exercised to its utmost extent, and acknowledges no limitations, other than are prescribed in the constitution. . . . If, as has always been understood, the sovereignty of Congress, though limited to specified objects, is plenary as to those objects, the power over commerce with foreign nations, and among the several States, is vested in Congress as absolutely as it would be in a single government, having in its constitution the same restrictions on the exercise of the power as are found in the constitution of the United States. The wisdom and the discretion of Congress, their identity with the people, and the influence which their constituents possess at elections, are, in this, as in many other instances, as that, for example, of declaring war, the sole restraints on which they have relied, to secure them from its abuse. They are the restraints on which the people must often rely solely, in all representative governments.

The power of Congress, then, comprehends navigation, within the limits of every State in the Union; so far as that navigation may be, in any manner, connected with "commerce with foreign nations, or among the several States, or with the Indian tribes." It may, of consequence, pass the jurisdictional line of New-York, and act upon the very waters to which the prohibition now under consideration applies.

But it has been urged with great earnestness, that, although the power of Congress to regulate commerce with foreign nations, and among the several States, be co-extensive with the subject itself, and have no other limits than are prescribed in the constitution, yet the States may severally exercise the same power, within their respective jurisdictions. In support of this argument, it is said, that they possessed it as an inseparable attribute of sovereignty, before the formation of the constitution, and still retain it, except so far as they have surrendered it by that instrument; that this principle results from the nature of the government, and is secured by the tenth amendment; that an affirmative grant of power is not exclusive, unless in its own nature it be such that the continued exercise of it by the former possessor is inconsistent with the grant, and that this is not of that description.

The appellant, conceding these postulates, except the last, contends, that full power to regulate a particular subject, implies the whole power, and leaves no residuum; that a grant of the whole is incompatible with the existence of a right in another to any part of it. . . .

In discussing the question, whether this power is still in the States, in the case under consideration, we may dismiss from it the inquiry, whether it is surrendered by the mere grant to Congress, or is retained until Congress shall exercise the power. We may dismiss that inquiry, because it has been exercised, and the regulations which Congress deemed it proper to make, are now in full operation. The sole question is, can a State regulate commerce with foreign nations and among the States, while Congress is regulating it?

The counsel for the respondent answer this question in the affirmative, and rely very much on the restrictions in the 10th section, as supporting their opinion. . . .

It has been contended by the general counsel for the appellant, that, as the word "to regulate" implies in its nature, full power over the thing to be regulated, it excludes, necessarily, the action of all others that would perform the same operation on the same thing. That regulation is designed for the entire result, applying to those parts which remain as they were, as well as to those which are altered. It produces a uniform whole, which is as much disturbed and deranged by changing what the regulating power designs to leave untouched, as that on which it has operated.

There is great force in this argument, and the Court is not satisfied that it has been refuted.

Since, however, in exercising the power of regulating their own purely internal affairs, whether of trading or police, the States may sometimes enact laws, the validity of which depends on their interfering with, and being contrary to, an act of Congress passed in pursuance of the constitution, the Court will enter upon the inquiry, whether the laws of New-York, as ex-

pounded by the highest tribunal of that State, have, in their application to this case, come into collision with an act of Congress, and deprived a citizen of a right to which that act entitles him. Should this collision exist, it will be immaterial whether those laws were passed in virtue of a concurrent power "to regulate commerce with foreign nations and among the several States," or, in virtue of a power to regulate their domestic trade and police. In one case and the other, the acts of New-York must yield to the law of Congress; and the decision sustaining the privilege they confer, against a right given by a law of the Union, must be erroneous. . . .

But the framers of our constitution foresaw this state of things, and provided for it, by declaring the supremacy not only of itself, but of the laws made in pursuance of it. The nullity of any act, inconsistent with the constitution, is produced by the declaration, that the constitution is the supreme law. The appropriate application of that part of the clause which confers the same supremacy on laws and treaties, is to such acts of the State Legislatures as do not transcend their powers, but, though enacted in the execution of acknowledged State powers, interfere with, or are contrary to the laws of Congress, made in pursuance of the constitution, or some treaty made under the authority of the United States. In every such case, the act of Congress, or the treaty, is supreme; and the law of the State, though enacted in the exercise of powers not controverted, must yield to it. . . .

But all inquiry into this subject seems to the Court to be put completely at rest, by the act already mentioned, entitled, "An act for the enrolling and licensing of steam boats."

This act authorizes a steam boat employed, or intended to be employed, only in a river or bay of the United States, owned wholly or in part by an alien, resident within the United States, to be enrolled and licensed as if the same belonged to a citizen of the United States.

This act demonstrates the opinion of Congress, that steam boats may be enrolled and licensed, in common with vessels using sails. They are, of course, entitled to the same privileges, and can no more be restrained from navigating waters, and entering ports which are free to such vessels, than if they were wafted on their voyage by the winds, instead of being propelled by the agency of fire. The one element may be as legitimately used as the other, for every commercial purpose authorized by the laws of the Union; and the act of a State inhibiting the use of either to any vessel having a license under the act of Congress, comes, we think, in direct collision with that act.

Like his opinions in *Marbury* and *McCulloch*, Marshall's opinion in *Gibbons* laid a constitutional foundation that remains in place today. The decision made several important points. First, commerce involves more than buying and selling. It includes the commercial intercourse between nations and states, and therefore transportation and navigation clearly fall within the definition of commerce. Second, the power to regulate commerce that occurs completely within the boundaries of a single state is reserved for the states. Third, commerce among the states begins in one state and ends in another. It does not stop when the act of crossing a state border is completed. Consequently, commerce that occurs within a state may be part of a larger interstate process. Fourth, once an act is considered part of interstate commerce, Congress is empowered by the Constitution to regulate it. The power to regulate interstate commerce is complete and has no limitation other than what may be found in other constitutional provisions.

Gibbons v. Ogden was a substantial victory for national power. It broadly construed the definitions of both commerce and interstate commerce. But Marshall did not go as far as Daniel Webster had urged. The opinion asserts only that Congress has complete power to regulate interstate commerce and that federal regulations are superior to any state laws. The decision does not answer the question of the legitimacy of states regulating interstate commerce in the absence of federal action. That controversy was left for future justices to decide.

Defining Interstate Commerce

The regulation of commerce by the federal government did not become a major item on the Supreme Court's agenda until the latter half of the nineteenth century. By this time, small intrastate businesses were giving way to large interstate corporations. Industrial expansion blossomed, and the interstate railroad and pipeline systems were well under way. The infamous captains of industry were creating large monopolistic trusts that dominated huge segments of the national economy, squeezing out small businesses and discouraging new entrepreneurs. The industrial combines that controlled the railroads also, in effect, ruled agriculture and other interests that relied on the rails to transport goods to market. This commercial growth brought great prosperity to some, but also caused horrendous social problems. Unsafe working conditions, sweat shops, child labor, and low wages plagued employees, who eventually formed labor unions.

In light of these developments, it was increasingly necessary for Congress to control interstate commerce. As the nineteenth century drew to a close, Congress passed two major pieces of legislation based on the commerce power. The first was the Interstate Commerce Act of 1887, which established a mechanism for regulating the nation's interstate railroads. The second was the Sherman Anti-Trust Act of 1890, which was designed to break up monopolies that restrained trade. Critics immediately attacked Congress for exceeding its constitutional authority. While the Commerce Clause and Marshall's interpretation of it clearly established congressional power, discriminating between inter- and intrastate commerce was not easy. The Supreme Court faced a significant number of appeals that asked the justices to clarify whether the national legislature had overstepped its bounds and regulated commerce that was purely intrastate. To say that the Court had difficulty developing a coherent doctrine is an understatement.

The regulation of the railroads provides a case in point. The first railroads were small local operations regulated by the states. But as the interstate systems developed, the justices held that their regulation was rightfully a federal responsibility.[3] Congress responded with the Interstate Commerce Act, which established the Interstate Commerce Commission (ICC) to regulate the rails and set rates. The Supreme Court approved the constitutionality of the commission, but later stripped it of its rate-setting powers.[4] In 1906 Congress revised the authority and procedures of the commission and reestablished its power to set rates. The Court generally supported this amended version of the regulatory plan.[5]

The Court's decision in *Houston, E. & W. Texas Railway Co. v. United States,* better known as the *Shreveport Rate Case* (1914), firmly established congressional power over the nation's rails. This dispute arose from competition among three railroad companies to serve various cities in Texas. Two were based in Texas, one in Houston and the other in Dallas, and the third competitor operated out of Shreveport, Louisiana. The Texas Railroad Commission regulated the Texas companies because their operations were exclusively in-state, but the Shreveport company came under the jurisdiction of the ICC. Difficulties arose when the Texas regulators set rates substantially lower than did the ICC. The motive behind these lower rates was clear: the Texas commission wanted to encourage intrastate trade and to discourage companies from taking their business to Shreveport. The rates placed the Shreveport railroad at a distinct disadvantage in competing for the Texas market. In response, the ICC ordered the intrastate Texas rates to be raised to the interstate levels. When the commission's authority to set intrastate rail rates was challenged, the Supreme Court ruled in favor of the ICC, articulating what became known as the "Shreveport Doctrine." The Court held that the federal government had the power to regulate intrastate commerce when a failure to regulate would cripple, retard, or destroy interstate commerce. According to Justice Charles Evans Hughes's opinion for the Court, whenever interstate and intrastate commercial activities are entwined so that the regulation of one controls the other, "it is Congress, and not the State, that is entitled to prescribe the final and dominant rule."

Manufacturing and Direct Effects on Interstate Commerce

The Court's endorsement of the federal power to regulate interstate transportation and distribution did not extend initially to the attempts by Congress to impose effective antitrust legislation. The target of the antitrust statutes were the monopolies that controlled basic industries and choked out all competition. During the late 1800s these trusts grew to capture and exercise dominance over many industries, including oil, meatpacking, sugar, and steel. The Sherman Act was Congress's first attempt to break up these anticompetitive combines. It outlawed all contracts and combinations of companies that had the effect of restraining trade and commerce or eliminating

3. *Wabash, St. Louis & Pacific Railway Co. v. Illinois,* 118 U.S. 557 (1886).

4. *Interstate Commerce Commission v. Brimson,* 154 U.S. 447 (1894); *Interstate Commerce Commission v. Cincinnati, New Orleans & Texas Pacific Railway Co.,* 167 U.S. 479 (1897); *Interstate Commerce Commission v. Alabama-Midland Railway Co.,* 168 U.S. 144 (1897).

5. See *Illinois Central Railroad Co. v. Interstate Commerce Commission,* 206 U.S. 41 (1907).

competition. The enforcement of the law, however, often focused on manufacturing and production activities, stages of commerce previously thought to be intrastate in nature.[6] Whether Congress had exceeded its constitutional authority by regulating manufacturing and production in the Sherman Act was tested in *United States v. E. C. Knight Co.* (1895), a battle over the federal government's attempts to break up the sugar trust.

6. See *Veazie v. Moor*, 14 How. 568 (1853); and *Kidd v. Pearson*, 128 U.S. 1 (1888).

United States v. E. C. Knight Co.
156 U.S. 1 (1895)

Vote: 8 (Brewer, Brown, Field, Fuller, Gray, Jackson, Shiras, White)
1 (Harlan)
Opinion of the Court: Fuller
Dissenting opinion: Harlan

In 1892, six companies dominated the American sugar refining industry. The American Sugar Refining Company was the largest, with control of about 65 percent of the nation's refining capacity. Thirty-three percent of the market was shared by four Pennsylvania refiners, and a scant 2 percent by a Boston company. In March of that year American Sugar entered into agreements that allowed it to acquire the four Pennsylvania refineries, including the E. C. Knight Company, giving it absolute control over 98 percent of the sugar refining business in the United States.

In response to this takeover, the federal government sued to have the acquisition agreements canceled. According to Justice Department attorneys, the sugar trust operated as a monopoly in restraint of trade in violation of the Sherman Anti-Trust Law. Attorneys for American Sugar and the acquired companies held that the Sherman Act did not apply to sugar refining because that activity is manufacturing subject to state, not federal, control.

Chief Justice Melville Fuller delivered the opinion of the Court:

The fundamental question is, whether conceding that the existence of a monopoly in manufacture is established by the evidence, that monopoly can be directly suppressed under the act of Congress in the mode attempted by this bill.

It cannot be denied that the power of a State to protect the lives, health, and property of its citizens, and to preserve good order and the public morals, "the power to govern men and things within the limits of its dominion," is a power originally and always belonging to the States, not surrendered by them to the general government, nor directly restrained by the Constitution of the United States, and essentially exclusive. The relief of the citizens of each State from the burden of monopoly and the evils resulting from the restraint of trade among such citizens was left with the States to deal with, and this court has recognized their possession of that power even to the extent of holding that an employment or business carried on by private individuals, when it becomes a matter of such public interest and importance as to create a common charge or burden upon the citizen; in other words, when it becomes a practical monopoly, to which the citizen is compelled to resort and by means of which a tribute can be exacted from the community, is subject to regulation by state legislative power. On the other hand, the power of Congress to regulate commerce among the several States is also exclusive. The Constitution does not provide that interstate commerce shall be free, but, by the grant of this exclusive power to regulate it, it was left free except as Congress might impose restraints. Therefore it has been determined that the failure of Congress to exercise this exclusive power in any case is an expression of its will that the subject shall be free from restrictions or impositions upon it by the several States, and if a law passed by a State in the exercise of its acknowledged powers comes into conflict with that will, the Congress and the

State cannot occupy the position of equal opposing sovereignties, because the Constitution declares its supremacy and that of the laws passed in pursuance thereof; and that which is not supreme must yield to that which is supreme. "Commerce, undoubtedly, is traffic," said Chief Justice Marshall, "but it is something more; it is intercourse. It describes the commercial intercourse between nations and parts of nations in all its branches, and is regulated by prescribing rules for carrying on that intercourse." That which belongs to commerce is within the jurisdiction of the United States, but that which does not belong to commerce is within the jurisdiction of the police power of the State.

The argument is that the power to control the manufacture of refined sugar is a monopoly over a necessary of life, to the enjoyment of which by a large part of the population of the United States interstate commerce is indispensable, and that, therefore, the general government in the exercise of the power to regulate commerce may repress such monopoly directly and set aside the instruments which have created it. But this argument cannot be confined to necessaries of life merely, and must include all articles of general consumption. Doubtless the power to control the manufacture of a given thing involves in a certain sense the control of its disposition, but this is a secondary and not the primary sense; and although the exercise of that power may result in bringing the operation of commerce into play, it does not control it, and affects it only incidentally and indirectly. Commerce succeeds to manufacture, and is not a part of it. The power to regulate commerce is the power to prescribe the rule by which commerce shall be governed, and is a power independent of the power to suppress monopoly. But it may operate in repression of monopoly whenever that comes within the rules by which commerce is governed or whenever the transaction is itself a monopoly of commerce.

It is vital that the independence of the commercial power and of the police power, and the delimitation between them, however sometimes perplexing, should always be recognized and observed, for while the one furnishes the strongest bond of union, the other is essential to the preservation of the autonomy of the States as required by our dual form of government; and acknowledged evils, however grave and urgent they may appear to be, had better be borne, than the risk be run, in the effort to suppress them, of more serious consequences by resort to expedients of even doubtful constitutionality.

It will be perceived how far-reaching the proposition is that the power of dealing with a monopoly directly may be exercised by the general government whenever interstate or international commerce may be ultimately affected. The regulation of commerce applies to the subjects of commerce and not to matters of internal police. Contracts to buy, sell, or exchange goods to be transported among the several States, the transportation and its instrumentalities, and articles bought, sold, or exchanged for the purposes of such transit among the States, or put in the way of transit, may be regulated, but this is because they form part of interstate trade or commerce. The fact that an article is manufactured for export to another State does not of itself make it an article of interstate commerce, and the intent of the manufacturer does not determine the time when the article or product passes from the control of the States and belongs to commerce. This was so ruled in *Coe v. Errol,* in which the question before the court was whether certain logs cut at a place in New Hampshire and hauled to a river town for the purpose of transportation to the State of Maine were liable to be taxed like other property in the State of New Hampshire. Mr. Justice Bradley, delivering the opinion of the court, said: "Does the owner's state of mind in relation to the goods, that is, his intent to export them, and his partial preparation to do so, exempt them from taxation? This is the precise question for solution. . . . There must be a point of time when they cease to be governed exclusively by the domestic law and begin to be governed and protected by the national law of commercial regulation, and that moment seems to us to be a legitimate one for this purpose, in which they commence their final movement from the State of their origin to that of their destination."

And again, in *Kidd v. Pearson,* where the question was discussed whether the right of a State to enact a statute prohibiting within its limits the manufacture of intoxicating liquors, except for certain purposes, could be overthrown by the fact that the manufacturer intended to export the liquors when made, it was held that the intent of the manufacturer did not determine the time when the article or product passed from the control of the State and belonged to commerce, and that, therefore, the statute, in omitting to except from its operation the manufacture of intoxicating liquors within the limits of the State for export, did not constitute an unauthorized interference with the right of Congress to regulate commerce. . . .

Contracts, combinations, or conspiracies to control domestic enterprise in manufacture, agriculture, mining, production in all its forms, or to raise or lower prices or wages, might unquestionably tend to restrain external as well as domestic trade, but the restraint would be an indirect result, however inevitable and whatever its extent, and such result would not necessarily determine the object of the contract, combination, or conspiracy.

Again, all the authorities agree that in order to vitiate a contract or combination it is not essential that its result should be a complete monopoly; it is sufficient if it really tends to that end and to deprive the public of the advantages which flow from free competition. Slight reflection will show that if the national power extends to all contracts and combinations in manufacture, agriculture, mining, and other productive industries, whose ultimate result may affect external commerce, comparatively little of business operations and affairs would be left for state control.

It was in the light of well-settled principles that the act of July 2, 1890, was framed. Congress did not attempt thereby to assert the power to deal with monopoly directly as such; or to limit and restrict the rights of corporations created by the States or the citizens of the States in the acquisition, control, or disposition of property; or to regulate or prescribe the price or prices at which such property or the products thereof should be sold; or to make criminal the acts of persons in the acquisition and control of property

which the States of their residence or creation sanctioned or permitted. Aside from the provisions applicable where Congress might exercise municipal power, what the law struck at was combinations, contracts, and conspiracies to monopolize trade and commerce among the several States or with foreign nations; but the contracts and acts of the defendants related exclusively to the acquisition of the Philadelphia refineries and the business of sugar refining in Pennsylvania, and bore no direct relation to commerce between the States or with foreign nations. The object was manifestly private gain in the manufacture of the commodity, but not through the control of interstate or foreign commerce. It is true that the bill alleged that the products of these refineries were sold and distributed among the several States, and that all the companies were engaged in trade or commerce with the several States and with foreign nations; but this was no more than to say that trade and commerce served manufacture to fulfil its function. Sugar was refined for sale, and sales were probably made at Philadelphia for consumption, and undoubtedly for resale by the first purchasers throughout Pennsylvania and other States, and refined sugar was also forwarded by the companies to other States for sale. Nevertheless it does not follow that an attempt to monopolize, or the actual monopoly of, the manufacture was an attempt, whether executory or consummated, to monopolize commerce, even though, in order to dispose of the product, the instrumentality of commerce was necessarily invoked. There was nothing in the proofs to indicate any intention to put a restraint upon trade or commerce, and the fact, as we have seen, that trade or commerce might be indirectly affected was not enough to entitle complainants to a decree. . . .

Decree affirmed.

Chief Justice Fuller's opinion shows the initial development of the Court's concern with the effects of various economic activities on interstate commerce. Proponents of federal regulation often argued that if an intrastate economic activity had an effect—any effect—on interstate commerce it

could be regulated by Congress. The Supreme Court rejected this position in *E. C. Knight*, holding that federal authority is not activated unless the intrastate activity has a direct effect on interstate commerce. In the sugar trust case, Fuller concluded that the challenged monopoly of refining facilities had only an indirect effect on interstate commerce and therefore was not subject to federal regulation. The distinction between direct and indirect effects is not very clear and can be interpreted various ways. In the hands of the Court's conservative majority, the direct effects test would later be used to strike down other federal regulatory attempts.

Although this decision removed manufacturing from the authority of the Sherman Act, the decision did not doom federal antitrust efforts. In fact, when the monopolistic activity was not manufacturing, the Court was quite willing to apply the law. For example, the Court held that companies engaged in production and interstate sale of pipe came under the sections of the Sherman Act.[7] In 1904 the Court went even further, ruling in *Northern Securities Company v. United States* that stock transactions creating a holding company (the result of an effective merger between the Northern Pacific and the Great Northern Railroad companies) were subject to Sherman Act scrutiny. In spite of these applications of the antitrust law, *E. C. Knight* set an important precedent, declaring manufacturing to be outside the definition of interstate commerce. This ruling later would be extended, with serious repercussions, to bar many of the New Deal programs passed to combat the Great Depression.

The Stream of Commerce Doctrine

Government efforts to break up the meatpacking trust presented a different constitutional challenge. The corporations that dominated the meat industry, such as Armour, Cudahy, and Swift,

7. *Addystone Pipe and Steel Co. v. United States,* 175 U.S. 211 (1899)

ruled the nation's stockyards, which stood at the throat of the meat distribution process. Western ranchers sent their livestock to the stockyards to be sold, butchered, and packed for shipment to consumers in the East. Livestock brokers, known as commission men, received the animals at the stockyards and sold them to the meatpacking companies for the ranchers. Consequently, when the meatpacking trust acquired control of the stockyards and the commission men who worked there, it was in a position to direct where the ranchers sent their stock, fix meat prices, demand unreasonably low rates for transporting stock, and decide when to withhold meat from the market. The government believed these actions constituted a restraint of trade in violation of the Sherman Act. The meatpackers argued that their control over the stockyards was an intrastate matter to be regulated by the states. The Court settled the dispute in *Swift & Company v. United States* (1905) in which Justice Oliver Wendell Holmes, Jr., for a unanimous Court, held that the Sherman Act applied to the stockyards. The commercial sale of beef, Holmes reasoned, began when the cattle left the range and did not terminate until final sale. The fact that the cattle stopped at the stockyards, midpoint in this commercial enterprise, did not mean that they were removed from interstate commerce. Holmes's opinion develops what has become known as the "stream of commerce doctrine," which allows federal regulation of interstate commerce from the point of its origin to the point of its termination. Interruptions in the course of that interstate commerce do not suspend the right of Congress to regulate. *Stafford v. Wallace* (1922), an appeal based on another federal assault on the meatpacking combines, develops the doctrine more fully.

Stafford v. Wallace

258 U.S. 495 (1922)

Vote: 7 (Brandeis, Clarke, Holmes, McKenna, Pitney,
*   Taft, Van Devanter)*
*   1 (McReynolds)*
Opinion of the Court: Taft
Not participating: Day

Armed with the *Swift & Company* precedent, Congress in 1921 passed the Packers and Stockyard Act. This legislation attempted to go beyond antitrust considerations in regulating the meatpacking industry. In addition to making it unlawful for the packers to fix prices or engage in monopolistic practices, the law forbade packers in interstate commerce to engage in any unfair, discriminatory, or deceptive practices. It required all stockyard dealers and commission men to register with the secretary of agriculture. The transactions at the stockyards had to conform to a schedule of charges open for public inspection. Fees and charges could be changed only after ten days' notice to the secretary. The Agriculture Department had the authority delegated by Congress to make rules and regulations to carry out the act, set stockyard rates, and prescribe recordkeeping procedures for stockyard officials.

Stafford and Company, a corporation engaged in commercial transactions of cattle, sued Secretary of Agriculture Henry Wallace asking the courts to enjoin his enforcement of the act. The lower court refused to issue the requested injunction, and the company appealed.

Chief Justice William Howard Taft delivered the opinion of the Court:

The object to be secured by the act is the free and unburdened flow of live stock from the ranges and farms of the West and the Southwest through the great stockyards and slaughtering centers on the borders of that region, and thence in the form of meat products to the consuming cities of the country in the Middle West and East, or, still as live stock, to the feeding places and fattening farms in the Middle West or East for further preparation for the market.

The chief evil feared is the monopoly of the packers, enabling them unduly and arbitrarily to lower prices to the shipper who sells, and unduly and arbitrarily to increase the price to the consumer who buys. Congress thought that the power to maintain this monopoly was aided by control of the stockyards. Another evil which it sought to provide against by the act, was exorbitant charges, duplication of commissions, deceptive practices in respect of prices, in the passage of the live stock through the stockyards, all made possible by collusion between the stockyards management and the commission men, on the one hand, and the packers and dealers on the other. Expenses incurred in the passage through the stockyards necessarily reduce the price received by the shipper, and increase the price to be paid by the consumer. If they be exorbitant or unreasonable, they are an undue burden on the commerce which the stockyards are intended to facilitate. Any unjust or deceptive practice or combination that unduly and directly enhances them is an unjust obstruction to that commerce. . . .

The stockyards are not a place of rest or final destination. Thousands of head of live stock arrive daily by carload and trainload lots, and must be promptly sold and disposed of and moved out to give place to the constantly flowing traffic that presses behind. The stockyards are but a throat through which the current flows, and the transactions which occur therein are only incident to this current from the West to the East, and from one State to another. Such transactions can not be separated from the movement to which they contribute and necessarily take on its character. The commission men are essential in making the sales without which the flow of the current would be obstructed, and this, whether they are made to packers or dealers. The dealers are essential to the sales to the stock farmers and feeders. The sales are not in this aspect merely local transactions. They create a local change of title, it is true, but they do not stop the flow; they merely change the private interests in the subject of the current, not interfering with, but, on the contrary, being indispensable to its continuity. The origin of the live stock is in the West, its ultimate destination known to, and intended by, all engaged in the business is in the Middle West and East either as meat products or stock for feeding and fattening. This is the definite and well-understood course of business. The stockyards and the sales are necessary factors in the middle of this current of commerce.

The act, therefore, treats the various stockyards of the country as great national public utilities to promote the flow of commerce from the ranges and farms of the West to the consumers in the East. It assumes that they conduct a business affected by a public use of a national character and subject to national regulation. That it is a business within the power of regulation by legislative action needs no discussion. . . . Nor is there any doubt that in the receipt of live stock by rail and in their delivery by rail the stockyards are an interstate commerce agency. The only question here is whether the business done in the stockyards between the receipt of the live stock in the yards and the shipment of them therefrom is a part of interstate commerce, or is so associated with it as to bring it within the power of national regulation. A similar question has been before this court and had great consideration in *Swift & Co.* v. *United States.* The judgment in that case gives a clear and comprehensive exposition which leaves to us in this case little but the obvious application of the principles there declared. . . .

The application of the commerce clause of the Constitution in the *Swift Case* was the result of the natural development of interstate commerce under modern conditions. It was the inevitable recognition of the great central fact that such streams of commerce from one part of the country to another which are ever flowing are in their very essence the commerce among the States and with foreign nations which historically it was one of the chief purposes of the Constitution to bring under national protection and control. This court declined to defeat this purpose in respect of such a stream and take it out of complete national regulation by a nice and technical inquiry into the non-interstate character of some of its necessary incidents and facilities when considered alone and without reference to their association with the movement of which they were an essential but subordinate part.

The principles of the *Swift Case* have become a fixed rule of this court in the construction and application of the commerce clause. . . .

Of course, what we are considering here is not a bill in equity or an indictment charging conspiracy to obstruct interstate commerce, but a law. The language of the law shows that what Congress had in mind primarily was to prevent such conspiracies by supervision of the agencies which would be likely to be employed in it. If Congress could provide for punishment or restraint of such conspiracies after their formation through the Anti-Trust Law as in the *Swift Case,* certainly it may provide regulation to prevent their formation. . . .

As already noted, the word "commerce" when used in the act is defined to be interstate and foreign commerce. Its provisions are carefully drawn to apply only to those practices and obstructions which in the judgment of Congress are likely to affect interstate commerce prejudicially. Thus construed and applied, we think the act clearly within congressional power and valid.

Other objections are made to the act and its provisions as violative of other limitations of the Constitution, but the only one seriously pressed was that based on the Commerce Clause and we do not deem it necessary to discuss the others.

The orders of the District Court refusing the interlocutory injunctions are

Affirmed.

The "stream of commerce" precedents set in the *Swift* and *Stafford* stockyards cases later were applied to other regulatory schemes. Most notable was *Chicago Board of Trade v. Olsen* (1923), which brought the grain exchanges under the rubric of interstate commerce. Such decisions broadened the power of the federal government to control the economy. But the Court still found that certain commercial activities exerted too little direct impact on interstate commerce to justify congressional control. The most prominent among these were manufacturing and processing.

The sugar trust case of *E. C. Knight* (1895) established this principle, and it was reinforced in 1918 by *Hammer v. Dagenhart,* the child labor case discussed in Chapter 5.

As the nation enjoyed the prosperity of the 1920s, the federal government had more power to regulate the economy than it had ever had, but not enough to cope effectively with a full-scale economic collapse. When the stock market crashed, the central government did not have the constitutional authority to impose adequate corrective measures, and the justices of the Supreme Court, at least initially, were unwilling to provide the political branches with that authority. This situation touched off history's most dramatic confrontation between the Court and the president, which permanently altered the distribution of government powers.

The Supreme Court and the New Deal

The New York Stock Exchange crash on October 29, 1929, set in motion a series of events that shook the American economy and drove the nation into a deep depression. For the next two years, the stock market continued to tumble, with the Standard and Poor's Industrial Averages falling 75 percent. The gross national product declined 27 percent over three years, and the unemployment rate rose from a healthy 3.2 percent in 1929 to a catastrophic 24.9 percent in 1933.

The Republican party, which had been victorious in the November 1928 elections, controlled the White House and both houses of Congress. The party attempted to cope with the depression by following philosophies of government that had been successful during the previous years of prosperity, with dismal results. The economic forces against which the Republicans fought were enormous. A different political approach was necessary to battle the collapse, and the American people were demanding such a change.

The Depression and Political Change

In the 1932 presidential election, Democratic candidate Franklin D. Roosevelt was swept into office by a huge margin as the voters rejected incumbent Herbert Hoover. With new Democratic majorities in the House and Senate, the president began combating the depression with his New Deal policies. The overwhelming Democratic margins in Congress gave Roosevelt all the political clout he needed to gain approval of his radical new approach to boosting the economy. His programs were so popular with the American people that in 1936 they reelected Roosevelt by an even greater margin and provided him with even larger Democratic majorities in Congress, reducing the Republicans almost to minor party status. Clearly, the severe economic events following the 1929 crash triggered substantial political change with the legislative and executive branches experiencing wholesale partisan shifts *(see Table 6-1)*.

The U.S. Supreme Court, however, did not change. In 1929, just before the stock market crashed, the Court had six Republicans and three Democrats. The economic conservatives (Taft, Van Devanter, McReynolds, Butler, Sutherland, and Sanford) held control and clearly outnumbered the justices more sympathetic to political and economic change (Holmes, Brandeis, and Stone). By 1932 the Court had three new justices. Charles Evans Hughes replaced Chief Justice Taft, Benjamin Cardozo took Justice Holmes's seat, and Owen Roberts replaced Edward Sanford. Although these changes reduced the Republican majority to five, there was no appreciable change in the ideological balance of the Court. Hoover filled all three of these vacancies, which occurred before Roosevelt took office. Inaugurated in March 1933, Roosevelt had no opportunity to name a Supreme Court justice until Willis Van Devanter retired in June 1937. Roosevelt's first appointment, Hugo L. Black, assumed his seat in August of that year. Not until 1940 did

Table 6-1   The Great Depression and Political Change

	1929	1931	1933	1935	1937
House of Representives					
No. of Democratic seats	163	216	313	332	333
No. of Republican seats	267	218	117	103	89
Senate					
No. of Democratic senators	39	47	59	69	75
No. of Republican senators	56	48	36	25	17
Presidency					
Incumbent	Hoover (R)	—	Roosevelt (D)	—	Roosevelt (D)
% of popular vote	58.2	—	57.4	—	60.8
Electoral vote margin	444-87	—	472-59	—	523-8
Supreme Court					
Republican justices	6	6	5	5	5
Number of new appointments over previous two years	0	2	1	0	0

Notes: Data depict the change in political representation in the three branches of the federal government following the 1929 stock market crash and the deepening depression that continued over the next several years.

Members of the House and one-third of the senators were elected the previous November. Data on presidential election margins are based on previous November's elections. Supreme Court information is as of January of the designated years.

the Court have a majority appointed from the period after Roosevelt's first election.

In the executive branch, Roosevelt assembled a cadre of young, creative people to devise novel ways of approaching the ailing economy, and these New Deal Democrats quickly set out to develop, enact, and implement their programs. Congress passed the first legislation, the Emergency Banking Act of 1933, just five days after Roosevelt's inauguration, and a string of statutes designed to control all major sectors of the nation's economy followed. In adopting these programs, Congress relied on a number of constitutional powers including the powers to tax, spend, and regulate interstate and foreign commerce *(see box, opposite).*

A new political majority dominated the legislative and executive branches, and it espoused philosophies that called for the government to take a significantly more active role in economic

regulation. The Supreme Court remained firmly in the control of representatives of the old order, with views on the relationship of government and the economy at odds with the political branches. This political scenario made a clash between the president and the Court inevitable.

The Court Attacks the New Deal

As soon as the New Deal programs came into being, conservative business interests began to challenge their constitutional validity. In just two years the appeals started to reach the Court's doorstep. Beginning in 1935 and lasting for two long, tense years, the Court and the New Deal Democrats fought over the constitutionality of an expanded federal role in managing the economy.

During this period, the justices struck down a number of important New Deal statutes. Of ten major programs, the Supreme Court approved

New Deal Legislation

The Roosevelt Democrats moved on the nation's economic problems with great speed. Roosevelt took the oath of office on March 4, 1933. Listed below are the major economic actions passed during his first term. Note how many were enacted within the first 100 days of the new administration.

March 9, 1933	Emergency Banking Act
March 31, 1933	Civilian Conservation Corps created
May 12, 1933	Agricultural Adjustment Act
May 12, 1933	Federal Emergency Relief Act
May 18, 1933	Tennessee Valley Authority created
June 5, 1933	Nation taken off gold standard
June 13, 1933	Home Owners Loan Corporation created
June 16, 1933	Federal Deposit Insurance Corporation created
June 16, 1933	Farm Credit Administration created
June 16, 1933	National Industrial Recovery Act
January 30, 1934	Dollar devalued
June 6, 1934	Securities and Exchange Commission authorized
June 12, 1934	Reciprocal Tariff Act
June 19, 1934	Federal Communications Commission created
June 27, 1934	Railroad Retirement Act
June 28, 1934	Federal Housing Administration authorized
April 8, 1935	Works Progress Administration created
July 5, 1935	National Labor Relations Act
August 14, 1935	Social Security Act
August 26, 1935	Federal Power Commission created
August 30, 1935	National Bituminous Coal Conservation Act
February 19, 1936	Soil Conservation and Domestic Allotment Act

only two—the Tennessee Valley Authority and the emergency monetary laws. Four hard-line conservative justices, Willis Van Devanter, James Clark McReynolds, George Sutherland, and Pierce Butler, formed the heart of the Court's opposition. Many thought their obstruction of New Deal initiatives would bring about the nation's ruin. As a consequence, they became known as the Four Horsemen of the Apocalypse, a reference to the end of the world in Revelations. Two of the four, McReynolds and Butler, were Democrats.

Naturally, these four justices by themselves could not declare void any act of Congress. They needed the vote of at least one other justice. As the box on page 284 indicates, they had little trouble attracting others to their cause. Of the eight major 1935-1936 decisions in which they were able to strike down congressional policies, three were by 5-4 votes in which the four were able to attract Justice Owen Roberts to their fold. In one additional case, both Roberts and Chief Justice Hughes voted against the legislation. But in three of these significant decisions, the Court was unanimous with even the more liberal Brandeis, Cardozo, and Stone voting to strike down the challenged legislation.

The first salvo in the war between the two branches occurred on January 7, 1935, when the Supreme Court by an 8-1 vote in *Panama Refining Company v. Ryan* struck down a section of the National Industrial Recovery Act (NIRA) as an improper delegation of congressional power to the executive branch. The section in question was a major New Deal weapon in regulating the oil industry. It gave the president the power to prohibit interstate shipment of oil and petroleum products that were produced or stored in a manner illegal under state law. The justices found fault with the act because it did not provide sufficiently clear standards to guide the executive branch; rather, it gave the president almost unlimited discretion in applying the prohibitions. *Panama*

The Supreme Court and the New Deal

Listed below are eight major decisions handed down by the Supreme Court in 1935 and 1936 declaring parts of the New Deal legislative program unconstitutional.

Case/Decision Date	Acts Ruled Unconstitutional/Grounds	Majority	Dissent
Panama Refining Co. v. Ryan (January 7, 1935)	Portions of the National Industrial Recovery Act. (Improper delegation of congressional powers)	Brandeis, Butler, Hughes, McReynolds, Roberts, Stone, Sutherland, Van Devanter	Cardozo
Railroad Retirement Board v. Alton Railroad Co. (May 6, 1935)	Railroad Retirement Act of 1934. (Exceeded Commerce Clause powers; Fifth Amendment due process violations)	Butler, McReynolds, Roberts, Sutherland, Van Devanter	Brandeis, Cardozo, Hughes, Stone
Schechter Poultry Corp. v. United States (May 27, 1935)	Portions of the National Industrial Recovery Act. (A regulation of intrastate commerce and improper delegation of congressional power)	Brandeis, Butler, Cardozo, Hughes, McReynolds, Roberts, Stone, Sutherland, Van Devanter	
Louisville Bank v. Radford (May 27, 1935)	Frazier-Lemke Act of 1934 extending bankruptcy relief. (Fifth Amendment property rights)	Brandeis, Butler, Cardozo, Hughes, McReynolds, Roberts, Stone, Sutherland Van Devanter	
Hopkins Savings Association v. Cleary (December 12, 1935)	Home Owners Loan Act of 1933 (Tenth Amendment)	Brandeis, Butler, Cardozo, Hughes, McReynolds, Roberts, Stone, Sutherland, Van Devanter	
United States v. Butler (January 6, 1936)	Agricultural Adjustment Act. (Taxing and spending power violations)	Butler, Hughes McReynolds, Roberts Sutherland, Van Devanter	Brandeis, Cardozo, Stone
Carter v. Carter Coal Co. (May 18, 1936)	Bituminous Coal Conservation Act. (A regulation of intrastate commerce; improper delegation of congressional power)	Butler, McReynolds, Roberts, Sutherland, Van Devanter	Brandeis, Cardozo, Hughes, Stone
Ashton v. Cameron County District Court (May 25, 1936)	Municipal Bankruptcy Act. (Tenth Amendment; Fifth Amendment property rights)	Butler, McReynolds, Roberts, Sutherland, Van Devanter	Brandeis, Cardozo, Hughes, Stone

The Four Horsemen

Willis Van Devanter
(1910–1937)

Republican from Wyoming. Born 1859. University of Cincinnati Law School. Wyoming state legislator and state supreme court judge. Federal appeals court judge. Appointed by William Howard Taft.

James Clark McReynolds
(1914–1941)

Democrat from Tennessee. Born 1862. University of Virginia Law School. United States Attorney General. Appointed by Woodrow Wilson.

George Sutherland
(1922–1938)

Republican from Utah. Born 1862. University of Michigan Law School. State legislator, U.S. Representative, U.S. Senator. Appointed by Warren G. Harding.

Pierce Butler
(1922–1939)

Democrat from Minnesota. Born 1866. No law school, studied privately. Corporate attorney. Appointed by Warren G. Harding.

Refining was the first case in which the Court struck down legislation because it was an improper delegation of power.

Although the decision in *Panama Refining* was restricted to the delegation question and did not focus on Congress's interstate commerce authority, it promised bad days ahead for the administration. Not only was the decision a disappointment for the president, but also the vote was lopsided. Only Justice Cardozo voted to approve the law.

The Supreme Court dropped its biggest bomb on the New Deal four months later in May 1935. The justices voted 5-4 on May 6 to declare the Railroad Retirement Act an unconstitutional violation of the Commerce Clause and the Due Process Clause of the Fifth Amendment.[8] Then on May 27, a date that became known as Black Monday, the justices announced three significant blows to the administration's efforts to fight the depression—all by unanimous votes. First, in *Humphrey's Executor v. United States,* the Court declared that the president did not have the power to remove a member of the Federal Trade Commission. Second, the justices invalidated the Frazier-Lemke Act that provided mortgage relief, especially to farmers.[9] Finally, in *Schechter Poultry Corp. v. United States* the Court handed the president his most stinging defeat when it declared major portions of the NIRA unconstitutional as an improper delegation of legislative power and a violation of the Commerce Clause.

8. *Railroad Retirement Board v. Alton Railroad Co.*, 295 U.S. 330 (1935).
9. *Louisville Bank v. Radford*, 295 U.S. 555 (1935).

Schechter Poultry Corp. v. United States

295 U.S. 495 (1935)

Vote: 9 (Brandeis, Butler, Cardozo, Hughes,
*   McReynolds, Roberts, Stone, Sutherland,*
*   Van Devanter)*
            0
Opinion of the Court: Hughes
Concurring opinion: Cardozo

Congress passed the NIRA, the most far-reaching and comprehensive of all the New Deal legislation, June 16, 1933. Applying to every sector of American industry, the NIRA called for the creation of codes of fair competition for business. The codes would regulate trade practices, wages, hours, and other business activities. Trade associations and other groups active in the industry had the responsibility for drafting the codes, which were submitted to the president for approval. In the absence of the private sector's recommendations, the president was authorized to draft codes himself. Once approved by the president, the codes had the force of law, and violators faced fines and even jail.

The NIRA was vulnerable to constitutional challenge on two grounds. First, it set virtually no standards for the president in approving or drafting the codes. Congress had handed Roosevelt a blank check to bring all of American industry into line with his views of what was best for the recovery of the economy. Second, the law regulated what at that time was considered intrastate commerce.

The *Schechter* case involved a challenge to the NIRA poultry codes, focusing on the industry in New York, the nation's largest chicken market.[10] This market clearly was operating in interstate commerce; 96 percent of the poultry sold was transported into New York from out-of-state sup-

pliers. The industry was riddled with graft and plagued by deplorable health and sanitary conditions. The Live Poultry Code approved by President Roosevelt set a maximum work week of forty hours and a minimum hourly wage of fifty cents. In addition, the code established a health inspection system, regulations to govern slaughtering procedures, and compulsory record-keeping.

The A. L. A. Schechter Poultry Corporation, owned by Joseph, Martin, Aaron, and Alex Schechter, was a poultry slaughtering business in Brooklyn. Slaughterhouse operators, such as the Schechters, purchased large numbers of live chickens from local poultry dealers who imported the fowl from out of state to be killed and dressed for sale.

Government officials found the Schechters in violation of the Poultry Code on numerous counts. They ignored the code's wage and hour provisions, failed to comply with government record-keeping requirements, and did not conform to the slaughter regulations. Their worst offense, however, was selling unsanitary poultry that the government found unfit for human consumption. For this reason, *Schechter Poultry* was known as the Sick Chicken case.

The government obtained indictments against the Schechter Poultry Corporation and the four brothers on sixty counts of violating the code, and the jury found them guilty of nineteen. Each of the brothers was sentenced to a short jail term. They appealed unsuccessfully to the court of appeals and then pressed their case to the U.S. Supreme Court, asserting that the NIRA was unconstitutional on improper delegation and Commerce Clause grounds.

Chief Justice Hughes delivered the opinion of the Court:

The question of the delegation of legislative power. We recently had occasion to review the pertinent decisions and the general principles which govern the determination of this question. The Constitution pro-

---

10. For a good discussion of the *Schechter* case, see Chapter 5 in *The New Deal Lawyers* by Peter H. Irons (Princeton, N.J.: Princeton University Press, 1982).

A. L. A. Schechter (center) of Schechter Poultry Corporation with his attorneys Joseph Heller (left) and Frederick Wood, May 2, 1935.

vides that "All legislative powers herein granted shall be vested in a Congress of the United States, which shall consist of a Senate and House of Representatives." Art I, § 1. And the Congress is authorized "To make all laws which shall be necessary and proper for carrying into execution" its general powers. Art. I, § 8, par. 18. The Congress is not permitted to abdicate or to transfer to others the essential legislative functions with which it is thus vested. . . .

Section 3 of the Recovery Act is without precedent. It supplies no standards for any trade, industry or activity. It does not undertake to prescribe rules of conduct to be applied to particular states of fact determined by appropriate administrative procedure. Instead of prescribing rules of conduct, it authorizes the making of codes to prescribe them. For that legislative undertaking, § 3 sets up no standards, aside from the statement of the general aims of rehabilitation, correction and expansion described in section one. In view of the scope of that broad declaration, and of the nature of the few restrictions that are imposed, the discretion of the President in approving or prescribing codes, and thus enacting laws for the government of trade and industry throughout the country, is virtually unfet-

tered. We think that the code-making authority thus conferred is an unconstitutional delegation of legislative power.

. . . *The question of the application of the provisions of the Live Poultry Code to intrastate transactions.* . . . This aspect of the case presents the question whether the particular provisions of the Live Poultry Code, which the defendants were convicted for violating and for having conspired to violate, were within the regulating power of Congress.

These provisions relate to the hours and wages of those employed by defendants in their slaughterhouses in Brooklyn and to the sales there made to retail dealers and butchers.

(1) Were these transactions *"in"* interstate commerce? Much is made of the fact that almost all the poultry coming to New York is sent there from other States. But the code provisions, as here applied, do not concern the transportation of the poultry from other States to New York, or the transactions of the commission men or others to whom it is consigned, or the sales made by such consignees to defendants. When defendants had made their purchases, whether at the West Washington Market in New York City or at the railroad

terminals serving the City, or elsewhere, the poultry was trucked to their slaughterhouses in Brooklyn for local disposition. The interstate transactions in relation to that poultry then ended. Defendants held the poultry at their slaughterhouse markets for slaughter and local sale to retail dealers and butchers who in turn sold directly to consumers. Neither the slaughtering nor the sales by defendants were transactions in interstate commerce.

The undisputed facts thus afford no warrant for the argument that the poultry handled by defendants at their slaughterhouse markets was in a *"current"* or *"flow"* of interstate commerce and was thus subject to congressional regulation. The mere fact that there may be a constant flow of commodities into a State does not mean that the flow continues after the property has arrived and has become commingled with the mass of property within the State and is there held solely for local disposition and use. So far as the poultry here in question is concerned; the flow in interstate commerce had ceased. The poultry had come to a permanent rest within the State. It was not held, used, or sold by defendants in relation to any further transactions in interstate commerce and was not destined for transportation to other States. Hence, decisions which deal with a stream of interstate commerce—where goods come to rest within a State temporarily and are later to go forward in interstate commerce—and with the regulations of transactions involved in that practical continuity of movement, are not applicable here.

(2) Did the defendants' transactions directly *"affect"* interstate commerce so as to be subject to federal regulation? The power of Congress extends not only to the regulation of transactions which are part of interstate commerce, but to the protection of that commerce from injury. It matters not that the injury may be due to the conduct of those engaged in intrastate operations. Thus, Congress may protect the safety of those employed in interstate transportation "no matter what may be the source of the dangers which threaten it." We said in *Second Employers' Liability Cases,* that it is the "effect upon interstate commerce," not "the source of the injury," which is "the criterion of congressional power." We have held that, in dealing with common carriers engaged in both interstate and intrastate commerce, the dominant authority of Con-

gress necessarily embraces the right to control their intrastate operations in all matters having such a close and substantial relation to interstate traffic that the control is essential or appropriate to secure the freedom of that traffic from interference or unjust discrimination and to promote the efficiency of the interstate service. And combinations and conspiracies to restrain interstate commerce, or to monopolize any part of it, are none the less within the reach of the Anti-Trust Act because the conspirators seek to attain their end by means of intrastate activities. . . .

In determining how far the federal government may go in controlling intrastate transactions upon the ground that they "affect" interstate commerce, there is a necessary and well-established distinction between direct and indirect effects. The precise line can be drawn only as individual cases arise, but the distinction is clear in principle. Direct effects are illustrated by the railroad cases we have cited, as *e.g.,* the effect of failure to use prescribed safety appliances on railroads which are the highways of both interstate and intrastate commerce, injury to an employee engaged in interstate transportation by the negligence of an employee engaged in an intrastate movement, the fixing of rates for intrastate transportation which unjustly discriminate against interstate commerce. But where the effect of intrastate transactions upon interstate commerce is merely indirect, such transactions remain within the domain of state power. If the commerce clause were construed to reach all enterprises and transactions which could be said to have an indirect effect upon interstate commerce, the federal authority would embrace practically all the activities of the people and the authority of the State over its domestic concerns would exist only by sufferance of the federal government. Indeed, on such a theory, even the development of the State's commercial facilities would be subject to federal control. As we said in the *Minnesota Rate Cases:* "In the intimacy of commercial relations, much that is done in the superintendence of local matters may have an indirect bearing upon interstate commerce. The development of local resources and the extension of local facilities may have a very important effect upon communities less favored and to an appreciable degree alter the course of trade. The freedom of local trade may stimulate interstate commerce, while restrictive measures within the police power of the State enacted exclusively with respect to internal business, as distinguished from interstate traffic, may in their reflex or indirect influence diminish the latter and reduce the volume of articles transported into or out of the State.''

The distinction between direct and indirect effects has been clearly recognized in the application of the Anti-Trust Act. Where a combination or conspiracy is formed, with the intent to restrain interstate commerce or to monopolize any part of it, the violation of the statute is clear. But where that intent is absent, and the objectives are limited to intrastate activities, the fact that there may be an indirect effect upon interstate commerce does not subject the parties to the federal statute, notwithstanding its broad provisions. . . .

[T]he distinction between direct and indirect effects of intrastate transactions upon interstate commerce must be recognized as a fundamental one, essential to the maintenance of our constitutional system. Otherwise, as we have said, there would be virtually no limit to the federal power and for all practical purposes we should have a completely centralized government. We must consider the provisions here in question in the light of this distinction.

The question of chief importance relates to the provisions of the Code as to the hours and wages of those employed in defendants' slaughterhouse markets. It is plain that these requirements are imposed in order to govern the details of defendants' management of their local business. The persons employed in slaughtering and selling in local trade are not employed in interstate commerce. Their hours and wages have no direct relation to interstate commerce. The question of how many hours these employees should work and what they should be paid differs in no essential respect from similar questions in other local businesses which handle commodities brought into a State and there dealt in as a part of its internal commerce. This appears from an examination of the considerations urged by the Government with respect to conditions in the poultry trade. Thus, the Government argues that hours and wages affect prices; that slaughterhouse men sell at a small margin above operating costs; that a slaughterhouse operator paying lower wages or reducing his cost by exacting long hours of work, translates his saving into lower prices; that this results in demands

for a cheaper grade of goods; and that the cutting of prices brings about a demoralization of the price structure. Similar conditions may be adduced in relation to other businesses. The argument of the Government proves too much. If the federal government may determine the wages and hours of employees in the internal commerce of a State, because of their relation to cost and prices and their indirect effect upon interstate commerce, it would seem that a similar control might be exerted over other elements of cost, also affecting prices, such as the number of employees, rents, advertising, methods of doing business, etc. All the processes of production and distribution that enter into cost could likewise be controlled. If the cost of doing an intrastate business is in itself the permitted object of federal control, the extent of the regulation of cost would be a question of discretion and not of power.

The Government also makes the point that efforts to enact state legislation establishing high labor standards have been impeded by the belief that unless similar action is taken generally, commerce will be diverted from the States adopting such standards, and that this fear of diversion has led to demands for federal legislation on the subject of wages and hours. The apparent implication is that the federal authority under the commerce clause should be deemed to extend to the establishment of rules to govern wages and hours in intrastate trade and industry generally throughout the country, thus overriding the authority of the States to deal with domestic problems arising from labor conditions in their internal commerce.

It is not the province of the Court to consider the economic advantages or disadvantages of such a centralized system. It is sufficient to say that the Federal Constitution does not provide for it. Our growth and development have called for wide use of the commerce power of the federal government in its control over the expanded activities of interstate commerce, and in protecting that commerce from burdens, interferences, and conspiracies to restrain and monopolize it. But the authority of the federal government may not be pushed to such an extreme as to destroy the distinction, which the commerce clause itself establishes, between commerce ''among the several States'' and the internal concerns of a State. The same answer must be made to the contention that is based upon the serious economic situation which led to the passage of the Recovery Act,—the fall in prices, the decline in wages and employment, and the curtailment of the market for commodities. Stress is laid upon the great importance of maintaining wage distributions which would provide the necessary stimulus in starting "the cumulative forces making for expanding commercial activity." Without in any way disparaging this motive, it is enough to say that the recuperative efforts of the federal government must be made in a manner consistent with the authority granted by the Constitution.

We are of the opinion that the attempt through the provisions of the Code to fix the hours and wages of employees of defendants in their intrastate business was not a valid exercise of federal power.

The other violations for which defendants were convicted related to the making of local sales. Ten counts, for violation of the provision as to "straight killing," were for permitting customers to make "selections of individual chickens taken from particular coops and half coops." Whether or not this practice is good or bad for the local trade, its effect, if any, upon interstate commerce was only indirect. The same may be said of violations of the Code by intrastate transactions consisting of the sale "of an unfit chicken" and of sales which were not in accord with the ordinances of the City of New York. The requirement of reports as to prices and volumes of defendants' sales was incident to the effort to control their intrastate business. . . .

On both the grounds we have discussed, the attempted delegation of legislative power, and the attempted regulation of intrastate transactions which affect interstate commerce only indirectly, we hold the code provisions here in question to be invalid and that the judgment of conviction must be reversed.

The decision in *Schechter* closely paralleled the *E. C. Knight* ruling and rejected the application of the stream of commerce doctrine. In *Knight* the Court held that sugar refining was a manufacturing stage not part of interstate commerce and, therefore, the federal government could not regulate it. Similarly, in *Schechter* the Court classified the slaughtering and local sale of chickens as intrastate commerce. The stream of commerce evident in the stockyards decisions did not apply. In *Schechter* the interstate movement of the poultry had ceased. Once the distributor had sold to local processors like the Schechter company, the chickens had reached their state of final destination and became a part of intrastate commerce. Also consistent with *E. C. Knight,* the justices concluded that the poultry slaughter business had only an indirect effect on interstate commerce.

Through the remaining months of 1935 and into 1936, the Court continued to strike down federal legislation designed to cope with the depression. In some cases the Court found the statutes defective for violating the federal taxing and spending power or for depriving individuals of their right to property without due process of law, topics covered in the next two chapters. But throughout this period, the Court was concerned with congressional actions that went beyond constitutional authority to regulate interstate commerce. Congress could not constitutionally legislate local business activity, such as manufacturing, processing, or refining, unless it had a direct effect on interstate commerce. The Court supported congressional regulation when the commerce was in movement from one state to another, but, as demonstrated in *Schechter,* the justices were unwilling to allow Congress to act on commerce after it had completed its interstate journey. *Schechter* examined when interstate commerce ends; in May 1936 the Court taught the administration a lesson in when interstate commerce begins.

Carter v. Carter Coal Company

298 U.S. 238 (1936)

Vote: 5 (Butler, McReynolds, Roberts, Sutherland,
Van Devanter)
4 (Brandeis, Cardozo, Hughes, Stone)
Opinion of the Court: Sutherland
Opinion dissenting in part: Hughes
Dissenting opinion: Cardozo

Congress passed the Bituminous Coal Conservation Act in August 1935, following the *Schechter* decision. This law replaced the NIRA coal codes, which had been reasonably effective in bringing some stability to the depressed coal industry. The new act called for the establishment of a commission empowered to develop regulations regarding fair competition, production, wages, hours, and labor relations. The commission included representatives from the coal producers, coal miners, and the public. To fund the program, Congress imposed a tax at the mines of 15 percent of the value of the coal produced. Unlike the NIRA codes, compliance with the new code regulations was voluntary. There was, however, an incentive for joining the program. Companies who participated were given a rebate of 90 percent of the taxes levied by the act.

James W. Carter and other shareholders urged their company not to participate in the program. The board of directors did not want to join, but it believed that the company could not afford to pay the 15 percent tax and forgo the participation rebate. The stockholders sued to prevent the company from joining the program on the grounds that the Coal Act was unconstitutional. Of Carter's several attacks on the law, the most deadly was the charge that coal mining was not in interstate commerce.

Justice Sutherland delivered the opinion of the Court:

Since the validity of the act depends upon whether it is a regulation of interstate commerce, the nature and extent of the power conferred upon Congress by the commerce clause becomes the determinative question in this branch of the case. The commerce clause vests in Congress the power—''To regulate Commerce with foreign Nations, and among the several States, and with the Indian Tribes.'' The function to be exercised is that of regulation. The thing to be regulated is the commerce described. In exercising the authority conferred by this clause of the Constitution, Congress is powerless to regulate anything which is not commerce, as it is powerless to do anything about commerce which is not regulation. We first inquire, then—What is commerce? . . .

As used in the Constitution, the word ''commerce'' is the equivalent of the phrase ''intercourse for the purposes of trade,'' and includes transportation, purchase, sale, and exchange of commodities between the citizens of the different states. And the power to regulate commerce embraces the instruments by which commerce is carried on. In *Adair* v. *United States* the phrase ''Commerce among the several States'' was defined as comprehending ''traffic, intercourse, trade, navigation, communication, the transit of persons and the transmission of messages by telegraph—indeed, every species of commercial intercourse among the several States.'' . . .

That commodities produced or manufactured within a state are intended to be sold or transported outside the state does not render their production or manufacture subject to federal regulation under the commerce clause. . . .

In *Heisler* v. *Thomas Colliery Co.* we held that the possibility, or even certainty of exportation of a product or article from a state did not determine it to be in interstate commerce before the commencement of its movement from the state. To hold otherwise ''would nationalize all industries, it would nationalize and withdraw from state jurisdiction and deliver to federal commercial control the fruits of California and the South, the wheat of the West and its meats, the cotton of the South, the shoes of Massachusetts and the woolen industries of other States, at the very inception of their production or growth, that is, the fruits unpicked, the cotton and wheat ungathered, hides and flesh of cattle yet 'on the hoof,' wool yet unshorn, and coal yet unmined, because they are in varying percentages destined for and surely to be exported to States other than those of their production."

In *Oliver Iron Co.* v. *Lord* we said on the authority of numerous cited cases: "Mining is not interstate commerce, but, like manufacturing, is a local business subject to local regulation and taxation. . . . Its character in this regard is intrinsic, is not affected by the intended use or disposal of the product, is not controlled by contractual engagements, and persists even though the business be conducted in close connection with interstate commerce."

The same rule applies to the production of oil. "Such production is essentially a mining operation and therefore is not a part of interstate commerce even though the product obtained is intended to be and in fact is immediately shipped in such commerce." One who produces or manufactures a commodity, subsequently sold and shipped by him in interstate commerce, whether such sale and shipment were originally intended or not, has engaged in two distinct and separate activities. So far as he produces or manufactures a commodity, his business is purely local. So far as he sells and ships, or contracts to sell and ship, the commodity to customers in another state, he engages in interstate commerce. In respect of the former, he is subject only to regulation by the state; in respect of the latter, to regulation only by the federal government. Production is not commerce; but a step in preparation for commerce.

We have seen that the word "commerce" is the equivalent of the phrase "intercourse for the purposes of trade." Plainly, the incidents leading up to and culminating in the mining of coal do not constitute such intercourse. The employment of men, the fixing of their wages, hours of labor and working conditions, the bargaining in respect of these things—whether carried on separately or collectively—each and all constitute intercourse for the purposes of production, not of trade. The latter is a thing apart from the relation of employer and employee, which in all producing occupations is purely local in character. Extraction of coal from the mine is the aim and the completed result of local activities. Commerce in the coal mined is not brought into being by force of these activities, but by negotiations, agreements, and circumstances entirely

apart from production. Mining brings the subject matter of commerce into existence. Commerce disposes of it.

A consideration of the foregoing, and of many cases which might be added to those already cited, renders inescapable the conclusion that the effect of the labor provisions of the act, including those in respect of minimum wages, wage agreements, collective bargaining, and the Labor Board and its powers, primarily falls upon production and not upon commerce; and confirms the further resulting conclusion that production is a purely local activity. It follows that none of these essential antecedents of production constitutes a transaction in or forms any part of interstate commerce. Everything which moves in interstate commerce has had a local origin. Without local production somewhere, interstate commerce, as now carried on, would practically disappear. Nevertheless, the local character of mining, of manufacturing and of crop growing is a fact, and remains a fact, whatever may be done with the products. . . .

Another group of cases, of which *Swift & Co.* v. *United States* is an example, rest upon the circumstance that the acts in question constituted direct interferences with the "flow" of commerce among the states. In the *Swift* case, livestock was consigned and delivered to the stockyards—not as a place of final destination, but, as the court said in *Stafford* v. *Wallace*, "a throat through which the current flows." The sales which ensued merely changed the private interest in the subject of the current without interfering with its continuity. It was nowhere suggested in these cases that the interstate commerce power extended to the growth or production of the things which, after production, entered the flow. If the court had held that the raising of the cattle, which were involved in the *Swift* case, including the wages paid to and working conditions of the herders and others employed in the business, could be regulated by Congress, that decision and decisions holding similarly would be in point; for it is that situation, and not the one with which the court actually dealt, which here concerns us. . . .

The restricted field covered by the *Swift* and kindred cases is illustrated by the *Schechter* case. There the commodity in question, although shipped from another state, had come to rest in the state of its destination, and, as the court pointed out, was no longer in a current or flow of interstate commerce. The *Swift* doctrine was rejected as inapposite. In the *Schechter* case the flow had ceased. Here it had not begun. The difference is one of substance. The applicable principle is the same. . . .

Whether the effect of a given activity or condition is direct or indirect is not always easy to determine. The word "direct" implies that the activity or condition invoked or blamed shall operate proximately—not mediately, remotely, or collaterally—to produce the effect. It connotes the absence of an efficient intervening agency or condition. And the extent of the effect bears no logical relation to its character. The distinction between a direct and an indirect effect turns, not upon the magnitude of either the cause or the effect, but entirely upon the manner in which the effect has been brought about. If the production by one man of a single ton of coal intended for interstate sale and shipment, and actually so sold and shipped, affects interstate commerce indirectly, the effect does not become direct by multiplying the tonnage, or increasing the number of men employed, or adding to the expense or complexities of the business, or by all combined. It is quite true that rules of law are sometimes qualified by considerations of degree, as the government argues. But the matter of degree has no bearing upon the question here, since that question is not—What is the *extent* of the local activity or condition, or the *extent* of the effect produced upon interstate commerce? but—What is the *relation* between the activity or condition and the effect?

Much stress is put upon the evils which come from the struggle between employers and employees over the matter of wages, working conditions, the right of collective bargaining, etc., and the resulting strikes, curtailment and irregularity of production and effect on prices; and it is insisted that interstate commerce is *greatly* affected thereby. But, in addition to what has just been said, the conclusive answer is that the evils are all local evils over which the federal government has no legislative control. The relation of employer and employee is a local relation. At common law, it is one of the domestic relations. The wages are paid for the doing of local work. Working conditions are obviously local conditions. The employees are not engaged in or about commerce, but exclusively in producing a commodity. And the controversies and evils, which it is the object of the act to regulate and minimize, are local controversies and evils affecting local work undertaken to accomplish that local result. Such effect as they may have upon commerce, however extensive it may be, is secondary and indirect. An increase in the greatness of the effect adds to its importance. It does not alter its character.

The government's contentions in defense of the labor provisions are really disposed of adversely by our decision in the *Schechter* case. The only perceptible difference between that case and this is that in the *Schechter* case the federal power was asserted with respect to commodities which had come to rest after their interstate transportation; while here, the case deals with commodities at rest before interstate commerce has begun. That difference is without significance. The federal regulatory power ceases when interstate commercial intercourse ends; and, correlatively, the power does not attach until interstate commercial intercourse begins. There is no basis in law or reason for applying different rules to the two situations. No such distinction can be found in anything said in the *Schechter* case. . . . A reading of the entire opinion makes clear, what we now declare, that the want of power on the part of the federal government is the same whether the wages, hours of service, and working conditions, and the bargaining about them, are related to production before interstate commerce has begun, or to sale and distribution after it has ended.

In *Carter* the five-justice majority held that coal mining was not interstate commerce because the activity occurred within a single state. The stream of commerce doctrine was inapplicable because the movement of the coal to other states had not yet begun. Furthermore, the justices concluded that the production of coal did not have a direct effect on interstate commerce. For these reasons, the Court invalidated federal regulation of coal mining, but *Carter v. Carter Coal* was Roosevelt's last major defeat at the hands of the Four Horsemen and their allies.

The Court-Packing Plan

The Court entered its summer recess in 1936 having completed a year and a half of dealing with Roosevelt's legislative program and striking down several of the New Deal's most significant programs. It was clear that the Four Horsemen constituted a solid block and in important cases could count on the support of at least one of the other members—usually Owen Roberts. Roosevelt was understandably frustrated with what he viewed as the Court's obstructionism and was impatient that no vacancies had occurred that he might fill with appointees sympathetic to the New Deal.

The national elections took center stage during the fall of 1936. There was little doubt that Roosevelt would be reelected and that the Democrats would continue to control Congress.[11] The only question was how big the margin was going to be. Roosevelt won by a landslide, capturing 98 percent of the electoral votes. His Republican opponent, Alf Landon of Kansas, carried only Maine and Vermont. The congressional elections also were a Democratic rout. When the legislature

11. Not everyone predicted a Roosevelt victory. The *Literary Digest* published a famous poll during that election year forecasting a Roosevelt defeat. The poll has become universally regarded as a classic case in defective research procedures. Within months after the election, the *Literary Digest* was defunct.

reconvened in early 1937, the Democrats controlled approximately 80 percent of the seats in both houses. With such an impressive mandate from the people and such strong party support in Congress, Roosevelt was willing to proceed with his planned attack on the Court. If no vacancies on the Supreme Court occurred naturally, Roosevelt would try to create some.

On February 5, 1937, the president announced his plan to reorganize the federal court system. His proposed legislation was predicated, at least formally, on the argument that the judiciary was too overworked and understaffed to carry out its duties effectively. His idea was to expand the number of lower court judgeships; streamline federal jurisdiction, especially with respect to cases having constitutional significance; and adopt a flexible method of temporarily moving lower court judges from their normal duties to districts with case backlogs.

To many observers these administrative reforms were little more than a smoke screen for Roosevelt's Supreme Court proposals. The president asked Congress to authorize the creation of one new seat on the Supreme Court for every justice who had attained the age of seventy but remained in active service. These expanded positions would have an upper limit of six, bringing the potential size of the Court to a maximum of fifteen. At the time of his proposal, six sitting justices were older than seventy. If Roosevelt could appoint six strong New Dealers to the Court, they probably could attract the votes of at least two others and form a majority that would give constitutional approval to the president's programs. Although Roosevelt attempted to justify his Supreme Court proposal on the grounds that the advanced age of several sitting justices called for the addition of younger, more vigorous colleagues, everyone saw the plan for what it was—an attempt to pack the Court.

Public reaction was not favorable, and even the Democratic majorities in Congress were badly

"To Furnish The Supreme Court Practical Assistance."

THIS ACT SHALL TAKE EFFECT ON THE 30TH DAY AFTER THE DATE OF ITS ENACTMENT.

CONGRESS

Editorial cartoon on President Roosevelt's Court-packing plan, Washington Post, *February 6, 1937.*

Precedent for the President

1789: CONGRESS DECIDED AT FIRST TO FIX THE NUMBER OF JUSTICES AT SIX.

1801: CONGRESS PLANNED ON A CHANGE TO FIVE, BUT THE SIX REMAINED VERY MUCH ALIVE.

1807: SIX HIGH JUDGES, SUPREME AS HEAVEN — AND JEFFERSON ADDED NUMBER SEVEN.

1837: SEVEN HIGH JUDGES, ALL IN A LINE — TWO MORE ADDED, AND THAT MADE NINE.

1863: NINE HIGH JUDGES WERE SITTING WHEN LINCOLN MADE THEM AN EVEN TEN.

1866: TEN HIGH JUDGES, VERY SEDATE; WHEN CONGRESS GOT THROUGH THERE WERE ONLY EIGHT.

1869: EIGHT HIGH JUDGES WHO WOULDN'T RESIGN; GRANT BROUGHT THE FIGURE BACK TO NINE.

1937: WOULD A JUSTICE FEEL LIKE A PACKED SARDINE IF THE NUMBER WAS RAISED TO — SAY — FIFTEEN?

A Washington Post *Herblock cartoon on the Court-packing plan, February 22, 1936.*

divided. Chief Justice Hughes wrote a public letter to Sen. Burton Wheeler of Montana, a leader of those Democrats opposing the president, criticizing the proposal.[12] The press expressed sharp disapproval. In spite of the general support the people gave Roosevelt and the New Deal, they did not appreciate his tampering with the structure of government to get his way. Roosevelt's response to this unexpected criticism was to go directly to the people to press his case, and in doing so he became a little more open about his objectives. In his radio broadcast *(see pages 296–*

12. Letter from Chief Justice Charles Evans Hughes to Sen. Burton K. Wheeler, March 21, 1937. The letter is reprinted in *Guide to the U.S. Supreme Court,* 2d ed., by Elder Witt (Washington, D.C.: Congressional Quarterly, 1990), 963-965.

300) the president explained his proposal and urged the American public to support it.

The Switch in Time

The battle in Congress over the president's plan was closely fought.[13] A continuation of the confrontation, however, was averted in large measure by the actions of the Supreme Court itself. On March 29, just twenty days after the president's broadcast, the Court signaled that

13. See William E. Leuchtenburg, "The Origins of Franklin D. Roosevelt's 'Court-Packing' Plan," *Supreme Court Review 1966* (Chicago: University of Chicago Press, 1966), 347-400; Leuchtenburg, *Franklin D. Roosevelt and the New Deal, 1932-1940* (New York: Harper & Row, 1963).

White House Broadcast

March 9, 1937

Last Thursday I described in detail certain economic problems which everyone admits now face the Nation. For the many messages which have come to me after that speech, and which it is physically impossible to answer individually, I take this means of saying "thank you."

Tonight, sitting at my desk in the White House, I make my first radio report to the people in my second term of office.

I am reminded of that evening in March, four years ago, when I made my first radio report to you. We were then in the midst of the great banking crisis.

Soon after, with the authority of the Congress, we asked the Nation to turn over all of its privately held gold, dollar for dollar, to the Government of the United States.

Today's recovery proves how right that policy was.

But when, almost two years later, it came before the Supreme Court its constitutionality was upheld only by a five-to-four vote. The change of one vote would have thrown all the affairs of this great Nation back into hopeless chaos. In effect, four Justices ruled that the right under a private contract to exact a pound of flesh was more sacred than the main objectives of the Constitution to establish an enduring Nation.

In 1933 you and I knew that we must never let our economic system get completely out of joint again—that we could not afford to take the risk of another great depression.

We also became convinced that the only way to avoid a repetition of those dark days was to have a government with power to prevent and to cure the abuses and the inequalities which had thrown that system out of joint.

We then began a program of remedying those abuses and inequalities—to give balance and stability to our economic system—to make it bomb-proof against the causes of 1929.

Today we are only part-way through that program—and recovery is speeding up to a point where the dangers of 1929 are again becoming possible, not this week or month perhaps, but within a year or two.

National laws are needed to complete that program. Individual or local or state effort alone cannot protect us in 1937 any better than ten years ago.

It will take time—and plenty of time—to work out our remedies administratively even after legislation is passed. To complete our program of protection in time, therefore, we cannot delay one moment in making certain that our National Government has power to carry through.

Four years ago action did not come until the eleventh hour. It was almost too late.

If we learned anything from the depression we will not allow ourselves to run around in new circles of futile discussion and debate, always postponing the day of decision.

The American people have learned from the depression. For in the last three national elections an overwhelming majority of them voted a mandate that the Congress and the President begin the task of providing that protection—not after long years of debate, but now.

The Courts, however, have cast doubts on the ability of the elected Congress to protect us against catastrophe by meeting squarely our modern social and economic conditions.

We are at a crisis in our ability to proceed with that protection. It is a quiet crisis. There are no lines of depositors outside closed banks. But to the far-sighted it is far-reaching in its possibilities of injury to America.

I want to talk with you very simply about the need for present action in this crisis—the need to meet the unanswered challenge of one-third of a Nation ill-nourished, ill-clad, ill-housed.

Last Thursday I described the American form of Government as a three horse team provided by the Constitution to the American people so that their field might be plowed. The three horses are, of course, the three branches of government—the Congress, the Executive and the Courts. Two of the horses are pulling in unison today; the third is not. Those who have intimated that the President of the United States is trying to drive that team overlook the simple fact that the President, as Chief Executive, is himself one of the three horses.

It is the American people themselves who are in the driver's seat.

It is the American people themselves who want the furrow plowed.

It is the American people themselves who expect the third horse to pull in unison with the other two.

I hope that you have re-read the Constitution of the United States. Like the Bible, it ought to be read again and again.

It is an easy document to understand when you remember that it was called into being because the Articles of Confederation under which the original thirteen States tried to operate after the Revolution showed the need of a National Government with power enough to handle national problems. In its Preamble, the Constitution states that it was intended to form a more perfect Union and promote the general welfare; and the powers given to the Congress to carry out those purposes can be best described by saying that they were all the powers needed to meet each and every problem which then had a national character and which could not be met by merely local action.

But the framers went further. Having in mind that in succeeding generations many other problems then undreamed of would become national problems, they gave to the Congress the ample broad powers "to levy taxes. . . and provide for the common defense and general welfare of the United States."

That, my friends, is what I honestly believe to have been the clear and underlying purpose of the patriots who wrote a Federal Constitution to create a National Government with national power, intended as they said, "to form a more perfect union . . . for ourselves and our posterity."

For nearly twenty years there was no conflict between the Congress and the Court. Then, in 1803, Congress passed a statute which the Court said violated an express provision of the Constitution. The Court claimed the power to declare it unconstitutional and did so declare it. But a little later the Court itself admitted that it was an extraordinary power to exercise and through Mr. Justice Washington laid down this limitation upon it: "It is but a decent respect due to the wisdom, the integrity and the patriotism of the Legislative body, by which any law is passed, to presume in favor of its validity until its violation of the Constitution is proved beyond all reasonable doubt."

But since the rise of the modern movement for social and economic progress through legislation, the Court has more and more often and more and more boldly asserted a power to veto laws passed by the Congress and State Legislatures in complete disregard of this original limitation.

In the last four years the sound rule of giving statutes the benefit of all reasonable doubt has been cast aside. The Court has been acting not as a judicial body, but as a policy-making body.

When the Congress has sought to stabilize national agriculture, to improve the conditions of labor, to safeguard business against unfair competition, to protect our national resources, and in many other ways, to serve our clearly national needs, the majority of the Court has been assuming the power to pass on the wisdom of these Acts of the Congress—and to approve or disapprove the public policy written into these laws.

That is not only my accusation. It is the accusation of most distinguished Justices of the present Supreme Court. I have not the time to quote to you all the language used by dissenting Justices in many of these cases. But in the case holding the Railroad Retirement Act unconstitutional, for instance, Chief Justice Hughes said in a dissenting opinion that the majority opinion was "a departure from sound principles," and placed "an unwarranted limitation upon the commerce clause." And three other Justices agreed with him.

In the case holding the A.A.A. unconstitutional, Justice Stone said of the majority opinion that it was a "tortured construction of the Constitution." And two other Justices agreed with him.

In the case holding the New York Minimum Wage Law unconstitutional, Justice Stone said that the majority were actually reading into the Constitution their own "personal economic predilections," and that if the legislative power is not left free to choose the methods of solving the problems of poverty, subsistence and health of large numbers in the community, then "government is to be rendered impotent." And two other Justices agreed with him.

In the face of these dissenting opinions, there is no basis for the claim made by some members of the Court that something in the Constitution has compelled them regretfully to thwart the will of the people.

In the face of such dissenting opinions, it is perfectly clear, that as Chief Justice Hughes has said: "We are under a Constitution but the Constitution is what the Judges say it is."

The Court in addition to the proper use of its judicial functions has improperly set itself up as a third House of the Congress—a super-legislature, as one of the Justices has called it—reading into the Constitution words and implications which are not there, and which were never intended to be there. *(continued)*

We have, therefore, reached the point as a Nation where we must take action to save the Constitution from the Court and the Court from itself. We must find a way to take an appeal from the Supreme Court to the Constitution itself. We want a Supreme Court which will do justice under the Constitution—not over it. In our Courts we want a government of laws and not of men.

I want—as all Americans want—an independent judiciary as proposed by the framers of the Constitution. That means a Supreme Court that will enforce the Constitution as written—that will refuse to amend the Constitution by the arbitrary exercise of judicial power—amendment by judicial say-so. It does not mean a judiciary so independent that it can deny the existence of facts universally recognized.

How then could we proceed to perform the mandate given us? It was said in last year's Democratic platform "If these problems cannot be effectively solved within the Constitution, we shall seek such clarifying amendment as will assure the power to enact those laws, adequately to regulate commerce, protect public health and safety, and safeguard economic security." In other words, we said we would seek an amendment only if every other possible means by legislation were to fail.

When I commenced to review the situation with the problem squarely before me, I came by a process of elimination to the conclusion that short of amendments the only method which was clearly constitutional, and would at the same time carry out other much needed reforms, was to infuse new blood into all our Courts. We must have men worthy and equipped to carry out impartial justice. But, at the same time, we must have Judges who will bring to the Courts a present-day sense of the Constitution—Judges who will retain in the Courts the judicial functions of a court, and reject the legislative powers which the Courts have today assumed.

In forty-five out of the forty-eight States of the Union, Judges are chosen not for life but for a period of years. In many States Judges must retire at the age of seventy. Congress has provided financial security by offering life pensions at full pay for Federal Judges on all Courts who are willing to retire at seventy. In the case of Supreme Court Justices, that pension is $20,000 a year. But all Federal Judges, once appointed, can, if they choose, hold office for life, no matter how old they may get to be.

What is my proposal? It is simply this: whenever a Judge or Justice of any Federal Court has reached the age of seventy and does not avail himself of the opportunity to retire on a pension, a new member shall be appointed by the President then in office, with the approval, as required by the Constitution, of the Senate of the United States.

That plan has two chief purposes. By bringing into the Judicial system a steady and continuing stream of new and younger blood, I hope, first, to make the administration of all Federal justice speedier and, therefore, less costly; secondly, to bring to the decision of social and economic problems younger men who have had personal experience and contact with modern facts and circumstances under which average men have to live and work. This plan will save our national Constitution from hardening of the judicial arteries.

The number of Judges to be appointed would depend wholly on the decision of present Judges now over seventy, or those who would subsequently reach the age of seventy.

If, for instance, any one of the six Justices of the Supreme Court now over the age of seventy should retire as provided under the plan, no additional place would be created. Consequently, although there never can be more than fifteen, there may be only fourteen, or thirteen, or twelve. And there may be only nine.

There is nothing novel or radical about this idea. It seeks to maintain the Federal bench in full vigor. It has been discussed and approved by many persons of high authority ever since a similar proposal passed the House of Representatives in 1869.

Why was the age fixed at seventy? Because the laws of many States, the practice of the Civil Service, the regulations of the Army and Navy, and the rules of many of our Universities and of almost every great private business enterprise, commonly fix the retirement age at seventy years or less.

The statute would apply to all the Courts in the Federal system. There is general approval so far as the lower Federal courts are concerned. The plan has met opposition only so far as the Supreme Court of the United States itself is concerned. If such a plan is good for the lower courts it certainly ought to be equally good for the highest Court from which there is no appeal.

Those opposing this plan have sought to arouse prejudice and fear by crying that I am seeking to "pack" the Supreme Court and that a baneful precedent will be established.

What do they mean by the words "packing the Court"?

Let me answer this question with a bluntness that will end all *honest* misunderstanding of my purposes.

If by that phrase "packing the Court" it is charged that I wish to place on the bench spineless puppets who would disregard the law and would decide specific cases as I wished them to be decided, I make this answer—that no President fit for his office would appoint, and no Senate of honorable men fit for their office would confirm, that kind of appointees to the Supreme Court.

But if by that phrase the charge is made that I would appoint and the Senate would confirm Justices worthy to sit beside present members of the Court who understand those modern conditions—that I will appoint Justices who will not undertake to override the judgment of the Congress on legislative policy—that I will appoint Justices who will act as Justices and not as legislators—if the appointment of such Justices can be called "packing the Courts," then I say that I and with me the vast majority of the American people favor doing just that thing—now.

Is it a dangerous precedent for the Congress to change the number of the Justices? The Congress has always had, and will have, that power. The number of Justices has been changed several times before—in the Administrations of John Adams and Thomas Jefferson,—both signers of the Declaration of Independence—Andrew Jackson, Abraham Lincoln and Ulysses S. Grant.

I suggest only the addition of Justices to the bench in accordance with a clearly defined principle relating to a clearly defined age limit. Fundamentally, if in the future, America cannot trust the Congress it elects to refrain from abuse of our Constitutional usages, democracy will have failed far beyond the importance to it of any kind of precedent concerning the Judiciary.

We think it so much in the public interest to maintain a vigorous judiciary that we encourage the retirement of elderly Judges by offering them a life pension at full salary. Why then should we leave the fulfillment of this public policy to chance or make it dependent upon the desire or prejudice of any individual Justice?

It is the clear intention of our public policy to provide for a constant flow of new and younger blood into the Judiciary. Normally every President appoints a large number of District and Circuit Judges and a few members of the Supreme Court. Until my first term practically every President of the United States had appointed at least one member of the Supreme Court. President Taft appointed five members and named a Chief Justice—President Wilson three—President Harding four including a Chief Justice—President Coolidge one—President Hoover three including a Chief Justice.

Such a succession of appointments should have provided a Court well-balanced as to age. But chance and the disinclination of individuals to leave the Supreme bench have now given us a Court in which five Justices will be over seventy-five years of age before next June and one over seventy. Thus a sound public policy has been defeated.

I now propose that we establish by law an assurance against any such ill-balanced Court in the future. I propose that hereafter, when a Judge reaches the age of seventy, a new and younger Judge shall be added to the Court automatically. In this way I propose to enforce a sound public policy by law instead of leaving the composition of our Federal Courts, including the highest, to be determined by chance or the personal decision of individuals.

If such a law as I propose is regarded as establishing a new precedent—is it not a most desirable precedent?

Like all lawyers, like all Americans, I regret the necessity of this controversy. But the welfare of the United States, and indeed of the Constitution itself, is what we all must think about first. Our difficulty with the Court today rises not from the Court as an institution but from human beings within it. But we cannot yield our constitutional destiny to the personal judgment of a few men who, being fearful of the future, would deny us the necessary means of dealing with the present.

This plan of mine is no attack on the Court; it seeks to restore the Court to its rightful and historic place in our system of Constitutional Government and to have it resume its high task of building anew on the Constitution "a system of living law."

I have thus explained to you the reasons that lie behind our efforts to secure results by legislation within the Constitution. I hope that thereby the difficult process of constitutional amendment may be rendered unnecessary. But let us examine that process.

There are many types of amendment proposed. Each one is radically different from the other. There is no substantial group within the Congress or outside it who are agreed on any single amendment.

(continued)

It would take months or years to get substantial agreement upon the type and language of an amendment. It would take months and years thereafter to get a two-thirds majority in favor of that amendment in *both* Houses of the Congress.

Then would come the long course of ratification by three-fourths of the States. No amendment which any powerful economic interests or the leaders of any powerful political party have had reason to oppose has ever been ratified within anything like a reasonable time. And thirteen States which contain only five percent of the voting population can block ratification even though the thirty-five States with ninety-five percent of the population are in favor of it.

A very large percentage of newspaper publishers, Chambers of Commerce, Bar Associations, Manufacturers' Associations, who are trying to give the impression that they really do want a constitutional amendment would be the first to exclaim as soon as an amendment was proposed "Oh! I was for an amendment all right, but this amendment that you have proposed is not the kind of an amendment that I was thinking about. I am, therefore, going to spend my time, my efforts and my money to block that amendment, although I would be awfully glad to help get some other kind of amendment ratified."

Two groups oppose my plan on the ground that they favor a constitutional amendment. The first includes those who fundamentally object to social and economic legislation along modern lines. This is the same group who during the campaign last Fall tried to block the mandate of the people.

Now they are making a last stand. And the strategy of that last stand is to suggest the time-consuming process of amendment in order to kill off by delay the legislation demanded by the mandate.

To them I say—I do not think you will be able long to fool the American people as to your purposes.

The other group is composed of those who honestly believe the amendment process is the best and who would be willing to support a reasonable amendment if they could agree on one.

To them I say—we cannot rely on an amendment as the immediate or only answer to our present difficulties. When the time comes for action, you will find that many of those who pretend to support you will sabotage any constructive amendment which is proposed. Look at these strange bedfellows of yours. When before have you found them really at your side in your fights for progress?

And remember one thing more. Even if an amendment were passed, and even if in the years to come it were to be ratified, its meaning would depend upon the kind of Justices who would be sitting on the Supreme Court bench. An amendment like the rest of the Constitution is what the Justices say it is rather than what its framers or you might hope it is.

This proposal of mine will not infringe in the slightest upon the civil or religious liberties so dear to every American.

My record as Governor and as President proves my devotion to those liberties. You who know me can have no fear that I would tolerate the destruction by any branch of government of any part of our heritage of freedom.

The present attempt by those opposed to progress to play upon the fears of danger to personal liberty brings again to mind that crude and cruel strategy tried by the same opposition to frighten the workers of America in a pay-envelope propaganda against the Social Security Law. The workers were not fooled by that propaganda then. The people of America will not be fooled by such propaganda now.

I am in favor of action through legislation:

First, because I believe that it can be passed at this session of the Congress.

Second, because it will provide a reinvigorated, liberal-minded Judiciary necessary to furnish quicker and cheaper justice from bottom to top.

Third, because it will provide a series of Federal Courts willing to enforce the Constitution as written, and unwilling to assert legislative powers by writing into it their own political and economic policies.

During the past half century the balance of power between the three great branches of the Federal Government, has been tipped out of balance by the Courts in direct contradiction of the high purposes of the framers of the Constitution. It is my purpose to restore that balance. You who know me will accept my solemn assurance that in a world in which democracy is under attack, I seek to make American democracy succeed.

changes were in the making. The first indication was the 5-4 decision in *West Coast Hotel v. Parrish* (1937), which upheld the validity of a Washington State law regulating wages and working conditions for women and children. Although this case involved a state law rather than a federal statute and concerned issues of substantive due process rather than the Commerce Clause, it had great significance. Aside from the doctrinal importance of the case, discussed in Chapter 9, the voting coalitions on the Court had changed. Justice Roberts, so long an ally of the Four Horsemen, deserted the conservatives and voted with the liberal bloc to approve the legislation. Just months earlier Roberts had voted with the conservatives in a 5-4 decision striking down a New York law that was nearly a carbon copy of the one he now approved.[14]

Two weeks later Roberts proved that his *West Coast Hotel* vote was not an aberration. On April 12 the Court issued its ruling in *National Labor Relations Board v. Jones & Laughlin Steel Corporation* (1937). Once again Roberts joined Hughes, Brandeis, Cardozo, and Stone to form a majority, this time upholding a major piece of New Deal legislation. The decision may be the most significant economic ruling handed down during this century. In it the Court announced a break from the past and ushered in a new era in the constitutional relationship between the government and the economy.

14. *Morehead v. New York ex rel. Tipaldo*, 298 U.S. 587 (1936).

NLRB v. Jones & Laughlin Steel Corporation

301 U.S. 1 (1937)

Vote: 5 (Brandeis, Cardozo, Hughes, Roberts, Stone)
4 (Butler, McReynolds, Sutherland, Van Devanter)
Opinion for the Court: Hughes
Dissenting opinion: McReynolds

In 1935 Congress passed the National Labor Relations Act, more commonly known as the Wagner Act. The purpose of the legislation was to help workers achieve gains in wages and working conditions through the collective bargaining process. The Act's primary aim was to protect the rights of employees to organize and join labor unions and to provide a means for the enforcement of those rights. The law authorized the creation of the National Labor Relations Board (NLRB), which was empowered to hear complaints of unfair labor practices and impose certain corrective measures. The act was based on the power of Congress to regulate interstate commerce and upon the assertion that labor unrest and strikes caused an interruption in such commerce that Congress had the right to prevent.

Jones & Laughlin was one of the nation's largest steel producers. Its operations were fully integrated, extending into many states and involving every aspect of steel production from mining through production and distribution. Complaints were filed against the company for engaging in unfair labor practices at its plant in Aliquippa, Pennsylvania. The charges included discriminating against workers who wanted to join a labor union. The NLRB ruled against the company and ordered it to reinstate ten workers who had been dismissed because of their union activities. The company refused, claiming that the National Labor Relations Act was unconstitutional. Steel production facilities, according to the company, were engaged in a manufacturing activity that had been declared by the Supreme Court to be intrastate commerce outside the regulatory authority of Congress. The lower courts, applying existing Supreme Court precedent, ruled in favor of the company, and the NLRB appealed.

Chief Justice Hughes delivered the opinion of the Court:

First. The scope of the Act.—The Act is challenged in its entirety as an attempt to regulate all industry, thus invading the reserved powers of the States over their local concerns. It is asserted that the references in the Act to interstate and foreign commerce are colorable at best; that the Act is not a true regulation of such commerce or of matters which directly affect it but on the contrary has the fundamental object of placing under the compulsory supervision of the federal government all industrial labor relations within the nation. . . .

If this conception of terms, intent and consequent inseparability were sound, the Act would necessarily fall by reason of the limitation upon the federal power which inheres in the constitutional grant, as well as because of the explicit reservation of the Tenth Amendment. The authority of the federal government may not be pushed to such an extreme as to destroy the distinction, which the commerce clause itself establishes, between commerce "among the several States" and the internal concerns of a State. That distinction between what is national and what is local in the activities of commerce is vital to the maintenance of our federal system. . . .

We think it clear that the National Labor Relations Act may be construed so as to operate within the sphere of constitutional authority. The jurisdiction conferred upon the Board, and invoked in this instance, is found in § 10 (a), which provides:

"Sec. 10 (a). The Board is empowered, as hereinafter provided, to prevent any person from engaging in any unfair labor practice (listed in section 8) affecting commerce."

The critical words of this provision, prescribing the limits of the Board's authority in dealing with the labor practices, are "affecting commerce." The Act specifically defines the "commerce" to which it refers (§ 2 (6)):

"The term 'commerce' means trade, traffic, commerce, transportation, or communication among the several States, or between the District of Columbia or any Territory of the United States and any State or other Territory, or between any foreign country and any State, Territory, or the District of Columbia, or

within the District of Columbia or any Territory, or between points in the same State but through any other State or any Territory or the District of Columbia or any foreign country."

There can be no question that the commerce thus contemplated by the Act (aside from that within a Territory or the District of Columbia) is interstate and foreign commerce in the constitutional sense. The Act also defines the term "affecting commerce" (§ 2 (7)):

"The term 'affecting commerce' means in commerce, or burdening or obstructing commerce or the free flow of commerce or having led or tending to lead to a labor dispute burdening or obstructing commerce or the free flow of commerce."

This definition is one of exclusion as well as inclusion. The grant of authority to the Board does not purport to extend to the relationship between all industrial employees and employers. Its terms do not impose collective bargaining upon all industry regardless of effects upon interstate and foreign commerce. It purports to reach only what may be deemed to burden or obstruct that commerce and, thus qualified, it must be construed as contemplating the exercise of control within constitutional bounds. It is a familiar principle that acts which directly burden or obstruct interstate or foreign commerce, or its free flow, are within the reach of the congressional power. Acts having that effect are not rendered immune because they grow out of labor disputes. It is the effect upon commerce, not the source of the injury, which is the criterion. Whether or not particular action does affect commerce in such a close and intimate fashion as to be subject to federal control, and hence to lie within the authority conferred upon the Board, is left by the statute to be determined as individual cases arise. We are thus to inquire whether in the instant case the constitutional boundary has been passed.

Second. The unfair labor practices in question.—
. . .

[T]he statute goes no further than to safeguard the right of employees to self-organization and to select representatives of their own choosing for collective bargaining or other mutual protection without restraint or coercion by their employer.

That is a fundamental right. Employees have as clear a right to organize and select their representatives for lawful purposes as the respondent has to organize its business and select its own officers and agents. Discrimination and coercion to prevent the free exercise of the right of employees to self-organization and representation is a proper subject for condemnation by competent legislative authority. Long ago we stated the reason for labor organizations. We said that they were organized out of the necessities of the situation; that a single employee was helpless in dealing with an employer; that he was dependent ordinarily on his daily wage for the maintenance of himself and family; that if the employer refused to pay him the wages that he thought fair, he was nevertheless unable to leave the employ and resist arbitrary and unfair treatment; that union was essential to give laborers opportunity to deal on an equality with their employer. We reiterated these views when we had under consideration the Railway Labor Act of 1926. Fully recognizing the legality of collective action on the part of employees in order to safeguard their proper interests, we said that Congress was not required to ignore this right but could safeguard it. Congress could seek to make appropriate collective action of employees an instrument of peace rather than of strife. We said that such collective action would be a mockery if representation were made futile by interference with freedom of choice. Hence the prohibition by Congress of interference with the selection of representatives for the purpose of negotiation and conference between employers and employees, "instead of being an invasion of the constitutional right of either, was based on the recognition of the rights of both." We have reasserted the same principle in sustaining the application of the Railway Labor Act as amended in 1934.

Third. The application of the Act to employees engaged in production.—The principle involved.— Respondent says that whatever may be said of employees engaged in interstate commerce, the industrial relations and activities in the manufacturing department of respondent's enterprise are not subject to federal regulation. The argument rests upon the proposition that manufacturing in itself is not commerce.

The Government distinguishes these cases. The various parts of respondent's enterprise are described as interdependent and as thus involving "a great movement of iron ore, coal and limestone along well-

defined paths to the steel mills, thence through them, and thence in the form of steel products into the consuming centers of the country—a definite and well-understood course of business." It is urged that these activities constitute a "stream" or "flow" of commerce, of which the Aliquippa manufacturing plant is the focal point, and that industrial strife at that point would cripple the entire government. Reference is made to our decision sustaining the Packers and Stockyards Act. . . .

We do not find it necessary to determine whether these features of defendant's business dispose of the asserted analogy to the "stream of commerce" cases. The instances in which that metaphor has been used are but particular, and not exclusive, illustrations of the protective power which the Government invokes in support of the present Act. The congressional authority to protect interstate commerce from burdens and obstructions is not limited to transactions which can be deemed to be an essential part of a "flow" of interstate or foreign commerce. Burdens and obstructions may be due to injurious action springing from other sources. The fundamental principle is that the power to regulate commerce is the power to enact "all appropriate legislation" for "its protection and advancement"; to adopt measures "to promote its growth and insure its safety"; "to foster, protect, control and restrain." That power is plenary and may be exerted to protect interstate commerce "no matter what the source of the dangers which threaten it." Although activities may be intrastate in character when separately considered, if they have such a close and substantial relation to interstate commerce that their control is essential or appropriate to protect that commerce from burdens and obstructions, Congress cannot be denied the power to exercise that control. . . .

It is thus apparent that the fact that the employees here concerned were engaged in production is not determinative. The question remains as to the effect upon interstate commerce of the labor practice involved. . . .

*Fourth. Effects of the unfair labor practice in respondent's enterprise.—*Giving full weight to respondent's contention with respect to a break in the complete continuity of the "stream of commerce" by reason of respondent's manufacturing operations, the fact remains that the stoppage of those operations by industrial strife would have a most serious effect upon interstate commerce. In view of respondent's far-flung activities, it is idle to say that the effect would be indirect or remote. It is obvious that it would be immediate and might be catastrophic. We are asked to shut our eyes to the plainest facts of our national life and to deal with the question of direct and indirect effects in an intellectual vacuum. Because there may be but indirect and remote effects upon interstate commerce in connection with a host of local enterprises throughout the country, it does not follow that other industrial activities do not have such a close and intimate relation to interstate commerce as to make the presence of industrial strife a matter of the most urgent national concern. When industries organize themselves on a national scale, making their relation to interstate commerce the dominant factor in their activities, how can it be maintained that their industrial labor relations constitute a forbidden field into which Congress may not enter when it is necessary to protect interstate commerce from the paralyzing consequences of industrial war? We have often said that interstate commerce itself is a practical conception. It is equally true that interferences with that commerce must be appraised by a judgment that does not ignore actual experience.

Experience has abundantly demonstrated that the recognition of the right of employees to self-organization and to have representatives of their own choosing for the purpose of collective bargaining is often an essential condition of industrial peace. Refusal to confer and negotiate has been one of the most prolific causes of strife. This is such an outstanding fact in the history of labor disturbances that it is a proper subject of judicial notice and requires no citation of instances. . . .

These questions have frequently engaged the attention of Congress and have been the subject of many inquiries. The steel industry is one of the great basic industries of the United States, with ramifying activities affecting interstate commerce at every point. The Government aptly refers to the steel strike of 1919-1920 with its far-reaching consequences. The fact that there appears to have been no major disturbance in that industry in the more recent period did not dispose of the possibilities of future and like dangers to interstate commerce which Congress was entitled to foresee and to exercise its protective power to forestall. It is not necessary again to detail the facts as to respondent's enterprise. Instead of being beyond the pale, we think that it presents in a most striking way the close and intimate relation which a manufacturing industry may have to interstate commerce and we have no doubt that Congress had constitutional authority to safeguard the right of respondent's employees to self-organization and freedom in the choice of representatives for collective bargaining. . . .

Reversed.

The decisions in *West Coast Hotel v. Parrish* and *NLRB v. Jones & Laughlin Steel* took the energy out of Roosevelt's drive to pack the Court. It no longer appeared necessary as the Court now was looking with greater approval at state and federal legislation to correct the failing economy. In addition, on May 18 Justice Willis Van Devanter, a consistent foe of the Roosevelt's New Deal programs, announced that he would retire from the Court at the end of the term. At long last the president would have an opportunity to put a justice of his own choosing on the Court.

On June 7 the Senate Judiciary Committee recommended that the Court-packing bill not be passed. To the president's great displeasure seven of the ten senators signing the report were Democrats. Majority Leader Joseph Robinson, D-Ark., mounted a last-ditch effort on behalf of the president, advocating a compromise plan that would have raised the threshold age for replacing the justices from seventy to seventy-five years. He made considerable progress in forging a coalition to pass this modified plan, but the effort stalled when Robinson died from a heart attack on July 14.[15]

Much has been said and written about Justice Roberts's change in position. At the time, it was described as "the switch in time that saved nine," because his move from the conservative to the liberal wing of the Court was largely responsible for killing the Court-packing plan and preserving the Court as a nine-justice institution. Such a characterization is not flattering for a judge, who is not supposed to make decisions on the basis of external political pressures. Nevertheless, it would certainly be understandable for a justice to rethink his views if the future of the Court as an institution were at stake.

More contemporary analyses of Roberts's switch point out that the notion that he caved in to the pressures of the president's plan is overly simplistic. Although the decision in *West Coast Hotel* was announced after Roosevelt sent his proposal to Congress, it was argued and initially voted upon weeks before the president made his plans public. Roosevelt had kept the Court-packing proposal carefully under wraps before he announced it, and there is little likelihood that the justices had advance knowledge of it. Furthermore, Owen Roberts was not a doctrinaire conservative. Although he joined the Court's right wing in several important decisions, he did not have the laissez-faire zeal of the Four Horsemen. In fact, Roberts had voted on a number of occasions in support of state efforts to combat economic problems.[16] Some observers now conclude that Roberts's change of position was primarily a matter of his growing disenchantment with the hard-line conservative view and that he followed "his sound judicial intuition to a well-reasoned posi-

Justice Owen Josephus Roberts who cast critical votes in 1937 Supreme Court cases that expanded the authority of the federal government to regulate the economy.

tion in keeping with the public interest."[17] As for Roberts's own explanation, he maintained traditional judicial silence. When asked in a 1946 interview why he had altered his position, he deflected the question by responding, "Who knows what causes a judge to decide as he does? Maybe the breakfast he had has something to do with it."[18] Whatever the real reasons for his switch, it broke the conservatives' domination of the Court.

15. For a full account of the events surrounding this compromise plan, see William E. Leuchtenburg, "FDR's Court Packing Plan: A Second Life, a Second Death," *Duke Law Journal* (June-September 1985): 673-689.

16. See, for example, his opinion for the Court in *Nebbia v. New York,* 291 U.S. 502 (1934).

17. Merlo J. Pusey, "Justice Roberts' 1937 Turnaround," *Yearbook of the Supreme Court Historical Society* (Washington, D.C.: The Supreme Court Historical Society, 1983), 107.

18. Ibid., 106.

Consolidating the New Interpretation of the Commerce Power

Van Devanter's retirement was followed over the next four years by the retirements of Justices Sutherland and Brandeis, and the deaths of Justices Cardozo and Butler. By 1940 Franklin Roosevelt had appointed a majority of the sitting justices. And in 1941 Justice James Clark McReynolds, the last of the Four Horsemen, also retired.

With *NLRB v. Jones and Laughlin Steel* showing the way, the increasingly liberal Court upheld a number of New Deal programs. It also continued to expand the concept of interstate commerce. Gone were the old notions that production, manufacturing, mining, and processing were exclusively intrastate affairs with insufficient direct

effects on interstate commerce to activate federal commerce powers. Precedents such as *E. C. Knight, Darby Lumber, Panama Refining, Schechter Poultry,* and *Carter Coal* were substantially overruled, discredited, or severely limited *(see box, page 307).*

Wickard v. Filburn (1942) illustrates how far the Court had moved from its pre-1937 idea of interstate commerce. As you compare this decision to earlier rulings, recall that in *E. C. Knight* a sugar trust controlling 98 percent of the nation's sugar refining was considered to be operating in intrastate commerce. And in *Carter v. Carter Coal* the entire coal mining industry was said to be outside the power of Congress to regulate interstate commerce. How do these industries compare with Filburn's farm?

Wickard v. Filburn

317 U.S. 111 (1942)
Vote: 9 (Black, Byrnes, Douglas, Frankfurter, Jackson, Murphy, Reed, Roberts, Stone)
0
Opinion of the Court: Jackson

The 1938 Agricultural Adjustment Act, as amended, allowed the Secretary of Agriculture to establish production limits for various grains. Under these limits, acreage allotments were assigned to the individual farmer. The purpose of the law was to stop the wild swings in grain prices by eliminating both surpluses and shortfalls.

Roscoe Filburn owned a small farm in Montgomery County, Ohio. For many years he raised dairy cattle and chickens, selling the milk, poultry, and eggs the farm produced. He also raised winter wheat on a small portion of his farm. He sold some wheat and used the rest to feed his cattle and chickens, make flour for home consumption, and produce seeds for the next planting.

In July 1940 Secretary of Agriculture Claude R. Wickard set the wheat production limits for the

1941 crop. Filburn was allotted 11.1 acres to be planted in wheat with a yield of 20.1 bushels per acre. He planted not only his allotted acres but also some other land to produce the wheat for home consumption. In total Filburn planted 23 acres in wheat from which he harvested 239 bushels more than the government allowed him. For this excess planting Filburn was fined $117.11. He refused to pay the fine claiming that Congress had exceeded its powers under the Commerce Clause by regulating an individual planting wheat on his own property for on-farm consumption. The lower court ruled in Filburn's favor, and Secretary Wickard appealed.

Justice Robert H. Jackson delivered the opinion of the Court:

It is urged that under the Commerce Clause of the Constitution, Article I, § 8, clause 3, Congress does not possess the power it has in this instance sought to exercise. The question would merit little consideration since our decision in *United States* v. *Darby* sustaining the federal power to regulate production of goods for commerce, except for the fact that this Act extends

Supreme Court Expansion of the Commerce Powers, 1937-1941

Decision	*Ruling*
NLRB v. Friedman-Harry Marks Clothing Company (1937)	The National Labor Relations Act applies to a company engaged in the manufacturing of clothing.
NLRB v. Fruehauf Trailer Company (1937)	The National Labor Relations Act applies to a company engaged in the manufacturing of trailers.
Steward Machine v. Davis (1937)	Unemployment provisions of the Social Security Act are constitutional.
Helvering v. Davis (1937)	Old-age benefits provisions of the Social Security Act are constitutional.
Santa Cruz Fruit Packing v. NLRB (1938)	The National Labor Relations Act applies to a fruit packing company although only 37 percent of its product is sold in interstate commerce.
Consolidated Edison Company v. NLRB (1938)	The National Labor Relations Act applies to a power company although all of its power is sold in state.
NLRB v. Fainblatt (1939)	The National Labor Relations Act applies to a small garment manufacturer even though all of its goods are sold in state.
United States v. Rock Royal Cooperative (1939)	Legislation allowing the secretary of agriculture to set milk prices paid to farmers is constitutional.
Mulford v. Smith (1939)	Tobacco production quotas set by secretary of agriculture under Agricultural Adjustment Act of 1938 are constitutional.
United States v. Darby Lumber Company (1941)	Congressional action prohibiting shipment in interstate commerce of goods in violation of federal wage and hour laws is constitutional.

federal regulation to production not intended in any part for commerce but wholly for consumption on the farm. The Act includes a definition of "market" and its derivatives, so that as related to wheat, in addition to its conventional meaning, it also means to dispose of "by feeding (in any form) to poultry or livestock which, or the products of which, are sold, bartered, or exchanged, or to be so disposed of." Hence, marketing quotas not only embrace all that may be sold without penalty but also what may be consumed on the premises. Wheat produced on excess acreage is designated as "available for marketing" as so defined, and the penalty is imposed thereon. Penalties do not depend upon whether any part of the wheat, either within or without the quota, is sold or intended to be sold. The sum of this is that the Federal Government fixes a quota including all that the farmer may harvest for sale or for his own farm needs, and declares that wheat produced on excess acreage may neither be disposed of nor used except upon payment of the penalty, or except it is stored as required by the Act or delivered to the Secretary of Agriculture.

Appellee says that this is a regulation of production and consumption of wheat. Such activities are, he urges, beyond the reach of Congressional power under the Commerce Clause, since they are local in character, and their effects upon interstate commerce are at most "indirect." In answer the Government argues that the statute regulates neither production nor consumption, but only marketing; and, in the alternative, that if the Act does go beyond the regulation of marketing it is sustainable as a "necessary and proper" implementation of the power of Congress over interstate commerce.

The Government's concern lest the Act be held to be a regulation of production or consumption, rather than of marketing, is attributable to a few dicta and decisions of this Court which might be understood to lay it down that activities such as "production," "manufacturing," and "mining" are strictly "local" and, except in special circumstances which are not present here, cannot be regulated under the commerce power because their effects upon interstate commerce are, as matter of law, only "indirect." Even today, when this power has been held to have great latitude, there is no decision of this Court that such activities may be regulated where no part of the product is intended for interstate commerce or intermingled with the subjects thereof. We believe that a review of the course of decision under the Commerce Clause will make plain, however, that questions of the power of Congress are not to be decided by reference to any formula which would give controlling force to nomenclature such as "production" and "indirect" and foreclose consideration of the actual effects of the activity in question upon interstate commerce.

At the beginning Chief Justice Marshall described the federal commerce power with a breadth never yet exceeded. *Gibbons* v. *Ogden*. He made emphatic the embracing and penetrating nature of this power by warning that effective restraints on its exercise must proceed from political rather than from judicial processes.

For nearly a century, however, decisions of this Court under the Commerce Clause dealt rarely with questions of what Congress might do in the exercise of

its granted power under the Clause, and almost entirely with the permissibility of state activity which it was claimed discriminated against or burdened interstate commerce. During this period there was perhaps little occasion for the affirmative exercise of the commerce power, and the influence of the Clause on American life and law was a negative one, resulting almost wholly from its operation as a restraint upon the powers of the states. In discussion and decision the point of reference, instead of being what was "necessary and proper" to the exercise by Congress of its granted power, was often some concept of sovereignty thought to be implicit in the status of statehood. Certain activities such as "production," "manufacturing," and "mining" were occasionally said to be within the province of state governments and beyond the power of Congress under the Commerce Clause.

It was not until 1887, with the enactment of the Interstate Commerce Act, that the interstate commerce power began to exert positive influence in American law and life. This first important federal resort to the commerce power was followed in 1890 by the Sherman Anti-Trust Act and, thereafter, mainly after 1903, by many others. These statutes ushered in new phases of adjudication, which required the Court to approach the interpretation of the Commerce Clause in the light of an actual exercise by Congress of its power thereunder.

When it first dealt with this new legislation, the Court adhered to its earlier pronouncements, and allowed but little scope to the power of Congress. *United States* v. *Knight Co.* These earlier pronouncements also played an important part in several of the five cases in which this Court later held that Acts of Congress under the Commerce Clause were in excess of its power.

Even while important opinions in this line of restrictive authority were being written, however, other cases called forth broader interpretations of the Commerce Clause destined to supersede the earlier ones, and to bring about a return to the principles first enunciated by Chief Justice Marshall in *Gibbons* v. *Ogden*. . . .

Whether the subject of the regulation in question was "production," "consumption," or "marketing" is . . . not material for purposes of deciding the question of federal power before us. That an activity is of local character may help in a doubtful case to determine whether Congress intended to reach it. The same consideration might help in determining whether in the absence of Congressional action it would be permissible for the state to exert its power on the subject matter, even though in so doing it to some degree affected interstate commerce. But even if appellee's activity be local and though it may not be regarded as commerce, it may still, whatever its nature, be reached by Congress if it exerts a substantial economic effect on interstate commerce, and this irrespective of whether such effect is what might at some earlier time have been defined as "direct" or "indirect." . . .

The effect of consumption of home-grown wheat on interstate commerce is due to the fact that it constitutes the most variable factor in the disappearance of the wheat crop. Consumption on the farm where grown appears to vary in an amount greater than 20 per cent of average production. The total amount of wheat consumed as food varies but relatively little, and use as seed is relatively constant.

The maintenance by government regulation of a price for wheat undoubtedly can be accomplished as effectively by sustaining or increasing the demand as by limiting the supply. The effect of the statute before us is to restrict the amount which may be produced for market and the extent as well to which one may forestall resort to the market by producing to meet his own needs. That appellee's own contribution to the demand for wheat may be trivial by itself is not enough to remove him from the scope of federal regulation where, as here, his contribution, taken together with that of many other similarly situated, is far from trivial.

It is well established by decisions of this Court that the power to regulate commerce includes the power to regulate the prices at which commodities in that commerce are dealt in and practices affecting such prices. One of the primary purposes of the Act in question was to increase the market price of wheat, and to that end to limit the volume thereof that could affect the market. It can hardly be denied that a factor of such volume and variability as home-consumed wheat would have a substantial influence on price and market conditions. This may arise because being in marketable condition such wheat overhangs the market and, if induced by rising prices, tends to flow into the market and check price increases. But if we assume that it is never marketed, it supplies a need of the man who grew it which would otherwise be reflected by purchases in the open market. Home-grown wheat in this sense competes with wheat in commerce. The stimulation of commerce is a use of the regulatory function quite as definitely as prohibitions or restrictions thereon. This record leaves us in no doubt that Congress may properly have considered that wheat consumed on the farm where grown, if wholly outside the scheme of regulation, would have a substantial effect in defeating and obstructing its purpose to stimulate trade therein at increased prices. . . .

Reversed.

Regulating Commerce as a Federal Police Power

During the battle over the meaning of interstate commerce, the stakes were almost exclusively economic. The regulation of commerce, however, also can be used as a way to regulate health, safety, and moral matters. If Congress may use the interstate commerce power to regulate essentially noneconomic activities, then the long line of decisions, beginning with the *Jones & Laughlin* *Steel* case, expands federal power far beyond that envisioned by the Framers. May Congress legitimately use the Commerce Clause as means of exercising an authority at the national level similar to the states' police powers?

Initial Rulings on Federal Police Powers

In 1903 the Court issued its first significant ruling on this question. At issue in *Champion v.*

Ames was a federal law prohibiting the movement of lottery tickets in interstate commerce. The case demonstrates that when applying police powers Congress usually attempts to prohibit or depress certain forms of commerce. This goal is much different from the commercial expansion goals that are present when Congress regulates commerce for economic reasons. In reading Justice John Marshall Harlan's opinion for the Court,

notice the expansive terms he uses to describe the commerce power. Does he convince you that the Commerce Clause can be stretched to include the power to prohibit what Congress thought was an immoral trade? The four dissenters did not think so. They argued that Congress was not regulating commerce at all, but was really trying to prohibit lotteries, a matter for the police powers of the state to address.

Champion v. Ames
188 U.S. 321 (1903)

Vote: 5 (Brown, Harlan, Holmes, McKenna, White)
   4 (Brewer, Fuller, Peckham, Shiras)
Opinion of the Court: Harlan
Dissenting opinion: Fuller

In 1895 Congress passed a statute prohibiting lottery tickets from interstate or foreign commerce and also from being sent through the U.S. mails. Federal authorities charged Charles Champion with violating this act. Champion had arranged for a shipment of lottery tickets, supposedly printed in Paraguay, to be transported from Texas to California by the Wells Fargo Company. He challenged his arrest on several grounds, arguing that he was not engaged in interstate commerce, that the power to regulate interstate commerce did not include the authority to prohibit items from such commerce, and that regulating lotteries should only be exercised through the police powers of the states.

Justice Harlan delivered the opinion of the Court:

What is the import of the word "commerce" as used in the Constitution? It is not defined by that instrument. Undoubtedly, the carrying from one State to another by independent carriers of things or commodities that are ordinary subjects of traffic, and which have in themselves a recognized value in money, constitutes interstate commerce. But does not com-

merce among the several States include something more? Does not the carrying from one State to another, by independent carriers, of lottery tickets that entitle the holder to the payment of a certain amount of money therein specified also constitute commerce among the States? . . .

The leading case under the commerce clause of the Constitution is *Gibbons* v. *Ogden*. Referring to that clause, Chief Justice Marshall said: ". . . This power, like all others vested in Congress, is *complete in itself,* may be exercised *to its utmost extent,* and acknowledges *no limitations, other than are prescribed in the Constitution.* These are expressed in plain terms, and do not affect the questions which arise in this case or which have been discussed at the bar. If, as has always been understood, the sovereignty of Congress, though limited to specified objects, is plenary as to those objects, the power over commerce with foreign nations, and among the several States, is vested in Congress *as absolutely as it would be in a single government, having in its constitution the same restrictions on the exercise of the power as are found in the Constitution of the United States.''* . . .

[P]rior adjudications . . . sufficiently indicate the grounds upon which this court has proceeded when determining the meaning and scope of the commerce clause. They show that commerce among the States embraces navigation, intercourse, communication, traffic, the transit of persons, and the transmission of messages by telegraph. They also show that the power to regulate commerce among the several States is vested in Congress as absolutely as it would be in a single government, having in its constitution the same restrictions on the exercise of the power as are found in the Constitution of the United States; that such power is plenary, complete in itself, and may be exerted by Congress to its utmost extent, subject *only* to such limitations as the Constitution imposes upon the exercise of the powers granted by it; and that in determining the character of the regulations to be adopted Congress has a large discretion which is not to be controlled by the courts, simply because, in their opinion, such regulations may not be the best or most effective that could be employed.

We come then to inquire whether there is any solid foundation upon which to rest the contention that Congress may not regulate the carrying of lottery tickets from one State to another, at least by corporations or companies whose business it is, for hire, to carry tangible property from one State to another. . . .

We are of opinion that lottery tickets are subjects of traffic and therefore are subjects of commerce, and the regulation of the carriage of such tickets from State to State, at least by independent carriers, is a regulation of commerce among the several States. . . .

It is to be remarked that the Constitution does not define what is to be deemed a legitimate regulation of interstate commerce. In *Gibbons* v. *Ogden* it was said that the power to regulate such commerce is the power to prescribe the rule by which it is to be governed. But this general observation leaves it to be determined, when the question comes before the court, whether Congress in prescribing a particular rule has exceeded its power under the Constitution. While our Government must be acknowledged by all to be one of enumerated powers, the Constitution does not attempt to set forth all the means by which such powers may be carried into execution. It leaves to Congress a large discretion as to the means that may be employed in executing a given power. . . .

If a State, when considering legislation for the suppression of lotteries within its own limits, may properly take into view the evils that inhere in the raising of money, in that mode, why may not Congress, invested with the power to regulate commerce among the several States, provide that such commerce shall not be polluted by the carrying of lottery tickets from one State to another? In this connection it must not be forgotten that the power of Congress to regulate commerce among the States is plenary, is complete in itself, and is subject to no limitations except such as may be found in the Constitution. What provision in that instrument can be regarded as limiting the exercise of the power granted? What clause can be cited which, in any degree, countenances the suggestion that one may, of right, carry or cause to be carried from one State to another that which will harm the public morals? We cannot think of any clause of that instrument that could possibly be invoked by those who assert their right to send lottery tickets from State to State except the one providing that no person shall be deprived of his liberty without the due process of law. We have said that the liberty protected by the Constitution embraces the right to be free in the enjoyment of one's faculties; "to be free to use them in all lawful ways; to live and work where he will; to earn his livelihood by any lawful calling; to pursue any livelihood or avocation, and for that purpose to enter into all contracts that may be proper." But surely it will not be said to be a part of any one's liberty, as recognized by the supreme law of the land, that he shall be allowed to introduce into commerce among the States an element that will be confessedly injurious to the public morals. . . .

Besides, Congress, by that act, does not assume to interfere with traffic or commerce in lottery tickets carried on exclusively within the limits of any State, but has in view only commerce of that kind among the several States. It has not assumed to interfere with the completely internal affairs of any State, and has only legislated in respect of a matter which concerns the people of the United States. As a State may, for the purpose of guarding the morals of its own people, forbid all sales of lottery tickets within its limits, so Congress, for the purpose of guarding the people of the United States against the "widespread pestilence of lotteries" and to protect the commerce which concerns all the States, may prohibit the carrying of lottery tickets from one State to another. . . .

The whole subject is too important, and the questions suggested by its consideration are too difficult of solution to justify any attempt to lay down a rule for determining in advance the validity of every statute that may be enacted under the commerce clause. We decide nothing more in the present case than that lottery tickets are subjects of traffic among those who choose to sell or buy them; that the carriage of such tickets by independent carriers from one State to another is therefore interstate commerce; that under its power to regulate commerce among the several States Congress—subject to the limitations imposed by the Constitution upon the exercise of the powers granted—has plenary authority over such commerce, and may prohibit the carriage of such tickets from State to State; and that legislation to that end, and of that character, is not inconsistent with any limitation or restriction imposed upon the exercise of the powers granted to Congress.

The judgment is

Affirmed.

Mr. Chief Justice Fuller . . . dissenting.

The naked question is whether the prohibition by Congress of the carriage of lottery tickets from one State to another by means other than the mails is within the powers vested in that body by the Constitution of the United States. That the purpose of Congress in this enactment was the suppression of lotteries cannot reasonably be denied. That purpose is avowed in the title of the act, and is its natural and reasonable effect, and by that its validity must be tested.

The power of the State to impose restraints and burdens on persons and property in conservation and promotion of the public health, good order and prosperity is a power originally and always belonging to the States, not surrendered by them to the General Government nor directly restrained by the Constitution of the United States, and essentially exclusive, and the suppression of lotteries as a harmful business falls within this power, commonly called of police.

It is urged, however, that because Congress is empowered to regulate commerce between the several States, it, therefore, may suppress lotteries by prohibiting the carriage of lottery matter. Congress may indeed make all laws necessary and proper for carrying the powers granted to it into execution, and doubtless an act prohibiting the carriage of lottery matter would be necessary and proper to the execution of a power to suppress lotteries; but that power belongs to the States and not to Congress. To hold that Congress has general police power would be to hold that it may accomplish objects not entrusted to the General Government, and to defeat the operation of the Tenth Amendment, declaring that: ''The powers not delegated to the United States by Constitution, nor prohibited by it to the States, are reserved to the States respectively, or to the people.''

The *Champion* case set the precedent that Congress may indeed use the Commerce Clause in much the same manner as states use their police powers. In the years following *Champion,* the legislature passed a number of laws designed to accomplish social, not economic, goals through the exercise of the commerce power. For example, in 1906 Congress approved the Meat Inspection Act and the Pure Food and Drug Act, which prohibited contaminated foods from interstate commerce. Five years later the Supreme Court upheld the food and drug act as a proper exercise of the commerce power.[19] In 1910, as a method of curtailing interstate prostitution rings, Congress passed the Mann Act, making it a criminal violation to take a female across state lines for immoral purposes. The Supreme Court unanimously ruled that the federal government has the authority under the Commerce Clause to prohibit such movement among the states.[20] In addition, Congress passed various criminal laws that federalized criminal activity that extends beyond the boundaries of a single state. Kidnapping that crosses state lines, interstate transportation of stolen property, or even interstate flight to avoid prosecution are all federal crimes because of

19. See *Hipolite Egg Company v. United States,* 220 U.S. 45 (1911).

20. *Hoke v. United States,* 227 U.S. 308 (1913)

Congress's power to regulate commerce among the states.

The most significant blow to the development of this police power was the Court's 1918 decision in *Hammer v. Dagenhart,* discussed in Chapter 5. The Court struck down the Keating-Owen Act of 1916, which barred from interstate commerce any goods produced by child labor. In the Court's thinking at that time, the manufacture of goods was intrastate commerce and therefore to be regulated only by the states. The justices saw the law as a regulation of the manufacturing stage rather than a regulation of interstate commerce. The decision was not so much a rejection of the power of Congress to regulate social matters as it was a reminder that the social problems must be a part of interstate commerce before Congress can use the Commerce Clause to justify action against them.

Modern Uses of the Commerce Power to Regulate Social Evils

With each expansion of the definition of interstate commerce that occurred after 1936, there was a commensurate expansion of the federal police powers. These changes gave Congress sufficient power to combat social problems that it otherwise would be unable to fight effectively. Modern civil rights laws provide a good example. The constitutional protections against discrimination are found primarily in the Equal Protection Clause of the Fourteenth Amendment and the Due Process Clause of the Fifth, which have erected powerful barriers against invidious discrimination. But their exclusive target is discrimination perpetuated by the government. The words of the Fourteenth Amendment are clear: "Nor shall any state . . . deny to any person within its jurisdiction the equal protection of the laws." Nothing in the Fifth or Fourteenth Amendments prohibits discrimination by private parties. They were not intended to prohibit a private citizen from being

discriminatory, but only to bar discriminatory government action. Although the Fourteenth Amendment includes a clause giving Congress the authority to enforce the provision with appropriate legislation, the Supreme Court has ruled that such enforcement legislation may not extend beyond the scope of the amendment itself. Consequently, the amendment does not empower Congress to regulate private discriminatory behavior.

When the civil rights movement of the 1950s and 1960s campaigned for the elimination of discriminatory conditions, high on its list was the eradication of discrimination by private parties who operated public accommodations. Targeted were the owners of hotels, restaurants, movies, theaters, recreation areas, and transportation systems. In the aftermath of *Brown v. Board of Education* (1954), governments could not maintain laws mandating segregation of such facilities, but private operators could still impose discrimination on their own. In the South, where segregation was the way of life, no one expected the states to pass civil rights statutes prohibiting private parties from discriminating. Therefore, civil rights advocates pressured Congress to do something about the situation.

Congress responded with passage of the Civil Rights Act of 1964, the most comprehensive legislation of its type ever passed. The act, as amended, is still the nation's most significant statute aimed at eliminating discrimination. However, the primary authority for passing this ground-breaking legislation was not a clause in the Bill of Rights or one of the Civil War amendments, but the Commerce Clause. Because the Court had treated Commerce Clause legislation favorably since 1937, members of Congress had confidence that the Civil Rights Act would withstand a legal challenge. Opponents of the legislation, however, argued that Congress had misused its power to regulate commerce by invoking it as justifying a civil rights law. Obviously, they said, the Framers, many of whom owned slaves, did not intend the power to regulate commerce among the states to be used to enact civil rights legislation.

Was Congress on solid grounds in doing so? The primary test of the law's constitutionality was *Heart of Atlanta Motel v. United States* (1964).

As you read this case, note Justice Tom C. Clark's description of how racial discrimination has a negative impact on interstate commerce. Also note the Court's expansive view of interstate commerce and its conclusion that the Commerce Clause can be used to combat moral wrongs.

Heart of Atlanta Motel v. United States

379 U.S. 241 (1964)

Vote: 9 (Black, Brennan, Clark, Douglas, Goldberg, Harlan, Stewart, Warren, White)

0

Opinion of the Court: Clark
Concurring opinions: Black, Douglas, Goldberg

Title II of the 1964 Civil Rights Act in its original form prohibited discrimination on the basis of race, color, religion, or national origin by certain public accommodations that operated in or affected interstate commerce. The accommodations specifically included were:

1. Inns, hotels, motels, or other lodging facilities of five rooms or more. Because they served the traveling public, these facilities were considered part of interstate commerce by definition.

2. Restaurants and cafeterias, if they served interstate travelers or if a substantial portion of their food or other products had moved in interstate commerce.

3. Motion picture houses, if they presented films that had moved in interstate commerce.

4. Any facility physically located within any of the other covered accommodations, which included operations such as hotel shops and theater snack bars.

The Heart of Atlanta Motel was a 216-room facility in Atlanta, Georgia. Located near the commercial center of the city, it had easy access to two interstate highways and two major state roads. The motel advertised for business in national publications and maintained more than

fifty billboards and highway signs around the state. Both the government and the motel agreed that the facility met the act's definition of a public accommodation in interstate commerce.

The motel admitted that prior to the enactment of the civil rights law it practiced a policy of racial discrimination. Furthermore, it acknowledged that it intended to continue its policy of not serving blacks. To secure its right to do so, the motel filed suit to have the 1964 Civil Rights Act declared unconstitutional.

Justice Clark delivered the opinion of the Court:

The Basis of Congressional Action.

While the Act as adopted carried no congressional findings the record of its passage through each house is replete with evidence of the burdens that discrimination by race or color places upon interstate commerce. This testimony included that fact that our people have become increasingly mobile with millions of people of all races traveling from State to State; that Negroes in particular have been the subject of discrimination in transient accommodations, having to travel great distances to secure the same; that often they have been unable to obtain accommodations and have had to call upon friends to put them up overnight; and that these conditions had become so acute as to require the listing of available lodging for Negroes in a special guidebook which was itself "dramatic testimony to the difficulties" Negroes encounter in travel. These exclusionary practices were found to be nationwide, the Under Secretary of Commerce testifying that there is "no question that this discrimination in the North still exists to a large degree" and in the West and Midwest as well. This testimony indicated a qualitative as well as a quantitative effect on interstate travel by Negroes. The former was the obvious impairment of the Negro traveler's pleasure and convenience that resulted when he continually was uncertain of finding lodging. As for the latter, there was evidence that this uncertainty stemming from racial discrimination had the effect of discouraging travel on the part of a substantial portion of the Negro community. This was the conclusion not only of the Under Secretary of Commerce but also of the Administrator of the Federal Aviation Agency who wrote the Chairman of the Senate Commerce Committee that it was his "belief that air commerce is adversely affected by the denial to a substantial segment of the traveling public of adequate and desegregated public accommodations." We shall not burden this opinion with further details since the voluminous testimony presents overwhelming evidence that discrimination by hotels and motels impedes interstate travel.

The Power of Congress Over Interstate Travel.

The power of Congress to deal with these obstructions depends on the meaning of the Commerce Clause. Its meaning was first enunciated 140 years ago by the great Chief Justice John Marshall in *Gibbons* v. *Ogden* (1824), in these words:

"The subject to be regulated is commerce; and . . . to ascertain the extent of the power, it becomes necessary to settle the meaning of the word. The counsel for the appellee would limit it to traffic, to buying and selling, or the interchange of commodities . . . but it is something more: it is intercourse . . . between nations, and parts of nations, in all its branches, and is regulated by prescribing rules for carrying on that intercourse.

"To what commerce does this power extend? The constitution informs us, to commerce 'with foreign nations and among the several States, and with the Indian tribes.'

"It has, we believe, been universally admitted, that these words comprehend every species of commercial intercourse. . . . No sort of trade can be carried on . . . to which this power does not extend.

"The subject to which the power is next applied, is to commerce 'among the several States.' The word 'among' means intermingled." . . .

In short, the determinative test of the exercise of power by the Congress under the Commerce Clause is simply whether the activity sought to be regulated is "commerce which concerns more States than one" and has a real and substantial relation to the national interest. Let us now turn to this facet of the problem.

That the "intercourse" of which the Chief Justice spoke included the movement of persons through more States than one was settled as early as 1849, in the *Passenger Cases,* where Mr. Justice McLean stated: "That the transportation of passengers is a part of commerce is not now an open question." Again in 1913 Mr. Justice McKenna, speaking for the Court, said: "Commerce among the States, we have said, consists of intercourse and traffic between their citizens, and includes the transportation of persons and property. . . . Nor does it make any difference whether the transportation is commercial in character." . . .

The same interest in protecting interstate commerce which led Congress to deal with segregation in interstate carriers and the white-slave traffic has prompted it to extend the exercise of its power to gambling; to criminal enterprises; to deceptive practices in the sale of products; to fraudulent security transactions; to misbranding of drugs; to wages and hours; to members of labor unions; to crop control; to discrimination against shippers; to the protection of small business from injurious price cutting; to resale price maintenance; to professional football; and to racial discrimination by owners and managers of terminal restaurants.

That Congress was legislating against moral wrongs in many of these areas rendered its enactments no less valid. In framing Title II of this Act Congress was also dealing with what it considered a moral problem. But that fact does not detract from the overwhelming evidence of the disruptive effect that racial discrimination has had on commercial intercourse. It was this burden which empowered Congress to enact appropriate legislation, and, given this basis for the exercise of its power, Congress was not restricted by the fact that the particular obstruction to interstate commerce with which it was dealing was also deemed a moral and social wrong.

It is said that the operation of the motel here is of a purely local character. But . . . the power of Congress to promote interstate commerce also includes the power to regulate the local incidents thereof, including local activities in both the States of origin and destination, which might have a substantial and harmful effect upon that commerce. One need only examine the evidence which we have discussed above to see that Congress may—as it has—prohibit racial discrimination by motels serving travelers, however ''local'' their operations may appear. . . .

We, therefore, conclude that the action of the Congress in the adoption of the Act as applied here to a motel which concededly serves interstate travelers is within the power granted it by the Commerce Clause of the Constitution, as interpreted by this Court for 140 years. It may be argued that Congress could have pursued other methods to eliminate the obstructions it found in interstate commerce caused by racial discrimination. But this is a matter of policy that rests entirely with the Congress not with the courts. How obstructions in commerce may be removed—what means are to be employed—is within the sound and exclusive discretion of the Congress. It is subject only to one caveat—that the means chosen by it must be reasonably adapted to the end permitted by the Constitution. We cannot say that its choice here was not so adapted. The Constitution requires no more.

Affirmed.

Employing the same sweeping language as the Court used in *Wickard v. Filburn* to declare wheat grown for home consumption to be in interstate commerce, Justice Clark's opinion gives Congress broad powers to use the Commerce Clause as authority to regulate moral wrongs that occur in interstate commerce. In this way, the Commerce Clause became one of the most powerful weapons in the federal government's arsenal not only to regulate the economy but also to use as a police power.

The Commerce Power of the States

Resolving the question of federal power over interstate and foreign commerce leaves unsettled the question of state commercial regulation. Marshall wrote in *Gibbons* that the ''completely internal commerce'' of a state was reserved for state regulation. This grant of power was substantial prior to the Civil War when most commercial activity was distinctly local and subject to state regulation. But with the industrial revolution and improved transportation systems, business became increasingly interstate in nature. Finally, the Supreme Court's 1937 redefinition of interstate commerce left little that met Marshall's notion of commerce that is ''completely internal.''

If the regulation of any business activity that affects interstate commerce were the exclusive preserve of the federal government, the role of the states would be minimal indeed. But this is not the case. The decisions of the Supreme Court have left a substantial sphere of authority for the states to regulate commerce. The dividing line between federal and state power, however, has varied over time as the Supreme Court has struggled in building an appropriate doctrine to govern this difficult area of federal-state relations.

The Doctrine of Selected Exclusiveness

Constructing the parameters of state power began in 1829 in the decision of *Willson v. BlackBird Creek Marsh Company*.[21] The dispute involved a Delaware law that authorized the building of a dam on a creek to stop water from entering a local marsh. Thompson Willson owned and operated a vessel that was federally licensed under the Coastal Licensing Act of 1793, the same legislation under which Thomas Gibbons had operated his steamboats. Willson objected to the dam as an impediment to commerce on a naviga-

---

21. Disputes over the power of the states to impose taxes on interstate and foreign commerce actually began two years earlier in *Brown v. Maryland*, 12 Wheat. 419 (1827). The taxation issues will be discussed in the next chapter where the fiscal authority to tax and spend is our focus.

ble stream. His ship purposefully rammed the dam causing it considerable damage. The company that owned the dam took legal action against Willson, and the state courts ruled in favor of the company. Willson appealed, claiming that the Delaware law authorizing the dam was in conflict with the federal Constitution. He argued that only Congress had the power to pass a law permitting the construction of an impediment to commerce on a navigable stream.

Chief Justice Marshall, speaking for the Court, rejected Willson's position. The justices concluded that, in the absence of federal laws to the contrary, the police powers of the state to regulate for the health and general welfare of its citizens were sufficient to authorize the construction of the dam. Indeed, Congress had not enacted any legislation dealing with commercial streams and the problems associated with marshland. "If congress had passed any act . . . the object of which was to control state legislation over those small navigable creeks into which the tide flows," Marshall's opinion stated, "we should feel not much difficulty in saying that a state law coming in conflict with such act would be void." The Court's decision in *Willson* began to carve out an area of state authority over commerce that is not purely intrastate, but the boundaries of that authority were not yet well developed.

With Marshall's death in 1835, his successor, Chief Justice Roger Taney, was left with the task of more sharply defining the commerce powers of the states. Taney was far more sympathetic to the states than was Marshall, and it is not surprising that the rulings of the Taney era strike a balance between federal and state authority. The Taney Court first grappled with the problem in *Mayor of New York v. Miln* (1837), a case that had been carried over from the last Marshall term. The dispute arose over the validity of New York's Passenger Act of 1824, which was designed to curb the flow of foreign indigents into the state.

The law required the masters of incoming ships to supply the mayor of New York with comprehensive information on all passengers. This material was necessary for the city to enforce a regulation that allowed it to keep out people likely to require public assistance. Ship captains who did not comply were liable for fines and penalties of $75 per passenger. In addition, the law required that passengers refused entry be returned to their point of origin at the shipowner's expense. George Miln, who had a financial interest in a ship called *The Emily,* was fined when the ship's master refused to comply with the law. Miln protested the stiff $7,500 penalty on the grounds that regulating foreign commerce was the exclusive jurisdiction of Congress, leaving no room for state action.

The Supreme Court upheld the New York law. In doing so, the justices did everything possible to avoid the complicated commerce issues the case presented. Instead, the Court followed the lead taken by Marshall in *Willson* and focused on the state's police powers. According to Philip Barbour's majority opinion, the states have the sovereign power to regulate for the well-being of their residents. That power is complete and unqualified. In the absence of federal commercial legislation to the contrary, there is nothing to bar the state from using its police authority, even if it affects foreign commerce as in the matter here. In fact, Barbour argued that it was the obligation of the state to protect its citizens from the financial obligations inevitably resulting from admitting "multitudes of poor persons, who come from foreign countries without possessing the means of supporting themselves." As a consequence, a state may use its police powers to ward off the "moral pestilence of paupers, vagabonds, and possibly convicts."

While the Court has long since abandoned this attitude toward the poor, the *Miln* decision revealed the Taney Court's readiness to support state regulations in the absence of federal action.[22] This thinking was consistent with the dual-federalism philosophy of that day (see Chapter 5). But, because the Court relied so heavily on the police powers, it failed to develop a complete doctrine of state commercial authority.

The License Cases of 1847 further revealed the difficulty the Taney Court had in crafting an adequate policy for the commerce powers of the states. These appeals came from New Hampshire, Rhode Island, and Massachusetts where the legislatures had passed statutes licensing and taxing alcoholic beverages.[23] The regulations applied to domestic liquors as well as imported alcoholic beverages. Once again the Supreme Court upheld the laws as exercises of state police power, but the Court was badly divided as to rationale. No majority opinion was reached, an unusual occurrence for that time. In fact, six justices wrote opinions. All supported the state laws, but the highly fractionalized opinions provided no authoritative guidance for the states.

Two years later the Court heard arguments in Smith v. Turner and Norris v. Boston, which are known as the Passenger Cases (1849). These appeals tested the constitutionality of laws passed by New York and Massachusetts to regulate foreigners coming into the United States. The legislation was intended to discourage indigent immigrants and to provide for the treatment of individuals who arrived for entry in a diseased condition. The laws included provisions for taxes, bonding, and record keeping. The New York law taxed each incoming ship $1.00-$1.50 per passenger. These fees were used to fund a hospital to treat arriving immigrants. The Massachusetts law prohibited the importation of passengers who were indigent or had physical or mental disabilities. In addition, Massachusetts charged arriving ships $2.00 for each passenger, with the proceeds going to a fund for immigrants who later required public assistance. George Smith and James Norris were British shipmasters. Smith landed in New York City with 290 immigrant passengers, and Norris docked in Boston with 19. Both protested the constitutionality of the taxes on Commerce Clause grounds.

The justices found these cases hard to resolve. In fact, they were argued three times, and still the justices had difficulty reaching a majority decision. Finally, by a 5-4 vote, the Court struck down the laws as being in conflict with the authority of Congress to regulate foreign commerce. The five justices in the majority each wrote separate opinions. The four dissenters, led by Taney, adhered to the view that such regulations to protect a state's citizens from indigent and ill immigrants were within the states' police powers.

The Passenger Cases left the law unsettled. Not only was the decision in conflict with previous rulings, but also the Court had failed to produce an opinion supported by a majority of the justices. This situation demanded a ruling that would authoritatively explain the constitutional division between federal and state commerce powers, but instead many questions remained unanswered. Did Congress have the exclusive power to regulate interstate and foreign commerce, leaving no authority for the states? Could the states regulate such commerce only if Congress had failed to enact any relevant legislation? Was the commerce power concurrent? Could Congress delegate its regulatory power to the states? Three years after the Passenger Cases, in Cooley v. Board of Wardens (1852), the justices issued a ruling resolving some of the confusion.

22. Edwards v. California, 314 U.S. 160 (1941) effectively overruled Miln. In Edwards the justices struck down an "anti-Okie" law passed to discourage large numbers of people from Oklahoma and neighboring states from moving into California. The Oklahomans were trying to escape the economic depression caused by the dust-bowl conditions in the central states. The Court found the law violated the right of citizens to travel freely among the various states.

23. Peirce v. New Hampshire, Fletcher v. Rhode Island, and Thurlow v. Massachusetts (The License Cases), 5 How. 504 (1847).

Cooley v. Board of Wardens

12 How. 299 (1852)

Vote: 7 (Catron, Curtis, Daniel, Grier, McKinley,
    Nelson, Taney)
  2 (McLean, Wayne)
Opinion of the Court: Curtis
Concurring opinion: Daniel
Dissenting opinion: McLean

Based on its power over interstate and foreign commerce, Congress passed a statute in 1789 pertaining to the regulation of ports. The legislation said that until Congress acted otherwise, state and local authorities would continue to control the nation's ports and harbors. In 1803 Pennsylvania passed a port regulation law requiring that all vessels hire a local pilot to guide ships in and out of the Port of Philadelphia. Ship owners who did not comply were fined. The money from these fines was placed in a "charitable fund for the distressed or decayed pilots, their widows and children."

Aaron Cooley owned a vessel that sailed into Philadelphia without hiring a local pilot. The port's Board of Wardens took legal action against him, and Cooley was fined. He responded by claiming that the Pennsylvania law was unconstitutional; only Congress, he asserted, could regulate the port because the harbor was an integral part of interstate and foreign commerce, and the states had no constitutional authority to set regulations for such commerce. By implication, Cooley also was challenging the 1789 act of Congress that had delegated such powers to the states. The Pennsylvania Supreme Court upheld the law and the fine, and Cooley pressed his case to the U.S. Supreme Court.

Justice Benjamin R. Curtis delivered the opinion of the Court:

That the power to regulate commerce includes the regulation of navigation, we consider settled. And when we look to the nature of the service performed by pilots, to the relations which that service and its compensations bear to navigation between the several States, and between the ports of the United States and foreign countries, we are brought to the conclusion, that the regulation of the qualifications of pilots, of the modes and times of offering and rendering their services, of the responsibilities which shall rest upon them, of the powers they shall possess, of the compensation they may demand, and of the penalties by which their rights and duties may be enforced, do constitute regulations of navigation, and consequently of commerce, within the just meaning of this clause of the Constitution. . . .

Nor should it be lost sight of, that this subject of the regulation of pilots and pilotage has an intimate connection with, and an important relation to the general subject of commerce with foreign nations and among the several States, over which it was one main object of the Constitution to create a national control. Conflicts between the laws of neighboring States, and discriminations favorable or adverse to commerce with particular foreign nations, might be created by State laws regulating pilotage, deeply affecting that equality of commercial rights, and that freedom from State interference, which those who formed the Constitution were so anxious to secure, and which the experience of more than half a century has taught us to value so highly. . . .

It becomes necessary, therefore, to consider whether this law of Pennsylvania, being a regulation of commerce, is valid.

The act of Congress of the 7th of August, 1789, sect. 4, is as follows:

"That all pilots in the bays, inlets, rivers, harbors, and ports of the United States shall continue to be regulated in conformity with the existing laws of the States, respectively, wherein such pilots may be, or with such laws as the States may respectively hereafter enact for the purpose, until further legislative provision shall be made by Congress."

If the law of Pennsylvania, now in question, had been in existence at the date of this act of Congress, we might hold it to have been adopted by Congress, and thus made a law of the United States, and so valid. Because this act does, in effect, give the force of an act of Congress, to the then existing State laws on this subject, so long as they should continue unrepealed by the State which enacted them.

But the law on which these actions are founded was not enacted till 1803. What effect then can be attributed to so much of the act of 1789, as declares, that pilots shall continue to be regulated in conformity, "with such laws as the States may respectively hereafter enact for the purpose, until further legislative provision shall be made by Congress"?

If the States were divested of the power to legislate on this subject by the grant of the commercial power to Congress, it is plain this act could not confer upon them power thus to legislate. If the Constitution excluded the States from making any law regulating commerce, certainly Congress cannot regrant, or in any manner reconvey to the States that power. And yet this act of 1789 gives its sanction only to laws enacted by the States. This necessarily implies a constitutional power to legislate; for only a rule created by the sovereign power of a State acting in its legislative capacity, can be deemed a law, enacted by a State; and if the State has so limited its sovereign power that it no longer extends to a particular subject, manifestly it cannot, in any proper sense, be said to enact laws thereon. Entertaining these views we are brought directly and unavoidably to the consideration of the question, whether the grant of the commercial power to Congress, did *per se* deprive the States of all power to regulate pilots. This question has never been decided by this court, nor, in our judgment, has any case depending upon all the considerations which must govern this one, come before this court. The grant of commercial power to Congress does not contain any terms which expressly exclude the States from exercising an authority over its subject-matter. If they are excluded it must be because of the nature of the power, thus granted to Congress, requires that a similar authority should not exist in the States. If it were conceded on the one side, that the nature of this power, like that to legislate for the District of Columbia, is absolutely and totally repugnant to the existence of similar power in the States, probably no one would deny that the grant of the power to Congress, as effectually and perfectly excludes the States from all future legislation on the subject, as if express words had been used to exclude them. And on the other hand,

if it were admitted that the existence of this power in Congress, like the power of taxation, is compatible with the existence of a similar power in the States, then it would be in conformity with the contemporary exposition of the Constitution, (Federalist, No. 32,) and with the judicial construction, given from time to time by this court, after the most deliberate consideration, to hold that the mere grant of such a power to Congress, did not imply a prohibition on the States to exercise the same power; that it is not the mere existence of such a power, but its exercise by Congress, which may be incompatible with the exercise of the same power by the States, and that the States may legislate in the absence of congressional regulations.

The diversities of opinion, therefore, which have existed on this subject, have arisen from the different views taken of the nature of this power. But when the nature of a power like this is spoken of, when it is said that the nature of the power requires that it should be exercised exclusively by Congress, it must be intended to refer to the subjects of that power, and to say they are of such a nature as to require exclusive legislation by Congress. Now the power to regulate commerce, embraces a vast field, containing not only many, but exceedingly various subjects, quite unlike in their nature; some imperatively demanding a single uniform rule, operating equally on the commerce of the United States in every port; and some, like the subject now in question, as imperatively demanding that diversity, which alone can meet the local necessities of navigation.

Either absolutely to affirm, or deny that the nature of this power requires exclusive legislation by Congress, is to lose sight of the nature of the subjects of this power, and to assert concerning all of them, what is really applicable but to a part. Whatever subjects of this power are in their nature national, or admit only of one uniform system, or plan of regulation, may justly be said to be of such a nature as to require exclusive legislation by Congress. That this cannot be affirmed of laws for the regulation of pilots and pilotage is plain. The act of 1789 contains a clear and authoritative declaration by the first Congress, that the nature of this subject is such, that until Congress should find it necessary to exert its power, it should be left to the legislation of the States; that it is local and not national;

that it is likely to be the best provided for, not by one system, or plan of regulations, but by as many as the legislative discretion of the several States should deem applicable to the local peculiarities of the ports within their limits.

Viewed in this light, so much of this act of 1789 as declares that pilots shall continue to be regulated "by such laws as the States may respectively hereafter enact for that purpose," instead of being held to be inoperative, as an attempt to confer on the States a power to legislate, of which the Constitution had deprived them, is allowed an appropriate and important signification. It manifests the understanding of Congress, at the outset of the government, that the nature of this subject is not such as to require its exclusive legislation. The practice of the States, and of the national government, has been in conformity with this declaration, from the origin of the national government to this time; and the nature of the subject when examined, is such as to leave no doubt of the superior fitness and propriety, not to say the absolute necessity, of different systems of regulation, drawn from local knowledge and experience, and conformed to local wants. How then can we say, that by the mere grant of power to regulate commerce, the States are deprived of all the power to legislate on this subject, because from the nature of the power the legislation of Congress must be exclusive. . . .

It is the opinion of a majority of the court that the mere grant to Congress of the power to regulate commerce, did not deprive the States of power to regulate pilots, and that although Congress has legislated on this subject, its legislation manifests an intention, with a single exception, not to regulate this subject, but to leave its regulation to the several States. To these precise questions, which are all we are called on to decide, this opinion must be understood to be confined. It does not extend to the question what other subjects, under the commercial power, are within the exclusive control of Congress, or may be regulated by the States in the absence of all congressional legislation; nor to the general question how far any regulation of a subject by Congress, may be deemed to operate as an exclusion of all legislation by the States upon the same subject. We decide the precise questions before us, upon what we deem sound principles, applicable to this particular subject in the state in which the legislation of Congress has left it. We go no further. . . .

We are of opinion that this State law was enacted by virtue of a power, residing in the State to legislate; that it is not in conflict with any law of Congress; that it does not interfere with any system which Congress has established by making regulations, or by intentionally leaving individuals to their own unrestricted action; that this law is therefore valid, and the judgment of the Supreme Court of Pennsylvania in each case must be affirmed.

Justice Curtis's opinion in *Cooley* nicely outlines the basic constitutional principles governing the state's power to regulate commerce. From this decision and those that preceded it, we can begin to build some understanding of how far the states may go in regulating commercial enterprise:

1. The states retain the power to regulate purely intrastate commerce.

2. Congress has the power to regulate interstate and foreign commerce. When it exercises this power any contrary state laws are preempted.

3. The power of Congress to regulate interstate and foreign commerce is exclusive over those elements of commercial activity that are national in scope or require uniform regulation.

4. Those elements of interstate and foreign commerce that are not national in scope or do not require uniformity, and which have not been regulated by Congress, may be subject to state authority including the state's police powers.

This division of authority is known as the doctrine of selected exclusiveness. It designates certain aspects of interstate and foreign commerce over which the powers of Congress are exclusive, allowing no state action. This exclusiveness, however, is not complete; in the absence of federal legislation, states may regulate some business activity affecting interstate commerce. The regulation of the Philadelphia port is an obvious part of interstate and foreign commerce where local harbor conditions require state supervision.

State Burdens on Interstate Commerce

The problem with the selected exclusiveness approach is that it leaves a great deal to interpretation. Those aspects of interstate commerce that require uniformity are not clear, nor are the essentially local aspects of interstate commerce. These and other issues of similar importance have been left to the judiciary to settle, a formidable task given the complexity of the nation's economy. The basic principles articulated in *Cooley* often cannot be neatly applied to contemporary conditions.

Among the essentially local aspects of interstate commerce are matters of public safety. Interstate trucking provides a good illustration. The use of trucks for the transportation of goods is an integral part of interstate commerce, but trucks use local roads that are the state's concern. One of the primary elements of a state's police powers is regulation to ensure the safety of its citizens- Safety regulations may impose a burden on interstate commerce.

The Supreme Court addressed this conflict in 1938 in *South Carolina State Highway Department v. Barnwell Brothers*. For purposes of public safety and to prevent damage to its highways, the South Carolina legislature passed a statute prohibiting certain trucks from using its highways. No truck with a gross weight in excess of 20,000 pounds or a width greater than ninety inches was permitted. The Barnwell Brothers Trucking Company challenged the regulation as an unreasonable burden on interstate commerce. Evidence presented at trial showed that between 85 percent and 90 percent of all interstate trucks were ninety-six inches wide and heavier than the 20,000 pound limit. Only four other states had weight limits as low as that imposed by South Carolina, and none had width restrictions as severe. Based on this information, the trial court ruled that South Carolina's law was an unconstitutional burden on the flow of interstate commerce.

The Supreme Court reversed. Justice Harlan F. Stone's opinion for the Court stressed that there were some state regulations affecting interstate commerce that were clearly unconstitutional. For example, states are prohibited from giving a preference to intrastate businesses at the expense of interstate commerce or placing unreasonable burdens on out-of-state businesses. However, ''there are matters of local concern, the regulation of which unavoidably involves some regulation of interstate commerce but which, because of their local character and their number and diversity, may never be fully dealt with by Congress.'' The regulation of such matters, in the absence of federal legislation, is left to the states. Congress has recognized this situation by not regulating parts of commerce such as the use of highways, ports, harbors, rivers, and docks. Congress also has not prohibited certain quarantine laws imposed by the states. Naturally, Congress may act in any of these areas when it determines that uniform national legislation is required. The justices, in a 7-0 decision, held that South Carolina's regulation of trucks using the state highways fell into this category. Because of an absence of federal legislation over highway safety and because the state regulations applied to vehicles in intra- and interstate commerce equally, the state law was not in violation of the Constitution.

Still, *Barnwell Brothers* left a number of issues unresolved. How far may a state go in regulating interstate commerce for safety purposes? How much of a burden may be imposed on the free flow of commerce among the states to achieve greater safety? Were the highways, which were built, owned, and maintained by the states, a special case, or did state authority similarly extend to other areas of interstate commerce? The justices took a second look at these issues in *Southern Pacific Co. v. Arizona* (1945). Once again Stone wrote the opinion for the Court, but this time the outcome was different. Was *Southern Pacific* consistent with *Barnwell Brothers,* or did the Court modify its position?

Southern Pacific Company v. Arizona

325 U.S. 761 (1945)

Vote: 7 (Frankfurter, Jackson, Murphy, Reed, Roberts, Rutledge, Stone)
2 (Black, Douglas)
Opinion for the Court: Stone
Dissenting opinions: Black, Douglas

On May 16, 1912, the Arizona legislature passed the Train Limit Law, making it unlawful for any individual or corporation to operate a train with more than fourteen passenger cars or seventy freight cars within the state. Violators were subject to fines. In 1940 the state brought a legal action against the Southern Pacific Company, which acknowledged operating passenger and freight trains in excess of the state limits. The company argued that the state law was unconstitutional because it conflicted with the Commerce Clause.

The jury returned a verdict for the company, but the state supreme court reversed, holding that Arizona was free to enact such regulations because Congress had not legislated the length of railroad trains. The Arizona law was a safety measure; it could be justified as an exercise of the state's police powers to act in the interests of local health, safety, and well-being. The railroad appealed the ruling to the U.S. Supreme Court, arguing that the state law placed an undue burden on the flow of interstate commerce. In presenting its case, Southern Pacific enjoyed the support of some powerful allies: the U.S. government and the Association of American Railroads submitted amicus curiae briefs attacking the constitutionality of the state law.

Chief Justice Stone delivered the opinion of the Court:

Although the commerce clause conferred on the national government power to regulate commerce, its possession of the power does not exclude all state power of regulation. Ever since *Willson* v. *Black-Bird Creek Marsh Co.* and *Cooley* v. *Board of Wardens*, it has been recognized that, in the absence of conflicting legislation by Congress, there is a residuum of power in the state to make laws governing matters of local concern which nevertheless in some measure affect interstate commerce or even, to some extent, regulate it. Thus the states may regulate matters which, because of their number and diversity, may never be adequately dealt with by Congress. *Cooley* v. *Board of Wardens, South Carolina Highway Dept.* v. *Barnwell Bros.* When the regulation of matters of local concern is local in character and effect, and its impact on the national commerce does not seriously interfere with its operation, and the consequent incentive to deal with them nationally is slight, such regulation has been generally held to be within state authority.

But ever since *Gibbons* v. *Ogden,* the states have not been deemed to have authority to impede substantially the free flow of commerce from state to state, or to regulate those phases of the national commerce which, because of the need of national uniformity, demand that their regulation, if any, be prescribed by a single authority. Whether or not this long-recognized distribution of power between the national and the state governments is predicated upon the implications of the commerce clause itself, or upon the presumed intention of Congress, where Congress has not spoken, the result is the same.

In the application of these principles some enactments may be found to be plainly within and others plainly without state power. But between these extremes lies the infinite variety of cases, in which regulation of local matters may also operate as a regulation of commerce, in which reconciliation of the conflicting claims of state and national power is to be attained only by some appraisal and accommodation of the competing demands of the state and national interests involved.

For a hundred years it has been accepted constitutional doctrine that the commerce clause, without the aid of Congressional legislation, thus affords some protection from state legislation inimical to the national commerce and that in such cases, where Congress has not acted, this Court, and not the state legislature, is under the commerce clause the final arbiter of the competing demands of state and national interests.

Congress has undoubted power to redefine the distribution of power over interstate commerce. It may either permit the states to regulate the commerce in a manner which would otherwise not be permissible, or exclude state regulation even of matters of peculiarly local concern which nevertheless affect interstate commerce.

But in general Congress has left it to the courts to formulate the rules thus interpreting the commerce clause in its application, doubtless because it has appreciated the destructive consequences to the commerce of the nation if their protection were withdrawn, and has been aware that in their application state laws will not be invalidated without the support of relevant factual material which will "afford a sure basis" for an informed judgment. Meanwhile, Congress has accommodated its legislation, as have the states, to these rules as an established feature of our constitutional system. There has thus been left to the states wide scope for the regulation of matters of local state concern, even though it in some measure affects the commerce, provided it does not materially restrict the free flow of commerce across state lines, or interfere with it in matters with respect to which uniformity of regulation is of predominant national concern.

Hence the matters for ultimate determination here are the nature and extent of the burden which the state regulation of interstate trains, adopted as a safety measure, imposes on interstate commerce, and whether the relative weights of the state and national interests involved are such as to make inapplicable the

rule, generally observed, that the free flow of interstate commerce and its freedom from local restraints in matters requiring uniformity of regulation are interests safeguarded by the commerce clause from state interference. . . .

The findings show that the operation of long trains, that is trains of more than fourteen passenger and more than seventy freight cars, is standard practice over the main lines of the railroads of the United States, and that, if the length of trains is to be regulated at all, national uniformity in the regulation adopted, such as only Congress can prescribe, is practically indispensable to the operation of an efficient and economical national railway system. On many railroads passenger trains of more than fourteen cars and freight trains of more than seventy cars are operated, and on some systems freight trains are run ranging from one hundred and twenty-five to one hundred and sixty cars in length. Outside of Arizona, where the length of trains is not restricted, appellant runs a substantial proportion of long trains. In 1939 on its comparable route for through traffic through Utah and Nevada from 66 to 85% of its freight trains were over seventy cars in length and over 43% of its passenger trains included more than fourteen passenger cars.

In Arizona, approximately 93% of the freight traffic and 95% of the passenger traffic is interstate. Because of the Train Limit Law appellant is required to haul over 30% more trains in Arizona than would otherwise have been necessary. The record shows a definite relationship between operating costs and the length of trains, the increase in length resulting in a reduction of operating costs per car. The additional cost of operation of trains complying with the Train Limit Law in Arizona amounts for the two railroads traversing that state to about $1,000,000 a year. The reduction in train lengths also impedes efficient operation. More locomotives and more manpower are required; the necessary conversion and reconversion of train lengths at terminals and the delay caused by breaking up and remaking long trains upon entering and leaving the state in order to comply with the law, delays the traffic and diminishes its volume moved in a given time, especially when traffic is heavy. . . .

The unchallenged findings leave no doubt that the Arizona Train Limit Law imposes a serious burden on the interstate commerce conducted by appellant. It materially impedes the movement of appellant's interstate trains through that state and interposes a substantial obstruction to the national policy proclaimed by Congress, to promote adequate, economical and efficient railway transportation service. Enforcement of the law in Arizona, while train lengths remain unregulated or are regulated by varying standards in other states, must inevitably result in an impairment of uniformity of efficient railroad operation because the railroads are subjected to regulation which is not uniform in its application. Compliance with a state statute limiting train lengths requires interstate trains of a length lawful in other states to be broken up and reconstituted as they enter each state according as it may impose varying limitations upon train lengths. The alternative is for the carrier to conform to the lowest train limit restriction of any of the states through which its trains pass, whose laws thus control the carriers' operations both within and without the regulating state.

Although the seventy car maximum for freight trains is the limitation which has been commonly proposed, various bills introduced in the state legislatures provided for maximum freight train lengths of from fifty to one hundred and twenty-five cars, and maximum passenger train lengths of from ten to eighteen cars. With such laws in force in states which are interspersed with those having no limit on train lengths, the confusion and difficulty with which interstate operations would be burdened under the varied system of state regulation and the unsatisfied need for uniformity in such regulation, if any, are evident. . . .

We think, as the trial court found, that the Arizona Train Limit Law, viewed as a safety measure, affords at most slight and dubious advantage, if any, over unregulated train lengths, because it results in an increase in the number of trains and train operations and the consequent increase in train accidents of a character generally more severe than those due to slack action. Its undoubted effect on the commerce is the regulation, without securing uniformity, of the length of trains operated in interstate commerce, which lack is itself a primary cause of preventing the free flow of commerce by delaying it and by substantially increasing its cost and impairing its efficiency. In these respects the case differs from those where a state, by regulatory measures affecting the commerce, has removed or reduced safety hazards without substantial interference with the interstate movement of trains. Such are measures abolishing the car stove, requiring locomotives to be supplied with electric headlights, providing for full train crews, and for the equipment of freight trains with cabooses. . . .

Here we conclude that the state does go too far. Its regulation of train lengths, admittedly obstructive to interstate train operation, and having a seriously adverse effect on transportation efficiency and economy, passes beyond what is plainly essential for safety since it does not appear that it will lessen rather than increase the danger of accident. Its attempted regulation of the operation of interstate trains cannot establish nationwide control such as is essential to the maintenance of an efficient transportation system, which Congress alone can prescribe. The state interest cannot be preserved at the expense of the national interest by an enactment which regulates interstate train lengths without securing such control, which is a matter of national concern. To this the interest of the state here asserted is subordinate. . . .

Reversed.

Stone's opinion in *Southern Pacific* is a strong declaration of how state requirements affect the flow of interstate traffic and commerce. The Commerce Clause leaves no room for state legislation that is inimical to national commerce, even if the subject of that regulation has not been touched by federal legislation. A state law that obstructs interstate commerce, going beyond what is clearly necessary for safety regulation, cannot stand in the face of the Commerce Clause.

Discriminating Against Interstate Commerce

Even though the Court's decisions in *Barnwell Brothers* and *Southern Pacific* deal with transportation and distribution activities, the principles set down in those cases also apply to state regulations that place burdens on other aspects of interstate commerce, especially a state's attempt to protect local businesses by discriminating against interstate commerce. In *Hunt v. Washington State Apple Advertising Commission* the justices confronted a state regulation that restricted the kind of information that could be displayed on containers of out-of-state agricultural products. The state claimed that the rule was an exercise of the police powers to protect its citizens from fraud and deception. Does the state make a convincing case, or is the regulation nothing more than a way to prevent interstate commerce from having a negative impact on local producers?

Hunt v. Washington State Apple Advertising Commission

432 U.S. 333 (1977)

Vote: 8 (Blackmun, Brennan, Burger, Marshall, Powell, Stevens, Stewart, White)

o

Opinion of the Court: Burger
Not participating: Rehnquist

In 1972 the North Carolina Board of Agriculture adopted a regulation that required all closed containers of apples shipped into the state to display either the United States Department of Agriculture (USDA) grade or nothing at all. It barred information based on the grading systems of the states in which the apples were grown. The reason for the regulation, according to North Carolina, which has a significant apple industry, was to ensure that all apples coming into the state used the same grading system, thereby removing the danger that multiple systems would confuse purchasers and lead to deception and fraud in the market. No other state had such a regulation.

Through their industry advertising commission, the Washington State apple growers challenged the North Carolina regulations. Washington grows approximately 30 percent of the nation's apples and is responsible for roughly half of all apples shipped in interstate commerce. Because the industry is so important to that state, it has taken steps to enhance its reputation by imposing a strict mandatory inspection and grading system. Washington's standards are higher the USDA's, and the grading system has widespread acceptance in the apple trade.

The Washington commission asked North Carolina to alter its regulation or to allow certain exceptions. When North Carolina refused, the commission sued to have the regulation declared unconstitutional. It asserted that interstate commerce was being unreasonably burdened in three ways. First, the law clearly discriminated against interstate commerce in favor of local growers. Second, denying Washington growers the ability to use the widely accepted quality grading system diminished the marketing advantage the state's industry had earned. Third, the unique North Carolina regulation increased the cost of interstate commerce by requiring out-of-state growers to package their North Carolina bound products differently from those being sent to the other states. The federal trial court found that the regulation violated the Commerce Clause, and North Carolina governor James Hunt, on behalf of the state, appealed to the U.S. Supreme Court.

Chief Justice Warren Burger delivered the opinion of the Court:

We turn . . . to the appellant's claim that the District Court erred in holding that the North Carolina statute violated the Commerce Clause insofar as it prohibited the display of Washington State grades on closed containers of apples shipped into the State. Appellants do not really contest the District Court's determination that the challenged statute burdened the Washington apple industry by increasing its costs of doing business in the North Carolina market and causing it to lose accounts there. Rather, they maintain that any such burdens on the interstate sale of Washington apples were far outweighed by the local benefits flowing from what they contend was a valid exercise of North Carolina's inherent police powers designed to protect its citizenry from fraud and deception in the marketing of apples.

Prior to the statute's enactment, appellants point out, apples from 13 different States were shipped into North Carolina for sale. Seven of those States, including the State of Washington, had their own grading system which, while differing in their standards, used similar descriptive labels (*e.g.,* fancy, extra fancy, etc.). This multiplicity of inconsistent grades, as the District Court itself found, posed dangers of deception and confusion not only in the North Carolina market, but in the Nation as a whole. The North Carolina statute, appellants claim, was enacted to eliminate this source of deception and confusion by replacing the numerous state grades with a single uniform standard. Moreover, it is contended that North Carolina sought to accomplish this goal of uniformity in an evenhanded manner as evidenced by the fact that its statute applies to all apples sold in closed containers in the State without regard to their point of origin. Nonetheless, appellants argue that the District Court gave "scant attention" to the obvious benefits flowing from the challenged legislation and to the long line of decisions from this Court holding that the State possesses "broad powers" to protect local purchasers from fraud and deception in the marketing of foodstuffs.

As the appellants properly point out, not every exercise of state authority imposing some burden on the free flow of commerce is invalid. Although the Commerce Clause acts as a limitation upon state power even without congressional implementation, our opinions have long recognized that,

"in the absence of conflicting legislation by Congress, there is a residuum of power in the state to make laws governing matters of local concern which nevertheless in some measure affect interstate commerce or even, to some extent, regulate it." *Southern Pacific Co.* v. *Arizona* (1945).

Moreover, as appellants correctly note, that "residuum" is particularly strong when the State acts to protect its citizenry in matters pertaining to the sale of foodstuffs. By the same token, however, a finding that state legislation furthers matters of legitimate local concern, even in the health and consumer protection areas, does not end the inquiry. Such a view, we have noted, "would mean that the Commerce Clause of itself imposes no limitations on state action . . . save for the rare instance where a state artlessly discloses an avowed purpose to discriminate against interstate goods." *Dean Milk Co.* v. *Madison* (1951). Rather, when such state legislation comes into conflict with the Commerce Clause's overriding requirement of a national "common market," we are confronted with the task of effecting an accommodation of the competing national and local interests. We turn to that task.

As the District Court correctly found, the challenged statute has the practical effect of not only burdening interstate sales of Washington apples, but also discriminating against them. This discrimination takes various forms. The first, and most obvious, is the statute's consequence of raising the costs of doing business in the North Carolina market for Washington apple growers and dealers, while leaving those of their North Carolina counterparts unaffected. As previously noted, this disparate effect results from the fact that North Carolina apple producers, unlike their Washington competitors, were not forced to alter their marketing practices in order to comply with the statute. They were still free to market their wares under the USDA grade or none at all as they had done prior to the statute's enactment. Obviously, the increased costs imposed by the statute would tend to shield the local apple industry from the competition of Washington apple growers and dealers who are already at a competitive disadvantage because of their great distance from the North Carolina market.

Second, the statute has the effect of stripping away from the Washington apple industry the competitive and economic advantages it has earned for itself through its expensive inspection and grading system. The record demonstrates that the Washington apple-grading system has gained nationwide acceptance in the apple trade. Indeed, it contains numerous affidavits from apple brokers and dealers located both inside and outside of North Carolina who state their preference, and that of their customers, for apples graded under the Washington, as opposed to the USDA, system because of the former's greater consistency, its emphasis on color, and its supporting mandatory inspections. Once again, the statute had no similar impact on the North Carolina apple industry and thus operated to its benefit.

Third, by prohibiting Washington growers and dealers from marketing apples under their State's grades, the statute has a leveling effect which insidiously operates to the advantage of local apple producers. As noted earlier, the Washington State grades are equal or superior to the USDA grades in all corresponding categories. Hence, with free market forces at work, Washington sellers would normally enjoy a distinct market advantage vis-à-vis local producers in those categories where the Washington grade is superior. However, because of the statute's operation, Washington apples which would otherwise qualify for and be sold under the superior Washington grades will now have to be marketed under their inferior USDA counterparts. Such "downgrading" offers the North Carolina apple industry the very sort of protection against competing out-of-state products that the Commerce Clause was designed to prohibit. At worst, it will have the effect of an embargo against those Washington apples in the superior grades as Washington dealers withhold them from the North Carolina market. At best, it will deprive Washington sellers of the market premium that such apples would otherwise command.

Despite the statute's facial neutrality, the Commission suggests that its discriminatory impact on interstate commerce was not an unintended byproduct and there are some indications in the record to that effect. The most glaring is the response of the North Carolina Agriculture Commissioner to the Commission's request for an exemption following the statute's passage in which he indicated that before he could support such an exemption, he would "want to have the sentiment

from our apple producers *since they were mainly responsible for this legislation being passed . . .*" (emphasis added). Moreover, we find it somewhat suspect that North Carolina singled out only closed containers of apples, the very means by which apples are transported in commerce, to effectuate the statute's ostensible consumer protection purpose when apples are not generally sold at retail in their shipping containers. However, we need not ascribe an economic protection motive to the North Carolina Legislature to resolve this case; we conclude that the challenged statute cannot stand insofar as it prohibits the display of Washington State grades even if enacted for the declared purpose of protecting consumers from deception and fraud in the marketplace.

When discrimination against commerce of the type we have found is demonstrated, the burden falls on the State to justify it both in terms of the local benefits flowing from the statute and the unavailability of nondiscriminatory alternatives adequate to preserve the local interests at stake. North Carolina has failed to sustain that burden on both scores.

The several States unquestionably possess a substantial interest in protecting their citizens from confusion and deception in the marketing of foodstuffs, but the challenged statute does remarkably little to further that laudable goal at least with respect to Washington apples and grades. The statute, as already noted, permits the marketing of closed containers of apples under *no* grades at all. Such a result can hardly be thought to eliminate the problems of deception and confusion created by the multiplicity of differing state grades; indeed, it magnifies them by depriving purchasers of all information concerning the quality of the contents of closed apple containers. Moreover, although the statute is ostensibly a consumer protection measure, it directs its primary efforts, not at the consuming public at large, but at apple wholesalers and brokers who are the principal purchasers of closed containers of apples. And those individuals are presumably the most knowledgeable individuals in this area. Since the statute does nothing at all to purify the flow of information at the retail level, it does little to protect consumers against the problems it was designed to eliminate. Finally, we note that any potential for confusion and deception created by the Washington grades was not of the type that led to the statute's enactment. Since Washington grades are in all cases equal or superior to their USDA counterparts, they could only "deceive" or "confuse" a consumer to his benefit, hardly a harmful result.

In addition, it appears that nondiscriminatory alternatives to the outright ban of Washington State grades are readily available. For example, North Carolina could effectuate its goal by permitting out-of-state growers to utilize state grades only if they also marked their shipments with the applicable USDA label. In that case, the USDA grade would serve as a benchmark against which the consumer could evaluate the quality of the various state grades. If this alternative was for some reason inadequate to eradicate problems caused by state grades inferior to those adopted by the USDA, North Carolina might consider banning those state grades which, unlike Washington's could not be demonstrated to be equal or superior to the corresponding USDA categories. Concededly, even in this latter instance, some potential for "confusion" might persist. However, it is the type of "confusion" that the national interest in the free flow of goods between the States demands be tolerated.

The judgment of the District Court is

Affirmed.

The *Southern Pacific* and *Hunt* cases are but two examples from a long line of decisions in which the Court has cast a disapproving eye on state laws that discriminate against interstate commerce or place an unreasonable burden on it. Other examples are summarized in the box, page 330.

It would be a mistake to conclude, however, that all state regulations that discriminate against interstate products are unconstitutional. In fact, the Court on occasion has ruled that states may ban certain products altogether. There is little problem with such regulations if the ban applies equally to goods produced inside the state as well as outside, and if the prohibition is reasonable, such as a ban against fireworks. These devices can be prohibited as a safety matter, but a state would be hard pressed to defend a law that prohibited only fireworks produced out of state.

But are there circumstances under which a state may constitutionally prohibit the importation of articles manufactured out of state but allow similar goods produced within its borders to be commercially traded? According to the state's arguments in *Maine v. Taylor,* such circumstances do exist. Does Maine offer a sufficiently strong case that its trade barrier is not offensive to the Constitution, or is the state using the police powers as a means of protecting a domestic industry against interstate competition?

Maine v. Taylor

477 U.S. 131 (1986)

Vote: 8 (Blackmun, Brennan, Burger, Marshall,
  O'Connor, Powell, Rehnquist, White)
  1 (Stevens)
Opinion of the Court: Blackmun
Dissenting opinion: Stevens

Maine passed a law prohibiting the importation of any live fish to be used as bait in any of the state's inland waters. The state said the law was to protect indigenous fish from parasites and diseases that are common among imported baitfish and to prevent the introduction of fish that might be detrimental to the state's ecology. Coupled with this state law was a federal statute (the Lacey Act) that, among other things, made it a crime to transport any fish or wildlife in violation of state laws.

Robert J. Taylor, operator of a bait business in Maine, imported 158,000 live golden shiners, a

Supreme Court Decisions Striking Down State Restrictions on Interstate Commerce

Case	State Law Declared Unconstitutional
Edwards v. California (1941)	California law making it a crime knowingly to bring an indigent into the state.
Dean Milk Company v. Madison (1951)	City ordinance discriminating against milk produced out of state.
Bibb v. Navajo Freight Lines (1959)	Illinois statute requiring a particular mudflap on all trucks and outlawing a conventional mudflap legal in forty-five other states.
Pike v. Bruce Church (1970)	Arizona law commanding that all Arizona-grown cantaloupes be packaged inside the state.
Great Atlantic and Pacific Tea Company v. Cottrell (1976)	Mississippi law banning milk produced in Louisiana in response to Louisiana's refusal to sign a reciprocity agreement.
Raymond Motor Transportation v. Rice (1978)	Wisconsin regulation prohibiting from the state's highways double trucks exceeding sixty-five feet in length.
Philadelphia v. New Jersey (1978)	New Jersey ban on the importation and dumping of out-of-state garbage.
Hughes v. Oklahoma (1979)	Law outlawing the transportation of Oklahoma-grown minnows for out-of-state sale.
Kassell v. Consolidated Freightways (1981)	Iowa law banning sixty-five foot double trucks.
New England Power Company v. New Hampshire (1982)	New Hampshire prohibition against selling domestically produced power to out-of-state interests.
Healy v. Beer Institute (1989)	Connecticut law requiring out-of-state beer distributors to show that the prices charged inside Connecticut are not higher than prices charged in bordering states.

species of minnow commonly used as bait in freshwater fishing. This act was in clear violation of the state statute. The fish were intercepted at the state border, and the federal government indicted Taylor for violating the Lacey Act. In his defense, Taylor attacked the constitutionality of the Maine law. He claimed that the ban on the interstate shipment of baitfish was a direct violation of the Commerce Clause. Maine intervened

to defend its statute. The federal district court upheld the constitutionality of the law, but the court of appeals reversed. The state of Maine and the United States petitioned the U.S. Supreme Court to review the case.

Justice Harry A. Blackmun delivered the opinion of the Court:

Once again, a little fish has caused a commotion. See *Hughes v. Oklahoma* (1979); *TVA v. Hill* (1978);

Cappaert v. United States (1976). The fish in this case is the golden shiner, a species of minnow commonly used as live bait in sport fishing. . . .

The Commerce Clause of the Constitution grants Congress the power "[t]o regulate Commerce with foreign Nations, and among the several States, and with the Indian Tribes." Art. I, § 8, cl. 3. "Although the Clause thus speaks in terms of powers bestowed upon Congress, the Court long has recognized that it also limits the power of the States to erect barriers against interstate trade." Maine's statute restricts interstate trade in the most direct manner possible, blocking all inward shipments of live baitfish at the State's border. Still, as both the District Court and the Court of Appeals recognized, this fact alone does not render the law unconstitutional. The limitation imposed by the Commerce Clause on state regulatory power "is by no means absolute," and "the States retain authority under their general police powers to regulate matters of 'legitimate local concern,' even though interstate commerce may be affected."

In determining whether a State has overstepped its role in regulating interstate commerce, this Court has distinguished between state statutes that burden interstate transactions only incidentally, and those that affirmatively discriminate against such transactions. While statutes in the first group violate the Commerce Clause only if the burdens they impose on interstate trade are "clearly excessive in relation to the putative local benefits," statutes in the second group are subject to more demanding scrutiny. The Court explained in *Hughes v. Oklahoma* that once a state law is shown to discriminate against interstate commerce "either on its face or in practical effect," the burden falls on the State to demonstrate both that the statute "serves a legitimate local purpose," and that this purpose could not be served as well by available nondiscriminatory means. . . .

No matter how one describes the abstract issue whether "alternative means could promote this local purpose as well without discriminating against interstate commerce," *Hughes v. Oklahoma,* the more specific question whether scientifically accepted techniques exist for the sampling and inspection of live baitfish is one of fact, and the District Court's finding that such techniques have not been devised cannot be

characterized as clearly erroneous. Indeed, the record probably could not support a contrary finding. Two prosecution witnesses testified to the lack of such procedures, and appellee's expert conceded the point, although he disagreed about the need for such tests. That Maine has allowed the importation of other freshwater fish after inspection hardly demonstrates that the District Court clearly erred in crediting the corroborated and uncontradicted expert testimony that standardized inspection techniques had not yet been developed for baitfish. . . .

After reviewing the expert testimony . . . we cannot say that the District Court clearly erred in finding that substantial scientific uncertainty surrounds the effect that baitfish parasites and nonnative species could have on Maine's fisheries. Moreover, we agree with the District Court that Maine has a legitimate interest in guarding against imperfectly understood environmental risks, despite the possibility that they may ultimately prove to be negligible. "[T]he constitutional principles underlying the commerce clause cannot be read as requiring the State of Maine to sit idly by and wait until potentially irreversible environmental damage has occurred or until the scientific community agrees on what disease organisms are or are not dangerous before it acts to avoid such consequences."

Nor do we think that much doubt is cast on the legitimacy of Maine's purposes by what the Court of Appeals took to be signs of protectionist intent. Shielding in-state industries from out-of-state competition is almost never a legitimate local purpose, and state laws that amount to "simple economic protectionism" consequently have been subject to a "virtually *per se* rule of invalidity." But there is little reason in this case to believe that the legitimate justifications the State has put forward for its statute are merely a sham or a "*post hoc* rationalization." . . .

The Commerce Clause significantly limits the ability of States and localities to regulate or otherwise burden the flow of interstate commerce, but it does not elevate free trade above all other values. As long as a State does not needlessly obstruct interstate trade or attempt to "place itself in a position of economic isolation," it retains broad regulatory authority to protect the health and safety of its citizens and the integrity of its natural resources. The evidence in this case amply supports the District Court's findings that Maine's ban on the importation of live baitfish serves legitimate local purposes that could not adequately be served by available nondiscriminatory alternatives. This is not a case of arbitrary discrimination against interstate commerce; the record suggests that Maine has legitimate reasons "apart from their origin, to treat [out-of-state baitfish] differently." The judgment of the Court of Appeals setting aside appellee's conviction is therefore reversed.

Justice STEVENS, dissenting.

There is something fishy about this case. Maine is the only State in the Union that blatantly discriminates against out-of-state baitfish by flatly prohibiting their importation. Although golden shiners are already present and thriving in Maine (and, perhaps not coincidentally, the subject of a flourishing domestic industry), Maine excludes golden shiners grown and harvested (and, perhaps not coincidentally sold) in other States. This kind of stark discrimination against out-of-state articles of commerce requires rigorous justification by the discriminating State. "When discrimination against commerce of the type we have found is demonstrated, the burden falls on the State to justify it both in terms of the local benefits flowing from the statute and the unavailability of nondiscriminatory alternatives adequate to preserve the local interests at stake." *Hunt v. Washington State Apple Advertising Comm'n* (1977).

. . . [T]he Court concludes that uncertainty about possible ecological effects from the possible presence of parasites and nonnative species in shipments of out-of-state shiners suffices to carry the State's burden of proving a legitimate public purpose. The Court similarly concludes that the State has no obligation to develop feasible inspection procedures that would make a total ban unnecessary. It seems clear, however, that the presumption should run the other way. Since the State engages in obvious discrimination against out-of-state commerce, it should be put to its proof. Ambiguity about dangers and alternatives should actually defeat, rather than sustain, the discriminatory measure.

This is not to derogate the State's interest in ecological purity. But the invocation of environmental protection or public health has never been thought to confer some kind of special dispensation from the general principle of nondiscrimination in interstate commerce. "A different view, that the ordinance is valid simply because it professes to be a health measure, would mean that the Commerce Clause of itself imposes no restraints on state action other than those laid down by the Due Process Clause, save for the rate instance where a state artlessly discloses an avowed purpose to discriminate against interstate goods." If Maine wishes to rely on its interest in ecological preservation, it must show that interest, and the infeasibility of other alternatives, with far greater specificity. Otherwise, it must further that asserted interest in a manner far less offensive to the notions of comity and cooperation that underlie the Commerce Clause.

Significantly, the Court of Appeals, which is more familiar with Maine's natural resources and with its legislation than we are, was concerned by the uniqueness of Maine's ban. That court felt, as I do, that Maine's unquestionable natural splendor notwithstanding, the State has not carried its substantial burden of proving why it cannot meet its environmental concerns in the same manner as other States with the same interest in the health of their fish and ecology.

I respectfully dissent.

The authority of the states to regulate interstate commerce remains consistent with the principles set out in *Cooley v. Board of Wardens*. The Constitution without doubt gives supremacy in this area to the national government. If Congress elects to regulate such commerce, the power of the state is preempted. But where Congress does not regulate, the states may have a role. When national uniformity is not necessary, states may pass reasonable forms of regulation to meet legitimate local needs. If these ordinances place unreasonable burdens on interstate commerce or discriminate against interstate commerce in favor of domestic business, the Court will view them with suspicion, requiring the state to meet a heavy obligation of proving their legitimacy. *Maine v. Taylor,* however, serves as an example that gaining Supreme Court approval for such statutes is not impossible.

READINGS

Baker, Leonard. *Back to Back: The Duel Between FDR and the Supreme Court.* New York: Macmillan, 1967.

Benson, Paul R., Jr. *The Supreme Court and the Commerce Clause, 1937-1970.* New York: Dunellen, 1970.

Cortner, Richard. *The Wagner Act Cases.* Knoxville: University of Tennessee Press, 1964.

Corwin, Edward S. *The Commerce Power versus States' Rights.* Princeton, N.J.: Princeton University Press, 1936.

Dawson, Nelson. *Louis D. Brandeis, Felix Frankfurter, and the New Deal.* Hamden, Conn.: Archon Books, 1980.

Frankfurter, Felix. *The Commerce Clause Under Marshall, Taney and Waite.* Chapel Hill: University of North Carolina Press, 1937.

Himmelberg, Robert. *The Origins of the National Recovery Administration.* New York: Fordham University Press, 1976.

Irons, Peter H. *New Deal Lawyers.* Princeton, N.J.: Princeton University Press, 1982.

McClosky, Robert. *American Conservatism in the Age of Enterprise, 1865-1910.* Cambridge, Mass.: Harvard University Press, 1951.

Pearson, Drew, and Robert S. Allen. *The Nine Old Men.* Garden City, N.Y.: Doubleday, 1936.

Pritchett, C. Herman. *The Roosevelt Court: A Study in Judicial Politics and Values.* New York: Macmillan, 1948.

Wood, Stephen B. *Constitutional Politics in the Progressive Era: Child Labor and the Law.* Chicago: University of Chicago Press, 1968.

CHAPTER 7

THE POWER TO TAX AND SPEND

Perhaps no government power affects Americans more directly than the authority to tax and spend. Each year federal, state, and local governments collect billions of dollars in taxes imposed on a wide variety of activities, transactions, and goods. The federal government reminds us of its power to tax when we receive our paychecks, to say nothing of every April 15, the deadline for filing tax returns. Many state governments lay taxes on our incomes as well, and a majority of them also impose a levy each time we make a retail purchase. If we own a house, we must annually pay a tax on its value. We pay state and/or federal excise taxes whenever we make a phone call, put gas in the car, or buy cigarettes or alcoholic beverages. When we buy goods from abroad, the price includes a duty imposed on imports.

Americans have strong opinions about the government's taxing and spending activities. Many people think they pay too much and receive too few of the government's services in return. The battles over spending priorities are neverending, especially when choices must be made between defense and social programs. In addition, there are constant complaints about inefficient and ineffective government agencies that waste tax dollars. The mere mention of the Internal Revenue Service (IRS) strikes fear in the hearts of many. Minor tax revolts at the state and local level are not unusual. In spite of this general

dissatisfaction, however, most Americans pay their taxes honestly and on time and accept the fact that taxation is a reality that will always be with us.

Today the government's power to tax and spend is firmly established with reasonably well defined contours, but this was not always the case. Some of the country's greatest constitutional battles were fought over the fiscal powers. The results of these legal disputes have significantly shaped the powers and constraints of our political institutions. In this chapter, we examine the Supreme Court's interpretations of the twin fiscal powers of taxation and spending.

The Constitutional Power to Tax and Spend

The power to tax was a fundamental issue at the Constitutional Convention. The government under the Articles of Confederation was ineffective in part because it had no authority to levy taxes. It could only request funds from the states and had no power to collect payments if the states refused to cooperate. The taxing authority resided solely with the states, which left the national government unable to execute public policies unless the states overwhelmingly supported them, a situation that did not occur with any regularity. It was clear that the central government would have to gain some revenue-gathering powers under the new constitution, while the states retained concurrent authority to impose taxes.

Article I, Section 8, of the Constitution enumerates the powers of the federal government, and the first of those listed is the power to tax and spend:

The Congress shall have the Power to lay and collect Taxes, Duties, Imposts and Excises, to pay the Debts and provide for the common Defence and general Welfare of the United States.

The wording of this grant of authority is quite broad. The revenue function breaks into three categories. The first is the general grant of taxation power. Second is the authority to collect duties and imposts, both of which are taxes levied on imports, the primary source of revenue at that time. The third is the power to impose excises, which are taxes on the manufacture, sale, or use of goods, or on occupational or other activities.

The power to spend is also broadly constructed. The revenues gathered through the various taxing mechanisms may be used to pay government debts, to fund the nation's defense, and to provide for the general welfare. Although James Madison (and others) argued that the Framers intended the spending power to be limited to funding those government activities explicitly authorized in the Constitution, the wording of Article I, Section 8, does not impose any such restriction. As we shall see later in this chapter, the fact that Congress may spend federal funds to provide for the *general welfare* is indeed a broad grant of authority.

This is not to say that the federal power to tax and spend is without limits. The Framers were sufficiently wary of the dangers of a strong central government that they imposed some restrictions. First, Article I, Section 8, stipulates that "all Duties, Imposts and Excises shall be uniform throughout the United States." The purpose of this provision was to prevent Congress from imposing different tax rates on various regions or requiring the citizens of one state to pay a tax rate higher than the citizens of other states. Geographical uniformity is the only stated constitutional requirement for excise taxes and taxes on imports. If this standard is met, the tax is likely to be valid.

Second, Article I, Section 9, holds that "No Tax or Duty shall be laid on Articles exported from any State." Consistent with the prevailing philosophy of increased commerce and trade, the Framers wanted to ensure that the products of the states would move freely without the burden of federal taxes being placed on them.

Third, Article I, Section 9, also dictates that "No capitation, or other direct, Tax shall be laid, unless in Proportion to the Census or Enumeration herein before directed to be taken." This same admonition is found in Article I, Section 2, where the Framers wrote "direct Taxes shall be apportioned among the several States . . . according to their respective Numbers" as determined by the national census. The term *direct tax* is not defined in the Constitution and is a difficult concept to understand. When the Framers referred to direct taxes they most likely meant a head tax—a tax imposed on each person—or a tax on land. As we shall see in the next section of this chapter, the requirement that direct taxes be apportioned on the basis of population has proved troublesome, and Congress has not often resorted to such levies.

The Framers generally allowed the states to retain their taxing authority as it existed prior to the ratification of the new Constitution. Consequently, state and local governments today tax a wide array of activities and goods, including individual and corporate incomes, personal property, real estate, retail sales, investments holdings, and inheritances. But the Constitution imposed some new restraints on state taxing authority. These limitations specifically removed from the states any power to place a tax on certain forms of commerce. Article I, Section 10, prohibits them from imposing any duty on imports or exports, as well as any tax on the cargo capacity of vessels using the nation's ports. The Framers were interested in the promotion of commerce, and these provisions precluded states from retarding commerce by using foreign trade as a source of tax revenue.

In addition to these specific restrictions, state and federal taxation must be consistent with the other provisions of the Constitution. It would be a violation of the Constitution, for example, if a state or the federal government taxed the exercise of a constitutional right, such as the freedom of speech or the exercise of religion. By the same token, if the government imposed varying tax rates based on a person's sex or race, such levies would be in violation of the constitutional rights of due process and equal protection of the laws.

Direct Taxes and the Power to Tax Income

The Constitution stipulates two standards for assessing federal taxes. The first is geographical uniformity. Duties, imposts, and excise taxes all must be applied according to this standard. If Congress taxes a particular product entering the ports of the United States, the tax rate on the article must be the same regardless of the point of entry. Excise taxes also must be applied uniformly throughout the nation. If an excise is placed on automobiles, for example, the amount assessed must be the same in California as it is in Tennessee.

The second standard for imposing taxes is population distribution. The Constitution says that all direct taxes must be apportioned among the states on the basis of population. The delegates from the sparsely populated states supported this provision because they feared that the larger states, with greater representation in the House of Representatives, would craft tax measures in such a way that the burden would fall disproportionately upon the citizens of the smaller states.

Unfortunately, the Framers did not explain what they meant by a direct tax. As the box on taxation methods illustrates, whether a tax is levied uniformly or is apportioned on the basis of population makes a great deal of difference as to who pays how much *(see page 337).* In *The Federalist Papers,* Alexander Hamilton claimed that direct taxes were only those imposed on land and buildings, but Hamilton's opinion did not settle the issue.[1] It required a Supreme Court decision to do that.

Defining Direct Taxation

In one of the Court's earliest cases, *Hylton v. United States* (1796), the justices defined the term *direct tax.* The dispute stemmed from a tax on carriages Congress passed June 5, 1794. The statute classified the tax as an excise and, therefore, applied the same rate on carriages nationwide. The Federalist majorities in Congress passed the statute over Anti-Federalist opposition, and the tax was completely partisan. The Federalists generally represented the states in the Northeast with large populations but relatively few carriages; the Anti-Federalist strongholds were the less densely populated and more agricultural states with larger numbers of carriages. Because the carriage tax was deemed an excise, the Anti-Federalist areas would pay a much greater share of it than would the residents of the Northeast. The Anti-Federalists would have preferred to classify the measure as a direct tax and apportion it on the basis of population.

Daniel Hylton, a resident of Virginia, challenged the constitutionality of the assessment, claiming that it was a direct tax, not an excise, and should have been apportioned on the basis of population. The government took the position

1. Alexander Hamilton, "Federalist No. 21," in *The Federalist Papers,* ed. Clinton Rossiter (New York: New American Library, 1961).

Direct and Indirect Taxes: Apportionment v. Geographical Uniformity

This example demonstrates the difference between direct and indirect taxing methods. The facts and figures used are purely hypothetical.

Assume that Congress decides to raise $1 million through a tax on the nation's 100,000 thoroughbred horses. If this tax is considered an excise tax, it must conform to the constitutional requirement of geographical uniformity. Congress would have to require that all thoroughbred horse owners pay a tax of ten dollars per horse. The rate would be the same in Maine as in Oregon. If, however, the tax on thoroughbred horses is classified as a direct tax, a different set of calculations would have to be made to meet the constitutionally required apportionment standard. Three factors would need to be known. First, the amount of money Congress intends to raise. Second, the proportion of the national population residing in each state. Third, the number of thoroughbred horses in each state. Apportionment means that the proportion of the revenue obtained from a state must equal the proportion of the country's population living there.

The impact of apportionment can be seen by the following calculations in applying the $1 million horse tax to three states. State A is a densely populated, urban state with few horses. State B is a moderately populated state with some ranching areas. And State C is a sparsely populated, primarily agricultural state, with a relatively large number of thoroughbreds.

State	Percentage of National Population	Taxes Due from State	Number of Horses in State	Tax Rate per Horse
State A	10	$100,000	100	$1,000
State B	5	$50,000	1,000	$50
State C	1	$10,000	10,000	$1

Obviously, the horse owners in State A would be greatly disadvantaged if the horse tax were classified as a direct tax and apportioned among the states on the basis of population. State C, on the other hand, would be greatly benefited. Because State C has only 1 percent of the nation's population, it would be responsible for raising only 1 percent of the tax revenues. Furthermore, that smaller tax obligation would be distributed over a disproportionately large number of horses.

Horse owners in State A clearly would prefer the tax on thoroughbreds to be defined as an excise tax with its required geographical uniformity. State C's thoroughbred owners obviously would argue for the horse tax to be considered a direct tax and be apportioned among the states on the basis of population.

---

that, as a tax on an article, the carriage tax was an excise.

By almost every rule of judicial authority developed since that time, the Court should have refused to hear the dispute.[2] The evidence showed that the case did not involve adverse parties. In fact, the suit appeared to be little more than a ploy by the government to obtain Court approval of its interpretation of the taxation provisions of the Constitution. Both sides to the dispute agreed that

Hylton owned 125 carriages exclusively for his private use. In reality, Hylton owned only 1, but the tax due on a single carriage was insufficient to meet the threshold for federal court jurisdiction. If Hylton owned 125 carriages, the taxes due would reach $2,000, enough for federal court action. This jurisdictional point was important because Federalist judges dominated the federal courts, and they were likely to give the law a sympathetic hearing. Administration officials also agreed that if the tax were found valid they would demand that Hylton pay only $16. Perhaps an even greater indication of collusion was that the government paid the fees of the attorneys for both sides.

2. See Melvin I. Urofsky, *A March of Liberty: A Constitutional History of the United States* (New York: Knopf, 1988), 146-148. See also Robert F. Cushman, *Cases in Constitutional Law,* 7th ed. (Englewood Cliffs, N.J.: Prentice-Hall, 1989), 177-178.

Former secretary of the Treasury Alexander Hamilton presented the government's case. Hamilton was one of the most vigorous supporters of a strong national government and of broad federal taxation powers. He understood the problems associated with apportioning taxes on the basis of population and consequently wanted the Court to set down a very narrow definition of direct taxes.

Hamilton's side was victorious. The three judges who participated in the decision each voted in favor of the statute and in agreement with Congress's determination that the carriage tax was an excise tax.[3] As was the custom in the years before John Marshall became chief justice, each justice wrote a separate opinion explaining his vote.[4] The opinions of James Iredell and Samuel Chase stressed the inappropriateness of attempting to apportion a tax on carriages and the inevitable inequities that would result. William Paterson's opinion emphasized the intention of the Framers. His opinion had particular credibility because Paterson, having been a New Jersey delegate to the Constitutional Convention, was one of the Framers. All three agreed that only two kinds of taxes fell into the direct tax category: capitation (or head) taxes and taxes on land.

Apportioning taxes on the basis of population is very cumbersome and almost inevitably leads to unjust tax burdens. The *Hylton* decision, by limiting the kinds of taxes that fell into the direct taxation category, significantly strengthened federal taxation powers. It freed Congress from having to apply unpopular apportionment standards to most taxes. So difficult is the apportionment problem that Congress only rarely has attempted to use a direct tax, and such efforts generally have been unsatisfactory.

Hylton was the first case in which the Supreme Court heard a challenge to the constitutionality of a federal statute; the decision predated *Marbury v. Madison* by seven years. It is clear from the arguments before the Court and the justices' opinions that the law was tested for its constitutionality. *Hylton* has not received the notoriety of *Marbury* because the act of Congress was found to be valid.

The Constitutionality of the Income Tax

From *Hylton* to the 1860s federal taxing authority remained generally unchanged. The government financed its activities largely through import duties and excise taxes. The Civil War, however, placed an incredible financial strain on the federal government. Between 1858 and the end of the war, it ran unusually high budget deficits and needed to find new sources of revenue to fund the war effort. In response, Congress in 1862 and 1864 imposed the first taxes on individual incomes. The 1881 case of *Springer v. United States* involved a challenge to the validity of that tax. William M. Springer, an attorney, claimed that the income tax was a direct tax and should have been apportioned on the basis of population. The justices unanimously rejected this position, once again holding that only capitation taxes and taxes on land were direct taxes. Although the challenged tax was a levy on the income of individuals, it could not be considered a capitation tax within the normal meaning of that term. *Springer,* then, set precedent that the federal government had the power to tax incomes.

As the government reduced its war debts, Congress in 1872 was able to repeal the income tax

3. The other three members of the Court were absent for various reasons. Oliver Ellsworth had just been sworn in as chief justice and, because he had missed some of the arguments, did not participate in the decision. Justice James Wilson heard arguments but did not vote in the case because he had participated in the lower court decision upholding the tax. Justice William Cushing was not present for the arguments and therefore did not vote on the merits.

4. The practice of each justice writing a separate opinion explaining individual views was borrowed from the British courts. When John Marshall became chief justice he moved away from the use of these seriatim opinions to the current practice of a single opinion explaining the views of the majority. Marshall believed that the use of a single opinion increased the Court's status and effectiveness.

law.[5] But the issue of taxing incomes did not go away. The Populist movement favored the use of the income tax as the primary method of raising federal revenues. In addition, labor groups and farm organizations began arguing that new revenue sources should be developed to shift the burden away from reliance on import duties. Members of the Democratic party criticized the regressive aspects of the tax structure of that time. In response to these demands, Congress enacted an income tax law in 1894. The statute, which was passed as part of the Wilson-Gorman Tariff Act, imposed a 2 percent tax on all corporate profits and on individual incomes. Income derived from salaries and wages, gifts, inheritances, dividends, rents, and interest, including interest from state and municipal bonds, all were subject

to this tax. People with incomes under $4,000 paid no tax. This exemption, set at a level much higher than the average worker earned, meant that most of the burden fell upon the wealthy. For this reason, the tax received overwhelming support from rank and file citizens, and bitter opposition from businesses and those individuals enjoying high incomes. The wealthy classes, in fact, claimed that the income tax would destroy the very fabric of the nation, replacing our historical principles of private property with communism and socialism.

The income tax law was promptly challenged in Court in an 1895 appeal, *Pollock v. Farmers' Loan & Trust Co.* One of the primary arguments of the law's opponents was that the income tax was a direct tax, and since Congress had not apportioned it, the law was unconstitutional. Given precedents such as *Hylton* and *Springer*, would you anticipate that this position would be successful?

5. For an excellent review of the history of the income tax in the United States, see John F. Witte, *The Politics and Development of the Federal Income Tax* (Madison: University of Wisconsin Press, 1985).

Pollock v. Farmers' Loan & Trust Co.

158 U.S. 601 (1895)

Vote: 5 (Brewer, Field, Fuller, Gray, Shiras)
     4 (Brown, Harlan, Jackson, White)
Opinion of the Court: Fuller
Dissenting opinions: Brown, Harlan, Jackson, White

Charles Pollock, a shareholder in the Farmers' Loan & Trust Company of New York, filed suit on behalf of himself and his fellow stockholders, to block the company from paying the national income tax on the grounds that the tax was unconstitutional. The lawsuit was obviously collusive: the company no more wanted to pay the tax than did its shareholders. Opponents of the law claimed (1) that taxing income from state and city bonds was an unconstitutional encroachment on the state's power to borrow money; (2) that a tax on income from real property was a direct tax and

must be apportioned on the basis of population; and (3) that these taxes were so integral to the entire tax act that the whole law should be declared unconstitutional.

The Court heard arguments on the *Pollock* case twice. In its first decision, the majority declared the tax on state and municipal bonds unconstitutional.[6] It further ruled that a tax on income from land was essentially the same as taxing land itself. Because a tax on land is a direct tax, so too is a tax on the income from land. Therefore, such taxes must be apportioned on the basis of population. But the Court was unable to reach a decision on whether the entire law should be declared unconstitutional. On this question the justices divided 4-4 because Justice Howell Jackson, ill with tuberculosis, was absent.

6. *Pollock v. Farmers' Loan & Trust Co.*, 157 U.S. 429 (1895).

Pollock filed a petition for a second hearing, and Jackson made it known that he would be present for it. The second decision reviewed much of what the Court concluded in the first, but this time the Court went on to rule on the question of the general constitutionality of the income tax act.

Chief Justice Melville Weston Fuller delivered the opinion of the Court:

Whenever this court is required to pass upon the validity of an act of Congress as tested by the fundamental law enacted by the people, the duty imposed demands in its discharge the utmost deliberation and care, and invokes the deepest sense of responsibility. And this is especially so when the question involves the exercise of a great governmental power, and brings into consideration, as vitally affected by the decision, that complex system of government, so sagaciously framed to secure and perpetuate ''an indestructible Union, composed of indestructible States.'' . . .

As heretofore stated, the Constitution divided Federal taxation into two great classes, the class of direct taxes, and the class of duties, imposts and excises; and prescribed two rules which qualified the grant of power as to each class.

The power to lay direct taxes apportioned among the several States in proportion to their representation in the popular branch of Congress, a representation based on population as ascertained by the census, was plenary and absolute; but to lay direct taxes without apportionment was forbidden. The power to lay duties, imposts, and excises was subject to the qualification that the imposition must be uniform throughout the United States.

Our previous decision was confined to the consideration of the validity of the tax on the income from real estate, and on the income from municipal bonds. The question thus limited was whether such taxation was direct or not, in the meaning of the Constitution; and the court went no farther, as to the tax on the income from real estate, than to hold that it fell within the same class as the source whence the income was derived, that is, that a tax upon the realty and a tax upon the receipts therefrom were alike direct; while as to the income from municipal bonds, that could not be taxed because of want of power to tax the source, and no reference was made to the nature of the tax as being direct or indirect.

We are now permitted to broaden the field of inquiry, and to determine to which of the two great classes a tax upon a person's entire income, whether derived from rents, or products, or otherwise, of real estate, or from bonds, stocks, or other forms of personal property, belongs; and we are unable to conclude that the enforced subtraction from the yield of all the owner's real or personal property, in the manner prescribed, is so different from a tax upon the property itself, that it is not a direct, but an indirect tax, in the meaning of the Constitution. . . .

The reasons for the clauses of the Constitution in respect of direct taxation are not far to seek. The States, respectively, possessed plenary powers of taxation. They could tax the property of their citizens in such manner and to such extent as they saw fit; they had unrestricted powers to impose duties or imposts on imports from abroad, and excises on manufactures, consumable commodities, or otherwise. They gave up the great sources of revenue derived from commerce; they retained the concurrent power o[f] levying excises, and duties if covering anything other than excises; but in respect of them the range of taxation was narrowed by the power granted over interstate commerce, and by the danger of being put at disadvantage in dealing with excises on manufactures. They retained the power of direct taxation, and to that they looked as their chief resource; but even in respect of that, they granted the concurrent power, and if the tax were placed by both governments on the same subject, the claim of the United States had preference. Therefore, they did not grant the power of direct taxation without regard to their own condition and resources as States; but they granted the power of apportioned direct taxation, a power just as efficacious to serve the needs of the general government, but securing to the States the opportunity to pay the amount apportioned, and to recoup from their own citizens in the most feasible way, and in harmony with their systems of local self-government. If, in the changes of wealth and population in particular States, apportionment produced inequality, it was an inequality stipulated for, just as the equal representation of the States, however small, in the Senate, was stipulated for. The Constitution ordains affirmatively that each State shall have two members of that body, and negatively that no State shall by amendment be deprived of its equal suffrage in the Senate without its consent. The Constitution ordains affirmatively that representatives and direct taxes shall be apportioned among the several States according to numbers, and negatively that no direct tax shall be laid unless in proportion to the enumeration.

The founders anticipated that the expenditures of the States, their counties, cities, and towns, would chiefly be met by direct taxation on accumulated property, while they expected that those of the Federal government would be for the most part met by indirect taxes. And in order that the power of direct taxation by the general government should not be exercised, except on necessity; and, when the necessity arose, should be so exercised as to leave the States at liberty to discharge their respective obligations, and should not be so exercised, unfairly and discriminatingly, as to particular States or otherwise, by a mere majority vote, possibly of those whose constituents were intentionally not subjected to any part of the burden, the qualified grant was made. . . .

It is said that a tax on the whole income of property is not a direct tax in the meaning of the Constitution, but a duty, and, as a duty, leviable without apportionment, whether direct or indirect. We do not think so. Direct taxation was not restricted in one breath, and the restriction blown to the winds in another. . . .

We have unanimously held in this case that, so far as this law operates on the receipts from municipal bonds, it cannot be sustained, because it is a tax on the power of the States, and on their instrumentalities to borrow money, and consequently repugnant to the Constitution. But if, as contended, the interest when received has become merely money in the recipient's pocket, and taxable as such without reference to the source from which it came, the question is immaterial whether it could have been originally taxed at all or not. This was admitted by the Attorney General with characteristic candor; and it follows that, if the revenue derived from municipal bonds cannot be taxed because the source cannot be, the same rule applies to revenue from any other source not subject to the tax; and the lack of power to levy any but an apportioned tax on real

and personal property equally exists as to the revenue therefrom.

Admitting that this act taxes the income of property irrespective of its source, still we cannot doubt that such a tax is necessarily a direct tax in the meaning of the Constitution. . . .

We are not here concerned with the question whether an income tax be or be not desirable, nor whether such a tax would enable the government to diminish taxes on consumption and duties on imports, and to enter upon what may be believed to be a reform of its fiscal and commercial system. Questions of that character belong to the controversies of political parties, and cannot be settled by judicial decision. In these cases our province is to determine whether this income tax on the revenue from property does or does not belong to the class of direct taxes. If it does, it is, being unapportioned, in violation of the Constitution, and we must so declare. . . .

We have considered the act only in respect of the tax on income derived from real estate, and from invested personal property, and have not commented on so much of it as bears on gains or profits from business, privileges, or employments, in view of the instances in which taxation on business, privileges, or employments has assumed the guise of an excise tax and been sustained as such.

Being of opinion that so much of the sections of this law as lays a tax on income from real and personal property is invalid, we are brought to the question of the effect of that conclusion upon these sections as a whole.

It is elementary that the same statute may be in part constitutional and in part unconstitutional, and if the parts are wholly independent of each other, that which is constitutional may stand while that which is unconstitutional will be rejected. And in the case before us there is no question as to the validity of this act, except sections twenty-seven to thirty-seven, inclusive, which relate to the subject which has been under discussion; and as to them we think . . . that if the different parts ''are so mutually connected with and dependent on each other, as to warrant a belief that the legislature intended them as a whole, and that, if all could not be carried into effect, the legislature would not pass the residue independently, and some parts are unconstitutional, all the provisions which are thus dependent, conditional or connected, must fall with them.'' . . .

According to the census, the true valuation of real and personal property in the United States in 1890 was $65,037,091,197, of which real estate with improvements thereon made up $39,544,544,333. Of course, from the latter must be deducted, in applying these sections, all unproductive property and all property whose net yield does not exceed four thousand dollars; but, even with such deductions, it is evident that the income from realty formed a vital part of the scheme for taxation embodied therein. If that be stricken out, and also the income from all invested personal property, bonds, stocks, investments of all kinds, it is obvious that by far the largest part of the anticipated revenue would be eliminated, and this would leave the burden of the tax to be borne by professions, trades, employments, or vocations; and in that way what was intended as a tax on capital would remain in substance a tax on occupations and labor. We cannot believe that such was the intention of Congress. We do not mean to say that an act laying by apportionment a direct tax on all real estate and personal property, or the income thereof, might not also lay excise taxes on business, privileges, employments, and vocations. But this is not such an act; and the scheme must be considered as a whole. Being invalid as to the greater part, and falling, as the tax would, if any part were held valid, in a direction which could not have been contemplated except in connection with the taxation considered as an entirety, we are constrained to conclude that sections twenty-seven to thirty-seven, inclusive, of the act, which became a law without the signature of the President on August 28, 1894, are wholly inoperative and void.

Our conclusions may, therefore, be summed up as follows:

First. We adhere to the opinion already announced, that, taxes on real estate being indisputably direct taxes, taxes on the rents or income of real estate are equally direct taxes.

Second. We are of opinion that taxes on personal property, or on the income of personal property, are likewise direct taxes.

Third. The tax imposed by sections twenty-seven to thirty-seven, inclusive, of the act of 1894, so far as it falls on the income of real estate and of personal property, being a direct tax within the meaning of the Constitution, and, therefore, unconstitutional and void because not apportioned according to representation, all those sections, constituting one entire scheme of taxation, are necessarily invalid.

The Sixteenth Amendment

The decision to invalidate the entire income tax act was quite unpopular. Because that statute had placed a greater obligation on the wealthy, the ruling convinced the middle and working classes that the Supreme Court was little more than the defender of the rich. Various political groups immediately began working to reverse the impact of the Court's decision by means of either a constitutional amendment or revised federal legislation. Labor and farming interests supported a new income tax, as did Progressive Republicans and Democratic populists. Opposition came primarily from conservative Republicans in the Northeast.

Finally, in 1909 Congress began serious work on an income tax measure. There were sufficient votes in the legislature to reform the tax structure, moving the federal government away from excessive reliance on regressive tariffs and excise taxes. The major question was whether to pass another income tax bill or to propose a constitutional amendment. Finding themselves in a minority, conservative Republicans threw their support to a constitutional amendment. They hoped the state legislatures would not ratify the proposed amendment, but, even if they did, the process would take several years to complete.

Congress proposed a constitutional amendment to authorize a federal income tax in July 1909, by overwhelming votes of 77 to 0 in the Senate and 318 to 14 in the House. The proposal received the required number of approvals from the state legislatures in February 1913 and became the Sixteenth Amendment to the United States Constitution:

The Congress shall have power to lay and collect taxes on incomes, from whatever source derived, without apportionment among the several states, and without regard to any census or enumeration.

The amendment effectively ended the debate over direct taxation and represents one of the four times in history that a constitutional amendment has been ratified to overturn a Supreme Court precedent. It gave Congress sufficient taxing authority to fund the federal government without having to resort to direct taxes. The Constitution now made all sources of income subject to Congress's taxing power and removed any requirement that a tax on income be apportioned on the basis of population.

Congress wasted no time. In 1913 the legislature imposed a 1 percent tax rate on individual incomes in excess of $3,000 and on incomes of married couples over $4,000. Not surprisingly, the statute's constitutionality was challenged in Court, but the justices upheld the law three years later in *Brushaber v. Union Pacific Railroad* (1916) by a 7-2 vote. As shown in Table 7-1, the income tax is now the primary source of federal revenue.

Intergovernmental Tax Immunity

The operation of a federal system carries within it inherent risks of conflict between the national government and the states. When both levels of government are authorized to tax, one government can use the power as a weapon against the other. No specific provision of the Constitution prohibits the federal government from taxing state governments or vice versa, but for the federal system to operate effectively, the entities need to avoid such conflicts.

Table 7-1   Federal Tax Revenues: The Impact of the Sixteenth Amendment

Source	1800	1850	1900	1950	1987
Customs duties	83.7	91.0	41.1	1.0	1.6
Excises	7.5	—	50.1	18.4	3.5
Gifts and inheritances	—	—	—	1.7	0.8
Individual incomes	—	—	—	38.5	41.2
Corporate incomes	—	—	—	25.5	8.8
Insurance trust (Social Security, etc.)	—	—	—	10.7	30.0
Other income	8.8	9.0	8.8	4.2	14.1

Sources: *Historical Statistics of the United States: Colonial Times to 1970* (Washington, D.C.: U.S. Bureau of the Census, 1975); *Statistical Abstract of the United States, 1990* (Washington, D.C.: U.S. Department of Commerce, Bureau of the Census, 1990).
Note: The data represent the proportion of total federal revenues for each of seven sources of taxation. The data prior to ratification of the Sixteenth Amendment in 1913 demonstrate the federal government's reliance on customs duties and excise taxes. Data from the period after 1913 illustrate the shift to income taxes as the primary sources for federal tax dollars.

Establishing the Tax Immunity Doctrine

The issue of intergovernmental tax immunity was first raised in *McCulloch v. Maryland* (1819), which tested the constitutional validity of the national bank. The Supreme Court's decision in *McCulloch* was tremendously important in a number of ways. We have already discussed its significance for the development of congressional power and the concept of federalism, but *McCulloch* also is relevant to the constitutional limitations on the power to tax.

McCulloch involved a challenge to a tax imposed by the state of Maryland on the national bank, a creation of the federal government. Supporters of federal power argued that the union could not be maintained if the states were permitted to place debilitating taxes on those operations of the federal government they did not approve. States' rights advocates claimed that the power of the states to tax within their own borders was absolute and there was no constitutional bar to such taxes. The Supreme Court ruled in favor of the federal government, declaring the state tax unconstitutional. Chief Justice Marshall's hard-hitting opinion for a unanimous Court put an immediate stop to a conflict that would have desperately weakened the union if allowed to continue.

In doing so, Marshall created the intergovernmental tax immunity doctrine. He wrote, "[T]he power to tax involves the power to destroy; . . . the power to destroy may defeat and render useless the power to create; . . . there is plain repugnance, in conferring on one government a power to control the constitutional measures of another." The ability of the states to tax the legitimate operations of the federal government is simply incompatible with the Framers' intent of creating viable government units at both the national and state levels.

Marshall's decision in *McCulloch* was consistent with his general philosophy of favoring a strong national government. But was the doctrine of intergovernmental tax immunity a two-way street? Marshall's opinion fell short of proclaiming that the national government was prohibited from taxing the legitimate operations of the states. He was more concerned in this case with reinforcing principles of federal supremacy. Yet a strong case can be made that it would also violate the principles of the Constitution for the federal government to be permitted to destroy the states through its taxing power.

The first case that tested whether the states enjoyed immunity from federal taxation was *Collector v. Day* (1871), which stemmed from an application of the Civil War federal income tax law. Judge J. M. Day of the probate court in Massachusetts objected to paying a federal tax on his income on intergovernmental tax immunity grounds. Three decades earlier the Supreme Court had ruled that the state governments could not tax the income of federal officeholders, and now Day was asking the Court to adopt the converse of that.[7] The Supreme Court, 8-1, held that Day's judicial income was immune from federal taxation. The Court reasoned that the Constitution protects the legitimate functions of the state. The federal government cannot use its taxation powers to curtail or destroy the operations or instruments of the state, and the probate court system is a legitimate and necessary agency of state government. To allow the federal government to tax the income of state judges would be to open the door for Congress to tax all state government functions.

For several decades the justices vigorously maintained the doctrine that the Constitution did not allow one government to tax the essential functions of another. In the *Pollock v. Farmers' Loan & Trust Co.* (1895) income tax decisions, as we have already seen, the Court struck down a federal tax on interest income from state and

7. *Dobbins v. Commissioners of Erie County,* 16 Pet. 435 (1842).

municipal bonds as an unconstitutional burden on the state's authority to borrow. The Court struck down state taxes on income from federal land leases and federally granted patents and copyrights, and on the sales of petroleum products to the federal government.[8] It also invalidated a federal tax on revenues derived from the sales of goods to state agencies.[9] The only significant standard imposed by the Court in this line of cases was that immunity covered only essential government functions. Consequently, the justices upheld a federal tax on the profits of South Carolina's state-run liquor stores.[10] As a merchant of alcoholic beverages, the state was acting as a private business, not exercising a government function, and therefore was not immune from federal taxation.

The Erosion of the Tax Immunity Doctrine

The Court's general support for the tax immunity doctrine was closely related to its conservatism; it opposed both big government and comprehensive regulation of the economy. When the more activist New Deal justices took control of the Court, however, support for the tax immunity doctrine began to wane. A series of Supreme Court decisions modified or reversed the earlier rulings that had established an almost impenetrable barrier against one government taxing the instruments or operations of another.

For example, in *Helvering v. Gerhardt* (1938) the Court overruled *Dobbins v. Commissioners of Erie County* (1842) and permitted states to tax the income of federal officials. The very next year the justices overruled *Collector v. Day* in *Graves v. New York ex rel. O'Keefe* (1939), holding that

there was no constitutional bar to the federal government taxing the income of state employees. "The theory," said the Court, "that a tax on income is legally or economically a tax on its source, is no longer tenable." Also falling were bans on taxing profits from doing business with state or federal government agencies. The Supreme Court went so far as to allow a state to impose taxes on a federal contractor even when those taxes were passed on to the federal government through a cost-plus contract.[11]

In all the cases limiting intergovernmental tax immunity, the Court repeatedly stressed one principle: to be valid, taxes must be nondiscriminatory. If a state wishes to tax a company's profits from a business transaction with the federal government, the tax obligation must be the same as that imposed on profits from business with nongovernmental parties. Consequently, in 1989 the Court invalidated a Michigan law that taxed the pensions of retired federal workers but not the benefits of those who retired from state government.[12]

Although these rulings seriously weakened the doctrine of intergovernmental tax immunity, the principle still has some vitality. It would be unconstitutional for a state to place a tax on cases filed in the federal courts operating within its boundaries, or for the federal government to impose an excise tax on the tickets issued by a state highway patrol. But aside from these obvious examples, where is the line between permissible and impermissible taxation? The Supreme Court helped answer that question in *South Carolina v. Baker* (1988), which involved a challenge to a federal law taxing the income from long-term state and city bonds. To uphold the federal tax would require the Court to overrule that portion of the *Pollock* decision that conferred immunity on such debt instruments of the state. The opinion by

8. *Gillespie v. Oklahoma,* 257 U.S. 501 (1922), and *Long v. Rockwood,* 277 U.S. 142 (1928) concerned patents and copyrights; *Panhandle Oil Co. v. Mississippi,* 277 U.S. 218 (1928) dealt with petroleum sales.

9. *Indian Motorcycle Co. v. United States,* 283 U.S. 501 (1931).

10. *South Carolina v. United States,* 199 U.S. 437 (1905).

11. *Alabama v. King and Boozer,* 314 U.S. 1 (1941).

12. *Davis v. Michigan Department of the Treasury,* 489 U.S. 803 (1989).

Justice William J. Brennan, Jr., not only answered the specific question presented to the Court but also provided an informative review of the status of the intergovernmental tax immunity doctrine. Also instructive is the dissenting opinion of Justice Sandra Day O'Connor, who vigorously defended the immunity position.

South Carolina v. Baker

485 U.S. 505 (1988)

Vote: 7 (Blackmun, Brennan, Marshall, Rehnquist,
Scalia, Stevens, White)
1 (O'Connor)
Opinion of the Court: Brennan
Concurring opinions: Rehnquist, Scalia, Stevens
Dissenting opinion: O'Connor
Not participating: Kennedy

Municipal and state bonds traditionally have been issued either as bearer bonds or as registered bonds. Interest from bearer bonds is presumed to belong to the person who owns the bonds, and the interest is paid when the owner redeems coupons attached to the bond. Owners of registered bonds are recorded on a central list, and if a bond is sold the transaction must be recorded. The owner of record automatically receives interest payments by check or electronic transfer of funds. State and municipal bonds of both types have been free from federal taxation since the Supreme Court's decision in *Pollock.*

In 1982 Congress passed the Tax Equity and Fiscal Responsibility Act (TEFRA). Section 310(b)(1) of that statute removed the federal income tax exemption for interest earned on publicly offered long-term bonds issued by state and local governments unless the bonds were issued in registered form. The primary purpose of Section 310 was to increase compliance with federal tax laws and thereby increase federal revenues. Congress estimated that income of $97 billion was going unreported. Bearer bonds became a target of reform efforts because of the ease with which they could be bought and sold. If the ownership transfer was not registered, the bondholder could evade income tax on capital gains. Unregistered bonds also were used to evade estate taxes. Other provisions in this law encouraged the federal government and private corporations to stop issuing nonregistered long-term bonds.

The state of South Carolina sued the United States, in the name of Secretary of the Treasury James Baker, to have the law declared unconstitutional as a violation of the Tenth Amendment and the intergovernmental tax immunity doctrine. The federal government responded that the law did not violate the Constitution or the immunity doctrine because it did not eliminate the state's power to issue bonds exempt from federal taxation. The law required only that for such bonds to be tax exempt, they must be issued in a particular format. The case was heard on original jurisdiction. A Special Master appointed by the Court to give preliminary consideration to the case recommended that the justices uphold the validity of the law.

Justice Brennan delivered the opinion of the Court:

South Carolina contends that even if a statute banning state bearer bonds entirely would be constitutional, § 310 unconstitutionally violates the doctrine of intergovernmental tax immunity because it imposes a tax on the interest earned on a state bond. We agree with South Carolina that § 310 is inconsistent with *Pollock v. Farmers' Loan & Trust Co.* (1895), which held that any interest earned on a state bond was immune from federal taxation. . . .

Under the intergovernmental tax immunity jurisprudence prevailing at the time, *Pollock* did not represent a unique immunity limited to income derived from state bonds. Rather, *Pollock* merely represented one application of the more general rule that neither the federal nor the state governments could tax income an individual directly derived from *any* contract with another government. Not only was it unconstitutional for the Federal Government to tax a bondowner on the interest she received on any state bond, but it was also unconstitutional to tax a state employee on the income earned from his employment contract, to tax a lessee on income derived from lands leased from a State, or to impose a sales tax on proceeds a vendor derived from selling a product to a state agency. Income derived from the same kinds of contracts with the Federal Government were likewise immune from taxation by the States. . . .

This general rule was based on the rationale that any tax on income a party received under a contract with the government was a tax on the contract and thus a tax "on" the government because it burdened the government's power to enter into the contract. . . . Thus, although a tax was collected from an independent private party, the tax was considered to be "on" the government because the tax burden might be passed on to it through the contract. This reasoning was used to define the basic scope of both federal and state tax immunities with respect to all types of government contracts. . . .

The rationale underlying *Pollock* and the general immunity for government contract income has been thoroughly repudiated by modern intergovernmental immunity caselaw. . . .

With the rationale for conferring a tax immunity on parties dealing with another government rejected, the government contract immunities recognized under prior doctrine were, one by one, eliminated. . . .

In sum, then, under current intergovernmental tax immunity doctrine the States can never tax the United States directly but can tax any private parties with whom it does business, even though the financial burden falls on the United States, as long as the tax does not discriminate against the United States or those with whom it deals. A tax is considered to be directly on the Federal Government only "when the levy falls on the United States itself, or on an agency or instrumentality so closely connected to the Government that the two cannot realistically be viewed as separate entities." The rule with respect to state tax immunity is essentially the same, except that at least some

nondiscriminatory federal taxes can be collected directly from the States even though a parallel state tax could not be collected directly from the Federal Government.

We thus confirm that subsequent caselaw has overruled the holding in *Pollock* that state bond interest is immune from a nondiscriminatory federal tax. We see no constitutional reason for treating persons who receive interest on government bonds differently than persons who receive income from other types of contracts with the government, and no tenable rationale for distinguishing the costs imposed on States by a tax on state bond interest from the costs imposed by a tax on the income from any other state contract. . . . Likewise, the owners of state bonds have no constitutional entitlement not to pay taxes on income they earn from state bonds, and States have no constitutional entitlement to issue bonds paying lower interest rates than other issuers. . . .

TEFRA § 310 thus clearly imposes no direct tax on the States. The tax is imposed on and collected from bondholders, not States, and any increased administrative costs incurred by States in implementing the registration system are not "taxes" within the meaning of the tax immunity doctrine. . . . Nor does § 310 discriminate against States. The provisions of § 310 seek to assure that *all* publicly offered long-term bonds are issued in registered form, whether issued by state or local governments, the Federal Government, or private corporations. Accordingly, the Federal Government has directly imposed the same registration requirement on itself that it has effectively imposed on States. The incentives States have to switch to registered bonds are necessarily different than those of corporate bond issuers because only state bonds enjoy any exemption from the federal tax on bond interest, but the sanctions for issuing unregistered corporate bonds are comparably severe. Removing the tax exemption for interest earned on state bonds would not, moreover, create a discrimination between state and corporate bonds since corporate bond interest is already subject to federal tax.

Because the federal imposition of a bond registration requirement on States does not violate the Tenth Amendment and because a nondiscriminatory federal tax on the interest earned on state bonds does not violate the intergovernmental tax immunity doctrine, we uphold the constitutionality of § 310. . . .

It is so ordered.

Justice O'CONNOR, dissenting.

The Court today overrules a precedent that it has honored for nearly a hundred years and expresses a willingness to cancel the constitutional immunity that traditionally has shielded the interest paid on state and local bonds from federal taxation. Henceforth the ability of state and local governments to finance their activities will depend in part on whether Congress voluntarily abstains from tapping this permissible source of additional income tax revenue. I believe that state autonomy is an important factor to be considered in reviewing the National Government's exercise of its enumerated powers. I dissent from the decision to overrule *Pollock* v. *Farmers' Loan & Trust Co.* (1895), and I would invalidate Congress' attempt to regulate the sovereign States by threatening to deprive them of this tax immunity, which would increase their dependence on the National Government. . . .

Long-term debt obligations are an essential source of funding for state and local governments. In 1974, state and local governments issued approximately $23 billion of new municipal bonds; in 1984, they issued $102 billion of new bonds. State and local governments rely heavily on borrowed funds to finance education, road construction, and utilities, among other purposes. As the Court recognizes, States will have to increase the interest rates they pay on bonds by 28-35% if the interest is subject to the federal income tax. Governmental operations will be hindered severely if the cost of capital rises by one-third. If Congress may tax the interest paid on state and local bonds, it may strike at the very heart of state and local government activities. . . .

Federal taxation of state activities is inherently a threat to state sovereignty. As Chief Justice Marshall observed long ago, "the power to tax involves the power to destroy." Justice Holmes later qualified this principle, observing that "[t]he power to tax is not the power to destroy while this Court sits." If this Court is the States' sole protector against the threat of crushing taxation, it must take seriously its responsibility to sit in judgment of federal tax initiatives. I do not think that the Court has lived up to its constitutional role in this case. The Court has failed to enforce the constitutional safeguards of state autonomy and self-sufficiency that may be found in the Tenth Amendment and the Guarantee Clause, as well as in the principles of federalism implicit in the Constitution. I respectfully dissent.

Taxation as a Regulatory Power

Normally, we think of taxation as a method of funding the government. Yet Marshall's well-known statement that the "power to tax involves the power to destroy" was an early recognition that taxes can be used for purposes other than raising revenue. Excessive taxation can make the targeted activities so unprofitable that it is no longer feasible to engage in them. The converse also is true. Favorable tax status, including tax exemptions, can encourage a preferred activity. These observations lead us to several important constitutional questions regarding the taxation powers of the federal government. Is it proper for the United States to impose taxes for reasons other than revenue raising? Is it constitutional for the government to use taxation as a method of regulation? Is it valid for Congress to enact tax laws as means of controlling activities not otherwise within the jurisdiction of the federal government?

Taxation for Nonrevenue Purposes

From the beginning, Congress has used its authority to tax for purposes other than raising revenue. Before the ratification of the Sixteenth Amendment, the federal government relied heavily on customs duties. In deciding what imported products to tax and at what level, the legislators clearly were guided by their policy preferences. Certain industries received protection from imports and were able to grow with little foreign competition. The practice of combining revenue gathering with other policy objectives continues to this day.

The only serious challenge to the use of import taxes as a regulatory mechanism came in *J. W. Hampton, Jr. & Co. v. United States* (1928). The Hampton Company imported into New York a quantity of barium dioxide that was assessed a duty of six cents per pound, two cents higher than the rate set by Congress. However, Congress had authorized the president to raise or lower tariff duties up to 50 percent of the amount set by Congress whenever the chief executive found that such adjustments were necessary for equitable foreign trade. In this case President Calvin Coolidge had concluded that an increased tariff was necessary to equalize the barium dioxide production costs between Germany and the United States. Hampton objected to the tax, claiming that the flexible tariff was an improper delegation of legislative power to the executive branch and that Congress violated the Constitution by using the taxation powers for reasons other than revenue gathering. As we saw in Chapter 3, the Supreme Court ruled that the delegation was proper.

The justices also held in *Hampton* that Congress did not have to rely exclusively on revenue needs in constructing tariff laws. In reaching this conclusion, the Court showed a deference to history. Chief Justice William Howard Taft, writing for the majority, noted that the very first revenue act in 1789 imposed import duties with an eye toward encouraging growth of domestic industry and protecting it from foreign competition. The Court was not likely to rule unconstitutional a practice that had been followed uninterrupted for almost a century and a half. "So long as the motive of Congress and the effect of its legislative action are to secure revenue for the benefit of the general government," Taft wrote, "the existence of other motives in the selection of the subjects of taxes cannot invalidate Congressional action."

Deciding that Congress may impose import duties with regulatory purposes does not necessarily answer a similar question with respect to excise taxes. Customs, after all, have a limited range. They can be applied only to those goods that are brought into the country from abroad. Excise taxes can be applied to the broad spectrum of domestic goods, services, and activities. The only restriction on such taxes explicitly mentioned in the Constitution is that they be geographically uniform. But is there an implied requirement that excise taxes can be generated only by revenue objectives or can Congress regulate through the use of the excise? If Congress is allowed to regulate domestic activities through the power to tax, does that not give the federal government the equivalent of a police power that the Framers reserved to the states?

Shortly after the Civil War, the Court heard *Veazie Bank v. Fenno* (1869), which presented a challenge to a federal excise tax that was imposed far more to regulate the economy than to raise revenue. In 1866 Congress passed a law placing a 10 percent tax on notes issued by state banks. The law was intended to protect the newly chartered national bank from state competition by making these notes far too costly for state banks to issue. Veazie Bank paid the tax under protest, claiming that Congress had no authority to issue such an excise. But in a 5-2 decision, the Court held that the tax was proper given the constitutional power of Congress to regulate the monetary system.

Did the *Veazie Bank* decision mean that Congress may impose excise taxes for any regulatory purpose or only as a means of promoting a power already granted to the federal government? The first major case to confront this question focused on a federal excise tax placed on margarine.

McCray v. United States

195 U.S. 27 (1904)

*Vote: 6 (Brewer, Day, Harlan, Holmes, McKenna,
    White)
    3 (Brown, Fuller, Peckham)
Opinion of the Court: White*

In the latter half of the nineteenth century, food producers developed a commercially marketable oleomargarine. The product was made of oleo oil, lard, milk, cream, and salt. It had a consistency and taste similar to butter but was less expensive. Especially successful was a margarine that was artificially colored to make the naturally white substance look like butter. As margarine grew in popularity, the dairy industry became concerned and demanded protection. In response, Congress passed the Oleomargarine Act of 1886 and amended it in 1902. In addition to licensing producers and retailers of margarine, the statute imposed an excise tax of one-quarter cent per pound on naturally colored margarine, and a tax of ten cents per pound on artificially colored margarine. The manufacturers of the product were responsible for payment of the tax. Although the Act raised revenue, its central purpose was to protect the dairy industry by raising the price of margarine and discouraging the sale of the artificially colored product.

McCray, a licensed retail seller of margarine, was assessed a $50 penalty for knowingly purchasing from the Ohio Butterine Company a fifty-pound package of margarine for resale upon which sufficient taxes had not been paid. The package bore the one-quarter cent tax stamps, but the margarine was artificially colored and subject to the higher tax. McCray challenged his fine, claiming that the federal tax was unconstitutional. Its defect, according to McCray, was that the law was a regulation on the intrastate manufacture of margarine, a sphere of authority reserved for the states. The federal government countered with the

argument that the margarine tax was an excise tax and as such the Constitution required only that it meet the standard of geographical uniformity. The lower courts upheld the validity of the tax.

Justice Edward White delivered the opinion of the Court:

Did Congress in passing the acts which are assailed, exert a power not conferred by the Constitution?

That the acts in question on their face impose excise taxes which Congress had the power to levy is so completely established as to require only statement. . . .

It is, however, argued if a lawful power may be exerted for an unlawful purpose, and thus by abusing the power it may be made to accomplish a result not intended by the Constitution, all limitations of power must disappear, and the grave function lodged in the judiciary, to confine all the departments within the authority conferred by the Constitution, will be of no avail. This, when reduced to its last analysis, comes to this, that, because a particular department of the government may exert its lawful powers with the object or motive of reaching an end not justified, therefore it becomes the duty of the judiciary to restrain the exercise of a lawful power wherever it seems to the judicial mind that such lawful power has been abused. But this reduces itself to the contention that, under our constitutional system, the abuse by one department of the government of its lawful powers is to be corrected by the abuse of its powers by another department.

The proposition, if sustained, would destroy all distinction between the powers of the respective departments of the government, would put an end to that confidence and respect for each other which it was the purpose of the Constitution to uphold, and would thus be full of danger to the permanence of our institutions. . . .

It is, of course, true, as suggested, that if there be no authority in the judiciary to restrain a lawful exercise of power by another department of the government, where a wrong motive or purpose has impelled to the exertion of the power, that abuses of a power conferred may be temporarily effectual. The remedy for this, however, lies, not in the abuse by the judicial authority of its functions, but in the people, upon whom, after all, under our institutions, reliance must be placed for the correction of abuses committed in the exercise of a lawful power. . . .

The decisions of this court from the beginning lend no support whatever to the assumption that the judiciary may restrain the exercise of lawful power on the assumption that a wrongful purpose or motive has caused the power to be exerted. As we have previously said, from the beginning no case can be found announcing such a doctrine, and on the contrary the doctrine of a number of cases is inconsistent with its existence. As quite recently pointed out by this court in *Knowlton* v. *Moore* (1900), the often quoted statement of Chief Justice Marshall in *McCulloch* v. *Maryland*, that the power to tax is the power to destroy, affords no support whatever to the proposition that where there is a lawful power to impose a tax its imposition may be treated as without the power because of the destructive effect of the exertion of the authority. . . .

It being thus demonstrated that the motive or purpose of Congress in adopting the acts in question may not be inquired into, we are brought to consider the contentions relied upon to show that the acts assailed were beyond the power of Congress, putting entirely out of view all considerations based upon purpose or motive.

1. Undoubtedly, in determining whether a particular act is within a granted power, its scope and effect are to be considered. Applying this rule to the acts assailed, it is self-evident that on their face they levy an excise tax. That being their necessary scope and operation, it follows that the acts are within the grant of power. The argument to the contrary rests on the proposition that, although the tax be within the power, as enforcing it will destroy or restrict the manufacture of artificially colored oleomargarine, therefore the power to levy the tax did not obtain. This, however, is but to say that the question of power depends, not upon the authority conferred by the Constitution but upon what may be the consequence arising from the exercise of the lawful authority.

Since, as pointed out in all the decisions referred to, the taxing power conferred by the Constitution knows no limits except those expressly stated in that instrument, it must follow, if a tax be within the lawful power, the exertion of that power may not be judicially

restrained because of the results to arise from its exercise. . . .

2. The proposition that where a tax is imposed which is within the grant of powers, and which does not conflict with any express constitutional limitation, the courts may hold the tax to be void because it is deemed that the tax is too high, is absolutely disposed of by the opinions in the cases hitherto cited, and which expressly hold . . . that "The judicial department cannot prescribe to the legislative department limitations upon the exercise of its acknowledged powers. The power to tax may be exercised oppressively upon persons; but the responsibility of the legislature is not to the courts, but to the people by whom its members are elected.''

3. Whilst undoubtedly both the Fifth and Tenth Amendments qualify, in so far as they are applicable, all the provisions of the Constitution, nothing in those amendments operates to take away the grant of power to tax conferred by the Constitution upon Congress. The contention on this subject rests upon the theory that the purpose and motive of Congress in exercising its undoubted powers may be inquired into by the courts, and the proposition is therefore disposed of by what has been said on that subject.

The right of Congress to tax within its delegated power being unrestrained, except as limited by the Constitution, it was within the authority conferred on Congress to select the objects upon which an excise should be laid. It therefore follows that, in exerting its power, no want of due process of law could possibly result, because that body chose to impose an excise on artificially colored oleomargarine and not upon natural butter artificially colored. . . .

4. Lastly we come to consider the argument that, even though as a general rule a tax of the nature of the one in question would be within the power of Congress, in this case the tax should be held not to be within such power, because of its effect. This is based on the contention that, as the tax is so large as to destroy the business of manufacturing oleomargarine artificially colored, to look like butter, it thus deprives the manufacturers of that article of their freedom to engage in a lawful pursuit, and hence, irrespective of the distribution of powers made by the Constitution, the taxing laws are void, because they violate those

fundamental rights which it is the duty of every free government to safeguard, and which, therefore, should be held to be embraced by implied though none the less potential guaranties, or in any event to be within the protection of the due process clause of the Fifth Amendment.

Let us concede, for the sake of argument only, the premise of fact upon which the proposition is based. Moreover, concede for the sake of argument only, that even although a particular exertion of power by Congress was not restrained by any express limitation of the Constitution, if by the perverted exercise of such power so great an abuse was manifested as to destroy fundamental rights which no free government could consistently violate, that it would be the duty of the judiciary to hold such acts to be void upon the assumption that the Constitution by necessary implication forbade them.

Such concession, however, is not controlling in this case. This follows when the nature of oleomargarine, artificially colored to look like butter, is recalled. As we have said, it has been conclusively settled by this court that the tendency of that article to deceive the public into buying it for butter is such that the States may, in the exertion of their police powers, without violating the due process clause of the Fourteenth Amendment, absolutely prohibit the manufacture of the article. It hence results, that even though it be true that the effect of the tax in question is to repress the manufacture of artificially colored oleomargarine, it cannot be said that such repression destroys rights which no free government could destroy, and, therefore, no ground exists to sustain the proposition that the judiciary may invoke an implied prohibition, upon the theory that to do so is essential to save such rights from destruction. And the same considerations dispose of the contention based upon the due process clause of the Fifth Amendment. That provision, as we have previously said, does not withdraw or expressly limit the grant of power to tax conferred upon Congress by the Constitution. From this it follows, as we have also previously declared, that the judiciary is without authority to avoid an act of Congress exerting the taxing power, even in a case where to the judicial mind it seems that Congress had in putting such power in motion abused its lawful authority by levying a tax which was unwise or oppressive, or the result of the enforcement of which might be to indirectly affect subjects not within the powers delegated to Congress.

Let us concede that if a case was presented where the abuse of the taxing power was so extreme as to be beyond the principles which we have previously stated, and where it was plain to the judicial mind that the power had been called into play not for revenue but solely for the purpose of destroying rights which could not be rightfully destroyed consistently with the principles of freedom and justice upon which the Constitution rests, that it would be the duty of the courts to say that such an arbitrary act was not merely an abuse of a delegated power, but was the exercise of an authority not conferred. This concession, however, like the one previously made, must be without influence upon the decision of this cause for the reasons previously stated; that is, that the manufacture of artificially colored oleomargarine may be prohibited by a free government without a violation of fundamental rights.

Affirmed.

With decisions such as *Veazie, McCray,* and others, Congress reasonably concluded that the power to tax could be employed as a regulatory weapon. The legislators were encouraged by statements such as that written by Justice White in *McCray:* ''The decisions of this court from the beginning lend no support whatever to the assumption that the judiciary may restrain the exercise of lawful power on the assumption that a wrongful purpose or motive has caused the power to be exerted.'' The Court seemed committed to a policy of approving legislation that took the proper form of an excise tax and met the geographical uniformity requirement regardless of the congressional motives behind it. If motives were not to be probed by the judiciary, the legislative branch would have a free hand in using taxation to regulate or even destroy certain activities considered by Congress to be detrimental to the nation.

The Rejection and Reestablishment of Regulatory Taxation

Among Congress's targets was child labor. As we saw in our discussions of federalism and the Commerce Clause, Congress first attempted to regulate child labor in the 1916 Keating-Owen Act, which prohibited articles produced by child labor from being shipped in interstate and foreign commerce. Just two years after that law was enacted, the Supreme Court in *Hammer v. Dagenhart* struck it down on the grounds that Congress, under the guise of interstate commerce regulation, was actually controlling manufacturing and mining, considered at that time to be intrastate activities the regulation of which was reserved to the states.

After suffering this defeat at the hands of the Supreme Court, Congress drafted a second statute to attack child labor, this time using the power to tax. Could the national legislature constitutionally use the excise tax as a means of eliminating child labor? Would the justices once again refuse to examine congressional motives? The answer to these questions came in *Bailey v. Drexel Furniture Co.* (1922). As you read Chief Justice Taft's opinion, note his distinction between a tax and a penalty. Does he make a compelling argument? And does it surprise you that progressive members of the Court, such as Oliver Wendell Holmes and Louis Brandeis, voted to strike down the law?

Young boys working a loom in Macon, Georgia, circa 1910. Conditions such as these were the target of reform legislation passed by Congress and declared unconstitutional by the Supreme Court in Hammer v. Dagenhart *(1918) and* Bailey v. Drexel Furniture Company *(1922).*

Bailey v. Drexel Furniture Co.

259 U.S. 20 (1922)

*Vote: 8 (Brandeis, Day, Holmes, McKenna,
    McReynolds, Pitney, Taft, Van Devanter)
    1 (Clarke)*

Opinion of the Court: Taft

Congress passed the Child Labor Tax Law on February 24, 1919. The statute imposed an excise tax of 10 percent on the net profits of any company hiring child labor. Under the law, child labor was defined as the employment of children under the age of sixteen in any mine or quarry, or under the age of fourteen in any mill, cannery, workshop, factory, or manufacturing establishment. The definition also included the use of children between the ages of fourteen and sixteen who worked more than eight hours a day or more than six days a week, or who worked between the hours of 7:00 p.m. and 6:00 a.m.

Drexel was a furniture manufacturing company in North Carolina. On September 20, 1921, it received from J. W. Bailey, the IRS collector for the Western District of North Carolina, a notice that it had been assessed $6,312.79 in excise taxes for having employed a boy under the age of fourteen during the 1919 tax year. The company paid the tax under protest and sued for a refund. Drexel argued that the tax was nothing more than an unconstitutional attempt to regulate manufacturing. The United States defended the statute as an excise tax that need meet no standard but geographical uniformity. The lower court ruled in favor of the company.

Chief Justice Taft delivered the opinion of the Court:

The law is attacked on the ground that it is a regulation of the employment of child labor in the States—an exclusively state function under the Federal Constitution and within the reservations of the Tenth Amendment. It is defended on the ground that it is a mere excise tax levied by the Congress of the United States under its broad power of taxation conferred by § 8, Article I, of the Federal Constitution. We must construe the law and interpret the intent and meaning of Congress from the language of the act. The words are to be given their ordinary meaning unless the context shows that they are differently used. Does this law impose a tax with only that incidental restraint and regulation which a tax must inevitably involve? Or does it regulate by the use of the so-called tax as a penalty? If a tax, it is clearly an excise. If it were an excise on a commodity or other thing of value we might not be permitted under previous decisions of this court to infer solely from its heavy burden that the act intends a prohibition instead of a tax. But this act is more. It provides a heavy exaction for a departure from a detailed and specified course of conduct in business. That course of business is that employers shall employ in mines and quarries, children of an age greater than sixteen years; in mills and factories, children of an age greater than fourteen years, and shall prevent children of less than sixteen years in mills and factories from working more than eight hours a day or six days in the week. If an employer departs from this prescribed course of business, he is to pay to the Government one-tenth of his entire net income in the business for a full year. The amount is not to be proportioned in any degree to the extent or frequency of the departures, but is to be paid by the employer in full measure whether he employs five hundred children for a year, or employs only one for a day. Moreover, if he does not know the child is within the named age limit, he is not to pay; that is to say, it is only where he knowingly departs from the prescribed course that payment is to be exacted. Scienter is associated with penalties not with taxes. The employer's factory is to be subject to inspection at any time not only by the taxing officers of the Treasury, the Department normally charged with the collection of taxes, but also by the Secretary of Labor and his subordinates whose normal function is the advancement and protection of the welfare of the workers. In the light of these features of the act, a court must be blind not to see that the so-called tax is imposed to stop the employment of children within the age limits prescribed. Its prohibitory and regulatory effect and purpose are palpable. All others can see and understand this. How can we properly shut our minds to it?

It is the high duty and function of this court in cases regularly brought to its bar to decline to recognize or enforce seeming laws of Congress, dealing with subjects not entrusted to Congress but left or committed by the supreme law of the land to the control of the States. We can not avoid the duty even though it require us to refuse to give effect to legislation designed to promote the highest good. The good sought in unconstitutional legislation is an insidious feature because it leads citizens and legislators of good purpose to promote it without thought of the serious breach it will make in the ark of our covenant or the harm which will come from breaking down recognized standards. In the maintenance of local self government, on the one hand, and the national power, on the other, our country has been able to endure and prosper for near a century and a half.

Out of a proper respect for the acts of a coordinate branch of the Government, this court has gone far to sustain taxing acts as such, even though there has been ground for suspecting from the weight of the tax it was intended to destroy its subject. But, in the act before us, the presumption of validity cannot prevail, because the proof of the contrary is found on the very face of its provisions. Grant the validity of this law, and all that Congress would need to do, hereafter, in seeking to take over to its control any one of the great number of subjects of public interest, jurisdiction of which the States have never parted with, and which are reserved to them by the Tenth Amendment, would be to enact a detailed measure of complete regulation of the subject and enforce it by a so-called tax upon departures from it. To give such magic to the word "tax" would be to break down all constitutional limitation of the powers of Congress and completely wipe out the sovereignty of the States.

The difference between a tax and a penalty is sometimes difficult to define and yet the consequences of the distinction in the required method of their collection often are important. Where the sovereign enacting the law has power to impose both tax and penalty the difference between revenue production and mere regulation may be immaterial, but not so when one sovereign can impose a tax only, and the power of regulation rests in another. Taxes are occasionally imposed in the discretion of the legislature on proper subjects with the primary motive of obtaining revenue from them and with the incidental motive of discouraging them by making their continuance onerous. They do not lose their character as taxes because of the incidental motive. But there comes a time in the extension of the penalizing features of the so-called tax when it loses its character as such and becomes a mere penalty with the characteristics of regulation and punishment. Such is the case in the law before us. Although Congress does not invalidate the contract of employment or expressly declare that the employment within the mentioned ages is illegal, it does exhibit its intent practically to achieve the latter result by adopting the criteria of wrongdoing and imposing its principal consequence on those who transgress its standard.

The case before us can not be distinguished from that of *Hammer* v. *Dagenhart*. Congress there enacted a law to prohibit transportation in interstate commerce of goods made at a factory in which there was employment of children within the same ages and for the same number of hours a day and days in a week as are penalized by the act in this case. This court held the law in that case to be void. It said:

"In our view the necessary effect of this act is, by means of a prohibition against the movement in interstate commerce of ordinary commercial commodities, to regulate the hours of labor of children in factories and mines within the States, a purely state authority."

In the case at the bar, Congress in the name of a tax which on the face of the act is a penalty seeks to do the same thing, and the effort must be equally futile.

The analogy of the *Dagenhart Case* is clear. The congressional power over interstate commerce is, within its proper scope, just as complete and unlimited as the congressional power to tax, and the legislative motive in its exercise is just as free from judicial suspicion and inquiry. Yet when Congress threatened to stop interstate commerce in ordinary and necessary commodities, unobjectionable as subjects of transportation, and to deny the same to the people of a State in order to coerce them into compliance with Congress's regulation of state concerns, the court said this was not in fact regulation of interstate commerce, but rather that of State concerns and was invalid. So here the so-called tax is a penalty to coerce people of a State to act as Congress wishes them to act in respect of a matter completely the business of the state government under the Federal Constitution. . . .

For the reasons given, we must hold the Child Labor Tax Law invalid and the judgment of the District Court is

Affirmed.

With the Court's rejection of both its attempts to regulate child labor through the commerce and taxation powers, Congress pursued yet another alternative. In 1924, two years after *Drexel,* Congress proposed a constitutional amendment that gave the national government power to regulate and prohibit child labor. Unlike most proposed amendments, Congress placed no deadline on the states for ratification. Slightly more than half of the state legislatures endorsed the amendment before support for it began to decline. In the final analysis, the amendment was unnecessary. Many states responded to decisions such as *Hammer* and *Drexel* by passing their own child labor laws. In addition, the 1937 constitutional revolution that redefined the concept of interstate commerce, along with subsequent employment regulation decisions such as *United States v. Darby Lumber* (1941), gave the federal government ample authority to control child labor.

The decision in *Drexel* was a reversal of the position on excise taxes the Court had held since the early 1800s. It generally proved to be out of line with Supreme Court rulings both before and after. The Court repeatedly has faced the question of taxation and regulation and generally has ruled in favor of the federal power to tax and even acknowledged that all taxes to some degree have regulatory effects. For example, in *United States v. Doremus* (1919) and *Nigro v. United States* (1928) the Court upheld federal excise taxes on narcotics, and in *United States v. Sanchez* (1950) it upheld a tax on marijuana. Similarly, an excise tax on objectionable firearms was declared valid in *Sonzinsky v. United States* (1937) even though the Court admitted that the law had an unmistakable "legislative purpose to regulate rather than to tax." The justices found no constitutional defects with an excise levied on professional gamblers in *United States v. Kahriger* (1953). These taxes expand federal regulatory powers. If Congress has the power to impose the tax, then the federal government also has the power to enforce the tax laws, creating, to an extent, "police powers" within the federal government that originally resided with the states.

The authority to use the excise tax as a regulatory power is not unlimited. Such taxes cannot be levied or enforced in a manner that violates other provisions of the Constitution. *Kahriger* provides an illustration. The tax imposed required those engaged in accepting bets to pay an annual excise of $50 and to register with the collector of internal revenue. Although it is constitutionally valid for Congress to impose an occupational excise tax, the law cannot compel a person to admit to criminal activity. To do so would be a violation of the Fifth Amendment's Self-Incrimination Clause. Although Joseph Kahriger raised these objections in his appeal, the majority upheld the statute's requirements that gamblers register with the government. Several years later, however, the Court reexamined this position in *Marchetti v. United States* (1968). Here the Court held that no laws, including tax laws, can constitutionally require a person to admit to criminal activities. To the extent that the *Kahriger* decision permitted such procedures, it was overruled.

Taxing and Spending for the General Welfare

The Constitution authorizes Congress to tax and spend for the general welfare. Whether the term *general welfare* was intended to expand the powers of Congress beyond those explicitly stated in the Constitution is subject to debate. James Madison, for example, argued that general welfare was only a reference to the other enumerated powers. Because the United States is a government of limited and specified powers, he asserted, the authority to tax and spend must be confined to those spheres of authority the Constitution explicitly granted. Alexander Hamilton took the opposite position. He interpreted the power to tax and spend for the general welfare to be a separate power altogether. For Hamilton taxing and spending authority was given in addition to the other granted powers, not limited by them. The conflict between these two opposing interpretations was the subject of legal disputes throughout much of the nation's history. During the constitutional crisis over legislation passed during the New Deal, however, the final battle between the two was waged.

A Restricted View of Taxing and Spending

Many of the programs recommended by Franklin Roosevelt to reestablish the nation's economic strength involved regulatory activity far more extensive than ever before proposed. Several depended on the power of the federal government to tax and spend for the general welfare. Opponents of the New Deal claimed that these programs, while ostensibly based upon the taxing and spending authority, in reality were regulations of matters the Constitution reserved for the states.

One of the most important objectives of the Roosevelt administration was to restore stability to the agricultural markets and to impose conditions that would make farms profitable. To accomplish these goals, Congress passed the Agricultural Adjustment Act of 1933. The constitutional test of the AAA, in the case of *United States v. Butler* (1936), was one of the most important of the New Deal era. Although the issues in this case were crucial both to the economic welfare of the nation and to the constitutional future of federalism, Justice Owen Roberts, writing for the majority, presented an uncomplicated formula for deciding the case: "Lay the article of the Constitution which is invoked beside the statute which is challenged and . . . decide whether the latter squares with the former." Do you believe the process of judicial review is that simple—especially when so much is riding on the outcome of the Court's deliberations?

United States v. Butler

297 U.S. 1 (1936)

Vote: 6 (Butler, Hughes, McReynolds, Roberts,
*   Sutherland, Van Devanter)*
*   3 (Brandeis, Cardozo, Stone)*
Opinion of the Court: Roberts
Dissenting opinion: Stone

During the Great Depression, agriculture was one of the hardest hit sectors of the economy. The nation's farmers were overproducing, which caused prices for farm products to drop. In many cases the cost of production was higher than the income from crop sales, leaving farmers in desperate straits. Most had their farms mortgaged, and all owed taxes on their lands. The more the farmers got behind economically, the more they attempted to produce to improve their situation. This strategy further increased production and made the overall situation even worse. At that time agriculture was responsible for a much larger proportion of the nation's economy than it is today, and conditions in the farming sector had dire effects on the general welfare of the entire country.

In response to this situation, Roosevelt proposed and Congress passed the AAA, a statute that combined the taxing and spending powers to combat the agricultural crisis. The central purpose of the plan was to reduce the amount of acreage being farmed. To accomplish this goal, the federal government would ''rent'' a percentage of the nation's farmland and leave this acreage unplanted. In effect, the government would pay the farmers not to farm. If the plan succeeded, agricultural production would drop, prices would rise, and the farmer would have a sufficient income. Making payments to the nation's farmers was an expensive proposition, and to fund these expenditures the AAA imposed an excise tax on the processing of agricultural products.

The program was a success until William M. Butler challenged the constitutionality of the law. Butler was the bankruptcy receiver for Hoosac Mills Corporation, a cotton processor. When the government imposed the processing tax on Hoosac, Butler took legal action to avoid payment, claiming that the AAA exceeded the taxing and spending powers granted to the federal government. The district court upheld the law, but the court of appeals reversed. The United States brought appeal to the Supreme Court.

Justice Roberts delivered the opinion of the Court:

The Government asserts that even if the respondents may question the propriety of the appropriation embodied in the statute their attack must fail because Article I, § 8 of the Constitution authorizes the contemplated expenditure of the funds raised by the tax. This contention presents the great and the controlling question in the case. We approach its decision with a sense of our grave responsibility to render judgment in accordance with the principles established for the government of all three branches of the Government.

There should be no misunderstanding as to the function of this court in such a case. It is sometimes said that the court assumes a power to overrule or control the action of the people's representatives. This is a misconception. The Constitution is the supreme law of the land ordained and established by the people. All legislation must conform to the principles it lays down. When an act of Congress is appropriately challenged in the courts as not conforming to the constitutional mandate the judicial branch of the Government has only one duty,—to lay the article of the Constitution which is invoked beside the statute which is challenged and to decide whether the latter squares with the former. All the court does, or can do, is to announce its considered judgment upon the question. The only power it has, if such it may be called, is the power of judgment. This court neither approves nor condemns any legislative policy. Its delicate and difficult office is to ascertain and declare whether the legislation is in accordance with, or in contravention of, the provisions of the Constitution; and, having done that, its duty ends.

The question is not what power the Federal Government ought to have but what powers in fact have been given by the people. It hardly seems necessary to reiterate that ours is a dual form of government; that in every state there are two governments,—the state and the United States. Each State has all governmental powers save such as the people, by their Constitution, have conferred upon the United States, denied to the States, or reserved to themselves. The federal union is a government of delegated powers. It has only such as are expressly conferred upon it and such as are reasonably to be implied from those granted. In this respect we differ radically from nations where all legislative power, without restriction or limitation, is vested in a parliament or other legislative body subject to no restrictions except the discretion of its members.

Article I, § 8, of the Constitution vests sundry powers in the Congress. But two of its clauses have any bearing upon the validity of the statute under review.

The third clause endows the Congress with power ''to regulate Commerce . . . among the several States.'' Despite a reference in its first section to a burden upon, and an obstruction of the normal currents of commerce, the act under review does not purport to regulate transactions in interstate or foreign commerce. Its stated purpose is the control of agricultural production, a purely local activity, in an effort to raise the prices paid the farmer. Indeed, the Government does not attempt to uphold the validity of the act on the basis of the commerce clause, which, for the purpose of the present case, may be put aside as irrelevant.

The clause thought to authorize the legislation,—

the first,—confers upon the Congress power "to lay and collect Taxes, Duties, Imposts and Excises, to pay the Debts and provide for the common Defence and general Welfare of the United States. . . ." It is not contended that this provision grants power to regulate agricultural production upon the theory that such legislation would promote the general welfare. The Government concedes that the phrase "to provide for the general welfare" qualifies the power "to lay and collect taxes." The view that the clause grants power to provide for the general welfare, independently of the taxing power, has never been authoritatively accepted. . . . The true construction undoubtedly is that the only thing granted is the power to tax for the purpose of providing funds for payment of the nation's debts and making provision for the general welfare.

Nevertheless the Government asserts that warrant is found in this clause for the adoption of the Agricultural Adjustment Act. The argument is that Congress may appropriate and authorize the spending of moneys for the "general welfare"; that the phrase should be liberally construed to cover anything conducive to national welfare; that decision as to what will promote such welfare rests with Congress alone, and the courts may not review its determination; and finally that the appropriation under attack was in fact for the general welfare of the United States.

The Congress is expressly empowered to lay taxes to provide for the general welfare. Funds in the Treasury as a result of taxation may be expended only through appropriation. (Art. I, § 9, cl. 7.) They can never accomplish the objects for which they were collected unless the power to appropriate is as broad as the power to tax. The necessary implication from the terms of the grant is that the public funds may be appropriated "to provide for the general welfare of the United States." These words cannot be meaningless, else they would not have been used. The conclusion must be that they were intended to limit and define the granted power to raise and to spend money. How shall they be construed to effectuate the intent of the instrument?

Since the foundation of the Nation sharp differences of opinion have persisted as to the true interpretation of the phrase. Madison asserted it amounted to no more than a reference to the other powers enumerated in the subsequent clauses of the same section; that, as the

United States is a government of limited and enumerated powers, the grant of power to tax and spend for the general national welfare must be confined to the enumerated legislative fields committed to the Congress. In this view the phrase is mere tautology, for taxation and appropriation are or may be necessary incidents of the exercise of any of the enumerated legislative powers. Hamilton, on the other hand, maintained the clause confers a power separate and distinct from those later enumerated, is not restricted in meaning by the grant of them, and Congress consequently has a substantive power to tax and to appropriate, limited only by the requirement that it shall be exercised to provide for the general welfare of the United States. Each contention has had the support of those whose views are entitled to weight. This court has noticed the question, but has never found it necessary to decide which is the true construction. Mr. Justice Story, in his Commentaries, espouses the Hamiltonian position. We shall not review the writings of public men and commentators or discuss the legislative practice. Study of all these leads us to conclude that the reading advocated by Mr. Justice Story is the correct one. While, therefore, the power to tax is not unlimited, its confines are set in the clause which confers it, and not in those of § 8 which bestow and define the legislative powers of the Congress. It results that the power of Congress to authorize expenditure of public moneys for public purposes is not limited by the direct grants of legislative power found in the Constitution. . . .

We are not now required to ascertain the scope of the phrase "general welfare of the United States" or to determine whether an appropriation in aid of agriculture falls within it. Wholly apart from that question, another principle embedded in our Constitution prohibits the enforcement of the Agricultural Adjustment Act. The act invades the reserved rights of the states. It is a statutory plan to regulate and control agricultural production, a matter beyond the powers delegated to the federal government. The tax, the appropriation of the funds raised, and the direction for their disbursement, are but parts of the plan. They are but means to an unconstitutional end.

From the accepted doctrine that the United States is a government of delegated powers, it follows that those not expressly granted, or reasonably to be implied from such as are conferred, are reserved to the states or to the people. To forestall any suggestion to the contrary, the Tenth Amendment was adopted. The same proposition, otherwise stated, is that powers not granted are prohibited. None to regulate agricultural production is given, and therefore legislation by Congress for that purpose is forbidden.

It is an established principle that the attainment of a prohibited end may not be accomplished under the pretext of the exertion of powers which are granted. . . .

The power of taxation, which is expressly granted, may, of course, be adopted as a means to carry into operation another power also expressly granted. But resort to the taxing power to effectuate an end which is not legitimate, not within the scope of the Constitution, is obviously inadmissible. . . .

. . . If the taxing power may not be used as the instrument to enforce a regulation of matters of state concern with respect to which the Congress has no authority to interfere, may it, as in the present case, be employed to raise the money necessary to purchase a compliance which the Congress is powerless to command? The Government asserts that whatever might be said against the validity of the plan if compulsory, it is constitutionally sound because the end is accomplished by voluntary cooperation. There are two sufficient answers to the contention. The regulation is not in fact voluntary. The farmer, of course, may refuse to comply, but the price of such refusal is the loss of benefits. The amount offered is intended to be sufficient to exert pressure on him to agree to the proposed regulation. The power to confer or withhold unlimited benefits is the power to coerce or destroy. If the cotton grower elects not to accept the benefits, he will receive less for his crops; those who receive payments will be able to undersell him. The result will be financial ruin. The coercive purpose and intent of the statute is not obscured by the fact that it has not been perfectly successful. It is pointed out that, because there still remained a minority whom the rental and benefit payments were insufficient to induce to surrender their independence of action, the Congress has gone further and, in the Bankhead Cotton Act, used the taxing power in a more directly minatory fashion to compel submission. This progression only serves more fully to expose the coercive purpose of the so-called tax imposed by the present act. It is clear that the Department of Agriculture has properly described the plan as one to keep a non-cooperating minority in line. This is coercion by economic pressure. The asserted power of choice is illusory. . . .

But if the plan were one for purely voluntary cooperation it would stand no better so far as federal power is concerned. At best it is a scheme for purchasing with federal funds submission to federal regulation of a subject reserved to the states. . . .

Congress has no power to enforce its commands on the farmer to the ends sought by the Agricultural Adjustment Act. It must follow that it may not indirectly accomplish those ends by taxing and spending to purchase compliance. The Constitution and the entire plan of our government negative any such use of the power to tax and to spend as the act undertakes to authorize. It does not help to declare that local conditions throughout the nation have created a situation of national concern; for this is but to say that whenever there is a widespread similarity of local conditions, Congress may ignore constitutional limitations upon its own powers and usurp those reserved to the states. If, in lieu of compulsory regulation of subjects within the states' reserved jurisdiction, which is prohibited, the Congress could invoke the taxing and spending power as a means to accomplish the same end, clause 1 of § 8 of Article I would become the instrument for total subversion of the governmental powers reserved to the individual states.

If the act before us is a proper exercise of the federal taxing power, evidently the regulation of all industry throughout the United States may be accomplished by similar exercises of the same power. It would be possible to exact money from one branch of an industry and pay it to another branch in every field of activity which lies within the province of the states. The mere threat of such a procedure might well induce the surrender of rights and the compliance with federal regulation as the price of continuance in business. . . .

The judgment is

Affirmed.

William M. Butler, receiver for Hoosac Mills, objected to paying the federal tax on processing cotton. His lawsuit successfully challenged the constitutionality of the Agricultural Adjustment Act of 1933.

Butler had a mixed outcome. The Court concluded that the federal government had broad powers to tax and spend for the general welfare. The justices decided, consistent with the position previously articulated by Alexander Hamilton, that Congress's fiscal authority was not limited to those subjects specifically enumerated in Article I. However, this philosophy did not mean

that congressional powers had no limits. The majority in *Butler* concluded that the law was unconstitutional because what it imposed was not truly a tax. Instead, the government was taking money from one group (the processors) to give to another (the farmers), and doing this to regulate farm production, a matter of intrastate commerce reserved for state regulation.

Expanding the Powers to Tax and Spend

The impact of the *Butler* case was short lived. Following the Court's dramatic change in position after Roosevelt's threat to add new members, the justices ruled that agriculture could be regulated under the commerce power.[13] As for the power to tax and spend for the general welfare, the position taken in *Butler* was reevaluated the very next year in *Steward Machine Co. v. Davis* (1937), a challenge to the constitutionality of the newly formed Social Security system. The Social Security Act (SSA) shared several characteristics with the Agricultural Adjustment Act the Court had condemned in *Butler*. Both used the taxing and spending powers to combat the effects of the depression; both took money from one group of people to give to another; and both regulated areas previously thought to be reserved to the states. But in *Steward Machine* the justices upheld the validity of the act. Note that in this case Justices Hughes and Roberts desert the *Butler* majority and join with the liberal wing of the Court to forge new constitutional interpretations.

13. See *Mulford v. Smith*, 307 U.S. 38 (1939); and *Wickard v. Filburn*, 317 U.S. 111 (1942).

Steward Machine Co. v. Davis

301 U.S. 548 (1937)
Vote: 5 (Brandeis, Cardozo, Hughes, Roberts, Stone)
    4 (Butler, McReynolds, Sutherland, Van Devanter)
Opinion of the Court: Cardozo
Dissenting opinions: Butler, McReynolds, Sutherland

On August 14, 1935, Congress passed the Social Security Act, a comprehensive law designed to provide economic security to groups of individuals who were particularly in need. Its three most important programs were the creation of an old age and survivors benefits program; the implementation of benefits for dependent children, the handicapped, and the sight-impaired; and the development of a cooperative federal-state unemployment compensation system. The unemployment provisions were the focus of the constitutional challenge in this case.

The act, as originally passed, imposed an excise tax on employers who hired more than eight workers. The tax was based on the total amount of wages paid. However, employers could receive a tax credit, not to exceed 90 percent of their unemployment tax obligations, for contributions made to an approved state unemployment compensation program.

The state programs had to meet federal specifications. The money employers contributed to these state funds was deposited with the secretary of the U.S. Treasury. The secretary would pay funds back to the states for their unemployment compensation programs. Congress also authorized additional federal funds to be used to assist the states in administering their compensation systems.

The Steward Machine Company, an Alabama corporation, paid the taxes due under the program and then sued the collector of internal revenue for a refund, claiming that the SSA violated the Constitution on a number of grounds. The amount of the contested refund was $46.14. The district court and the court of appeals upheld the validity of the act.

Justice Cardozo delivered the opinion of the Court:

The assault on the statute proceeds on an extended front. Its assailants take the ground that the tax is not an excise; that it is not uniform throughout the United States as excises are required to be; that its exceptions are so many and arbitrary as to violate the Fifth Amendment; that its purpose was not revenue, but an unlawful invasion of the reserved powers of the states; and that the states in submitting to it have yielded to coercion and have abandoned governmental functions which they are not permitted to surrender.

The objections will be considered seriatim with such further explanation as may be necessary to make their meaning clear.

First. The tax, which is described in the statute as an excise, is laid with uniformity throughout the United States as a duty, an impost or an excise upon the relation of employment. . . .

The subject matter of taxation open to the power of the Congress is as comprehensive as that open to the power of the states, though the method of apportionment may at times be different. . . . The statute books of the states are strewn with illustrations of taxes laid on occupations pursued of common right. We find no basis for a holding that the power in that regard which belongs by accepted practice to the legislatures of the states, has been denied by the Constitution to the Congress of the nation.

The tax being an excise, its imposition must conform to the canon of uniformity. There has been no departure from this requirement. According to the settled doctrine the uniformity exacted is geographical, not intrinsic.

Second. The excise is not invalid under the provisions of the Fifth Amendment by force of its exemptions.

The statute does not apply, as we have seen, to employers of less than eight. It does not apply to agricultural labor, or domestic service in a private home or to some other classes of less importance. Petitioner contends that the effect of these restrictions is an arbitrary discrimination vitiating the tax. . . .

The classifications and exemptions directed by the statute now in controversy have support in considerations of policy and practical convenience that cannot be condemned as arbitrary. . . . The act of Congress is therefore valid, so far at least as its system of exemptions is concerned, and this though we assume that discrimination, if gross enough, is equivalent to confiscation and subject under the Fifth Amendment to challenge and annulment.

Third. The excise is not void as involving the coercion of the States in contravention of the Tenth Amendment or of restrictions implicit in our federal form of government.

The proceeds of the excise when collected are paid into the Treasury at Washington, and thereafter are subject to appropriation like public moneys generally. No presumption can be indulged that they will be misapplied or wasted. Even if they were collected in the hope or expectation that some other and collateral good would be furthered as an incident, that without more would not make the act invalid. This indeed is hardly questioned. The case for the petitioner is built on the contention that here an ulterior aim is wrought into the very structure of the act, and what is even more important that the aim is not only ulterior, but essentially unlawful. In particular, the 90 per cent credit is relied upon as supporting that conclusion. But before the statute succumbs to an assault upon these lines, two propositions must be made out by the assailant. There must be a showing in the first place that separated from the credit the revenue provisions are incapable of standing by themselves. There must be a showing in the second place that the tax and the credit in combination are weapons of coercion, destroying or impairing the autonomy of the states. The truth of each proposition being essential to the success of the assault, we pass for convenience to a consideration of the second, without pausing to inquire whether there has been a demonstration of the first.

To draw the line intelligently between duress and inducement there is need to remind ourselves of facts as to the problem of unemployment that are now matters of common knowledge. The relevant statistics are gathered in the brief of counsel for the Government. Of the many available figures a few only will be mentioned. During the years 1929 to 1936, when the country was passing through a cyclical depression, the number of the unemployed mounted to unprecedented heights. Often the average was more than 10 million; at times a peak was attained of 16 million or more. Disaster to the breadwinner meant disaster to dependents. Accordingly the roll of the unemployed, itself formidable enough, was only a partial roll of the destitute or needy. The fact developed quickly that the states were unable to give the requisite relief. The problem had become national in area and dimensions. There was need of help from the nation if the people were not to starve. It is too late today for the argument to be heard with tolerance that in a crisis so extreme the use of the moneys of the nation to relieve the unemployed and their dependents is a use for any purpose narrower than the promotion of the general welfare. . . .

In the presence of this urgent need for some remedial expedient, the question is to be answered whether the expedient adopted has overlept the bounds of power. The assailants of the statute say that its dominant end and aim is to drive the state legislatures under the whip of economic pressure into the enactment of unemployment compensation laws at the bidding of the central government. Supporters of the statute say that its operation is not constraint, but the creation of a larger freedom, the states and the nation joining in a coöperative endeavor to avert a common evil. . . .

The Social Security Act is an attempt to find a method by which all these public agencies may work together to a common end. Every dollar of the new taxes will continue in all likelihood to be used and needed by the nation as long as states are unwilling, whether through timidity or for other motives, to do what can be done at home. At least the inference is permissible that Congress so believed, though retaining undiminished freedom to spend the money as it pleased. On the other hand fulfilment of the home duty will be lightened and encouraged by crediting the taxpayer upon his account with the Treasury of the nation to the extent that his contributions under the laws of the locality have simplified or diminished the problem of relief and the probable demand upon the resources of the fisc. Duplicated taxes, or burdens that approach them, are recognized hardships that government, state or national, may properly avoid. If Congress believed that the general welfare would better be promoted by relief through local units than by the system then in vogue, the cooperating localities ought not in all fairness to pay a second time.

Who then is coerced through the operation of this statute? Not the taxpayer. He pays in fulfilment of the mandate of the local legislature. Not the state. Even now she does not offer a suggestion that in passing the unemployment law she was affected by duress. For all that appears she is satisfied with her choice, and would be sorely disappointed if it were now to be annulled. The difficulty with the petitioner's contention is that it confuses motive with coercion. "Every tax is in some measure regulatory. To some extent it interposes an economic impediment to the activity taxed as compared with others not taxed." In like manner every rebate from a tax when conditioned upon conduct is in some measure a temptation. But to hold that motive or temptation is equivalent to coercion is to plunge the law in endless difficulties. The outcome of such a doctrine is the acceptance of a philosophical determinism by which choice becomes impossible. Till now the law has been guided by a robust common sense which assumes the freedom of the will as a working hypothesis in the solution of its problems. . . .

United States v. *Butler,* is cited by petitioner as a decision to the contrary. There a tax was imposed on processors of farm products, the proceeds to be paid to farmers who would reduce their acreage and crops under agreements with the Secretary of Agriculture, the plan of the act being to increase the prices of certain farm products by decreasing the quantities produced. The court held (1) that the so-called tax was not a true one, the proceeds being earmarked for the benefit of farmers complying with the prescribed conditions, (2) that there was an attempt to regulate production without the consent of the state in which production was affected, and (3) that the payments to farmers were coupled with coercive contracts, unlawful in their aim and oppressive in their consequences. The decision was by a divided court, a minority taking the view that the objections were untenable. None of them is applicable to the situation here developed.

(a) The proceeds of the tax in controversy are not earmarked for a special group.

(b) The unemployment compensation law which is a condition of the credit has had the approval of the state and could not be a law without it.

(c) The condition is not linked to an irrevocable agreement, for the state at its pleasure may repeal its unemployment law, terminate the credit, and place itself where it was before the credit was accepted.

(d) The condition is not directed to the attainment of an unlawful end, but to an end, the relief of unemployment, for which nation and state may lawfully cooperate.

Fourth. The statute does not call for a surrender by the states of powers essential to their quasi-sovereign existence. . . .

The judgment is

Affirmed.

In a second case decided the same day, the Court upheld the old age benefits provisions of the Social Security Act.[14] From that point on, the Social Security program became a permanent fixture in the lives of American workers. The Social Security cases also firmly established that the taxing and spending powers are to be broadly construed. If Congress decides that the general welfare of the United States demands a program requiring the use of these fiscal powers, the Supreme Court likely will find it constitutionally valid unless parts of the law violate specific provisions of the Constitution. In fact, *United States v. Butler* was the last case in which the Supreme Court ruled that Congress had exceeded its spending powers. Since these 1937 decisions, Congress has used the spending authority to expand greatly the role of the federal government.

14. *Helvering v. Davis,* 301 U.S. 609 (1937)

Federal-State Fiscal Tensions

Serious challenges to a federal spending program are now unusual. Yet a battle over federal and state authority with respect to spending programs does occasionally flare up. One such case was *South Dakota v. Dole* (1987). This dispute involved a conflict over federal spending power and the state's authority to regulate highway safety and alcoholic beverages. The use of federal funds to coerce the states into taking particular policy positions was attacked in much the same manner as *Steward Machine* attacked the establishment of state unemployment compensation programs. It is interesting to note that Chief Justice William Rehnquist, normally considered a strong defender of states' rights, wrote the majority opinion upholding the exercise of federal authority over the states. A dissenting vote was cast by Justice Brennan, another surprise because Brennan usually could be counted on to support federal power. Not surprising was the stinging dissent registered by Justice O'Connor on behalf of state interests.

South Dakota v. Dole

483 U.S. 203 (1987)

Vote: 7 (Blackmun, Marshall, Powell, Rehnquist, Scalia, Stevens, White)
2 (Brennan, O'Connor)
Opinion of the Court: Rehnquist
Dissenting opinions: Brennan, O'Connor

In 1984 Congress passed a statute directing the secretary of transportation to withhold a portion of federal highway funds from any state that did not establish a minimum drinking age of twenty-one years. The purpose of the law was to decrease the number of serious automobile accidents among a group that statistics showed had a high percentage of accidents. The legislators correctly believed that withholding federal dollars would be an effective way of encouraging the states to comply with the federal program.

South Dakota, which allowed the purchase of beer containing 3.2 percent alcohol by persons nineteen years or older, objected to the statute, arguing that Congress was infringing on the rights of the states. The Twenty-first Amendment, which repealed prohibition in 1933, gave full authority to the states to regulate alcoholic beverages; therefore, South Dakota claimed that Congress had no authority to set minimum drinking ages. According to the state, the federal government was using its considerable spending power to coerce the states into enacting laws that were otherwise outside congressional authority.

The state sued Secretary of Transportation Elizabeth Dole, asking the courts to declare the law unconstitutional. Both the district court and the court of appeals ruled against the state and upheld the law.

Chief Justice Rehnquist delivered the opinion of the Court:

The Constitution empowers Congress to "lay and collect Taxes, Duties, Imposts, and Excises, to pay the Debts and provide for the common Defence and general Welfare of the United States." Art. I, § 8, cl. 1. Incident to this power, Congress may attach conditions on the receipt of federal funds, and has repeatedly employed the power "to further broad policy objectives by conditioning receipt of federal moneys upon compliance by the recipient with federal statutory and administrative directives." The breadth of this power was made clear in *United States v. Butler* (1936), where the Court, resolving a longstanding debate over the scope of the Spending Clause, determined that "the power of Congress to authorize expenditure of public moneys for public purposes is not limited by the direct grants of legislative power found in the Constitution." Thus, objectives not thought to be within Article I's "enumerated legislative fields" may neverthe-less be attained through the use of the spending power and the conditional grant of federal funds.

The spending power is of course not limited, but is instead subject to several general restrictions articu-lated in our cases. The first of these limitations is derived from the language of the Constitution itself: the exercise of the spending power must be in pursuit of "the general welfare." In considering whether a particular expenditure is intended to serve general public purposes, courts should defer substantially to the judgment of Congress. Second, we have required that if Congress desires to condition the States' receipt of federal funds, it "must do so unambiguously . . ., enabl[ing] the States to exercise their choice know-ingly, cognizant of the consequences of their participa-tion." Third, our cases have suggested (without signif-icant elaboration) that conditions on federal grants might be illegitimate if they are unrelated "to the federal interest in particular national projects or pro-grams." Finally, we have noted that other constitu-tional provisions may provide an independent bar to the conditional grant of federal funds.

South Dakota does not seriously claim that § 158 is inconsistent with any of the first three restrictions mentioned above. We can readily conclude that the provision is designed to serve the general welfare, especially in light of the fact that "the concept of welfare or the opposite is shaped by Congress. . . ." Congress found that the differing drinking ages in the States created particular incentives for young persons to combine their desire to drink with their ability to drive, and that this interstate problem required a na-tional solution. The means it chose to address this dangerous situation were reasonably calculated to ad-vance the general welfare. The conditions upon which States receive the funds, moreover, could not be more clearly stated by Congress. And the State itself, rather than challenging the germaneness of the condition to federal purposes, admits that it "has never contended that the congressional action was . . . unrelated to a national concern in the absence of the Twenty-first Amendment." Indeed, the condition imposed by Con-gress is directly related to one of the main purposes for which highway funds are expended—safe interstate travel. This goal of the interstate highway system had been frustrated by varying drinking ages among the States. . . . By enacting § 158, Congress condi-tioned the receipt of federal funds in a way reasonably calculated to address this particular impediment to a purpose for which the funds are expended.

The remaining question about the validity of § 158—and the basic point of disagreement between the parties—is whether the Twenty-first Amendment constitutes an "independent constitutional bar" to the conditional grant of federal funds. Petitioner, relying on its view that the Twenty-first Amendment prohibits *direct* regulation of drinking ages by Congress, asserts that "Congress may not use the spending power to regulate that which it is prohibited from regulating directly under the Twenty-first Amendment." But our cases show that this "independent constitutional bar" limitation on the spending power is not of the kind petitioner suggests. *United States v. Butler,* for exam-ple, established that the constitutional limitations on Congress when exercising its spending power are less exacting than those on its authority to regulate di-rectly. . . .

[T]he "independent constitutional bar" limitation on the spending power is not, as petitioner suggests, a prohibition on the indirect achievement of objectives which Congress is not empowered to achieve directly. Instead, we think that the language in our earlier opinions stands for the unexceptionable proposition that the power may not be used to induce the States to engage in activities that would themselves be uncon-stitutional. Thus, for example, a grant of federal funds conditioned on invidiously discriminatory state action or the infliction of cruel and unusual punishment would be an illegitimate exercise of the Congress' broad spending power. But no such claim can be or is made here. Were South Dakota to succumb to the blandish-ments offered by Congress and raise its drinking age to 21, the State's action in so doing would not violate the constitutional rights of anyone.

Our decisions have recognized that in some circum-stances the financial inducement offered by Congress might be so coercive as to pass the point at which "pressure turns into compulsion." Here, however, Congress has directed only that a State desiring to establish a minimum drinking age lower than 21 lose a relatively small percentage of certain federal highway funds. Petitioner contends that the coercive nature of this program is evident from the degree of success it has achieved. We cannot conclude, however, that a conditional grant of federal money of this sort is unconstitutional simply by reason of its success in achieving the congressional objective.

When we consider, for a moment, that all South Dakota would lose if she adheres to her chosen course as to a suitable minimum drinking age is 5% of the funds otherwise obtainable under specified highway grant programs, the argument as to coercion is shown to be more rhetoric than fact. . . .

Here Congress has offered relatively mild encouragement to the States to enact higher minimum drinking ages than they would otherwise choose. But the enactment of such laws remains the prerogative of the States not merely in theory but in fact. Even if Congress might lack the power to impose a national minimum drinking age directly, we conclude that encouragement to state action found in § 158 is a valid use of the spending power. Accordingly, the judgment of the Court of Appeals is

Affirmed.

Justice O'CONNOR, dissenting.

The Court today upholds the National Minimum Drinking Age Amendment, 23 U.S.C. § 158, as a valid exercise of the spending power conferred by Article I, § 8. But § 158 is not a condition on spending reasonably related to the expenditure of federal funds and cannot be justified on that ground. Rather, it is an attempt to regulate the sale of liquor, an attempt that lies outside Congress' power to regulate commerce because it falls within the ambit of § 2 of the Twenty-first Amendment. . . .

When Congress appropriates money to build a highway, it is entitled to insist that the highway be a safe one. But it is not entitled to insist as a condition of the use of highway funds that the State impose or change regulations in other areas of the State's social and economic life because of an attenuated or tangential relationship to highway use or safety. Indeed, if the rule were otherwise, the Congress could effectively regulate almost any area of a State's social, political, or economic life on the theory that use of the interstate transportation system is somehow enhanced. If, for example, the United States were to condition highway

moneys upon moving the state capital, I suppose it might argue that interstate transportation is facilitated by locating local governments in places easily accessible to interstate highways—or, conversely, that highways might become overburdened if they had to carry traffic to and from the state capital. In my mind, such a relationship is hardly more attenuated than the one which the Court finds supports § 158.

There is a clear place at which the Court can draw the line between permissible and impermissible conditions on federal grants. It is the line identified in the Brief for the National Conference of State Legislatures et al. as *Amici Curiae:*

"Congress has the power to *spend* for the general welfare, it has the power to *legislate* only for the delegated purposes." . . .

This approach harks back to *United States v. Butler* (1936), the last case in which this Court struck down an Act of Congress as beyond the authority granted by the Spending Clause. . . .

While *Butler's* authority is questionable insofar as it assumes that Congress has no regulatory power over farm production, its discussion of the spending power and its description of both the power's breadth and its limitations remain sound. The Court's decision in *Butler* also properly recognizes the gravity of the task of appropriately limiting the spending power. If the spending power is to be limited only by Congress' notion of the general welfare, the reality, given the vast financial resources of the Federal Government, is that the Spending Clause gives "power to the Congress to tear down the barriers, to invade the states' jurisdiction, and to become a parliament of the whole people, subject to no restrictions save such as are self-imposed." This, of course, as *Butler* held, was not the Framers' plan and it is not the meaning of the Spending Clause. . . .

The immense size and power of the Government of the United States ought not obscure its fundamental character. It remains a Government of enumerated powers. Because 23 U.S.C. § 158 cannot be justified as an exercise of any power delegated to the Congress, it is not authorized by the Constitution. The Court errs in holding it to be the law of the land, and I respectfully dissent.

Rehnquist's opinion gave strong support to the federal spending power. The majority held that there are only four basic requirements that must be met for a federal spending statute to be valid: (1) the expenditure must be for the general welfare; (2) any conditions imposed on the expenditure must be unambiguous; (3) the conditions must be reasonably related to the purpose of the expenditure; and (4) the legislation must not violate any independent constitutional provision. These are minimal requirements indeed, especially since the Court acknowledged a policy of deferring to the legislature as to determinations of what promotes the general welfare. O'Connor's dissent, which praised much of what the Court concluded in *Butler,* is not likely to find a great deal of support today; rather, since 1937 the Court repeatedly has given approval to an expansive interpretation of the powers of the federal government to tax and spend for the general welfare.

Restrictions on the Revenue Powers of the States

Taxation is a concurrent power: the states exercised the power to tax prior to the ratification of the Constitution and retain that authority today. The powers of the states to tax are very broad, limited primarily by provisions in their own constitutions and laws. Taxes on property, income, and sales provide the bulk of funds for state government activities.

The federal Constitution, however, removed certain sources of revenue from the states. Article I, Section 10, explicitly prohibits the states from taxing imports. In addition, the Commerce Clause blocks the states from placing taxes that impose an unreasonable burden on interstate or foreign commerce. Aside from these limitations, the states remain free to develop their own tax structures and sources of revenue.

State Taxes on Foreign Commerce

In *Brown v. Maryland* (1827) the Supreme Court first faced a question of the validity of state taxes on imports. The dispute centered on a Maryland law that required importers of foreign goods to pay a license fee. The Supreme Court struck down the statute as a tax on imports and as infringing on the authority of the federal government to regulate foreign commerce. An important part of the Court's opinion, however, dealt with the following question: When does an imported article cease to be an import and become part of the taxable goods within a state? The Court's answer to this question was the "original package" doctrine. For the majority, John Marshall wrote, "While [the imported article remains] the property of the importer, in his warehouse, in the original form or package in which it was imported, a tax upon it is too plainly a duty on imports to escape the prohibition in the constitution."

The original package doctrine meant that goods flowing into the United States remained within the federal government's taxing and regulating power until they were sold, processed, or broken out of their original packaging. Once any of those events took place, the articles became normal property within the state and subject to state taxation. The impact of this interpretation was that large warehouses filled with imported goods ready for shipment to other parts of the United States were free from state taxation as long as no sale took place and the materials remained in their original packages. The states balked at this rule, arguing that they should be able to levy property taxes on such goods as long as the tax was nondiscriminatory—that is, if imported articles stored in warehouses were taxed on exactly the same basis as other property within the state. In *Low v. Austin* (1872) the Court rejected the constitutionality of such nondiscriminatory taxes, adhering to Marshall's rationale in *Brown.*

Although attacked by legal scholars and those promoting the interests of the states, the original package doctrine survived until 1976 when the justices accepted an appeal from a decision by the Georgia Supreme Court that approved certain nondiscriminatory taxes on warehoused imports. After reanalyzing the issues involved, the Court altered a rule of law that had been in effect for more than a century.

Michelin Tire Corp. v. Wages

423 U.S. 276 (1976)

Vote: 8 (Blackmun, Brennan, Burger, Marshall, Powell, Rehnquist, Stewart, White)

0

Opinion of the Court: Brennan
Concurring opinion: White
Not participating: Stevens

The Michelin Tire Corporation operated a warehouse in Gwinnett County, Georgia, just outside of Atlanta. The company imported tires and tire products into the United States from France and Nova Scotia and stored them in the Georgia warehouse for later distribution to retail outlets. When the county tax assessors levied a nondiscriminatory ad valorem property tax on the inventory, the company sued W. L. Wages, the county tax commissioner, for relief, claiming that, except for some tire tubes that had been removed from their original containers, the warehouse contents were constitutionally free from state taxation. The local court granted the relief requested, and the Georgia Supreme Court heard the county's appeal. The state high court ruled that the tires were subject to tax because after being imported in bulk they had been sorted and arranged for sale. Michelin sought a reversal by the U.S. Supreme Court, which ignored subtle questions regarding the application of the original package doctrine and instead focused on the fundamental issue of whether any warehoused imports are subject to state taxation.

Justice Brennan delivered the opinion of the Court:

Low v. Austin [1872] is the leading decision of this Court holding that the States are prohibited by the Import-Export Clause from imposing a nondiscriminatory ad valorem property tax on imported goods until they lose their character as imports and become incorporated into the mass of property in the State. The Court there reviewed a decision of the California Supreme Court that had sustained the constitutionality of California's nondiscriminatory ad valorem tax on the ground that the Import-Export Clause only prohibited taxes upon the character of the goods as imports and therefore did not prohibit nondiscriminatory taxes upon the goods as property. This Court reversed on its reading of the seminal opinion construing the Import-Export Clause, *Brown v. Maryland* (1827), as holding that "[w]hilst retaining their character as imports, a tax upon them, in any shape, is within the constitutional prohibition."

Scholarly analysis has been uniformly critical of *Low v. Austin.* It is true that Mr. Chief Justice Marshall, speaking for the Court in *Brown v. Maryland* said that "while [the thing imported remains] the property of the importer, in his warehouse, in the original form or package in which it was imported, a tax upon it is too plainly a duty on imports to escape the prohibition in the constitution." Commentators have uniformly agreed that *Low v. Austin* misread this dictum in holding that the Court in *Brown* included nondiscriminatory ad valorem property taxes among prohibited "imposts" or "duties," for the contrary conclusion is plainly to be inferred from consideration of the specific abuses which led the Framers to include the Import-Export Clause in the Constitution.

Our independent study persuades us that a nondiscriminatory ad valorem property tax is not the type of state exaction which the Framers of the Constitution or the Court in *Brown* had in mind as being an "impost" or "duty" and that *Low v. Austin*'s reliance upon the *Brown* dictum to reach the contrary conclusion was misplaced.

One of the major defects of the Articles of Confederation, and a compelling reason for the calling of the Constitutional Convention of 1787, was the fact that the Articles essentially left the individual States free to burden commerce both among themselves and with foreign countries very much as they pleased. Before 1787 it was commonplace for seaboard States with port facilities to derive revenue to defray the costs of state and local government by imposing taxes on imported goods destined for customers in other States. At the same time, there was no secure source of revenue for the central government. . . .

The Framers of the Constitution thus sought to alleviate three main concerns by committing sole power to lay imposts and duties on imports in the Federal Government, with no concurrent state power: the Federal Government must speak with one voice when regulating commercial relations with foreign governments, and tariffs, which might affect foreign relations, could not be implemented by the States consistently with that exclusive power; import revenues were to be the major source of revenue of the Federal Government and should not be diverted to the States; and harmony among the States might be disturbed unless seaboard States, with their crucial ports of entry, were prohibited from levying taxes on citizens of other States by taxing goods merely flowing through their ports to the other States not situated as favorably geographically.

Nothing in the history of the Import-Export Clause even remotely suggests that a nondiscriminatory ad valorem property tax which is also imposed on imported goods that are no longer in import transit was the type of exaction that was regarded as objectionable by the Framers of the Constitution. For such an exaction, unlike discriminatory state taxation against imported goods as imports, was not regarded as an impediment that severely hampered commerce or constituted a form of tribute by seaboard States to the disadvantage of the other States.

It is obvious that such nondiscriminatory property taxation can have no impact whatsoever on the Federal Government's exclusive regulation of foreign commerce, probably the most important purpose of the Clause's prohibition. By definition, such a tax does not fall on imports as such because of their place of origin. It cannot be used to create special protective tariffs or particular preferences for certain domestic goods, and it cannot be applied selectively to encourage or discourage any importation in a manner inconsistent with federal regulation.

Nor will such taxation deprive the Federal Government of the exclusive right to all revenues from imposts and duties on imports and exports, since that right by definition only extends to revenues from exactions of a particular category; if nondiscriminatory ad valorem taxation is not in that category, it deprives the Federal Government of nothing to which it is entitled. Unlike imposts and duties, which are essentially taxes on the commercial privilege of bringing goods into a country, such property taxes are taxes by which a State apportions the cost of such services as police and fire protection among the beneficiaries according to their respective wealth; there is no reason why an importer should not bear his share of these costs along with his competitors handling only domestic goods. The Import-Export Clause clearly prohibits state taxation based on the foreign origin of the imported goods, but it cannot be read to accord imported goods preferential treatment that permits escape from uniform taxes imposed without regard to foreign origin for services which the State supplies. . . .

Finally, nondiscriminatory ad valorem property taxes do not interfere with the free flow of imported goods among the States, as did the exactions by States under the Articles of Confederation directed solely at imported goods. . . .

[S]ince prohibition of nondiscriminatory ad valorem property taxation would not further the objectives of the Import-Export Clause, only the clearest constitutional mandate should lead us to condemn such taxation. . . .

The Court in *Low v. Austin* nevertheless expanded the prohibition of the Clause to include nondiscriminatory ad valorem property taxes, and did so with no analysis, but with only the statement that *Brown v. Maryland* had marked the line "where the power of Congress over the goods imported ends, and that of the State begins, with as much precision as the subject admits.'' But the opinion in *Brown v. Maryland* cannot properly be read to propose such a broad definition of ''imposts'' or ''duties.'' The tax there held to be prohibited by the Import-Export Clause was imposed under a Maryland statute that required importers of foreign goods, and wholesalers selling the same by bale or package, to obtain a license and pay a $50 fee therefor, subject to certain forfeitures and penalties for noncompliance. The importers contested the validity of the statute, arguing that the license was a ''palpable evasion'' of the Import-Export Clause because it was essentially equivalent to a duty on imports. Since the power to impose a license on importers would also entail a power to price them out of the market or prohibit them entirely, the importers concluded that such a power must be repugnant to the exclusive federal power to regulate foreign commerce.

The Attorney General of Maryland, Roger Taney, later Chief Justice, defended the constitutionality of Maryland's law. He argued that the fee was not a prohibited ''impost'' or ''duty'' because the license fee was not a tax upon the imported goods, but on the importers, a tax upon the occupation and nothing more, and the Import-Export Clause prohibited only exactions on the right of importation and not an exaction upon the occupation of importers. . . .

The Court in *Brown* refused to define ''imposts'' or ''duties'' comprehensively, since the Maryland statute presented only the question ''whether the legislature of a State can constitutionally require the importer of foreign articles to take out a license from the State, before he shall be permitted to sell a bale or package so imported.'' However, in holding that the Maryland license fee was within prohibited ''imposts, or duties on imports . . .'' the Court significantly characterized an impost or duty as ''a custom or a tax levied on articles brought into a country,'' although also holding that, while normally levied before the articles are permitted to enter, the exactions are no less within the prohibition if levied upon the goods as imports after entry; since ''imports'' are the goods imported, the prohibition of imposts or duties on ''imports'' was more than a prohibition of a tax on the act of importation; it ''extends to a duty levied after [the thing imported] has entered the country.'' And since the power to prohibit sale of an article is the power to prohibit its introduction into the country, the privilege of sale must be a concomitant of the privilege of importation, and licenses on the right to sell must therefore also fall within the constitutional prohibition.

Taney's argument was persuasive, however, to the extent that the Court ''was prompted to declare that the words of the prohibition ought not to be pressed to their utmost extent; . . . in our complex system, the object of the powers conferred on the government of the Union, and the nature of the often conflicting powers which remain in the States, must always be taken into view. . . . [T]here must be a point of time when the prohibition ceases, and the power of the State to tax commences. . . .''

Despite the language and objectives of the Import-Export Clause, and despite the limited nature of the holding in *Brown v. Maryland,* the Court in *Low v. Austin,* ignored the warning that the boundary between the power of States to tax persons and property within their jurisdictions and the limitations on the power of the States to impose imposts or duties with respect to ''imports'' was a subtle and difficult line which must be drawn as the cases arise. *Low v. Austin* also ignored the cautionary remark that, for those reasons, it ''might be premature to state any rule as being universal in its application.'' Although it was ''sufficient'' in the context of Maryland's license tax on the right to sell imported goods to note that a tax imposed directly on imported goods which have not been acted upon in any way would clearly fall within the constitutional prohibition, that observation did not apply, as the foregoing analysis indicates, to a state tax which treated those same goods without regard to the fact of their foreign origin. . . .

It follows from the foregoing that *Low v. Austin* was wrongly decided. That decision must be, and is, overruled.

Petitioner's tires in this case were no longer in transit. They were stored in a distribution warehouse from which petitioner conducted a wholesale operation, taking orders from franchised dealers and filling them from a constantly replenished inventory. The warehouse was operated no differently than would be a distribution warehouse utilized by a wholesaler dealing solely in domestic goods, and we therefore hold that the nondiscriminatory property tax levied on petitioner's inventory of imported tires was not interdicted by the Import-Export Clause of the Constitution. The judgment of the Supreme Court of Georgia is accordingly

Affirmed.

State Taxes on Interstate Commerce

State taxes on interstate commerce have provided another source of constitutional disputes. A state has the right to tax commerce that occurs within its borders, but it cannot impose taxes that discriminate against or place an undue burden on interstate commerce. In the nation's formative years this rule of constitutional interpretation was relatively easy to apply, but, given the changes in economic realities and the significant alterations in the definition of interstate commerce, the situation is now much more complex.

Today, relatively little commercial activity is purely intrastate. Consequently, whenever a state imposes a tax on business activity, it can be charged that the state is placing a burden on interstate commerce. The Supreme Court has attempted to fashion a rule that copes with modern economic conditions and yet is mindful of three important considerations. First, if the states are to remain viable entities, they must retain the ability to tax commercial activities. Second, true burdens on interstate commerce, as well as taxes that discriminate against it, must be avoided. Third, simply engaging in an interstate commercial activity should not suffice to exempt a company from paying its fair share in state taxes. Naturally, these principles are far easier to state than to apply to real situations.

In *Complete Auto Transit v. Brady* (1977) the justices concluded that their previous decisions were inconsistent with contemporary conditions and that a new statement on the authority of states to tax activities affecting interstate commerce was required. In his opinion for the Court Justice Harry A. Blackmun found fault with some leading precedents and replaced them with a four-pronged test to determine the validity of state taxation.

Complete Auto Transit v. Brady

430 U.S. 274 (1977)

Vote: 9 (Blackmun, Brennan, Burger, Marshall, Powell, Rehnquist, Stevens, Stewart, White)

o

Opinion of the Court: Blackmun

Complete Auto Transit was a Michigan corporation doing business in Mississippi. Under its contract with General Motors, Complete trucked new vehicles manufactured out of state and brought into Mississippi by rail. The automobiles were loaded onto Complete's trucks in the Jackson, Mississippi, rail yards and delivered to GM dealerships around the state. There is no doubt that Complete's business was interstate commerce. The company provided the last segment in the transportation of goods manufactured out of state to their retail destinations within the state.

Mississippi imposed a tax on transportation companies for the privilege of doing business in the state at a rate of 5 percent of gross income from state business. The state applied the tax to businesses operating in intra- and interstate commerce. In 1971 the Mississippi Tax Commission informed Complete that it owed $122,160.59 in taxes from a three-year period beginning in 1968. In 1972 Complete received a second bill for $42,990.89 for taxes due over the previous year.

Compete paid the taxes under protest and sued for a refund.

Complete based its case on a 1951 Supreme Court precedent, *Spector Motor Service v. O'Connor,* which held that a state tax on the privilege of doing business is unconstitutional if imposed on any activity that is part of interstate commerce. The Mississippi Supreme Court upheld the tax, holding that Complete enjoyed the various services of the state and should be obliged to pay its fair share of state taxes. Because the tax did not discriminate against interstate commerce and was based exclusively on income derived from Mississippi sources, it was not constitutionally defective. Complete appealed to the U.S. Supreme Court, asking it to strike down the tax on the basis of the *Spector* precedent.

Justice Blackmun delivered the opinion of the Court:

Once again we are presented with " 'the perennial problem of the validity of a state tax for the privilege of carrying on within a state, certain activities' related to a corporation's operation of an interstate business.'' The issue in this case is whether Mississippi runs afoul of the Commerce Clause when it applies the tax it imposes on "the privilege of . . . doing business" within the State to appellant's activity in interstate commerce. The Supreme Court of Mississippi unanimously sustained the tax against appellant's constitutional challenge. We noted probable jurisdiction in order to consider anew the applicable principles in this troublesome area. . . .

Appellant's attack is based solely on decisions of this Court holding that a tax on the "privilege" of engaging in an activity in the State may not be applied to an activity that is part of interstate commerce. See, *e.g., Spector Motor Service v. O'Connor* (1951); *Freeman v. Hewit* (1946). This rule looks only to the fact that the incidence of the tax is the "privilege of doing business"; it deems irrelevant any consideration of the practical effect of the tax. The rule reflects an underlying philosophy that interstate commerce should enjoy a sort of "free trade" immunity from state taxation.

Appellee, in its turn, relies on decisions of this Court stating that "[i]t was not the purpose of the commerce clause to relieve those engaged in interstate commerce from their just share of state tax burden even though it increases the cost of doing the business," *Western Live Stock v. Bureau of Revenue* (1938). These decisions have considered not the formal language of the tax statute but rather its practical effect, and have sustained a tax against Commerce Clause challenge when the tax is applied to an activity with a substantial nexus with the taxing State, is fairly apportioned, does not discriminate against interstate commerce, and is fairly related to the services provided by the State.

Over the years, the Court has applied this practical analysis in approving many types of tax that avoided running afoul of the prohibition against taxing the "privilege of doing business," but in each instance it has refused to overrule the prohibition. Under the present state of the law, the *Spector* rule, as it has come to be known, has no relationship to economic realities. Rather it stands only as a trap for the unwary draftsman.

The modern origin of the *Spector* rule may be found in *Freeman v. Hewit. . . .*

Mr. Justice Frankfurter, speaking for five Members of the Court, announced a blanket prohibition against any state taxation imposed directly on an interstate transaction. He explicitly deemed unnecessary to the decision of the case any showing of discrimination against interstate commerce or error in apportionment of the tax. He recognized that a State could constitutionally tax local manufacture, impose license taxes on corporations doing business in the State, tax property within the State, and tax the privilege of residence in the State and measure the privilege by net income, including that derived from interstate commerce. Nevertheless, a direct tax on interstate sales, even if fairly apportioned and nondiscriminatory, was held to be unconstitutional *per se.* . . .

The rule announced in *Freeman* was viewed in the commentary as a triumph of formalism over substance, providing little guidance even as to formal requirements. . . .

The prohibition against state taxation of the "privilege" of engaging in commerce that is interstate was reaffirmed in *Spector Motor Service v. O'Connor* (1951), a case similar on its facts to the instant case. The taxpayer there was a Missouri corporation engaged exclusively in interstate trucking. Some of its shipments originated or terminated in Connecticut. Connecticut imposed on a corporation a "tax or excise upon its franchise for the privilege of carrying on or doing business within the state," measured by apportioned net income. Spector brought suit in federal court to enjoin collection of the tax as applied to its activities. The District Court issued the injunction. The Second Circuit reversed. This Court, with three Justices in dissent, in turn reversed the Court of Appeals and held the tax unconstitutional as applied. . . .

In this case, of course, we are confronted with a situation like that presented in *Spector*. The tax is labeled a privilege tax "for the privilege of . . . doing business" in Mississippi, and the activity taxed is, or has been assumed to be, interstate commerce. We note again that no claim is made that the activity is not sufficiently connected to the State to justify a tax, or that the tax is not fairly related to benefits provided the taxpayer, or that the tax discriminates against interstate commerce, or that the tax is not fairly apportioned.

The view of the Commerce Clause that gave rise to the rule of *Spector* perhaps was not without some substance. Nonetheless, the possibility of defending it in the abstract does not alter the fact that the Court has rejected the proposition that interstate commerce is immune from state taxation:

"It is a truism that the mere act of carrying on business in interstate commerce does not exempt a corporation from state taxation. 'It was not the purpose of the commerce clause to relieve those engaged in interstate commerce from their just share of state tax burden even though it increases the cost of doing business.' *Western Live Stock v. Bureau of Revenue* (1938)."

Not only has the philosophy underlying the rule been rejected, but the rule itself has been stripped of any practical significance. If Mississippi had called its tax one on "net income" or on the "going concern value" of appellant's business, the *Spector* rule could not invalidate it. There is no economic consequence that follows necessarily from the use of the particular words, "privilege of doing business," and a focus on that formalism merely obscures the question whether the tax produces a forbidden effect. Simply put, the *Spector* rule does not address the problems with which the Commerce Clause is concerned. Accordingly, we now reject the rule of *Spector Motor Service, Inc. v. O'Connor,* that a state tax on the "privilege of doing business" is *per se* unconstitutional when it is applied to interstate commerce, and that case is overruled.

There being no objection to Mississippi's tax on appellant except that it was imposed on nothing other than the "privilege of doing business" that is interstate, the judgment of the Supreme Court of Mississippi is affirmed.

It is so ordered.

The *Complete Auto Transit* decision established four criteria that must be met for a state tax on interstate commerce to be valid: (1) the targeted activity must be sufficiently connected to the state to justify a tax; (2) the tax must be fairly apportioned so that the levy is based on intrastate activity or income not subject to taxation by other states; (3) the tax must not discriminate against interstate commerce; and (4) the tax must be fairly related to the services provided by the state. These criteria assume that Congress has not preempted the state tax by imposing conflicting regulations on the interstate commerce activities involved.

In an unusual occurrence by today's standards,

the entire Court supported Justice Blackmun's opinion in *Complete Auto Transit*. There were no concurring or dissenting views. Given this unanimity, it is not surprising that the Court has applied the precedent to subsequent disputes over the validity of state taxes on activities affecting interstate and foreign commerce. In *Wardair Canada v. Florida Department of Revenue* (1986) the justices ruled that a state tax on the sale of aviation fuel to an airline engaged in foreign commerce satisfied the four requirements. Similarly, in *Goldberg v. Sweet* (1989) the Court concluded that an Illinois excise tax on interstate telephone calls did not violate the constitutional principles established in *Complete Auto Transit.* Therefore, the four-pronged test established in 1977 constitutes the Court's current policy on state taxation of interstate activities. It appears to provide a workable compromise between the needs of the states to secure revenue and the Constitution's mandate that interstate commerce not be unreasonably burdened.

READINGS

Carson, Gerald. "The Income Tax and How it Grew." *American Heritage* 25 (December 1973), 4-7, 79-88.

Corwin, Edward S. "The Spending Power of Congress—Apropos the Maternity Act." *Harvard Law Review* 36 (1923): 548-582.

Dakin, Melvin G. "The Protective Cloak of the Export-Import Clause: Immunity for the Goods or Immunity for the Process?" *Louisiana Law Review* 19 (1959): 747-776.

Dunne, Gerald T. *Monetary Decisions of the Supreme Court.* New Brunswick, N.J.: Rutgers University Press, 1960.

Early, Alexander R., and Robert G. Weitzman. "A Century of Dissent: The Immunity of Goods Imported for Resale from Nondiscriminatory State Personal Property Taxes." *Southwestern University Law Review* 7 (1975): 247-272.

Hurst, James Willard. *A Legal History of Money in the United States, 1774-1970.* Lincoln: University of Nebraska Press, 1973.

Lund, Nelson. "Congressional Power over Taxation and Commerce: The Supreme Court's Lost Chance to Devise a Consistent Doctrine." *Texas Tech Law Review* 18 (1987): 729-760.

McCoy, Thomas R., and Barry Friedman. "Conditional Spending: Federalism's Trojan Horse." *The Supreme Court Review* (1988): 85-127.

Powell, Thomas Reed. "State Taxation of Imports—When Does an Import Cease to Be an Import?" *Harvard Law Review* 58 (1945): 858-876.

Witte, John F. *The Politics and Development of the Federal Income Tax.* Madison: University of Wisconsin Press, 1985.

PART IV

ECONOMIC LIBERTIES

PART IV

ECONOMIC LIBERTIES AND INDIVIDUAL RIGHTS

If asked what we admire about the United States, many Americans would answer the freedoms of speech, press, and religion. But when asked to make political decisions—to choose elected officials, for example—we Americans may put other considerations ahead of the freedoms we cherish. As the old adage goes, people tend to vote their pocketbooks. Americans might not admit that the state of the economy drives their behavior, but it is perhaps the single most important determinant in choosing the nation's leaders.

That we hold economic well-being as a priority is not surprising. In Part III we saw that economic issues—commerce, taxing, and spending—were major sources of friction between the federal government and the states virtually from the beginning of U.S. history.

Economic questions, however, are not the exclusive domain of the federalism cases. Quite the contrary. The Supreme Court often has heard constitutional challenges in which individuals claim that their personal economic liberties have been violated by government actions. In such cases the justices must determine how much power federal and state governments have to seize private property, to alter freely made contracts, and to restrict private employment agreements as to wages and hours. Seen in this way, a strong relationship exists between civil liberties, such as

the freedom of speech, and economic liberties, such as the right to private property. Indeed, both provoke the same fundamental question: To what extent can government enact legislation that infringes on personal rights? Both also involve the same perennial conflict between the interests of the individual and those of the common good.

Even so, most people, including elected officials and even Supreme Court justices, tend to separate economic liberties from other civil liberties. We consider the right to express our views as significantly different from the right to conduct business. The Framers, however, viewed both as vested rights, "those so fundamental to an individual that they must remain beyond governmental control," and they were very much on the minds of those who gathered to write the Constitution in 1787.[1] According to James Madison, one of the most important objectives of the Framers was to provide

more effectively for the security of private rights and the steady dispensement of justice within the states. Interference with these were the evils which had, more perhaps than anything else, produced this convention.

But, as Madison's comment implies, the Framers' conception of liberties and what interfered with their exercise was somewhat different from

1. Ralph A. Rossum and G. Alan Tarr, *American Constitutional Law*, 3d ed. (New York: St. Martin's Press, 1991), 285.

ours. They equated liberty with the protection of private property, and in their view the states, not the new government, posed the greater threat. Given the economic chaos under the Articles of Confederation, we can easily understand the Founders' concerns. They believed the states had "crippled" both the government and the economy, and they wanted to create a national government strong enough to protect economic liberty from aggressive state governments. We must also keep in mind that many who attended the convention were wealthy men who, "having accumulated property . . . wanted to keep it."[2] In short, the Framers were concerned about the nonpropertied masses taking control of state legislatures and using "their numerical strength" to advance their interests, "to abrogate debts, tax industry," and so forth.[3] Indeed, in an important (albeit controversial) work, *An Economic Interpretation of the Constitution,* historian Charles A. Beard depicted the Founders as self-serving, even greedy, men, who viewed the Constitution as a vehicle for the protection of their property interests.

Other analysts have taken issue with Beard's interpretation. Some contend that we cannot necessarily equate modern definitions of property with those used by the Framers; that is, the property interests they sought to protect were probably more encompassing than those we envision today. While we might consider property as something tangible, or of clear monetary value, to at least some of the Framers, property was "shorthand for an expanse of personal freedoms that need[ed] only be tangentially related, if at all, to economic activity."[4]

To protect these paramount property rights,

however conceptualized, the Framers inserted several provisions into the Constitution, two of which we examine in Chapter 8, the Contract Clause and the Takings Clause.

Under Article I, Section 10, "No State shall . . . pass any . . . Law impairing the Obligation of Contracts." To understand the meaning of the clause, we must consider its language within the context of the day. As one source suggests:

For the generation of 1787, property was a natural right. And if men were to be able to use their property, they had to have an equal right to make pledges about their property—to contract. Thus the right to contract was of the same sacredness as the right to property itself, and the obligation to keep one's contracts was a duty required by the natural right to property.[5]

In the Contract Clause the Framers sought to prevent governments from infringing on contractual agreements; in the Takings Clause of the Fifth Amendment they tried to protect private property from government seizure: "nor shall private property be taken for public use without just compensation." In so doing the Founders recognized that the government could confiscate property, for example, to construct roads or erect government buildings. Through the Takings Clause, they wanted to protect property owners from abusive governmental practices. And, as we shall see in Chapter 8, if the Contract and Takings Clauses were the Framers' way of protecting property interests against the "evils" of government interference, they were effective, at least initially. For the Marshall Court the Contract Clause, in particular, "served as one of the most effective instruments for establishing federal control over state actions."[6] That Court read Article I, Section 10, to prohibit state action that infringed on property rights, which in turn impeded economic development.

2. Malcolm M. Feeley and Samuel Krislov, *Constitutional Law* (Glenview, Ill.: Scott/Foresman, 1990), 328.

3. Ibid.

4. Walter F. Murphy, James E. Fleming, and William F. Harris II, *American Constitutional Interpretation* (Mineola, N.Y.: Foundation Press, 1986), 939.

5. Ibid., 940.

6. Elder Witt, *Guide to the U.S. Supreme Court,* 2d ed. (Washington, D.C.: Congressional Quarterly, 1990), 305.

But that interpretation was short-lived. With the end of the Marshall Court and the ascendancy of the Taney Court in the mid-1830s, use of the Contract Clause as a vehicle to protect property interests waned. Why that occurred is something we consider fully in Chapter 8; for now, it is important to note that the "death" of the Contract Clause did not mean that courts were no longer interested in protecting economic liberties. They simply turned to another section of the Constitution to do so. The Fourteenth Amendment's Due Process Clause says no state shall "deprive any person of life, liberty, or property, without due process of law." Under a doctrine called substantive due process, which is reviewed in Chapter 9, between the 1890s and 1930s, the Supreme Court used the Fourteenth Amendment to prohibit states from interfering with "liberty" interests. For example, it struck down legislation mandating maximum work hours on the ground that it interfered with the rights of employers to enter into contracts with their employees.

Like the earlier Court's interpretations of the Takings and Contract Clauses, this treatment of the Fourteenth Amendment eventually fell into disrepute. In Chapter 9 we examine the reasons for its decline. But, before turning to those chapters, let us look at some general issues arising from the economic liberties contained in the Contract and Takings Clauses and those that the Court read into the Fourteenth Amendment's Due Process Clause. One issue is this: as we mentioned, today Americans tend to think of liberties and rights as guarantees of the right to free speech or press or even equality under law. But for most of its history, the Court was far more preoccupied with economics. Elder Witt wrote, "For the first 150 years of its history, the Supreme Court exerted its greatest influence . . . through its decisions on matters of economic interest."[7]

We can attribute the Court's role to several

7. Ibid.

factors. For example, as depicted in Table IV-1, cases involving economic liberties dominated the Court's agenda during its early years. In 1825 fully one-third of the business of the Court involved economic issues. Today, less than 3 percent of the Court's cases deal with such issues. Another factor is the complex relationship between "vested rights" and "community interests." As we have suggested, many of the nation's Founders were quite concerned about individual liberty, particularly the protection of property. But in a democratic society, it is often true that the pursuit of such individual interests impinges on those of the collective good. For example, if a state enacts a law setting a minimum wage, that statute affects the individual liberty of employers: it would be in their best interest, economically speaking, to pay their employees as little as possible. They would argue that minimum wage laws violate their constitutional guarantees. But is there another interest at stake? What are the results of paying workers a substandard wage? Does the state have a responsibility to enact legislation for the "health, safety, and welfare" of all its citizens?

Table IV-1 Business of the Supreme Court, 1793–1825 (Selected Years)

Subject Matter	1793–1800 %	1800–1816 %	1825 %
Admiralty/Maritime	47.5	25.0	15.4
Slave trade/Slavery	—	3.0	11.5
Jurisdiction/Procedure	—	15.0	15.4
Construction of statutes	—	4.5	15.4
Common law	44.3	42.5	34.6
Contracts/Debt	[18.0]		[3.8]
Property	[14.8]		[15.4]
Other	[11.5]		[15.4]
Equity	6.6		3.8
Probate	1.6		—
Total number of cases	61	400	26

Source: Sheldon Goldman, *Constitutional Law* (New York: Harper & Row, 1987), 167

It is the clash between the two interests—individual liberty (vested rights) and the state (police powers)—that has been a primary cause of the Court's involvement in this area and that brings us to a second interesting issue emerging from the economic liberties guarantees. Different Courts approached the task of balancing vested rights and police powers in very different ways: some exalted liberty interests above those of the community; others took precisely the opposite approach. Indeed, some analysts suggest that the Rehnquist Court may be heading in yet another doctrinal direction. They argue that the Court will begin to use the Takings Clause as a mechanism for protecting property rights. What political, legal, and historical factors contributed to these varying approaches to economic liberties are things to think about as you read the material that follows.

READINGS

Ackerman, Bruce A. *Private Property and the Constitution.* New Haven, Conn.: Yale University Press, 1977.

Beard, Charles A. *An Economic Interpretation of the Constitution.* New York: Macmillan, 1935.

Brown, Robert E. *Charles Beard and the Constitution.* Princeton, N.J.: Princeton University Press, 1956.

Dorn, James, and Henry G. Manne, eds., *Economic Liberties and the Judiciary.* Fairfax, Va.: George Mason University Press, 1987.

McDonald, Forrest. *We the People: The Economic Origins of the Constitution.* Chicago: University of Chicago Press, 1958.

Miller, Arthur Selwyn. *The Supreme Court and American Capitalism.* New York: Free Press, 1968.

Semonche, John E. *Charting the Future: The Supreme Court Responds to a Changing Society, 1890-1920.* Westport, Conn.: Greenwood Press, 1978.

CHAPTER **8**

THE CONTRACT AND TAKINGS CLAUSES

Suppose a friend of yours graduated from college some years ago and accepted a position with a large corporation. One of the reasons she took this particular job was that the company offered an attractive savings plan as a fringe benefit. Under the terms of the savings plan contract, your friend regularly placed a portion of her income into the fund, and the company matched her contributions. Money deposited in the fund belonged to the individual savers, and the company had no authority to use the funds for any corporate purpose. Over the years her savings account grew steadily. Then, due to a national recession, the company's fortunes reversed, and it, along with many others, faced bankruptcy. The state rushed to the relief of the troubled businesses by passing a law that allowed them unilaterally to use the assets in employee savings plans to finance operations until the economy regained its strength. The company took advantage of this statute, but, after spending all of the savings plan funds, the company still went under.

This story raises some basic questions. How can the state pass a law that releases a company from its contractual obligations? The company's employees were cheated out of their money, and the state was involved. How can one participate in any investment or commercial activity without some protection against a state granting similar special considerations to corporations or other parties?

If you were outraged by your friend's fate, your reaction would be quite understandable. One of the hallmarks of a society that values commercial activity is the right to enter into contracts. It would be hard to imagine a market-based economy that did not recognize and protect legally binding agreements. In most instances, we would expect the government to enforce contracts and not encourage parties who wish to break them. In fact, the individuals who drafted the U.S. Constitution felt much the same way.

In addition to favoring protections against government infringement on contractual agreements, the Framers were concerned about a related and perhaps more fundamental issue—the protection of private property from government seizure. Although economic philosophies promoting the socialization of private property were not well developed at the time of the Constitution's creation, the Framers were aware that governments could confiscate private property for public purposes. Such actions often were necessary to build roads, erect public buildings, and for other reasonable purposes. But the power to take private property for public purposes may be abused, and the Framers wanted to ensure that the Constitution protected citizens' private property rights.

Two significant provisions in the federal Constitution—the Contract Clause and the Takings Clause—limit the government's power to infringe on contracts and seize private property. Together they underscore the importance the Framers placed on private property rights and free enterprise.

The Framers and the Contract Clause

It might be difficult to find a group of people more supportive of the right to enter into binding agreements than the delegates to the Constitutional Convention. For the most part, these individuals represented the propertied classes, and they assembled in Philadelphia at a time of economic turmoil. Many of them feared that as the nation coped with its economic problems it might suspend the obligation to honor contracts.

Following the Revolutionary War the economy was very unstable, and the government under the Articles of Confederation was unable to correct the situation. Hardest hit were the small farmers, many of whom had taken out large amounts in loans that they could not repay. When creditors started foreclosing on real estate and debtors were jailed for failing to pay, farmers and others faced with unmanageable obligations began to agitate for relief. Several states responded to this pressure by passing laws to help them. Among these acts were bankruptcy laws that erased certain debt obligations or extended the time to pay debts, legal obstacles that blocked creditors from asserting their contractual rights against their debtors, and state currencies of dubious value that were declared legal tender to satisfy debt obligations.

These state policies hurt the creditors, many of whom were wealthy landowners. They called for a strengthening of the national government to deal with economic problems and a ban on the state governments' practice of nullifying contractual obligations. In response, Congress authorized a convention to propose changes in the Articles.

Once assembled, the delegates went much further than originally authorized and created the Constitution of the United States.

The document drafted in Philadelphia clearly reflected the economic interests of the delegates. Among the provisions they placed in the document was a protection of contracts against state government infringement. Article I, Section 10, declares: "No State shall . . . pass any . . . Law impairing the obligation of contracts."

The eighteenth century understanding of the term *contract* was no different from today's. A contract is an agreement voluntarily entered into by two or more parties in which a promise is made and something of value is given or pledged. Contractual agreements are made in almost every commercial transaction, such as a mining company's promise to deliver a quantity of iron ore to a steel mill in return for a particular fee, or a lawyer's promise to represent a client at a specified rate of compensation.

For the Framers, the right to enter into contracts was an important freedom closely tied to the right of private property. The ownership of private property implies the right to buy, sell, divide, occupy, lease, and use it; but one cannot effectively exercise these various property rights without the ability to enter into legally binding arrangements with others. In commercial transactions the parties rely on each other to carry out the contractual provisions. During the nation's formative years, those who failed to live up to contractual promises were dealt with harshly. In the minds of the propertied classes of the eighteenth century, this is how it should be, and the government should not be allowed to intervene in such private arrangements.

Evidence from the convention indicates that the Framers adopted the Contract Clause as a means of protecting agreements between private parties from state interference. However, at that time contracts also were a means of carrying out public policy. Because governments then were much more limited than they are today, the states regularly entered into contracts with individuals or corporations to carry out government policy or to distribute government benefits. These state actions included land grants, commercial monopolies, and licenses to construct roads and bridges. Individuals who entered into a contractual agreement with the state expected it to live up to its obligations and not abrogate the arrangement or unilaterally change the terms. In spite of what the Framers might have intended, the Contract Clause is generally worded and therefore offers protection both to contracts among private parties and to agreements made between private parties and the government.

The Contract Clause was not a major point of controversy at the convention; rather, the records show that the delegates accepted its wisdom with little debate. The clause was one of several prohibitions the Framers imposed on state economic regulation. For example, states could no longer coin money, issue bills of credit, create tender for payment of debts, or tax and regulate certain forms of interstate or foreign commerce.

The debates over ratification of the Constitution also made little reference to the Contract Clause. In *The Federalist Papers,* Alexander Hamilton justified the prohibition against state impairment of contract obligations by claiming that "Laws in violation of private contracts . . . may be considered as another probable source of hostility."[1] James Madison declared, "[L]aws impairing the obligation of contracts are contrary to the first principles of the social compact and to every principle of sound legislation."[2]

In spite of this lack of attention at the drafting and ratification stages, the Contract Clause became an important legal force in the early years of the nation's development. As political majorities changed from election to election, it was not unusual for state legislatures to enter into contracts with private parties only to break or change those agreements in subsequent legislative sessions. In addition, state governments often would adopt policies that ran contrary to contracts among private individuals. When such actions occurred, injured parties would challenge the state in court. Because the states were not obliged to follow principles of due process of law until after ratification of the Fourteenth Amendment in 1868, the Contract Clause was the primary constitutional grounds to challenge state policies. As a result, it was one of the most litigated constitutional provisions in the first decades of U.S. history. One study concluded that roughly 40 percent of all Supreme Court cases prior to 1889 that attacked the validity of state legislation did so on the basis of Contract Clause arguments.[3]

John Marshall and the Contract Clause

The significance of the Contract Clause increased dramatically through the Marshall Court's interpretations of its meaning. Chief Justice John Marshall had strong views on private property, economic development, and the role of the federal government. He consistently supported aggressive policies that would result in vigorous economic expansion. Underlying this position was a philosophy that elevated private property to the level of a natural right that government had little authority to limit. Furthermore, Marshall firmly believed that the nation's interests could be served best by the federal government becoming the primary agent for economic policy making rather than relying on the states to supply this leadership. As we have seen in the areas of federalism and commerce, Marshall

1. Alexander Hamilton, "Federalist No. 7," in *The Federalist Papers,* ed. Clinton Rossiter (New York: New American Library, 1961).
2. James Madison, "Federalist No. 44," in *The Federalist Papers.*

3. Benjamin F. Wright, *The Contract Clause of the Constitution* (Cambridge, Mass.: Harvard University Press, 1938).

could be counted on to uphold actions taken by the federal government and to favor it over competing state interests. Marshall's ideology predisposed him to champion the Contract Clause, which he viewed as essential to the right to private property. Moreover, the clause's restriction of the regulatory powers of the states appealed to his views on federalism. Given Marshall's domination of the Court for more than three decades, it is not surprising that the Contract Clause achieved an elevated status during those years.

Establishing the Importance of the Contract Clause

The first Supreme Court decision to consider the Contract Clause was *Fletcher v. Peck* (1810),

which concerned the validity of a state nullifying a public contract. The suit flowed from one of the most notorious incidents of corruption and bribery in the nation's early history—the Yazoo River land fraud. In this litigation the beneficiaries of the scheme sought to use the Contract Clause to protect their gains.

Chief Justice Marshall was caught in a bind. To give force to the Contract Clause would be to rule in favor of those who profited from state government corruption. To rule against the unpopular fraudulent transactions would be to hand down a precedent significantly curtailing the meaning of the provision. Which option did Marshall choose?

Fletcher v. Peck

6 Cranch 87 (1810)

Vote: 5 (Johnson, Livingston, Marshall, Todd, Washington)

o

Opinion of the Court: Marshall
Concurring opinion: Johnson
Not participating: Chase, Cushing

This dispute had its roots in the 1795 session of the Georgia legislature. Clearly motivated by wholesale bribery, the legislators sold about 35 million acres of public lands to several land companies. The territory in question encompassed most of what is now Mississippi and Alabama. Some of the nation's most prominent public figures, including a number of members of Congress, supported this transaction or invested in it. The citizens of Georgia were outraged by the sale and turned out most of the legislators in the next election. In 1796 the newly elected legislature promptly rescinded the sales contract and moved to repossess the land. Unfortunately, by this time the original land companies had sold numerous

parcels to third party investors and settlers. A massive and complicated set of legal actions ensued to determine ownership of the disputed lands. Attempts to negotiate a settlement proved unsuccessful. Even President Thomas Jefferson was drawn into the controversy as he tried to work out a compromise settlement that would satisfy the state of Georgia as well as the investors.

Fletcher v. Peck was a lawsuit filed to obtain a judicial determination of the ownership question. John Peck acquired a parcel of the land in question from James Gunn, one of the original recipients of the Georgia land sales. Peck in turn sold the land to Robert Fletcher. When the state repealed the sale and resumed control of the land, Fletcher sued Peck for return of the purchase price. The real issue, however, rested squarely on the meaning of the Contract Clause: May a state that has entered into a valid contract later rescind that contract? Joseph Story, who was to become the youngest man appointed to the Supreme Court, represented those who had purchased the land and wanted clear title to it. He argued that the Contract Clause barred the state from rescinding the original sales agreements. Attorneys supporting Georgia's repudiation of the land sale held that the state was empowered to declare it void because the original transaction was based on fraud. Furthermore, they contended that the Contract Clause was intended to protect against the abrogation of private contracts, not those made by the states.

Chief Justice Marshall delivered the opinion of the Court:

The importance and the difficulty of the questions, presented by these pleadings, are deeply felt by the court.

The lands in controversy vested absolutely in James Gunn and others, the original grantees, by the conveyance of the governor, made in pursuance of an act of assembly to which the legislature was fully competent. Being thus in full possession of the legal estate, they, for a valuable consideration, conveyed portions of the land to those who were willing to purchase. If the original transaction was infected with fraud, these purchasers did not participate in it, and had no notice of it. They were innocent. Yet the legislature of Georgia has involved them in the fate of the first parties to the transaction, and, if the act be valid, has annihilated their rights also. . . .

If a suit be brought to set aside a conveyance obtained by fraud, and the fraud be clearly proved, the conveyance will be set aside, as between the parties; but the rights of third persons, who are purchasers without notice, for a valuable consideration, cannot be disregarded. Titles, which according to every legal test, are perfect, are acquired with that confidence which is inspired by the opinion that the purchaser is safe. If there be any concealed defect, arising from the conduct of those who had held the property long before he acquired it, of which he had no notice, that concealed defect cannot be set up against him. He has paid the money for a title good at law, he is innocent, whatever may be the guilt of others, and equity will not subject him to the penalties attached to that guilt. All titles would be insecure, and the intercourse between man and man would be very seriously obstructed if this principle be overturned. . . .

If the legislature felt itself absolved from those rules of property which are common to all the citizens of the United States, and from those principles of equity which are acknowledged in all our courts, its act is to be supported by its power alone, and the same power may devest any other individual of his lands, if it shall be the will of the legislature so to exert it. . . .

Is the power of the legislature competent to the annihilation of such title, and to a resumption of the property thus held?

The principle asserted is, that one legislature is competent to repeal any act which a former legislature was competent to pass; and that one legislature cannot abridge the powers of a succeeding legislature.

The correctness of this principle, so far as respects general legislation, can never be controverted. But, if an act be done under a law, a succeeding legislature cannot undo it. The past cannot be recalled by the most absolute power. Conveyances have been made, those conveyances have vested legal estates, and, if those estates may be seized by the sovereign authority, still, that they originally vested is a fact, and cannot cease to be a fact.

When, then, a law is in its nature a contract, when absolute rights have vested under that contract, a repeal of the law cannot devest those rights; and the act of annulling them, if legitimate, is rendered so by a power applicable to the case of every individual in the community.

It may well be doubted whether the nature of society and of government does not prescribe some limits to the legislative power; and, if any be prescribed, where are they to be found, if the property of an individual, fairly and honestly acquired, may be seized without compensation.

To the legislature all legislative power is granted; but the question, whether the act of transferring the property of an individual to the public, be in the nature of the legislative power, is well worthy of serious reflection.

It is the peculiar province of the legislature to prescribe general rules for the government of society; the application of those rules to individuals in society would seem to be the duty of other departments. How far the power of giving the law may involve every other power, in cases where the constitution is silent, never has been, and perhaps never can be, definitely stated.

The validity of this rescinding act, then, might well be doubted, were Georgia a single sovereign power. But Georgia cannot be viewed as a single, unconnected, sovereign power, on whose legislature no other restrictions are imposed than may be found in its own constitution. She is a part of a large empire; she is a member of the American union; and that union has a constitution the supremacy of which all acknowledge, and which imposes limits to the legislature of the several states, which none claim a right to pass. The constitution of the United States declares that no state shall pass any bill of attainder, *ex post facto* law, or law impairing the obligation of contracts.

Does the case now under consideration come within this prohibitory section of the constitution?

In considering this very interesting question, we immediately ask ourselves what is a contract? Is a grant a contract?

A contract is a compact between two or more parties, and is either executory or executed. An executory contract is one in which a party binds himself to do, or not to do, a particular thing; such was the law under which the conveyance was made by the governor. A contract executed is one in which the object of contract is performed; and this, says Blackstone, differs in nothing from a grant. The contract between Georgia and the purchasers was executed by the grant. A contract executed, as well as one which is executory, contains obligations binding on the parties. A grant, in its own nature, amounts to an extinguishment of the right of the grantor, and implies a contract not to reassert that right. A party is, therefore, always estopped by his own grant.

Since, then, in fact, a grant is a contract executed, the obligation of which still continues, and since the constitution uses the general term contract, without distinguishing between those which are executory and those which are executed, it must be construed to comprehend the latter as well as the former. A law annulling conveyances between individuals, and declaring that the grantors should stand seised of their former estates, notwithstanding those grants, would be as repugnant to the constitution as a law discharging the vendors of property from the obligation of executing their contracts by conveyances. It would be strange if a contract to convey was secured by the constitution, while an absolute conveyance remained unprotected.

If, under a fair construction [of] the constitution, grants are comprehended under the term contracts, is a grant from the state excluded from the operation of the provision? Is the clause to be considered as inhibiting the state from impairing the obligation of contracts between two individuals, but as excluding from that inhibition contracts made with itself?

The words themselves contain no such distinction. They are general, and are applicable to contracts of every description. If contracts made with the state are to be exempted from their operation, the exception must arise from the character of the contracting party, not from the words which are employed.

Whatever respect might have been felt for the state sovereignties, it is not to be disguised that the framers of the constitution viewed, with some apprehension, the violent acts which might grow out of the feelings of the moment; and that the people of the United States, in adopting that instrument, have manifested a determination to shield themselves and their property from the effects of those sudden and strong passions to which men are exposed. The restrictions on the legislative power of the states are obviously founded in this sentiment; and the constitution of the United States contains what may be deemed a bill of rights for the people of each state.

No state shall pass any bill of attainder, *ex post facto* law, or law impairing the obligation of contracts.

A bill of attainder may affect the life of an individual, or may confiscate his property, or may do both.

In this form the power of the legislature over the lives and fortunes of individuals is expressly restrained. What motive, then, for implying, in words which import a general prohibition to impair the obligation of contracts, an exception in favour of the right to impair the obligation of those contracts into which the state may enter?

The state legislatures can pass no *ex post facto* law. An *ex post facto* law is one which renders an act punishable in a manner in which it was not punishable when it was committed. Such a law may inflict penalties on the person, or may inflict pecuniary penalties which swell the public treasury. The legislature is then prohibited from passing a law by which a man's estate, or any part of it, shall be seized for a crime which was not declared, by some previous law, to render him liable to that punishment. Why, then, should violence be done to the natural meaning of words for the purpose of leaving to the legislature the power of seizing, for public use, the estate of an individual in the form of a law annulling the title by which he holds that estate? The court can perceive no sufficient grounds for making this distinction. This rescinding act would have the effect of an *ex post facto* law. It forfeits the estate of Fletcher for a crime not committed by himself, but by those from whom he purchased. This cannot be effected in the form of an *ex post facto* law, or bill of attainder; why, then, is it allowable in the form of a law annulling the original grant?

The argument in favour of presuming an intention to except a case, not excepted by the words of the constitution, is susceptible of some illustration from a principle originally ingrafted in that instrument, though no longer a part of it. The constitution, as passed, gave the courts of the United States jurisdiction in suits brought against individual states. A state,

then, which violated its own contract was suable in the courts of the United States for that violation. Would it have been a defence in such a suit to say that the state had passed a law absolving itself from the contract? It is scarcely to be conceived that such a defence could be set up. And yet, if a state is neither restrained by the general principles of our political institutions, nor by the words of the constitution, from impairing the obligation of its own contracts, such a defence would be a valid one. This feature is no longer found in the constitution; but it aids in the construction of those clauses with which it was originally associated.

It is, then, the unanimous opinion of the court, that, in this case, the estate having passed into the hands of a purchaser for a valuable consideration, without notice, the state of Georgia was restrained, either by general principles which are common to our free institutions, or by the particular provisions of the constitution of the United States, from passing a law whereby the estate of the plaintiff in the premises so purchased could be constitutionally and legally impaired and rendered null and void.

Marshall's opinion gave considerable force to the Contract Clause. Although he acknowledged that the original transactions were based on bribery and corruption, Marshall concluded that such matters are beyond the power of the courts to control. He concentrated instead on the validity of a state rescinding a previously passed, binding agreement. According to the Court's holding in this case, the Constitution prohibits the states from impairing the obligation of any contract, even those contracts contrary to the public good. In striking down the 1796 Georgia statute, the Supreme Court for the first time nullified a state law on constitutional grounds. *Fletcher v. Peck* established the Contract Clause as an important provision of the new Constitution and encouraged its use in challenging economic regulations of the states.

Marshall's initial interpretation of the Contract

Clause was reinforced just two years later in *New Jersey v. Wilson* (1812). This dispute can be traced back to 1758 when the remnants of the Delaware Indian tribe settled its land claims with the state of New Jersey. The Delawares consented to give up their claim to the disputed lands if the state would purchase a tract for the tribe to inhabit. The agreement included a provision that the land granted to the tribe would be free from state taxation. In 1801 members of the tribe decided to move to New York, and New Jersey granted them permission to sell their land. Three years later the state passed a law subjecting the property to state taxes. The new owners objected, claiming that the repeal of tax exempt status was an impairment of the 1758 contract. Chief Justice Marshall, for a unanimous Court, ruled in favor of the landowners. The legislature granted the tax exemption to the land as part of a legally binding contract.

That contractual obligation cannot later be impaired by the state. The tax status conferred in 1758 remained with the land even though the original parties to the agreement had sold it.

In 1819 the Court heard *Sturges v. Crowninshield,* an appeal that presented issues hitting squarely on the concerns expressed by the delegates at the Constitutional Convention. Richard Crowninshield, whose business enterprises had suffered hard times, received two loans from Josiah Sturges totaling approximately $1,500. The loans were secured by promissory notes. When Crowninshield became insolvent, he sought relief from his debts by invoking New York's recently passed bankruptcy law. Sturges objected, claiming that the New York law was a state impairment of the obligation of contracts in violation of the Constitution. The New York bankruptcy law was an example of just what the Framers had intended to prohibit—states interfering with debtor-creditor agreements.

The case presented two issues to the Supreme Court. The first was whether a state may enact a bankruptcy law at all. Article I, Section 8, Clause 4, of the Constitution expressly gave the federal government power to enact such legislation. Did this power preclude the states from acting? A unanimous Court, again through an opinion written by Chief Justice Marshall, held that in the absence of any federal action the states were free to enact bankruptcy laws. The second issue was whether the New York law was invalid as an impairment of contracts. Here the Court found the law defective. The New York law discharged Crowninshield's contractual indebtedness entered into prior to the passage of the statute, which, according to the Court, was beyond the power of the state.[4]

Corporate Charters as Contracts

The same year the Court decided *Sturges,* the justices announced their decision in *Trustees of Dartmouth College v. Woodward* (1819), perhaps the most famous of the Marshall-era Contract Clause cases. The Dartmouth College case presented a question of particular significance to the business community: Is a corporation charter a contract protected against state impairment? The case had added intrigue because it involved a bitter partisan battle between the Jeffersonian Republicans and the Federalists.

4. Eight years later, however, the Court held in *Ogden v. Saunders,* 12 Wheat. 213 (1827) that state bankruptcy laws did not violate the Contract Clause if the contract was entered into after the enactment of the bankruptcy statute.

Trustees of Dartmouth College v. Woodward

4 Wheat. 518 (1819)

Vote: 5 (Johnson, Livingston, Marshall, Story, Washington)
1 (Duvall)
Opinion of the Court: Marshall
Concurring opinions: Story, Washington
Not participating: Todd

In 1769 King George III issued a corporate charter establishing Dartmouth College in New Hampshire. The charter designated a board of trustees as the ultimate governing body, and the board's authority extended to the college president. The board was self-perpetuating with the power to fill its own vacancies. The founder and first president of Dartmouth was Eleazar Wheelock, who also had authority to designate his own successor. He chose his son, John Wheelock, who assumed the presidency upon Eleazar's death. John Wheelock was ill-suited for the position, and for years friction existed between him and the board.

To shore up his position, Wheelock made political alliances with the Jeffersonian Republicans who had gained control of the state legislature in 1816. The Republicans gladly took his side in the dispute with the Federalist-dominated board of trustees and passed a law radically changing the governing structure of the college. The law called for an expansion of the board from twelve to twenty-one members to be appointed by the governor, and it created a supervisory panel with veto power over the actions of the trustees. The new officials removed the old trustees from office. In effect, the legislature had converted Dartmouth College, renamed Dartmouth University under the new law, from a private to a public institution. The result was chaos. The students and faculty for the most part remained loyal to the old trustees, but the state essentially took over the buildings and records of the college. As might be expected, the college soon found itself on the edge of fiscal collapse.

To resolve the situation, the old trustees hired Daniel Webster to represent them. Webster, a 1801 Dartmouth graduate, agreed to take the case for a fee of $1,000, a considerable sum of money in those days. The trustees sued William Woodward, the secretary of the college, who had in his possession the college charter, records, and seal. Webster and the old trustees lost in the state courts and then appealed to the U.S. Supreme Court. When the case was argued in March 1818, Webster engaged in four hours of brilliant oratory before the justices. At times his argument was quite emotional, and he is said to have brought tears to the eyes of those present when he spoke his often quoted line, "It is, sir, as I have said, a small college, and yet there are those that love it." The justices, however, did not act in the heat of emotion. Instead, almost a full year went by before the Court announced its decision. By the time the opinion was released, both John Wheelock and William Woodward had died.

Chief Justice Marshall delivered the opinion of the Court:

This Court can be insensible neither to the magnitude nor delicacy of this question. The validity of a legislative act is to be examined; and the opinion of the highest law tribunal of a State is to be revised: an opinion which carries with it intrinsic evidence of the diligence, of the ability, and the integrity, with which it was formed. On more than one occasion, this Court has expressed the cautious circumspection with which it approaches the consideration of such questions; and has declared, that, in no doubtful case, would it pronounce a legislative act to be contrary to the constitution. But the American people have said, in the constitution of the United States, that "no State shall pass any bill of attainder, *ex post facto* law, or law impairing the obligation of contracts." In the same instrument they have also said, "that the judicial power shall extend to all cases in law and equity arising under the constitution." On the judges of this Court, then, is imposed the high and solemn duty of protecting, from even legislative violation, those contracts which the constitution of our country has placed beyond legislative control; and, however irksome the task may be, this is a duty from which we dare not shrink. . . .

It can require no argument to prove, that the circumstances of this case constitute a contract. An application is made to the crown for a charter to incorporate a religious and literary institution. In the application, it is stated that large contributions have been made for the object, which will be conferred on the corporation, as soon as it shall be created. The charter is granted, and on its faith the property is conveyed. Surely in this transaction every ingredient of a complete and legitimate contract is to be found.

The points for consideration are,

1. Is this contract protected by the constitution of the United States?

2. Is it impaired by the acts under which the defendant holds? . . .

1. . . . [T]he term "*contract*" must be understood in a . . . limited sense. . . . [I]t must be understood as intended to guard against a power of at least doubtful utility, the abuse of which had been extensively felt; and to restrain the legislature in future

Rev. Eleazar Wheelock (left) was the founder and first president of Dartmouth College; John Wheelock (middle), son of Eleazar, was the second president, and his dispute with the college board of trustees led to the famed litigation. William H. Woodward (right) was the secretary-treasurer of the college and the defendant in the Contract Clause case of Dartmouth College v. Woodward.

from violating the right to property. That anterior to the formation of the constitution, a course of legislation had prevailed in many, if not in all, of the States, which weakened the confidence of man in man, and embarrassed all transactions between individuals, by dispensing with a faithful performance of engagements. To correct this mischief, by restraining the power which produced it, the State legislatures were forbidden "to pass any law impairing the obligation of contracts," that is, of contracts respecting property, under which some individual could claim a right to something beneficial to himself; and that since the clause in the constitution must in construction receive some limitation, it may be confined, and ought to be confined, to cases of this description; to cases within the mischief it was intended to remedy. . . .

The parties in this case differ less on general principles, less on the true construction of the constitution in the abstract, than on the application of those principles to this case, and on the true construction of the charter of 1769. This is the point on which the cause essentially depends. If the act of incorporation be a grant of political power, if it create a civil institution to be employed in the administration of the government, or if the funds of the college be public property, or if the State of New-Hampshire, as a government, be alone interested in its transactions, the subject is one in which the legislature of the State may act according to its own judgment, unrestrained by any limitation of its power imposed by the constitution of the United States.

But if this be a private eleemosynary institution, endowed with a capacity to take property for objects unconnected with government, whose funds are bestowed by individuals on the faith of the charter; if the donors have stipulated for the future disposition and management of those funds in the manner prescribed by themselves; there may be more difficulty in the case. . . .

It becomes then the duty of the Court most seriously to examine this charter, and to ascertain its true character. . . .

Whence, then, can be derived the idea, that Dartmouth College has become a public institution, and its trustees public officers, exercising powers conferred by the public for public objects? Not from the source whence its funds were drawn; for its foundation is purely private and eleemosynary—Not from the application of those funds; for money may be given for education, and the persons receiving it do not, by being employed in the education of youth, become members of the civil government. Is it from the act of incorporation? Let this subject be considered.

A corporation is an artificial being, invisible, intangible, and existing only in contemplation of law. Being the mere creature of law, it possesses only those properties which the charter of its creation confers upon it, either expressly, or as incidental to its very existence. These are such as are supposed best calculated to effect the object for which it was created. Among the most important are immortality, and, if the expression may be allowed, individuality; properties, by which a perpetual succession of many persons are considered as the same, and may act as a single individual. They enable a corporation to manage its own affairs, and to hold property without the perplexing intricacies, the hazardous and endless necessity of perpetual conveyances for the purpose of transmitting it from hand to hand. It is chiefly for the purpose of clothing bodies of men, in succession, with these qualities and capacities, that corporations were invented, and are in use. By these means, a perpetual succession of individuals are capable of acting for the promotion of the particular object, like one immortal being. But this being does not share in the civil government of the country, unless that be the purpose for which it was created. Its immortality no more confers on it political power, or a political character,

Drawing of Dartmouth College, 1803.

than immortality would confer such power or character on a natural person. It is no more a State instrument, than a natural person exercising the same powers would be. If, then, a natural person, employed by individuals in the education of youth, or for the government of a seminary in which youth is educated, would not become a public officer, or be considered as a member of the civil government, how is it, that this artificial being, created by law, for the purpose of being employed by the same individuals for the same purposes, should become a part of the civil government of the country? Is it because its existence, its capacities, its powers, are given by law? Because the government has given it the power to take and to hold property in a particular form, and for particular purposes, has the government a consequent right substantially to change that form, or to vary the purposes to which the property is to be applied? This principle has never been asserted or recognized, and is supported by no authority. Can it derive aid from reason? . . .

From the fact, then, that a charter of incorporation has been granted, nothing can be inferred which changes the character of the institution, or transfers to the government any new power over it. The character of civil institutions does not grow out of their incorporation, but out of the manner in which they are formed, and the objects for which they are created. The right to change them is not founded on their being incorporated, but on their being the instruments of government, created for its purposes. The same institutions, created for the same objects, though not incorporated, would be public institutions, and, of course, be controllable by the legislature. The incorporating act neither gives nor prevents this control. Neither, in reason, can the incorporating act change the character of a private eleemosynary institution. . . .

From this review of the charter, it appears, that Dartmouth College is an eleemosynary institution, incorporated for the purpose of perpetuating the application of the bounty of the donors, to the specified objects of that bounty; that its trustees or governors were originally named by the founder, and invested with the power of perpetuating themselves; that they are not public officers, nor is it a civil institution, participating in the administration of government; but a charity school, or a seminary of education, incorporated for the preservation of its property, and the perpetual application of that property to the objects of its creation. . . .

This is plainly a contract to which the donors, the trustees, and the crown, (to whose rights and obligations New-Hampshire succeeds,) were the original parties. It is a contract made on a valuable consideration. It is a contract for the security and disposition of property. It is a contract, on the faith of which, real and personal estate has been conveyed to the corporation. It is then a contract within the letter of the constitution, and within its spirit also. . . .

The opinion of the Court, after mature deliberation, is, that this is a contract, the obligation of which cannot be impaired, without violating the constitution of the United States. This opinion appears to us to be equally supported by reason, and by the former decisions of this Court.

2. We next proceed to the inquiry, whether its obligation has been impaired by those acts of the legislature of New-Hampshire. . . .

From the review of this charter, which has been taken, it appears, that the whole power of governing the college, of appointing and removing tutors, of fixing their salaries, of directing the course of study to be pursued by the students, and of filling up vacancies created in their own body, was vested in the trustees. On the part of the crown it was expressly stipulated, that this corporation, thus constituted, should continue forever; and that the number of trustees should forever consist of twelve, and no more. By this contract the crown was bound, and could have made no violent alteration in its essential terms, without impairing its obligation.

By the revolution, the duties, as well as the powers, of government devolved on the people of New-Hampshire. . . . It is too clear to require the support of argument, that all contracts, and rights, respecting property, remained unchanged by the revolution. The obligations then, which were created by the charter to Dartmouth College, were the same in the new, that they had been in the old government. The power of the government was also the same. A repeal of this charter at any time prior to the adoption of the present constitution of the United States, would have been an extraordinary and unprecedented act of power, but one which could have been contested only by the restrictions upon the legislature, to be found in the constitution of the State. But the constitution of the United States has imposed this additional limitation, that the legislature of a State shall pass no act "impairing the obligation of contracts." . . .

The whole power of governing the college is transferred from trustees appointed according to the will of the founder, expressed in the charter, to the executive of New-Hampshire. The management and application of the funds of this eleemosynary institution, which are placed by the donors in the hands of trustees named in the charter, and empowered to perpetuate themselves, are placed by this act under the control of the government of the State. The will of the State is substituted for the will of the donors, in every essential operation of the college. This is not an immaterial change. The founders of the college contracted, not merely for the perpetual application of the funds which they gave, to the objects for which those funds were given; they contracted also, to secure that application by the constitution of the corporation. They contracted for a system, which should, as far as human foresight can provide, retain forever the government of the literary institution they had formed, in the hands of persons approved by themselves. This system is totally changed. The charter of 1769 exists no longer. It is reorganized; and reorganized in such a manner, as to convert a literary institution, moulded according to the will of its founders, and placed under the control of private literary men, into a machine entirely subservient to the will of the government. This may be for the advantage of this college in particular, and may be for the advantage of literature in general; but it is not according to the will of the donors, and is subversive of that contract, on the faith of which their property was given. . . .

It results from this opinion, that the acts of the legislature of New-Hampshire . . . are repugnant to the constitution of the United States. . . . The judgment of the State Court must, therefore, be reversed.

The Dartmouth College case was a clear victory for Webster and the board. The old trustees regained control of the college, and Webster's reputation as one of the nation's leading legal advocates was firmly established. The decision was also a victory for business interests. By holding that corporate charters were contracts under the meaning of Article I, Section 10, the Court gave businesses considerable protection against state regulation. The decision, however, was not totally one-sided. Marshall acknowledged the power of the state to include within its contracts and charters provisions reserving the right to make future changes.

The importance of the Contract Clause reached its zenith under the Marshall Court. These early decisions protecting contractual agreements helped spur economic development and expansion. But an inevitable battle was on the horizon, a battle between the constitutional sanctity of contracts and a state's authority to regulate for the public good.

The Decline of the Contract Clause: From the Taney Court to the New Deal

The Marshall years ended when the chief justice died July 6, 1835, at the age of seventy-nine. Marshall had been appointed in 1801 in one of the last acts of the once-dominant Federalist party, and he had imposed his political philosophy on the Court's constitutional interpretations for more than three decades. His decisions in Contract Clause disputes, as well as in other areas of federalism and economic regulation, encouraged economic development and fostered entrepreneurial activity.

Elevating the Importance of the Public Good

The days of the Federalist philosophy sympathetic to the interests of business and the economic elite had long since passed. Andrew Jackson now occupied the White House. Jackson came from the American frontier and was committed to policies beneficial to ordinary citizens; he had little sympathy for the moneyed classes of the Northeast. Within a short period, Jackson had the opportunity to change the course of the Supreme Court. He filled not only the center chair left vacant by Marshall's death, but also those of five associate justices during his presidency.[5] The new appointees all held ideologies consistent with principles of Jacksonian democracy, especially the new chief justice, Roger Brooke Taney, a Maryland Democrat who had served in a number of posts in the Jackson administration *(see profile of Taney, page 233)*. Changes in constitutional interpretation were inevitable, although in the final analysis the Taney Court did not veer as far from Marshall precedents as many had predicted.

5. This number includes Associate Justice John Catron, who was nominated on Jackson's last day in office and whose appointment is often credited to Jackson's successor, Martin Van Buren.

Given the differences between Federalist and Jacksonian values, however, the Court was likely to reevaluate the Contract Clause. The Taney Court's first opportunity to do so came in *Charles River Bridge v. Warren Bridge* (1837). As you read the Court's opinion, compare it to the positions Marshall stated in the *Fletcher* and *Dartmouth College* cases. While Taney certainly did not repudiate Marshall's rulings, his opinion in *Charles River Bridge* struck a new balance between the power of the state to legislate for the public good and the inviolability of contracts. The Court also held that contracts should be strictly construed, a position at odds with Marshall's rather expansive interpretations of contractual obligations. Justice Joseph Story, who had appeared as an attorney in *Fletcher* and had supported Marshall's views of the Contract Clause since he joined the Court in 1811, dissented from this change in doctrine.

Charles River Bridge v. Warren Bridge

11 Pet. 420 (1837)

Vote: 5 *(Baldwin, Barbour, McLean, Taney, Wayne)*
    2 *(Story, Thompson)*
Opinion of the Court: Taney
Concurring opinion: McLean
Dissenting opinions: Story, Thompson

In 1785 the Massachusetts legislature created by charter the Charles River Bridge Company. The charter gave the company the right to construct a bridge between Boston and Charlestown and to collect tolls for its use. This agreement replaced a ferry franchise between the two cities that the colonial legislature had granted to Harvard College in 1650. In 1792 the legislature extended the charter. Because of the population growth in the Boston area, the bridge received heavy use, and its investors prospered. In 1828, when traffic congestion on the bridge became a significant problem, the legislature decided that a second bridge was necessary. Consequently, the

state incorporated the Warren Bridge Company and authorized it to construct a bridge to be located about a hundred yards from the first. The Warren Bridge investors had authority to collect tolls to pay for the expense of construction plus an agreed-upon profit. However, in no more than six years the state was to assume ownership of the Warren Bridge and then operate it on a toll-free basis.

The Charles River Bridge Company opposed the construction of a second bridge. It claimed that its charter conferred the exclusive right to build and operate a bridge between Boston and Charlestown. A second bridge, eventually to be operated without tolls, would deprive the company of the profits from its investment. The second charter, the company claimed, was a violation of the Contract Clause. To represent it, the Charles River Bridge Company hired Daniel Webster, who had won the Dartmouth College case two decades earlier. When the Massachu-

The Charles River Bridge ran from Prince Street in Boston to Charlestown. The bridge, considered of very advanced design at the time of its construction, was built on seventy-five oak piers and was more than 1,500 feet long.

setts courts failed to grant relief, Charles River Bridge took its case to the U.S. Supreme Court.

The case was first argued in March 1831. John Marshall still led the Court at that time, and Webster understandably felt confident of victory. However, the justices could not agree on a decision, and the case was scheduled for reargument in 1833. Once again, no decision was reached. Before a third hearing could be scheduled, deaths and resignations had changed the ideological complexion of the Court. When Jackson announced Taney as his choice for chief justice, Webster is said to have proclaimed, "The Constitution is gone." From Webster's perspective perhaps that was true. The Taney justices scheduled the bridge case to be reargued in 1837, and Webster no longer had a sympathetic audience for his strong Contract Clause position.

Chief Justice Taney delivered the opinion of the Court:

The plaintiffs in error insist . . . [t]hat . . . the acts of the legislature of Massachusetts . . . by their true construction, necessarily implied that the legislature would not authorize another bridge, and especially a free one, by the side of this, and placed in the same line of travel, whereby the franchise granted to the "proprietors of the Charles River Bridge" should be rendered of no value; and the plaintiffs in error contend, that the grant of the ferry to the college, and of the charter to the proprietors of the bridge, are both contracts on the part of the state; and that the law authorizing the erection of the Warren Bridge in 1828, impairs the obligation of one or both of these contracts. . . .

[W]e are not now left to determine, for the first time, the rules by which public grants are to be construed in this country. The subject has already been considered in this Court . . . and the principle recognized, that in grants by the public, nothing passes by implication. . . .

[T]he object and end of all government is to promote the happiness and prosperity of the community by which it is established; and it can never be assumed, that the government intended to diminish its power of accomplishing the end for which it was created. And in a country like ours, free, active, and enterprising, continually advancing in numbers and wealth; new channels of communication are daily found necessary, both for travel and trade; and are essential to the comfort, convenience, and prosperity of the people. A state ought never to be presumed to surrender this power, because, like the taxing power, the whole community have an interest in preserving it undiminished. And when a corporation alleges, that a state has surrendered for seventy years, its power of improvement, and public accommodation, in a great and important line of travel, along which a vast number of its citizens must daily pass; the community have a right to insist, in the language of this Court above quoted, ''that its abandonment ought not to be presumed, in a case, in which the deliberate purpose of the state to abandon it does not appear.'' The continued existence of a government would be of no great value, if by implications and presumptions, it was disarmed of the powers necessary to accomplish the ends of its creation; and the functions it was designed to perform, transferred to the hands of privileged corporations. The rule of construction announced by the Court, was not confined to the taxing power; nor is it so limited in the opinion delivered. On the contrary, it was distinctly placed on the ground that the interests of the community were concerned in preserving, undiminished, the power then in question; and whenever any power of the state is said to be surrendered or diminished, whether it be the taxing power or any other affecting the public interest, the same principle applies, and the rule of construction must be the same. No one will question that the interests of the great body of the people of the state, would, in this instance, be affected by the surrender of this great line of travel to a single corporation, with the right to exact toll, and exclude competition for seventy years. While the rights of private property are sacredly guarded, we must not forget that the community also have rights, and that the happiness and well being of every citizen depends on their faithful preservation.

Adopting the rule of construction above stated as the settled one, we proceed to apply it to the charter of 1785, to the proprietors of the Charles River Bridge. This act of incorporation is in the usual form, and the privileges such as are commonly given to corporations of that kind. It confers on them the ordinary faculties of a corporation, for the purpose of building the bridge; and establishes certain rates of toll, which the company are authorized to take. This is the whole grant. There is no exclusive privilege given to them over the waters of Charles river, above or below their bridge. No right to erect another bridge themselves, nor to prevent other persons from erecting one. No engagement from the state, that another shall not be erected; and no undertaking not to sanction competition, nor to make improvements that may diminish the amount of its income. Upon all these subjects the charter is silent; and nothing is said in it about a line of travel, so much insisted on in the argument, in which they are to have exclusive privileges. No words are used, from which an intention to grant any of these rights can be inferred. If the plaintiff is entitled to them, it must be implied, simply, from the nature of the grant; and cannot be inferred from the words by which the grant is made.

The relative position of the Warren Bridge has already been described. It does not interrupt the passage over the Charles River Bridge, nor make the way to it or from it less convenient. None of the faculties or franchises granted to that corporation, have been revoked by the legislature; and its right to take the tolls granted by the charter remains unaltered. In short, all the franchises and rights of property enumerated in the charter, and there mentioned to have been granted to it, remain unimpaired. But its income is destroyed by the Warren Bridge; which, being free, draws off the passengers and property which would have gone over it, and renders their franchise of no value. This is the gist of the complaint. For it is not pretended, that the erection of the Warren Bridge would have done them any injury, or in any degree affected their right of property; if it had not diminished the amount of their tolls. In order then to entitle themselves to relief, it is necessary to show, that the legislature contracted not to do the act of which they complain; and that they impaired, or in other words, violated that contract by the erection of the Warren Bridge.

The inquiry then is, does the charter contain such a contract on the part of the state? Is there any such stipulation to be found in that instrument? It must be admitted on all hands, that there is none—no words that even relate to another bridge or to the diminution of their tolls, or to the line of travel. If a contract on that subject can be gathered from the charter, it must be by implication; and cannot be found in the words used. Can such an agreement be implied? The rule of construction before stated is an answer to the question. In charters of this description, no rights are taken from the public, or given to the corporation, beyond those which the words of the charter, by their natural and proper construction, purport to convey. There are no words which import such a contract as the plaintiffs in error contend for, and none can be implied. . . .

Indeed, the practice and usage of almost every state in the Union, old enough to have commenced the work of internal improvement, is opposed to the doctrine contended for on the part of the plaintiffs in error. Turnpike roads have been made in succession, on the same line of travel; the later ones interfering materially with the profits of the first. These corporations have, in some instances, been utterly ruined by the introduction of newer and better modes of transportation, and travelling. In some cases, rail roads have rendered the turnpike roads on the same line of travel so entirely useless, that the franchise of the turnpike corporation is not worth preserving. Yet in none of these cases have the corporations supposed that their privileges were invaded, or any contract violated on the part of the state. Amid the multitude of cases which have occurred, and have been daily occurring for the last forty or fifty years, this is the first instance in which such an implied contract has been contended for, and this Court called upon to infer it from an ordinary act of incorporation, containing nothing more than the usual stipulations and provisions to be found in every such law. The absence of any such controversy, when there must have been so many occasions to give rise to it, proves that neither states, nor individuals, nor corporations, ever imagined that such a contract could be implied from such charters. It shows that the men who voted for these laws, never imagined that they were forming such a contract; and if we maintain that they have made it, we must create it by a legal fiction, in opposition to the truth of the fact, and the obvious intention of the party. We cannot deal thus with the rights reserved to the states; and by legal intendments and mere technical reasoning, take away from them any portion of that power over their own internal police and improvement, which is so necessary to their well being and prosperity. . . .

The judgment of the supreme judicial court of the commonwealth of Massachusetts, dismissing the plaintiff's bill, must, therefore, be affirmed, with costs.

Mr. Justice Story, dissenting.

I maintain, that, upon the principles of common reason and legal interpretation, the present grant carries with it a necessary implication that the legislature shall do no act to destroy or essentially to impair the franchise; that, (as one of the learned judges of the state court expressed it,) there is an implied agreement that the state will not grant another bridge between Boston and Charlestown, so near as to draw away the custom from the old one; and, (as another learned judge expressed it,) that there is an implied agreement of the state to grant the undisturbed use of the bridge and its tolls so far as respects any acts of its own, or of any persons acting under its authority. In other words, the state, impliedly, contracts not to resume its grant, or to do any act to the prejudice or destruction of its grant. I maintain, that there is no authority or principle established in relation to the construction of crown grants, or legislative grants; which does not concede and justify this doctrine. Where the thing is given, the incidents, without which it cannot be enjoyed, are also given. . . . I maintain that a different doctrine is utterly repugnant to all the principles of the common law, applicable to all franchises of a like nature; and that we must overturn some of the best securities of the rights of property, before it can be established. I maintain, that the common law is the birthright of every citizen of Massachusetts, and that he holds the title deeds of his property, corporeal, and incorporeal, under it. I maintain, that under the principles of the common law, there exists no more right in the legislature of Massachusetts, to erect the Warren Bridge, to the ruin of the franchise of the Charles River Bridge than exists to transfer the latter to the former, or to authorize the former to demolish the latter. If the legislature does not mean in its grant to give any exclusive rights, let it say so, expressly; directly; and in terms admitting of no misconstruction. The grantees will then take at their peril, and must abide the results of their overweening confidence, indiscretion, and zeal.

My judgment is formed upon the terms of the grant, its nature and objects, its design and duties; and, in its interpretation, I seek for no new principles, but I apply such as are as old as the very rudiments of the common law.

Daniel Webster
(1782-1852)

Monroe delegate to Electoral College, 1820
United States representative, Massachusetts,
    1823–1827
United States senator, Massachusetts, 1827–1841
Presidential candidate, 1836
Secretary of state (Harrison-Tyler administrations),
    1841–1843
United States senator, Massachusetts, 1845–1850
Secretary of state (Fillmore administration),
    1850–1852

Webster was perhaps best known for his role as an advocate before the Supreme Court and the brilliant oratorical skills he displayed in both Congress and the courts. Webster appeared before the Supreme Court in 168 cases, winning about half of them. In twenty four of his appearances he was an advocate in a major constitutional dispute. Among his most celebrated cases were:

McCulloch v. Maryland (1819)
Dartmouth College v. Woodward (1819)
Cohens v. Virginia (1821)
Gibbons v. Ogden (1824)
Osborn v. Bank of the United States (1824)
Ogden v. Saunders (1827)
Wheaton v. Peters (1834)
Charles River Bridge v. Warren Bridge (1837)
Swift v. Tyson (1842)
West River Bridge v. Dix (1848)
Luther v. Borden (1849)

D aniel Webster played an influential role in the development of American law and politics during a public career that spanned almost fifty years. He was born in Salisbury, New Hampshire, January 18, 1782, and educated at Phillips Exeter Academy and Dartmouth College. He was admitted to the bar in 1805 and immediately began the practice of law in his home state.

In 1813 Webster was first elected to Congress as a Federalist representative from New Hampshire. This office was only the beginning of an illustrious series of important positions:

United States representative, New Hampshire,
    1813–1817

For a review of Webster's legal career, see Maurice G. Baxter, *Daniel Webster and the Supreme Court* (Amherst: University of Massachusetts Press, 1966).

In spite of Justice Story's protest that the majority had rendered the Contract Clause meaningless, the Taney Court continued to allow the states more leeway in regulating for the public good. As Taney noted in his *Charles River Bridge* opinion, "While the rights of private property are sacredly guarded, we must not forget that the community also have rights, and that the happiness and well being of every citizen depends on their faithful preservation." For example, in *West River Bridge Company v. Dix* (1848) the Court upheld the state's right to exercise eminent domain authority even when it conflicted with existing contracts. In that case Vermont had previously granted to a private company a charter to construct a bridge and collect tolls. When the state later decided to build a public highway to be used without tolls, it canceled the company's charter. The state offered to compensate the company for its loss, but the owners were not satisfied with the amount. In an opinion by Justice Peter V. Daniel, the Court rejected the bridge company's claim that the state had violated the Constitution, holding that the Contract Clause did not restrict the state's right to regulate for the public good under the power of eminent domain.

The Taney justices, however, did not totally abandon the Marshall Court's posture favoring business, nor did they repeal the Contract Clause by judicial fiat; the Court instead took a more balanced position. In a number of cases, especially when the contractual provisions were clear, the Taney Court struck down state regulations on Contract Clause grounds. For example, in *Bronson v. Kinzie* (1843) the Court invalidated Illinois laws that expanded the rights of debtors. The challenged statutes placed certain limits on mortgage debt, including protecting the rights of owners to repurchase properties lost to foreclosure. To the extent that these laws were applied to contracts in existence before their passage, the laws were unconstitutional. In *Piqua Branch of the State Bank of Ohio v. Knoop* (1854) the justices declared void the assessment of state taxes on a bank because, in calculating the taxes, Ohio had used a basis different from that specified under the state charter establishing the bank.

Continued Contract Clause Decline in the Post–Civil War Period

After the Taney years, the Court continued to move away from strong enforcement of the Contract Clause and to accord the states increased freedom to exercise their police powers. *Fertilizing Company v. Hyde Park* (1878) provides a good illustration. The Illinois state legislature passed a statute March 8, 1867, creating the Northwest Fertilizing Company. The charter authorized the company within a designated territory to operate a facility that converted dead animals to fertilizer and other products. The charter also gave the company the right to transport dead animals and animal parts (offal) through the territory. Based on this authority, the company operated its plant in a sparsely populated, swampy area. However, the facility was located within the boundaries of the village of Hyde Park, which was beginning to experience considerable population growth. In 1869 the legislature upgraded the village charter, giving it full powers of local government including the authority to "define or abate nuisances which are, or may be, injurious to the public health." Recognizing its charter with the Fertilizing Company, the legislature stipulated that no village regulations could be applied to the company for at least two years. At the end of the two years, the village passed an ordinance that said, "No person shall transfer, carry, haul, or convey any offal, dead animals, or other offensive or unwholesome matter or material, into or through the village of Hyde Park." Parties in violation of the law were subject to fines. In 1873, following the arrest and conviction of railroad workers hauling dead animals to its plant, the Fertilizing Company filed suit claiming that their original charter was a contract that could not be abrogated by the state or its local governments. The company was unsuccessful in the state courts and appealed to the U.S. Supreme Court.

Justice Noah Swayne's opinion made clear at the outset that the company faced a difficult task in its attempt to convince the justices:

The rule of construction in this class of cases is that it shall be most strongly against the corporation. Every reasonable doubt is to be resolved adversely. Nothing is to be taken as conceded but what is given in unmistakable terms, or by an implication equally clear. The affirmative must be shown. Silence is negation, and doubt is fatal to the claim. This doctrine is vital to the public welfare.

The Court then went on to rule against the Contract Clause arguments of the company. The justices had no doubt that the transportation of offal was a public nuisance. Nor was there any doubt that the state had ample police power to combat such an offensive practice. According to Swayne, "That power belonged to the States when the Federal Constitution was adopted. They did not surrender it, and they all have it now. . . . It rests upon the fundamental principle that every one shall so use his own as not to wrong and injure another. To regulate and abate nuisances is one of its ordinary functions.'' The states, the Court was implying, could not contract away their inherent powers to regulate for their citizens' health, safety, and welfare.

Two years following the *Fertilizing Company* case, the justices addressed a similar appeal, this time dealing with questions of public morality. *Stone v. Mississippi* (1880) focused on the use of the state's police power to combat lotteries, a form of gambling that large portions of the population considered evil at that time. As you read Chief Justice Morrison Waite's opinion for the Court, compare it with the decisions written during the Marshall era. Note how much the Court's interpretation of the Contract Clause had changed.

Stone v. Mississippi

101 U.S. 814 (1880)

Vote: 9 (Bradley, Clifford, Field, Harlan, Hunt, Miller, Strong, Swayne, Waite)

0

Opinion of the Court: Waite

In 1867 the post–Civil War provisional state legislature chartered the Mississippi Agricultural, Educational, and Manufacturing Aid Society. In spite of its name, the society's only purpose was to operate a lottery. The charter gave the society authority to run a lottery in Mississippi for twenty-five years, and, in return, the society paid an initial sum of cash to the state, an additional annual payment for each year of operation, plus a percentage of the lottery receipts. In 1868, however, a state convention drafted a new constitution, which the people ratified the next year. This constitution contained provisions explicitly outlawing lotteries. On July 16, 1870, the legislature passed a statute providing for enforcement of the antilottery provisions, and four years later, on March 17, 1874, the state attorney general filed charges against John B. Stone and others associated with the Mississippi Agricultural, Educational and Manufacturing Aid Society for being in violation of state law. The state admitted that the company was operating within the provisions of its 1867 charter, but contended that the new constitution and subsequent enforcement legislation effectively repealed that grant. Stone countered that the federal Contract Clause explicitly prohibits the state from negating the provisions of the charter.

Chief Justice Waite delivered the opinion of the Court:

It is now too late to contend that any contract which a State actually enters into when granting a charter to a private corporation is not within the protection of the clause in the Constitution of the United States that prohibits States from passing laws impairing the obligation of contracts. Art. 1, sect. 10. The doctrines of *Trustees of Dartmouth College* v. *Woodward* [1819], announced by this court more than sixty years ago, have become so imbedded in the jurisprudence of the United States as to make them to all intents and purposes a part of the Constitution itself. In this connection, however, it is to be kept in mind that it is not the charter which is protected, but only any contract the charter may contain. If there is no contract, there is nothing in the grant on which the Constitution can act. Consequently, the first inquiry in this class of cases always is, whether a contract has in fact been entered into, and if so, what its obligations are.

In the present case the question is whether the State of Mississippi, in its sovereign capacity, did by the charter now under consideration bind itself irrevocably by a contract to permit "the Mississippi Agricultural, Educational, and Manufacturing Aid Society," for twenty-five years, "to receive subscriptions, and sell and dispose of certificates of subscription which shall entitle the holders thereof to" "any lands, books, paintings, antiques, scientific instruments or apparatus, or any other property or thing that may be ornamental, valuable, or useful," "awarded to them" "by casting of lots, or by lot, chance, or otherwise." There can be no dispute but that under this form of words the legislature of the State chartered a lottery company, having all the powers incident to such a corporation, for twenty-five years, and that in consideration thereof the company paid into the State treasury $5,000 for the use of a university, and agreed to pay, and until the commencement of this suit did pay, an annual tax of $1,000 and "one-half of one per cent on the amount of receipts derived from the sale of certificates or tickets." If the legislature that granted this charter had the power to bind the people of the State and all succeeding legislatures to allow the corporation to continue its corporate business during the whole term of its authorized existence, there is no doubt about the sufficiency of the language employed to effect that object, although there was an evident purpose to conceal the vice of the transaction by the phrases that were used. Whether the alleged contract exists, therefore, or not, depends on the authority of the legislature to bind the State and the people of the State in that way.

All agree that the legislature cannot bargain away the police power of a State. "Irrevocable grants of property and franchises may be made if they do not impair the supreme authority to make laws for the right government of the State; but no legislature can curtail the power of its successors to make such laws as they may deem proper in matters of police." Many attempts have been made in this court and elsewhere to define the police power, but never with entire success. It is always easier to determine whether a particular case comes within the general scope of the power, than to give an abstract definition of the power itself which will be in all respects accurate. No one denies, however, that it extends to all matters affecting the public health or the public morals. Neither can it be denied that lotteries are proper subjects for the exercise of this power. We are aware that formerly, when the sources of public revenue were fewer than now, they were used in some or all of the States, and even in the District of Columbia, to raise money for the erection of public buildings, making public improvements, and not infrequently for educational and religious purposes; but this court said, more than thirty years ago, speaking through Mr. Justice Grier, that "experience has shown that the common forms of gambling are comparatively innocuous when placed in contrast with the widespread pestilence of lotteries. The former are confined to a few persons and places, but the latter infests the whole community; it enters every dwelling; it reaches every class; it preys upon the hard earnings of the poor; and it plunders the ignorant and simple." Happily, under the influence of restrictive legislation, the evils are not so apparent now; but we very much fear that with the same opportunities of indulgence the same results would be manifested.

If lotteries are to be tolerated at all, it is no doubt better that they should be regulated by law, so that the people may be protected as far as possible against the inherent vices of the system; but that they are demoralizing in their effects, no matter how carefully regulated, cannot admit of a doubt. When the government is untrammelled by any claim of vested rights or chartered privileges, no one has ever supposed that lotteries could not lawfully be suppressed, and those who manage them punished severely as violators of the rules of social morality. From 1822 to 1867, without any constitutional requirement, they were prohibited by law in Mississippi, and those who conducted them punished as a kind of gamblers. During the provisional government of that State, in 1867, at the close of the late civil war, the present act of incorporation, with more of like character, was passed. The next year, 1868, the people, in adopting a new constitution with a view to the resumption of their political rights as one of the United States, provided that "the legislature shall never authorize any lottery, nor shall the sale of lottery-tickets be allowed, nor shall any lottery heretofore authorized be permitted to be drawn, or tickets therein to be sold." . . .

The question is therefore directly presented, whether, in view of these facts, the legislature of a State can, by the charter of a lottery company, defeat the will of the people, authoritatively expressed, in relation to the further continuance of such business in their midst. We think it cannot. No legislature can bargain away the public health or the public morals. The people themselves cannot do it, much less their servants. The supervision of both these subjects of governmental power is continuing in its nature, and they are to be dealt with as the special exigencies of the moment may require. Government is organized with a view to their preservation, and cannot divest itself of the power to provide for them. For this purpose the largest legislative discretion is allowed, and the discretion cannot be parted with any more than the power itself. . . .

[T]he power of governing is a trust committed by the people to the government, no part of which can be granted away. The people, in their sovereign capacity, have established their agencies for the preservation of the public health and the public morals, and the protection of public and private rights. These several agencies can govern according to their discretion, if within the scope of their general authority, while in power;

but they cannot give away nor sell the discretion of those that are to come after them, in respect to matters the government of which, from the very nature of things, must "vary with varying circumstances." They may create corporations, and give them, so to speak, a limited citizenship; but as citizens, limited in their privileges, or otherwise, these creatures of the government creation are subject to such rules and regulations as may from time to time be ordained and established for the preservation of health and morality.

The contracts which the Constitution protects are those that relate to property rights, not governmental. It is not always easy to tell on which side of the line which separates governmental from property rights a particular case is to be put; but in respect to lotteries there can be no difficulty. They are not, in the legal acceptation of the term, *mala in se*, [wrong by its very nature] but, as we have just seen, may properly be made *mala prohibita* [wrong by government declaration]. They are a species of gambling, and wrong in their influences. They disturb the checks and balances of a well-ordered community. Society built on such a foundation would almost of necessity bring forth a population of speculators and gamblers, living on the expectation of what, "by the casting of lots, or by lot, chance, or otherwise," might be "awarded" to them from the accumulations of others. Certainly the right to suppress them is governmental, to be exercised at all times by those in power, at their discretion. Any one, therefore, who accepts a lottery charter does so with the implied understanding that the people, in their sovereign capacity, and through their properly constituted agencies, may resume it at any time when the public good shall require, whether it be paid for or not. All that one can get by such a charter is a suspension of certain governmental rights in his favor, subject to withdrawal at will. He has in legal effect nothing more than a license to enjoy the privilege on the terms named for the specified time, unless it be sooner abrogated by the sovereign power of the State. It is a permit, good as against existing laws, but subject to future legislative and constitutional control or withdrawal.

On the whole, we find no error in the record.

Judgment affirmed.

Following *Stone v. Mississippi* it was clear that the Court would no longer be sympathetic to Contract Clause attacks on state regulatory statutes. With Contract Clause avenues closing, opponents of state regulation of business and commercial activities turned to another provision of the Constitution, the Due Process Clause of the Fourteenth Amendment. From the late 1880s to the 1930s, the Court heard and often responded favorably to these substantive due process arguments, a period of Court history discussed in Chapter 9.

National Emergencies and the Abrogation of Contracts

The Contract Clause reached its lowest status during the Great Depression of the 1930s. With the stock market crash of 1929, the nation entered its worst economic crisis; most Americans were placed in serious financial jeopardy. The 1932 election of Franklin Roosevelt ushered in the New Deal, and the federal government began innovative economic programs to combat the depression. At the same time, various states were developing their own programs to protect their citizens against the economic ravages the country was experiencing.

What people feared the most during the depression was losing the family home. Homeowners did what they could to meet their mortgage obligations, but, because so many were out of work, they were unable to make their payments. Financial institutions had little choice but to foreclose on these properties as stipulated in the mortgage contracts. To provide relief, several states passed statutes to expand homeowners' chances of saving their houses. Banks and other creditors opposed these assistance measures. For them, intervention by the state was a direct violation of the constitutional ban against impairment of contracts. The showdown between the Contract Clause and the government's authority to cope with economic crisis occurred in *Home Building and Loan Association v. Blaisdell* (1934). As you read Chief Justice Charles Evans Hughes's opinion for the Court, think about the Constitutional Convention and the concerns that led the Framers to adopt the Contract Clause. Would they agree with the Court that the Constitution should bend in the face of national crises; or would they side with Justice George Sutherland's dissent that the provisions of the Constitution should be interpreted the same way regardless of the conditions of the times?

Home Building and Loan Association v. Blaisdell

290 U.S. 398 (1934)

Vote: 5 (Brandeis, Cardozo, Hughes, Roberts, Stone)
    4 (Butler, McReynolds, Sutherland,
      Van Devanter)
Opinion of the Court: Hughes
Dissenting opinion: Sutherland

During the Great Depression, the people of Minnesota faced high unemployment, low prices for agricultural and manufactured products, a stagnation of business, and a scarcity of credit. In response to these conditions, the legislature declared that a state of economic emergency existed that demanded the use of extraordinary police powers for the protection of the people. One of the legislature's actions was passage of the Minnesota Mortgage Moratorium Act, which was designed to prevent homeowners from losing their houses when they could not make their mortgage payments. The act allowed homeowners who were behind in their payments to petition a state court for an extension of time to meet their mortgage obligations. During the period of the extension, the homeowners would not make normal mortgage payments but instead would pay a reasonable rental amount to the mortgage holder. The maximum extension was two years. The act was to be in effect only so long as the economic emergency continued. Its provisions applied to all mortgages, including those signed prior to the passage of the statute.

John Blaisdell and his wife owned a house in Minneapolis that was mortgaged to the Home Building and Loan Association. They lived in one part of the house and rented the other part. When the Blaisdells were unable to keep their payments current or to obtain additional credit, they requested an extension in accordance with the moratorium law. After initially denying the request and then being reversed by the state supreme court, the trial court granted the Blaisdells a two-year moratorium on mortgage payments. During this period the Blaisdells were ordered to pay $40.00 per month, which would be applied to taxes, insurance, interest, and mortgage principle. The Home Building and Loan Association opposed the extension and appealed to the Minnesota Supreme Court on the grounds that the law was an impairment of contracts in violation of the Contract Clause of the federal Constitution. The Minnesota court conceded that the law impaired the obligation of contracts, but concluded that the statute was within the police powers of the state because of the severe economic emergency. Home Building and Loan appealed to the U.S. Supreme Court.

Chief Justice Hughes delivered the opinion of the Court:

In determining whether the provision for this temporary and conditional relief exceeds the power of the State by reason of the clause in the Federal Constitution prohibiting impairment of the obligations of contracts, we must consider the relation of emergency to constitutional power, the historical setting of the contract clause, the development of the jurisprudence of this Court in the construction of that clause, and the principles of construction which we may consider to be established.

Emergency does not create power. Emergency does not increase granted power or remove or diminish the restrictions imposed upon power granted or reserved. The Constitution was adopted in a period of grave emergency. Its grants of power to the Federal Government and its limitations of the power of the States were determined in the light of emergency and they are not altered by emergency. What power was thus granted and what limitations were thus imposed are questions which have always been, and always will be, the subject of close examination under our constitutional system.

While emergency does not create power, emergency may furnish the occasion for the exercise of power. "Although an emergency may not call into life a power which has never lived, nevertheless emergency may afford a reason for the exertion of a living power already enjoyed." The constitutional question presented in the light of an emergency is whether the power possessed embraces the particular exercise of it in response to particular conditions. Thus, the war power of the Federal Government is not created by the emergency of war, but it is a power given to meet that emergency. It is a power to wage war successfully, and thus it permits the harnessing of the entire energies of the people in a supreme coöperative effort to preserve the nation. But even the war power does not remove constitutional limitations safeguarding essential liberties. When the provisions of the Constitution, in grant or restriction, are specific, so particularized as not to admit of construction, no question is presented. Thus, emergency would not permit a State to have more than two Senators in the Congress, or permit the election of President by a general popular vote without regard to the number of electors to which the States are respectively entitled, or permit the States to "coin money" or to "make anything but gold and silver coin a tender in payment of debts." But where constitutional grants and limitations of power are set forth in general clauses, which afford a broad outline, the process of construction is essential to fill in the details. That is true of the contract clause. The necessity of construction is not obviated by the fact that the contract clause is associated in the same section with other and more specific prohibitions. Even the grouping of subjects in the same clause may not require the same application to each of the subjects, regardless of differences in their nature.

In the construction of the contract clause, the debates in the Constitutional Convention are of little aid. But the reasons which led to the adoption of that clause, and of the other prohibitions of Section 10 of Article I, are not left in doubt and have frequently been described with eloquent emphasis. The widespread distress following the revolutionary period, and the plight of debtors, had called forth in the States an ignoble array of legislative schemes for the defeat of creditors and the invasion of contractual obligations. Legislative interferences had been so numerous and extreme that the confidence essential to prosperous trade had been undermined and the utter destruction of credit was threatened. "The sober people of America" were convinced that some "thorough reform" was needed which would "inspire a general prudence and industry, and give a regular course to the business of society." *The Federalist*, No. 44. It was necessary to impose the restraining power of a central authority in order to secure the foundations even of "private faith." . . .

But full recognition of the occasion and general purpose of the clause does not suffice to fix its precise scope. Nor does an examination of the details of prior legislation in the States yield criteria which can be considered controlling. To ascertain the scope of the constitutional prohibition we examine the course of judicial decisions in its application. These put it beyond question that the prohibition is not an absolute one and is not to be read with literal exactness like a mathematical formula. . . .

The legislature cannot "bargain away the public health or the public morals." Thus, the constitutional provision against the impairment of contracts was held not to be violated by an amendment of the state constitution which put an end to a lottery theretofore authorized by the legislature. The lottery was a valid enterprise when established under express state authority, but the legislature in the public interest could put a stop to it. A similar rule has been applied to the control

by the State of the sale of intoxicating liquors. The States retain adequate power to protect the public health against the maintenance of nuisances despite insistence upon existing contracts. Legislation to protect the public safety comes within the same category of reserved power. This principle has had recent and noteworthy application to the regulation of the use of public highways by common carriers and "contract carriers," where the assertion of interference with existing contract rights has been without avail. . . .

It is manifest from this review of our decisions that there has been a growing appreciation of public needs and of the necessity of finding ground for a rational compromise between individual rights and public welfare. The settlement and consequent contraction of the public domain, the pressure of a constantly increasing density of population, the interrelation of the activities of our people and the complexity of our economic interests, have inevitably led to an increased use of the organization of society in order to protect the very bases of individual opportunity. Where, in earlier days, it was thought that only the concerns of individuals or of classes were involved, and that those of the State itself were touched only remotely, it has later been found that the fundamental interests of the State are directly affected; and that the question is no longer merely that of one party to a contract as against another, but of the use of reasonable means to safeguard the economic structure upon which the good of all depends.

It is no answer to say that this public need was not apprehended a century ago, or to insist that what the provision of the Constitution meant to the vision of that day it must mean to the vision of our time. If by the statement that what the Constitution meant at the time of its adoption it means to-day, it is intended to say that the great clauses of the Constitution must be confined to the interpretation which the framers, with the conditions and outlook of their time, would have placed upon them, the statement carries its own refutation. It was to guard against such a narrow conception that Chief Justice Marshall uttered the memorable warning—"We must never forget that it is *a constitution* we are expounding": (*McCulloch* v. *Maryland*)— "a constitution intended to endure for ages to come, and consequently, to be adapted to the various *crises* of human affairs." When we are dealing with the words of the Constitution, said this Court in *Missouri* v. *Holland*, "we must realize that they have called into life a being the development of which could not have been foreseen completely by the most gifted of its begetters. . . . The case before us must be considered in the light of our whole experience and not merely in that of what was said a hundred years ago."

Nor is it helpful to attempt to draw a fine distinction between the intended meaning of the words of the Constitution and their intended application. When we consider the contract clause and the decisions which have expounded it in harmony with the essential reserved power of the States to protect the security of their peoples, we find no warrant for the conclusion that the clause has been warped by these decisions from its proper significance or that the founders of our Government would have interpreted the clause differently had they had occasion to assume that responsibility in the conditions of the later day. The vast body of law which has been developed was unknown to the fathers, but it is believed to have preserved the essential content and the spirit of the Constitution. With a growing recognition of public needs and the relation of individual right to public security, the court has sought to prevent the perversion of the clause through its use as an instrument to throttle the capacity of the States to protect their fundamental interests. This development is a growth from the seeds which the fathers planted. . . . The principle of this development is . . . that the reservation of the reasonable exercise of the protective power of the State is read into all contracts and there is no greater reason for refusing to apply this principle to Minnesota mortgages than to New York leases.

Applying the criteria established by our decisions we conclude:

1. An emergency existed in Minnesota which furnished a proper occasion for the exercise of the reserved power of the State to protect the vital interests of the community. . . .

2. The legislation was addressed to a legitimate end, that is, the legislation was not for the mere advantage of particular individuals but for the protection of a basic interest of society.

3. In view of the nature of the contracts in question—mortgages of unquestionable validity—the relief afforded and justified by the emergency, in order not to contravene the constitutional provision, could only be of a character appropriate to that emergency and could be granted only upon reasonable conditions.

4. The conditions upon which the period of redemption is extended do not appear to be unreasonable. . . .

5. The legislation is temporary in operation. It is limited to the exigency which called it forth. . . .

We are of the opinion that the Minnesota statute as here applied does not violate the contract clause of the Federal Constitution. Whether the legislation is wise or unwise as a matter of policy is a question with which we are not concerned. . . .

The judgment of the Supreme Court of Minnesota is affirmed.

Mr. Justice Sutherland, dissenting.

Few questions of greater moment than that just decided have been submitted for judicial inquiry during this generation. He simply closes his eyes to the necessary implications of the decision who fails to see in it the potentiality of future gradual but ever-advancing encroachments upon the sanctity of private and public contracts. The effect of the Minnesota legislation, though serious enough in itself, is of trivial significance compared with the far more serious and dangerous inroads upon the limitations of the Constitution which are almost certain to ensue as a consequence naturally following any step beyond the boundaries fixed by that instrument. And those of us who are thus apprehensive of the effect of this decision would, in a matter so important, be neglectful of our duty should we fail to spread upon the permanent records of the court the reasons which move us to the opposite view.

A provision of the Constitution, it is hardly necessary to say, does not admit of two distinctly opposite interpretations. It does not mean one thing at one time and an entirely different thing at another time. If the contract impairment clause, when framed and adopted, meant that the terms of a contract for the payment of money could not be altered . . . by a state statute enacted for the relief of hardly pressed debtors to the end and with the effect of postponing payment or enforcement during and because of an economic or financial emergency, it is but to state the obvious to say that it means the same now. This view, at once so rational in its application to the written word, and so necessary to the stability of constitutional principles, though from time to time challenged, has never, unless recently, been put within the realm of doubt by the decisions of this court. . . .

The provisions of the Federal Constitution, undoubtedly, are pliable in the sense that in appropriate cases they have the capacity of bringing within their grasp every new condition which falls within their meaning. But, their *meaning* is changeless; it is only their *application* which is extensible. . . .

A statute which materially delays enforcement of the mortgagee's contractual right of ownership and possession does not modify the remedy merely; it destroys, for the period of delay, *all* remedy so far as the enforcement of that right is concerned. The phrase, "obligation of a contract," in the constitutional sense imports a legal duty to perform the specified obligation of *that* contract, not to substitute and perform, against the will of one of the parties, a different, albeit equally valuable, obligation. And a state, under the contract

impairment clause, has no more power to accomplish such a substitution than has one of the parties to the contract against the will of the other. It cannot do so either by acting directly upon the contract, or by bringing about the result under the guise of a statute in form acting only upon the remedy. If it could, the efficacy of the constitutional restriction would, in large measure, be made to disappear. . . .

I quite agree with the opinion of the court that whether the legislation under review is wise or unwise is a matter with which we have nothing to do. Whether it is likely to work well or work ill presents a question entirely irrelevant to the issue. The only legitimate inquiry we can make is whether it is constitutional. If it is not, its virtues, if it have any, cannot save it; if it is, its faults cannot be invoked to accomplish its destruction. If the provisions of the Constitution be not upheld when they pinch as well as when they comfort, they may as well be abandoned. Being unable to reach any other conclusion than that the Minnesota statute infringes the constitutional restriction under review, I have no choice but to say so.

The Court upheld the Minnesota statute because the majority concluded that the economic emergency justified the state's use of extensive police powers. Does the Contract Clause retain any vitality under such an interpretation? Or did the *Home Building and Loan Association* decision render it virtually meaningless? After all, there would be little reason to pass such a statute in good economic times.

The Revitalization of the Contract Clause

For four decades following the Minnesota Mortgage Moratorium decision, parties challenging state laws rarely rested their arguments on the Contract Clause. It made little practical sense to do so when the justices were reluctant to use the provision to strike down state legislation designed

to promote the economic welfare of the citizens. Litigants who attempted to invoke the clause usually were unsuccessful. For example, in *El Paso v. Simmons* (1965) the Contract Clause was used to attack a Texas statute governing defaults on land sales agreements with the state. Consistent with the trend that began with *Charles River Bridge* more than a century earlier, the justices turned a deaf ear to the Contract Clause claims and upheld the challenged legislation. The justices made it quite clear that they were not eager to interfere with the sovereign right of the state to protect the general welfare of the people and would give the state legislatures wide discretion in determining proper public policy over economic matters. The Contract Clause, once the most litigated constitutional provision, had lost much of its relevance.

To conclude, however, that the Contract

Clause had been erased from the Constitution effectively and forever would be incorrect. In the decades following the New Deal, the Court was dominated by justices who took generally liberal positions on economic matters. They were philosophically opposed to allowing business interests to use the clause as a weapon to strike down legislation benefiting the people at large. But the Court's liberal majority began to unravel following the resignation of Chief Justice Earl Warren and Richard Nixon's appointment of Warren E. Burger to replace him in 1969. As succeeding appointments brought more conservative and business-oriented justices to the Court, the prospects for a revitalized Contract Clause grew. This fact was not lost on enterprising lawyers, who

began to consider raising Contract Clause issues once again.

Finally, in 1977 and 1978 the Court handed down two Contract Clause decisions: *United States Trust Co. v. New Jersey* and *Allied Structural Steel Co. v. Spannaus*. In both instances the justices struck down state legislation intended to promote the general welfare because the statutes were found to impair the obligation of contracts. Each time the Court's liberal justices voiced strong objections. As you read the opinions in these cases, try to determine if they represent a sharp break from the position the Court had taken over the preceding century or if they possibly can be reconciled with decisions such as *Home Building and Loan Association v. Blaisdell*.

United States Trust Co. v. New Jersey

431 U.S. 1 (1977)

Vote: 4 (Blackmun, Burger, Rehnquist,
Stevens)
3 (Brennan, Marshall, White)
Opinion of the Court: Blackmun
Concurring opinion: Burger
Dissenting opinion: Brennan
Not participating: Powell, Stewart

In 1921 the states of New York and New Jersey entered into a compact to establish the Port Authority of New York, a body responsible for developing and coordinating transportation and commerce. The Port Authority was financially independent, with funds primarily derived from private investors. It had the power to mortgage its facilities and to pledge its revenues as payment for bonds issued to its investors. In 1962, in response to increased interest in mass transit, the Port Authority took control of the financially ailing Hudson & Manhattan Railroad. As part of the acquisition, the states agreed that none of the authority's revenues pledged as security for exist-

ing bonds would be used for any additional railroad expenditures.

Between 1972 and 1974, with the nation in the midst of an energy crisis and under intense pressure to develop mass transit, New York and New Jersey moved to expand their system. Because money was difficult to raise, the states decided that they would use revenues previously pledged as security for existing bonds. To free such funds both state legislatures passed statutes in 1974 repealing retroactively their pledge not to use these moneys for increased mass transit expenditures. United States Trust Company, a holder of the affected bonds, sued to invalidate the repeal as an unconstitutional impairment of the obligation of contracts. The New Jersey courts ruled against the company on the grounds that the repeal was a proper exercise of state police powers. The company sought U.S. Supreme Court review.

Justice Harry A. Blackmun delivered the opinion of the Court:

At the time the Constitution was adopted, and for nearly a century thereafter, the Contract Clause was one of the few express limitations on state power. The many decisions of this Court involving the Contract Clause are evidence of its important place in our constitutional jurisprudence. Over the last century, however, the Fourteenth Amendment has assumed a far larger place in constitutional adjudication concerning the States. We feel that the present role of the Contract Clause is largely illuminated by two of this Court's decisions. In each, legislation was sustained despite a claim that it had impaired the obligations of contracts.

Home Building & Loan Assn. v. *Blaisdell* (1934) is regarded as the leading case in the modern era of Contract Clause interpretation. At issue was the Minnesota Mortgage Moratorium Law, enacted in 1933, during the depth of the Depression and when that State was under severe economic stress, and appeared to have no effective alternative. . . . A closely divided Court, in an opinion by Mr. Chief Justice Hughes, observed that "emergency may furnish the occasion for the exercise of power" and that the "constitutional question presented in the light of an emergency is whether the power possessed embraces the particular exercise of it in response to particular conditions." . . .

This Court's most recent Contract Clause decision is *El Paso* v. *Simmons* (1965). That case concerned a 1941 Texas statute that limited to a 5-year period the reinstatement rights of an interest-defaulting purchaser of land from the State. . . . This Court held that "it is not every modification of a contractual promise that impairs the obligation of contract under federal law." It observed that the State "has the 'sovereign right . . . to protect the . . . general welfare of the people' "and " 'we must respect the "wide discretion on the part of the legislature in determining what is and what is not necessary." ' " . . .

Both of these cases eschewed a rigid application of the Contract Clause to invalidate state legislation. Yet neither indicated that the Contract Clause was without meaning in modern constitutional jurisprudence, or that its limitation on state power was illusory. Whether or not the protection of contract rights comports with current views of wise public policy, the Contract Clause remains a part of our written Constitution. We therefore must attempt to apply that constitutional

provision to the instant case with due respect for its purpose and the prior decisions of the Court. . . .

Although the Contract Clause appears literally to proscribe "any" impairment, this Court observed in *Blaisdell* that "the prohibition is not an absolute one and is not to be read with literal exactness like a mathematical formula." Thus, a finding that there has been a technical impairment is merely a preliminary step in resolving the more difficult question whether that impairment is permitted under the Constitution. In the instant case, as in *Blaisdell,* we must attempt to reconcile the strictures of the Contract Clause with the "essential attributes of sovereign power" necessarily reserved by the States to safeguard the welfare of their citizens.

The trial court concluded that repeal of the 1962 covenant was a valid exercise of New Jersey's police power because repeal served important public interests in mass transportation, energy conservation, and environmental protection. Yet the Contract Clause limits otherwise legitimate exercises of state legislative authority, and the existence of an important public interest is not always sufficient to overcome that limitation. "Undoubtedly, whatever is reserved of state power must be consistent with the fair intent of the constitutional limitation of that power." Moreover, the scope of the State's reserved power depends on the nature of the contractual relationship with which the challenged law conflicts.

The States must possess broad power to adopt general regulatory measures without being concerned that private contracts will be impaired, or even destroyed, as a result. Otherwise, one would be able to obtain immunity from state regulation by making private contractual arrangements. This principle is summarized in Mr. Justice Holmes' well-known dictum: "One whose rights, such as they are, are subject to state restriction, cannot remove them from the power of the State by making a contract about them."

Yet private contracts are not subject to unlimited modification under the police power. The Court in *Blaisdell* recognized that laws intended to regulate existing contractual relationships must serve a legitimate public purpose. A State could not "adopt as its policy the repudiation of debts or the destruction of contracts or the denial of means to enforce them."

Legislation adjusting the rights and responsibilities of contracting parties must be upon reasonable conditions and of a character appropriate to the public purpose justifying its adoption. As is customary in reviewing economic and social regulation, however, courts properly defer to legislative judgment as to the necessity and reasonableness of a particular measure.

When a State impairs the obligation of its own contract, the reserved-powers doctrine has a different basis. The initial inquiry concerns the ability of the State to enter into an agreement that limits its power to act in the future. As early as *Fletcher* v. *Peck,* the Court considered the argument that "one legislature cannot abridge the powers of a succeeding legislature." It is often stated that "the legislature cannot bargain away the police power of a State." *Stone* v. *Mississippi* (1880). This doctrine requires a determination of the State's power to create irrevocable contract rights in the first place, rather than an inquiry into the purpose or reasonableness of the subsequent impairment. In short, the Contract Clause does not require a State to adhere to a contract that surrenders an essential attribute of its sovereignty. . . .

In applying this standard, however, complete deference to a legislative assessment of reasonableness and necessity is not appropriate because the State's self-interest is at stake. A governmental entity can always find a use for extra money, especially when taxes do not have to be raised. If a State could reduce its financial obligations whenever it wanted to spend the money for what it regarded as an important public purpose, the Contract Clause would provide no protection at all. . . .

Mass transportation, energy conservation, and environmental protection are goals that are important and of legitimate public concern. Appellees contend that these goals are so important that any harm to bondholders from repeal of the 1962 covenant is greatly outweighed by the public benefit. We do not accept this invitation to engage in a utilitarian comparison of public benefit and private loss. . . . [A] State cannot refuse to meet its legitimate financial obligations simply because it would prefer to spend the money to promote the public good rather than the private welfare of its creditors. We can only sustain the repeal of the 1962 covenant if that impairment was both reasonable and necessary to serve the admittedly important purposes claimed by the State.

The more specific justification offered for the repeal of the 1962 covenant was the States' plan for encouraging users of private automobiles to shift to public transportation. The States intended to discourage private automobile use by raising bridge and tunnel tolls and to use the extra revenue from those tolls to subsidize improved commuter railroad service. Appellees contend that repeal of the 1962 covenant was necessary to implement this plan because the new mass transit facilities could not possibly be self-supporting and the covenant's "permitted deficits" level had already been exceeded. We reject this justification because the repeal was neither necessary to achievement of the plan nor reasonable in light of the circumstances.

The determination of necessity can be considered on two levels. First, it cannot be said that total repeal of the covenant was essential; a less drastic modification would have permitted the contemplated plan without entirely removing the covenant's limitations on the use of Port Authority revenues and reserves to subsidize commuter railroads. Second, without modifying the covenant at all, the States could have adopted alternative means of achieving their twin goals of discouraging automobile use and improving mass transit. Appellees contend, however, that choosing among these alternatives is a matter for legislative discretion. But a State is not completely free to consider impairing the obligations of its own contract on a par with other policy alternatives. Similarly, a State is not free to impose a drastic impairment when an evident and more moderate course would serve its purposes equally well. . . .

[T]he need for mass transportation in the New York metropolitan area was not a new development, and the likelihood that publicly owned commuter railroads would produce substantial deficits was well known. As early as 1922, over a half century ago, there were pressures to involve the Port Authority in mass transit. It was with full knowledge of these concerns that the 1962 covenant was adopted. Indeed, the covenant was specifically intended to protect the pledged revenues and reserves against the possibility that such concerns would lead the Port Authority into greater involvement in deficit mass transit.

During the 12-year period between adoption of the covenant and its repeal, public perception of the importance of mass transit undoubtedly grew because of increased general concern with environmental protection and energy conservation. But these concerns were not unknown in 1962, and the subsequent changes were of degree and not of kind. We cannot say that these changes caused the covenant to have a substantially different impact in 1974 than when it was adopted in 1962. And we cannot conclude that the repeal was reasonable in the light of changed circumstances.

We therefore hold that the Contract Clause of the United States Constitution prohibits the retroactive repeal of the 1962 covenant. The judgment of the Supreme Court of New Jersey is reversed.

Mr. Justice Brennan . . . dissenting.

Decisions of this Court for at least a century have construed the Contract Clause largely to be powerless in binding a State to contracts limiting the authority of successor legislatures to enact laws in furtherance of the health, safety, and similar collective interests of the polity. In short, those decisions established the principle that lawful exercises of a State's police powers stand paramount to private rights held under contract. Today's decision, in invalidating the New Jersey Legislature's 1974 repeal of its predecessor's 1962 covenant, rejects this previous understanding and remolds the Contract Clause into a potent instrument for overseeing important policy determinations of the state legislature. At the same time, by creating a constitutional safe haven for property rights embodied in a contract, the decision substantially distorts modern constitutional jurisprudence governing regulation of private economic interests. I might understand, though I do not accept, this revival of the Contract Clause were it in accordance with some coherent and constructive view of public policy. But elevation of the Clause to the status of regulator of the municipal bond market at the heavy price of frustration of sound legislative policymaking is as demonstrably unwise as it is unnecessary. The justification for today's decision, therefore, remains a mystery to me, and I respectfully dissent.

The legislation challenged in *U.S. Trust* was passed for the general welfare of the people of New York and New Jersey and in large measure was a response to a national energy crisis. These factors seemed similar to the conditions prompting the Court to approve the Minnesota Mortgage Moratorium Act. Therefore, many were surprised by the Court's resurrection of the Contract Clause, and there was considerable interest in what the case meant for the future. Although the decision invalidated state laws based on the Contract Clause, the opinion was a moderate one without the absolutist tones of the Marshall era. Did the Court's decision signal a change in policy or was it an aberration? How solid was this newly expressed support for the Contract Clause? After all, only seven justices participated in the decision, and the majority consisted of just four. Would the outcome have been different had the full Court voted? The justices provided some answers to these questions the very next year in *Allied Structural Steel Co. v. Spannaus* (1978).

Allied Structural Steel Co. v. Spannaus

438 U.S. 234 (1978)

Vote: 5 (Burger, Powell, Rehnquist, Stevens,
        Stewart)
    3 (Brennan, Marshall, White)
Opinion of the Court: Stewart
Dissenting opinion: Brennan
Not participating: Blackmun

Although its principal place of business was Illinois, Allied Structural Steel Company maintained an office with thirty employees in Minnesota. In 1963 the company adopted a general pension plan, in which employees became vested after working the required number of years and reaching the specified age. Employees who quit or were terminated before meeting these requirements did not acquire any pension rights. The company, which made annual payments to a pension trust fund, was the sole contributor to the plan. The company retained a virtually unrestricted right to modify the plan or to terminate it at any time.

On April 9, 1974, Minnesota enacted the Private Pension Benefits Protection Act. Under the provisions of that law, a company that terminated a pension plan or closed down its Minnesota operations would be subject to a charge to the extent that its retirement funds did not assure full pensions to all workers employed by the company for ten or more years. During the summer of 1974, Allied began closing its Minnesota office and discharged a number of its employees. Nine of the terminated workers had been with the company longer than ten years, but they did not qualify for a pension under Allied's plan. The state invoked the Private Pension Benefits Protection Act and assessed Allied $185,000 for the employees' pensions. Claiming that the Minnesota law impaired the obligation of its pension contract with its employees, Allied filed suit in federal district court against state attorney general

Warren Spannaus. The court ruled in favor of the state, and Allied continued its attack on the statute in the U.S. Supreme Court.

Justice Potter Stewart delivered the opinion of the Court:

There can be no question of the impact of the Minnesota Private Pension Benefits Protection Act upon the company's contractual relationships with its employees. The Act substantially altered those relationships by superimposing pension obligations upon the company conspicuously beyond those that it had voluntarily agreed to undertake. But it does not inexorably follow that the Act as applied to the company, violates the Contract Clause of the Constitution.

The language of the Contract Clause appears unambiguously absolute: ''No State shall . . . pass any . . . Law impairing the Obligation of Contracts.'' U.S. Const., Art. I, § 10. The Clause is not, however, the Draconian provision that its words might seem to imply. As the Court has recognized, ''literalism in the construction of the contract clause . . . would make it destructive of the public interest by depriving the State of its prerogative of self-protection.''

Although it was perhaps the strongest single constitutional check on state legislation during our early years as a Nation, the Contract Clause receded into comparative desuetude with the adoption of the Fourteenth Amendment, and particularly with the development of the large body of jurisprudence under the Due Process Clause of that Amendment in modern constitutional history. Nonetheless, the Contract Clause remains part of the Constitution. It is not a dead letter. . . .

If the Contract Clause is to retain any meaning at all . . . it must be understood to impose *some* limits upon the power of a State to abridge existing contractual relationships, even in the exercise of its otherwise legitimate police power. The existence and nature of those limits were clearly indicated in a series of cases in this Court arising from the efforts of the States to deal with the unprecedented emergencies brought on by the severe economic depression of the early 1930's.

In *Home Building & Loan Assn.* v. *Blaisdell* the Court upheld against a Contract Clause attack a mortgage moratorium law that Minnesota had enacted to provide relief for homeowners threatened with foreclosure. Although the legislation conflicted directly with lenders' contractual foreclosure rights, the Court there acknowledged that, despite the Contract Clause, the States retain residual authority to enact laws "to safeguard the vital interests of [their] people." In upholding the state mortgage moratorium law, the Court found five factors significant. First, the state legislature had declared in the Act itself that an emergency need for the protection of homeowners existed. Second, the state law was enacted to protect a basic societal interest, not a favored group. Third, the relief was appropriately tailored to the emergency that it was designed to meet. Fourth, the imposed conditions were reasonable. And, finally, the legislation was limited to the duration of the emergency.

The *Blaisdell* opinion thus clearly implied that if the Minnesota moratorium legislation had not possessed the characteristics attributed to it by the Court, it would have been invalid under the Contract Clause of the Constitution. . . .

In applying these principles to the present case, the first inquiry must be whether the state law has, in fact, operated as a substantial impairment of a contractual relationship. The severity of the impairment measures the height of the hurdle the state legislation must clear. Minimal alteration of contractual obligations may end the inquiry at its first stage. Severe impairment, on the other hand, will push the inquiry to a careful examination of the nature and purpose of the state legislation.

The severity of an impairment of contractual obligations can be measured by the factors that reflect the high value the Framers placed on the protection of private contracts. Contracts enable individuals to order their personal and business affairs according to their particular needs and interests. Once arranged, those rights and obligations are binding under the law, and the parties are entitled to rely on them.

Here, the company's contracts of employment with its employees included as a fringe benefit or additional form of compensation, the pension plan. The company's maximum obligation was to set aside each year an amount based on the plan's requirements for vesting. The plan satisfied the current federal income tax code and was subject to no other legislative requirements. And, of course, the company was free to amend or terminate the pension plan at any time. The company thus had no reason to anticipate that its employees' pension rights could become vested except in accordance with the terms of the plan. It relied heavily, and reasonably, on this legitimate contractual expectation in calculating its annual contributions to the pension fund.

The effect of Minnesota's Private Pension Benefits Protection Act on this contractual obligation was severe. The company was required in 1974 to have made its contributions throughout the pre-1974 life of its plan as if employees' pension rights had vested after 10 years, instead of vesting in accord with the terms of the plan. Thus a basic term of the pension contract—one on which the company had relied for 10 years—was substantially modified. The result was that, although the company's past contributions were adequate when made, they were not adequate when computed under the 10-year statutory vesting requirement. The Act thus forced a current recalculation of the past 10 years' contributions based on the new, unanticipated 10-year vesting requirement.

Not only did the state law thus retroactively modify the compensation that the company had agreed to pay its employees from 1963 to 1974, but also it did so by changing the company's obligations in an area where the element of reliance was vital—the funding of a pension plan. . . .

Moreover, the retroactive state-imposed vesting requirement was applied only to those employers who terminated their pension plans or who, like the company, closed their Minnesota offices. The company was thus forced to make all the retroactive changes in its contractual obligations at one time. By simply proceeding to close its office in Minnesota, a move that had been planned before the passage of the Act, the company was assessed an immediate pension funding charge of approximately $185,000.

Thus, the statute in question here nullifies express terms of the company's contractual obligations and imposes a completely unexpected liability in potentially disabling amounts. . . . Yet there is no showing in the record before us that this severe disruption of contractual expectations was necessary to meet an important general social problem. The presumption favoring "legislative judgment as to the necessity and reasonableness of a particular measure" simply cannot stand in this case. . . .

Moreover, in at least one other important respect the Act does not resemble the mortgage moratorium legislation whose constitutionality was upheld in the *Blaisdell* case. This legislation, imposing a sudden, totally unanticipated, and substantial retroactive obligation upon the company to its employees, was not enacted to deal with a situation remotely approaching the broad and desperate emergency economic conditions of the early 1930's—conditions of which the Court in *Blaisdell* took judicial notice.

Entering a field it had never before sought to regulate, the Minnesota Legislature grossly distorted the company's existing contractual relationships with its employees by superimposing retroactive obligations upon the company substantially beyond the terms of its employment contracts. And that burden was imposed upon the company only because it closed its office in the State.

This Minnesota law simply does not possess the attributes of those state laws that in the past have survived challenge under the Contract Clause of the Constitution. The law was not even purportedly enacted to deal with a broad, generalized economic or social problem. It did not operate in an area already subject to state regulation at the time the company's contractual obligations were originally undertaken, but invaded an area never before subject to regulation by the State. It did not effect simply a temporary alteration of the contractual relationships of those within its coverage, but worked a severe, permanent, and immediate change in those relationships—irrevocably and retroactively. And its narrow aim was leveled, not at every Minnesota employer, not even at every Minnesota employer who left the State, but only at those who had in the past been sufficiently enlightened as voluntarily to agree to establish pension plans for their employees.

. . . [I]f the Contract Clause means anything at all, it means that Minnesota could not constitutionally do what it tried to do to the company in this case.

The judgment of the District Court is reversed.

Mr. Justice Brennan . . . dissenting.

In cases involving state legislation affecting private contracts, this Court's decisions over the past half century, consistently with both the constitutional text and its original understanding, have interpreted the Contract Clause as prohibiting state legislative Acts which, "[w]ith studied indifference to the interests of the [contracting party] or to his appropriate protection," effectively diminished or nullified the obligation due him under the terms of a contract. But the Contract Clause has not, during this period, been applied to state legislation that, while creating new duties, in nowise diminished the efficacy of any contractual obligation owed the constitutional claimant. . . .

Today's decision greatly expands the reach of the Clause. The Minnesota Private Pension Benefits Protection Act (Act) does not abrogate or dilute any obligation due a party to a private contract; rather, like all positive social legislation, the Act imposes new, additional obligations on a particular class of persons. . . .

The Act does not relieve either the employer or his employees of any existing contract obligation. Rather, the Act simply creates an additional, supplemental duty of the employer, no different in kind from myriad duties created by a wide variety of legislative measures which defeat settled expectations but which have nonetheless been sustained by this Court. For this reason, the Minnesota Act, in my view, does not implicate the Contract Clause in any way. The basic fallacy of today's decision is its mistaken view that the Contract Clause protects all contract-based expectations, including that of an employer that his obligations to his employees will not be legislatively enlarged beyond those explicitly provided in his pension plan. . . .

[I]n my view, the Contract Clause has no applicability whatsoever to the Act. . . . I would affirm the judgment of the District Court.

Justice Stewart's opinion provides insight into the meaning of the Contract Clause in the contemporary era. First, although the Court invalidated the charges assessed against Allied Steel, the Court did not restore the Contract Clause to the prominence it had during the Marshall era. Second, the Contract Clause places some limits on the exercise of the state's police powers, but it does not obliterate those powers. Third, the Contract Clause applies to laws that either increase or decrease the duties of a party to a contract. Fourth, the clause is not limited to creditor-debtor contracts. Fifth, in applying the Contract Clause, the Court will first examine the extent of the impairment of contractual obligations, and "the severity of the impairment measures the height of the hurdle the state legislation must clear." If there has been substantial impairment of a contractual relationship, the Court will consider with care the nature and purpose of the legislation. In short, the majority assumed a position that balanced the importance of contractual relationships against the need of the state to exercise its police powers for the public welfare. Such a position neither returns the Contract Clause to the preferred position it enjoyed during the Marshall era nor substantially strips it of its meaning as occurred in later years.

The Takings Clause

When the Bill of Rights is mentioned, we almost automatically think of liberties such as freedom of speech, press, and religion, or the protections against unfair criminal procedures. But when the members of the First Congress proposed a listing of those rights considered so important as to merit constitutional protection, they included in the Fifth Amendment a significant private property guarantee—the Takings Clause, which states, "nor shall private property be taken for public use, without just compensation."

This provision acknowledges that government programs sometimes require the seizure of private property. The authority to do so is called the power of eminent domain. Without it, attempts to build courthouses, post offices, or military bases could be blocked by a single property owner who refuses to sell a needed parcel of land to the government. Such an owner could demand unreasonable compensation, holding the government project for ransom. Think of how impossible it would have been to build the interstate highway system if the government did not have the power to take private property when owners refused to cooperate. The Takings Clause ensures that property owners will not be unduly disadvantaged when the government seizes their land; it guarantees that the owner will be fairly compensated for the loss.

The power of eminent domain also may be exercised by state and local governments. Although the Takings Clause was drafted only to protect private landowners from property seizures by the federal government, the Supreme Court ruled in the 1890s that the Due Process Clause of the Fourteenth Amendment required state and local governments to abide by the Takings Clause as well.[6]

The most common issue that flows from government takings cases is the question of what constitutes "just compensation." In the normal course of events, the government attempts to buy the necessary land from the owners. If negotiations fail, the government may declare the power of eminent domain and take the property, giving the owners what it thinks is a fair price. Usually fair market value is the appropriate standard. It is not uncommon, however, for the owners to argue that what the government wants to pay is inadequate. In such situations the owners may go to court to challenge the amount. Questions of just

6. See *Missouri Pacific Railway v. Nebraska,* 164 U.S. 403 (1896), and *Chicago, Burlington & Quincy Railroad v. Chicago,* 166 U.S. 226 (1897).

compensation are normally settled through negotiation or trial court action and rarely involve issues of significance beyond the specific land under dispute.[7] While legal battles may be fought over whether the offered compensation is just, there is no doubt about the power of the government to seize the property.

Of greater importance are two questions of more general significance in understanding the meaning of the Fifth Amendment Takings Clause: What is a taking and what constitutes a public use? Both questions have required authoritative answers by the Supreme Court.

The Taking of Private Property

In most cases it is relatively easy to determine that a taking has occurred. If the federal government decides to build a new post office and must acquire a piece of privately owned property upon which to build, a taking is necessary if a voluntary sale is not negotiated. Similarly, a taking occurs when, in designing a water control project, the government finds it necessary to dam certain streams and cause privately owned land to become permanently flooded. In these situations private land is totally taken by the government and is used for a public purpose. There is no question that the individual has been deprived of ownership rights over the property.

Often, however, the government regulates in such a way as to infringe only incidentally on the owner's use of property. Obvious examples are zoning laws or other regulatory ordinances that make certain land uses unlawful. Owners may be distressed that they can no longer use their property in particular ways, but the Supreme Court generally has held that such statutes do not constitute a Fifth Amendment taking. For example, the justices ruled that takings did not occur when a state ordered property owners to cut down standing cedar trees because of a disease they carried, when a local government passed an ordinance removing an individual's right to use his land as a brickyard, and when a city prohibited a person from mining sand and gravel on his land.[8] In these and numerous similar cases the government's action significantly reduced the way the land could be used and decreased its commercial value; yet the Court held that a taking had not occurred. Instead, these policies were applications of the government's police powers.

Penn Central Transportation Co. v. New York City (1978) provides another example. New York City, like many other localities, passed a Landmarks Preservation Law designed to protect historic buildings and places. According to this statute, owners of buildings designated by the Landmarks Preservation Commission as being historic landmarks were required to keep the exterior of the buildings in good repair and to obtain the approval of the city before altering the exterior in any significant way. In 1967 the Commission declared Grand Central Station, owned by the Penn Central company, to be a historic building. Later, Penn Central and UGP Properties entered into an arrangement to construct an office building above the station. They presented two different plans to the city, one calling for a fifty-five-story office building to be cantilevered over the terminal with the bottom of the new structure

---

7. Although disputes over compensations levels normally are settled at the trial court level, occasionally such controversies involve significant issues and large amounts of money. For example, in *United States v. Sioux Nation of Indians,* 448 U.S. 371 (1980) the Supreme Court settled a longstanding dispute over the abrogation of the Fort Laramie Treaty of 1868. The treaty had established the right of the Sioux nation to the Black Hills, but an 1877 act of Congress essentially took back those lands. The Supreme Court ruled that the treaty abrogation was governed by the Takings Clause and that the Sioux were entitled to the value of the land in 1877 plus 5 percent annual interest since that year, amounting to a total claim of some $100,000,000.

8. *Miller v. Schoene,* 276 U.S. 272 (1928); *Hadacheck v. Los Angeles,* 239 U.S. 394 (1915); *Goldblatt v. Hempstead,* 369 U.S. 590 (1962), respectively.

resting on the top of the station. The city denied the construction plans on the grounds that the office building would destroy the historic setting of the terminal. Penn Central filed suit to have the city's actions declared a taking under the Fifth Amendment and to demand just compensation. In a 6-3 vote, however, the Supreme Court held that the historic preservation legislation did not constitute a taking. It, like zoning, health, and safety regulations, was a reasonable public law that did not take the owner's property, although it may have restricted its use and decreased the potential income the property might produce.

Does a seizure of private property by the government have to be complete and total before the Takings Clause applies? What happens when a government program so severely curtails the possible uses of a piece of property that its value almost disappears? *United States v. Causby* (1946), a case involving a North Carolina couple whose modest chicken farm was ruined by the U.S. military, answers these questions. Did a taking occur even though the Causbys retained title to their property? The majority held that it did. But pay attention to the dissent by Justice Hugo Black, which is interesting on two counts. First, it reflects Black's generally sympathetic attitude toward federal government programs, and, second, it demonstrates the importance he placed on applying the words as written. Here he attempts to apply the word "taking" as he believes the Framers intended it to be used.

United States v. Causby

328 U.S. 256 (1946)

Vote: 5 (Douglas, Frankfurter, Murphy, Reed,
        Rutledge)
        2 (Black, Burton)
Opinion of the Court: Douglas
Dissenting opinion: Black
Not participating: Jackson

The Causbys owned 2.8 acres outside Greensboro, North Carolina. On this land was their house and the various outbuildings they needed for their chicken business. In 1942 the federal government leased a local airfield for use by army and navy aircraft. Bombers, fighters, and transport planes regularly flew in and out of this facility at all hours of the day and night. Planes often flew in close formation and in considerable numbers. The end of the airport runway was only 2,220 feet from the Causbys' property. The authorized flight patterns allowed planes to fly at an altitude of 83 feet over the Causbys' land, just 67 feet over their house, and within 18 feet of the highest tree on their property.

This activity caused the couple considerable discomfort as well as economic loss. The noise was described as startling, and the Causbys found it difficult to sleep at night. Although there were no aircraft accidents on their property, there had been several near the airport, which made the Causbys fearful and nervous. In addition, the productivity of their chickens decreased. Significant numbers of them died when they flew into the walls of their coops out of fear and panic when the planes flew particularly close. The property could no longer be used as a commercial chicken farm.

The Causbys filed suit in the federal court of claims arguing that the government had taken their land without just compensation in violation of the Takings Clause. The court agreed and ordered the government to pay them $2,000 for their loss. The federal government appealed to the Supreme Court claiming that there had been no taking because there had been no physical violation of the landowners' property.

Justice William O. Douglas delivered the opinion of the Court:

It is ancient doctrine that at common law ownership of the land extended to the periphery of the universe. . . . But that doctrine has no place in the modern world. The air is a public highway, as Congress has declared. Were that not true, every transcontinental flight would subject the operator to countless trespass suits. Common sense revolts at the idea. To recognize such private claims to the airspace would clog these highways, seriously interfere with their control and development in the public interest, and transfer into private ownership that to which only the public has a just claim.

But that general principle does not control the present case. For the United States conceded on oral argument that if the flights over respondents' property rendered it uninhabitable, there would be a taking compensable under the Fifth Amendment. It is the owner's loss, not the taker's gain, which is the measure of the value of the property taken. Market value fairly determined is the normal measure of the recovery. And that value may reflect the use to which the land could readily be converted, as well as the existing use. If, by reason of the frequency and altitude of the flights, respondents could not use this land for any purpose, their loss would be complete. It would be as complete as if the United States had entered upon the surface of the land and taken exclusive possession of it.

. . . The owner's right to possess and exploit the land—that is to say, his beneficial ownership of it—would be destroyed. It would not be a case of incidental damages arising from a legalized nuisance. . . .

There is no material difference between the supposed case and the present one, except that here enjoyment and use of the land are not completely destroyed. But that does not seem to us to be controlling. The path of glide for airplanes might reduce a valuable factory site to grazing land, an orchard to a vegetable patch, a residential section to a wheat field. Some value would remain. But the use of the airspace immediately above the land would limit the utility of the land and cause a diminution in its value. . . .

We have said that the airspace is a public highway. Yet it is obvious that if the landowner is to have full enjoyment of the land, he must have exclusive control of the immediate reaches of the enveloping atmosphere. Otherwise buildings could not be erected, trees could not be planted, and even fences could not be run. The principle is recognized when the law gives a remedy in case overhanging structures are erected on adjoining land. The landowner owns at least as much of the space above the ground as he can occupy or use in connection with the land. The fact that he does not occupy it in a physical sense—by the erection of buildings and the like—is not material. As we have said, the flight of airplanes, which skim the surface but do not touch it, is as much an appropriation of the use of the land as a more conventional entry upon it. We would not doubt that, if the United States erected an elevated railway over respondents' land at the precise altitude where its planes now fly, there would be a partial taking, even though none of the supports of the structure rested on the land. The reason is that there would be an intrusion so immediate and direct as to subtract from the owner's full enjoyment of the property and to limit his exploitation of it. While the owner does not in any physical manner occupy that stratum of airspace or make use of it in the conventional sense, he does use it in somewhat the same sense that space left between buildings for the purpose of light and air is used. The superadjacent airspace at this low altitude is so close to the land that continuous invasions of it affect the use of the surface of the land itself. We think that the landowner, as an incident to his ownership, has a claim to it and that invasions of it are in the same category as invasions of the surface. . . .

The airplane is part of the modern environment of life, and the inconveniences which it causes are normally not compensable under the Fifth Amendment. The airspace, apart from the immediate reaches above the land, is part of the public domain. We need not determine at this time what those precise limits are. Flights over private land are not a taking, unless they are so low and so frequent as to be a direct and immediate interference with the enjoyment and use of the land. We need not speculate on that phase of the present case. For the findings of the Court of Claims plainly establish that there was a diminution in value of the property and that the frequent, low-level flights were the direct and immediate cause. We agree with the Court of Claims that a servitude has been imposed upon the land.

Mr. Justice Black, dissenting.

The Fifth Amendment provides that "private property" shall not "be taken for public use without just compensation." The Court holds today that the Government has "taken" respondents' property by repeatedly flying Army bombers directly above respondents' land at a height of eighty-three feet where the light and noise from these planes caused respondents to lose sleep and their chickens to be killed. Since the effect of the Court's decision is to limit, by the imposition of relatively absolute constitutional barriers, possible future adjustments through legislation and regulation which might become necessary with the growth of air transportation, and since in my view the Constitution does not contain such barriers, I dissent. . . .

The Court's opinion seems to indicate that the mere flying of planes through the column of air directly above respondents' land does not constitute a "taking." Consequently, it appears to be noise and glare, to the extent and under the circumstances shown here, which make the Government a seizer of private property. . . . The concept of taking property as used in the Constitution has heretofore never been given so sweeping a meaning. The Court's opinion presents no case where a man who makes noise or shines light onto his neighbor's property has been ejected from that property for wrongfully taking possession of it. Nor would anyone take seriously a claim that noisy automobiles passing on a highway are taking wrongful possession of the homes located thereon, or that a city elevated train which greatly interferes with the sleep of those who live next to it wrongfully takes their property. . . . I am not willing, nor do I think the Constitution and the decisions authorize me, to extend that phrase so as to guarantee an absolute constitutional right to relief not subject to legislative change, which is based on averments that at best show mere torts committed by government agents while flying over land. The future adjustment of the rights and remedies of property owners, which might be found necessary because of the flight of planes at safe altitudes, should, especially in view of the imminent expansion of air navigation, be left where I think the Constitution left it, with Congress. . . .

No greater confusion could be brought about in the coming age of air transportation than that which would result were courts by constitutional interpretation to hamper Congress in its efforts to keep the air free. Old concepts of private ownership of land should not be introduced into the field of air regulation. I have no doubt that Congress will, if not handicapped by judicial interpretations of the Constitution, preserve the freedom of the air, and at the same time, satisfy the just claims of aggrieved persons. The noise of newer, larger, and more powerful planes may grow louder and louder and disturb people more and more. But the solution of the problems precipitated by these technological advances and new ways of living cannot come about through the application of rigid constitutional restraints formulated and enforced by the courts. What adjustments may have to be made, only the future can reveal. It seems certain, however, that courts do not possess the techniques or the personnel to consider and act upon the complex combinations of factors entering into the problems. . . . Today's opinion is, I fear, an opening wedge for an unwarranted judicial interference with the power of Congress to develop solutions for new and vital national problems. In my opinion this case should be reversed on the ground that there has been no "taking" in the constitutional sense.

The Public Use Requirement

Although the Fifth Amendment recognizes the government's power to take private property, it does not allow all such seizures. Quite explicitly, the Takings Clause stipulates that the government may take private property only for a "public use." Even if the government provides adequate compensation, it may not take property against the owner's will for the sole benefit of a private individual or organization. When the government plans to build a new courthouse, road, or park, the public use is clear, but it would be of doubtful constitutionality, for example, if a state seized a piece of private property under the power of eminent domain and gave it to a fraternal organization to construct a new lodge. Occasionally, government seizure of land is challenged as not based on a truly public purpose. *Hawaii Housing Authority v. Midkiff* (1984) concerned the state

of Hawaii's plan to redistribute land, using the power of eminent domain to force large landowners to sell their properties to the people who leased them. Was this program a benefit to the public generally, or did it serve only the private interests of those who now were able to become landowners?

Hawaii Housing Authority v. Midkiff
467 U.S. 229 (1984)

*Vote: 8 (Blackmun, Brennan, Burger, O'Connor,
Powell, Rehnquist, Stevens, White)*

0

*Opinion of the Court: O'Connor
Not participating: Marshall*

The Hawaiian Islands were settled by Polynesians who developed an economic system based upon principles of feudalism. Ownership and control of the land rested with the islands' high chief, who distributed parcels to various lower-ranking chiefs. At the end of the chain, tenant farmers and their families lived on the land and worked it. Private ownership of real property was not permitted. Ultimate ownership of all lands rested with the royal family.

The monarchy was overthrown in 1893, and, after a brief period as a republic, the islands were annexed by the United States in 1898. When Hawaii became the fiftieth state in 1959, the land still remained in the hands of a few. In the mid-1960s the federal government owned 49 percent of the land in the Hawaiian Islands, and just seventy-two private landowners held another 47 percent. On Oahu, the most commercially developed island, twenty-two landowners controlled more than 72 percent of the private real estate. The Hawaiian legislature determined that this land concentration condition was detrimental to the state's economy and general welfare.

The legislature first decided to compel landowners to sell a large portion of their holdings to those individuals who leased the land from them. The landowners opposed this plan because it would result in exceedingly high capital gains that would be subject to significant federal taxation. In response, the legislature revised its plans and enacted the Land Reform Act of 1967. This legislation allowed the state to condemn tracts of residential real estate. The Hawaii Housing Authority (HHA) would then seize the condemned property, compensate the landowners for their loss, and resell the parcels to the private individuals who had been leasing the land. Compensation for land seized by the government enjoyed a more favorable tax status than did profits from outright sales, making the legislation more acceptable to the landowners.

Frank Midkiff and others owned a large tract of land that was condemned under the land reform program. Midkiff and the HHA could not agree on a fair price for the land. He and others filed suit in federal district court to have the Land Reform Act declared unconstitutional as a violation of Takings Clause. Among the arguments presented was the claim that redistributing land ownership was not an appropriate ''public use'' under the meaning of the Fifth Amendment. The district court rejected this argument, but the Court of Appeals for the Ninth Circuit reversed. The housing authority appealed to the Supreme Court.

Justice Sandra Day O'Connor delivered the opinion of the Court:

The Fifth Amendment of the United States Constitution provides, in pertinent part, that "private property [shall not] be taken for public use, without just compensation." These cases present the question whether the Public Use Clause of that Amendment, made applicable to the States through the Fourteenth Amendment, prohibits the State of Hawaii from taking, with just compensation, title in real property from lessors and transferring it to lessees in order to reduce the concentration of ownership of fees simple in the State. We conclude that it does not. . . .

The majority of the Court of Appeals . . . determined that the Act violates the "public use" requirement of the Fifth and Fourteenth Amendments. On this argument, however, we find ourselves in agreement with the dissenting judge in the Court of Appeals.

The starting point for our analysis of the Act's constitutionality is the Court's decision in *Berman v. Parker* (1954). In *Berman,* the Court held constitutional the District of Columbia Redevelopment Act of 1945. That Act provided both for the comprehensive use of the eminent domain power to redevelop slum areas and for the possible sale or lease of the condemned lands to private interests. In discussing whether the takings authorized by that Act were for a "public use," the Court stated:

"We deal, in other words, with what traditionally has been known as the police power. An attempt to define its reach or trace its outer limits is fruitless, for each case must turn on its own facts. The definition is essentially the product of legislative determinations addressed to the purposes of government, purposes neither abstractly nor historically capable of complete definition. Subject to specific constitutional limitations, when the legislature has spoken, the public interest has been declared in terms well-nigh conclusive. In such cases the legislature, not the judiciary, is the main guardian of the public needs to be served by social legislation, whether it be Congress legislating concerning the District of Columbia . . . or the States legislating concerning local affairs. . . . This principle admits of no exception merely because the power of eminent domain is involved. . . ."

The Court explicitly recognized the breadth of the principle it was announcing, noting:

"Once the object is within the authority of Congress, the right to realize it through the exercise of eminent domain is clear. For the power of eminent domain is merely the means to the end. . . . Once the object is within the authority of Congress, the means by which it will be attained is also for Congress to determine. Here one of the means chosen is the use of private enterprise for redevelopment of the area. Appellants argue that this makes the project a taking from one businessman for the benefit of another businessman. But the means of executing the project are for Congress and Congress alone to determine, once the public purpose has been established."

The "public use" requirement is thus coterminous with the scope of a sovereign's police powers.

There is, of course, a role for courts to play in reviewing a legislature's judgment of what constitutes a public use, even when the eminent domain power is equated with the police power. But the Court in *Berman* made clear that it is "an extremely narrow" one. The Court in *Berman* cited with approval the Court's decision in *Old Dominion Co. v. United States* (1925), which held that deference to the legislature's "public use" determination is required "until it is shown to involve an impossibility." The *Berman* Court also cited to *United States ex rel. TVA v. Welch* (1946), which emphasized that "[a]ny departure from this judicial restraint would result in courts deciding on what is and is not a governmental function and in their invalidating legislation on the basis of their view on that question at the moment of decision, a practice which has proved impracticable in other fields." In short, the Court has made clear that it will not substitute its judgment for a legislature's judgment as to what constitutes a public use "unless the use be palpably without reasonable foundation."

To be sure, the Court's cases have repeatedly stated that "one person's property may not be taken for the benefit of another private person without a justifying public purpose, even though compensation be paid." Thus, in *Missouri Pacific R. Co. v. Nebraska* (1896), where the "order in question was not, *and was not claimed to be,* . . . a taking of private property for a public use under the right of eminent domain," the Court invalidated a compensated taking of property for lack of a justifying public purpose. But where the exercise of the eminent domain power is rationally related to a conceivable public purpose, the Court has never held a compensated taking to be proscribed by the Public Use Clause.

On this basis, we have no trouble concluding that the Hawaii Act is constitutional. The people of Hawaii have attempted, much as the settlers of the original 13 Colonies did, to reduce the perceived social and economic evils of a land oligopoly traceable to their monarchs. The land oligopoly has, according to the Hawaii Legislature, created artificial deterrents to the normal functioning of the State's residential land market and forced thousands of individual homeowners to lease, rather than buy, the land underneath their homes. Regulating oligopoly and the evils associated with it is a classic exercise of a State's police powers. We cannot disapprove of Hawaii's exercise of this power.

Nor can we condemn as irrational the Act's approach to correcting the land oligopoly problem. The Act presumes that when a sufficiently large number of persons declare that they are willing but unable to buy lots at fair prices the land market is malfunctioning. When such a malfunction is signalled, the Act authorizes HHA to condemn lots in the relevant tract. The Act limits the number of lots any one tenant can purchase and authorizes HHA to use public funds to ensure that the market dilution goals will be achieved. This is a comprehensive and rational approach to identifying and correcting market failure.

Of course, this Act, like any other, may not be successful in achieving its intended goals. But ''whether *in fact* the provision will accomplish its objectives is not the question: the [constitutional requirement] is satisfied if . . . the . . . [state] Legislature *rationally could have believed* that the [Act] would promote its objective.'' When the legislature's purpose is legitimate and its means are not irrational, our cases make clear that empirical debates over the wisdom of takings—no less than debates over the wisdom of other kinds of socioeconomic legislation—are not to be carried out in the federal courts. Redistribution of fees simple to correct deficiencies in the market determined by the state legislature to be attributable to land oligopoly is a rational exercise of the eminent domain power. Therefore, the Hawaii statute must pass the scrutiny of the Public Use Clause. . . .

The mere fact that property taken outright by eminent domain is transferred in the first instance to private beneficiaries does not condemn that taking as having only a private purpose. The Court long ago rejected any literal requirement that condemned property be put into use for the general public. ''It is not essential that the entire community, nor even any considerable portion, . . . directly enjoy or participate in any improvement in order [for it] to constitute a public use.'' As the unique way titles were held in Hawaii skewed the land market, exercise of the power of eminent domain was justified. The Act advances its purposes without the State's taking actual possession of the land. In such cases, government does not itself have to use property to legitimate the taking; it is only the taking's purpose, and not its mechanics, that must pass scrutiny under the Public Use Clause. . . .

The State of Hawaii has never denied that the Constitution forbids even a compensated taking of property when executed for no reason other than to confer a private benefit on a particular private party. A purely private taking could not withstand the scrutiny of the public use requirement; it would serve no legitimate purpose of government and would thus be void. But no purely private taking is involved in these cases. The Hawaii Legislature enacted its Land Reform Act not to benefit a particular class of identifiable individuals but to attack certain perceived evils of concentrated property ownership in Hawaii—a legitimate public purpose. Use of the condemnation power to achieve this purpose is not irrational. Since we assume for purposes of these appeals that the weighty demand of just compensation has been met, the requirements of the Fifth and Fourteenth Amendments have been satisfied. Accordingly, we reverse the judgment of the Court of Appeals, and remand these cases for further proceedings in conformity with this opinion.

It is so ordered.

The Rehnquist Court and the Takings Clause

Today, the Supreme Court continues to grapple with the problem of determining an appropriate balance between the rights of private property and the government's ability to legislate for the public good. In deciding such cases, the justices of the Rehnquist Court often have divided along ideological lines. Conservative justices have been more prone to conclude that a taking has occurred, and liberals are more likely to determine that government regulatory policies impose only an incidental burden on the rights of the property owner.

Nollan v. California Coastal Commission (1987) illustrates how the justices' political philosophies influence case outcomes. Behind this dispute were California's regulations to increase the public's access to the ocean beaches. To help accomplish this objective, the state would allow the Nollans to construct a house on their beachfront property only if they granted the public the right to use a portion of their land to walk from one public beach to another. The five justices who were considered the Court's conservative bloc thought the state regulation was a taking of the Nollans' property. The four liberals said it was not. What do you think? Was the Nollan property partially taken from them by the public access requirement and, therefore, was California bound by the Fifth Amendment to pay just compensation?

Nollan v. California Coastal Commission

483 U.S. 825 (1987)

Vote: 5 (O'Connor, Powell, Rehnquist, Scalia, White)
   4 (Blackmun, Brennan, Marshall, Stevens)
Opinion of the Court: Scalia
Dissenting opinions: Blackmun, Brennan, Stevens

James Patrick Nollan and his wife owned a beachfront lot in Ventura County, California. One-quarter mile north of their property was Faria County Park, an oceanside public beach and recreation area. Another public beach, known as The Cove, was located 1,800 feet south of the Nollan lot. A concrete sea wall, eight feet high, separated the beach part of the Nollan property from the rest of the land. Originally, a small bungalow that was rented to summer vacationers stood on the property. The house, however, fell into serious disrepair and could no longer be rented. The Nollans decided to replace the bungalow with a new structure, and, to do so, they needed a building permit from the California Coastal Commission.

The commission granted the Nollans permission to build their new house, but with one significant condition: a strip of their property was to be set aside for use by the public to move between the two public beaches. The Nollans protested. On rehearing, the commission reaffirmed the requirement, finding that the easement was necessary because the new house would reduce the view of the beach from the street and prevent the public "psychologically . . . from realizing a stretch of coastline exists nearby that they have every right to visit." The Nollans then filed suit claiming that the public access condition constituted a taking under the Fifth Amendment. The California Supreme Court ruled in favor of the coastal commission, and the Nollans took their case to the U.S. Supreme Court.

Justice Antonin Scalia delivered the opinion of the Court:

Had California simply required the Nollans to make an easement across their beachfront available to the public on a permanent basis in order to increase public access to the beach, rather than conditioning their permit to rebuild their house on their agreeing to do so, we have no doubt there would have been a taking. To say that the appropriation of a public easement across a landowner's premises does not constitute the taking of a property interest but rather . . . "a mere restriction on its use" is to use words in a manner that deprives them of all their ordinary meaning. Indeed, one of the principal uses of the eminent domain power is to assure that the government be able to require conveyance of just such interests, so long as it pays for them. Perhaps because the point is so obvious, we have never been confronted with a controversy that required us to rule upon it, but our cases' analysis of the effect of other governmental action leads to the same conclusion. We have repeatedly held that, as to property reserved by its owner for private use, "the right to exclude [others is] 'one of the most essential sticks in the bundle of rights that are commonly characterized as property.'" In *Loretto* [*v. Teleprompter Manhattan CATV*, 1982] we observed that where governmental action results in "[a] permanent physical occupation" of the property, by the government or others, our cases uniformly have found a taking to the extent of the occupation, without regard to whether the action achieves an important public benefit or has only minimal economic impact on the owner." We think a "permanent physical occupation" has occurred, for purposes of that rule, where individuals are given a permanent and continuous right to pass to and fro, so that the real property may continuously be traversed, even though no particular individual is permitted to station himself permanently upon the premises. . . .

Given, then, that requiring uncompensated conveyance of the easement outright would violate the Fourteenth Amendment, the question becomes whether requiring it to be conveyed as a condition for issuing a land-use permit alters the outcome. We have long recognized that land-use regulation does not effect a taking if it "substantially advance[s] legitimate state interests" and does not "den[y] an owner economically viable use of his land." . . . Our cases have not elaborated on the standards for determining what constitutes a "legitimate state interest" or what type of connection between the regulation and the state interest satisfies the requirement that the former "substan-

tially advance" the latter. They have made clear, however, that a broad range of governmental purposes and regulations satisfies these requirements. The Commission argues that among these permissible purposes are protecting the public's ability to see the beach, assisting the public in overcoming the "psychological barrier" to using the beach created by a developed shorefront, and preventing congestion on the public beaches. We assume, without deciding, that this is so—in which case the Commission unquestionably would be able to deny the Nollans their permit outright if their new house (alone, or by reason of the cumulative impact produced in conjunction with other construction) would substantially impede these purposes, unless the denial would interfere so drastically with the Nollans' use of their property as to constitute a taking.

. . . Thus, if the Commission attached to the permit some condition that would have protected the public's ability to see the beach notwithstanding construction of the new house—for example, a height limitation, a width restriction or a ban on fences—so long as the Commission could have exercised its police power (as we have assumed it could) to forbid construction of the house altogether, imposition of the condition would also be constitutional. Moreover (and here we come closer to the facts of the present case), the condition would be constitutional even if it consisted of the requirement that the Nollans provide a viewing spot on their property for passersby with whose sighting of the ocean their new house would interfere. Although such a requirement, constituting a permanent grant of continuous access to the property, would have to be considered a taking if it were not attached to a development permit, the Commission's assumed power to forbid construction of the house in order to protect the public's view of the beach must surely include the power to condition construction upon some concession by the owner, even a concession of property rights, that serves the same end. If a prohibition designed to accomplish that purpose would be a legitimate exercise of the police power rather than a taking, it would be strange to conclude that providing the owner an alternative to that prohibition which accomplishes the same purpose is not.

The evident constitutional propriety disappears, however, if the condition substituted for the prohibition utterly fails to further the end advanced as the justification for the prohibition. . . . The purpose then becomes, quite simply, the obtaining of an easement to serve some valid governmental purpose, but without payment of compensation. Whatever may be the outer limits of "legitimate state interests" in the takings and land-use context, this is not one of them. In short, unless the permit condition serves the same governmental purpose as the development ban, the building restriction is not a valid regulation of land use but "an out-and-out plan of extortion." . . .

It is quite impossible to understand how a requirement that people already on the public beaches be able to walk across the Nollans' property reduces any obstacles to viewing the beach created by the new house. It is also impossible to understand how it lowers any "psychological barrier" to using the public beaches, or how it helps to remedy any additional congestion on them caused by construction of the Nollans' new house. We therefore find that the Commission's imposition of the permit condition cannot be treated as an exercise of its land-use power for any of these purposes. Our conclusion on this point is consistent with the approach taken by every other court that has considered the question, with the exception of the California state courts. . . .

California is free to advance its "comprehensive program," if it wishes, by using its power of eminent domain for this "public purpose," but if it wants an easement across the Nollans' property, it must pay for it.

Reversed.

Justice BRENNAN . . . dissenting.

The Court's conclusion that the permit condition imposed on appellants is unreasonable cannot withstand analysis. First, the Court demands a degree of exactitude that is inconsistent with our standard for reviewing the rationality of a State's exercise of its police power for the welfare of its citizens. Second, even if the nature of the public-access condition imposed must be identical to the precise burden on access created by appellants, this requirement is plainly satisfied.

There can be no dispute that the police power of the States encompasses the authority to impose conditions on private development. It is also by now commonplace that this Court's view of the rationality of a State's exercise of its police power demands only that the State *"could rationally have decided"* that the measure adopted might achieve the State's objective. In this case, California has employed its police power in order to condition development upon preservation of public access to the ocean and tidelands. The Coastal Commission, if it had so chosen, could have denied the Nollans' request for a development permit, since the property would have remained economically viable without the requested new development. Instead, the State sought to accommodate the Nollans' desire for new development, on the condition that the development not diminish the overall amount of public access to the coastline. Appellants' proposed development would reduce public access by restricting visual access to the beach, by contributing to an increased need for community facilities, and by moving private development closer to public beach property. The Commission sought to offset this diminution in access, and thereby preserve the overall balance of access, by requesting a deed restriction that would ensure "lateral" access: the right of the public to pass and repass along the dry sand parallel to the shoreline in order to reach the tidelands and the ocean. In the expert opinion of the Coastal Commission, development conditioned on such a restriction would fairly attend to both public and private interests.

The Court finds fault with this measure because it regards the condition as insufficiently tailored to address the precise type of reduction in access produced by the new development. The Nollans' development blocks visual access, the Court tells us, while the Commission seeks to preserve lateral access along the coastline. Thus, it concludes, the State acted irrationally. Such a narrow conception of rationality, however, has long since been discredited as a judicial arrogation of legislative authority. . . .

Imposition of the permit condition in this case represents the State's reasonable exercise of its police power. The Coastal Commission has drawn on its expertise to preserve the balance between private development and public access, by requiring that any project that intensifies development on the increasingly crowded California coast must be offset by gains in public access. Under the normal standard for review of the police power, this provision is eminently reasonable. . . .

State agencies . . . require considerable flexibility in responding to private desires for development in a way that guarantees the preservation of public access to the coast. They should be encouraged to regulate development in the context of the overall balance of competing uses of the shoreline. The Court today does precisely the opposite, overruling an eminently reasonable exercise of an expert state agency's judgment, substituting its own narrow view of how this balance should be struck. Its reasoning is hardly suited to the complex reality of natural resource protection in the 20th century. I can only hope that today's decision is an aberration, and that the broader vision ultimately prevails.

I dissent.

Whether the *Nollan* decision was an aberration, as Justice Brennan hoped, or a signal of decisions to come from the Rehnquist Court has yet to be determined. Clearly, however, the changing composition of the Court during the early 1990s provides reason to suspect that the justices may well give increased protection to private property rights. The retirements of William Brennan and Thurgood Marshall removed the two justices most prone to side with public interests over private property. It is quite possible that the decidedly conservative Court of the 1990s might breathe renewed life into the Constitution's private property protections. If so, the Contract and Takings Clauses may take on greater constitutional importance in the coming years.

READINGS

Ackerman, Bruce. *Private Property and the Constitution.* New Haven, Conn.: Yale University Press, 1977.

Dowd, Morgan D. "Justice Story, the Supreme Court, and the Obligation of Contract." *Case Western Reserve Law Review* 19 (1968): 493-527.

Epstein, Richard A. *Takings: Private Property and the Power of Eminent Domain.* Cambridge, Mass.: Harvard University Press, 1985.

Hagin, Horace H. "Fletcher vs. Peck." *Georgetown Law Journal* 16 (November 1927): 1-40.

Horowitz, Morton J. *The Transformation of American Law, 1780-1860.* Cambridge, Mass.: Harvard University Press, 1977.

Hunting, Warren B. *The Obligation of Contracts Clause of the United States Constitution.* Baltimore: The Johns Hopkins University Press, 1919.

Isaacs, Nathan. "John Marshall on Contracts: A Study in Early American Juristic Theory." *Virginia Law Review* 7 (March 1921): 413-428.

Magrath, C. Peter. *Yazoo: Law and Politics in the New Republic.* Providence, R.I.: Brown University Press, 1966.

Schwartz, Bernard. "Old Wine in New Bottles? The Renaissance of the Contract Clause." *Supreme Court Review 1979* (1980): 95-121.

Stites, Francis N. *Private Interest and Public Gain: The Dartmouth College Case.* Amherst: University of Massachusetts Press, 1972.

Trimble, Bruce. "Chief Justice Waite and the Limitations on the Dartmouth College Decision." *University of Cincinnati Law Review* 9 (January 1935): 41-66.

Wright, Benjamin F. *The Contract Clause of the Constitution.* Cambridge, Mass.: Harvard University Press, 1938.

CHAPTER 9

ECONOMIC SUBSTANTIVE
DUE PROCESS

L et us say that federal and state agents receive a tip that the owners of a factory are violating the federal law that prohibits the employment of children younger than fourteen. Without stopping to obtain a warrant, the agents enter the factory and observe that underage employees are indeed working there. The agents arrest the owners, and a court convicts them. But the factory owners challenge their conviction on two similarly named, but distinct grounds—procedural due process and substantive due process.

Citing the first ground, the factory owners allege that the procedure the agents used, entering the factory without a warrant, violated guarantees in the Constitution, including sections of the Fifth (and the Fourteenth) Amendment that prohibit government from depriving persons of life, liberty, and property without due process of law. For many, the term *due process* is synonymous with fairness. The American system of justice is based on the idea that even people guilty of violating the law deserve fair treatment. What fair treatment means often is in dispute, but what is not in dispute is this particular characterization of due process. Known as *procedural due process,* it is the most traditional and widely accepted use of the term. It suggests that governments must proceed in fair ways, but it does not bar their action completely. If the government had proceeded

fairly against the factory owners, their conviction was justified.

What is the second ground on which the factory owners base their appeal? None other than due process. Under this approach to the Due Process Clause, the owners argue that the law prohibiting the employment of minors violated due process guarantees because, in an unreasonable way, it took away their "liberty," their right to do business. In their appeal, the owners say that due process implies something more than procedural fairness; they seek to inject into it some substantive meaning. In other words, in their view, the term not only covers the way government operates, but also it provides a concrete right that government cannot violate. Under this interpretation, often called *substantive due process,* the guarantee places a limit on government activity: it suggests, using the example above, that the federal law cannot stand because it "is inherently unfair and unjust and therefore can never meet the requirement of due process of law. The substance of the law must be just and must not unfairly deny persons their life, liberty, or property."[1] *(See box, page 430.)*

This chapter examines whether this reading of the due process clauses is reasonable. We shall

1. Sheldon Goldman, *Constitutional Law,* 2d ed. (New York: HarperCollins, 1991), 378.

Procedural and Substantive Due Process

The U.S. Constitution contains two clauses—in the Fifth and Fourteenth Amendments—prohibiting the federal government and the states from depriving any person of life, liberty, or property without due process of law. When James Madison included the clause in the Fifth Amendment—part of the Bill of Rights—the meaning of the words "due process" was considered in its literal sense as guaranteeing only that government would follow fair and proper procedure in its dealings with private individuals. This became known in law as procedural due process—essentially a requirement that those who were adversely affected by particular government action had to be given fair notice, as well as proper opportunity to be heard, before the government could take action against them. Observance of procedural due process, or fair procedure, was actually as old as Magna Carta, if not older. As an English judge noted in 1723: "Even God himself did not pass sentence upon Adam, before he [Adam] was called upon to make his defence. Adam [says God] where art thou? Has thou not eaten of the tree, whereof I commanded thee that thou shouldst not eat?"

In the years prior to the Civil War, state courts also began to interpret due process as a protection against arbitrary or unjust laws. In other words, even where the fairest procedure was followed, legislation could deprive a person of life, liberty, or property unless he were protected by limitations imposed by due process on the substance of that legislation. As Supreme Court Justice John Marshall Harlan defined this aspect of due process at a later time, substantive due process "includes a freedom from all substantial arbitrary impositions."

Since arbitrary action is synonymous with unreasonable action, due process requires a determination of reasonableness. Substantive due process thus allowed courts to decide on the reasonableness of challenged government action in relation to the ends which may be legitimately furthered by government, a procedure that permitted judges to substitute their own opinions for those of legislatures on the question of what

Justice Stephen J. Field

constituted reasonable government acts. This, in fact, is what occurred toward the close of the nineteenth century when the Supreme Court, at the urging of Justices Stephen J. Field and Joseph P. Bradley, adopted the substantive due process approach in its decisions. Particularly after the turn of the century, in cases following that of *Lochner v. New York* in 1905, the Court relied on its independent judgment to determine the reasonableness of challenged statutes. In those cases, the Court came close to exercising the functions of what dissenting Justice Louis D. Brandeis called a "superlegislature," setting itself up as virtual supreme censor of the wisdom of legislation.

Under the *Lochner* approach, substantive due process became the great instrument of judicially imposed laissez faire and was employed to invalidate a host of laws, particularly those seeking to regulate economic abuses. As the twentieth century went on, the justices themselves came to see that *Lochner* went too far and that due process was not intended to make them judges of the wisdom or desirability of government measures. Eventually, they adopted a view urged by Justice Oliver Wendell Holmes on the proper judicial role in due process cases. The Holmes test was whether a reasonable legislator—the legislative version of the "reasonable man"—could have adopted the law at issue. The legislative judgment might well be debatable. But that was the whole point about the Holmes approach. Under it, the courts left debatable issues, as respects business, economic, and social affairs, to legislative decision.

Source: Bernard Schwartz, *The Law in America* (New York: McGraw-Hill, 1974), 137.

see that modern Supreme Courts, for the most part, have rejected substantive due process as it applies to laws governing economic relationships. In contrast, for approximately forty years between the 1890s and the 1930s, the Court read due process in substantive terms and used it to strike down many laws allegedly infringing on economic rights. Even if the agents had obtained a search warrant, these earlier Courts might have ruled in favor of the factory owners.

If economic substantive due process is now a discredited doctrine, why should we devote an entire chapter to it? There are several reasons. First, its rise and fall from the Court's grace is an intriguing part of legal history. The adoption of substantive due process came about gradually and resulted from the push and pull of the legal and political environment of the day. Second, it provides us with an opportunity to revisit the concept of judicial activism. Today, that term is most often associated with liberalism, with Courts that overturned restrictive government laws and practices, such as those requiring segregation of public facilities or prohibiting seditious speech. But, as we pointed out in Chapter 2, activism does not always mean liberalism. Indeed, the Courts of the 1890s–1930s were activist in overturning many laws, but that activism was conservative, not liberal.

A third reason is that substantive due process is a way to reexamine the cycles of history we have already discussed. As depicted in Table 9-1, substantive due process was another weapon in the Court's laissez-faire arsenal. While it was using delegation of power doctrines (Chapter 3), the Tenth Amendment (Chapter 5), the Commerce Clause (Chapter 6), and taxing and spending provisions (Chapter 7) to strike down federal regulations of business, the Court also invoked substantive due process to hold against similar legislation passed by the states. This use was particularly ironic because, at the time, the Court

Table 9-1 The Legal Tools of the Laissez-Faire Courts, 1890s to 1930s: Some Examples

	1890–1899	1900–1909	1910–1919	1920–1929	1930–1939
Used to Strike State Laws					
Substantive Due Process	Allgeyer v. Louisiana (1897)	Lochner v. New York (1905)			Morehead v. Tipaldo (1936)
Used to Strike Federal Laws					
Delegation of Powers					Panama Refining Co. v. Ryan (1935)
					Schechter Poultry v. United States (1935)
Commerce Clause			Hammer v. Dagenhart (1918)		Panama Refining Co. v. Ryan (1935)
					Schechter Poultry v. United States (1935)
					Carter v. Carter Coal (1936)
Taxing and Spending				Bailey v. Drexel Furniture (1922)	United States v. Butler (1936)
Tenth Amendment			Hammer v. Dagenhart (1918)		

was espousing notions of dual federalism and invoking the Tenth Amendment. In other words, the Court found ways to strike down all sorts of economic regulation, even though, in so doing, it often took contradictory stances. Therefore, substantive due process provides a way to tie together much of what we have covered in this book.

Finally, the doctrine of substantive due process has relevance today, even if it no longer governs economic relationships. The Court continues to apply due process guarantees to noneconomic relations, legislation that allegedly infringes on privacy rights. Moreover, it always is possible that the Court will return to endorsing a laissez-faire philosophy. Should the justices be so inclined, they may find economic substantive due process or other constitutional provisions equally useful. We shall consider these issues at the end of the chapter, but first, let us review substantive due process chronologically—how it developed, why the Court embraced it, and what led to its demise.

The Development of Substantive Due Process

In general terms, prior to the adoption of the Fourteenth Amendment, judges interpreted due process guarantees contained in the Fifth Amendment and in state constitutions as procedural in intent and nature. Historian Kermit L. Hall wrote, "Before the Civil War [due process] had essentially one meaning," that people were "entitled" to fair and orderly proceedings, particularly criminal proceedings.[2]

There were some exceptions. Writing in *Dred Scott v. Sandford,* Chief Justice Roger B. Taney invoked the specter of due process to strike government interference in "property rights":

An act of Congress which deprives a citizen of the United States of his liberty or property [a slave], merely because he came himself or brought his property into

a particular Territory . . . could hardly be dignified with the name of due process of law.

Around the same time, a New York state court in *Wynehamer v. People* (1856) invoked a substantive interpretation of the state's due process requirement in striking down an alcohol prohibition law. It asserted that due process guarantees "prohibit, regardless of the matter of procedure, a certain kind or degree of exertion of legislative power altogether" and that the "substantive content of legislation" is covered, not simply the "mode of procedure."[3]

But decisions like *Wynehamer* represented the exception, not the rule. Neither state court judges interpreting their due process clauses, nor their federal court counterparts treating the Fifth Amendment, read them to possess a substantive right and, therefore, a bar on interventionist government legislation. Rather, they viewed them through a procedural lens and for good reason: it was simply unclear whether due process clauses were meant to have substance. More to the point, some argue that the country needed the kinds of regulations that substantive due process would find so offensive. As the country changed from an agrarian to an industrial society, economic abuses called for limits. In Chapter 8 we saw that this perceived need provided one explanation as to why the Contract Clause—as a mechanism for protecting economic interests—vanished from the legal scene.

Initial Interpretation of the Fourteenth Amendment Due Process Clause

The federal and state governments' recognition of the need for limits on individual liberties, especially economic liberties, caused at least one sector of American life, business, intense displeasure. As the Court weakened its major source of protection—the Contract Clause—business was

2. Kermit L. Hall, *The Magic Mirror* (New York: Oxford University Press, 1989), 232.

3. See Gerald Gunther, *Constitutional Law* (Mineola, N.Y.: Foundation Press, 1991), 436.

subjected to increasing regulation by the states, and these regulations decreased profits. This growing concern coincided with the end of the Civil War. Louis Fisher wrote that "the climate" after the war "promoted the pursuit of material goals, especially after the heavy sacrifices demanded by the war."[4] Not surprisingly, business interests looked to other parts of the Constitution for protection.

4. Louis Fisher, *American Constitutional Law* (New York: McGraw-Hill, 1990), 474.

As *The Slaughterhouse Cases* (1873) reveal, business thought it had found an answer in the newly ratified Fourteenth Amendment. Although the Court's majority did not see it their way, some of the dissenters surely did. As you read *Slaughterhouse,* pay careful attention to the Court's opinion and the dissents. Justice Joseph P. Bradley's dissent sets the tone for many majority opinions that follow.

The Slaughterhouse Cases

(Butchers' Benevolent Association v. Crescent City Livestock Landing & Slaughter House Company)

16 Wall. 36 (1873)

Vote: 5 (Clifford, Davis, Hunt, Miller, Strong)
*   4 (Bradley, Chase, Field, Swayne)*
Opinion of the Court: Miller
Dissenting opinions: Bradley, Field, Swayne

After the Civil War, the United States experienced an industrial revolution, an economic diversification that touched the entire country. Along with the benefits of industrialization came some negative side effects. For example, the Louisiana state legislature claimed that the Mississippi River had become polluted because New Orleans butchers dumped garbage into it. To remedy this problem (or, as some have suggested, to use it as an excuse to create a monopolistic enterprise), the legislature created a company—the Crescent City Live Stock Landing & Slaughter House Company—to receive and slaughter all city livestock for twenty-five years.

Because the butchers were forced to use the company facilities and to pay top dollar for the privilege, they formed their own organization, the Butchers' Benevolent Association, and hired an attorney, former U.S. Supreme Court justice John A. Campbell, to sue the corporation. In his arguments, Campbell sought to apply the Fourteenth Amendment to the butchers' case. In general terms, he asserted that the amendment—although passed in the wake of the Civil War—was not meant solely to protect blacks. Rather, its language was broad enough to encompass all citizens. He used that as a base from which to launch his more specific argument, that Louisiana's law deprived his clients of their right to pursue their business, a basic guarantee granted by the Fourteenth Amendment's Privileges and Immunities Clause:

No State shall make or enforce any law which shall abridge the privileges or immunities of citizens of the United States.

For good measure, he noted that the Louisiana law also violated the amendment's two other central guarantees, due process and equal protection, and that it was involuntary servitude outlawed by the Thirteenth Amendment.

Justice Samuel F. Miller delivered the opinion of the Court:

The plaintiffs in error . . . allege that the statute is a violation of the Constitution of the United States in these several particulars:

That it creates an involuntary servitude forbidden by the 13th article of amendment;

That it abridges the privileges and immunities of citizens of the United States;

That it denies to the plaintiffs the equal protection of the laws; and,

That it deprives them of their property without due process of law; contrary to the provisions of the 1st section of the 14th article of amendment.

This court is thus called upon for the first time to give construction to these articles.

We do not conceal from ourselves the great responsibility which this duty devolves upon us. No questions so far reaching and pervading in their consequences, so profoundly interesting to the people of this country, and so important in their bearing upon the relations of the United States and of the several states to each other, and to the citizens of the states, and of the United States, have been before this court during the official life of any of its present members. We have given every opportunity for a full hearing at the bar; we have discussed it freely and compared views among ourselves; we have taken ample time for careful deliberation, and we now propose to announce the judgments which we have formed in the construction of those articles, so far as we have found them necessary to the decision of the cases before us, and beyond that we have neither the inclination nor the right to go. . . .

The most cursory glance at these articles discloses a unity of purpose, when taken in connection with the history of the times, which cannot fail to have an important bearing on any question of doubt concerning their true meaning. Nor can such doubts, when any reasonably exist, be safely and rationally solved without a reference to that history; for in it is found the occasion and the necessity for recurring again to the great source of power in this country, the people of the states, for additional guaranties of human rights; additional powers to the Federal government; additional restraints upon those of the states. Fortunately that history is fresh within the memory of us all, and its leading features, as they bear upon the matter before us, free from doubt.

The institution of African slavery, as it existed in about half the states of the Union, and the contests pervading the public mind for many years, between those who desired its curtailment and ultimate extinction and those who desired additional safeguards for its security and perpetuation, culminated in the effort, on the part of most of the states in which slavery existed, to separate from the Federal government, and to resist its authority. This constituted the War of the Rebellion, and whatever auxiliary causes may have contributed to bring about this war, undoubtedly the overshadowing and efficient cause was African slavery. . . .

The language is: "No state shall make or enforce any law which shall abridge the privileges or immunities of citizens of the United States." . . .

"The inquiry," . . . "is, what are the privileges and immunities of citizens of the several states? We feel no hesitation in confining these expressions to those privileges and immunities which are fundamental; which belong of right to the citizens of all free governments, and which have at all times been enjoyed by citizens of the several states which compose this Union, from the time of their becoming free, independent, and sovereign. What these fundamental principles are, it would be more tedious than difficult to enumerate." "They may all, however, be comprehended under the following general heads: protection by the government, with the right to acquire and possess property of every kind, and to pursue and obtain happiness and safety, subject, nevertheless, to such restraints as the government may prescribe for the general good of the whole." . . .

"All persons born or naturalized in the United States, and subject to the jurisdiction thereof, are citizens of the United States and of the state, wherein they reside. No state shall make or enforce any law which shall abridge the privileges or immunities of citizens of the United States, nor shall any state deprive any person of life, liberty or property without due process of law, nor deny to any person within its jurisdiction the equal protection of the laws."

The argument has not been much pressed in these cases that the defendant's charter deprives the plaintiffs of their property without due process of law, or that it denies to them the equal protection of the law. The first of these paragraphs has been in the Constitution since the adoption of the 5th Amendment, as a restraint upon the Federal power. It is also to be found in some form of expression in the constitutions of nearly all the states, as a restraint upon the power of the states. This law, then, has practically been the same as it now is during the existence of the government, except so far as the present Amendment may place the restraining power over the states in this matter in the hands of the Federal government.

We are not without judicial interpretation, therefore, both state and national, of the meaning of this clause. And it is sufficient to say that under no construction of that provision that we have ever seen, or any that we deem admissible, can the restraint imposed by the state of Louisiana upon the exercise of their trade by the butchers of New Orleans be held to be a deprivation of property within the meaning of that provision.

"Nor shall any state deny to any person within its jurisdiction the equal protection of the laws."

In the light of the history of these amendments, and the pervading purpose of them, . . . it is not difficult to give a meaning to this clause. The existence of laws in the states where the newly emancipated negroes resided, which discriminated with gross injustice and hardship against them as a class, was the evil to be remedied by this clause, and by it such laws are forbidden.

If, however, the states did not conform their laws to its requirements, then by the 5th section of the article of amendment Congress was authorized to enforce it by suitable legislation. We doubt very much whether any action of a state not directed by way of discrimination against the negroes as a class, or on account of their race, will ever be held to come within the purview of this provision. It is so clearly a provision for that race and that emergency, that a strong case would be necessary for its application to any other. But as it is a state that is to be dealt with, and not alone the validity of its laws, we may safely leave that matter until Congress shall have exercised its power, or some case of state oppression, by denial of equal justice in its courts, shall have claimed a decision at our hands. We find no such case in the one before us, and we do not deem it necessary to go over the argument again, as it may have relation to this particular clause of the Amendment.

In the early history of the organization of the government, its statesmen seem to have divided on the line which should separate the powers of the national government from those of the state governments, and though this line has never been very well defined in public opinion, such a division has continued from that day to this.

The adoption of the first eleven amendments to the Constitution so soon after the original instrument was accepted shows a prevailing sense of danger at that time from the Federal power and it cannot be denied that such a jealousy continued to exist with many patriotic men until the breaking out of the late Civil War. It was then discovered that the true danger to the perpetuity of the Union was in the capacity of the state organizations to combine and concentrate all the powers of the state, and of contiguous states, for a determined resistance to the general government.

Unquestionably this has given great force to the argument, and added largely to the number of those who believe in the necessity of a strong national government.

But, however pervading this sentiment, and however it may have contributed to the adoption of the Amendments we have been considering, we do not see in those Amendments any purpose to destroy the main features of the general system. Under the pressure of all the excited feeling growing out of the war, our statesmen have still believed that the existence of the states with powers for domestic and local government, including the regulation of civil rights, the rights of person and of property, was essential to the perfect working of our complex form of government, though they have thought proper to impose additional limitations on the states, and to confer additional power on that of the nation.

But whatever fluctuations may be seen in the history of public opinion on this subject during the period of our national existence, we think it will be found that this court, so far as its functions required, has always held, with a steady and an even hand, the balance between state and Federal power, and we trust that such may continue to be the history of its relation to that subject so long as it shall have duties to perform which demand of it a construction of the Constitution, or of any of its parts.

The judgments of the Supreme Court of Louisiana in these cases are affirmed.

Mr. Justice Field, dissenting:

The question presented is . . . one of the gravest importance, not merely to the parties here, but to the whole country. It is nothing less than the question whether the recent Amendments to the Federal Constitution protect the citizens of the United States against the deprivation of their common rights by state legislation. In my judgment the 14th Amendment does afford such protection, and was so intended by the Congress which framed and the states which adopted it. . . .

The provisions of the Fourteenth Amendment, which is properly a supplement to the thirteenth, cover, in my judgment, the case before us, and inhibit any legislation which confers special and exclusive privileges like these under consideration. The Amendment was adopted to obviate objections which had been raised and pressed with great force to the validity of the civil rights act, and to place the common rights of the American citizens under the protection of the National government. It first declares that "all persons born or naturalized in the United States, and subject to the jurisdiction thereof, are citizens of the United States and of the state wherein they reside." It then declares that "No state shall make or enforce any law which shall abridge the privileges or immunity of citizens of the United States, nor shall any state deprive any person of life, liberty or property, without due process of law, nor deny to any person within its jurisdiction the equal protection of the laws." . . .

The first clause of the fourteenth Amendment . . . removes it from the region of discussion and doubt. It recognizes in express terms, if it does not create, citizens of the United States, and it makes their citizenship dependent upon the place of their birth, or the fact of their adoption, and not upon the Constitution or laws of any state or the condition of their ancestry. A citizen of a state is now only a citizen of the United States residing in that state. The fundamental rights, privileges, and immunities which belong to him as a free man and a free citizen, now belong to him as a citizen of the United States, and are not dependent upon his citizenship of any state. The exercise of these rights and privileges, and the degree of enjoyment received from such exercise, are always more or less affected by the condition and the local institutions of the state, or city, or town where he resides. They are thus affected in a state by the wisdom of its laws, the ability of its officers, the efficiency of its magistrates, the education and morals of its people, and by many other considerations. This is a result which follows from the constitution of society, and can never be avoided, but in no other way can they be affected by the action of the

state, or by the residence of the citizen therein. They do not derive their existence from its legislation, and cannot be destroyed by its power. . . .

[G]rants of exclusive privileges, such as is made by the act in question, are opposed to the whole theory of free government, and it requires no aid from any bill of rights to render them void. That only is a free government, in the American sense of the term, under which the inalienable right of every citizen to pursue his happiness is unrestrained, except by just, equal, and impartial laws.

Mr. Justice Bradley, dissenting:

The [Fourteenth] Amendment . . . prohibits any state from depriving any person (citizen or otherwise) of life, liberty or property, without due process of law.

In my view, a law which prohibits a large class of citizens from adopting a lawful employment, or from following a lawful employment previously adopted, does deprive them of liberty as well as property, without due process of law. Their right of choice is a portion of their liberty; their occupation is their property. Such a law also deprives those citizens of the equal protection of the laws, contrary to the last clause of the section.

The constitutional question is distinctly raised in these cases; the constitutional right is expressly claimed; it was violated by state law, which was sustained by the state court, and we are called upon in a legitimate and proper way to afford redress. Our jurisdiction and our duty are plain and imperative.

It is futile to argue that none but persons of the African race are intended to be benefited by this Amendment. They may have been the primary cause of the Amendment, but its language is general, embracing all citizens, and I think it was purposely so expressed.

The mischief to be remedied was not merely slavery and its incidents and consequences; but that spirit of insubordination and disloyalty to the national government which had troubled the country for so many years in some of the states, and that intolerance of free speech and free discussion which often rendered life and property insecure, and led to much unequal legislation. The Amendment was an attempt to give voice to the strong national yearning for that time and that condition of things, in which American citizenship should be a sure guaranty of safety, and in which every citizen of the United States might stand erect in every portion of its soil, in the full enjoyment of every right and privilege belonging to a freeman, without fear of violence or molestation.

But great fears are expressed that this construction of the Amendment will lead to enactments by Congress interfering with the internal affairs of the states, and establishing therein civil and criminal codes of law for the government of the citizens, and thus abolishing the state governments in everything but name; or else, that it will lead the Federal courts to draw to their cognizance the supervision of state tribunals on every subject of judicial inquiry, on the plea of ascertaining whether the privileges and immunities of citizens have not been abridged.

In my judgment no such practical inconveniences would arise. Very little, if any, legislation on the part of Congress would be required to carry the Amendment into effect. Like the prohibition against passing a law impairing the obligation of a contract, it would execute itself. The point would be regularly raised in a suit at law, and settled by final reference to the Federal Court. As the privileges and immunities protected are only those fundamental ones which belong to every citizen, they would soon become so far defined as to cause but a slight accumulation of business in the Federal Courts. Besides, the recognized existence of the law would prevent its frequent violation. But even if the business of the national courts should be increased, Congress could easily supply the remedy by increasing their number and efficiency. The great question is: what is the true construction of the Amendment? When once we find that, we shall find the means of giving it effect. The argument from inconvenience ought not to have a very controlling influence in questions of this sort. The national will and national interest are of far greater importance.

In my opinion the judgment of the Supreme Court of Louisiana ought to be reversed.

The *Slaughterhouse* opinions are significant for several reasons. First, as Sheldon Goldman noted, "It was supreme irony that the first case to confront the Court with putting concrete meaning into the Fourteenth Amendment was brought by whites, not blacks."[5] This irony did not escape Miller, who relied "strongly on historical memory" to stress the true purpose of the amendment—to protect blacks. By using the "history of the day . . . fresh within the memory of us all," Miller refuted Campbell's basic position.[6] Next, he demolished the attorney's application of the specific guarantees to the dispute at hand. He spent the most energy on the primary claim of privileges and immunities (truly emasculating the clause), but he also rejected the Due Process Clause claim. Why did Miller take such a hard-

line position? In large measure, he did not want to see the Court become a "super legislature," a censor on what states could and could not do.

The Beginning of Substantive Due Process: The Court Opens a Window

Miller's opinion in *Slaughterhouse*, taken in conjunction with Bradley's (and Field's) dissent, are clear statements of the Court's initial rejection and acceptance of substantive due process. Indeed, Bradley and Miller (and later Field) are considered to represent the epitome of opposing views on the subject *(see box, page 430)*.

It was Miller's view, however, that for the moment carried the day—there was no substance in due process. Given the terse language of the opinion, we might suspect that it closed the book on the subject forever. But that was not the case. He observed just five years later:

5. Goldman, *Constitutional Law,* 195
6. Gunther, *Constitutional Law,* 408.

It is not a little remarkable, that while [due process] has been in the Constitution . . . as a restraint upon the authority of the Federal government, for nearly a century . . . its powers ha[d] rarely been invoked in the judicial forum or the more enlarged theatre of public discussion. But while it has been a part of the Constitution, as a restraint upon the power of the States, only a very few years, the docket of this court is crowded with cases in which we are asked to hold that State courts and State legislatures have deprived their own citizens of life, liberty, or property without due process of law. There is here abundant evidence that there exists some strange misconception of the scope of this provision as found in the fourteenth amendment.[7]

Why was it necessary for Miller to write this? Had not *Slaughterhouse* eradicated the notion of the Fourteenth Amendment's Due Process Clause as a prohibition of state economic regulation?

It had, but that did not prevent attorneys, representing increasingly desperate business interests, from making substantive due process arguments. From their perspective, the current environment held promise for the eventual adoption of such arguments. Within legal circles, for example, there was much discussion of several theories that lent themselves to Bradley's dissenting position in *Slaughterhouse*. One was expressed in Thomas M. Cooley's influential *Constitutional Limitations,* which elevated the word *liberty* within the Due Process Clause as an important constitutional right. The protection of this right, in Cooley's eyes, required a substantive reading of the Fourteenth Amendment, which, in turn, would serve as a mechanism for protecting property rights and "as a much-needed barrier to unwarranted government interference with pri-

vate enterprise."[8] While Cooley's theory was rather specific, Herbert Spencer offered a more general view. Called "social Darwinism," it treated social evolution in the same terms as Darwin wrote about biological evolution: "If left to themselves, the best of mankind, 'the fittest' would survive and prosper."[9] This proposition had a natural compatibility with laissez-faire economic theories: if government leaves business alone, the best will prosper. Applying substantive due process would persuade government to leave business alone.

But perhaps the most important factor contributing to the vitality of substantive due process was the Court. Social Darwinism may have influenced some scholars, the social elite, and business, but most Americans did not buy its tenets.[10] If they had, states would not have kept on trying to regulate businesses; the public would have demanded policies of noninterference. But they did continue. To a large extent, the crowded docket to which Miller referred was the Court's own doing.

An important, and certainly vivid, example of how the Court encouraged substantive due process arguments came in *Munn v. Illinois*. This decision cut both ways: the Court upheld the state's regulation but provided enough of a loophole for clever attorneys to exploit later. What was that loophole? One way to answer this question is to reconsider Miller's opinion in *Slaughterhouse* as you read *Munn*. Do you spot any differences?

7. *Davidson v. New Orleans*, 96 U.S. 97 (1878).

8. Goldman, *Constitutional Law*, 380.
9. Walter F. Murphy, James E. Fleming, and William F. Harris II, *American Constitutional Interpretation* (Mineola, N.Y.: Foundation Press, 1986), 942.
10. Ibid.

Munn v. Illinois

94 U.S. 113 (1877)

*Vote: 7 (Bradley, Clifford, Davis, Hunt,
        Miller, Swayne, Waite)
      2 (Field, Strong)
Opinion of the Court: Waite
Dissenting opinion: Field*

While the industrial revolution affected much of the nation, its impact on the city of Chicago was monumental. Primarily because of its status as a "key transfer point for transcontinental trade," particularly for the grain market, Chicago was becoming the "New York of the West."[11] Grain produced by farmers in the Midwest would flow into Chicago and then be shipped to merchants throughout the United States. As a result, a "most lucrative business" developed in Chicago—the "storing of grain . . . until it was sold and shipped." Typically, companies stored the goods in warehouses that looked like huge skyscrapers. They were called grain elevators because of the way the grain "was mechanically loaded by dump baskets fastened to conveyor belts."

A dozen or more grain storage companies sprang up in Chicago. Among the most successful was Munn & Scott, co-owned by Ira Munn. He started with one warehouse able to store 8,000 bushels of grain, but within a few short years, Munn was overseeing an enterprise with four elevators and a storage capacity of 2,700,000 bushels. He was, in short, a very successful entrepreneur.

Despite his success, Munn (along with many others) grew corrupt and engaged in fraudulent business practices. He charged exorbitantly high fees, mixed inferior with superior grain, and engaged in price fixing with other companies. As

11. We adapt this discussion largely from C. Peter Magrath's "The Case of the Unscrupulous Warehouseman," in *Quarrels that Have Shaped the Constitution,* ed. John A. Garraty (New York: Harper & Row, 1987).

these abuses became more obvious, farmers and merchants pleaded with city officials to regulate the industry. After several ineffective attempts by a local board to do so, the state—under continued pressure from farmers' organizations (known as the Granger movement)—in 1871 enacted a law that included provisions establishing boards to regulate, among other aspects of the business, the maximum rates grain elevators could charge. The state justified the law as quite compatible with its constitution, which specified that public warehouses were subject to regulation.[12] Shortly after the act took effect, Munn went into bankruptcy, amid allegations of ethical and professional violations. The company that took over his warehouses also refused to comply with the act and challenged it as a violation of the Fourteenth Amendment's Due Process Clause.

Chief Justice Morrison R. Waite delivered the opinion of the Court:

The question to be determined in this case is whether the General Assembly of Illinois can, under the limitations upon the legislative power of the States imposed by the Constitution of the United States, fix by law the maximum of charges for the storage of grain in warehouses at Chicago and other places in the State having not less than one hundred thousand inhabitants, "in which grain is stored in bulk, and in which the grain of different owners is mixed together, or in which grain is stored in such a manner that the identity of different lots or parcels cannot be accurately preserved."

It is claimed that such a law is repugnant. . . .

To that part of amendment 14, which ordains that no State shall "Deprive any person of life, liberty or property, without due process of law, nor deny to any person within its jurisdiction the equal protection of the laws." . . .

The Constitution contains no definition of the word "deprive," as used in the Fourteenth Amendment. To determine its signification, therefore, it is necessary to

12. See Goldman, *Constitutional Law,* 387.

In the late nineteenth century, grain elevators, used to store grain until it was sold, were a common sight on the Chicago River. Ira Munn and George Scott's grain elevators (at right) were among the most successful, until Munn's corrupt business practices brought the industry under government scrutiny.

ascertain the effect which usage has given it, when employed in the same or a like connection.

While this provision of the Amendment is new in the Constitution of the United States as a limitation upon the powers of the States, it is old as a principle of civilized government. It is found in Magna Charta, and, in substance if not in form, in nearly or quite all the constitutions that have been from time to time adopted by the several States of the Union. By the 5th Amendment, it was introduced into the Constitution of the United States as a limitation upon the powers of the National Government, and by the Fourteenth, as a guaranty against any encroachment upon an acknowledged right of citizenship by the Legislatures of the States. . . .

[I]t is apparent that, down to the time of the adoption of the Fourteenth Amendment, it was not supposed that statutes regulating the use, or even the price of the use, of private property necessarily deprived an owner of his property without due process of law. Under some circumstances they may, but not under all. The Amendment does not change the law in this particular; it simply prevents the States from doing that which will operate as such a deprivation.

This brings us to inquire as to the principles upon which this power of regulation rests, in order that we may determine what is within and what without its operative effect. Looking, then, to the common law, from whence came the right which the Constitution protects, we find that when private property is "affected with a public interest, it ceases to be juris privati only." . . . Property does become clothed with a public interest when used in a manner to make it of public consequence, and affect the community at large. When, therefore, one devotes his property to a use in which the public has an interest, he, in effect, grants to the public an interest in that use, and must submit to be controlled by the public for the common good, to the extent of the interest he has thus created. He may withdraw his grant by discontinuing the use; but, so long as he maintains the use, he must submit to the control. . . .

[W]hen private property is devoted to a public use, it is subject to public regulation. It remains only to ascertain whether the warehouses of these plaintiffs in error, and the business which is carried on there, come within the operation of this principle.

For this purpose, we accept as true the statements of fact contained in the elaborate brief of one of the counsel of the plaintiffs in error. From this it appears that ". . . the trade in grain is carried on by the inhabitants of seven or eight of the great States of the West with four or five of the States lying on the seashore, and forms the largest part of interstate commerce in these States. The grain warehouses or elevators in Chicago are immense structures, holding from 300,000 to 1,000,000 bushels at one time, according to size. They are divided into bins of large capacity and great strength. . . . They are located with the river harbor on one side and the railway tracks on the other; and the grain is run through them from car to vessel, or boat to car, as may be demanded in the course of business. It has been found impossible to preserve each owner's grain separate, and this has given rise to a system of inspection and grading, by which the grain of different owners is mixed, and receipts issued for the number of bushels which are negotiable, and redeemable in like kind, upon demand. This mode of conducting the business was inaugurated more than twenty years ago, and has grown to immense proportions. The railways have found it impracticable to own such elevators, and public policy forbids the transaction of such business by the carrier; the ownership has, therefore, been by private individuals, who have embarked their capital and devoted their industry to such business as a private pursuit." . . .

Under such circumstances it is difficult to see why, if the common carrier, or the miller, or the ferryman, or the innkeeper, or the wharfinger, or the baker, or the cartman, or the hackney-coachman, pursues a public employment and exercises "a sort of public office," these plaintiffs in error do not. They stand, to use again the language of their counsel, in the very "gateway of commerce," and take toll from all who pass. Their business most certainly "tends to a common charge, and is become a thing of public interest and use." Every bushel of grain for its passage "pays a toll, which is a common charge," and, therefore . . . every such warehouseman "ought to be under public regulation, viz.: that he . . . take but reasonable toll." Certainly, if any business can be clothed "with a public interest, and cease to be juris privati only," this has been. It may not be made so by the operation of the Constitution of Illinois or this statute, but it is by the facts. . . .

We conclude, therefore, that the statute in question is not repugnant to the Constitution of the United States, and that there is no error in the judgment. In passing upon this case we have not been unmindful of the vast importance of the questions involved. This and cases of a kindred character were argued before us more than a year ago by the most eminent counsel, and in a manner worthy of their well earned reputations. We have kept the cases long under advisement, in order that their decision might be the result of our mature deliberations.

The judgment is affirmed.

To return to our question, what was the loophole in Waite's opinion? Like Miller, he seemed to reject substantive due process completely, asserting that most regulatory legislation should be presumed valid; indeed, the American Bar Association, which was then a newly formed organization and full of business-oriented attorneys, denounced the ruling as "barbarous" and vowed to see it overturned.[13] Also consider the statement in Justice Stephen J. Field's acrimonious dissent, which largely reflected Bradley's in *Slaughterhouse:* the law was "nothing less than a bold assertion of absolute power by the state to control at its discretion the property and business of the citizen." So it is not surprising that Waite's majority opinion "has generally been regarded as a great victory for liberalism and a judicial refusal to recognize due process as a limit on the substance of legislative regulatory power."[14]

But is that description precise? Not exactly. Although Waite could have taken the same approach as Miller in *Slaughterhouse*—the complete rejection of the due process claim—he did not. Instead, Waite qualified his opinion, asserting first that state regulations of private property were "not supposed" to deprive owners of their right to due process, but that "under some circumstances they may." What differentiated "some circumstances" from others? In Waite's opinion, the answer lay in the nature of the subject of the regulation: "We find that when private property is 'affected with a public interest it ceases to be [of private right] only.'" Waite used this doctrine, often called the business-affected-with-a-public-interest doctrine (BAPI), to find against Munn's claim.

But is not the doctrine also the source of the problem? Could it not be used to support the claim as well? Justice Field thought so, for in his dissent he found BAPI useless: "There is hardly an

enterprise or business engaging the attention and labor of any considerable portion of the community, in which the public has not an interest in the sense in which that term is used by the court." Hence, however unwittingly, Waite's opinion (with Field's dissent) provided the loophole "lawyers with business clients unhappy with state regulation" attempted to open even further.[15] By avoiding a hard-line stance of the sort taken by Miller in *Slaughterhouse,* Waite's "maybe yes, maybe no" approach in the end *"seemed* to concede *some* scope for the concept of substantive due process."[16]

In two cases, coming a decade or so after *Munn,* the Court moved closer to the concession only implied by Waite. In the first, *Mugler v. Kansas* (1887), the Court considered a state law that prohibited the manufacture and sale of liquor. Although the majority upheld the regulation against a substantive due process challenge, the Court's opinion represented something of a break from *Munn.* First, it articulated the view that not "every statute enacted ostensibly for the promotion of [the public interest] is to be accepted as a legitimate exertion of police powers of the state." This opinion was far more explicit than Waite's: there were clear limits of state regulatory power. Second, and more important, it took precisely the opposite position from the majority in *Slaughterhouse.* Recall that Justice Miller wanted to avoid the Court being placed in the position of a "super legislature," scrutinizing and perhaps censoring state action. But in *Mugler,* that is precisely what the Court said it would do:

There are . . . limits beyond which legislation cannot rightfully go. . . . If, therefore, a statute purporting to have been enacted to protect the public health, the public morals, or the public safety, has no real or substantial relation to those objects, or is a palpable invasion of rights secured by the fundamental law, *it is* the

---

13. C. Herman Pritchett, *The American Constitution* (New York: McGraw-Hill, 1959), 558.
14. Ibid., 557.

15. Hall, *The Magic Mirror,* 234.
16. Goldman, *Constitutional Law,* 385.

duty of the *courts to so adjudge,* and thereby give effect to the Constitution. (Emphasis added.)

In *Mugler* the Court did not fully adopt the doctrine of substantive due process; it even upheld the state regulation on liquor. It also established its intent to review legislation to determine whether it was a "reasonable" exercise of state power. In essence, the Court would balance the interests of the state against those of individual due process guarantees.

The legislation tested in *Mugler* was deemed reasonable, but in *Chicago, Milwaukee & St. Paul Railway v. Minnesota* (1890), decided three years after *Mugler,* the Court went the other way. For the first time, the justices struck down a state regulation on the grounds that it interfered with due process guarantees. At first glance, *Chicago, Milwaukee & St. Paul Railway* bears a distinct resemblance to *Munn v. Illinois.* Strong lobbying efforts by farm groups led Minnesota in 1887 to establish a commission to set "equal and reasonable" rates for railroad transportation of goods and for warehouse storage. The commission received a complaint that the Chicago, Milwaukee, and St. Paul Railway Company was charging dairy farmers unreasonable rates to ship their milk. It held hearings to investigate the claim and ruled against the railroad. When the company refused to abide by the ruling and reduce its rates, the commission went to the state supreme court. In the opinion of that tribunal, the commission's enabling legislation intended that the rates it "recommended and published" were to be "not simply advisory . . . but final and conclusive as to what are equal and reasonable charges." The railroad took its case to the U.S. Supreme Court, where it argued that the commission had interfered with "its property" without providing it with due process of law.

Writing for the majority, Justice Samuel Blatchford held for the railroad on two grounds, both centering on the Fourteenth Amendment's Due Process Clause. Procedurally, he found the law—at least as construed by the state supreme court—defective. Because courts could not review the rates the commission set, the law deprived the railroad of a certain degree of fairness. On this point, the Court took a "traditional" approach to due process, asserting that "procedural safeguards" must be "attached to public expropriations of private property."[17] But Blatchford did not stop there; rather, he examined the law in terms of the reasonableness standard promulgated in *Mugler:*

The question of the reasonableness of a rate of charge for transportation by a railroad company . . . is eminently a question for judicial investigation, requiring due process of law for its determination.

In so doing, he found that it deprived the company of its property in an unfair way:

If the company is deprived of the power of charging reasonable rates . . . and such deprivation takes place in the absence of an investigation by judicial machinery, it is deprived of the lawful use of its property, and thus, in substance and effect, of the property itself, without due process of law.

The *Chicago, Milwaukee & St. Paul Railway* case was not all that extraordinary: it merely applied the standard articulated in *Mugler,* a standard that obviously cut both ways. Sometimes the Court, in its attempt to inquire (balance interests), would find a law a "reasonable" use of state power *(Mugler),* and sometimes it would find it violative of substantive due process guarantees, as it did here. But this case and, to a lesser extent, *Mugler,* were remarkable if we consider how different they were from *Slaughterhouse.* Over a seventeen-year period, the Court had moved from a refusal to inject substance into due process to a near affirmation of the doctrine of substantive due process; it had moved from the assertion that it would not become a censor to one arguing that

17. Hall, *The Magic Mirror,* 236.

Table 9-2 The U.S. Supreme Court: From *Slaughterhouse* to *Mugler*

The *Slaughterhouse* Court (1873)	The *Mugler* Court (1887)
Chase[1]	Waite
Hunt	Blatchford
Clifford	Gray
Strong	Woods
Miller	Miller
Bradley[1]	Bradley
Swayne[1]	Matthews
Davis	Harlan
Field[1]	Field

1. In minority in *Slaughterhouse*.

judicial inquiry was necessary, if not mandated, by the Constitution. And although, as we shall see, it did not fully endorse Thomas Cooley's position defining due process "liberty" in economic terms until seven years later, Blatchford's ruling "cleared the ground" for exactly that.[18]

This change in position prompts us to ask why the Court did such a turnabout over two decades. The most obvious answer is personnel changes. As the data in Table 9-2 show, by the time the Court decided *Mugler,* only one member of the *Slaughterhouse* majority, Miller, remained. By 1890 Miller also was gone, as was Chief Justice Waite, who, despite the loophole in the *Munn* opinion, generally favored state regulatory power. Their replacements were quite different. Many had been corporate attorneys schooled in the philosophies of Cooley and Herbert Spencer and quite willing to borrow "liberally from the briefs" of their former colleagues who argued against state regulation.[19] Justice David J. Brewer, who replaced Stanley Matthews, a moderate-conservative states' rights advocate, had "refused to follow" *Munn* as a court of appeals judge. It is not surprising that many

18. Ibid.
19. Ibid., 234.

eagerly awaited the *Chicago, Milwaukee & St. Paul Railway* decision as "the first indication of how recent changes in personnel might have affected the Court's view."[20] Given the backgrounds of the new appointees, it also is not surprising to find that the views of the *Slaughterhouse* dissenters—especially Field and Bradley—went on to rule the day.

But there may have been more to it. By asserting the standard they did, the Court was engaging in extreme judicial activism. Peter Woll wrote:

By substituting its judgment for that of state legislators in determining the fairness of regulations of property and liberty under the due process clause of the Fourteenth Amendment, the Court was acting contrary to the public opinion that spurred state regulation. Political pressures upon state legislatures throughout the country had resulted in laws regulating business which courts were unwilling to sustain.[21]

It seems fair to say that the justices did not see it this way. Rather, they viewed these "political pressures" as just that, as particularized, radical "socialistic" elements that did not reflect majority interests. If this was their perception, it had a solid foundation. Some legislation had resulted from the lobbying efforts of farm and labor movements and later, as we shall see, of the Progressives and New Dealers. In the minds of many conservatives of the day, including some of the justices, such pressures were illegitimate because they sought to subvert the free enterprise system. In short, while the Populists, Progressives, and New Dealers, in the opinion of conservatives, tried to put the brakes on businesses and inculcate the government with socialistic legislation, the conservatives strongly believed that the best interests of the country lay with "an utterly free market, unfettered by governmental regulation."

20. Arnold M. Paul, *Conservative Crisis and the Rule of Law* (Ithaca, N.Y.: Cornell University Press, 1960), 42.
21. Peter Woll, *Constitutional Law* (Englewood Cliffs, N.J.: Prentice-Hall, 1981), 486.

This, not the plans of radicals, was "more just and socially useful" because in the end all would benefit financially.[22]

A fundamental change was in the wind, and

22. Craig R. Ducat and Harold W. Chase, *Constitutional Interpretation* (St. Paul, Minn.: West Publishing, 1988), 559.

many point to the Court's decision in *Allgeyer v. Louisiana* (1897) as the turning point. What did the Court say here that it had not fully articulated in cases like *Mugler* and *Chicago, Milwaukee & St. Paul Railway?*

Allgeyer v. Louisiana

165 U.S. 578 (1897)

Vote: 9 (Brewer, Brown, Field, Fuller, Gray, Harlan, Peckham, Shiras, White)

0

Opinion of the Court: Peckham

With the alleged purpose of protecting against fraud, Louisiana enacted a law that barred its citizens and corporations from doing business with out-of-state insurance companies, unless they complied with a specified set of requirements. State attorneys alleged that the Allgeyer Company had violated the law by maintaining an insurance policy with a New York mail order agency.

Rather than argue that it was innocent of the charge, the company challenged the constitutionality of the law on Fourteenth Amendment due process grounds. In its view, the term *liberty* included the right to use and enjoy all "endowments" without constraint and that the term *property* included the right to acquire it and engage in business. Here, Allgeyer's attorney alleged, the law acts as a significant and unconstitutional curtailment of the business activity of the company.

Justice Rufus W. Peckham delivered the opinion of the Court:

The question presented is the simple proposition whether under the act a party while in the state can insure property in Louisiana in a foreign insurance company, which has not complied with the laws of the state, under an open policy, the special contract or

insurance and the open policy being contracts made and entered into beyond the limits of the state. . . .

It is natural that the state court should have remarked that there is in this "statute an apparent interference with the liberty of defendants in restricting their rights to place insurance on property of their own whenever and in what company they desired." Such interference is not only apparent, but it is real, and we do not think that it is justified for the purpose of upholding what the state says is its policy with regard to foreign insurance companies which had not complied with the laws of the state for doing business within its limits. In this case the company did no business within the state, and the contracts were not therein made.

The supreme court of Louisiana says that the act of writing, within that state, the letter of notification, was an act therein done to effect an insurance on property then in the state, in a marine insurance company which had not complied with its laws, and such act was therefore prohibited by the statute. As so construed we think the statute is a violation of the 14th Amendment of the Federal Constitution, in that it deprives the defendants of their liberty without due process of law. The statute which forbids such act does not become due process of law, because it is inconsistent with the provisions of the Constitution of the Union. The liberty mentioned in that amendment means, not only the right of the citizen to be free from the mere physical restraint of his person, as by incarceration, but the term is deemed to embrace the right of the citizen to be free in the enjoyment of all his faculties; to be free to use them in all lawful ways; to live and work where he will; to earn his livelihood by any lawful calling; to pursue any livelihood or avocation, and for that purpose to enter into all contracts which may be proper, necessary, and essential to his carrying out to a successful conclusion the purposes above mentioned.

It was said by Mr. Justice Bradley in *Butchers' Union S. H. & L. S. L. Co.* v. *Crescent City L. S. L. & S. H. Co. [Slaughterhouse Cases]*, in the course of his concurring opinion in that case, that "the right to follow any of the common occupations of life is an inalienable right. It was formulated as such under the phrase 'pursuit of happiness' in the Declaration of Independence, which commenced with the fundamental proposition that 'all men are created equal, that they are endowed by their Creator with certain inalienable rights; and among these are life, liberty, and the pursuit of happiness.' This right is a large ingredient in the civil liberty of the citizen." Again, the learned justice said: "I hold that the liberty of pursuit—the right to follow any of the ordinary callings of life—is one of the privileges of a citizen of the United States." And again, "But if it does not abridge the privileges and immunities of a citizen of the United States to prohibit him from pursuing his chosen calling, and giving to others the exclusive right of pursuing it, it certainly does deprive him, to a certain extent, of his liberty; for it takes from him the freedom of adopting and following the pursuit which he prefers; which, as already intimated, is a material part of the liberty of the citizen." It is true that these remarks were made in regard to questions of monopoly, but they well describe the rights which are covered by the word "liberty" as contained in the 14th Amendment. . . .

The foregoing extracts have been made for the purpose of showing what general definitions have been given in regard to the meaning of the word "liberty" as used in the amendment, but we do not intend to hold that in no such case can the state exercise its police power. When and how far such power may be legitimately exercised with regard to these subjects may be left for determination to each case as it arises.

Has not a citizen of a state, under the provisions of the Federal Constitution above mentioned, a right to contract outside of the state for insurance on his property—a right of which state legislation cannot deprive him? We are not alluding to acts done within the state by an insurance company or its agents doing business therein, which are in violation of the state statutes . . . and would be controlled by it. When we speak of the liberty to contract for insurance or to do an act to effectuate such a contract already existing, we refer to and have in mind the facts of this case, where the contract was made outside the state, and as such was a valid and proper contract. The act done within the limits of the state under the circumstances of this case and for the purpose therein mentioned, we hold a proper act, one which the defendants were at liberty to perform and which the state legislature had no right to prevent, at least with reference to the Federal Constitution. To deprive the citizen of such a right as herein described without due process of law is illegal. Such a statute as this in question is not due process of law, because it prohibits an act which under the Federal Constitution the defendants had a right to perform. This does not interfere in any way with the acknowledged right of the state to enact such legislation in the legitimate exercise of its police or other powers as to it may seem proper. In the exercise of such right, however, care must be taken not to infringe upon those other rights of the citizen which are protected by the Federal Constitution.

In the privilege of pursuing an ordinary calling or trade and of acquiring, holding, and selling property must be embraced the right to make all proper contracts in relation thereto, and although it may be conceded that this right to contract in relation to persons or property or to do business within the jurisdiction of the state may be regulated and sometimes prohibited when the contracts or business conflict with the policy of the state as contained in the statutes, yet the power does not and cannot extend to prohibiting the citizen from making contracts of the nature involved in this case outside of the limits and jurisdiction of the state, and which are also to be performed outside of such jurisdiction; nor can the state legally prohibit its citizens from doing such an act as writing this letter of notification, even though the property which is the subject of the insurance may at the time when such insurance attaches be within the limits of the state. The mere fact that a citizen may be within the limits of a particular state does not prevent his making a contract outside its limits while he himself remains within it. The contract in this case was thus made. It was a valid contract, made outside of the state, to be performed outside of the state, although the subject was property temporarily within the state. As the contract was valid in the place where made and where it was to be performed, the party to the contract upon whom is devolved the right or duty to send the notification in order that the insurance provided for by the contract may attach to the property specified in the shipment mentioned in the notice, must have the liberty to do that act and to give that notification within the limits of the state, any prohibition of the state statute to the contrary notwithstanding.

Peckham's opinion is not so different from the majority's opinion in *Chicago, Milwaukee & St. Paul Railway.* He struck down the state law in part on the grounds that it was not reasonable. But he went much further. By merging substantive due process with freedom of contract, by reading the term *liberty* to mean economic liberty, encompassing the right to "enter into all contracts," Peckham's opinion was "forceful," to say the least.[23] He adopted the position that businesses had been pressing since the demise of the Contract Clause as a source of protection. Now their right to do business, to set their own rates and enter into contracts with other businesses and perhaps even with employees, had the highest level of legal protection. In just under twenty-five years, business interests had pushed the Court from *Slaughterhouse,* in which it refused to review state legislation for its compatibility with due process guarantees to *Munn,* in which legislation was presumed valid *generally,* but was open to judicial inquiry into its "reasonableness." The Court then moved from a balancing of state versus individual interests *(Chicago, Milwaukee & St. Paul Railway)* to placing state regulations in a less exalted position than the fundamental liberty of contract *(Allgeyer).*

The Roller Coaster Ride of Substantive Due Process: 1898-1923

However explicit *Allgeyer* was, the true test of its importance would come in its application.

23. Melvin I. Urofsky, *A March of Liberty* (New York: Knopf, 1988), 500.

Some read it to mean that the Court rarely would uphold legislation that infringed on economic "liberty," but *Holden v. Hardy,* decided the very next year, dispelled this notion. In this case, the Court examined a Utah law prohibiting companies engaged in the excavation of mines from working its employees more than eight hours a day, except in emergency situations. Attorneys challenging the law claimed that

[i]t is . . . not within the power of the legislature to prevent persons who are . . . perfectly competent to contract, from entering into employment and voluntarily making contracts in relation thereto merely because the employment . . . may be considered by the legislature to be dangerous or injurious to the health of the employee; and if such right to contract cannot be prevented, it certainly cannot be restricted by the legislature to suit its own ideas of the ability of the employee to stand the physical and mental strain incident to the work.

The state asserted that the challenged statute was a "health regulation" and within the state's power because it was aimed at "preserving to a citizen his ability to work and support himself."

In *Holden* the Court reiterated its *Mugler* position:

The question in each case is whether the legislature has adopted the statute in exercise of a reasonable discretion or whether its actions be a mere excuse for an unjust discrimination.

The Supreme Court, now acting as the nation's "super legislature," deemed the legislation "reasonable"; that is, it did not impinge on the liberty of contract because the state had well justified its interest in the ''special health problems'' of mine workers.[24]

Holden was a victory for emerging labor groups and the still-forming Progressive Movement, which were vigorously lobbying state legislatures to pass laws protecting workers. As the industrial revolution wore on, they argued, such laws were becoming increasingly important because corporations were even more profit-oriented and, as a result, more likely to exploit

24. Goldman, *Constitutional Law*, 381.

employees. While they succeeded in convincing many state legislatures to enact laws like Utah's, the possibility that courts would strike them down remained a threat. *Holden* had proven otherwise.

That ruling, however, took on a different gloss once the Court decided *Lochner v. New York* (1905). Although the law at issue varied only slightly from Utah's, the justices reached a wholly different conclusion. Why? Does the case fit compatibly with the logic of *Holden,* as Justice Peckham implies, or does it reveal the true reach of his ruling in *Allgeyer?*

Lochner v. New York

198 U.S. 45 (1905)

Vote: 5 (Brewer, Brown, Fuller, McKenna, Peckham)
4 (Day, Harlan, Holmes, White)
Opinion of the Court: Peckham
Dissenting opinions: Harlan, Holmes

In 1897 New York enacted a law that prohibited employees of bakeries from working more than ten hours per day and sixty hours per week. The state justified the law on the following grounds:

(1) Police power is necessarily invoked to control work conditions in a ''great commercial and manufacturing State'' like New York. The police power here reflects community standards and is properly exercised by an elected body that is aware of unique local conditions.

(2) New York, through its use of the police power, protects both consumers and workers from bad health and sickness; therefore, this law is a health measure.

After he was convicted of violating the law, Joseph Lochner, the owner of a New York bakery, challenged it on Fourteenth Amendment due process grounds. In part, he alleged that

(1) Employees and employer have the right to agree upon hours and wages, and the use of the

police power by New York to interfere with such agreements is so ''paternal'' as to violate the Fourteenth Amendment.

(2) Regardless of the state's asserted interests, the ''most cherished rights of American citizenship''—freedom of contract and property rights—''should be most closely and jealously scrutinized by this court.'' Since the interests here are not sufficiently ''clear and apparent,'' the Court should strike the law.

Justice Peckham delivered the opinion of the Court:

The mandate of the statute, that ''no employee shall be required or permitted to work,'' is the substantial equivalent of an enactment that ''no employee shall contract or agree to work,'' more than ten hours per day; and, as there is no provision for special emergencies, the statute is mandatory in all cases. It is not an act merely fixing the number of hours which shall constitute a legal day's work, but an absolute prohibition upon the employer permitting, under any circumstances, more than ten hours' work to be done in his establishment. The employee may desire to earn the extra money which would arise from his working more than the prescribed time, but this statute forbids the employer from permitting the employee to earn it.

The statute necessarily interferes with the right of

After Joseph Lochner, the owner of a bakery located in Utica, New York, was convicted of violating a state maximum hour work law, he asked the U.S. Supreme Court to strike it down as violative of his constitutional rights. In Lochner v. New York (1905), the justices agreed. The majority found that the law impermissibly interfered with the right of employers to enter into contracts with their employees.

contract between the employer and employees, concerning the number of hours in which the latter may labor in the bakery of the employer. The general right to make a contract in relation to his business is part of the liberty of the individual protected by the 14th Amendment of the Federal Constitution. *Allgeyer* v. *Louisiana*. Under that provision no state can deprive any person of life, liberty, or property without due process of law. The right to purchase or to sell labor is part of the liberty protected by this amendment, unless there are circumstances which exclude the right. There are, however, certain powers, existing in the sovereignty of each state in the Union, somewhat vaguely termed police powers, the exact description and limitation of which have not been attempted by the courts. Those powers, broadly stated, and without, at present, any attempt at a more specific limitation, relate to the safety, health, morals, and general welfare of the public. Both property and liberty are held on such reasonable conditions as may be imposed by the governing power of the state in the exercise of those powers, and with such conditions the 14th Amendment was not designed to interfere.

The state, therefore, has power to prevent the individual from making certain kinds of contracts, and in regard to them the Federal Constitution offers no protection. If the contract be one which the state, in the legitimate exercise of its police power, has the right to prohibit, it is not prevented from prohibiting it by the 14th Amendment. Contracts in violation of a statute, either of the Federal or state government, or a contract to let one's property for immoral purposes, or to do any other unlawful act, could obtain no protection from the Federal Constitution, as coming under the liberty of person or of free contract. Therefore, when the state, by its legislature, in the assumed exercise of its police powers, has passed an act which seriously limits the right to labor or the right of contract in regard to their means of livelihood between persons who are *sui juris* (both employer and employee), it becomes of great importance to determine which shall prevail,—the right of the individual to labor for such time as he may choose, or the right of the state to prevent the individual from laboring, or from entering into any contract to labor, beyond a certain time prescribed by the state.

This court has recognized the existence and upheld the exercise of the police powers of the states in many cases which might fairly be considered as border ones, and it has, in the course of its determination of questions regarding the asserted invalidity of such statutes, on the ground of their violation of the rights secured by the Federal Constitution, been guided by rules of a very liberal nature, the application of which has resulted, in numerous instances, in upholding the validity of state statutes thus assailed. Among the later cases where the state law has been upheld by this court is that of *Holden* v. *Hardy*. A provision in the act of the legislature of Utah was there under consideration, the act limiting the employment of workmen in all underground mines or workings, to eight hours per day, "except in cases of emergency, where life or property is in imminent danger." It also limited the hours of labor in smelting and other institutions for the reduction or refining of ores or metals to eight hours per day, except in like cases of emergency. The act was held to be a valid exercise of the police powers of the state . . . [because the] law applies only to the classes subjected by their employment to the peculiar conditions and effects attending underground mining and work in smelters, and other works for the reduction and refining of ores. Therefore it is not necessary to discuss or decide whether the legislature can fix the hours of labor in other employments. . . .

It must, of course, be conceded that there is a limit to the valid exercise of the police power by the state. There is no dispute concerning this general proposition. Otherwise the 14th Amendment would have no efficacy and the legislatures of the states would have unbounded power, and it would be enough to say that any piece of legislation was enacted to conserve the morals, the health, or the safety of the people; such legislation would be valid, no matter how absolutely without foundation the claim might be. The claim of the police power would be a mere pretext,—become another and delusive name for the supreme sovereignty of the state to be exercised free from constitutional restraint. This is not contended for. In every case that comes before this court, therefore, where legislation of this character is concerned, and where the protection of the Federal Constitution is sought, the question necessarily arises: Is this a fair, reasonable, and appropriate exercise of the police power of the state, or is it an unreasonable, unnecessary, and arbitrary interference with the right of the individual to his personal liberty, or to enter into those contracts in relation to labor which may seem to him appropriate or necessary for the support of himself and his family? Of course the liberty of contract relating to labor includes both parties to it. The one has as much right to purchase as the other to sell labor.

This is not a question of substituting the judgment of the court for that of the legislature. If the act be within the power of the state it is valid, although the judgment of the court might be totally opposed to the enactment of such a law. But the question would still remain: Is it within the police power of the state? and that question must be answered by the court.

The question whether this act is valid as a labor law, pure and simple, may be dismissed in a few words. There is no reasonable ground for interfering with the liberty of person or the right of free contract, by determining the hours of labor, in the occupation of a baker. There is no contention that bakers as a class are not equal in intelligence and capacity to men in other trades or manual occupations, or that they are not able to assert their rights and care for themselves without the protecting arm of the state, interfering with their independence of judgment and of action. They are in no sense wards of the state. Viewed in the light of a purely labor law, with no reference whatever to the question of health, we think that a law like the one before us involves neither the safety, the morals, nor the welfare, of the public, and that the interest of the public is not in the slightest degree affected by such an act. The law must be upheld, if at all, as a law pertaining to the health of the individual engaged in the occupation of a baker. It does not affect any other portion of the public than those who are engaged in that occupation. Clean and wholesome bread does not depend upon whether the baker works but ten hours per day or only sixty hours a week. The limitation of the hours of labor does not come within the police power on that ground.

It is a question of which of two powers or rights shall prevail,—the power of the state to legislate or the right of the individual to liberty of person and freedom of contract. The mere assertion that the subject relates, though but in a remote degree, to the public health,

does not necessarily render the enactment valid. The act must have a more direct relation, as a means to an end, and the end itself must be appropriate and legitimate, before an act can be held to be valid which interferes with the general right of an individual to be free in his person and in his power to contract in relation to his own labor. . . .

We think the limit of the police power has been reached and passed in this case. There is, in our judgment, no reasonable foundation for holding this to be necessary or appropriate as a health law to safeguard the public health, or the health of the individuals who are following the trade of a baker. If this statute be valid, and if, therefore, a proper case is made out in which to deny the right of an individual, *sui juris,* as employer or employee, to make contracts for the labor of the latter under the protection of the provisions of the Federal Constitution, there would seem to be no length to which legislation of this nature might not go. The case differs widely, as we have already stated, from the expressions of this court in regard to laws of this nature, as stated in *Holden* v. *Hardy.* . . .

We think that there can be no fair doubt that the trade of a baker, in and of itself, is not an unhealthy one to that degree which would authorize the legislature to interfere with the right to labor, and with the right of free contract on the part of the individual, either as employer or employee. In looking through statistics regarding all trades and occupations, it may be true that the trade of a baker does not appear to be as healthy as some other trades, and is also vastly more healthy than still others. To the common understanding the trade of a baker has never been regarded as an unhealthy one. Very likely physicians would not recommend the exercise of that or of any other trade as a remedy for ill health. Some occupations are more healthy than others, but we think there are none which might not come under the power of the legislature to supervise and control the hours of working therein, if the mere fact that the occupation is not absolutely and perfectly healthy is to confer that right upon the legislative department of the government. It might be safely affirmed that almost all occupations more or less affect the health. There must be more than the mere fact of the possible existence of some small amount of unhealthiness to warrant legislative interference with liberty. It is unfortunately true that labor, even in any department, may possibly carry with it the seeds of unhealthiness. But are we all, on that account, at the mercy of legislative majorities? A printer, a tinsmith, a locksmith, a carpenter, a cabinetmaker, a dry goods clerk, a bank's, a lawyer's, or a physician's clerk, or a clerk in almost any kind of business, would all come under the power of the legislature, on this assumption. No trade, no occupation, no mode of earning one's living, could escape this all-pervading power, and the acts of the legislature in limiting the hours of labor in all employments would be valid, although such limitation might seriously cripple the ability of the laborer to support himself and his family. In our large cities there are many buildings into which the sun penetrates for but a short time in each day, and these buildings are occupied by people carrying on the business of bankers, brokers, lawyers, real estate, and many other kinds of business, aided by many clerks, messengers, and other employees. Upon the assumption of the validity of this act under review, it is not possible to say that an act, prohibiting lawyers' or bank clerks, or others, from contracting to labor for their employers more than eight hours a day would be invalid. It might be said that it is unhealthy to work more than that number of hours in an apartment lighted by artificial light during the working hours of the day; that the occupation of the bank clerk, the lawyer's clerk, the real-estate clerk, or the broker's clerk, in such offices is therefore unhealthy, and the legislature, in its paternal wisdom, must, therefore, have the right to legislate on the subject of, and to limit, the hours for such labor; and, if it exercises that power, and its validity be questioned, it is sufficient to say, it has reference to the public health; it has reference to the health of the employees condemned to labor day after day in buildings where the sun never shines; it is a health law, and therefore it is valid, and cannot be questioned by the courts.

It is also urged, pursuing the same line of argument, that it is to the interest of the state that its population should be strong and robust, and therefore any legislation which may be said to tend to make people healthy must be valid as health laws, enacted under the police power. If this be a valid argument and a justification for this kind of legislation, it follows that the protection of the Federal Constitution from undue interference with liberty of person and freedom of contract is visionary, wherever the law is sought to be justified as a valid exercise of the police power. Scarcely any law but might find shelter under such assumptions, and conduct, properly so called, as well as contract, would come under the restrictive sway of the legislature. Not only the hours of employees, but the hours of employers, could be regulated, and doctors, lawyers, scientists, all professional men, as well as athletes and artisans, could be forbidden to fatigue their brains and bodies by prolonged hours of exercise, lest the fighting strength of the state be impaired. We mention these extreme cases because the contention is extreme. We do not believe in the soundness of the views which uphold this law. On the contrary, we think that such a law as this, although passed in the assumed exercise of the police power, and as relating to the public health, or the health of the employees named, is not within that power, and is invalid. The act is not, within any fair meaning of the term, a health law, but is an illegal interference with the rights of individuals, both employers and employees, to make contracts regarding labor upon such terms as they may think best, or which they may agree upon with the other parties to such contracts. Statutes of the nature of that under review, limiting the hours in which grown and intelligent men may labor to earn their living, are mere meddlesome interferences with the rights of the individual and they are not saved from condemnation by the claim that they are passed in the exercise of the police power and upon the subject of the health of the individual whose rights are interfered with, unless there be some fair ground, reasonable in and of itself, to say that there is material danger to the public health, or to the health of the employees, if the hours of labor are not curtailed. If this be not clearly the case, the individuals whose rights are thus made the subject of legislative interference are under the protection of the Federal Constitution regarding their liberty of contract as well as of person; and the legislature of the state has no power to limit their right as proposed in this statute. All that it could properly do has been done by it with regard to the conduct of bakeries, as provided for in the other sections of the act, above set forth. These several sections provide for the inspection of the premises where the bakery is carried on, with regard to furnishing proper wash rooms and waterclosets, apart from the bake room, also with regard to providing proper drainage, plumbing, and painting; the sections, in addition, provide for the height of the ceiling, the cementing or tiling of floors, where necessary in the opinion of the factory inspector, and for other things of that nature; alterations are also provided for and are to be made where necessary in the opinion of the inspector, in order to comply with the provisions of the statute. These various sections may be wise and valid regulations, and they certainly go to the full extent of providing for the cleanliness and the healthiness, so far as possible, of the quarters in which bakeries are to be conducted. Adding to all these requirements a prohibition to enter into any contract of labor in a bakery for more than a certain number of hours a week is, in our judgment, so wholly beside the matter of a proper, reasonable, and fair provision as to run counter to that liberty of person and of free contract provided for in the Federal Constitution.

It was further urged on the argument that restricting the hours of labor in the case of bakers was valid because it tended to cleanliness on the part of the workers, as a man was more apt to be cleanly when not overworked, and if cleanly then his "output" was also more likely to be so. What has already been said applies with equal force to this contention. We do not admit the reasoning to be sufficient to justify the claimed right of such interference. The state in that case would assume the position of a supervisor, or *pater familias,* over every act of the individual, and its right of governmental interference with his hours of labor, his hours of exercise, the character thereof, and the extent to which it shall be carried would be recognized and upheld. In our judgment it is not possible in fact to discover the connection between the number of hours a baker may work in the bakery and the healthful quality of the bread made by the workman. The connection, if any exist, is too shadowy and thin to build any argument for the interference of the legislature. If the man works ten hours a day it is all right, but if ten and a half or eleven his health is in danger and his bread may be unhealthy, and, therefore, he shall not be permitted to do it. This, we think, is unreasonable and entirely arbitrary. When assertions such as we have adverted to become necessary in order to give, if possible, a plausible foundation for the contention that the law is a "health law," it gives rise to at least a suspicion that there was some other motive dominating the legislature than the purpose to subserve the public health or welfare.

This interference on the part of the legislatures of the several states with the ordinary trades and occupations of the people seems to be on the increase. . . .

It is impossible for us to shut our eyes to the fact that many of the laws of this character, while passed under what is claimed to be the police power for the purpose of protecting the public health or welfare, are, in reality, passed from other motives. We are justified in saying so when, from the character of the law and the subject upon which it legislates, it is apparent that the public health or welfare bears but the most remote relation to the law. The purpose of a statute must be determined from the natural and legal effect of the language employed; and whether it is or is not repugnant to the Constitution of the United States must be determined from the natural effect of such statutes when put into operation, and not from their proclaimed purpose.

It is manifest to us that the limitation of the hours of labor provided for in this section of the statute under which the indictment was found, and the plaintiff in error convicted, has no such direct relation to, and no such substantial effect upon, the health of the employee, as to justify us in regarding the section as really a health law. It seems to us that the real object and purpose were simply to regulate the hours of labor between the master and his employees (all being men, *sui juris*), in a private business, not dangerous in any degree to morals, or in any real and substantial degree to the health of the employees. Under such circumstances the freedom of master and employee to contract with each other in relation to their employment, and in defining the same, cannot be prohibited or interfered with, without violating the Federal Constitution.

The judgment of the Court of Appeals of New York, as well as that of the Supreme Court and the County Court of Oneida County, must be reversed and the case remanded to the County Court for further proceedings not inconsistent with this opinion.

Reversed.

Lochner has been called the Court's "clearest expression" of economic substantive due process.[25] Although the Court said the question to be asked in this case is the same one it had been addressing since *Mugler* (Is the law a fair, reasonable, and appropriate exercise of police power?), its answer is quite different. By distinguishing *Holden* to the point of nonexistence and by narrowing the definition of what constitutes reasonable state regulations, the Court moved away from a strict "reasonableness" approach to one that reflected *Allgeyer:* an employer's right "to make a contract" with employees is virtually sacrosanct.

That the Court accomplished this feat not by changing the legal question but by changing the answer creates something of a puzzle, particularly with regard to the immediate subject of the dispute—maximum work hours. Think about it this way: it upheld the Utah law at issue in *Holden* on

the grounds that the "kind of employment . . . and the character of the employees . . . were such as to make [the state law] reasonable and proper"; it struck the *Lochner* law because bakers can "care for themselves" (despite evidence to the contrary) and that the production of "clean and wholesome bread" is not affected. Was this distinction significant? Or was it merely a way to mask what the Court wanted to do: narrow the grounds on which states could reasonably regulate and, thereby, strike protective legislation as a violation of the right to contract?

These questions moved into prominence in *Muller v. Oregon* (1908). As you read this most interesting case, think about the following. Some scholars argue that the Court's decision in *Muller* merely echoed the logic of *Holden* and *Lochner;* that is, the Court followed the "reasonableness" approach. Others suggest that there were extralegal factors at work that had a great influence on the Court. With which view do you agree?

25. Ralph A. Rossum and G. Alan Tarr, *American Constitutional Law* (New York: St. Martin's Press, 1991), 313.

Muller v. Oregon

208 U.S. 412 (1908)

*Vote: 9 (Brewer, Day, Fuller, Harlan, Holmes,
    McKenna, Moody, Peckham, White)*
        0
Opinion of the Court: Brewer

At the forefront of the Progressive Movement was an organization called the National Consumers' League (NCL). Through the efforts of the NCL and others, the drive for maximum hour legislation had succeeded in many states, which, by the early 1900s, had imposed some type of restriction. After *Lochner,* however, all of their efforts were threatened by employers who sought to use that ruling to challenge state regulations.

This case began when the state of Oregon brought charges against Curt Muller for working

his female laundresses longer than the state maximum of ten hours per day. Once convicted, Muller decided to challenge the law. In the view of his attorneys, Oregon's regulation, which prohibited women, but not men, from working in laundries more than ten hours violated his right to enter into a contract with his employees.

Recognizing that in light of *Lochner*, Muller's argument rested on strong grounds, the NCL grew concerned. It was reluctant to see its hard work to attain passage of the Oregon law nullified by the Supreme Court. To defend the law, the NCL contacted Louis D. Brandeis, a well-known attorney of the day and a future U.S. Supreme Court justice *(see box page 456).* Because his philosophical position was very much akin to the NCL's, he agreed to help the organization with the

Curt Muller (with arms folded) made constitutional history when he asked the U.S. Supreme Court to strike down as violative of his rights an Oregon law regulating the number of hours his laundresses could work at his cleaning establishment. In Muller v. Oregon *(1908), however, the Court held that states may constitutionally enact maximum hour work laws for women.*

Muller case, but only if it could convince Oregon's attorneys to give him complete control over its course.

When NCL leaders managed to accomplish this, Brandeis got down to work. Because of the decision in *Lochner* and the stability of the Court's membership, he decided that bold action was necessary. Instead of filling his brief with legal arguments, he would provide the Court with *"facts,* published by anyone with expert knowledge of industry in its relation to women's hours

of labor,'' which indicated the evils of Muller's actions. In particular, the brief pointed out that forcing women to work long hours affected their health and their reproductive systems.[26] In the end, with the help of the NCL, Brandeis produced an incredible document. Known in legal history as the Brandeis Brief, it contained 113 pages of sociological data and only 2 pages of legal argument.

26. Clement E. Vose, *Constitutional Change* (Lexington, Mass.: Lexington Books, 1972), 172.

Louis Dembitz Brandeis (1916–1939)

Louis Dembitz Brandeis, born November 13, 1856, in Louisville, Kentucky, was the son of Adolph and Fredericka Dembitz Brandeis, Jews who had emigrated from Bohemia after the unsuccessful democratic revolts of 1848. His father was a prosperous grain merchant who provided his family with comfort, education, and culture. Having completed two years of preparatory studies at the Annen-Realschule in Dresden, but without a college degree, Brandeis enrolled at Harvard Law School when he was eighteen years of age. He graduated in 1877 with the highest average in the law school's history. After eight months practicing law in St. Louis, Brandeis returned to Cambridge—for him "the world's center"—and with Bostonian Samuel D. Warren, Jr., second in their law school class, opened a one-room office downtown.

Warren and Brandeis and the successor firm Brandeis, Dunbar, and Nutter handled a variety of cases and were highly successful. By the time he was thirty-five, Brandeis was earning more than $50,000 a year. He married Alice Goldmark of New York, March 23, 1891, and the couple had two daughters. Despite his earnings, the family preferred to live simply, setting a ceiling on their personal expenditures of $10,000 a year. As a young lawyer Brandeis devoted many hours to his alma mater. He helped raise funds for a teaching post for Oliver Wendell Holmes, Jr., and was one of the founders of the *Harvard Law Review.*

The turn of the century marked the rapid growth in America of corporate monopolies—the "curse of bigness," as Brandeis described it. He chose to protect the rights not of special interest groups but of the general public, and usually without a fee for his services. Brandeis initiated sliding scale gas rates in Boston that lowered consumer costs while raising corporate dividends, and he instituted savings bank insurance policies, another reform later implemented in the rest of the country. He defended municipal control of Boston's subway system and opposed the monopolistic practices of the New Haven Railroad. He arbitrated labor disputes in New York's garment industry, serving as chairman of an arbitration board from 1910 to 1916, and established the constitutionality of state maximum hour and minimum wage statutes. For thirty-seven years Brandeis devoted his time, energy, and talents to a host of public causes. He called himself an "attorney for the situation," but the press adopted the popular title "people's attorney."

President Wilson respected Brandeis and often sought his opinion. He nominated him associate justice of the Supreme Court January 28, 1916, to fill the vacancy left by Justice Joseph R. Lamar's death. Vicious opposition to his appointment ensued. One particularly vituperative critic described Brandeis as a "business-baiter, stirrer up of strife, litigious lover of hate and unrest, destroyer of confidence, killer of values, commercial coyote, spoiler of pay envelopes."

Factory owners paying higher wages, New Haven Railroad stockholders, moguls in the Boston transit system, insurance and gas industries—in short, all the losers in court—united to voice their objections to the appointment. Among those seeking satisfaction for past injuries was William Howard Taft. His administration had been embarrassed by an investigation led in part by Brandeis of the conservation practices of Secretary of the Interior Richard A. Ballinger.

The former president, ambitious for a justiceship himself, described the nomination as "one of the deepest wounds that I have had as an American and a lover of the Constitution" and spoke of the "indelible stain" on the Wilson administration that confirmation would bring.

Another critic, Clarence W. Barron, editor and publisher of the *Wall Street Journal,* also felt the choice was unwise: "There is only one redeeming feature in the nomination and that is that it will assist to bury Mr. Wilson in the next Presidential election." The president viewed the political climate differently. He believed Brandeis was a smart choice who would attract the needed Progressive vote. Wilson could not count on a divided Republican party to ensure his reelection.

During four months of acrimonious debate over his appointment, Brandeis quietly pursued his legal practice. He went to the office every day and did not resort to personal attacks against his opponents. "Your attitude while the wolves yelp is sublime," his young nephew wrote.

The hearings in the Senate Judiciary Committee turned up no valid grounds for rejection. According to Senator Thomas J. Walsh, Brandeis's only "real crime" was that "he had not stood in awe of the majesty of wealth." One of his supporters from the Harvard Law School, Arthur Hill, attributed the opposition to the fact that "Mr. Brandeis is an outsider, successful and a Jew."

Brandeis was confirmed by the Senate on June 1, 1916, by a vote of 47–22, becoming the first Jewish justice.

On February 13, 1939, Brandeis, aged eighty-two, resigned from the Court but not from public service. After twenty-two years on the bench, he devoted the last years of his life to the Zionist movement and a boycott of German products. As the *New York Times* noted upon his retirement in 1939, "the storm against him. . . seems almost incredible now." He died October 5, 1941, in Washington, D.C.

Source: Elder Witt, *Guide to the U.S. Supreme Court,* 2d ed. (Washington, D.C.: Congressional Quarterly, 1990), 852–853.

Justice Brewer delivered the opinion of the Court:

We held in Lochner v. New York that a law providing that no laborer shall be required or permitted to work in bakeries more than sixty hours in a week or ten hours in a day was not, as to men, a legitimate exercise of the police power of the state, but an unreasonable, unnecessary and arbitrary interference with the right and liberty of the individual to contract in relation to his labor, and as such was in conflict with, and void under, the Federal Constitution. That decision is invoked by plaintiff in error as decisive of the question before us. But this assumes that the difference between the sexes does not justify a different rule respecting a restriction of the hours of labor.

In patent cases counsel are apt to open the argument with a discussion of the state of the art. It may not be amiss, in the present case, before examining the constitutional question, to notice the course of legislation, as well as expressions of opinion from other than judicial sources. In the brief filed by Mr. Louis D. Brandeis for the defendant in error is a very copious collection of all these matters, an epitome of which is found in the margin.[†] . . .

[†]The following . . . states impose . . . restrictions in some form or other upon the hours of labor that may be required of women: Massachusetts, Rhode Island, Louisiana, Connecticut, Maine, New Hampshire, Maryland, Virginia, Pennsylvania, New York, Nebraska, Washington, Colorado, New Jersey, Oklahoma, North Dakota, South Dakota, Wisconsin, [and] South Carolina.

In foreign legislation Mr. Brandeis calls attention to . . . Great Britain, France, Switzerland, Austria, Holland, Italy, [and] Germany.

Then follow extracts from over ninety reports of committees, bureaus of statistics, commissioners of hygiene, inspectors of factories, both in this country and in Europe, to the effect that long hours of labor are dangerous for women primarily because of their special physical organization. The matter is discussed in these reports in different aspects, but all agree as to the danger. It would, of course, take too much space to give these reports in detail. Following them are extracts from similar reports discussing the general benefits of short hours from an economic aspect of the question. In many of these reports individual instances are given tending to support the general conclusion. Perhaps the general scope and character of all these reports may be summed up in what an inspector for Hanover says: "The reasons for the reduction of the working day to ten hours—(a) the physical organization of women, (b) her maternal functions, (c) the rearing and education of the children, (d) the maintenance of the home—are all so important and so far-reaching that the need for such reduction need hardly be discussed."

The legislation and opinions referred to in the margin may not be, technically speaking, authorities, and in them is little or no discussion of the constitutional question presented to us for determination, yet they are significant of a widespread belief that woman's physical structure, and the functions she performs in consequence thereof, justify special legislation restricting or qualifying the conditions under which she should be permitted to toil. Constitutional questions, it is true, are not settled by even a consensus of present public opinion, for it is the peculiar value of a written constitution that it places in unchanging form limitations upon legislative action, and thus gives a permanence and stability to popular government which otherwise would be lacking. At the same time, when a question of fact is debated and debatable, and the extent to which a special constitutional limitation goes is affected by the truth in respect to that fact, a widespread and long-continued belief concerning it is worthy of consideration. We take judicial cognizance of all matters of general knowledge.

It is undoubtedly true, as more than once declared by this court, that the general right to contract in relation to one's business is part of the liberty of the individual, protected by the 14th Amendment to the Federal Constitution; yet it is equally well settled that this liberty is not absolute and extending to all contracts, and that a state may, without conflicting with the provisions of the 14th Amendment, restrict in many respects the individual's power of contract. Without stopping to discuss at length the extent to which a state may act in this respect, we refer to the following cases in which the question has been considered: *Allgeyer v. Louisiana; Holden v. Hardy; Lochner v. New York.*

That woman's physical structure and the performance of maternal functions place her at a disadvantage in the struggle for subsistence is obvious. This is especially true when the burdens of motherhood are upon her. Even when they are not, by abundant testimony of the medical fraternity continuance for a long time on her feet at work, repeating this from day to day, tends to injurious effects upon the body, and, as healthy mothers are essential to vigorous offspring, the physical well-being of woman becomes an object of public interest and care in order to preserve the strength and vigor of the race.

Still again, history discloses the fact that woman has always been dependent upon man. He established his control at the outset by superior physical strength, and this control in various forms, with diminishing intensity, has continued to the present. As minors, though not to the same extent, she has been looked upon in the courts as needing especial care that her rights may be preserved. Education was long denied her, and while now the doors of the schoolroom are opened and her opportunities for acquiring knowledge are great, yet even with that and the consequent increase of capacity for business affairs it is still true that in the struggle for subsistence she is not an equal competitor with her brother. Though limitations upon personal and contractual rights may be removed by legislation, there is that in her disposition and habits of life which will operate against a full assertion of those rights. She will still be where some legislation to protect her seems necessary to secure a real equality of right. Doubtless there are individual exceptions, and there are many respects in which she has an advantage over him; but looking at it from the viewpoint of the effort to maintain an independent position in life, she is not upon an equality. Differentiated by these matters from the other sex, she is properly placed in a class by herself, and legislation designed for her protection may be sustained, even when like legislation is not necessary for men, and could not be sustained. It is impossible to close one's eyes to the fact that she still looks to her brother and depends upon him. Even though all restrictions on political, personal, and contractual rights were taken away, and she stood, so far as statutes are concerned, upon an absolutely equal plane with him, it would still be true that she is so constituted that she will rest upon and look to him for protection; that her physical structure and a proper discharge of her maternal functions—having in view not merely her own health, but the well-being of the race—justify legislation to protect her from the greed as well as the passion of man. The limitations which this statute places upon her contractual powers, upon her right to agree with her employer as to the time she shall labor, are not imposed solely for her benefit, but also largely for the benefit of all. Many words cannot make this plainer. The two sexes differ in structure of body, in the functions to be performed by each, in the amount of physical strength, in the capacity for long-continued labor, particularly when done standing, the influence of vigorous health upon the future well-being of the race, the self-reliance which enables one to assert full rights, and in the capacity to maintain the struggle for subsistence. This difference justifies a difference in legislation, and upholds that which is designed to compensate for some of the burdens which rest upon her.

We have not referred in this discussion to the denial of the elective franchise in the state of Oregon, for while that may disclose a lack of political equality in all things with her brother, that is not of itself decisive. The reason runs deeper, and rests in the inherent difference between the two sexes, and in the different functions in life which they perform.

For these reasons, and without questioning in any respect the decision in Lochner v. New York, we are of the opinion that it cannot be adjudged that the act in question is in conflict with the Federal Constitution, so far as it respects the work of a female in a laundry, and the judgment of the Supreme Court of Oregon is affirmed.

Why did the justices affirm the Oregon law? One answer is that the Court did not depart from *Lochner*: it merely found that Oregon's regulations, unlike New York's, were a "reasonable exercise" of the state's power.[27] But the Court applied the reasonableness approach both in *Lochner* and *Holden* and came to completely different conclusions. So, despite the Court's attempt to distinguish *Lochner,* how much can the application of that standard possibly explain about *Muller*'s outcome? Another possibility is that Brandeis forced the Court to see the reasonableness of the Oregon regulation. By presenting such a mass of statistical data, he kept the justices riveted on the law and diverted their attention from a substantive due process approach. The strategy worked: not only did the Court "commend" Brandeis's brief, but also it did not even cite *Lochner*.

Winning *Muller* gave a big boost to the Progressive Movement. Some worried, however, that the decision depended on the fact that the law covered only women and that, when the Court had an opportunity to review a law covering all workers, it would apply *Lochner*. This fear in-creased when the Court agreed to review *Bunting v. Oregon* (1917), which involved another Oregon law providing that "no person shall be employed in any mill, factory, or manufacturing establishment in this state more than ten hours in any one day." Compounding the NCL's concern was that Brandeis now sat on the Supreme Court and, since he had participated in oral argument, would almost certainly disqualify himself from the case.

In 1917, however, the Supreme Court dispelled their concerns. In a 5-3 decision, with Brandeis not participating, the majority upheld the Oregon law. Writing for the Court, Justice Joseph McKenna explained that, although Bunting contended that "the law . . . is not either necessary or useful 'for the preservation of the health of employees,'" no evidence was provided to support that contention. Moreover, the judgment of the Oregon legislature and supreme court was that "'it cannot be held, as a matter of law, that the legislative requirement is unreasonable or arbitrary.'" McKenna concluded, therefore, that no further discussion was "necessary" and upheld the law.

Once again the Court failed even to mention *Lochner*. But, given its holding, many predicted

27. Rossum and Tarr, *American Constitutional Law,* 314.

the death of that decision; after all, it was wholly incompatible with *Bunting*. Perhaps the demise of substantive due process would follow. Indeed, throughout the period between *Mugler* (1890) and up to about *Bunting*, it appeared that *Lochner* was more the exception than the rule. Between 1887 and 1910, the Court heard 558 cases involving due process claims challenging state regulations and upheld 83 percent of the laws. It seemed that *Lochner,* not *Muller,* was the unusual case.[28]

28. Alfred H. Kelly, Winfred A. Harbison, and Herman Belz, *The American Constitution,* 7th ed. (New York: W. W. Norton, 1991), 405.

The Heyday of Substantive Due Process: 1923-1936

The *Bunting* funeral for *Lochner* proved to be premature. Within six years, not only did the Court virtually overrule *Bunting*, but also it seemed to be more committed to the *Lochner* version of due process than ever before. *Adkins v. Children's Hospital* (1923) provides an excellent illustration of the magnitude of this resurgence. As you read the Court's ruling, compare it to *Muller.* Is there any way, legally speaking, to justify the two decisions? Or do you suspect that other, extralegal factors came into play?

Adkins v. Children's Hospital

261 U.S. 525 (1923)

Vote: 5 (Butler, McKenna, McReynolds,
  Sutherland, Van Devanter)
 3 (Holmes, Sanford, Taft)
Opinion of the Court: Sutherland
Dissenting opinions: Holmes, Taft
Not participating: Brandeis

In 1918 Congress, with the support of the progressive-oriented president, Woodrow Wilson, enacted a law "providing for the fixing of minimum wages for women and children in the District of Columbia."[29] The act authorized the establishment of the Minimum Wage Board to set pay rates. The board, staffed by progressives, ordered that restaurants and hospitals pay women workers a minimum wage of 34.5 cents per hour, $16.50 per week, or $71.50 per month. According to the board, these rates would "supply the necessary cost of living to . . . women workers to maintain them in good health and morals."

Children's Hospital of the District of Columbia, which employed "a large number of women

29. We adopt this account from Vose, *Constitutional Change,* 190-196.

in various capacities," refused to comply. In its opinion, the law violated the Due Process Clause of the Fifth Amendment encompassing the liberty to enter into salary contracts with employees.[30]

Because of delay at the lower court level, the case did not reach the Supreme Court until 1923. An attorney for the board, assisted by then-NCL attorney (and future Supreme Court justice) Felix Frankfurter and other NCL staffers, sought to defend the 1918 law on grounds similar to Brandeis's in *Muller.* They offered the Court "impressive documentation on the cost of living and the desirability of good wages."

Justice George Sutherland delivered the opinion of the Court:

The statute now under consideration is attacked upon the ground that it authorizes an unconstitutional interference with the freedom of contract included within the guaranties of the due process clause of the 5th Amendment. That the right to contract about one's affairs is a part of the liberty of the individual protected by this clause is settled by the decisions of this court, and is no longer open to question. . . .

30. Because the District of Columbia is not a state, the Due Process Clause of the Fourteenth Amendment did not apply.

There is, of course, no such thing as absolute freedom of contract. It is subject to a great variety of restraints. But freedom of contract is, nevertheless, the general rule and restraint the exception; and the exercise of legislative authority to abridge it can be justified only by the existence of exceptional circumstances. . . .

[The statute under consideration] is simply and exclusively a price-fixing law, confined to adult women . . . who are legally as capable of contracting for themselves as men. It forbids two parties having lawful capacity—under penalties as to the employer—to freely contract with one another in respect of the price for which one shall render service to the other in a purely private employment. . . .

The feature of this statute which, perhaps more than any other, puts upon it the stamp of invalidity is that it exacts from the employer an arbitrary payment for a purpose and upon a basis having no causal connection with his business, or the contract, or the work the employee engages to do. The declared basis . . . is not the value of the service rendered, but the extraneous circumstance that the employee needs to get a prescribed sum of money to insure her subsistence, health, and morals. . . . The moral requirement, implicit in every contract of employment, viz., that the amount to be paid and the service to be rendered shall bear to each other some relation of just equivalence, is completely ignored. The necessities of the employee are alone considered, and these arise outside of the employment, are the same when there is no employment, and as great in one occupation as in another. Certainly the employer, by paying a fair equivalent for the service rendered, though not sufficient to support the employee, has neither caused nor contributed to her poverty. . . . A statute requiring an employer to pay in money, to pay at prescribed and regular intervals, to pay the value of the services rendered, even to pay with fair relation to the extent of the benefit obtained from the service, would be understandable. But a statute which prescribes payment without regard to any of these things, and solely with relation to circumstances apart from the contract of employment, the business affected by it, and the work done under it, is so clearly the product of a naked, arbitrary exercise of power,

that it cannot be allowed to stand under the Constitution of the United States. . . .

It has been said that legislation of the kind now under review is required in the interest of social justice, for whose ends freedom of contract may lawfully be subjected to restraint. The liberty of the individual to do as he pleases, even in innocent matters, is not absolute. It must frequently yield to the common good, and the line beyond which the power of interference may not be pressed is neither definite nor unalterable, but may be made to move, within limits not well defined, with changing need and circumstance. Any attempt to fix a rigid boundary would be unwise as well as futile. But, nevertheless, there are limits to the power, and when these have been passed, it becomes the plain duty of the courts, in the proper exercise of their authority, to so declare. To sustain the individual freedom of action contemplated by the Constitution is not to strike down the common good, but to exalt it; for surely the good of society as a whole cannot be better served than by the preservation against arbitrary restraint of the liberties of its constituent members.

It follows from what has been said that the act in question passes the limit prescribed by the Constitution, and, accordingly, the decrees of the court below are affirmed.

Mr. Justice Holmes, dissenting:

The question in this case is the broad one, whether Congress can establish minimum rates of wages for women in the District of Columbia, with due provision for special circumstances, or whether we must say that Congress has no power to meddle with the matter at all. To me, notwithstanding the deference due to the prevailing judgment of the court, the power of Congress seems absolutely free from doubt. The end—to remove conditions leading to ill health, immorality, and the deterioration of the race—no one would deny to be within the scope of constitutional legislation. The means are means that have the approval of Congress, of many states, and of those governments from which we have learned our greatest lessons. When so many intelligent persons, who have studied the matter more than any of us can, have thought that the means are effective and are worth the price, it seems to me impossible to deny that the belief reasonably may be held by reasonable men. . . . [T]he only objection that can be urged is found within the vague contours of the 5th Amendment, prohibiting the depriving any person of liberty or property without due process of law. To that I turn.

The earlier decisions upon the same words in the 14th Amendment began within our memory, and went no farther than an unpretentious assertion of the liberty to follow the ordinary callings. Later that innocuous generality was expanded into the dogma, Liberty of Contract. Contract is not specially mentioned in the text that we have to construe. It is merely an example of doing what you want to do, embodied in the word "liberty." But pretty much all law consists in forbidding men to do some things that they want to do, and contract is no more exempt from law than other acts. . . .

I confess that I do not understand the principle on which the power to fix a minimum for the wages of women can be denied by those who admit the power to fix a maximum for their hours of work. I fully assent to the proposition that here, as elsewhere, the distinctions of the law are distinctions of degree; but I perceive no difference in the kind or degree of interference with liberty, the only matter with which we have any concern, between the one case and the other. The bargain is equally affected whichever half you regulate. . . .

I am of opinion that the statute is valid.

Adkins represented the return of substantive due process; indeed, it made clear that *"Muller* and *Bunting* did not represent a repudiation"* of that doctrine.[31] If anything, as Justice Holmes's dissent noted, it had come back stronger than ever with the term "due process of law" evolving into the "dogma, Liberty of Contract."

Why the change? In large measure, it can be traced back to the political climate of the day, which affected the Court. Following World War I, the U.S. economy boomed, and voters elected one president after another who were committed to a free market economy. These presidents, in turn, appointed justices, at least some of whom shared those beliefs. As Table 9-3 indicates, one president, Warren G. Harding, made the first four of these new Supreme Court appointments. Clement E. Vose notes that "the most important single fact about the Harding appointments was that he named two ardent conservatives of the old school—Sutherland and Butler—to serve along with two justices similarly committed who were already sitting—Van Devanter and McReynolds."[32] The Four Horsemen were all in place.

The entrenchment of substantive due process, as we mentioned at the beginning of this chapter, was but one manifestation of the impact of Republican appointments to the Court. With their stronger commitment to an "utterly free market," these conservative justices also invoked creative theories of the limits of national power, especially dual federalism, to strike down federal regulatory efforts. "Taken together" the doctrines of dual federalism and substantive due process constituted "a lethal sequence of knockout punches which killed all [regulatory] legislation."[33]

The Depression, the New Deal, and the Decline of Substantive Due Process

The laissez-faire approach of the Court through the 1920s was in keeping with the times. The nation continued to boom and to elect politicians, President Herbert Hoover, for example, who were committed to a private-sector-based economy that they were convinced would remain

31. Rossum and Tarr, *American Constitutional Law*, 314.
32. Vose, *Constitutional Change*, 194.

33. Ducat and Chase, *Constitutional Interpretation*, 554.

Table 9-3   From *Bunting* to *Adkins*

Justice	Bunting Vote (1917)	Harding Appointments (1921–1922)	Adkins Vote (1923)
McKenna	Upheld law	No change	Struck law
Holmes	Upheld law	No change	Upheld law
Day	Upheld law	Replaced by Butler------------>Struck law	
Pitney	Upheld law	Replaced by Sanford---------->Upheld law	
Clarke	Upheld law	Replaced by Sutherland ------>Struck law	
White	Struck law	Replaced by Taft ------------->Upheld law	
Van Devanter	Struck law	No change	Struck law
McReynolds	Struck law	No change	Struck law
Brandeis	No participation	No change	No participation

successful if left free from regulation. The Great Depression, triggered by the stock market crash of 1929, and the subsequent election of Franklin D. Roosevelt demonstrates just how quickly that perception changed. The depression "shattered the dream of a self-correcting free economy."[34] Roosevelt's election indicated the desire of the citizenry for greater regulation to get the nation back on its feet.

At first, it appeared as if the Court, although dominated by Republican-appointed justices, might go along with the depression-fighting regulatory efforts of the new administration and of the states, which in part required that it repudiate substantive due process. How could states exercise any control on employers if the Court continued to strike down the legislatures' efforts on "liberty of contracts" grounds?

In the 1934 case of *Nebbia v. New York*, the Court seemed willing to relent. At issue here was the authority of the New York Milk Control Board to fix milk prices. The owner of a grocery store, Leo Nebbia, sold milk at a rate higher than allowed and was convicted of violating the board's order.

In arguing against the law, Nebbia invoked the Fourteenth Amendment's Due Process Clause: the establishment of maximum prices interfered with his ability to conduct business. In a 5-4 decision, the Court rejected this claim. Writing for the majority, Justice Owen Roberts seemed to return in earnest to Waite's business-affected-with-public-interest doctrine:

The phrase "affected with a public interest" can, in the nature of things, mean no more than that an industry, for adequate reason, is subject to control for the public good. [There] can be no doubt that upon proper occasion and by appropriate measures the state may regulate a business in any of its aspects, including the prices to be charged for the products or commodities it sells.

Although *Nebbia,* in retrospect, was "a harbinger of the limited future ahead for substantive due process," that was hardly the case in the context of the day.[35] As you will recall from the chapters on the Commerce Clause and federalism, for the next two years the Court generally continued along its laissez-faire path of the 1920s—seemingly in ignorance of the political, economic, and social events transpiring around it.

34. Fisher, *American Constitutional Law,* 476.

35. Ducat and Chase, *Constitutional Interpretation.*

To help stabilize the market, the New York Milk Control Board fixed the price of a quart of milk at nine cents. When Leo Nebbia, pictured above, the owner of a grocery store, sold two quarts of milk and a loaf of bread for eighteen cents, the state convicted him of violating the board's order. In 1934 the Supreme Court rejected Nebbia's claim that the order violated his constitutional rights, ruling that it was a valid exercise of state power.

In particular, it refused to let go of the doctrine of substantive due process.

Just two years after *Nebbia,* it decided another New York case, but in quite a different way. At issue in *Morehead v. New York ex rel. Tipaldo* (1936) was a 1933 minimum wage law that "declared it to be against public policy for any employer to employ any woman at an oppressive and unreasonable wage." It defined as unreasonable a wage that was "both less than the fair and reasonable value of the services rendered and less than sufficient to meet the minimum cost of living necessary for health."[36] If a woman thought that her employer was paying her inadequate wages, she could file a complaint with a state board. Women employees of a laundry invoked this procedure against Joseph Tipaldo, the manager of

36. See Vose, *Constitutional Change,* 204.

the operation. In 1934 Tipaldo was found guilty: he paid his employees only seven to ten dollars per week, when the board had set $12.40 as a minimum wage.

When the case reached the Supreme Court, Tipaldo received some support from an unexpected source: the feminist National Woman's Party (NWP). Although it did not agree with his substantive due process claim, the NWP argued that the New York law violated the Constitution on the grounds that it treated the sexes differently and fostered inequality. As NWP leaders explained,

The Woman's Party stands for equality between men and women in all laws. This includes laws affecting the position of women in industry as well as all other laws. The Woman's Party does not take any position with regard to the merits of minimum wage legislation, but it does demand that such legislation, if passed, shall be for both sexes. It is opposed to all legislation having a sex basis and applying to one sex alone.[37]

Attorneys defending the state's action, including National Consumers' League representatives, therefore, faced a difficult challenge. The constituency benefiting from the law—women—was divided over the issue, but more important, the attorneys had to deal with the *Adkins* precedent. In part, they did so by trying to distinguish this law from the one at issue in *Adkins;* they also tried to demonstrate that economic conditions had changed considerably since 1923 and required this kind of regulation. Moreover, they had the *Nebbia* ruling in hand. It was just possible that the Court might go along with the state. But it was not to be. In keeping with their rulings on federal New Deal legislation and as a result of Justice Roberts's defection from the *Nebbia* majority, the Court struck the New York law. Writing for a majority of five, Justice Pierce Butler was just as emphatic on the subject of substantive due process as the *Adkins* Court had been: "Freedom of contract is the general rule and restraint the exception."

37. Quoted by Vose in *Constitutional Change*, 212

West Coast Hotel v. Parrish: The End of Substantive Due Process

The Court's refusal to uphold federal New Deal legislation, as you recall from Chapter 6, provoked President Roosevelt's anger. Its ruling in *Morehead* cut even deeper. Peter Irons wrote, "More than any other decision by the Court during the New Deal period, *Morehead* unleashed a barrage of criticism from conservatives as well as from liberals," who sympathized with the plight of women and children workers.[38] Even the Republican party's 1936 platform included a plank supporting adoption of minimum wage and maximum hour laws of the sort struck in *Morehead*.

Amid all this pressure, including Roosevelt's Court-packing scheme, the Court did a major about-face on the constitutionality of New Deal programs *(see Chapter 6).* As part of that change came what would be the demise of the doctrine of substantive due process in *West Coast Hotel v. Parrish*.

38. Peter H. Irons, *The New Deal Lawyers* (Princeton, N.J.: Princeton University Press, 1982), 278.

West Coast Hotel v. Parrish

300 U.S. 379 (1937)

Vote: 5 (Brandeis, Cardozo, Hughes, Roberts, Stone)
     4 (Butler, McReynolds, Sutherland, Van Devanter)
Opinion of the Court: Hughes
Dissenting opinion: Sutherland

Elsie Parrish had worked as a chambermaid in an Oregon hotel for a wage of twenty-two cents to twenty-five cents per hour.[39] When she was discharged in 1935, she asked the management for

39. We derive this account from William E. Leuchtenburg, "The Case of the Wenatchee Chambermaid," in *Quarrels That Have Shaped the Constitution,* by John Garraty.

back pay of $216.19, "the difference between what she had received and what she would have gotten" if the hotel had abided by the Oregon wage board's minimum wage rate of $14.30 per week.

The hotel offered her $17, but Parrish refused to settle and brought suit against it. She found an attorney willing to represent her, but the attorney could not generate much interest in her case among outside organizations. Even the National Consumers' League declined to participate, viewing it as a waste of time in light of *Morehead*.

Chief Justice Hughes delivered the opinion of the Court:

This case presents the question of the constitutional validity of the minimum wage law of the State of Washington. . . .

The appellant relies upon the decision of this Court in Adkins v. Children's Hospital, which held invalid the District of Columbia Minimum Wage Act which was attacked under the due process clause of the Fifth Amendment. On the argument at bar, counsel for the appellees attempted to distinguish the Adkins Case upon the ground that the appellee was employed in a hotel and that the business of an innkeeper was affected with a public interest. That effort at distinction is obviously futile, as it appears that in one of the cases ruled by the Adkins opinion the employee was a woman employed as an elevator operator in a hotel.

The recent case of Morehead v. New York came here on certiorari to the New York court which had held the New York minimum wage act for women to be invalid. A minority of this Court thought that the New York statute was distinguishable in a material feature from that involved in the Adkins Case and that for that and other reasons the New York statute should be sustained. But the Court of Appeals of New York had said that it found no material difference between the two statutes and this Court held that the "meaning of the statute" as fixed by the decisions of the state court "must be accepted here as if the meaning had been specifically expressed in the enactment." That view led to the affirmance by this Court of the judgment in the Morehead Case, as the Court considered that the only question before it was whether the Adkins Case was distinguishable and that reconsideration of that decision had not been sought. Upon that point the Court said: "The petition for the writ sought review upon the ground that this case [Morehead] is distinguishable from that one [Adkins]. No application has been made for reconsideration of the constitutional question there decided. The validity of the principles upon which that decision rests is not challenged. This court confines itself to the ground upon which the writ was asked or granted. . . . Here the review granted was no broader than that sought by the petitioner. . . . He is not entitled and does not ask to be heard upon the question whether the Adkins Case should be overruled. He maintains that it may be distinguished on the ground that the statutes are vitally dissimilar."

We think that the question which was not deemed to be open in the Morehead Case is open and is necessarily presented here. The Supreme Court of Washington has upheld the minimum wage statute of that State. It has decided that the statute is a reasonable exercise of the police power of the State. In reaching that conclusion the state court has invoked principles long established by this Court in the application of the Fourteenth Amendment. The state court has refused to regard the decision in the Adkins Case as determinative and has pointed to our decisions both before and since that case as justifying its position. We are of the opinion that this ruling of the state court demands on our part a reexamination of the Adkins Case. The importance of the question, in which many States having similar laws are concerned, the close division by which the decision in the Adkins Case was reached, and the economic conditions which have supervened, and in the light of which the reasonableness of the exercise of the protective power of the State must be considered, make it not only appropriate, but we think imperative, that in deciding the present case the subject should receive fresh consideration. . . .

The principle which must control our decision is not in doubt. The constitutional provision invoked is the due process clause of the Fourteenth Amendment governing the States, as the due process clause invoked in the Adkins Case governed Congress. In each case the violation alleged by those attacking minimum wage regulation for women is deprivation of freedom of contract. What is this freedom? The Constitution does not speak of freedom of contract. It speaks of liberty and prohibits the deprivation of liberty without due process of law. In prohibiting that deprivation the Constitution does not recognize an absolute and uncontrollable liberty. Liberty in each of its phases has its history and connotation. But the liberty safeguarded is liberty in a social organization which requires the protection of law against the evils which menace the health, safety, morals and welfare of the people. Liberty under the Constitution is thus necessarily subject to the restraints of due process, and regulation which is reasonable in relation to its subject and is adopted in the interests of the community is due process.

This essential limitation of liberty in general governs freedom of contract in particular. More than twenty-five years ago we set forth the applicable principle in these words after referring to the cases where the liberty guaranteed by the Fourteenth Amendment had been broadly described:

"But it was recognized in the cases cited, as in many others, that freedom of contract is a qualified and not an absolute right. There is no absolute freedom to do as one wills or to contract as one chooses. The guaranty of liberty does not withdraw from legislative supervision that wide department of activity which consists of the making of contracts, or deny to government the power to provide restrictive safeguards. Liberty implies the absence of arbitrary restraint, not immunity from reasonable regulations and prohibitions imposed in the interests of the community."

This power under the Constitution to restrict freedom of contract has had many illustrations. That it may be exercised in the public interest with respect to contracts between employer and employee is undeniable. . . . In dealing with the relation of employer and employed, the legislature has necessarily a wide field of discretion in order that there may be suitable protection of health and safety, and that peace and good order may be promoted through regulations designed to insure wholesome conditions of work and freedom from oppression.

The point that has been strongly stressed that adult employees should be deemed competent to make their own contracts was decisively met nearly forty years ago in Holden v. Hardy, where we pointed out the inequality in the footing of the parties. . . .

It is manifest that this established principle is peculiarly applicable in relation to the employment of women in whose protection the State has a special interest. That phase of the subject received elaborate consideration in Muller v. Oregon (1908). . . . In later rulings this Court sustained the regulation of hours of work of women employees.

This array of precedents and the principles they applied were thought by the dissenting Justices in the Adkins Case to demand that the minimum wage statute be sustained. The validity of the distinction made by

the Court between a minimum wage and a maximum of hours in limiting liberty of contract was especially challenged. That challenge persists and is without any satisfactory answer. As Chief Justice Taft observed: "In absolute freedom of contract the one term is as important as the other, for both enter equally into the consideration given and received; a restriction as to one is not any greater in essence than the other, and is of the same kind. One is the multiplier and the other the multiplicand." And Mr. Justice Holmes, while recognizing that "the distinctions of the law are distinctions of degree," could "perceive no difference in the kind or degree of interference with liberty, the only matter with which we have any concern, between the one case and the other. The bargain is equally affected whichever half you regulate."

One of the points which was pressed by the Court in supporting its ruling in the Adkins Case was that the standard set up by the District of Columbia Act did not take appropriate account of the value of the services rendered. In the Morehead Case, the minority thought that the New York statute had met that point in its definition of a "fair wage" and that it accordingly presented a distinguishable feature which the Court could recognize within the limits which the Morehead petition for certiorari was deemed to present. The Court, however, did not take that view and the New York Act was held to be essentially the same as that for the District of Columbia. The statute now before us is like the latter, but we are unable to conclude that in its minimum wage requirement the State has passed beyond the boundary of its broad protective power.

The minimum wage to be paid under the Washington statute is fixed after full consideration by representatives of employers, employees and the public. It may be assumed that the minimum wage is fixed in consideration of the services that are performed in the particular occupations under normal conditions. Provision is made for special licenses at less wages in the case of women who are incapable of full service. The statement of Mr. Justice Holmes in the Adkins Case is pertinent: "This statute does not compel anybody to pay anything. It simply forbids employment at rates below those fixed as the minimum requirement of health and right living. It is safe to assume that women will not be employed at even the lowest wages allowed unless they earn them, or unless the employer's business can sustain the burden. In short the law in its character and operation is like hundreds of so-called police laws that have been upheld.'' . . .

We think that the views thus expressed are sound and that the decision in the Adkins Case was a departure from the true application of the principles governing the regulation by the State of the relation of employer and employed. Those principles have been reenforced by our subsequent decisions. . . .

With full recognition of the earnestness and vigor which characterize the prevailing opinion in the Adkins Case, we find it impossible to reconcile that ruling with these well-considered declarations. What can be closer to the public interest than the health of women and their protection from unscrupulous and overreaching employers? And if the protection of women is a legitimate end of the exercise of state power, how can it be said that the requirement of the payment of a minimum wage fairly fixed in order to meet the very necessities of existence is not an admissible means to that end? The legislature of the State was clearly entitled to consider the situation of women in employment, the fact that they are in the class receiving the least pay, that their bargaining power is relatively weak, and that they are the ready victims of those who would take advantage of their necessitous circumstances. The legislature was entitled to adopt measures to reduce the evils of the "sweating system," the exploiting of workers at wages so low as to be insufficient to meet the bare cost of living, thus making their very helplessness the occasion of a most injurious competition. The legislature had the right to consider that its minimum wage requirements would be an important aid in carrying out its policy of protection. The adoption of similar requirements by many States evidences a deep-seated conviction both as to the presence of the evil and as to the means adapted to check it. Legislative response to the conviction cannot be regarded as arbitrary or capricious and that is all we

have to decide. Even if the wisdom of the policy be regarded as debatable and its effects uncertain, still the legislature is entitled to its judgment.

There is an additional and compelling consideration which recent economic experience has brought into a strong light. The exploitation of a class of workers who are in an unequal position with respect to bargaining power and are thus relatively defenceless against the denial of a living wage is not only detrimental to their health and well-being but casts a direct burden for their support upon the community. What these workers lose in wages the taxpayers are called upon to pay. The bare cost of living must be met. We may take judicial notice of the unparalleled demands for relief which arose during the recent period of depression and still continue to an alarming extent despite the degree of economic recovery which has been achieved. It is unnecessary to cite official statistics to establish what is of common knowledge through the length and breadth of the land. While in the instant case no factual brief has been presented, there is no reason to doubt that the State of Washington has encountered the same social problem that is present elsewhere. The community is not bound to provide what is in effect a subsidy for unconscionable employers. The community may direct its law-making power to correct the abuse which springs from their selfish disregard of the public interest. The argument that the legislation in question constitutes an arbitrary discrimination, because it does not extend to men, is unavailing. This Court has frequently held that the legislative authority, acting within its proper field, is not bound to extend its regulation to all cases which it might possibly reach. The legislature "is free to recognize degrees of harm and it may confine its restrictions to those classes of cases where the need is deemed to be clearest." . . .

Our conclusion is that the case of Adkins v. Children's Hospital should be, and it is, overruled. The judgment of the Supreme Court of the State of Washington is affirmed.

The Aftermath of West Coast Hotel

West Coast Hotel was an explicit repudiation of economic substantive due process. In one fell swoop, the justices overruled *Adkins* and forever changed the way the Court would view state regulatory efforts. But the period stretching from 1890 through 1936 continues to have an impact on Supreme Court rulings. Although the Court has not revitalized economic due process, neither has it returned to the hard-line position of Justice Miller in *Slaughterhouse*. How then does it examine state regulatory efforts? In some ways, its approach is not all that different, at least in theory, from Waite's in *Munn*. Recall that he promulgated a standard by which the Court should presume state legislation valid. Today's Court has adopted a rational basis test that also "starts with the assumption that legislation bears some rational relation to a state's legitimate powers and places the burden on opponents to prove there is no conceivable rational relationship between the statute or regulation and a legitimate function of government."[40] The difference between Waite's

standard and that of today's Court lies generally in application. The Waite Court and its successors allowed incursions into their standard, and we should remember that the standard was amenable to exceptions; modern Courts have not done so. Indeed, since 1937, the Court has rejected virtually all challenges to state economic regulatory efforts. One reason for these decisions is the nature of the current legal test: it is extremely difficult for attorneys to demonstrate "no conceivable rational relationship." Another reason is the Court's reluctance to apply even that standard to state regulation. Unlike the Waite Court, for example, it simply refuses to determine what is and is not in the public interest or what is rational and what is not.[41]

Williamson v. Lee Optical Company (1955) provides a good example of how the Court now treats Fourteenth Amendment economic claims. This case can be compared with the classic statements for and against a substantive interpretation of the due process clause: Miller's in *Slaughterhouse*, Waite's in *Munn*, Peckham's in *Lochner*, and so forth.

40. Malcolm M. Feeley and Samuel Krislov, *Constitutional Law*, 2d ed. (Glenview, Ill.: Scott, Foresman, 1990), 336.

41. Rossum and Tarr, *American Constitutional Law*, 315.

Williamson v. Lee Optical Company

348 U.S. 483 (1955)

Vote: 8 (Black, Burton, Clark, Douglas, Frankfurter, Minton, Reed, Warren)

0

Opinion of the Court: Douglas
Not participating: Harlan

In 1953 Oklahoma passed a law that made it "unlawful for any person . . . to fit, adjust, adapt, or to apply . . . lenses, frames . . . or any other optical appliances to the face," unless that person was a licensed ophthalmologist, "a physician who specializes in the care of eyes," or

an optometrist, "one who examines eyes for refractory error . . . and fills prescriptions." An optician, an "artisan qualified to grind lenses to fill prescriptions," could do so only from a written prescription from an ophthalmologist or optometrist.

Lee Optical Company challenged the law. The state argued that it was a constitutional exercise of state police power; the company maintained that the statute bore no reasonable relation to a public health and welfare interest and unconstitutionally deprived opticians of their right to perform their craft.

Justice William O. Douglas delivered the opinion of the Court:

The effect of [the act] is to forbid the optician from fitting or duplicating lenses without a prescription from an ophthalmologist or optometrist. In practical effect, it means that no optician can fit old glasses into new frames or supply a lens, whether it be a new lens or one to duplicate a lost or broken lens, without a prescription. The District Court conceded that it was in the competence of the police power of a State to regulate the examination of the eyes. But it rebelled at the notion that a State could require a prescription from an optometrist or ophthalmologist "to take old lenses and place them in new frames and then fit the completed spectacles to the *face* of the eyeglass wearer."
. . . It was, accordingly, the opinion of the court that this provision of the law violated the Due Process Clause by arbitrarily interfering with the optician's right to do business. . . .

The Oklahoma law may exact a needless, wasteful requirement in many cases. But it is for the legislature, not the courts, to balance the advantages and disadvantages of the new requirement. It appears that in many cases the optician can easily supply the new frames or new lenses without reference to the old written prescription. It also appears that many written prescriptions contain no directive data in regard to fitting spectacles to the face. But in some cases the directions contained in the prescription are essential, if the glasses are to be fitted so as to correct the particular defects of vision or alleviate the eye condition. The legislature might have concluded that the frequency of occasions when a prescription is necessary was sufficient to justify this regulation of the fitting of eyeglasses. Likewise, when it is necessary to duplicate a lens, a written prescription may or may not be necessary. But the legislature might have concluded that one was needed often enough to require one in every case. Or the legislature may have concluded that eye examinations were so critical, not only for correction of vision but also for detection of latent ailments or diseases, that every change in frames and every duplication of a lens should be accompanied by a prescription from a medical expert. To be sure, the present law does not require a new examination of the eyes every time the frames are changed or the lenses duplicated. For if the old prescription is on file with the optician, he can go ahead and make the new fitting or duplicate the lenses. But the law need not be in every respect logically consistent with its aims to be constitutional. It is enough that there is an evil at hand for correction, and that it might be thought that the particular legislative measure was a rational way to correct it.

The day is gone when this Court uses the Due Process Clause of the Fourteenth Amendment to strike down state laws, regulatory of business and industrial conditions, because they may be unwise, improvident, or out of harmony with a particular school of thought. . . . We emphasize again what Chief Justice Waite said in Munn v. Illinois, . . . "For protection against abuses by legislatures the people must resort to the polls, not to the courts."

Although *Williamson* was decided in 1955, it continues to characterize the Court's thinking on substantive due process. In *Pennell v. City of San Jose* (1988), the Court rejected the claims of a landlord who sought to invalidate a city rent control scheme on substantive due process grounds. In applying a rational basis standard, Chief Justice William H. Rehnquist concluded, "We have long recognized that a legitimate and rational goal of price or rate regulation is the protection of consumer welfare."

For the moment, therefore, individual economic claims against state regulation lack the protection they once had under the Contract Clause and later under the Fourteenth Amendment. We say "for the moment" because some observers suggest that the justices of the Rehnquist Court have uncovered a new source for the elevation of such "rights": the Takings Clause, as interpreted in *Nollan v. California Coastal Commission* (1987). For now, we can safely assume that the days of *Lochner* have come to a close, at least as they bear on economic rights.

But the demise of the doctrine of substantive due process may have another effect. It may no longer apply to individual economic-state relations, but it currently remains alive as a mode of governance of individual privacy-state relations. Indeed, at least some of the justices in the majority of *Griswold v. Connecticut* (1965), in which the Court struck a Connecticut law prohibiting the disbursement of birth control and established a right to privacy, did so on substantive due process grounds. Justice John Marshall Harlan wrote in a concurring opinion:

In my view, the proper constitutional inquiry in this case is whether this Connecticut statute infringes the Due Process Clause of the Fourteenth Amendment because the enactment violates basic values ''implicit in the concept of ordered liberty.'' . . . The Due Process Clause of the Fourteenth Amendment stands, in my opinion, on its own bottom.

Furthermore, Justice Harry A. Blackmun's opinion in 1973 legalizing abortion *(Roe v. Wade)* during the first two trimesters of pregnancy also invoked the Due Process Clause:

[The] right of privacy, whether it be founded in *the Fourteenth Amendment's concept of personal liberty and restrictions upon state action, as we feel it is,* or [another clause] . . . is broad enough to encompass a woman's decision whether or not to terminate her pregnancy. (Emphasis added.)

That the *Roe* right rests, in part, on the Due Process Clause has been a source of contention among legal scholars. There are those, like John Hart Ely, who accuse Blackmun of ''*Lochnering*,'' of returning to a discredited theory of individual rights as the peg on which to hang abortion rights. Others point out the difference between *Lochner* and *Roe* in the nature of the rights at issue.

Either way, it is true that the doctrine—so exalted at the turn of the century and so despised by its middle—has had a significant effect on the course of the law. What could have simply faded out of existence with Miller's *Slaughterhouse* opinion became the source of one of the most interesting episodes in constitutional law.

READINGS

Berger, Raoul. *Government by Judiciary.* Cambridge, Mass.: Harvard University Press, 1977.

Beth, Loren P. *The Development of the American Constitution.* New York: Harper & Row, 1971.

Jacobs, Clyde E. *Law Writers and the Courts.* Berkeley: University of California Press, 1954.

Keller, Morton. *Affairs of State.* Cambridge, Mass.: Harvard University Press, 1977.

Paul, Arnold M. *Conservative Crisis and the Rule of Law.* Ithaca, N.Y.: Cornell University Press, 1960.

Swindler, William F. *Court and Constitution in the Twentieth Century.* 3 vols. Indianapolis: Bobbs-Merrill, 1970.

Twiss, Benjamin R. *Lawyers and the Constitution.* Princeton, N.J.: Princeton University Press, 1942.

Vose, Clement E. *Constitutional Change.* Lexington, Mass.: Lexington Books, 1972.

Wolfe, Christopher. *The Rise of Modern Judicial Review.* New York: Basic Books, 1986.

APPENDIX

APPENDIX

CONSTITUTION OF THE UNITED STATES

We the People of the United States, in Order to form a more perfect Union, establish Justice, insure domestic Tranquility, provide for the common defence, promote the general Welfare, and secure the Blessings of Liberty to ourselves and our Posterity, do ordain and establish this Constitution for the United States of America.

ARTICLE I

Section 1. All legislative Powers herein granted shall be vested in a Congress of the United States, which shall consist of a Senate and House of Representatives.

Section 2. The House of Representatives shall be composed of Members chosen every second Year by the People of the several States, and the Electors in each State shall have the Qualifications requisite for Electors of the most numerous Branch of the State Legislature.

No Person shall be a Representative who shall not have attained to the age of twenty five Years, and been seven Years a Citizen of the United States, and who shall not, when elected, be an Inhabitant of that State in which he shall be chosen.

[Representatives and direct Taxes shall be apportioned among the several States which may be included within this Union, according to their respective Numbers, which shall be determined by adding to the whole Number of free Persons, including those bound to Service for a Term of Years, and excluding Indians not taxed, three fifths of all other Persons.][1] The actual Enumeration shall be made within three Years after the first Meeting of the Congress of the United States, and within every subsequent Term of ten Years, in such Manner as they shall by Law direct. The Number of Representatives shall not exceed one for every thirty Thousand, but each State shall have at Least one Representative; and until such enumeration shall be made, the State of New Hampshire shall be entitled to chuse three, Massachusetts eight, Rhode-Island and Providence Plantations one, Connecticut five, New-York six, New Jersey four, Pennsylvania eight, Delaware one, Maryland six, Virginia ten, North Carolina five, South Carolina five, and Georgia three.

When vacancies happen in the Representation from any State, the Executive Authority thereof shall issue Writs of Election to fill such Vacancies.

The House of Representatives shall chuse their Speaker and other Officers; and shall have the sole Power of Impeachment.

Section 3. The Senate of the United States shall be composed of two Senators from each State, [chosen by the Legislature thereof,][2] for six Years; and each Senator shall have one Vote.

Immediately after they shall be assembled in Consequence of the first Election, they shall be divided as equally as may be into three Classes. The Seats of the Senators of the first Class shall be vacated at the Expiration of the second Year, of the second Class at the Expiration of the fourth Year, and of the third Class at the Expiration of the sixth Year, so that one third may be chosen every second Year; [and if Vacancies happen by Resignation, or otherwise, during the Recess of the Legislature of any State, the Executive thereof may make temporary Appointments until the next Meeting of the Legislature, which shall then fill such Vacancies.][3]

No Person shall be a Senator who shall not have attained to the Age of thirty Years, and been nine Years a Citizen of the United States, and who shall not, when elected, be an Inhabitant of that State for which he shall be chosen.

The Vice President of the United States shall be President of the Senate, but shall have no Vote, unless they be equally divided.

The Senate shall chuse their other Officers, and also a President pro tempore, in the Absence of the Vice President, or when he shall exercise the Office of President of the United States.

The Senate shall have the sole Power to try all Impeachments. When sitting for that Purpose, they shall be on Oath or Affirmation. When the President of the United States is tried the Chief Justice shall preside: And no Person shall be convicted without the Concurrence of two thirds of the Members present.

Judgment in Cases of Impeachment shall not extend further than to removal from Office, and disqualification to hold and enjoy any Office of honor, Trust or Profit under the United States: but the Party convicted shall nevertheless be liable and subject to Indictment, Trial, Judgment and Punishment, according to Law.

Section 4. The Times, Places and Manner of holding Elections for Senators and Representatives, shall be prescribed in each State by the Legislature thereof; but the Congress may at any time by Law make or alter such Regulations, except as to the Places of chusing Senators.

The Congress shall assemble at least once in every Year, and such Meeting shall [be on the first Monday in December],[4] unless they shall by Law appoint a different Day.

Section 5. Each House shall be the Judge of the Elections, Returns and Qualifications of its own Members, and a Majority of each shall constitute a Quorum to do Business; but a smaller Number may adjourn from day to day, and may be authorized to compel the Attendance of absent Members, in such Manner, and under such Penalties as each House may provide.

Each House may determine the Rules of its Proceedings, punish its Members for disorderly Behaviour, and, with the Concurrence of two thirds, expel a Member.

Each House shall keep a Journal of its Proceedings, and from time to time publish the same, excepting such Parts as may in their Judgment require Secrecy; and the Yeas and Nays of the Members of either House on any question shall, at the Desire of one fifth of those Present, be entered on the Journal.

Neither House, during the Session of Congress, shall, without the Consent of the other, adjourn for more than three days, nor to any other Place than that in which the two Houses shall be sitting.

Section 6. The Senators and Representatives shall receive a Compensation for their Services, to be ascertained by Law, and paid out of the Treasury of the United States. They shall in all Cases, except Treason, Felony and Breach of the Peace, be privileged from Arrest during their Attendance at the Session of their respective Houses, and in going to and returning from the same; and for any Speech or Debate in either House, they shall not be questioned in any other Place.

No Senator or Representative shall, during the Time for which he was elected, be appointed to any civil Office under the Authority of the United States, which shall have been created, or the Emoluments whereof shall have been encreased during such time; and no Person holding any Office under the United States, shall be a Member of either House during his Continuance in Office.

Section 7. All Bills for raising Revenue shall originate in the House of Representatives; but the Senate may propose or concur with amendments as on other Bills.

Every Bill which shall have passed the House of Representatives and the Senate, shall, before it become a Law, be presented to the President of the United States; If he approve he shall sign it, but if not he shall return it, with his Objections to that House in which it shall have originated, who shall enter the Objections at large on their Journal, and proceed to reconsider it. If after such Reconsideration two thirds of that House shall agree to pass the Bill, it shall be sent, together with the Objections, to the other House, by which it shall likewise be reconsidered, and if approved by two thirds of that House, it shall become a Law. But in all such Cases the Votes of both Houses shall be determined by yeas and Nays, and the Names of the Persons voting for and against the Bill shall be entered on the Journal of each House respectively. If any Bill shall not be returned by the President within ten Days (Sundays excepted) after it shall have been presented to him, the Same shall be a Law, in like Manner as if he had signed it, unless the Congress by their Adjournment prevent its Return, in which Case it shall not be a Law.

Every Order, Resolution, or Vote to which the Concurrence of the Senate and House of Representatives may be necessary (except on a question of Adjournment) shall be presented to the President of the United States; and before the Same shall take Effect, shall be approved by him, or being disapproved by him, shall be repassed by two thirds of the Senate and House of Representatives, according to the Rules and Limitations prescribed in the Case of a Bill.

Section 8. The Congress shall have Power To lay and collect Taxes, Duties, Imposts and Excises, to pay the Debts and provide for the common Defence and general Welfare of the United States; but all Duties, Imposts and Excises shall be uniform throughout the United States;

To borrow Money on the credit of the United States;

To regulate Commerce with foreign Nations, and among the several States, and with the Indian Tribes;

To establish an uniform Rule of Naturalization, and uniform Laws on the subject of Bankruptcies throughout the United States;

To coin Money, regulate the Value thereof, and of foreign Coin, and fix the Standard of Weights and Measures;

To provide for the Punishment of counterfeiting the Securities and current Coin of the United States;

To establish Post Offices and post Roads;

To promote the Progress of Science and useful Arts, by securing for limited Times to Authors and Inventors the exclusive Right to their respective Writings and Discoveries;

To constitute Tribunals inferior to the supreme Court;

To define and punish Piracies and Felonies commited on the high Seas, and Offences against the Law of Nations;

To declare War, grant Letters of Marque and Reprisal, and make Rules concerning Captures on Land and Water;

To raise and support Armies, but no Appropriation of Money to that Use shall be for a longer Term than two Years;

To provide and maintain a Navy;

To make Rules for the Government and Regulation of the land and naval Forces;

To provide for calling forth the Militia to execute the Laws of the Union, suppress Insurrections and repel Invasions;

To provide for organizing, arming, and disciplining, the Militia, and for governing such Part of them as may be employed in the Service of the United States, reserving to the States respectively, the Appointment of the Officers, and the Authority of training the Militia according to the discipline prescribed by Congress;

To exercise exclusive Legislation in all Cases whatsoever, over such District (not exceeding ten Miles square) as may, by Cession of Particular States, and the Acceptance of Congress, become the Seat of the Government of the United States, and to exercise like Authority over all Places purchased by the Consent of the Legislature of the State in which the Same shall be, for the Erection of Forts, Magazines, Arsenals, dock-Yards, and other needful Buildings; —And

To make all Laws which shall be necessary and proper for carrying into Execution the foregoing Powers, and all other Powers vested by this Constitution in the Government of the United States, or in any Department or Officer thereof.

Section 9. The Migration or Importation of such Persons as any of the States now existing shall think proper to admit, shall not be prohibited by the Congress prior to the Year one thousand eight hundred and eight, but a Tax or duty may be imposed on such Importation, not exceeding ten dollars for each Person.

The Privilege of the Writ of Habeas Corpus shall not be suspended, unless when in Cases of Rebellion or Invasion the public Safety may require it.

No Bill of Attainder or ex post facto Law shall be passed.

No capitation, or other direct, Tax shall be laid, unless in Proportion to the Census of Enumeration herein before directed to be taken.[5]

No Tax or Duty shall be laid on Articles exported from any State.

No Preference shall be given by any Regulation of Commerce or Revenue to the Ports of one State over those of another; nor shall Vessels bound to, or from, one State, be obliged to enter, clear or pay Duties in another.

No Money shall be drawn from the Treasury, but in Consequence of Appropriations made by Law; and a regular Statement and Account of the Receipts and Expenditures of all public Money shall be published from time to time.

No Title of Nobility shall be granted by the United States: And no Person holding any Office of Profit or Trust under them, shall, without the Consent of the Congress, accept of any present, Emolument, Office, or Title, of any kind whatever, from any King, Prince or foreign State.

Section 10. No State shall enter into any Treaty, Alliance, or Confederation; grant Letters of Marque and Reprisal; coin Money; emit Bills of Credit; make any Thing but gold and silver Coin a Tender in Payment of Debts; pass any Bill of Attainder, ex post facto Law, or Law impairing the Obligation of Contracts, or grant any Title of Nobility.

No State shall, without the Consent of the Congress, lay any Imposts or Duties on Imports or Exports, except what may be absolutely necessary for executing it's inspection Laws: and the net Produce of all Duties and Imposts, laid by any State on Imports or Exports, shall be for the Use of the Treasury of the United States; and all such Laws shall be subject to the Revision and Controul of the Congress.

No State shall, without the Consent of Congress, lay any Duty of Tonnage, keep Troops, or Ships of War in time of Peace, enter into any Agreement or Compact with another State, or with a foreign Power, or engage in War, unless actually invaded, or in such imminent Danger as will not admit of delay.

ARTICLE II

Section 1. The executive Power shall be vested in a President of the United States of America. He shall hold his Office during the Term of four Years, and, together with the Vice President, chosen for the same Term, be elected, as follows.

Each State shall appoint, in such Manner as the Legislature thereof may direct, a Number of Electors, equal to the whole Number of Senators and Representatives to which the State may be entitled in the Congress: but no Senator or Representative, or Person holding an Office of Trust or Profit under the United States, shall be appointed an Elector.

[The Electors shall meet in their respective States, and vote by Ballot for two Persons, of whom one at least shall not be an Inhabitant of the same State with themselves. And they shall make a List of all the Persons voted for, and of the Number of Votes for each; which List they shall sign and certify, and transmit sealed to the Seat of the Government of the United States, directed to the President of the Senate. The President of the Senate shall, in the Presence of the Senate and House of Representatives, open all the Certificates, and the Votes shall then be counted. The Person having the greatest Number of Votes shall be the President, if such Number be a Majority of the whole Number of Electors appointed; and if there be more than one who have such Majority, and have an equal Number of Votes, then the House of Representatives shall immediately chuse by Ballot one of them for President; and if no Person have a Majority, then from the five highest on the list the said House shall in like Manner chuse the President. But in chusing the President, the Votes shall be taken by States, the Representation from each State having one Vote; a quorum for this Purpose shall consist of a Member or Members from two thirds of the States, and a Majority of all the States shall be necessary to a Choice. In every Case, after the Choice of the President, the Person having the greatest Number of Votes of the Electors shall be the Vice President. But if there should remain two or more who have equal Votes, the Senate shall chuse from them by Ballot the Vice President.][6]

The Congress may determine the Time of chusing the Electors, and the Day on which they shall give their Votes; which Day shall be the same throughout the United States.

No Person except a natural born Citizen, or a Citizen of the United States, at the time of the Adoption of this Constitution, shall be eligible to the Office of President; neither shall any Person be eligible to that Office who shall not have attained to the Age of thirty five Years, and been fourteen Years a Resident within the United States.

In Case of the Removal of the President from Office, or of his Death, Resignation, or Inability to discharge the Powers and Duties of the said Office,[7] the Same shall devolve on the Vice President, and the Congress may by Law provide for the Case of Removal, Death, Resignation or Inability, both of the President and Vice President, declaring what Officer shall then act as President, and such Officer shall act accordingly, until the Disability be removed, or a President shall be elected.

The President shall, at stated Times, receive for his Services, a Compensation, which shall neither be encreased nor diminished during the Period for which he shall have been elected, and he shall not receive within that Period any other Emolument from the United States, or any of them.

Before he enter on the Execution of his Office, he shall take the following Oath or Affirmation: —"I do solemnly swear (or affirm) that I will faithfully execute the Office of President of the United States, and will to the best of my Ability, preserve, protect and defend the Constitution of the United States."

Section 2. The President shall be Commander in Chief of the Army and Navy of the United States, and of the Militia of the several States, when called into the actual Service of the United States; he may require the Opinion, in writing, of the principal Officer in each of the executive Departments, upon any Subject relating to the Duties of their respective Offices, and he shall have Power to grant Reprieves and Pardons for Offenses against the United States, except in Cases of Impeachment.

He shall have Power, by and with the Advice and Consent of the Senate, to make Treaties, provided two thirds of the Senators present concur; and he shall nominate, and by and with the Advice and Consent of the Senate, shall appoint Ambassadors, other public Ministers and Consuls, Judges of the supreme Court, and all other Officers of the United States, whose Appointments are not herein otherwise provided for, and which shall be established by Law: but the Congress may by Law vest the Appointment of such inferior Officers, as they think proper, in the President alone, in the Courts of Law, or in the Heads of Departments.

The President shall have Power to fill up all Vacancies that may happen during the Recess of the Senate, by granting Commissions which shall expire at the End of their next Session.

Section 3. He shall from time to time give to the Congress Information of the State of the Union, and recommend to their Consideration such Measures as he shall judge necessary and expedient; he may, on extraordinary Occasions, convene both Houses, or either of them, and in Case of Disagreement between them, with Respect to the Time of Adjournment, he may adjourn them to such Time as he shall think proper; he shall receive Ambassadors and other public Ministers; he shall take Care that the Laws be faithfully executed, and shall Commission all the Officers of the United States.

Section 4. The President, Vice President and all Civil Officers of the United States, shall be removed from office on Impeachment for, and Conviction of, Treason, Bribery, or other high Crimes and Misdemeanors.

ARTICLE III

Section 1. The judicial Power of the United States, shall be vested in one supreme Court, and in such inferior Courts as the Congress may from time to time ordain and establish. The Judges, both of the supreme and inferior Courts, shall hold their Offices during good Behaviour, and shall, at stated Times, receive for their Services, a Compensation, which shall not be diminished during their Continuance in Office.

Section 2. The judicial Power shall extend to all Cases, in Law and Equity, arising under this Constitution, the Laws of the United States, and Treaties made, or which shall be made, under their Authority; —to all Cases affecting Ambassadors, other public Ministers and Consuls; —to all Cases of admiralty and maritime Jurisdiction; —to Controversies to which the United States shall be a Party; —to Controversies between two or more States; —between a State and Citizens of another State;[8] —between Citizens of different States; —between Citizens of the same State claiming Lands under Grants of different States, and between a State, or the Citizens thereof, and foreign States, Citizens or Subjects.[8]

In all Cases affecting Ambassadors, other public Ministers and Consuls, and those in which a State shall be Party, the supreme Court shall have original Jurisdiction. In all the other Cases before mentioned, the supreme Court shall have appellate Jurisdiction, both as to Law and Fact, with such Exceptions, and under such Regulations as the Congress shall make.

The Trial of all Crimes, except in cases of Impeachment, shall be by Jury; and such Trial shall be held in the State where the said Crimes shall have been committed; but when not committed within any State, the Trial shall be at such Place or Places as the Congress may by Law have directed.

Section 3. Treason against the United States, shall consist only in levying War against them, or in adhering to their Enemies, giving them Aid and Comfort. No Person shall be convicted of Treason unless on the Testimony of two Witnesses to the same overt Act, or on Confession in open Court.

The Congress shall have Power to declare the Punishment of Treason, but no Attainder of Treason shall work Corruption of Blood, or Forfeiture except during the Life of the Person attainted.

ARTICLE IV

Section 1. Full Faith and Credit shall be given in each State to the public Acts, Records, and judicial Proceedings of every other State. And the Congress may by general Laws prescribe the Manner in which such Acts, Records and Proceedings shall be proved, and the Effect thereof.

Section 2. The Citizens of each State shall be entitled to all Privileges and Immunities of Citizens in the several States.

A Person charged in any State with Treason, Felony, or other Crime, who shall flee from Justice, and be found in another State, shall on Demand of the executive Authority of the State from which he fled, be delivered up, to be removed to the State having Jurisdiction of the Crime.

[No Person held to Service or Labour in one State, under the Laws thereof, escaping into another, shall, in Consequence of any Law or Regulation therein, be discharged from such Service or Labour, but shall be delivered up on Claim of the Party to whom such Service or Labour may be due.]⁹

Section 3. New States may be admitted by the Congress into this Union; but no new State shall be formed or erected within the Jurisdiction of any other State; nor any State be formed by the Junction of two or more States, or Parts of States, without the Consent of the Legislatures of the States concerned as well as of the Congress.

The Congress shall have Power to dispose of and make all needful Rules and Regulations respecting the Territory or other Property belonging to the United States; and nothing in this Constitution shall be so construed as to Prejudice any Claims of the United States, or of any particular State.

Section 4. The United States shall guarantee to every State in this Union a Republican Form of Government, and shall protect each of them against Invasion; and on Application of the Legislature, or of the Executive (when the Legislature cannot be convened) against domestic Violence.

ARTICLE V

The Congress, whenever two thirds of both Houses shall deem it necessary, shall propose Amendments to this Constitution, or, on the Application of the Legislatures of two thirds of the several States, shall call a Convention for proposing Amendments, which, in either Case, shall be valid to all Intents and Purposes, as Part of this Constitution, when ratified by the Legislatures of three fourths of the several States, or by Conventions in three fourths thereof, as the one or the other Mode of Ratification may be proposed by the Congress; Provided [that no Amendment which may be made prior to the Year One thousand eight hundred and eight shall in any Manner affect the first and fourth Clauses in the Ninth Section of the first Article; and]¹⁰ that no State, without its Consent, shall be deprived of its equal Suffrage in the Senate.

ARTICLE VI

All Debts contracted and Engagements entered into, before the Adoption of this Constitution, shall be as valid against the United States under this Constitution, as under the Confederation.

This Constitution, and the Laws of the United States which shall be made in Pursuance thereof; and all Treaties made, or which shall be made, under the Authority of the United States, shall be the supreme Law of the Land; and the Judges in every State shall be bound thereby, any Thing in the Constitution or Laws of any State to the Contrary notwithstanding.

The Senators and Representatives before mentioned, and the Members of the several State Legislatures, and all executive and judicial Officers, both of the United States and of the several States, shall be bound by Oath or Affirmation, to support this Constitution; but no religious Test shall ever be required as a Qualification to any Office or public Trust under the United States.

ARTICLE VII

The Ratification of the Conventions of nine States, shall be sufficient for the Establishment of this Constitution between the States so ratifying the Same. Done in Convention by the Unanimous Consent of the States present the Seventeenth Day of September in the Year of our Lord one thousand seven hundred and Eighty seven and of the Independence of the United States of America the Twelfth. In witness whereof We have hereunto subscribed our Names, George Washington, President and deputy from Virginia.

New Hampshire:	John Langdon,
	Nicholas Gilman.
Massachusetts:	Nathaniel Gorham,
	Rufus King.
Connecticut:	William Samuel Johnson,
	Roger Sherman.
New York:	Alexander Hamilton.
New Jersey:	William Livingston,
	David Brearley,
	William Paterson,
	Jonathan Dayton.
Pennsylvania:	Benjamin Franklin,
	Thomas Mifflin,
	Robert Morris,
	George Clymer,
	Thomas FitzSimons,
	Jared Ingersoll,
	James Wilson,
	Gouverneur Morris.
Delaware:	George Read,
	Gunning Bedford Jr.,
	John Dickinson,
	Richard Bassett,
	Jacob Broom.
Maryland:	James McHenry,
	Daniel of St. Thomas Jenifer,
	Daniel Carroll.

Virginia:	John Blair, James Madison Jr.
North Carolina:	William Blount, Richard Dobbs Spaight, Hugh Williamson.
South Carolina:	John Rutledge, Charles Cotesworth Pinckney, Charles Pinckney, Pierce Butler.
Georgia:	William Few, Abraham Baldwin.

[The language of the original Constitution, not including the Amendments, was adopted by a convention of the states on Sept. 17, 1787, and was subsequently ratified by the states on the following dates: Delaware, Dec. 7, 1787; Pennsylvania, Dec. 12, 1787; New Jersey, Dec. 18, 1787; Georgia, Jan. 2, 1788; Connecticut, Jan. 9, 1788; Massachusetts, Feb. 6, 1788; Maryland, April 28, 1788; South Carolina, May 23, 1788; New Hampshire, June 21, 1788.

Ratification was completed on June 21, 1788.

The Constitution subsequently was ratified by Virginia, June 25, 1788; New York, July 26, 1788; North Carolina, Nov. 21, 1789; Rhode Island, May 29, 1790; and Vermont, Jan. 10, 1791.]

AMENDMENTS

Amendment I

(First ten amendments ratified December 15, 1791.)

Congress shall make no law respecting an establishment of religion, or prohibiting the free exercise thereof; or abridging the freedom of speech, or of the press; or the right of the people peaceably to assemble, and to petition the Government for a redress of grievances.

Amendment II

A well regulated Militia, being necessary to the security of a free State, the right of the people to keep and bear Arms, shall not be infringed.

Amendment III

No Soldier shall, in time of peace be quartered in any house, without the consent of the Owner, nor in time of war, but in a manner to be prescribed by law.

Amendment IV

The right of the people to be secure in their persons, houses, papers, and effects, against unreasonable searches and seizures, shall not be violated, and no Warrants shall issue, but upon probable cause, supported by Oath or affirmation, and particularly describing the place to be searched, and the persons or things to be seized.

Amendment V

No person shall be held to answer for a capital, or otherwise infamous crime, unless on a presentment or indictment of a Grand Jury, except in cases arising in the land or naval forces, or in the Militia, when in actual service in time of War or public danger; nor shall any person be subject for the same offence to be twice put in jeopardy of life or limb; nor shall be compelled in any criminal case to be a witness against himself, nor be deprived of life, liberty, or property, without due process of law; nor shall private property be taken for public use, without just compensation.

Amendment VI

In all criminal prosecutions, the accused shall enjoy the right to a speedy and public trial, by an impartial jury of the State and district wherein the crime shall have been committed, which district shall have been previously ascertained by law, and to be informed of the nature and cause of the accusation; to be confronted with the witnesses against him; to have compulsory process for obtaining witnesses in his favor, and to have the Assistance of Counsel for his defence.

Amendment VII

In Suits at common law, where the value in controversy shall exceed twenty dollars, the right of trial by jury shall be preserved, and no fact tried by a jury, shall be otherwise reexamined in any Court of the United States, than according to the rules of the common law.

Amendment VIII

Excessive bail shall not be required, nor excessive fines imposed, nor cruel and unusual punishments inflicted.

Amendment IX

The enumeration in the Constitution, of certain rights, shall not be construed to deny or disparage others retained by the people.

Amendment X

The powers not delegated to the United States by the Constitution, nor prohibited by it to the States, are reserved to the States respectively, or to the people.

Amendment XI

(Ratified February 7, 1795)

The Judicial power of the United States shall not be construed to extend to any suit in law or equity, commenced or prosecuted against one of the United States by Citizens of another State, or by Citizens or Subjects of any Foreign State.

Amendment XII

(Ratified June 15, 1804)

The Electors shall meet in their respective states and vote by ballot for President and Vice-President, one of whom, at least, shall not be an inhabitant of the same state with themselves; they shall name in their ballots the person voted for as President, and in distinct ballots the person voted for as Vice-President, and they shall make distinct lists of all persons voted for as President, and of all persons voted for as Vice-President, and of the number of votes for each, which lists they shall sign and certify, and transmit sealed to the seat of the government of the United States, directed to the President of the Senate; —The President of the Senate shall, in the presence of the Senate and House of Representatives, open all the certificates and the votes shall then be counted; —The person having the greatest number of votes for President, shall be the President, if such number be a majority of the whole number of Electors appointed; and if no person have such majority, then from the persons having the highest numbers not exceeding three on the list of those voted for as President, the House of Representatives shall choose immediately, by ballot, the President. But in choosing the President, the votes shall be taken by states, the representation from each state having one vote; a quorum for this purpose shall consist of a member or members from two-thirds of the states, and a majority of all the states shall be necessary to a choice. [And if the House of Representatives shall not choose a President whenever the right of choice shall devolve upon them, before the fourth day of March next following, then the Vice-President shall act as President, as in the case of the death or other constitutional disability of the President—][11] The person having the greatest number of votes as Vice-President, shall be the Vice-President, if such number be a majority of the whole number of Electors appointed, and if no person have a majority, then from the two highest numbers on the list, the Senate shall choose the Vice-President; a quorum for the purpose shall consist of two-thirds of the whole number of Senators, and a majority of the whole number shall be necessary to a choice. But no person constitutionally ineligible to the office of President shall be eligible to that of Vice-President of the United States.

Amendment XIII
(Ratified December 6, 1865)

Section 1. Neither slavery nor involuntary servitude, except as a punishment for crime whereof the party shall have been duly convicted, shall exist within the United States, or any place subject to their jurisdiction.

Section 2. Congress shall have power to enforce this article by appropriate legislation.

Amendment XIV
(Ratified July 9, 1868)

Section 1. All persons born or naturalized in the United States and subject to the jurisdiction thereof, are citizens of the United States and of the State wherein they reside. No State shall make or enforce any law which shall abridge the privileges or immunities of citizens of the United States; nor shall any State deprive any person of life, liberty, or property, without due process of law; nor deny to any person within its jurisdiction the equal protection of the laws.

Section 2. Representatives shall be apportioned among the several States according to their respective numbers, counting the whole number of persons in each State, excluding Indians not taxed. But when the right to vote at any election for the choice of electors for President and Vice President of the United States, Representatives in Congress, the Executive and Judicial officers of a State, or the members of the Legislature thereof, is denied to any of the male inhabitants of such State, being twenty-one years of age,[12] and citizens of the United States, or in any way

abridged, except for participation in rebellion, or other crime, the basis of representation therein shall be reduced in the proportion which the number of such male citizens shall bear to the whole number of male citizens twenty-one years of age in such State.

Section 3. No person shall be a Senator or Representative in Congress, or elector of President and Vice President, or hold any office, civil or military, under the United States, or under any State, who, having previously taken an oath, as a member of Congress, or as an officer of the United States, or as a member of any State legislature, or as an executive or judicial officer of any State, to support the Constitution of the United States, shall have engaged in insurrection or rebellion against the same, or given aid or comfort to the enemies thereof. But Congress may by a vote of two-thirds of each House, remove such disability.

Section 4. The validity of the public debt of the United States, authorized by law, including debts incurred for payment of pensions and bounties for services in suppressing insurrection or rebellion, shall not be questioned. But neither the United States nor any State shall assume or pay any debt or obligation incurred in aid of insurrection or rebellion against the United States, or any claim for the loss or emancipation of any slave; but all such debts, obligations and claims shall be held illegal and void.

Section 5. The Congress shall have power to enforce, by appropriate legislation, the provisions of this article.

Amendment XV
(Ratified February 3, 1870)

Section 1. The right of citizens of the United States to vote shall not be denied or abridged by the United States or by any State on account of race, color, or previous condition of servitude.

Section 2. The Congress shall have power to enforce this article by appropriate legislation.

Amendment XVI
(Ratified February 3, 1913)

The Congress shall have power to lay and collect taxes on incomes, from whatever source derived, without apportionment among the several States, and without regard to any census or enumeration.

Amendment XVII
(Ratified April 8, 1913)

The Senate of the United States shall be composed of two Senators from each State, elected by the people thereof, for six years; and each Senator shall have one vote. The electors in each State shall have the qualifications requisite for electors of the most numerous branch of the State legislatures.

When vacancies happen in the representation of any State in the Senate, the executive authority of such State shall issue writs of election to fill such vacancies: *Provided,* That the legislature of any State may empower the executive thereof to make temporary appointments until the people fill the vacancies by election as the legislature may direct.

This amendment shall not be so construed as to affect the election or term of any Senator chosen before it becomes valid as part of the Constitution.

[Amendment XVIII

(Ratified January 16, 1919)

Section 1. After one year from the ratification of this article the manufacture, sale, or transportation of intoxicating liquors within, the importation thereof into, or the exportation thereof from the United States and all territory subject to the jurisdiction thereof for beverage purposes is hereby prohibited.

Section 2. The Congress and the several States shall have concurrent power to enforce this article by appropriate legislation.

Section 3. This article shall be inoperative unless it shall have been ratified as an amendment to the Constitution by the legislatures of the several States, as provided in the Constitution, within seven years from the date of the submission hereof to the States by the Congress.][13]

Amendment XIX

(Ratified August 18, 1920)

The right of citizens of the United States to vote shall not be denied or abridged by the United States or by any State on account of sex.

Congress shall have power to enforce this article by appropriate legislation.

Amendment XX

(Ratified January 23, 1933)

Section 1. The terms of the President and Vice President shall end at noon on the 20th day of January, and the terms of Senators and Representatives at noon on the 3d day of January, of the years in which such terms would have ended if this article had not been ratified; and the terms of their successors shall then begin.

Section 2. The Congress shall assemble at least once in every year, and such meeting shall begin at noon on the 3d day of January, unless they shall by law appoint a different day.

Section 3.[14] If, at the time fixed for the beginning of the term of the President, the President elect shall have died, the Vice President elect shall become President. If a President shall not have been chosen before the time fixed for the beginning of his term, or if the President elect shall have failed to qualify, then the Vice President elect shall act as President until a President shall have qualified; and the Congress may by law provide for the case wherein neither a President elect nor a Vice President elect shall have qualified, declaring who shall then act as President, or the manner in which one who is to act shall be selected, and such person shall act accordingly until a President or Vice President shall have qualified.

Section 4. The Congress may by law provide for the case of the death of any of the persons from whom the House of Representatives may choose a President whenever the right of choice shall have devolved upon them, and for the case of the death of any of the persons from whom the Senate may choose a Vice President whenever the right of choice shall have devolved upon them.

Section 5. Sections 1 and 2 shall take effect on the 15th day of October following the ratification of this article.

Section 6. This article shall be inoperative unless it shall have been ratified as an amendment to the Constitution by the legislatures of three-fourths of the several States within seven years from the date of its submission.

Amendment XXI

(Ratified December 5, 1933)

Section 1. The eighteenth article of amendment to the Constitution of the United States is hereby repealed.

Section 2. The transportation or importation into any State, Territory or possession of the United States for delivery or use therein of intoxicating liquors, in violation of the laws thereof, is hereby prohibited.

Section 3. This article shall be inoperative unless it shall have been ratified as an amendment to the Constitution by conventions in the several States, as provided in the Constitution, within seven years from the date of the submission hereof to the States by the Congress.

Amendment XXII

(Ratified February 27, 1951)

Section 1. No person shall be elected to the office of the President more than twice, and no person who has held the office of President, or acted as President, for more than two years of a term to which some other person was elected President shall be elected to the office of the President more than once. But this Article shall not apply to any person holding the office of President when this Article was proposed by the Congress, and shall not prevent any person who may be holding the office of President, or acting as President, during the term within which this Article become operative from holding the office of President or acting as President during the remainder of such term.

Section 2. This Article shall be inoperative unless it shall have been ratified as an amendment to the Constitution by the legislatures of three-fourths of the several States within seven years from the date of its submission to the States by the Congress.

Amendment XXIII

(Ratified March 29, 1961)

Section 1. The District constituting the seat of Government of the United States shall appoint in such manner as the Congress may direct:

A number of electors of President and Vice President equal to the whole number of Senators and Representatives in Congress to which the District would be entitled if it were a State, but in no event more than the least populous State;

they shall be in addition to those appointed by the States, but they shall be considered, for the purposes of the election of President and Vice President, to be electors appointed by a State; and they shall meet in the District and perform such duties as provided by the twelfth article of amendment.

Section 2. The Congress shall have power to enforce this article by appropriate legislation.

Amendment XXIV
(Ratified January 23, 1964)

Section 1. The right of citizens of the United States to vote in any primary or other election for President or Vice President, for electors for President or Vice President, or for Senator or Representative in Congress, shall not be denied or abridged by the United States or any State by reason of failure to pay any poll tax or other tax.

Section 2. The Congress shall have power to enforce this article by appropriate legislation.

Amendment XXV
(Ratified February 10, 1967)

Section 1. In case of the removal of the President from office or of his death or resignation, the Vice President shall become President.

Section 2. Whenever there is a vacancy in the office of the Vice President, the President shall nominate a Vice President who shall take office upon confirmation by a majority vote of both Houses of Congress.

Section 3. Whenever the President transmits to the President pro tempore of the Senate and the Speaker of the House of Representatives his written declaration that he is unable to discharge the powers and duties of his office, and until he transmits to them a written declaration to the contrary, such powers and duties shall be discharged by the Vice President as Acting President.

Section 4. Whenever the Vice President and a majority of either the principal officers of the executive departments or of such other body as Congress may by law provide, transmit to the President pro tempore of the Senate and the Speaker of the House of Representatives their written declaration that the President is unable to discharge the powers and duties of his office, the Vice President shall immediately assume the powers and duties of the office as Acting President.

Thereafter, when the President transmits to the President pro tempore of the Senate and the Speaker of the House of Representatives his written declaration that no inability exists, he shall resume the powers and duties of his office unless the Vice President and a majority of either the principal officers of the executive department or of such other body as Congress may by law provide, transmit within four days to the President pro tempore of the Senate and the Speaker of the House of Representatives their written declaration that the President is unable to discharge the powers and duties of his office. Thereupon Congress shall decide the issue, assembling within forty-eight hours for that purpose if not in session. If the Congress, within twenty-one days after receipt of the latter written declaration, or, if Congress is not in session, within twenty-one days after Congress is required to assemble, determines by two-thirds vote of both houses that the President is unable to discharge the powers and duties of his office, the Vice President shall continue to discharge the same as Acting President; otherwise, the President shall resume the powers and duties of his office.

Amendment XXVI
(Ratified July 1, 1971)

Section 1. The right of citizens of the United States, who are eighteen years of age or older, to vote shall not be denied or abridged by the United States or by any State on account of age.

Section 2. The Congress shall have power to enforce this article by appropriate legislation.

Notes

1. The part in brackets was changed by Section 2 of the Fourteenth Amendment.
2. The part in brackets was changed by Section 1 of the Seventeenth Amendment.
3. The part in brackets was changed by the second paragraph of the Seventeenth Amendment.
4. The part in brackets was changed by Section 2 of the Twentieth Amendment.
5. The Sixteenth Amendment gave Congress the power to tax incomes.
6. The material in brackets has been superseded by the Twelfth Amendment.
7. This provision has been affected by the Twenty-fifth Amendment.
8. These clauses were affected by the Eleventh Amendment.
9. This paragraph has been superseded by the Thirteenth Amendment.
10. Obsolete.
11. The part in brackets has been superseded by Section 3 of the Twentieth Amendment.
12. See the Twenty-sixth Amendment.
13. This Amendment was repealed by Section 1 of the Twenty-first Amendment.
14. See the Twenty-fifth Amendment.

U.S. PRESIDENTS

PRESIDENT	POLITICAL PARTY	TERM OF SERVICE
George Washington	Federalist	April 30, 1789–March 4, 1793
George Washington	Federalist	March 4, 1793–March 4, 1797
John Adams	Federalist	March 4, 1797–March 4, 1801
Thomas Jefferson	Democratic Republican	March 4, 1801–March 4, 1805
Thomas Jefferson	Democratic Republican	March 4, 1805–March 4, 1809
James Madison	Democratic Republican	March 4, 1809–March 4, 1813
James Madison	Democratic Republican	March 4, 1813–March 4, 1817
James Monroe	Democratic Republican	March 4, 1817–March 4, 1821
James Monroe	Democratic Republican	March 4, 1821–March 4, 1825
John Q. Adams	Democratic Republican	March 4, 1825–March 4, 1829
Andrew Jackson	Democrat	March 4, 1829–March 4, 1833
Andrew Jackson	Democrat	March 4, 1833–March 4, 1837
Martin Van Buren	Democrat	March 4, 1837–March 4, 1841
W. H. Harrison	Whig	March 4, 1841–April 4, 1841
John Tyler	Whig	April 6, 1841–March 4, 1845
James K. Polk	Democrat	March 4, 1845–March 4, 1849
Zachary Taylor	Whig	March 4, 1849–July 9, 1850
Millard Fillmore	Whig	July 10, 1850–March 4, 1853
Franklin Pierce	Democrat	March 4, 1853–March 4, 1857
James Buchanan	Democrat	March 4, 1857–March 4, 1861
Abraham Lincoln	Republican	March 4, 1861–March 4, 1865
Abraham Lincoln	Republican	March 4, 1865–April 15, 1865
Andrew Johnson	Republican	April 15, 1865–March 4, 1869
Ulysses S. Grant	Republican	March 4, 1869–March 4, 1873
Ulysses S. Grant	Republican	March 4, 1873–March 4, 1877
Rutherford B. Hayes	Republican	March 4, 1877–March 4, 1881
James A. Garfield	Republican	March 4, 1881–Sept. 19, 1881
Chester A. Arthur	Republican	Sept. 20, 1881–March 4, 1885
Grover Cleveland	Democrat	March 4, 1885–March 4, 1889
Benjamin Harrison	Republican	March 4, 1889–March 4, 1893
Grover Cleveland	Democrat	March 4, 1893–March 4, 1897
William McKinley	Republican	March 4, 1897–March 4, 1901
William McKinley	Republican	March 4, 1901–Sept. 14, 1901
Theodore Roosevelt	Republican	Sept. 14, 1901–March 4, 1905

PRESIDENT	POLITICAL PARTY	TERM OF SERVICE
Theodore Roosevelt	Republican	March 4, 1905–March 4, 1909
William H. Taft	Republican	March 4, 1909–March 4, 1913
Woodrow Wilson	Democrat	March 4, 1913–March 4, 1917
Woodrow Wilson	Democrat	March 4, 1917–March 4, 1921
Warren G. Harding	Republican	March 4, 1921–Aug. 2, 1923
Calvin Coolidge	Republican	Aug. 3, 1923–March 4, 1925
Calvin Coolidge	Republican	March 4, 1925–March 4, 1929
Herbert Hoover	Republican	March 4, 1929–March 4, 1933
Franklin D. Roosevelt	Democrat	March 4, 1933–Jan. 20, 1937
Franklin D. Roosevelt	Democrat	Jan. 20, 1937–Jan. 20, 1941
Franklin D. Roosevelt	Democrat	Jan. 20, 1941–Jan. 20, 1945
Franklin D. Roosevelt	Democrat	Jan. 20, 1945–April 12, 1945
Harry S Truman	Democrat	April 12, 1945–Jan. 20, 1949
Harry S Truman	Democrat	Jan. 20, 1949–Jan. 20, 1953
Dwight D. Eisenhower	Republican	Jan. 20, 1953–Jan. 20, 1957
Dwight D. Eisenhower	Republican	Jan. 20, 1957–Jan. 20, 1961
John F. Kennedy	Democrat	Jan. 20, 1961–Nov. 22, 1963
Lyndon B. Johnson	Democrat	Nov. 22, 1963–Jan. 20, 1965
Lyndon B. Johnson	Democrat	Jan. 20, 1965–Jan. 20, 1969
Richard Nixon	Republican	Jan. 20, 1969–Jan. 20, 1973
Richard Nixon	Republican	Jan. 20, 1973–Aug. 9, 1974
Gerald R. Ford	Republican	Aug. 9, 1974–Jan. 20, 1977
Jimmy Carter	Democrat	Jan. 20, 1977–Jan. 20, 1981
Ronald Reagan	Republican	Jan. 20, 1981–Jan. 20, 1985
Ronald Reagan	Republican	Jan. 20, 1985–Jan. 20, 1989
George Bush	Republican	Jan. 20, 1989–

THUMBNAIL SKETCH OF THE SUPREME COURT'S HISTORY

COURT ERA	CHIEF JUSTICES	DEFINING CHARACTERISTICS	MAJOR COURT CASES
Developmental Period (1789–1800)	John Jay (1789–1795) John Rutledge (1795) Oliver Ellsworth (1796–1800)	Low prestige: spotty attendance by justices, resignations for more "prestigious positions," hears about fifty cases Business of the Court: largely admiralty and maritime disputes Use of seriatim opinion practice	*Chisolm v. Georgia* (1793) *Ware v. Hylton* (1796) *Hylton v. United States* (1796)
The Marshall Court (1801–1835)	John Marshall (1801–1835)	Establishment of Court's role in governmental process Strong Court support for national powers (especially commerce) over states' rights Use of "Opinions of the Court," rather than seriatim practice Beginning of systematic reporting of Court opinions Despite the importance of its opinions interpreting the Constitution, the business of the Court continues to involve private law issues (maritime, property, contracts)	*Marbury v. Madison* (1803) *Fletcher v. Peck* (1810) *Dartmouth College v. Woodward* (1819) *McCulloch v. Maryland* (1819) *Cohens v. Virginia* (1821) *Gibbons v. Ogden* (1824)
Taney and Civil War Courts (1836–1888)	Roger Taney (1836–1864) Salmon Chase (1864–1873) Morrison Waite (1874–1888)	Continued assertion of federal power over states (with some accommodation for state police powers) Growing North-South splits on the Court Court showdowns with Congress at the onset and conclusion of the Civil War Growth of Court's caseload, with the majority of post–Civil War cases involving private law issues and war litigation Congress fixes Court size at nine	*Charles River Bridge v. Warren Bridge* (1837) *New York v. Miln* (1837) *Luther v. Borden* (1849) *Dred Scott v. Sandford* (1857) *Ex parte Milligan* (1866) *Ex parte McCardle* (1869) *Civil Rights Cases* (1883)
Conservative Court Eras (1889–1937)	Melville Fuller (1888–1910) Edward White (1910–1921) William Howard Taft (1921–1930) Charles Evans Hughes (1930–1937)	But for a brief period reflecting progressivism, the Courts of this era tended to protect business interests over governmental police powers Court sets "civil rights" policy of "separate but equal" Congress relieves justices of circuit riding duty Congress, in 1925 Judiciary Act, gives Court greater discretion over its docket Despite Judiciary Act, Court's docket continues to grow, with many cases reflecting economic issues (e.g., congressional power under the Commerce Clause) Some important construction of Bill of Rights guarantees (protection of rights increases after WW I) Showdown with FDR over New Deal legislation: Court continues to strike down New Deal	*United States v. E. C. Knight* (1895) *Pollack v. Farmers' Loan* (1895) *Plessy v. Ferguson* (1896) *Allegeyer v. Louisiana* (1897) *Lochner v. New York* (1905) *Hammer v. Dagenhart* (1918) *Schenck v. United States* (1919) *Adkins v. Children's Hospital* (1923) *Near v. Minnesota* (1931)

COURT ERA	CHIEF JUSTICES	DEFINING CHARACTERISTICS	MAJOR COURT CASES
		laws, leading the president to propose a Court packing plan	*Powell v. Alabama* (1932) *Schecter Poultry v. United States* (1935)
The Roosevelt and World War II Court Eras (1937–1953)	Charles Evans Hughes (1937–1941) Harlan Fiske Stone (1941–1946) Fred Vinson (1946–1953)	With the "switch in time that saved nine" the Court begins to uphold federal regulations under the Commerce Clause, as well as state use of police powers Expansion of rights and liberties, until WW II and ensuing cold war Increases in nonconsensual behavior (dissents and concurrences) among the justices	*NLRB v. Jones & Laughlin Steel* (1937) *United States v. Carolene Products* (1938) *Korematsu v. United States* (1944) *Dennis v. United States* (1951) *Youngstown Sheet & Tube v. Sawyer* (1952)
The Warren Court Era (1953–1969)	Earl Warren (1953–1969)	Expansion of rights, liberties, and criminal justice Establishment of the right to privacy Emergence of Court as national policy maker Continued increase in Court's docket, with steady growth in the number of *in forma pauperis* petitions Growth in the percentage of constitutional cases on Court's plenary docket First black appointed to the Court (Marshall)	*Brown v. Board of Education* (1954) *Roth v. United States* (1957) *Mapp v. Ohio* (1961) *Baker v. Carr* (1962) *Abington School District v. Schempp* (1963) *Gideon v. Wainwright* (1963) *Heart of Atlanta Motel v. United States* (1964) *New York Times v. Sullivan* (1964) *Griswold v. Connecticut* (1965) *Miranda v. Arizona* (1966)
Republican Court Eras (1969–)	Warren Burger (1969–1986) William Rehnquist (1986–)	Attempts in some areas (e.g., criminal law) to limit or rescind Warren Court rulings Expansion of women's rights, including right to abortion Some attempt to increase state power Legitimation of affirmative action policies Court increasingly called on to resolve intergovernmental disputes, involving separation of powers or the authority of one branch of government over another Appointment of first woman to the Court (O'Connor)	*Reed v. Reed* (1971) *New York Times v. United States* (1971) *Roe v. Wade* (1973) *Miller v. California* (1973) *United States v. Nixon* (1974) *Buckley v. Valeo* (1976) *Gregg v. Georgia* (1976) *Regents of the University of California v. Bakke* (1978) *United States v. Leon* (1984) *Garcia v. SAMTA* (1985) *Webster v. Reproductive Health Services* (1989)

THE JUSTICES

The justices of the Supreme Court are listed below in order of appointment, with the dates of their lives, state from which appointed, political party affiliation at time of appointment, educational institutions attended, appointing president, confirmation date and vote, date of service termination, and significant pre-appointment offices and activities.

Jay, John (1745–1829). New York. Federalist. King's College (Columbia University). Nominated chief justice by George Washington; confirmed 1789 by voice vote; resigned 1795. Delegate to Continental Congress, chief justice of New York, minister to Spain and Great Britain, secretary of foreign affairs.

Rutledge, John (1739–1800). South Carolina. Federalist. Middle Temple (England). Nominated associate justice by George Washington; confirmed 1789 by voice vote; resigned 1791. Nominated chief justice by George Washington August 1795 and served as recess appointment; confirmation denied and service terminated December 1795. South Carolina legislator, state attorney general, governor, chief justice of South Carolina, delegate to Continental Congress and Constitutional Convention.

Cushing, William (1732–1810). Massachusetts. Federalist. Harvard. Nominated associate justice by George Washington; confirmed 1789 by voice vote; died in office 1810. Massachusetts state court judge, electoral college delegate.

Wilson, James (1742–1798). Pennsylvania. Federalist. University of St. Andrews (Scotland). Nominated associate justice by George Washington; confirmed 1789 by voice vote; died in office 1798. Delegate to Continental Congress and Constitutional Convention.

Blair, John, Jr. (1732–1800). Virginia. Federalist. College of William and Mary; Middle Temple (England). Nominated associate justice by George Washington; confirmed 1789 by voice vote; resigned 1796. Virginia legislator, state court judge, delegate to Constitutional Convention.

Iredell, James (1751–1799). North Carolina. Federalist. English schools. Nominated associate justice by George Washington; confirmed 1790 by voice vote; died in office 1799. Customs official, state court judge, state attorney general.

Johnson, Thomas (1732–1819). Maryland. Federalist. Privately educated. Nominated associate justice by George Washington; confirmed 1791 by voice vote; resigned 1793. Delegate to Annapolis Convention and Continental Congress, governor, state legislator, state court judge.

Paterson, William (1745–1806). New Jersey. Federalist. Princeton. Nominated associate justice by George Washington; confirmed 1793 by voice vote; died in office 1806. New Jersey attorney general, delegate to Constitutional Convention, U.S. senator, governor.

Chase, Samuel (1741–1811). Maryland. Federalist. Privately educated. Nominated associate justice by George Washington; confirmed 1796 by voice vote; died in office 1811. Maryland state legislator, delegate to Continental Congress, state court judge.

Ellsworth, Oliver (1745–1807). Connecticut. Federalist. Princeton. Nominated chief justice by George Washington; confirmed 1796 by 21-1 vote; resigned 1800. Connecticut state legislator, delegate to Continental Congress and Constitutional Convention, state court judge, U.S. senator.

Washington, Bushrod (1762–1829). Virginia. Federalist. College of William and Mary. Nominated associate justice by John Adams; confirmed 1798 by voice vote; died in office 1829. Virginia state legislator.

Moore, Alfred (1755–1810). North Carolina. Federalist. Privately educated. Nominated associate justice by John Adams; confirmed 1799 by voice vote; resigned 1804. North Carolina legislator, state attorney general, state court judge.

Marshall, John (1755–1835). Virginia. Federalist. Privately educated, College of William and Mary.

Nominated chief justice by John Adams; confirmed 1801 by voice vote; died in office 1835. Virginia state legislator, minister to France, U.S. representative, U.S. secretary of state.

Johnson, William (1771–1834). South Carolina. Democratic/Republican. Princeton. Nominated associate justice by Thomas Jefferson; confirmed 1804 by voice vote; died in office 1834. South Carolina state legislator, state court judge.

Livingston, Henry Brockholst (1757–1823). New York. Democratic/Republican. Princeton. Nominated associate justice by Thomas Jefferson; confirmed 1806 by voice vote; died in office 1823. New York state legislator, state court judge.

Todd, Thomas (1765–1826). Kentucky. Democratic/Republican. Liberty Hall (Washington and Lee). Nominated associate justice by Thomas Jefferson; confirmed 1807 by voice vote; died in office 1826. Kentucky state court judge, state chief justice.

Story, Joseph (1779–1845). Massachusetts. Democratic/Republican. Harvard. Nominated associate justice by James Madison; confirmed 1811 by voice vote; died in office 1845. Massachusetts state legislator, U.S. representative.

Duvall, Gabriel (1752–1844). Maryland. Democratic/Republican. Privately educated. Nominated associate justice by James Madison; confirmed 1811 by voice vote; resigned 1835. Maryland state legislator, U.S. representative, state court judge, presidential elector, comptroller of the U.S. Treasury.

Thompson, Smith (1768–1843). New York. Democratic/Republican. Princeton. Nominated associate justice by James Monroe; confirmed 1823 by voice vote; died in office 1843. New York state legislator, state court judge, secretary of the navy.

Trimble, Robert (1776–1828). Kentucky. Democratic/Republican. Kentucky Academy. Nominated associate justice by John Quincy Adams; confirmed 1826 by 27-5 vote; died in office 1828. Kentucky state legislator, state court judge, U.S. attorney, federal district court judge.

McLean, John (1785–1861). Ohio. Democrat. Privately educated. Nominated associate justice by Andrew Jackson; confirmed 1829 by voice vote; died in office 1861. U.S. representative, Ohio Supreme Court, commissioner of U.S. General Land Office, U.S. postmaster general.

Baldwin, Henry (1780–1844). Pennsylvania. Democrat. Yale. Nominated associate justice by Andrew Jackson; confirmed 1830 by 41-2 vote; died in office 1844. U.S. representative.

Wayne, James Moore (1790–1867). Georgia. Democrat. Princeton. Nominated associate justice by Andrew Jackson; confirmed 1835 by voice vote; died in office 1867. Georgia state legislator, mayor of Savannah, state court judge, U.S. representative.

Taney, Roger Brooke (1777–1864). Maryland. Democrat. Dickinson College. Nominated associate justice by Andrew Jackson; nomination not confirmed 1835; nominated chief justice by Andrew Jackson; confirmed 1836 by 29-15 vote; died in office 1864. Maryland state legislator, state attorney general, acting secretary of war, secretary of the Treasury (nomination later rejected by Senate).

Barbour, Philip Pendleton (1783–1841). Virginia. Democrat. College of William and Mary. Nominated associate justice by Andrew Jackson; confirmed 1836 by 30-11 vote; died in office 1841. Virginia state legislator, U.S. representative, U.S. Speaker of the House, state court judge, federal district court judge.

Catron, John (1786–1865). Tennessee. Democrat. Self-educated. Nominated associate justice by Andrew Jackson; confirmed 1837 by 28-15 vote; died in office 1865. Tennessee state court judge, state chief justice.

McKinley, John (1780–1852). Alabama. Democrat. Self-educated. Nominated associate justice by Martin Van Buren; confirmed 1837 by voice vote; died in office 1852. Alabama state legislator, U.S. senator, U.S. representative.

Daniel, Peter Vivian (1784–1860). Virginia. Democrat. Princeton. Nominated associate justice by Martin Van Buren; confirmed 1841 by 22-5 vote; died in office 1860. Virginia state legislator, state Privy Council, federal district court judge.

Nelson, Samuel (1792–1873). New York. Democrat. Middlebury College. Nominated associate justice by John Tyler; confirmed 1845 by voice vote; retired 1872. Presidential elector, state court judge, New York Supreme Court chief justice.

Woodbury, Levi (1789–1851). New Hampshire. Democrat. Dartmouth, Tapping Reeve Law School. Nominated associate justice by James Polk; confirmed 1846 by voice vote; died in office 1851. New Hampshire state legislator, state court judge, governor, U.S. senator, secretary of the navy, secretary of the Treasury.

Grier, Robert Cooper (1794–1870). Pennsylvania. Democrat. Dickinson College. Nominated associate justice by James Polk; confirmed 1846 by voice vote; retired 1870. Pennsylvania state court judge.

Curtis, Benjamin Robbins (1809–1874). Massachusetts. Whig. Harvard. Nominated associate justice by Millard Fillmore; confirmed 1851 by voice vote; resigned 1857. Massachusetts state legislator.

Campbell, John Archibald (1811–1889). Alabama. Democrat. Franklin College (University of Georgia), U.S. Military Academy. Nominated associate justice by Franklin Pierce; confirmed 1853 by voice vote; resigned 1861. Alabama state legislator.

Clifford, Nathan (1803–1881). Maine. Democrat. Privately educated. Nominated associate justice by James Buchanan; confirmed 1858 by 26-23 vote; died in office 1881. Maine state legislator, state attorney general, U.S. representative, U.S. attorney general, minister to Mexico.

Swayne, Noah Haynes (1804–1884). Ohio. Republican. Privately educated. Nominated associate justice by Abraham Lincoln; confirmed 1862 by 38-1 vote; retired 1881. Ohio state legislator, local prosecutor, U.S. attorney for Ohio, Columbus city council.

Miller, Samuel Freeman (1816–1890). Iowa. Republican. Transylvania University. Nominated associate justice by Abraham Lincoln; confirmed 1862 by voice vote; died in office 1890. Medical doctor, private law practice, justice of the peace.

Davis, David (1815–1886). Illinois. Republican. Kenyon College, Yale. Nominated associate justice by Abraham Lincoln; confirmed 1862 by voice vote; resigned 1877. Illinois state legislator, state court judge.

Field, Stephen J. (1816–1899). California. Democrat. Williams College. Nominated associate justice by Abraham Lincoln; confirmed 1863 by voice vote; retired 1897. California state legislator, California Supreme Court.

Chase, Salmon Portland (1808–1873). Ohio. Republican. Dartmouth. Nominated chief justice by Abraham Lincoln; confirmed 1864 by voice vote; died in office 1873. U.S. senator, Ohio governor, U.S. secretary of the Treasury.

Strong, William (1808–1895). Pennsylvania. Republican. Yale. Nominated associate justice by Ulysses S. Grant; confirmed 1870 by voice vote; retired 1880. U.S. representative, Pennsylvania Supreme Court.

Bradley, Joseph P. (1813–1892). New Jersey. Republican. Rutgers. Nominated associate justice by Ulysses S. Grant; confirmed 1870 by 46-9 vote; died in office 1892. Private law practice.

Hunt, Ward (1810–1886). New York. Republican. Union College. Nominated associate justice by Ulysses S. Grant; confirmed 1872 by voice vote; retired 1882. New York state legislator, mayor of Utica, state court judge.

Waite, Morrison Remick (1816–1888). Ohio. Republican. Yale. Nominated chief justice by Ulysses S. Grant; confirmed 1874 by 63-0 vote; died in office 1888. Private practice, Ohio state legislator.

Harlan, John Marshall (1833–1911). Kentucky. Republican. Centre College, Transylvania University. Nominated associate justice by Rutherford B. Hayes; confirmed 1877 by voice vote; died in office 1911. Kentucky attorney general.

Woods, William B. (1824–1887). Georgia. Republican. Western Reserve College, Yale. Nominated associate justice by Rutherford B. Hayes; confirmed 1880 by 39-8 vote; died in office 1887. Ohio state legislator, Alabama chancellor, federal circuit court judge.

Matthews, Stanley (1824–1889). Ohio. Republican. Kenyon College. Nominated associate justice by Rutherford B. Hayes; no Senate action on nomination; renominated associate justice by James A. Garfield; confirmed 1881 by 24-23 vote; died in office 1889. Ohio state legislator, state court judge, U.S. attorney for southern Ohio, U.S. senator.

Gray, Horace (1828–1902). Massachusetts. Republican. Harvard. Nominated associate justice by Chester A. Arthur; confirmed 1881 by 51-5 vote; died in office 1902. Massachusetts Supreme Court.

Blatchford, Samuel (1820–1893). New York. Republican. Columbia. Nominated associate justice by Chester A. Arthur; confirmed 1882 by voice vote; died in office 1893. Federal district court judge, federal circuit court judge.

Lamar, Lucius Quintus Cincinnatus (1825–1893). Mississippi. Democrat. Emory College. Nominated associate justice by Grover Cleveland; confirmed

1888 by 32-28 vote; died in office 1893. Georgia state legislator, U.S. representative from Mississippi, U.S. senator from Mississippi, U.S. secretary of the interior.

Fuller, Melville Weston (1833–1910). Illinois. Democrat. Bowdoin College, Harvard. Nominated chief justice by Grover Cleveland; confirmed 1888 by 41-20 vote; died in office 1910. Illinois state legislator.

Brewer, David Josiah (1837–1910). Kansas. Republican. Wesleyan, Yale, Albany Law School. Nominated associate justice by Benjamin Harrison; confirmed 1889 by 53-11 vote; died in office 1910. Kansas state court judge, federal circuit court judge.

Brown, Henry B. (1836–1913). Michigan. Republican. Yale, Harvard. Nominated associate justice by Benjamin Harrison; confirmed 1890 by voice vote; retired 1906. Michigan state court judge, federal district court judge.

Shiras, George, Jr. (1832–1924). Pennsylvania. Republican. Ohio University, Yale. Nominated associate justice by Benjamin Harrison; confirmed 1892 by voice vote; retired 1903. Private practice.

Jackson, Howell Edmunds (1832–1895). Tennessee. Democrat. West Tennessee College, University of Virginia, Cumberland University. Nominated associate justice by Benjamin Harrison; confirmed 1893 by voice vote; died in office 1895. Tennessee state legislator, U.S. senator, federal circuit court judge, federal court of appeals judge.

White, Edward Douglass (1845–1921). Louisiana. Democrat. Mount St. Mary's College, Georgetown. Nominated associate justice by Grover Cleveland; confirmed 1894 by voice vote; nominated chief justice by William Howard Taft; confirmed 1910 by voice vote; died in office 1921. Louisiana state legislator, Louisiana Supreme Court, U.S. senator.

Peckham, Rufus Wheeler (1838–1909). New York. Democrat. Albany Boys' Academy. Nominated associate justice by Grover Cleveland; confirmed 1895 by voice vote; died in office 1909. New York local district attorney, city attorney, state court judge.

McKenna, Joseph (1843–1926). California. Republican. Benicia Collegiate Institute. Nominated associate justice by William McKinley; confirmed 1898 by voice vote; retired 1925. California state legislator, U.S. representative, federal court of appeals judge, U.S. attorney general.

Holmes, Oliver Wendell, Jr. (1841–1935). Massachusetts. Republican. Harvard. Nominated associate justice by Theodore Roosevelt; confirmed 1902 by voice vote; retired 1932. Professor, Massachusetts Supreme Court.

Day, William Rufus (1849–1923). Ohio. Republican. University of Michigan. Nominated associate justice by Theodore Roosevelt; confirmed 1903 by voice vote; resigned 1922. Ohio state court judge, U.S. secretary of state, federal court of appeals judge.

Moody, William Henry (1853–1917). Massachusetts. Republican. Harvard. Nominated associate justice by Theodore Roosevelt; confirmed 1906 by voice vote; retired 1910. Massachusetts local district attorney, U.S. representative, secretary of the navy, U.S. attorney general.

Lurton, Horace Harmon (1844–1914). Tennessee. Democrat. University of Chicago, Cumberland. Nominated associate justice by William Howard Taft; confirmed 1909 by voice vote; died in office 1914. Tennessee Supreme Court, federal court of appeals judge.

Hughes, Charles Evans (1862–1948). New York. Republican. Colgate, Brown, Columbia. Nominated associate justice by William Howard Taft; confirmed 1910 by voice vote; resigned 1916; nominated chief justice by Herbert Hoover; confirmed 1930 by 52-26 vote; retired 1941. New York governor, U.S. secretary of state, Court of International Justice judge.

Van Devanter, Willis (1859–1941). Wyoming. Republican. Indiana Ashbury University, University of Cincinnati. Nominated associate justice by William Howard Taft; confirmed 1910 by voice vote; retired 1937. Cheyenne city attorney, Wyoming territorial legislature. Wyoming Supreme Court, assistant U.S. attorney general, federal court of appeals judge.

Lamar, Joseph Rucker (1857–1916). Georgia. Democrat. University of Georgia, Bethany College, Washington and Lee. Nominated associate justice by William Howard Taft; confirmed 1910 by voice vote; died in office 1916. Georgia state legislator, Georgia Supreme Court.

Pitney, Mahlon (1858–1924). New Jersey. Republican. Princeton. Nominated associate justice by William Howard Taft; confirmed 1912 by 50-26 vote; retired 1922. U.S. representative, New Jersey state legislator, New Jersey Supreme Court, Chancellor of New Jersey.

McReynolds, James Clark (1862–1946). Tennessee. Democrat. Vanderbilt, University of Virginia. Nominated associate justice by Woodrow Wilson; confirmed 1914 by 44-6 vote; retired 1941. U.S. attorney general.

Brandeis, Louis Dembitz (1856–1941). Massachusetts. Democrat. Harvard. Nominated associate justice by Woodrow Wilson; confirmed 1916 by 47-22 vote; retired 1939. Private practice.

Clarke, John Hessin (1857–1945). Ohio. Democrat. Western Reserve University. Nominated associate justice by Woodrow Wilson; confirmed 1916 by voice vote; resigned 1922. Federal district judge.

Taft, William Howard (1857–1930). Ohio. Republican. Yale, Cincinnati Law School. Nominated chief justice by Warren G. Harding; confirmed 1921 by voice vote; retired 1930. Ohio local prosecutor, state court judge, U.S. solicitor general, federal court of appeals judge, governor of the Philippines, secretary of war, president.

Sutherland, George (1862–1942). Utah. Republican. Brigham Young, University of Michigan. Nominated associate justice by Warren G. Harding; confirmed 1922 by voice vote; retired 1938. Utah state legislator, U.S. representative, U.S. senator.

Butler, Pierce (1866–1939). Minnesota. Democrat. Carleton College. Nominated associate justice by Warren G. Harding; confirmed 1922 by 61-8 vote; died in office 1939. Minnesota county attorney, private practice.

Sanford, Edward Terry (1865–1930). Tennessee. Republican. University of Tennessee, Harvard. Nominated associate justice by Warren G. Harding; confirmed 1923 by voice vote; died in office 1930. Assistant U.S. attorney general, federal district court judge.

Stone, Harlan Fiske (1872–1946). New York. Republican. Amherst College, Columbia. Nominated associate justice by Calvin Coolidge; confirmed 1925 by 71-6 vote; nominated chief justice by Franklin Roosevelt; confirmed 1941 by voice vote; died in office 1946. Law professor, U.S. attorney general.

Roberts, Owen Josephus (1875–1955). Pennsylvania. Republican. University of Pennsylvania. Nominated associate justice by Herbert Hoover; confirmed 1930 by voice vote; resigned 1945. Private practice, Pennsylvania local prosecutor, special U.S. attorney.

Cardozo, Benjamin Nathan (1870–1938). New York. Democrat. Columbia. Nominated associate justice by Herbert Hoover; confirmed 1932 by voice vote; died in office 1938. State court judge.

Black, Hugo Lafayette (1886–1971). Alabama. Democrat. Birmingham Medical College, University of Alabama. Nominated associate justice by Franklin Roosevelt; confirmed 1937 by 63-16 vote; retired 1971. Alabama police court judge, county solicitor, U.S. senator.

Reed, Stanley Forman (1884–1980). Kentucky. Democrat. Kentucky Wesleyan, Yale, Virginia, Columbia, University of Paris. Nominated associate justice by Franklin Roosevelt; confirmed 1938 by voice vote; retired 1957. Federal Farm Board general counsel, Reconstruction Finance Corporation general counsel, U.S. solicitor general.

Frankfurter, Felix (1882–1965). Massachusetts. Independent. College of the City of New York, Harvard. Nominated associate justice by Franklin Roosevelt; confirmed 1939 by voice vote; retired 1962. Law professor, War Department law officer, assistant to secretary of war, assistant to secretary of labor, War Labor Policies Board chairman.

Douglas, William Orville (1898–1980). Connecticut. Democrat. Whitman College, Columbia. Nominated associate justice by Franklin Roosevelt; confirmed 1939 by 62-4 vote; retired 1975. Law professor, Securities and Exchange Commission.

Murphy, Francis William (1890–1949). Michigan. Democrat. University of Michigan, London's Inn (England), Trinity College (Ireland). Nominated associate justice by Franklin Roosevelt; confirmed 1940 by voice vote; died in office 1949. Michigan state court judge, mayor of Detroit, governor of the Philippines, governor of Michigan, U.S. attorney general.

Byrnes, James Francis (1879–1972). South Carolina. Democrat. Privately educated. Nominated associate justice by Franklin Roosevelt; confirmed 1941 by voice vote; resigned 1942. South Carolina local solicitor, U.S. representative, U.S. senator.

Jackson, Robert Houghwout (1892–1954). New York. Democrat. Albany Law School. Nominated associate justice by Franklin Roosevelt; confirmed 1941 by voice vote; died in office 1954. Counsel for Internal Revenue Bureau and Securities and Exchange Commission, U.S. solicitor general, U.S. attorney general.

Rutledge, Wiley Blount (1894–1949). Iowa. Democrat. Maryville College, University of Wisconsin, University of Colorado. Nominated associate justice by Franklin Roosevelt; confirmed 1943 by voice vote; died in office 1949. Law professor, federal court of appeals judge.

Burton, Harold Hitz (1888–1964). Ohio. Republican. Bowdoin College, Harvard. Nominated associate justice by Harry Truman; confirmed 1945 by voice vote; retired 1958. Ohio state legislator, mayor of Cleveland, U.S. senator.

Vinson, Frederick Moore (1890–1953). Kentucky. Democrat. Centre College. Nominated chief justice by Harry Truman; confirmed 1946 by voice vote; died in office 1953. U.S. representative, federal appeals court judge, director of Office of Economic Stabilization, secretary of the Treasury.

Clark, Tom Campbell (1899–1977). Texas. Democrat. University of Texas. Nominated associate justice by Harry Truman; confirmed 1949 by 73-8 vote; retired 1967. Texas local district attorney, U.S. attorney general.

Minton, Sherman (1890–1965). Indiana. Democrat. Indiana University, Yale. Nominated associate justice by Harry Truman; confirmed 1949 by 48-16 vote; retired 1956. U.S. senator, federal court of appeals judge.

Warren, Earl (1891–1974). California. Republican. University of California. Recess appointment as chief justice by Dwight Eisenhower 1953; confirmed 1954 by voice vote; retired 1969. California local district attorney, state attorney general, governor.

Harlan, John Marshall (1899–1971). New York. Republican. Princeton, Oxford, New York Law School. Nominated associate justice by Dwight Eisenhower; confirmed 1955 by 71-11 vote; retired 1971. Chief counsel for New York State Crime Commission, federal court of appeals.

Brennan, William Joseph, Jr. (1906–). New Jersey. Democrat. University of Pennsylvania, Harvard. Received recess appointment from Dwight Eisenhower to be associate justice 1956; confirmed 1957 by voice vote; retired 1990. New Jersey Supreme Court.

Whittaker, Charles Evans (1901–1973). Missouri. Republican. University of Kansas City. Nominated associate justice by Dwight Eisenhower; confirmed 1957 by voice vote; retired 1962. Federal district court judge, federal appeals court judge.

Stewart, Potter (1915–1985). Ohio. Republican. Yale, Cambridge. Received recess appointment from Dwight Eisenhower to be associate justice in 1958; confirmed 1959 by 70-17 vote; retired 1981. Cincinnati city council, federal court of appeals judge.

White, Byron Raymond (1917–). Colorado. Democrat. University of Colorado, Oxford, Yale. Nominated associate justice by John Kennedy; confirmed 1962 by voice vote. Deputy U.S. attorney general.

Goldberg, Arthur J. (1908–1990). Illinois. Democrat. Northwestern. Nominated associate justice by John Kennedy; confirmed 1962 by voice vote; resigned 1965. Secretary of labor.

Fortas, Abe (1910–1982). Tennessee. Democrat. Southwestern College, Yale. Nominated associate justice by Lyndon Johnson; confirmed 1965 by voice vote; resigned 1969. Counsel for numerous federal agencies, private practice.

Marshall, Thurgood (1908–). New York. Democrat. Lincoln University, Howard University. Nominated associate justice by Lyndon Johnson; confirmed 1967 by 69-11 vote. Retired 1991. NAACP Legal Defense Fund, federal court of appeals judge, U.S. solicitor general.

Burger, Warren Earl (1907–). Minnesota. Republican. University of Minnesota, St. Paul College of Law. Nominated chief justice by Richard Nixon; confirmed 1969 by 74-3 vote; retired 1986. Assistant U.S. attorney general, federal appeals court judge.

Blackmun, Harry Andrew (1908–). Minnesota. Republican. Harvard. Nominated associate justice by Richard Nixon; confirmed 1970 by 94-0 vote. Federal appeals court judge.

Powell, Lewis Franklin, Jr. (1907–). Virginia. Democrat. Washington and Lee, Harvard. Nominated associate justice by Richard Nixon; confirmed 1971 by 89-1 vote; retired 1987. Private practice, Virginia State Board of Education, American Bar Association president, American College of Trial Lawyers president.

Rehnquist, William Hubbs (1924–). Arizona.

Republican. Stanford, Harvard. Nominated associate justice by Richard Nixon; confirmed 1971 by 68-26 vote; nominated chief justice by Ronald Reagan; confirmed 1968 by 65-33 vote. Private practice, assistant U.S. attorney general.

Stevens, John Paul (1920–). Illinois. Republican. Chicago, Northwestern. Nominated associate justice by Gerald Ford; confirmed 1975 by 98-0 vote. Federal court of appeals judge.

O'Connor, Sandra Day (1930–). Arizona. Republican. Stanford. Nominated associate justice by Ronald Reagan; confirmed 1981 by 99-0 vote. Arizona state legislator, state court judge.

Scalia, Antonin (1936–). District of Columbia. Republican. Georgetown, Harvard. Nominated associate justice by Ronald Reagan; confirmed 1986 by 98-0 vote. Assistant U.S. attorney general, federal court of appeals judge.

Kennedy, Anthony McLeod (1936–). California. Republican. Stanford, London School of Economics, Harvard. Nominated associate justice by Ronald Reagan; confirmed 1988 by 97-0 vote. Federal appeals court judge.

Souter, David Hackett (1939–). New Hampshire. Republican. Harvard, Oxford. Nominated associate justice by George Bush; confirmed 1990 by 90-9 vote. New Hampshire attorney general, state court judge, federal appeals court judge.

Thomas, Clarence (1948–). Georgia. Republican. Immaculate Conception Seminary, Holy Cross, Yale. Nominated associate justice by George Bush; confirmed 1991 by 52-48 vote. Equal Employment Opportunity Commission chairman, federal appeals court judge.

SEAT CHART OF THE JUSTICES

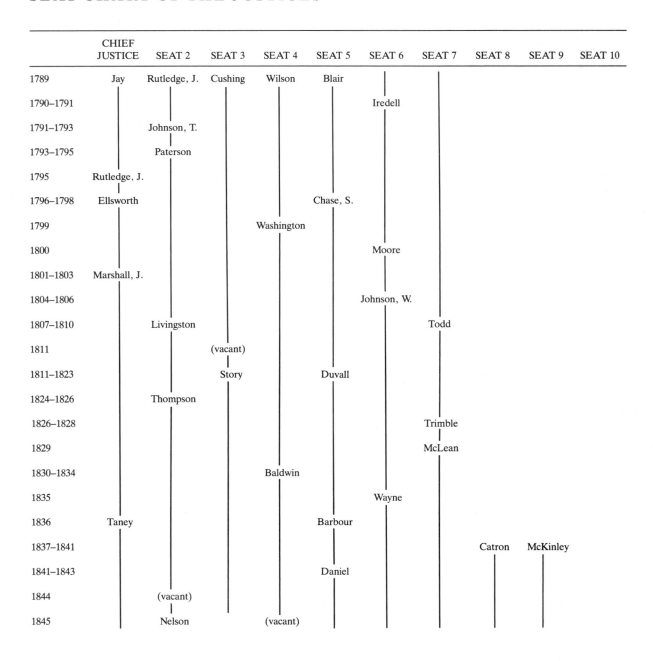

	CHIEF JUSTICE	SEAT 2	SEAT 3	SEAT 4	SEAT 5	SEAT 6	SEAT 7	SEAT 8	SEAT 9	SEAT 10
1789	Jay	Rutledge, J.	Cushing	Wilson	Blair					
1790–1791						Iredell				
1791–1793		Johnson, T.								
1793–1795		Paterson								
1795	Rutledge, J.									
1796–1798	Ellsworth				Chase, S.					
1799				Washington						
1800						Moore				
1801–1803	Marshall, J.									
1804–1806						Johnson, W.				
1807–1810		Livingston					Todd			
1811			(vacant)							
1811–1823			Story		Duvall					
1824–1826		Thompson								
1826–1828							Trimble			
1829							McLean			
1830–1834				Baldwin						
1835						Wayne				
1836	Taney				Barbour					
1837–1841								Catron	McKinley	
1841–1843					Daniel					
1844		(vacant)								
1845		Nelson		(vacant)						

	CHIEF JUSTICE	SEAT 2	SEAT 3	SEAT 4	SEAT 5	SEAT 6	SEAT 7	SEAT 8	SEAT 9	SEAT 10
1846–1851			Woodbury	Grier						
1852			Curtis							
1853–1857									Campbell	
1858–1860			Clifford							
1861					(vacant)					
1862					Miller		Swayne		Davis	
1863–1864										Field
1865	Chase, S. P.									
1866–1867								(seat abolished)		
1868–1869						(vacant)				
1870–1872				Strong		Bradley				
1873		Hunt								
1874–1877	Waite									
1877–1880									Harlan I	
1881				Woods			Matthews			
1882–1887		Blatchford	Gray							
1888				Lamar, L.						
1888–1889	Fuller									
1889–1890							Brewer			
1891					Brown					
1892						Shiras				
1893				Jackson, H.						
1894–1895		White, E.								
1896–1897				Peckham						
1898–1902										McKenna
1903–1906			Holmes			Day				

	CHIEF JUSTICE	SEAT 2	SEAT 3	SEAT 4	SEAT 5	SEAT 6	SEAT 7	SEAT 8	SEAT 9	SEAT 10
1907–1909					Moody					
1910				Lurton						
1910–1911	White, E.	Van Devanter			Lamar, J.		Hughes			
1912–1914									Pitney	
1914–1916				McReynolds						
1916–1921					Brandeis		Clarke			
1921–1922	Taft									
1922						Butler	Sutherland			
1923–1924									Sanford	
1925–1930										Stone
1930–1931	Hughes								Roberts	
1932–1937			Cardozo							
1937		Black								
1938							Reed			
1939			Frankfurter		Douglas					
1940–1941						Murphy				
1941–1942	Stone			Byrnes						Jackson, R.
1943–1945				Rutledge, W.						
1945–1946									Burton	
1946–1949	Vinson									
1949–1953				Minton		Clark				
1953–1954	Warren									
1955–1956										Harlan II
1957–1958				Brennan			Whittaker			
1959–1962									Stewart	
1962–1965			Goldberg				White, B.			

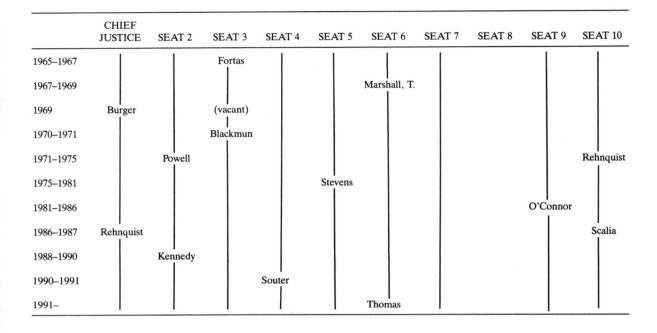

	CHIEF JUSTICE	SEAT 2	SEAT 3	SEAT 4	SEAT 5	SEAT 6	SEAT 7	SEAT 8	SEAT 9	SEAT 10
1965–1967			Fortas							
1967–1969						Marshall, T.				
1969	Burger		(vacant)							
1970–1971			Blackmun							
1971–1975		Powell								Rehnquist
1975–1981					Stevens					
1981–1986									O'Connor	
1986–1987	Rehnquist									Scalia
1988–1990		Kennedy								
1990–1991				Souter						
1991–						Thomas				

THE AMERICAN LEGAL SYSTEM

FEDERAL COURTS	STATE COURTS

HIGHEST APPELLATE COURTS

U.S. Supreme Court	State Supreme Court[1]

INTERMEDIATE APPELLATE COURTS

U.S. Courts of Appeals Court of Appeals for the Federal Circuit Temporary Emergency Court of Appeals	Courts of Appeals[2]

TRIAL COURTS OF GENERAL JURISDICTION

U.S. District Courts	District Courts[3]

TRIAL COURTS OF LIMITED JURISDICTION

Tax Court Rail Reorganization Court Claims Court Court of International Trade Court of Veterans Appeals	*Examples include:* Juvenile Court, Family Court, Traffic Court, Small Claims Court, Justice of the Peace, Magistrate Court

1. Sometimes called Supreme Judicial Court or Court of Appeals
2. These courts exist in about two-thirds of all states. They are sometimes called Superior or District Courts.
3. Sometimes called circuit courts, courts of common pleas, superior courts.

SUPREME COURT PROCEDURES

Procedure	Time
Court receives requests for review, between 4,000 and 5,000 per year.	Throughout term.

Appeal: request for review of case in which a federal or state court struck down a federal law; U.S. government is a party.
Certification: request by lower court for definitive answers to legal questions.
Petitions: usually a request for a writ of certiorari; all others.

Procedure	Time
Cases are docketed.	Throughout term.

Original docket: cases coming to the Court under its original jurisdiction.
Appellate docket: all other cases, including *in forma pauperis* petitions, which receive special docket numbers.

Procedure	Time
Justices review docketed cases.	Throughout term.

Chief justice prepares discuss list, approximately one-fourth of docketed cases; chief justice circulates discuss list prior to conferences.

Procedure	Time
Conferences.	Fridays (see Supreme Court Calendar).

Selection of cases for review, for denial of review; Rule of Four in effect (four or more justices must agree to review a case).

Procedure	Time
Announcement of action on cases.	Mondays following Friday conference.

Procedure	Time
Clerk sets date for oral argument.	Usually not less than three months after Court has granted review.

Procedure	Time
Attorneys file briefs.	Appellant/petitioner must file within forty-five days from the day the Court has granted review; appellee/respondent must file within thirty days of receipt of appellant/petitioner's brief.

Procedure	Time
Oral arguments.	Seven two-week sessions from October through April on Mondays, Tuesdays, and Wednesdays.

Court hears four cases per day; each case *generally* receiving one hour of the Court's time.

Procedure	Time
Conferences.	Wednesday afternoons, Fridays (in weeks with oral arguments and before two-week oral argument period).
Discussion of cases; tentative votes; assignment of majority opinion.	

Procedure	Time
Drafting and circulating of opinions.	One week to six months after assignment.

Procedure	Time
Issuing and announcement of opinions.	Usually Mondays.

Procedure	Time
Reporting of opinions.	Concurrent with announcement.

Sources of opinions: U.S. Reports (U.S.), official reporter system; Lawyers' Edition (L.Ed.); Supreme Court Reporter (S.Ct.); U.S. Law Week (U.S.L.W.); electronic reporter systems (WESTLAW, LEXIS).

SUPREME COURT CALENDAR

Activity	Time
Start of Term	First Monday in October
Oral Argument Cycle	October–April: Mondays, Tuesdays, Wednesdays in seven two-week sessions
Recess Cycle	October–April: two or more consecutive weeks after two weeks of oral; Christmas, Easter
Conferences	Wednesday afternoon following Monday orals (discussion of four Monday cases) Friday following Tuesday, Wednesday orals (discussion of eight Tuesday–Wednesday cases; cert. petitions) Friday before two-week oral period
Opinion Announcement	Throughout term with bulk coming in Spring/Summer
Summer Recess	Late June/early July
Initial Conference	Late September (resolve old business, consider cert. petitions from the summer)

BRIEFING SUPREME COURT CASES

1. What is the name of the case?
   The name is important because it *generally* reveals which party is asking the Court to review the case. The name appearing first is usually (but not always) the appellant/petitioner, the party that lost in the court below.

2. In what year did the Supreme Court decide the case?
   The year is important because it will help to put the case into a legal and historical context. See Thumbnail Sketch of the Supreme Court's History for more detail.

3. What circumstances triggered the dispute?

4. What statute or action triggered the dispute?

5. What provision of the Constitution is at issue?

6. What is the basic legal question(s) the Court is being asked to address?

7. What was the outcome of the dispute?

8. How did the majority reach its decision? What was its legal reasoning?

9. What legal doctrine, standards, or policy did the majority announce?

10. What other views (dissents, concurrences) were expressed?

AN EXAMPLE: *National League of Cities v. Usery* (1976)

1. Case Name. *National League of Cities v. Usery*

2. Year Case Decided by Supreme Court. *1976*

3. Facts that Triggered the Dispute. *In 1974 Congress required the states and their subdivisions to abide by established minimum wage and maximum hour work requirements. The National League of Cities, along with another organization and various cities and states, brought this action against Secretary of Labor W. J. Usery to challenge the constitutionality of the congressional enactment.*

4. Statute. *National League of Cities et al. launched this suit to challenge 1974 amendments to the Fair Labor Standards Act of 1938 (FLSA). This amendment expanded the scope of the FLSA's minimum wage and maximum hour provisions so that virtually all state public employees, who were excluded in the original legislation, were brought under its reach.*

5. Provision of the Constitution. *National League of Cities et al. alleged that the 1974 amendments, enacted by Congress under its power to regulate commerce, infringed on states' rights under the Tenth Amendment.*

6. Legal Question. *Do the 1974 amendments to the Fair Labor Standards Act constitute an infringement on states' rights?*

7. Outcome. *In a 5-4 ruling, the Court held for National League of Cities et al.*

8. Legal Reasoning of the Majority. *In delivering the opinion of the Court, Justice William H. Rehnquist held that:*
   a. there are "attributes of sovereignty attaching to every state government which may not be impaired by Congress, not because Congress may lack an affirmative grant of legislative authority to reach the matter, but because the Constitution prohibits it from exercising the authority in that manner."
   b. in this instance, the amendments fall within the reach of the commerce clause. But they infringe, to an impermissible degree, on State sovereignty. That is, they impair the State's "ability to function effectively in a federal system."

9. Legal Doctrine. *The majority:*
   a. established a legal standard that prohibited the exercise of congressional power "so as to force directly upon the States its choices as to how essential decisions regarding the conduct of integral governmental function are to be made."
   b. did not specify precisely the meaning of the term "integral governmental functions," but wrote that Congress could not displace functions that are "es-

sential to [the] separate and independent existence of the states.'' It also provided some examples of activities outside of congressional authority: fire prevention, police protection, sanitation, public health, and parks and recreation.

c. overruled a previous decision (Maryland v. Wirtz, 1968) in which the Court ruled that Congress could prescribe regulations for employees, regardless of whether their employer is a state.

10. Other Points of View.

a. Justice Blackmun concurred: the Court is adopting a ''balancing approach'' to federal-state relations.

b. Justice Brennan (joined by White and Marshall) dissented: the majority repudiates well-settled principles of constitutional interpretation.

1. ''Nothing in the Tenth Amendment constitutes a limitation on congressional exercise powers delegated by the Constitution to Congress,'' including the authority to regulate commerce.

2. The majority opinion is a ''usurpation of the role reserved for the political process by their purported discovery in the Constitution of a restraint derived'' from state sovereignty on congressional power under the commerce clause. It ''can only be regarded as a transparent cover for invalidating a congressional judgment with which they disagree.''

c. Justice Stevens dissented: the majority's opinion means that Congress ''may not interfere with a sovereign State's inherent right to pay a substandard wage to the janitor at the state capitol. The principle on which the holding rests is difficult to perceive.''

GLOSSARY

A fortiori With greater force or reason.

Abstention A doctrine or policy of the federal courts to refrain from deciding a case so that the issues involved may first be definitively resolved by state courts.

Acquittal A decision by a court that a person charged with a crime is not guilty.

Advisory opinion An opinion issued by a court indicating how it would rule on a question of law should such a question come before it in an actual case. Federal courts do not hand down advisory opinions, but some state courts do.

Affidavit A written statement of facts voluntarily made under oath or affirmation.

Affirm To uphold a decision of a lower court.

Aggravating circumstances Conditions that increase the seriousness of a crime but are not a part of its legal definition.

Amicus curiae "Friend of the court." A person (or group), not a party to a case, who submits views (usually in the form of written briefs) on how the case should be decided.

Ante Prior to.

Appeal The procedure by which a case is taken to a superior court for a review of the lower court's decision.

Appellant The party dissatisfied with a lower court ruling who appeals the case to a superior court for review.

Appellate jurisdiction The legal authority of a superior court to review and render judgment on a decision by a lower court.

Appellee The party usually satisfied with a lower court ruling against whom an appeal is taken.

Arguendo In the course of argument.

Arraignment A formal stage of the criminal process in which the defendants are brought before a judge, confronted with the charges against them, and they enter a plea to those charges.

Arrest Physically taking into custody or otherwise depriving freedom of a person suspected of violating the law.

Attainder, Bill of A legislative act declaring a person or easily identified group of people guilty of a crime and imposing punishments without the benefit of a trial. Such legislative acts are prohibited by the United States Constitution.

Bail A security deposit, usually in the form of cash or bond, which allows those accused of crimes to be released from jail and guarantees their appearance at trial.

Balancing test A process of judicial decision making in which the court weighs the relative merits of the rights of the individual against the interests of the government.

Bench trial A trial, without a jury, conducted before a judge.

Bicameral A legislature, such as the U.S. Congress, with two houses.

Bona fide Good faith.

Brandeis brief A legal argument that stresses economic and sociological evidence along with traditional legal authorities. Named after Louis Brandeis, who pioneered its use.

Brief A written argument of law and fact submitted to the court by an attorney representing a party having an interest in a lawsuit.

Case law Law that has evolved from past court decisions, as opposed to law created by legislative acts.

Case or controversy rule The constitutional requirement that courts may only hear real disputes brought by adverse parties.

Case A legal dispute or controversy brought to a court for resolution.

Certification A procedure whereby a lower court requests that a superior court rule on specified legal questions so that the lower court may correctly apply the law.

Certiorari, Writ of   An order of an appellate court to an inferior court to send up the records of a case that the appellate court has elected to review. The primary method by which the U.S. Supreme Court exercises its discretionary jurisdiction to accept appeals for a full hearing.

Circuit courts of appeal   The intermediate level appellate courts in the federal system having jurisdiction over a particular region.

Civil law   Law that deals with the private rights of individuals (e.g., property, contracts, negligence), as contrasted with criminal law.

Class action   A lawsuit brought by one or more persons who represent themselves and all others similarly situated.

Collateral estoppel   A rule of law that prohibits an already settled issue from being relitigated in another form.

Comity   The principle by which the courts of one jurisdiction give respect and deference to the laws and legal decisions of another jurisdiction.

Common law   Law that has evolved from usage and custom as reflected in the decisions of courts.

Concurrent powers   Authority that may be exercised by both the state and federal governments.

Concurring opinion   An opinion that agrees with the result reached by the majority, but disagrees as to the appropriate rationale for reaching that result.

Consent decree   A court-ratified agreement voluntarily reached by parties to settle a lawsuit.

Constitutional court   A court created under authority of Article III of the Constitution. Judges serve for terms of good behavior and are protected against having their salaries reduced by the legislature.

Contempt   A purposeful failure to carry out an order of a court (civil contempt) or a willful display of disrespect for the court (criminal contempt).

Contraband   Articles that are illegal to possess.

Criminal law   Law governing the relationship between individuals and society. Deals with the enforcement of laws and the punishment of those who, by breaking laws, commit crimes.

Curtilage   The land and outbuildings immediately adjacent to a home and regularly used by its occupants.

De facto   In fact, actual.

De jure   As a result of law or official government action.

De minimis   Small or unimportant. A *de minimis* issue is considered one too trivial for a court to consider.

De novo   New, from the beginning.

Declaratory judgment   A court ruling determining a legal right or interpretation of the law, but not imposing any relief or remedy.

Defendant   A party at the trial level being sued in a civil case or charged with a crime in a criminal case.

Demurrer   A motion to dismiss a lawsuit in which the defendant admits to the facts alleged by the plaintiff but contends that those facts are insufficient to justify a legal cause of action.

Deposition   Sworn testimony taken out of court.

Dicta; Obiter dicta   Those portions of a judge's opinion that are not essential to deciding the case.

Directed verdict   An action by a judge ordering a jury to return a specified verdict.

Discovery   A pretrial procedure whereby one party to a lawsuit gains access to information or evidence held by the opposing party.

Dissenting opinion   A formal written expression by a judge who disagrees with the result reached by the majority.

Distinguish   A court's explanation of why a particular precedent is inapplicable to the case under consideration.

District courts   The trial courts of general jurisdiction in the federal system.

Diversity jurisdiction   The authority of federal courts to hear cases in which a party from one state is suing a party from another state.

Docket   The schedule of cases to be heard by a court.

Double jeopardy   The trying of a defendant a second time for the same offense. Prohibited by the Fifth Amendment to the Constitution.

Due process   Government procedures that follow principles of essential fairness.

Enjoin An order from a court requiring a party to do or refrain from doing certain acts.

En banc An appellate court hearing with all the judges of the court participating.

Equity Law based on principles of fairness rather than strictly applied statutes.

Error, Writ of An order issued by an appeals court commanding a lower court to send up the full record of a case for review.

Ex parte A hearing in which only one party to a dispute is present.

Ex post facto law A criminal law passed by the legislature and made applicable to acts committed prior to passage of the law. Prohibited by the U.S. Constitution.

Ex rel Upon information from. Used to designate a court case instituted by the government but instigated by a private party.

Ex vi termini From the force or very meaning of the term or expression.

Exclusionary rule A principle of law that illegally gathered evidence may not be admitted in court.

Exclusive powers Powers reserved for either the federal government or the state governments, but not exercised by both.

Federal question A legal issue based on the U.S. Constitution, laws, or treaties.

Felony A serious criminal offense, usually punishable by incarceration of one year or more.

Grand jury A panel of twelve to twenty-three citizens who review prosecutorial evidence to determine if there are sufficient grounds to issue an indictment binding an individual over for trial on criminal charges.

Guilty A determination that a person accused of a criminal offense is legally responsible as charged.

Habeas corpus "You have the body." A writ issued to determine if a person held in custody is being unlawfully detained or imprisoned.

Harmless error An error occurring in a court proceeding that is insufficient in magnitude to justify the overturning of the court's final determination.

Immunity An exemption from prosecution granted in exchange for testimony.

In camera A legal hearing held in the judge's chambers or otherwise in private.

Incorporation The process whereby provisions of the Bill of Rights are declared to be included in the due process guarantee of the Fourteenth Amendment and made applicable to state and local governments.

Indictment A document issued by a grand jury officially charging an individual with criminal violations and binding the accused over for trial.

Information A document, serving the same purpose as an indictment, but issued directly by the prosecutor.

In forma pauperis "In the form of a pauper." A special status granted to indigents that allows them to proceed without payment of court fees and to be exempt from certain procedural requirements.

Infra Below.

Injunction A writ prohibiting the person to whom it is directed from committing certain specified acts.

In re "In the matter of." The designation used in a judicial proceeding in which there are no formal adversaries.

In rem An act directed against a thing and not against a person.

Interlocutory decree A provisional action that temporarily settles a legal question pending the final determination of a dispute.

Inter alia Among other things.

Judgment of the court The final ruling of a court, independent of the legal reasoning supporting it.

Judicial activism A philosophy that courts should not be reluctant to review and if necessary strike down legislative and executive actions.

Judicial restraint A philosophy that courts should defer to the legislative and executive branches whenever possible.

Judicial review The authority of a court to determine the constitutionality of acts committed by the legislative and executive branches and to strike down acts judged to be in violation of the Constitution.

Jurisdiction The authority of a court to hear and decide legal disputes and to enforce its rulings.

Justiciable Capable of being heard and decided by a court.

Legislative court A court created by Congress under authority of Article I of the Constitution to assist in carrying out the powers of the legislature.

Litigant A party to a lawsuit.

Magistrate A low level judge with limited authority.

Mandamus "We command." A writ issued by a court commanding a public official to carry out a particular act or duty.

Mandatory jurisdiction A case that a court is required to hear.

Marque and reprisal An order from the government of one country requesting and legitimizing the seizure of persons and property of another country. Prohibited by the Constitution.

Merits The central issues of a case.

Misdemeanor A less serious criminal act, usually punishable by less than one year of incarceration.

Mistrial A trial that is prematurely ended by a judge because of procedural irregularities.

Mitigating circumstances Conditions that lower the moral blame of a criminal act, but do not justify or excuse it.

Moot Unsettled or undecided. A question presented in a lawsuit that cannot be answered by a court either because the issue has resolved itself or conditions have so changed that the court is unable to grant the requested relief.

Motion A request made to a court for a certain ruling or action.

Natural law Laws considered applicable to all persons in all nations because they are thought to be basic to human nature.

Nolle prosequi The decision of a prosecutor to drop criminal charges against an accused.

Nolo contendere No contest. A plea entered by a criminal defendant in which the accused does not admit guilt but submits to sentencing and punishment as if guilty.

Opinion of the court An opinion announcing the judgment and reasoning of a court endorsed by a majority of the judges participating.

Order A written command issued by a judge.

Original jurisdiction The authority of a court to try a case and to decide it, as opposed to appellate jurisdiction.

Per curiam An unsigned or collectively written opinion issued by a court.

Per se In and of itself.

Petitioner A party seeking relief in court.

Petit jury A trial court jury to decide criminal or civil cases.

Plaintiff The party who brings a legal action to court for resolution or remedy.

Plea bargain An arrangement in a criminal case in which the defendant agrees to plead guilty in return for the prosecutor reducing the criminal charges or recommending a lenient sentence.

Plurality opinion An opinion announcing the judgment of a court with supporting reasoning that is not endorsed by a majority of the justices participating.

Police powers The power of the state to regulate for the health, safety, morals, and general welfare of its citizens.

Political question An issue more appropriate for determination by the legislative or executive branch than the judiciary.

Precedent A previously decided case that serves as a guide for deciding a current case.

Preemption A doctrine under which an area of authority previously left to the states is, by act of Congress, brought into the exclusive jurisdiction of the federal government.

Prima facie "At first sight." A case that is sufficient to prevail unless effectively countered by the opposing side.

Pro bono publico "For the public good." Usually refers to legal representation done without fee for some charitable or public purpose.

Pro se A person who appears in court without an attorney.

Quash To annul, vacate, or totally do away with.

Ratio decidendi A court's primary reasoning for deciding a case the way it did.

Recuse The action of a judge not to participate in a case because of conflict of interest or other disqualifying condition.

Remand To send a case back to an inferior court

for additional action.

Res judicata A legal issue that has been finally settled by a court judgment.

Respondent The party against whom a legal action is filed.

Reverse An action by an appellate court setting aside or changing a decision of a lower court.

Ripeness A condition in which a legal dispute has evolved to the point where the issues it presents can be effectively resolved by a court.

Selective incorporation The policy of the Supreme Court to decide incorporation issues on a case by case, right by right basis.

Solicitor general Justice Department official whose office represents the federal government in all litigation before the U.S. Supreme Court.

Standing; standing to sue The right of parties to bring legal actions because they are directly affected by the legal issues raised.

Stare decisis "Let the decision stand." The doctrine that once a legal issue has been settled it should be followed as precedent in future cases presenting the same question.

State action An action taken by an agency or official of a state or local government.

Stay To stop or suspend.

Strict construction Narrow interpretation of the provisions of laws.

Subpoena An order compelling a person to testify or to produce evidence before a court, legislative hearing, or grand jury.

Sub silentio "Under silence." A court action taken without explicit notice or indication.

Summary judgment A decision by a court made without a full hearing or without receiving briefs or oral arguments.

Supra Above.

Temporary restraining order A judicial order prohibiting certain challenged actions from being taken prior to a full hearing on the question.

Test A criterion or set of criteria used by courts to determine if certain legal thresholds have been met or constitutional provisions violated.

Three judge court A special federal court made up of appellate and trial court judges created to expedite the processing of certain issues made eligible for such priority treatment by congressional statute.

Ultra vires Actions taken that exceed the legal authority of the person or agency performing them.

Usus loquendi The common usage of ordinary language.

Vacate To void or rescind.

Vel non "Or not."

Venireman A juror.

Venue The geographical jurisdiction in which a case is heard.

Voir dire "To speak the truth." The stage of a trial in which potential jurors are questioned to determine their competence to sit in judgment of a case.

Warrant A judicial order authorizing an arrest or search and seizure.

Writ A written order of a court commanding the recipient to perform or not to perform certain specified acts.

SUBJECT INDEX

CASE INDEX

ACKNOWLEDGMENTS

5 Steffen W. Schmidt, Mack C. Shelley II, and Barbara A. Bardes, *American Government and Politics Today.* Copyright © 1989 by West Publishing Company. Used with permission. **7** Paul E. Johnson, John H. Miller, Gary J. Ostrom, Jr., and David W. Rohde, *American Government,* 2d ed. Copyright © 1990 by Houghton Mifflin Company. Used with permission. **9** Janet A. Flammang et al., *American Politics in a Changing World.* Copyright © 1990 by Brooks/Cole. Used with permission. **40, 79, 113, 176, 233, 456** Elder Witt, *Guide to the U.S. Supreme Court,* 2d ed. Copyright © 1990 by Congressional Quarterly Inc. Pages 810–811, 171, 855–856, 854–855, 819–820, 852–853. Used with permission. **54** Lawrence Baum, *The Supreme Court,* 4th ed. Copyright © 1992 by CQ Press. Used with permission. **67** *Equal Justice Under Law.* Copyright © 1965 by Foundation of the Federal Bar Association. Used with permission. **81, 127** *Guide to Congress,* 3d ed. Copyright © 1982 by Congressional Quarterly Inc. Pages 823, 825, 198. Used with premission. **93–94** Melvin I. Urofsky, ed. *Documents of American Constitutional History,* vol. I. Copyright © 1989 by Alfred A. Knopf. Used with permission. **104** *Guide to Congress,* 4th ed., ed. Mary Cohn. Copyright © 1991 by Congressional Quarterly Inc. Reprinted with permission. **119** *Revolution in Civil Rights.* Copyright © 1965 by Congressional Quarterly Inc. Used with permission. **141** *Guide to the Presidency,* ed. Michael Nelson. Copyright © 1989 by Congressional Quarterly Inc. Used with permission. **248** Harold W. Stanley and Richard G. Niemi, *Vital Statistics on American Politics,* 3d ed. Copyright © 1992 by CQ Press. Used with permission. **381** Sheldon Goldman, *Constitutional Law,* Copyright © 1987 by Harper & Row. Used with permission. **430** Bernard Schwartz, *The Law in America* (New York: McGraw-Hill, 1974), 137. Reprinted by permission of the author.

PHOTOGRAPHS

34 Lisa Biganzoli, National Geographic Staff; **40, 113, 176, 285, 400, 430, 456** Library of Congress; **62** Courtesy of the Rhode Island Historical Society; **82, 206** Wide World Photos; **105, 161, 163, 211, 287, 361** UPI/Bettmann; **142** LBJ Library; **145** (left), **233, 305** Collection of the Supreme Court of the United States; **145** (middle and right), **146** Bancroft Library, University of California (Berkeley); **160, 353** National Archives; **201** Indiana State Library; **202** Indiana Historical Society Library; **234, 269** (bottom), **440, 455, 464** Supreme Court Historical Society; **269** (top) Courtesy of The New-York Historical Society, New York City; **270** Drew University Library Archives; **295** (left) Washington Post; (right) A Copyright 1936 Cartoon by Herblock; **392, 393,** Dartmouth College; **397** Goodspeed's Book Shop/Supreme Court Historical Society; **449** From the Collection of Joseph Lochner, Jr. by Dante Tranquille.